JOURNALISM
ETHICS

D1518353

JOURNALISM ETHICS

Arguments and Cases

Martin Hirst and Roger Patching

OXFORD
UNIVERSITY PRESS

OXFORD
UNIVERSITY PRESS

253 Normanby Road, South Melbourne, Victoria 3205, Australia

Oxford University Press is a department of the University of Oxford.
It furthers the University's objective of excellence in research, scholarship,
and education by publishing worldwide in

Oxford New York

Auckland Bangkok Buenos Aires Cape Town Chennai
Dar es Salaam Delhi Hong Kong Istanbul Karachi Kolkata
Kuala Lumpur Madrid Melbourne Mexico City Mumbai Nairobi
São Paulo Shanghai Taipei Tokyo Toronto

OXFORD is a trade mark of Oxford University Press
in the UK and in certain other countries

National Library of Australia
Cataloguing-in-Publication data:

Hirst, Martin.
    Journalism ethics: arguments and cases.

    Bibliography.
    Includes index.
    For undergraduates.
    ISBN 0 19 555039 0.

    1. Journalistic ethics—Textbooks. 2. Journalistic ethics—Case studies—Textbooks.
    I. Patching, Roger, 1944-. II. Title.

    174.9074

Typeset by OUPANZS
Printed by Bookpac Production Services, Singapore

Contents

Table of Cases

Acknowledgments

This book had its genesis in the mid 1990s while both authors were teaching at Charles Sturt University in Bathurst, in the central west of New South Wales. It was originally planned as a collaborative effort with other journalism staff and ethics lecturers at CSU. The authors at that stage worked on the case studies part of the project. The text never eventuated, but the authors resurrected the idea when Martin joined the journalism staff at the University of Queensland in 2002. Roger had earlier joined the journalism staff at nearby Queensland University of Technology.

The theoretical framework, especially the development of the concept of 'ethical fault lines', owes much to Martin's 2003 doctorate, 'Grey Collar Journalism: The Social Relations of News Production'. The book can be seen in two distinct sections. The first five chapters establish the theoretical framework needed to discuss the various ethical aspects of journalism, while the remaining seven chapters look at the practical applications. Martin wrote the initial drafts of the first six chapters. Roger produced the original draft of the introduction, the majority of the case studies, and the first drafts of the last six chapters.

The authors realise that because many of the case studies came from 'yesterday's headlines', the stories may have changed or developed further since they completed the text. Ethics is never static. As the stories continue to evolve, further ethical dilemmas may present themselves, giving rise to more opportunities for discussion and reflection.

The authors appreciate the support of their respective wives during the production of the book, and in Roger's case, the support of his children.

They also acknowledge the help of colleagues at UQ and QUT, and among the wider journalism education community in Australia. They also appreciate the help of the staff at Oxford University Press, in particular commissioning editor Debra James, Chris Wyness, and their always helpful and insightful copy-editor, Liz Filleul.

All illustrations in this text have been used with the permission of the copyright holders. The authors express their thanks to News Limited and Fairfax Publications.

Martin Hirst and Roger Patching
Brisbane, 2004

Abbreviations

ABC	Australian Broadcasting Corporation (Australia)
ABC	American Broadcasting Company (USA)
ACP	Australian Consolidated Press
AFR	*The Australian Financial Review*
AJA	Australian Journalists' Association
AP	Associated Press
APC	Australian Press Council
ASIO	Australian Security Intelligence Organisation
ATSIC	Aboriginal and Torres Strait Islander Commission
BBC	British Broadcasting Corporation
BECTU	Broadcasting Entertainment Cinematograph and Theatre Union (UK)
CBS	Columbia Broadcasting System (USA)
CMC	Crime and Misconduct Commission (Queensland)
CNN	Cable News Network (USA)
CNNNN	Chaser Non-stop News Network (Australia)
CTVA	Commercial Television Australia (formerly FACTS, now Free TV Australia)
DFAT	Department of Foreign Affairs and Trade (Australia)
DPP	Director of Public Prosecutions (Australian states)
FACTS	Federation of Australian Commercial Television Stations (now Free TV Australia)
FARB	Federation of Australian Radio Broadcasters (in 2002 FARB changed its name to Commercial Radio Australia)
HWT	Herald and Weekly Times group (Melbourne)
ICAC	Independent Commission Against Corruption (NSW)
MEAA	Media Entertainment and Arts Alliance
MoD	Ministry of Defence (UK)
NBC	National Broadcasting Corporation (USA)
NESB	Non English-speaking Background
NYT	*The New York Times*
PANPA	Pacific Area Newspaper Publishers' Association
SA	South Australia (Australian state)

SBS	Special Broadcasting Service
SMH	*The Sydney Morning Herald*
TAFE	Technical and Further Education (Australian post-secondary education sector)
UPI	United Press International
WA	Western Australia (Australian state)

Preface

Arguments, cases, and fault lines

Where to begin?

A discussion of ethical practice in the media can unexpectedly begin in your living room at the end of a busy day. It can be in response to an item broadcast on the evening news. How often do you come home, watch the news, and see something that upsets or enrages you? 'Foot in the door' journalism has become standard practice and hardly a night goes by without at least one national TV current affairs program making at least one ethical blunder (Hirst et al. 1995). In the mid 1990s Channel Nine personality Ray Martin, and the show he was hosting at the time, *A Current Affair*, were investigated over an alleged fraudulent bail application for someone they interviewed 'exclusively'. *ACA* reporter Chris Smith was placed on a two-year $4000 good behaviour bond after pleading guilty to forging the signature of a program executive to obtain the release of a prisoner from jail so she could be interviewed ('TV Reporter Admits Jail Release Forgery' 1995).

One place to begin an exploration of journalism ethics is with the Media Entertainment and Arts Alliance (MEAA) Australian Journalists' Association Code of Ethics. In the Preamble to the Code it is written that 'Respect for truth and the public's right to information are overriding principles for all journalists'. As we shall see, many journalists and journalism educators believe that this opening statement immediately leads to problems because it contradicts other clauses of the Code.

Or we could start our exploration of journalism ethics by first examining the principles that have informed debates about ethics from the time of Aristotle, or even earlier. For example, we could turn to Peter Singer's monumental edited volume of nearly 600 pages, *A Companion to Ethics* (Singer 1991) in which it is suggested that the first written documents concerning ethics were inscribed in Mesopotamia sometime around 3000 BC. And let's not forget Moses and the tablets of stone.

We have chosen to begin with this last point, the philosophical principles of ethics and a little bit of history. This is not because we think that theory is more important than practice, but because we think they're virtually inseparable. Each chapter is a blend of theory (arguments) and practical examples (cases) because in our experience, one doesn't make sense without the other.

Everyday fault lines in the news

For anyone familiar with the daily news, whether through newspapers, radio, television, or online, it is not surprising that sometimes things seem to go horribly wrong, are judged to be in poor taste, or too explicit. Often the context is important when we make value judgments about ethics. Take, for example, the arguments about publishing photographs of Saddam Hussein's dead sons, Uday and Qusay, in July 2003. The men had been killed in a gunfight with American troops in the Iraqi city of Mosul. In this case, what appears to be a simple argument about publishing potentially disturbing images becomes a matter of international diplomacy and strategic brinkmanship in a battle for hearts and minds. Writing originally in the *Washington Post*, Ken Ringle (2003) illustrated the news media's dilemma and how the American Secretary of Defence, Donald Rumsfeld, decided to resolve it: 'The issue is the sanitation of imagery. How does a Government or a media outlet decide on the treatment of the visual images of the shattered corpses that are part of war? ... The dilemma was solved ... through the release of the pictures ... not by the military but by the US government' (Ringle 2003, p. 17).

From the military's point of view, the propaganda value of the gruesome deaths was enormous. But what was the journalistic reason for showing the pictures? Could there be a valid reason for showing them—especially after the furore in the US, UK, and Australia when the Arab television network Al Jazeera showed British corpses during the war? Was it being done, from the media's point of view, for the sake of audience voyeurism?

One obvious retort to this question is that the role of objective journalism is to establish the facts. In this case there is obvious public interest in knowing whether Saddam's sons are in fact dead, or not. This answer removes all traces of responsibility from the journalist or editor involved. After all, a reporter has no right to stand in the way of the public's right to know. In the abstract this is true. However, reality is always more concrete, and therefore more complex than an abstract argument about ideals, rights, and responsibilities.

Should the news media have allowed itself to be used as a propaganda tool by the American Government in the case of Uday and Qusay? Secretary of Defence Rumsfeld told the world's media he felt comfortable with his decision to release the images. 'I feel it was the right decision and I'm glad I made it,' Rumsfeld said, before adding that the people of Iraq had 'been waiting for confirmation' that Uday and Qusay were dead (Rumsfeld cited in Ringle 2003).

Indeed, publication of the dramatic and shocking photos occurred simultaneously around the world, and media organisations in most countries carried a version of them. Yes, they had some news value—importance, consequence, drama, conflict, and death—and the Iraqi people had a material interest in knowing the fate of the long-feared Hussein brothers. But for the rest of the world there's an element of curiosity and voyeurism attached to seeing the images. An editorial in a German newspaper summed up this argument in terms of the respect our culture normally affords to the dead: 'We're talking about human dignity ... independent of [their] crimes ... the display represents a violation of the basic principles of the civilised world' (editorial in the *Frankfurter Rundschau* cited in Ringle 2003).

Another common ethical dilemma arose with the capture of Uday and Qusay's father Saddam several months later. The American military commanders could hardly contain their glee—'We got him' they announced to the media in Baghdad (Griffith, Jones, Coorey, and wire services 2003). The media wanted pictures of the captured Iraqi leader and the American military obliged. He was shown having a medical examination, and having swabs taken from his mouth, used for DNA testing to prove he was the real Saddam, the military said (Griffith et al., 2003). But did the Americans need to humiliate the former dictator by showing him being medically examined? We feel that the ethics of reporting during wars and military conflict are so important that we've dedicated a whole chapter in this book to examining the issues raised in more detail.

Fault lines

In peacetime, as in war, there are daily occurrences in news reporting that can have an impact on the lives of subjects and audiences due to the editorial decision to cover a particular story in a certain way. One of our central concerns in this book is to demonstrate just how often such dilemmas arise and importantly, how seemingly singular, and often random events, can be traced back to the ethical issues identified in the following chapters.

The cases discussed in this book, and many others like them, represent what we call the major fault lines in journalism today. Think of fault lines as being like the fissures in the ground caused by earth tremors; some are quite mild, leaving cracks that are hardly noticeable; others can be quite strong, with almost earthquake intensity. The latter can cause massive structural damage, such as the fall-out from the case of the serial fabricator and plagiarist Jayson Blair in 2003, which shook one of the world's most respected newspapers, the *New York Times*, so hard that the masthead nearly crumbled. This case also illustrates the fact that once a fault line is opened up, it very rarely, if ever, heals completely. A year after his sacking, Jayson Blair released a book, *Burning Down My Master's House*, in which he describes cocaine abuse, PR operatives exchanging sexual favours for favourable mentions, and his own attempted suicide. The contents of the book were so explosive that the *NYT*'s senior editors were once again forced into damage control. They were quoted as saying that Blair's book 'does not merit much attention', and 'ends up spewing imaginary blame in all directions' (Bone 2004). Blair's book is worth reading; it is a strong cautionary tale for young reporters.

The most problematic schism, the deepest fissure and the widest crack, is perhaps the fault line at the centre of the professional world views of journalists, reporters and editors. It is along this particular fault line that the most pressing of ethical issues in journalism today are most obviously and openly expressed. As you will see from chapter 3, the fault lines in journalism are the ongoing processes of contradiction, resolution, and change. The fault lines also represent a continuum along which the various social, moral, and ideological attitudes of reporters and editors might lie. On one side of this fault line lie the ideals of the 'fourth estate' (Schultz 1994, 1998) and on the other, the economic and social relations of the news commodity (Hirst 2000; McChesney 2000; McChesney & Scott 2002; Oakham 1998). This particular fault line represents a central contradiction in the way most reporters and editors see the world and it is manifest as the public interest versus the profit motive. It is a dialectical relationship between the *idea* that good journalism is about reporting matters in the public interest, and the *reality* of a global and monopolistic group of interlocking and competing business interests whose product is 'the news' (Hirst 1997a,

2001, 2003). Often this fault line is expressed as a paradox, an apparent contradiction between the influence of journalism on one hand, and 'widespread attack' from politicians, the public, and even journalists themselves on the other (Hargreaves 2003, p. 2).

The fault lines in journalism manifest themselves every day in a million small decisions about what to write about, how to write it and whether it goes on the front page or gets spiked. The sub-editors at the *Weekend Australian* must have been thinking something along these lines when they gave a story the headline 'History's fault line' (Jackson 2003a). Sally Jackson's piece was about how reporters had to revise their stories about the looting of the Baghdad museum during the 2003 Iraq War. When the US marines first got to Baghdad a major international story broke about the alleged looting of the city's famous museum. It turned out it didn't happen quite that way: 'While there was stealing, the bulk of the ancient collection had been safely squirreled away in a secret vault' (Jackson 2003a).

On the same weekend the *Australian*'s editorial highlighted the contradictions in the Federal Government's attempts to once again re-align national media policy. Given the editorial was in one of Rupert Murdoch's papers, you can read between the lines when the editorialist writes: 'We want the world's best media, but lock out some of the world's great media companies. We want diversity, but it's illegal to set up another free-to-air television network' ('Media Policy is Still a Shambles' 2003). The editorial ends by arguing that Murdoch's (then) Australian company, News Limited, should be allowed to purchase and manage television stations in markets where it already has newspaper interests. This passage once again highlights the contradictions and fault lines: 'Perhaps it's more comfortable for some to process media policy through the magnifying glass of the supposed power of media moguls—as if they aren't answerable to their readers and viewers every day of the week' ('Media Policy is Still a Shambles' 2003). Can you spot the genius of this argument? The power of media giants like Murdoch is not real, it is only 'supposed'. The real power, according to this self-serving argument, is with 'readers and viewers'. We will be driving several truckloads of arguments and cases down that particular fault line. Only a couple of months later, the Murdoch-owned Fox network in the USA was in court attempting to sue a writer for using the words 'fair and balanced' in a book title. Why? Because Fox claims to have copyrighted the words, and also claims that their use in a satirical book would devalue them (Goldenberg 2003). The irony was not lost on Goldenberg. She reported that while the Fox cable network claims to be 'fair and balanced', it has a reputation as being home to a boots-and-all, right-wing commentariat: 'The vehemence of the network's attachment to the phrase may come as a surprise to some viewers. The channel has been enthusiastic in its support of the Bush Administration and America's past two wars' (Goldenberg 2003).

How to use this book

The purpose of this book is to position the arguments about fault lines and the philosophical traditions in which ethics are usually discussed within an overall theoretical framework. A framework that we think will help you both as a student and as a working reporter. A framework that provides you with the analytical skills and sound arguments for ethical decision-making. Within these pages you will find a critique of some competing and complementary ethical philosophies and the case for an holistic approach, which we have broadly defined as the dialectic of ethics following the work of American journalism scholar John C. Merrill (1989). Each general and specific argument is assessed using the dialectical method and then measured through its application to specific cases from Australia and around the globe. We hope that the arguments, and the case studies, will provide material for you to consider, and to debate with your classmates, your reporter friends, and with anyone who wishes to either attack, or defend, a particular incident as either ethical or unethical. Just remember that journalism ethics is hardly ever black and white, but rather varying shades of grey. Throughout this book we'll be using many examples of ethical conflict to illustrate our arguments and in case studies for discussion. International cases will dominate the arguments at the beginning of each chapter, and Australian incidents will dominate the case studies.

There is one certainty about the subject of ethics in journalism: There's always plenty to talk about. As we were writing this book, ethical issues were occurring in the media on almost a daily basis—from the justification of the 2003 Iraq War, its reporting and aftermath, to issues of chequebook journalism, trial by media, and invasion of privacy. There are constant arguments about cases of alleged misbehaviour by reporters, editors, and media proprietors. In this book we've tried to demonstrate that arguments and cases are linked and that to best examine individual cases, we first have to understand the arguments. As we develop a better understanding of past and recent cases, the more we are able to argue and debate the merits, or demerits, of a particular ethical question.

Arguments and cases carries a series of arguments and examples that illustrate the contradictions in the ways journalism is practised in the English-speaking capitalist democracies and offers some guidance in negotiating the fault lines in ethics.

We have chosen the title carefully and deliberately and the logical order, arguments *and then* cases, reflects the way in which we believe that working reporters, editors, and students of journalism can best develop their own thinking about ethical issues and fault lines. The process of becoming and being a reporter is also a process of lifelong learning. Our ideas, attitudes, and knowledge are constantly developing in a cycle that educational theorists call 'action learning'. Very simply, this is the process of adapting and changing our behaviour in response to our experiences of and in the world around us (Bunning 1991). Action learning involves a circular, or spiral, process of thinking about how to do something, doing the task, reflecting on our actions, and then another round of doing and so on. Such a method is almost intrinsic to journalism, as well as being the foundation of journalism education because news reporting represents what Etienne Wenger calls a 'community of practice'. This is not a difficult concept to grasp; it basically means a group of people involved in a common purpose (in our case producing the news) 'who share a concern, a set of problems, or a passion about a topic'. Members of this community learn by interacting 'on an ongoing basis' (Wenger, McDermott et al. 2002, p. 4). In this way learning—the gaining of new knowledge and insight—relies on a combination of both theory and practice and the application of one to the other.

Each chapter is structured in such a way that it mirrors this logic. First of all, you are invited to read, consider, and debate the contexts and arguments put in the essay that opens each chapter. Second, you are asked to reflect on the real-life cases that we've chosen to illustrate the main themes of each section. Finally, to reinforce the arguments we invite you to put yourself into the situation with some provocative questions about the principles, arguments, and context of each case. Since the case studies involve actual reported events, we have drawn on the media coverage of the time for the background. After all it is *what* the reporter chose to report and *how* they chose to report it that gives rise to the ethical dilemma. The questions at the end of each case study run the range of differing opinions on the various issues, and as such don't necessary reflect the opinions of the authors. In most of the chapters there are scenarios for you to consider individually, or in a group. Some are loosely based on the authors' experiences, while others were developed from fictitious ethical dilemmas suggested by QUT journalism students as part of their ethics course in 2004.

We believe it is important for tertiary journalism students to consider ethical dilemmas they may face in the future while still at university, where they can weigh up the merits of each case and arrive at a logical conclusion.

We believe you should have developed an ethical framework for how you will conduct yourself as a journalist before you do too many major journalism assignments as part of your degree and certainly before you enter the media workforce. Once you are *in the media* you will need to make ethical decisions quickly. Rarely will you have time to reflect for too long on the various competing aspects of an ethical dilemma. In the classroom you need to take an ethical position on each issue under discussion, and be prepared to defend it. As you'll see time and again through this book, there are never black and white answers to ethical dilemmas. If there were, then they wouldn't be dilemmas. In each instance you need to weigh up the pros and cons (using the various tools and methods we discuss in the following pages) and reach a decision on the information before you—much as you will once you join the media workforce. Don't be afraid to express your opinion.

In most Australian university journalism courses, media ethics are usually taught using a combination of historical critique and case studies (Sheridan Burns 1995; Richards 2003); even the occasional hypothetical (Sheridan Burns 1994). This approach, which follows the principles of problem-based learning (Sheridan Burns 1996, 1997), allows both personal and critical reflection on the development of first principles and the discussion of topical issues taken from current media practice.

In this book we adopt a combination of these approaches and begin by looking at a philosophical system (dialectics) and ways of examining ethical dilemmas. This philosophical overview and critical methodology will then be linked to a series of case studies taken from recent stories in the media. By examining the case studies in the light of a framework for thinking about ethics and a careful assessment of historical precedents, we can begin to argue about, and discuss the validity of, different systems in a contemporary context.

As you read through this book and discuss the case studies you will soon begin to realise that there are no simple solutions to ethical dilemmas in the media. At all times editors, reporters, subs, and producers all need to be aware of both the practical and the philosophical issues. We certainly advocate a familiarity with both approaches in preparing for the privilege and responsibility that comes with ethical editorial decision-making.

This introduction has set out how *arguments and cases* can be used in journalism programs to enhance the learning of ethics. In this section we explained the structure of the book and the purpose behind each chapter. The central themes of the book are noted, though not discussed in detail to illustrate two fundamental points:

The first is that the news and information media is a complex and contradictory mix of institutions and social relations, each of which generates many pressures on journalists. From time to time this causes fault lines to appear in the way reporters think about things. This shakes things up a bit and there's change. This introduces the central element of the emotional dialectic of journalism, which is discussed in the following chapters. Dialectics is a system of thinking derived from the Latin word *dialectica*, meaning logic (Williams 1989, p. 106). The dialectic is also the elemental process of contradiction, synthesis, and change—which basically means that from time to time, the news media tends to get dragged in all sorts of interesting but unpredictable directions.

This leads to the second major point that the culture of the newsroom and hence how journalists think about the world (including ethics) is influenced by events that go on in the 'real world'. The process of gathering, writing, and publishing the news is a process of social interaction. This necessarily involves journalists in a range of contradictory and sometimes difficult social relationships with individuals, organisations, populations, and ideas (Williams 1989, p. 106). This is also a form of dialectics: a process of contradiction, combination, and resolution, a force that shapes both ideas and our material world—the social conditions which make humans what we are today (Bullock & Trombley 2000, pp. 222–3).

THE DIALECTIC IN JOURNALISM:

ETHICS AND PHILOSOPHY

Objectives

When you have read and discussed this chapter you should be familiar with the following ideas and methods:

- An understanding of why ethics is important in journalism.
- An understanding of how we are using the terms 'dialectic' and 'dialectics'.
- Familiarity with some of the important philosophical trends and thinking around journalism ethics.
- An ability to engage in practical reasoning and critical reflection about arguments, cases, and issues in journalism ethics.
- The application of theory and philosophy to the practical tasks of thinking and acting ethically.

Introduction: Contradictions in journalism

This chapter introduces the study of ethics in general, and media ethics in particular by introducing and explaining the framing system we've adopted in the text—the application of dialectics and the dialectic to a study of journalism ethics. We begin the chapter with an explanation of the constant process of dialectical motion and change within journalism and the idea that ethics lies across one of the major fault lines in journalism. The critical argument here is about the contradiction between the principles of the public good and journalism practised within a free-market economic model (Wayne 2003). In other words it is about the very real contradiction between the theory and practice of ethics in journalism. This introduces the central idea that ethics should be considered as part of a set of social relations that govern the way news is gathered, written, and published. When you've read this section, read the two case studies and see if you can identify the dialectic in action.

A number of standard philosophical distinctions are made and illustrated in this chapter, including those between normative and descriptive philosophical methods—between duties and obligations on the one hand, and between intrinsic good and consequentialist good on the other. The growing field of virtue ethics is also briefly examined. This section establishes the baseline on which the rest of the book rests. In subsequent chapters you will be asked to consider some of these principles in relation to specific case studies and at the end of this chapter is a series of tasks to get you started on this process. There is also a section on practical reasoning, which will help you to work out your own ethical position in relation to issues that you might confront as a journalist.

Why we need a philosophy of ethics

As we will see in the case studies at the end of the chapter, ethical dilemmas do not just occur in single, remarkable moments, such as the night Princess Diana died, or in a character weakness like former US President Bill Clinton's lust for a particular young intern. Some fault lines can take decades to form and one of these longer-term pressure points is the so-called 'Information Revolution'. The information super-highway is taking us into the age of multimedia, while virtual reality and the convergence of newsroom technologies are having a huge impact on journalism (Pavlik 2003). Their impact is not only on the business models for modern media, and on the bottom line of profitability, on staffing structures, and newsroom workloads. They are also having an effect on the very definition of who (and what) is a journalist and on how news is delivered into our homes. The 'Information Revolution' also brings with it a new set of problems, and these pressures create new fault lines, some we haven't even thought of yet (Hargreaves 2003, p. 18). We'll be addressing these in chapter 11.

At the same time the world is facing major environmental, economic, scientific, and political problems. We only have to recall recent events, like the 11 September 2001 attacks on the World Trade Centre buildings in New York, or the bomb blasts in Bali in October 2002 and Madrid in March 2004, to begin grasping the enormity of the international social, political, and economic questions confronting us. The issues of famine, pollution, terrorism, war, inequality, and poverty cannot be solved unless we have access to vast amounts of information and are able to process it in logical ways. The news media plays a crucial role in this process. Human societies must cooperate to find and implement solutions. We expect to have access to accurate information on which to base political and social decisions on things that affect us. We expect the news media to provide this information, but in the global crises we face today, people are constantly asking: 'Is the news media doing a good job?' Given that we rely so heavily on the news media to keep us informed, we have a right to ask: 'Can the media respond effectively?' As we shall see, this is both an immediate question and an issue of history and philosophy.

Many people today, from students to factory workers and chief executives, are questioning the media's role in our public and political life. British journalist and academic Ian Hargreaves (2003) describes it as a public crisis in media confidence. In the end it matters to all of us whether or not the news media provides a true and useful picture of the world around us. We rely on its information to make decisions in all sorts of ways—from what to wear each day (weather reports) to how to vote. If the news media doesn't get the story right, the impact on the lives of many people could be great, not to mention catastrophic.

This may seem like a harsh introduction to a chapter about philosophy, but at the core of the news media's ability to get it right is a question of ethics. A reporter's ability to tell the truth, to be accurate, to be fair, and to act without fear or favour are all affected by everyday decisions that are often related to what we call journalism ethics.

For example:

- Would you accept a bribe? What would you consider a bribe? A free lunch, theatre tickets, a bottle of wine, insider tips on the share market?
- Would you turn a blind eye to police bashing a suspect if you thought s/he was guilty of a serious crime, like child abuse?
- Would the emotion of a murder trial, or your sympathy for the families of victims, cloud your judgment about how a story is reported?
- Would you always give sources from different ethnic, racial, and religious backgrounds the same amount of space and credibility in your reporting?
- Would you secretly tape an interview with a corrupt official because you think the story is more important than revealing you are a reporter?

Whatever your answer to these questions, you need to consider the arguments, and review the case studies in this book. As you read the text, you will find the tools, and gain the confidence to explore the relationship between practical and philosophical concepts of ethics. These issues are bound up within the professional ideology of journalism, and the associated issues of quality reporting, truth, objectivity, fairness, accuracy, democracy, citizenship, and the social role of the news in our society.

One central concern of this book, and an idea that has stood the test of time in relation to the new media, is the idea of 'freedom'. What is meant by the famous, and often abused slogan 'freedom of the press'? One common belief is that freedom of the press is meaningless unless it encompasses the freedom of 'ordinary people to receive full and fair information on all issues that are likely to affect their lives and their interests' (Belsey & Chadwick 1992, p. 5). This issue will be taken up in some detail in the following chapter.

It is the media's pursuit of this noble aim—to process, publish, and broadcast useful, accurate, and balanced information—that begins to draw together the strands of the argument presented in the following pages. In this chapter we have chosen to start with some philosophical principles and concepts, the theories that underpin any practical demonstration of ethics in the newsroom.

A note about the dialectic and emotional attitudes

Throughout this book we often mention the dialectic and its operation in journalism. We also write frequently about emotional attitudes and the ideas that journalists hold in their heads and which inform their work in news reporting. Before we go any further, we need to define and explain our use of these terms.

What is the dialectic?

Like much of the theoretical work underpinning a study of journalism ethics, the concept of the dialectic is a very old one. Raymond Williams (1989) traced it back to the Greek philosopher Plato (427–347 BC), and noted that it has been used in modern philosophical discourse since the fifteenth century. Harsh Narain (1973, pp. 1–25) disputes Williams's attribution to Plato, though he agrees the dialectic is almost as old as philosophy itself. The word dialectic originally stood for logic and systematic thinking; later it came also to mean the process of contradiction and resolution between conflicting sets of ideas. In modern European philosophy the roots of the dialectic as a method of reasoning can be traced to the philosopher Immanuel Kant (1724–1804), and later to Georg Hegel (1770–1831), who hypothesised that the inherent contradictions between an idea and its opposite would be resolved at a higher level of meaning. It was in the hands of German philosopher Hegel that the concept of the dialectic came to refer to the principles of contradiction, and constant tension between competing ideas or social forces. What Kant, Hegel, and later Karl Marx believed possible using the concept of the dialectic was to 'make sense of the connection between the material world and consciousness, in both its theoretical and practical forms' (Hunt 1993, p. 6).

According to the philosophy of dialectics, everything tends to clash and merge with its opposite (the 'unity of opposites'). Development and change is everywhere in nature, and in society. Dialectically, the development of nature and human discourse proceeds by the process of an idea (thesis) conflicting with its opposite (antithesis) to produce a new idea which combines elements of the previous ideas (synthesis), which in turn produces a new thesis, and the process begins again. For Hegel, and later for Karl Marx (1818–83), the dialectic was a way of understanding the processes of natural development, and the processes of change in human history (Bullock & Trombley 2000, p. 222; Hunt 1993). For Kant the philosophy of 'pure reason' could resolve the apparent contradictions between human beings (nature) and their metaphysical selves (their intelligence or spirit). In his important work on the dialectic, *Foundations of the Metaphysics of Morals* (published in 1785), Kant argued that on one side there is 'freedom of will' and on the other the 'laws of nature'. He believed that the contradiction could be resolved if it was assumed that both freedom and determination are in essence the same thing. He wrote that 'there is not the least contradiction between a thing in appearance … being subject to certain [natural] laws of which it is [at the same time] independent' (Kant 1959, p. 76).

Merrill's dialectic of journalism

The first theoretician to introduce the dialectic into the study of journalism was the American scholar John C. Merrill (1989) in *The Dialectic in Journalism*. In this text Merrill writes of the 'triadic movement that pushes thought forward and to higher levels through the recognition of flux and the merger of conflicting concepts'. According to Merrill, journalism is filled with such concepts needing reconciliation, two of the chief among them being 'freedom' and 'responsibility'. Merrill argues that in a debate about journalistic ethics, the notion of freedom is in contradiction to, and clashes with, the idea of responsibility, and the synthesis is a new ideology: social responsibility in journalism. This interpretation of the new synthesis is of course itself open to debate, challenge, and eventual mutation into something else. One of the key ideas we are keen to generate through this text is to ask: What is the next synthesis? Or, put another way: What are the forces and ideas that will challenge and eventually overturn the ideal of 'responsibility' in journalism? Is it, for example, the notion of 'accountability'?

The reason we can pose these questions, rather than think that 'responsibility' is the end of the line, is that one important aspect of the dialectic is that no contradiction between opposing ideals is permanent. At each stage of synthesis, resolution creates a new conflict, a new set of contradictions, and the inevitable further clash of ideals and ideas.

The contradictory elements of any dialectic in journalism will necessarily revolve around social issues, each impacting on news media ethics. Merrill emphasises changes in ideas driving a change in practice, and the philosophical heart of his dialectic in journalism is Aristotle's idea of the 'Golden Mean'. That is between two extremes there lies a more reasonable and acceptable middle path, one that avoids the excesses of timidity and recklessness. The application of the 'Golden Mean' to debates around ethics implies that the resolution of the conflict lies in a synthesis that is somewhere in the middle, between the two extremes. We can see this in how Merrill attempts to solve the contradiction between the individual freedoms that news workers enjoy and the need for some form of social control over the news media. In Merrill's synthesis it is responsible journalism that takes a middle way, through a process of gentle reform, rather than massive upheaval, or revolution.

The dialectic: Idealism versus materialism

In Merrill's account, the dialectic clash between two ideals creates the triadic movement in journalism, and we argue that this as an idealist philosophy based on Kant's and Hegel's conceptions of the dialectic. Idealism is the theory that the only things that can really exist are mental constructs—ideas (Narain 1973, p. 26). Hegel's eighteenth century idealism, articulated in his books *Phenomenology of Mind* and *Philosophy of Nature*, centred around the notion that there has only ever been one all-encompassing mind, or spirit, and that our individual thoughts are dependent fragments (Bullock & Trombley 2000, p. 412). Narain (1973, p. 29) quotes from *Philosophy of Nature*: 'God has two revelations, as nature and as spirit, and both manifestations are temples which He fills and in which He is present'. Of course, as true dialecticians, we would expect that this thesis is itself challenged by its opposite, or antithesis.

The antithesis of idealism is the philosophical tradition of materialism, or dialectical materialism, developed by two more German philosophers who both studied the work of Hegel. Karl Marx and Friedrich Engels extended the scope of dialectics to the natural world and to the formation and transformation of human society (Bullock & Trombley 2000, p. 222). According to a materialist dialectic, gradual quantitative changes will generally lead to a qualitative (revolutionary) change. Further, the unity of any synthesis is inherently unstable, leading to new contradictions and further dialectic development. Marx and Engels argued that historically and empirically measurable changes, such as between modes of production—from slavery to feudalism, and from feudalism to capitalism—were the result of cumulative changes brought about by the clash of economic, social, and political forces. In their view this clash was based on the existence of antagonistic social classes and real social forces, not just a clash of ideas, and ideals (Callinicos 1995, p. 101). From a materialist perspective the important clashes in the world are the 'fettering of the productive forces by the relations of production', and 'the class struggle between exploiters and exploited' (Callinicos 1995, p. 102). We can apply this analysis to journalism to demonstrate that the major contradiction, the fault line, in the news media today is based on the relations of production in the newsroom—that is, how the news commodity is produced (see chapter 4). Briefly, what drives the development of a dialectic in journalism is not a clash between ideals (freedom and responsibility) but a clash of material forces (Wayne 2003). The contradiction in the news media is the gulf between the need for the news commodity to sell and produce a profit for the owning class, and the supposedly democratic function of the news media to provide information to the public without fear or favour (Hirst 2000, 2003). These issues are taken up at many points throughout this text, particularly in chapter 4, which covers the political economy of ethics.

An emotional attitude

In 'Why I Write', the British journalist and author George Orwell (1984, p. 9) says that most journalists and writers will develop a world view, an outlook on life from which they 'will never completely escape'. Orwell calls this an 'emotional attitude' to the world around the individual. It is fabricated from all the social relationships that a person is involved in, including their working life. The term 'emotional attitude' is perhaps synonymous with what others have called the 'world view', or the 'ideology' of journalists. We like to use the term 'emotional attitude' because it evokes the important idea that the way we think and what we think are very clearly linked to our human emotions. This is doubly important in a discussion about ethics, which involves important emotions like empathy, disgust, love, respect, hate, and fear.

All reporters have an emotional attitude towards what they consider to be 'news' events. This attitude will vary depending on the experiences of each individual. It will also have to do with their social background, how they were brought up, their education, and their feelings towards other groups in society. News workers today will display a range of emotional attitudes. It might be no more than an uneasy feeling about some ethical dilemma they might face, or it could be as strong questioning, or understanding the social relations that weave around and through journalism. The fault lines in emotional attitudes of journalism today centre around questions of ethics: the 'right' way to gather news; the values of 'accuracy' and 'objectivity'; notions of 'bias' versus public service; and the impact of 'infotainment' genres on 'serious' news values. These are the fault lines, or what John Merrill (1989) calls the 'antinomes', the contradictory positions and ideas within journalism.

The emotional attitudes that reporters and editors hold, and which colour their view of news, are created in a dialectic, the interplay of opposing ideas (Merrill 1989) and opposing social forces (Hirst 2001). Thus we can talk about an 'emotional dialectic' (Hirst 2003), the fluid, contested, and challenging continuum of ideas, attitudes, and ideologies that reporters and editors hold and work within. The emotional dialectic is the process that determines a person's view of the world and forms their consciousness. In news media, the 'interplay' of opposing forces—the emotional dialectic—carries over into the news agenda and into decisions about how and why a story should be reported. It might even have a direct impact on where the news item is published. This is what co-author Martin Hirst (2003) in his doctoral thesis called the 'dialectic of the front-page'.

For the purposes of arguments and cases in journalism ethics, an ideology of journalism (see chapter 2) is best understood as the sum total of individual and shared assumptions, and emotional attitudes that make up an informal, but powerful common sense approach to life. As Paul Scott argues, it is these common sense and seemingly mainstream views that can often 'legitimise and privilege' some ideologies over others. Scott argues that 'through omission, neglect or ridicule—other ideas, lifestyles, or behaviours can either be marginalised or become part of the spectacle of the bizarre' (2001, p. 137).

It stands to reason that reporters and editors, like every other citizen, have a range of opinions about many issues. In the case of journalists, the important additional point is that these attitudes have a direct bearing on the work they do. As George Orwell (1984) argued in 'Why I Write', the emotional attitudes, or the ideology of any reporter, or writer, will determine their approach to news, current affairs, politics, history, and the affairs of state. By and large, these attitudes will be the product of their age and therefore subject to change according to the epoch. By linking the concept of ideologies to the dialectic, we can account for the ways in which old ideas and practices of journalism might be challenged by new forces. Therefore we can argue that at any given time in history, there is a strong relationship between the dominant ideology in journalism and the economic forces that exert their social control over news production (see chapter 4). Raymond Williams (1989, p. 156) concludes that the ideological content of what we call news both expresses and supports the social values of those powerful interests who control the 'economic conditions of production'.

In order to fully understand and appreciate the emotional dialectic of journalism and its relationship to media ethics we have to question not just the words and the images of the news text itself, but also the social relations under which the text was produced. Michael Schudson (1997, pp. 7–22) outlines several useful approaches to the study of news as work under the following headings:

- the political economy of news
- the social organisation of news work
- textual and cultural approaches; including the techniques of content and discourse analysis.

You will find that we have adopted, modified, and taken advantage of all these methods throughout this text. We believe that an interdisciplinary approach such as this is the most appropriate way to discuss ethics in journalism. We must understand the philosophical roots of the ideas and concepts, we must understand how the news product is produced and the conditions of its production. We must also understand the social context in which the news is both produced and consumed and the significance of embedded (ideological) meanings.

Theories and origins of ethics

There are many variations in theories and systems of ethical thought, discussion, and, ultimately, decision-making. A broad distinction can be made between systems that simply describe situations, and those that end up codifying a list of rules, recommendations, or proposals. The 'descriptive' methods are those which merely lay out the facts for our consideration. They describe a situation and invite us to make up our own minds, or to imitate the good behaviour as it is described. On the other hand, systems of ethics that are 'normative' are generally ones that define 'good' and 'bad' behaviour and demand that we stay within the rules and boundaries (norms) of good behaviour. Normative systems are also sometimes described as 'evaluative', or 'prescriptive' (Bullock & Trombley 2000, pp. 594–5).

It is fairly obvious then that Codes of Ethics in the media might usually be normative: they set out in reasonably precise terms the 'rights' and 'wrongs' of ethical behaviour. One final point about normative systems—they tend to be socially determined. That is, the standards and values prescribed in the Code tend to be those of a particular group, or are based on standards of behaviour that are broadly acceptable to 'mainstream' society (whatever that is defined as). In journalism and the news media, most Codes of Ethics, Charters of Editorial Independence, and other written instruments of classifying ethics are said to be normative. They are systems that recommend, and sometimes enforce, the standards that are deemed valid by the drafters of the Code.

In this section we ask and answer the questions:
- Where do ethics come from?
- Are there universal principles from which ethics can be derived and applied?

There is no doubt that debates about 'how we live' are as old as human society itself and in fact are perhaps one of the defining characteristics of such societies. The grandson of the great Chinese philosopher Confucius (500 BC) is said to have beaten Aristotle (400 BC) by a century to the articulation of one famous dictum of ethics—the so-called 'Golden Mean' (Christians, Rotzoll & Fackler 1991, p. 12).

Anthropologists have concerned themselves with examining the ethical systems of primitive, small-scale societies in an attempt to find a universal prescription for human behaviour. Whatever we may think of this project it is obviously important to understand how our earliest ancestors coped with such issues as: Who has the right to live, the right to wealth, and to power? More importantly, as philosophers and as journalists we have to ask the follow-up question: Why?

The earliest written records of ethical debate are about 5000 years old—developed in Mesopotamia, Egypt, and the Hebrew world. It is therefore no surprise that ethical traditions are often historically associated with religious movements, churches, and philosophies. For example, Hindu, Buddhist, Taoist, Jewish, Christian, and Islamic thinkers have all proposed life codes that suggest ethical ways of existing in harmony with other human beings, often in a relationship with a spiritual world. Each poses and answers in its own way questions such as:
- How can I know what is right?
- What is the ultimate criterion for right action?

- Why should I do what is right?
- What sanctions and/or punishments should apply for transgressions of the moral code?

All of these questions are applicable in a study of journalism ethics, at both a philosophical and a practical level. For example, most Codes of Ethics contain some type of enforcement clause that includes penalties for non-compliance. These issues are taken up in a later chapter about Codes and Charters in the newsroom.

We have prepared the following very brief outline of the major themes and divisions that have been formally labelled to mark out territory in the debate about ethical decision-making. The list is roughly divided into what we term 'idealist' theories (based on the individual) and 'materialist' (based on social relations). After examining this list you will see that elements from many entries are still relevant today and inform several positions in the discussion. Where possible we have included examples that relate to ethical questions we continue to ask each other and society. If you want to know more about various philosophical trends and historical debates you can read some of the sources we've referenced in this chapter.

Deontological versus teleological systems of ethics

We want to begin this discussion by continuing with the concepts of contradiction and dialectics in arguments about ethics. The first distinction to be made is between deontological and teleological systems of ethical thought and decision-making. Deontology is primarily concerned with obligations and duties that are imposed upon individuals. Teleological ethics is primarily concerned with consequences. This 'obligations' versus 'consequences' contradiction then leads us to a discussion of the distinction between 'intention' and 'foresight'.

- Do we intend to always act in an ethical manner, in accordance with the duties and obligations (responsibilities) of being a journalist? A deontological approach is one that makes us always consider our actions ahead of any consequences.
- What do we intend our actions to achieve? This is a teleological approach in which we look at possible consequences, both positive and negative.
- Can we foresee any unethical consequences? In considering teleological questions, can we look ahead and predict both good and bad results of our actions?
- Can we predict outcomes before they happen? If we always behave ethically following the principles of deontology, can we apply a predictive teleology to double our chances of being ethically good?

Contemporary deontology

Deontology is derived from the Greek word *deon* meaning duty (Christians, Rotzoll & Fackler 1991, p. 14). Deontological systems of ethics are the dialectical opposite of teleological models. Deontology is concerned with moral duties, teleology with the consequences of our actions. Deontology is a prescriptive and normative approach to ethics that regards moral duties and good actions as 'self-evident and not necessarily derived from any higher, or more fundamental truths' (Bullock & Trombley 2000, p. 213).

A key aspect of deontological systems is their implication that we ought to live by moral rules, and that these rules should not be broken—even if better things may come from breaking them. In other words, unlike teleological, or 'goal-oriented' ethics, it is not the consequences of our actions, but their inherent moral value that should determine what we do (Hurst & White 1994, p. 10). Hence, we need to know how rules are to be framed, and what actions constitute a breach of these rules. The theories of Immanual Kant (whom we've already met) are often described as deontological. In Kant's schema there is a 'categorical imperative' derived from a universal law of freedom and there are no exceptions— for example, 'Do not lie', or 'Do not commit suicide'. Kantian ethics is then, quite clearly, a form of deontological ethics.

The formulation adopted by Kant in his manuscript, *Groundwork on the Metaphysics of Morals* (1785), is that all our actions should be 'willed without contradiction as a universal law' (Bullock & Trombley 2000, p. 108). Kant's system is prescriptive and therefore in the normative tradition, and it is overridden by the 'categorical imperative', and must have 'universal application' (Sanders 2003, p. 18). Further, the Kantian imperative implies that we should never treat people as a 'means to an end', but as an 'end in themselves'. In other words, we should never take advantage of other people. This is crucial for journalistic ethics because it implies that reporters must not take advantage of people, or put them at risk just to get a story published or broadcast. Karen Sanders's (2003, p. 19) critique of Kantian ethics is that it leaves 'the moral significance of the emotions insufficiently explained'. We will come back to this point about reporters and their emotions when talking about the dialectics of journalism towards the end of this chapter.

Teleology and utility

The utilitarian model, most closely identified with John Stuart Mill, is the classic teleological model. It directs us to first know, and understand, all the possible consequences of our actions. This is obviously important in journalism, particularly in situations where the consequences of publishing, or broadcasting, a story can be life-threatening. A classic case of this model in practice was the apparent suicide in 2003 of former United Nations weapons inspector David Kelly in the wake of the heated confrontation between Britain's Blair Government and the British Broadcasting Corporation (BBC). BBC reporter Andrew Gilligan quoted an unnamed source as saying that the Prime Minister's office had 'sexed up' a report about Iraq's weapons of mass destruction to justify the 2003 US-led invasion of Iraq. The BBC had not identified Kelly as the source of the story (his employers—Britain's Ministry of Defence—did that), but the result was that Kelly was found dead with his wrists slashed (Bita 2003, p. 2). Could Andrew Gilligan have foreseen the consequence of his actions—David Kelly's death? We'll revisit this case in different contexts in later chapters.

The well-known English philosopher of the nineteenth century John Stuart Mill (1806–73) is credited with modifying, or at least articulating, the utility principle, first proposed by Jeremy Bentham (1748–1832). We know of J.S. Mill through the aphorism 'the greatest good for the greatest number of people'. J.S. Mill's work provides a handy guide to utilitarian action, which we can call the calculation of utility.

To calculate the consequences of your actions apply the following formula:
- First, 'in the most conscientious manner possible' (Christians, Rotzoll & Fackler 1991, p. 16) examine all possible consequences of all possible actions in a given situation.
- Second, work out how much good and how much harm are created through the pursuit of your various options.

- Third, follow the course that maximises the good, and creates the least amount of harm.

Mill's utility principle is altruistic—that is, it does not rely on us being motivated by an egoistic impulse to act in our own best interest. Instead, as individuals we are encouraged to act in pursuit of certain collective, or social, benefits. But this begs a further question: What things are good in themselves? Are you familiar with the Divinyls' song with the chorus, 'It's a fine, fine line between pleasure and pain'? It was the theme of a TV advertising campaign for Mylanta antacid in 2004. How do we reconcile pleasure for the many with pain for the few? How do we determine the greatest good for the greatest number? What do we do about those who fall outside these parameters?

To satisfy ourselves that we are on the right track at all, we need to look at the *content* and *context* of the pleasure/pain dichotomy. Hence we must begin putting our ethical considerations into a socially constructed framework. What feels good to one person may cause excruciating agony to another person with different sensibilities and thresholds. Ethical questions cannot be separated from questions of social structure, and therefore cannot be easily separated from questions of social control, or from institutions of power. We will come back to these questions in subsequent chapters.

The tradition of the social contract

It goes without saying that one of the primary directives for journalists is to honour their contract with readers, viewers, and listeners—to give them the truth, the facts and the context for the stories they report. The social contract implies that, at the level of ethical behaviour, morality is an implicit agreement we make with other human beings. In general terms a social contract implies an unwritten agreement that we will all behave responsibly towards each other (Bullock & Trombley 2000, p. 799). We do this voluntarily, in good faith, and in order to collectively gain a share of any benefits derived from human endeavours towards establishing and sustaining a healthy society. In ethical systems constructed on the basis of a social contract, we begin to get the first sense of a materialist ethic separated from the spiritual elements of the ancients and an infallible, or unquestioning, belief in the divine omnipotence of a God.

Bullock and Trombley (2000, p. 800) note that the argument around a social contract was an important weapon in ideological debates between an emergent secular system of nation states and the old feudal and religious social systems of sixteenth and seventeenth century Western Europe. Though the original proponents of this tradition—the philosophers Thomas Hobbes (1588–1679) and John Locke (1632–1704)—may themselves have been very religious in keeping with the social codes of their time, their work on developing new and relevant ethical and moral codes was taken up in the later debates, and dialectically pushed following generations of ethicists towards accounting for material circumstance, rather than God's will, in their explanation and prescriptions for behaviour in the social world.

This is an important development in philosophy because it begins to assume that human beings are capable of materialised thought and action *independent* of a higher authority. Karl Marx was an early writer in this tradition, and as noted earlier it was Marx who turned Hegel's view of dialectics on its head. This forms an important point of departure for the arguments presented in the rest of this book and requires some explanation. A key thought from Marx, and one that sets him apart from the Hegelians, is his belief that it is human action, not divine intervention, which makes the world go round. In particular, Marx argued that it is a human being's ability to work as an individual, and also to work collectively, which sets our societies apart from those of other animals on the planet. This might, at this point, seem a little obscure for a text about journalism ethics, but it is at the very core of our arguments and cases. As we demonstrate in following chapters, it is the ways in which reporters and editors go about their daily tasks in the newsroom—the social organisation of the news production process—that finally impacts upon and helps determine many ethical, and unethical, attitudes in the newsroom.

Rights-based ethics systems

The concept, if not the practice, of universal human rights is a core principle of most systems of ethics. 'Liberty, equality, fraternity' were the buzzwords of the most successful revolution in history. The eighteenth century overthrow of feudal theocracy for the bourgeois ethics of individualism, private property, and the rule of law laid the philosophical and ideological foundations for the growth of capitalism as the global system of economic and social organisation. Bourgeois laws, ethics, and systems of government have evolved into the market-driven mass societies we inhabit today. No revolution since has even come close to being so thorough, successful, and long-lived. As the power and influence of bourgeois philosophers grew in direct proportion to the economic and political power of their class from the eighteenth century through to the twentieth, so did the power of their arguments. Central to their world view was the separation of church and state. This new ruling class took over from the old feudal lords and began to take control of all the important national economies in the old world and the new. They moulded these economies and the systems of government that grew out of them to best suit their own financial and political interests.

One of their key propositions was that in a nation state, under a secular system of government, all citizens would have equal rights. One important contributor to this political theorising was John Locke who argued that these individual and collective rights included the preservation of life, a certain degree of personal liberty, the rights to health and to personal possessions, and a right to punish those who transgress. Similar ideals are coded into one of the founding documents of bourgeois rule, the American Declaration of Independence: 'life, liberty and the pursuit of happiness' (cited in Hurst & White 1994, p. 9).

The systems of ethics that base themselves on the exercise of certain rights can only function according to the rule that we should always respect the rights of other individuals. However, we need to ask and answer the following question before proceeding to a discussion of application: Can ethics and morals be based on rights, or are rights derived from more fundamental moral principles? In a very concrete sense what is the 'right to life'? Or, perhaps more applicably we should ask: What is the right to freedom of expression? Is it a right that everyone has regardless of its conflict with other 'rights', such as a 'right to peace and quiet'? In other words: Are rights universal, or relative?

Universal prescriptions about the value, sanctity, and application of human rights have some weight in Australian and international law. They are becoming increasingly important and incorporated into descriptions of ethical behaviour. For example, federal and state anti-vilification laws exist on the basis of Australia's signature on the International Covenant on Civil and Political Rights.

On the other hand, the Australian constitution, unlike the American, does not include a 'right' to freedom of expression. However, the Australian High Court has ruled that the constitution contains an 'implied' right to freedom of political speech. As we move forward in a new century, we need to address these questions in relation to changing the Australian constitution and in relation to such issues as what value we place on human rights and freedoms in the context of an ongoing threat of terrorism and war. Should the media, under circumstances of crisis, be prepared to suspend its freedom in the name of a more important cause—that of national security?

One line of argument suggests there might be contradictions and pitfalls associated with a rights-based approach to media ethics. For example, if people have a right not to be deceived, then deception in investigative journalism, even for results which would be for the general benefit of the public, would not be permitted at all (Belsey & Chadwick 1992, p. 11). In capitalist societies these issues are at the core of debates about ethics.

Rawls's veil of ignorance

It is axiomatic that there has to be fairness in the social contract if it is going to effectively hold any given society together (Christians, Rotzoll & Fackler 1991, p. 17). But how can we strike a fair bargain 'contract' in a world full of inequality? According to American ethicist John Rawls's so-called 'veil of ignorance' theory, to achieve this social cohesion it is necessary for people to divorce themselves from their social surroundings—for example, their sex, race, religion, or social and economic class. In other words, we have to believe that there are no social conditions, or relations, which establish a hierarchy, or structural inequalities between individuals.

We therefore have to imagine that we are all equal in order to behave ethically and equally to all individuals. We have to stand behind a veil of ignorance about a person's actual social standing, and important information about the situation is also notionally hidden (Hurst & White 1994, p. 12). From what we've said so far, you should be starting to see that the veil of ignorance idea is a subtle feature of many ethical systems, both deontological and teleological.

In an example given by Hurst and White, that of a reporter deciding whether or not they should do a 'death-knock' (where the journalist knocks on the door of the family home hoping for an interview about the loved one who is in the news because of a tragedy), the journalist would have to ignore their own self-interest (to get the story) in coming to a decision. In less theoretical terms than Rawls, Hurst and White call this 'putting oneself in someone else's shoes' (1994, p. 12). There are two principles that inform Rawls's theoretical curtain:

• Liberty is paramount and cannot be traded for possessions and/or wealth.
• Inequality in distribution of the social wealth is OK, if it acts to benefit the least advantaged party.

However, we think there is an important contradiction in Rawls's theory: we don't, unfortunately, live in the best of all possible worlds, one in which we can pretend not to know about racism, sexism, homophobia, economic inequality, and so on. Even more importantly, at one level all of us realise that there are many structural inequalities that exist in our everyday world. It is precisely these inequalities that determine social position: ethnicity, class, gender and assumed sexuality being just four of the most important ones. And it is precisely these inequalities that drive many people to become crusading journalists.

In our view, Rawls's veil of ignorance attempts to deny the validity of social ethics and the importance of social relations (especially relations of unequal power) in ethical reasoning. If we were to forget that we are reporters, with a job to do, it makes any ethical decision meaningless. It is OK to put yourself in someone else's shoes and imagine how they might feel, but as journalists we have to put some kind of situational context around our ethical thinking. We cannot ignore our role as a journalist. We can easily imagine situations where, as a reporter, you might be asked to write a story that will result in some harm to one or more people. If you were to simply put yourself in their position, it stands to reason that you wouldn't write the story. However, greater issues must be brought to bear. Is the story likely to result in some larger social good—an outcome that will benefit many more people than are hurt? Is the person whose reputation, or happiness, is compromised someone who deserves their fate because of some previous antisocial, illegal, or unethical behaviour? You will notice that these and similar questions are present in nearly all the case studies we'll present in later chapters. One thing that you will learn very quickly is that there is usually no black and white in journalism ethics, only those ever-present 'shades of grey'.

Universal versus relative ethics

In philosophical terms we can make the distinction between 'universal', and 'particular'. Something is universal if it has abstract properties and abstract relations with other things or ideas. For example, 'redness' is a universal value, while 'tomato' is particular (though it contains 'redness') (Bullock & Trombley 2000, p. 897). We can say then, that universal prescription is a form of normative and deontological ethics in which there is a prominent role for human reasoning about ethical judgments.

Universal prescription is perhaps the first attempt to locate the rationale for ethics in the material, rather than the spiritual, or idealist world. This is particularly the case when combined with 'realism', the idea that the real world can be understood as a series of verifiable, material facts (Bullock & Trombley 2000, p. 732). Universal prescription is a system that attempts to combine elements of Immanuel Kant's 'categorical imperative' with John Stuart Mill's 'utilitarianism'.

Relativism and universalism are, of course, contradictory and it is therefore difficult for one person to be at the same time a universalist and a relativist—at least not without causing him/herself a headache. According to the relativists, there are no universal truths, and all forms of morality are particular to specific social formations and cultures that are historically determined. For example, just because a statement holds true for you, here and now, does not mean it will be true for other people under different circumstances. Relativism is usually associated with cultural differences that exist over distances, and between various nations or societies (Bullock & Trombley 2000, p. 742). This leads relativists to advance the argument that we should not pass judgment on, nor should we attempt to change, the moral, social, and ethical values freely expressed in other cultures. By the same token, they should not interfere in our world either.

In other words, we might choose to do things one way, but if another individual or cultural group chooses a different way, it doesn't matter. In a relativist world there are no universals such as fundamental human rights.

To illustrate this point, let's consider a relativist argument that was adopted by Australian Prime Minister John Howard in August 2003 when an Indonesian court condemned convicted Bali bomber, Amrozi, to death by firing squad. Nearly all the Australian politicians interviewed about the issue backed the PM's position that he would not interfere in the Indonesian legal system's internal workings, nor would he seek a commuting of Amrozi's sentence. For John Howard, despite the fact that Australia fundamentally and universally opposes the death penalty, if, in this case, the Indonesian courts wanted to sentence Amrozi to death that would be OK by him. Only one federal Labor politician pointed out that the relativist argument in this case would come back to haunt Australia. Shadow Attorney-General, Duncan Kerr, argued that if an Australian citizen was subsequently sentenced to death in a country whose legal system was questionable, then the Australian Government and the Australian people would not be able to complain or intercede for clemency without sounding and looking like hypocrites. It didn't take long: in mid 2004 the first case involving an Australian sentenced to death for drug-trafficking in Thailand was reported by the media, in a very low-key way.

This question of relativity in ethics raises questions about practices that might be considered harmful in one society, but perfectly acceptable behaviour in another context. For example, there are laws in Australia against female circumcision, but in some societies (and indeed in some Australian communities) this practice has persisted, sometimes in secret, for strong religious and cultural reasons. Australian governments have taken an educational, rather than legalistic approach to the issue, though the practice has been outlawed in most states and territories. Since 1985 the World Health Organization has taken a universal approach and condemns the practice as an abuse of the human rights of women and children (Laurie 2003). In the context of an ethic of normative relativism Australians should not condemn those groups who wish to carry out this action in the belief that it is 'right' for their women. Conversely, our universalist approach to human rights for women would indicate we should condemn all cases of female circumcision. You can see that there is a fundamental clash here between concepts of a rights-based system and a position of cultural relativism.

On the one hand, women have the right to choose what to do with their own bodies, and the right not to have their bodies mutilated by others. On the other hand, the relativists would argue, we cannot condemn cultural rites, and religious practices we don't agree with, just because they're different. Is it fair to say that most of us don't feel quite so strongly about circumcision for male babies? It was once a common practice and routine for male babies born up to the late 1960s. Now it doesn't happen automatically in most births. But do we object so strongly to male circumcision in all circumstances?

Determinism versus free will

Determinism generally means a belief in an overriding causal law—that every event has a cause and effect. In a vernacular shorthand it boils down to something like 'for every action, there is an equal and opposite reaction'. For ethicists and political thinkers like J.S.

Mill, the law of determination is the 'most general and comprehensive of all the laws of nature' (Bullock & Trombley 2000, p. 217). As we noted above, the very nature of the dialectic implies a tension between what is predetermined (nature) and what is an act of free will (the human intelligence). It is an ethical dilemma that we cannot ignore. The argument about determinism in ethics says there is a causal explanation for everything that happens in the universe, hence we have no freedom of choice, and therefore we are not morally responsible for our actions. In other words, we cannot do other than what we do, because it is pre-determined for us, through nature. We might, for the sake of remembering, characterise the determinist position as 'the Devil made me do it!'

On the other hand, the free will argument is that moral decision-making is based on an assumption that individuals are responsible, and should therefore be held responsible, for what they freely choose to do. The concept of free will is very important in bourgeois ideologies and therefore, one could argue, central to any discussion of media ethics in a normative, capitalist society. If we are free to choose our actions, we must accept responsibility for their inherent moral value and the consequences that flow. As Bullock and Trombley note, 'determinism and free will seem, on the face of it, to be incompatible' (2000, p. 337). In our view the apparent contradiction between freedom and responsibility in journalistic practice (Merrill 1989), as characterised in the determinism versus free will debate, is crucial to an understanding of the fault lines in contemporary journalism theory and practice.

Social ethics

Christians et al. (1991, p. 23) mention social ethics as being the 'particular social context or a specific set of institutional arrangements' in which meaning is given to ethical decisions. In a social sense then, ethical judgments are therefore, 'woven into a set of obligations one assumes towards certain segments of society' (Christians, Rotzoll & Fackler 1991, p. 21). Our interpretation is slightly different and is set out in the following paragraph.

Society at any time sets the general moral standards, but always with reference to the dominant political/economic structures. Over time these standards are subject to change when they are put under various material and ideological pressures. This approach comes closest to satisfying our concern that all ethical decisions should be made with full knowledge of all the social conditions which might apply, or have some impact upon the decision or consequences for some or all of the actors concerned. Social ethics is not, strictly speaking, a *method* of ethics (in the sense that the principle of utility is a method), rather social ethics is a state of mind, an awareness of situation and context. Having adopted this approach we can use various methods to plot an ethical path.

Virtue theory

A virtue is described in the *Australian Concise Oxford Dictionary* (Moore 1997, p. 1532) as 'moral excellence; uprightness, goodness'. The dictionary also tells us that virtue is a 'good quality'.

Instead of asking 'What ought I do?' virtue theory asks, 'What kind of person should I be?' Virtue theory puts the ethical spotlight on characteristics that compose a 'good' individual, rather than the social consequences of our actions. In this tradition it is argued that a virtuous character will always act ethically.

Aristotle's ethical guide, the 'Golden Mean', is a good example of virtue theory, where moral virtue is the *mean* (or middle ground) between two extremes. Aristotle referred to virtues as 'dispositions' and believed they could be developed over time through education and repetition. Assuming, of course, that we are prepared to be rational and intelligent in our choice-making (Sanders 2003, p. 15). In Aristotle's case, the 'Golden Mean' is that space of comfort between excess and deficiency. For example, *courage* is the mean between *cowardice* and *temerity*. This process emphasises character over action, believing that actions are the result of innate attributes (Christians, Rotzoll & Fackler 1991, p. 12).

Andrew Belsey and Ruth Chadwick (1992) suggest that, while not necessarily being always temperate in their behaviour, particularly where the consumption of alcohol is concerned, a good journalist should display the positive virtues of 'fairness, truthfulness, trustworthiness and non-malevolence'. They then go on to ask whether this is in fact a good foundation for ethical behaviour because virtue might also be defined as respecting the rights of others or promoting the general good, both of which might conflict with what journalists actually do (1992, pp. 11–12).

John O'Neill (1992, pp. 19–20) suggests that the virtues of truth-telling, honesty, and integrity might be appropriate for media professionals. At the same time O'Neill recognises that the oft-cited journalistic virtue of 'objectivity', 'is often rejected by some of the best journalists of our day' (1992, p. 20). Indeed, we'll be returning to the problematic issue of objectivity at the conclusion of this chapter, and in subsequent chapters.

Finally, it is important to note a caveat on the idea of virtue ethics and Aristotle's 'Golden Mean', which is not a fixed capacity and can vary according to circumstances. Sanders (2003, p. 16) uses the example of a war correspondent who takes risks to get a story from the frontlines. Depending on the circumstances—the precautions taken, the news value of the story—one could imagine the reporter being either brave or stupid.

Is moral reasoning an adequate basis for media ethics?

There can be no doubt that a system of sustained moral reasoning is one fundamental requirement of a healthy society. The authors of an influential text from the 1980s that has been reprinted many times, *Media Ethics: Cases and Moral Reasoning* (Christians, Rotzoll & Fackler 1991), appear to adopt an almost theological approach to ethical issues, and we feel that in the secular years of the early twenty-first century this is a little out of date. However, a recent Australian text (Hendtlass & Nichols 2003) has firmly put itself into the Judaeo–Christian camp, and articulates what it describes as Christian normative principles:

- every situation, however grim, can be redeemed in the light of Jesus Christ;
- that people can be forgiven and can make a fresh start with God; and
- that the gospel both judges and liberates situations of repression or captivity.

Hendtlass & Nichols 2003, p. 71

While it is your freedom and your responsibility to work out your own position on this and other ethical frameworks, we believe that any situation in which dilemmas in media ethics are likely to arise will always be complicated by social and personal value systems. We generally refer to these value systems as ideologies, and in this text prefer to talk about emotional attitudes. We can add that everyone has one, and that every society also constructs a collective set of emotional attitudes around a hierarchy of beliefs and ideas. Hallin (1989) calls this inner core of ideologies the 'sphere of consensus'. Christians, Rotzoll, and Fackler (1991) suggest that we can never fully understand the situation of every individual, and their entire belief system. However, in a general sense, we can get an orientation to the values of our own society—at least to those that appear to form an uncontroversial consensus: 'No exhaustive list of the values held by participants is ever possible, but attention to them helps prevent us from basing our decisions on personal biases or unexamined prejudices' (Christians, Rotzoll & Fackler 1991, p. 10). As we have seen, George Orwell also believed that journalists and writers of every social and political persuasion should pay attention to their own value systems, particularly when writing about contentious issues:

> Everyone writes of them in one guise or another. It is simply a question of which side one takes and what approach one follows. And the more one is conscious of one's political bias, the more chance one has of acting politically without sacrificing one's aesthetic and intellectual integrity.
>
> Orwell 1984

These individual and collective value systems, which we share, and often disagree about, are the sum total of emotional attitudes held by individuals and groups. These are the ideologies that constitute the 'frame of reference' to help us make sense of the world around us. Ideologies are belief systems that constitute our way of viewing the world, a little like rose-coloured glasses. We must remember that the lens can be a distorting, as well as a clarifying, prism through which to view the world. In other words, the ideas in our heads can be true, or false (Williams 1989, p. 156). Ideologies are in our heads, but they are produced through the process of our interactions with the world around us—the social relations within which we exist on a daily basis. The nineteenth century German philosopher Friedrich Engels described the creation of ideologies thus: 'the material life-conditions of the persons inside whose heads this thought process goes on in the last resort determine the course of this process' (Engels, *Theses on Feuerbach*, cited in Williams 1989, p. 155). For news workers, the most important social relations are those that surround, shape, influence, and ultimately determine the ways in which we work. These social relations exist both within and outside the newsroom, and we cannot escape them.

In the context of clashing, or competing ideologies, Christians et al. insist that no decision can be justified without reference to an 'ethical principle' (1991 p. 11), but take a look at their examples of applying Aristotle's 'Golden Mean' to the questions of tobacco regulation and nuclear arms control. Can we say that the simple notion of 'virtue standing between two vices' has any real explanatory value in these cases? What would be the 'Golden

Mean' in relation to tobacco given that we know smoking is one of the major health concerns of the century? Could it be five a day, ten, fifteen? How many nuclear warheads would constitute a 'Golden Mean', and who should have control of them? Sometimes it seems there's no logic at all in such ethical dilemmas.

If this is not enough to throw doubt on this approach, perhaps you should consider the example that Christians, Rotzoll, and Fackler use themselves: 'There were slaves in [Aristotle's] Greece; Aristotle opted for treating them well and fairly but not for the radical change of releasing them altogether' (1991, p. 13).

Today we would condemn Aristotle for the application of his own 'Golden Mean' to the question of owning slaves. For Aristotle, the economic imperative, the need to own the wealth created by the slaves (from whom it is stolen) would outweigh the moral imperative that every human being has a universal right to pursue life, liberty, and happiness. In Ancient Greece slavery was a cornerstone of the whole empire and paid for the way of life enjoyed by nobles such as Aristotle. Under such circumstances it would be unthinkable from within their ideology to abolish slavery. After all, who would then prepare Aristotle's hot bath or cook his meals? The point here is simply that we cannot separate such individual emotional attitudes from the social value system (ideology) that gives them life and substance, or from the social system (mode of production) in which they occur.

Similar objections may arise in relation to deontological ethics based on Kant's categorical imperative (Christians, Rotzoll & Fackler 1991, p. 14) and a blanket application of the 'utilitarian principles' outlined by J.S. Mill (Christians, Rotzoll & Fackler 1991, p. 15). Again one example from their text *Media Ethics: Cases and Moral Reasoning* will suffice. In a situation where the principle of 'the greatest good for the greatest number is to be applied' (p. 16), the authors raise a serious objection that quite frankly brings a wry smile to our lips: 'In a society of ten people, nine sadists cannot justly persecute the tenth person even though it yields the greatest happiness' (p. 17). All we can do is ask: Why not? The line between pleasure and pain is very fine, and there's plenty of room for improvement on both sides.

Two final points need to be mentioned before we turn to a serious study of ethics in the media. In the last pages of their introduction, Christians, Rotzoll, and Fackler (1991) turn to the questions of moral duty and who gets to make decisions. On pages 21 and 22 they outline five duties that we might consider in a media context. We have added our own thoughts (in brackets) under each heading to illustrate the problematic nature of 'duty':

Duty to ourselves:
- integrity and conscience (adherence to our own belief system)
- careerism and self-interest (the economic imperative of individual success in a competitive economic system)
- fear of reprisal or consequence (being sacked for breaking or even sticking to principles; not knowing how to react when those around us don't appear to hold onto their own ideals).

Duty to clients/audience/supporters:
- an obligation to those who pay the bills (they make the rules, we just do our job)

- an obligation to audience (do we give them what they want, what they need, or what we think they want/need?)
- an obligation to the talent (protecting the source, not invading their privacy).

Duty to our employer or organisation:
- blindly following company policy (even if we disagree)
- loyalty to an organisation can be morally good and satisfying (what if the organisation has poor ethical standards and lacks principles?)
- always striving to give your employer a competitive edge (if the company goes bust you're out of a job)
- reporting whistle-blowing may override loyalty to employer (the greater social good is served by going outside the accepted norms of company policy/behaviour)
- protection of sources may override duty to organisation/society (are you prepared to break a law you don't agree with, or a company policy?).

Duty to colleagues:
- professional loyalties to self and to organisations (this appears to contradict the idea of getting ahead through competition with workmates)
- pulling your weight in the newsroom (nobody likes a slacker in the workplace)
- helping out with information that might be useful to someone working on a story (would you collaborate with a colleague or protect information in order to beat them to a scoop?)
- adherence to the Code of Ethics, and membership of a union (united we stand, divided we fall)
- protecting colleagues from persecution or unfair dismissal (loyalty to colleagues when they're being unfairly treated is honourable, but sometimes dangerous).

Duty to society:
- always telling the truth (this is a cornerstone of journalism and should never be overridden)
- a responsibility towards the social group (how do we avoid falling into line with something we don't agree with when there is strong peer pressure to conform?)
- respecting the privacy of vulnerable individuals (is it just human nature to take advantage of the weak, especially in journalism?)
- adhering to the normative rules and values (even if you disagree? What are the consequences for standing out from the crowd?)
- respecting the confidentiality of sources (what if you're legally obliged to break the confidence?).

As you can see we again face the dialectic of conflict, confusion, and contradiction when attempting to prioritise these 'duties'. In order to paper over these contradictions, Christians and his co-authors rely on an individualistic approach. They suggest that any ultimate responsibility lies with individuals because they alone can act as 'existing and responsible agents' who must accept praise or blame for their actions (Christians, Rotzoll & Fackler 1991, p. 24). This is backed up by their assertion at the end of their introductory chapter that corporate obligations are less than those of individuals. John Merrill adopts a similar approach when he argues for a form of 'existential' journalism and *individual,* rather than *collective,* responsibility:

The journalist, if an existentialist, is committed to expanding his or her individuality and to acting in the face of personal risk. It is only in this way that the forces of enslavement and depersonalization can be frustrated.

Merrill 1989, p. 26

It is difficult to agree with this statement in the age of monopoly media ownership and control (see chapter 3). An individual is in a very weak position when confronted by the power of the corporation. How could anyone possibly resist an order from someone as powerful as Rupert Murdoch? Murdoch has been resisted, though not very often by a lone, brave, existential reporter, but by the power of the union, which encourages everyone to stick together. We currently live in a social system in which freedom of the press simply means freedom for the media giants and multinational conglomerates. One might expect, under such conditions, that the obligations on the media owners might be greater, not less than those of individual reporters and editors.

What do you think? Does this approach abstract us too much from a social context in much the same way as Rawls's veil of ignorance? However you feel in relation to this question it cannot be denied that our economic, social, cultural, and political relationships with other individuals and organisations have an impact on our decision-making as editors, reporters, and journalists. We will leave this section with an observation from Andrew Belsey and Ruth Chadwick, which highlights the on-going dilemma of solving ethical disputes and conundrums:

Clearly, the matter of providing a reasoned basis in ethical theory for a code of conduct is neither simple nor something on which consensus is likely, and so this question, together with the other issues raised … will continue to be debated. The important thing is to keep the discussion going.

Belsey & Chadwick 1992, p. 12

Now we're left with the all-important question, given all you've read earlier in this chapter about various views of ethical behaviour: How do you go about making an ethical decision, given there are so many often-conflicting ideas? If you're discussing an ethical dilemma in a university assignment or tutorial there are a number of aspects to consider. Among them are:

- What factors will have the most bearing on the decision—personal, social, economic, legal, or political?
- Who are the various parties involved? Do you have any obligation to each of them (for example, respecting their confidence, or loyalty to a source)?
- What are the relative merits of the various people involved?
- Will justice be served for all by your action?
- Will you be helping someone who deserves assistance by your action?
- Is the action prompted by a wrong you have committed and need to make amends for?
- What outcome would satisfy each of those involved? How will your chosen course of action affect each of them? (And that includes your boss.)

- What are the 'power dynamics' of the situation? Who might have power over you, or others involved in the issue, and what's your relationship with them? This could be colleagues, your employer, the sources you're using, or even someone close to you, like a lover, spouse, or close friend.
- What courses of action are open to you? What are the best and worst possible outcomes for the various scenarios?
- Will anyone be harmed by your preferred choice of action? And by how much? Is the 'good' brought about by your action outweighed by the potential harm?
- How can you minimise unnecessary harm to all concerned?
- Are you just using a person as a means to an end without considering the effect your action will have on them?
- Would honouring any ideal or value you hold invalidate your chosen course of action?
- Are there any rules or principles—like Codes of Ethics or Charters of Editorial Independence—that would automatically invalidate your proposed course of action?
- Which of the alternative courses of action would generate the greatest benefit or the least harm for the greatest number?
- Are any of the alternative courses of action based on your or your organisation's best interests?
- And after reviewing all that, what would you do?

We believe these guidelines for ethical decision-making were first developed by the journalism staff at the University of Oregon in the United States and have been adapted by others over time, but the fundamentals remain the same.

There are lots of issues to consider in making one ethical decision, which is why we say you need to have decided on your ethical boundaries before you enter the media workforce. You'll need to distil those issues down to a manageable group to guide you in ethical decision-making in the future. As we mentioned earlier, once you are working in the mass media, there'll be precious little time for mulling over the ramifications of your actions. You'll need to make your decisions relatively quickly, and be prepared to justify them, if necessary.

Case studies

→ ## Case study 1
Monica and Bill

News of the affair between the then US President and the White House intern first came to light on the *Drudge Report*, the Internet gossip sheet established and edited by Californian freelancer Matt Drudge on 21 January 1998. What followed was a 'media feeding frenzy' that drew as much attention to the journalists covering the story as it did to the President of the United States. While the scandal of the presidential affair consumed the final years of the Clinton Administration and led to Congressional hearings on possible impeachment, it also showed the changing face of journalism ethics in the US. 'What it reveals is a profession struggling to cope with the pressure of increasing competition, rapidly changing technology and shifting ethical standards' (Potter 1998). We are not interested here in further exposing yet another dubious episode in the sex life of a US President, but rather in the behaviour of the US media.

While the *Drudge Report* may have had problems with accuracy in the past, in this case the gist of the report was accurate. The respected magazine *Newsweek* had known of the affair, but had held back publication because it was unable to confirm some details to its editors' satisfaction (Potter 1998). However, the reporting that followed exposure of the affair was media overkill. The scent of political blood was in the air and much of the media in the US acted as if they were judge and jury of the man holding the nation's highest office. Jennifer Hewitt, Washington correspondent for the *Sydney Morning Herald,* characterised the coverage as a 'raging flood' and wrote that: 'Nothing can withstand the force—not taste, not privacy, not reputation, not silence. Allegations burst into view and are then spread everywhere instantly' (Hewitt 1998). The respected Washington journalist Sam Donaldson instantly declared that Clinton might be out of office in a matter of days. Another talked in those first days of the possibility of impeachment (Rieder 1998).

The competitive nature of so many journalists chasing so few facts on such a massive story meant that allegations and rumours all made their way into the public view very quickly (Hewitt 1998). The painful lesson being learned in the era of Internet news, 24-hour news channels, and the public's insatiable appetite for scandal was not to jump to conclusions. When did the senior executives in newsrooms across America decide that it was acceptable to talk about presidential semen on the nightly news? That and whether the President considered oral sex to be adultery were to this point hardly the normal fare of political coverage in the US. Another low point in the coverage came with a lawyer for one of Ms Lewinsky's former boyfriends saying she was obsessed with sex and had announced she would take presidential knee pads to the White House (Hewitt 1998). 'Sources' in stories sometimes simply meant what someone else was reporting. A *Dallas Morning News* story about a Secret Service agent supposedly seeing Mr Clinton and Ms Lewinsky in a compromising position appeared on the Internet, was repeated by others, and then retracted—all before it even made it into the newspaper's printed version (Hewitt 1998). Nearly all the mainstream American news organisations, and a large number in other countries, felt under pressure to keep up with the latest angles in the story. But was that an excuse for reporting hearsay as fact, or accusations as charges? From the point of view of journalism, the casualty of the episode was media credibility. It was a sorry chapter in American journalism. Within months, the American public had turned against the media and its continuous coverage of the presidential sex scandal. In November 1998, 10 months after the story first broke, a survey in *New York* magazine found that 50 per cent of respondents thought the coverage had been irresponsible, while nine out of ten people didn't want to hear any more, and 60 per cent thought the media deluge was prompted purely by ratings and sales (Strickland 1998). In hindsight most will acknowledge that the media went too far in its coverage. But with Internet deadlines every minute, 24-hour news channels clamouring for the latest, is that recognition likely to prevent it from happening when the next big story comes along?

→ ## Case study 2
The death of Princess Di

The death of Diana, the Princess of Wales, was in every way a modern-day tragedy. Diana was every press photographer's favourite subject and her death on 30 August 1997 after a car crash in an underground tunnel in Paris occurred while she was fleeing from the paparazzi who had hounded her for so long. A week before her death, the princess had said: 'The press is savage. It doesn't forgive anything. They only track the mistakes. Each intention is miss-read, every gesture criticised' (Henning 1997). For the 17 years of her 'public' life, right from the time she was catapulted into the international limelight as a 20-year-old kindergarten teacher chosen as the bride of the future King of England, Diana had been hounded by the media, some would say hounded to death. Her death in a car driven by a person who was alleged to have more than three times the legal alcohol limit in his blood (Gledhill & Henning 1997) would initially lead to seven photographers being charged with manslaughter and eventually acquitted. Diana's death also renewed debate about the individual's right to privacy from continuous media scrutiny—particularly individuals who are also 'celebrities', at least in the eyes of millions of magazine readers. At the time, Princess Diana was the most famous woman alive. Pictures of her, and snippets of news or scandal about her, had filled the news media for years. After her death came that amazing outpouring of grief worldwide, and the internationally televised funeral. The British author and journalist William Shawcross (1997) captured the essence of the love–hate relationship between Diana and the media: 'She lived for publicity and she both loved and hated publicity. She exploited the press and the press exploited her'. She was the world media's most prized asset—Diana on the front page of a glossy magazine guaranteed thousands of extra sales. No journalists' lives were more dramatically affected by Diana's tragic death that those of the royal 'rat pack'—the British newspaper teams that had charted the princess's every move since her engagement to the Prince of Wales. And there has been no royal since that has attracted such media attention. Like the Monica–Bill affair, we're interested here in the lessons the media should learn from the tragedy (not the tragedy itself) and in the way the media covered the life of Diana. *SMH* reporter Ian Verrender (1996) characterised the Princess of Wales (POW) as a Prisoner of War, and asked the paparazzi what they looked for in their incessant attention to Diana.

'Anything that resembles a moment of human weakness—or normal. Bending over would be great, guv. A skirt blowing up. Maybe the faint outline of a nipple against a blouse, or even some VPL (visible panty line). The ultimate goal, obviously, is to shoot POW and a male in the same frame.'

Verrender 1996

Little wonder she was fleeing from the paparazzi on that fateful night in Paris. There's more discussion of privacy and the public person in chapter 7. Finally, before moving on, it is interesting to note, as an aside, that more than 6 years later, in 2003, the ABC aired a documentary that alleged the driver of Diana's car was not drunk, and that no autopsy had been carried out on his body at the time. The program also suggested the driver was working for a British intelligence agency, and may have been involved in a plot to assassinate Diana. In the same year, a former Royal butler came forward with a letter, said to be from Diana, which indicated she feared someone (later revealed to be Prince Charles) was plotting to kill her in a car accident. This story was sold exclusively to a British tabloid newspaper, and was dutifully reported by all other media outlets. Seven years after her tragic death, the British Coroner referred the case to Scotland Yard (the home of Britain's police force) for investigation. Prince Charles, and possibly sons William and Harry, are to be interviewed over the allegation that Charles planned to kill her ('Charles in Kill Probe', 2004). Whether any of this new speculation is true or not hardly seems to matter. The important thing is that 'news' about the late Princess of Wales and her tragic death will still grab attention, headlines, and audiences. We ask you to consider whether a picture of Diana on that fateful night would be worth endangering a life for. Perhaps in the cut-throat world of the global paparazzi, some made the decision that it was. Why? Because pictures of Diana were traditionally very valuable and in the end she may well have been a victim of poor ethical decisions by the photographers who chased her car into that Paris tunnel.

Issues and questions raised by case studies 1 and 2

1   Naturally the whole of America (and most of the world for that matter) is interested in what their President does, but what should be considered 'off limits'?

2   Is the most powerful man in the Western world entitled to any privacy?

3   Much has been made of the love life of President Kennedy since his assassination in 1963. Should his private life be open to public scrutiny after his death?

4   Isn't it just as hurtful then to the immediate family?

5   President Clinton's involvement with Monica Lewinsky was a big story, but wasn't the media in the early stages hiding behind an ethical technicality in reporting what another media outlet (the *Drudge Report*) was saying?

6   Once the story was 'in the open', every media outlet wanted a part of it. What ethical dangers did that expose?

7   Is it a story only if it affects the President's decisions (i.e. involves corruption)?

8   Maybe some of the Washington journalists saw themselves in the mould of Woodward and Bernstein of Watergate fame, and maybe forcing the resignation of a President.

9   President Clinton's wife, Hillary, now a New York Senator, has written about how she felt when she found out about Bill's relationship with Monica. How would you feel under the circumstances?

10   Would you want to see your partner's relationships featured in the daily newspapers or on the TV?

11   Why is the Clinton situation different?

12   Should the paparazzi have chased Diana's car through the streets of Paris?

13   Was it really that important that they get 'one more' picture of Diana with her rich lover?

14   Has anyone the right to endanger human life to get a picture?

15   Is it any different if the photographer chooses to risk their own life?

16   Why not just wait and see what the 'happy couple' was up to on the Sunday?

17   Is anyone such 'public property' that they are not entitled to any privacy at all?

18   And what of the 'upmarket' media—the network news services and broadsheets—who look down their noses at the tabloids, glossy magazines, and daily TV current affairs programs and say it's not them, but the 'trashies' that hound public figures?

19   Where does the blame lie—with the media? Or the public, with their insatiable appetite for gossip about a President or Princess?

20   Celebrities, as opposed to Presidents and Royalty, need publicity to continuously reinforce their celebrity status, so are they fair game for the paparazzi?

2

JOURNALISTS AND IDEOLOGY:

FREEDOM OF THE PRESS, ACCURACY, BALANCE, BIAS, FAIRNESS, AND OBJECTIVITY

Objectives

After reading and discussing this chapter you should have an understanding of the following:

■ The concept of ideology and its importance to a debate about journalists' ethics.
■ The definitions of common terms in the debate: accuracy, balance, bias, fairness, and objectivity.
■ The place of these constructs in a discussion of journalism ethics.
■ The importance of historical and contemporary debates among journalists, their supporters, and their many critics.
■ The role of journalists and editors as public intellectuals—with a role in the production and circulation of ideologies.

Introduction: Can journalists be trusted?

Journalists tend to think of themselves as the Good Guys doing the Right Thing for a Better World, even as they lie their way through undercover investigations, corner grief-stricken parents after school shootings and stake out politicians' love nests. So they're often shaken when people treat them as vultures and parasites.

Stepp 1999

The American quotation above holds true for the Australian news media and the public's view of it. A 2001 Morgan Poll of honesty and ethics in Australian occupations found that although the image of print journalists had improved over the previous year—up from seven per cent of people thinking they were honest and ethical to 13 per cent—newspaper reporters still rated fourth lowest in the rankings (AAP 2001). Television reporters also surged from six per cent to 18 per cent, ahead of their print colleagues, but around 80 per cent of people (about four out of five) didn't think they were honest or ethical (AAP 2001). Nurses rated the highest at 90 per cent, followed by pharmacists at 83 per cent, and doctors on 75 per cent. The survey upheld the newsroom belief that journalists are about as popular as used-car salesmen and real estate agents. Car salesmen, with an honesty/ethics rating of two per cent, estate agents at eight per cent, and advertising people, also on eight per cent, were the only occupations to rate lower than print journalists in the 2001 honesty survey (AAP 2001). The other occupational group that journalists are often compared to in the honesty and ethical stakes is politicians. Another survey in 2001, by *Readers Digest,* ranked politicians as the least trustworthy of the twenty-five professions in their survey, below used-car salesmen (cited in Jasmen 2001). Journalists came in at number 20 in that survey, above bankers and trade unionists, but below lawyers, builders, taxi drivers, and car mechanics (Jasmen 2001). In a similar survey in 2004, journalists had dropped another two places and only out-ranked politicians, car salesmen, real estate agents and, interestingly, CEOs (*Reader's Digest* cited in AAP 2004).

In 2002 nothing much had changed in the annual Morgan Poll. Car salesmen were still on the bottom of the 'most trusted' list (this time there were twenty-eight professions in the survey), and print journalists had dropped another two spots to be twenty-sixth, only ahead of estate agents and car salesmen (Rood 2002). Television journalists maintained their 18 per cent approval rating, but newspaper journalists slipped back to only nine per cent—less than one in 10 of those surveyed considered them to be honest and ethical (AAP 2002a). Another poll, this one commissioned by the *Courier-Mail* in 2003 after the Queensland Premier, Peter Beattie, suggested the State needed 'truth in media' laws, found that only 16 per cent of Queenslanders trusted politicians more than journalists. Asked whom they trusted more to tell the truth, the media or politicians, 84 per cent of the 300 Queenslanders polled nominated the media (Parnell 2003a). Many might suggest that's not a fair choice—having to pick only between journalists and politicians—but it suited the *Courier-Mail*'s story. The latest version of the Roy Morgan 'trust' poll saw nurses top the list for the tenth consecutive year, with 94 per cent of the public rating them the most respected of the twenty-eight professions in the survey (Arlington 2004). Newspaper journalists were again the least trusted of the members of the media, being considered honest and ethical by only 13 per cent of those surveyed. Talkback radio announcers (21 per cent) and television reporters (17 per cent) fared a little better (The most and least trusted jobs survey, 2004). Back in 1996, in a cover story titled 'Why people hate the media', the *Bulletin* magazine released its own *Bulletin* Morgan poll showing 85 per cent of people believed the Australian media puts too much focus on sensational subjects like sex and violence; 80 per cent thought the media does not care about people's feelings and their right to privacy; and 36 per cent said journalists and commentators are poor at behaving in a trustworthy manner in preparing and getting stories (Murphy 1996). Journalists have plenty to do to raise their reputations in the eyes of the general public. They can start by being accurate, balanced or free of bias, and fair and by striving to be objective in what they publish.

The fault lines in journalistic ideologies

In order to fully explore arguments and cases in media ethics we need to discuss and explain the relationship between journalism and ideology. We also need to understand how conflicting ideologies compete for attention and influence in the ongoing debate about media ethics (Richards 2002a). Ideological positions and arguments don't impact on journalism ethics in an abstract way; they manifest themselves in very real fault lines. Not only between the news media and the public it serves, but also in arguments between reporters about personal conviction, political beliefs, and loyalties. Drinks have been spilled often, and blood occasionally, in disputes between reporters. Understanding this conflict, or dialectic, and debate at the heart of journalism is a necessary step to an understanding of the role and power of the assumptions and ideas embedded in journalists' heads. Each day, in the newsroom, or out on a job, every news worker carries with them, as items in their 'tool-kit', a set of emotional and intellectual attitudes towards sources, their audience, and the news they report. This emotional and intellectual tool-kit has been gathered since early childhood— it's how they see the world, and will vary from journalist to journalist depending on their family background, their upbringing, their education, their friends, the area and environment in which they grew up etc. Without being too elitist about it, tertiary-trained journalists are a privileged group and may, because of their upbringing, have difficulty coping with some of the things they'll report upon. Their attitudes will colour their approach to a story, the way they choose to tell it, and how they go about obtaining the information to write it.

Journalists, like everyone else in any given society, will hold in their heads a series of ideas about politics, religion, economics, and a whole range of social issues like abortion, ANZAC day, cutting down the forests, gay liberation, refugees, and women's rights. News workers will share ideologies with some colleagues, family and friends, and they may hold completely opposite views to many more. Things can get quite heated when journalists disagree with each other; some even describe it as a 'culture war' (Glover 2003). Such ideological conflicts are around most of the time, but they really seem to come to the fore during times of crisis, when rival media opinioneers are clamouring for public attention, and profess to hold the key to solving whatever problem it is they're talking about.

The conflicting ideologies of journalism

Everyday ethical concepts such as free speech, freedom of the press, truth, objectivity, accuracy, balance, fairness, and (lack of) bias form an ideology of journalism (Simper 1995a). So too does the notion that journalism is a profession (Hargreaves 2003; Schultz 1994, 1998, 1999). Most of the time there is some level of agreement about these terms and their application, but there are also periods of intense dispute both among news workers and within the wider community.

A common ideological belief is that journalists are part of some supposed 'elite' of opinion-formers, wise figures, and pundits who are basically courtesans in an 'electronic whorehouse' (Sheehan 2003). Whichever way you slice it there are great fault lines within and around these journalistic ideologies (Glover 2003). In *The Electronic Whorehouse*, author and *SMH* columnist Paul Sheehan (2003) argues that Australia is dominated by a 'left and liberal media establishment'. Another senior journalist and editor, Max Suich (2003, p. 14) contends that Sheehan's argument is at best 'unpersuasive'. Suich (2003, p. 15) goes on to suggest that the 'noise of all these opinions, including Sheehan's, may be the reason … there is growing disillusion … with the quality press'. In supporting the public role of journalists in creating and shaping public opinion, Mark Davis (2002) argues that Australia, like any society, needs people with ideas, 'especially those humanitarian elites that conservative commentators love to disparage'. Davis is making the argument that journalists are among the group of general public intellectuals that encourage, challenge, and lead debates. We agree—the very fact that reporters and columnists engage, often loudly, in public debate and the circulation of opinion, means they deserve to be taken seriously as public intellectuals. That there is such a wide gulf between 'Right' and 'Left' is then no real surprise. These political tensions inform many debates in journalism ethics.

Journalists in conflict: The ideological fallout from '9/11'

In the confusing aftermath of the terrorist attacks on New York and Washington in September 2001, rival American journalists and columnists were quick to condemn each other. Given the high levels of emotion and rhetoric surrounding the news media's coverage of September 11, it's not surprising that a wide Left–Right split appeared between journalists (Blair 2001). Richard Ackland (2001) reported a spat between two female correspondents in which one called the other a 'war slut' in print. Rupert Murdoch himself issued an apology (of sorts) before it got any worse.

Ackland's column, in which he reports this insider gossip, itself takes a general swipe at Murdoch correspondents in Australia who had been quick to jump on the 'anti-terrorist' bandwagon. He notes how regular contributors to the opinion and editorial pages in a Murdoch paper were 'trying to pass themselves off' as fair-minded, and not part of the very 'chattering classes', and so-called 'elites' that they claim to despise.

It would be fair to assume that Ackland was having a go at someone like Piers Akerman, who had, the day before, written an opinion piece on the November 2001 Australian federal election. It was an election in which the issues of 'border security', and 'refugees' were very controversial and Akerman (2001) had taken a shot at what he often described as the 'commentariat', a vaguely left-wing and ill-defined group of reporters whom Akerman happened to disagree with. In this instance it was columnists and reporters who had accused Prime Minister John Howard of using the asylum-seeker issue to whip up fear in the campaign. 'Commentariat' has become a common collective noun of abuse in Australia, the same way conservative columnists in the United States accuse those they disagree with of being 'liberal' (Hannity 2002). Sean Hannity is an American radio talk host, the classic 'shock-jock'. He claims to be a proud American, a native of New York and to hate the 'Left', which he claims has 'foolishly and relentlessly attacked and undermined the very policies and institutions that have made [America] a beacon of liberty and prosperity' (Hannity 2002, p. 6). The Australian equivalents, at least in attitude and tone, are columnists like Piers Akerman in Sydney's *Daily Telegraph*, and the *Australian*'s Greg Sheridan (Hirst & Schutze 2004). What they share is a real hatred for the ideology they describe as 'modern liberalism, feel-good feminism, or radical environmentalism' (Hannity 2002, p. 7). 'Liberal' or 'Left' is an epithet usually aimed at more 'humanitarian' columnists, those who Akerman (2001) labels 'predictable bores'. There is a sense in which this is a straight Right–Left split between reporters and commentators, but it clearly demonstrates how political fault lines can impact on journalistic ethics. Dennis Glover, in his book *Orwell's Australia* (2003, p. 39), argues that while 'truth has become contested and politics more ruthless', at the same time 'the whole notion of objectivity has itself been undermined and too few journalists do anything to call our politicians to account'.

In a negative sense, the term ideology has come to mean, 'abstract, impractical, or fanatical theory' (Williams 1989, p. 154). It is in this sense that Piers Akerman might from time to time call individual members of the 'commentariat' 'ideologues', the implication being that they hold fanatical and impractical ideas. It is in this sense that some governments and politicians are now referring to an abstract, fanatical ideology of terrorism, often associated with Islam under the term 'Jihadism' (see chapter 6). There is no doubt that since 11 September 2001 the media has been dragged into an ideological battle. It is a conflict in which, according to Glover (2003, pp. 72–3), the conservative opinions of 'right-wing commentators' have 'finally become the new orthodoxy', which pretends to be brave by questioning 'politically correct' supporters of more liberal, or left-wing ideas. Davis (2002) describes this form of abuse by conservative commentators as 'clever', because 'it helps mask the fact that those who attack elites are themselves part of an elite'. He goes on to ask how many 'ordinary' people have radio shows, or newspaper columns that they are free to use against their ideological opponents. It is an ideological attack by one side on those it disagrees with. According to Davis this means that 'liberal-minded' commentators are demonised in an ultimately 'irrational' way. On the other side, Davis describes a new phenomenon of even more conservative commentators as the rise of the 'neoconservatives, who ... seem to be able to do little but set up and knock down straw men'.

As Andrew Dodd (2001a) has pointed out, the 'war on terror' marked a turning point in American media history, with greater introspection by journalists and the development of clearly ideological positions: one became either a 'patriot', or an 'appeaser' of terrorists. It is clear that any discussion of journalism and ethics must be aware of these fault lines in ideology. We then need to ask a further question: Why is there such a clear schism within journalism about political and social issues, such as war and refugee policy? The answer, we believe, can be found by examining the emotional attitudes of journalists in relation to various 'points' on a dialectic continuum that marks out a journalistic ideology.

In their pioneering work on what ideologies are, and how they come into being, Karl Marx and Friedrich Engels defined one aspect of ideology as the ruling ideas of the class that controls the economy and production. In his pamphlet, *Theses on Feuerbach*, Engels wrote that ideology is 'nothing more than the ideal expression of the dominant material relationships, the dominant material relationships grasped as ideas' (Engels, *Theses on Feurbach*, cited in Williams 1989, p. 115). One would therefore expect, in a capitalist society, that the wealthy class that owns most of the economic resources, including the news media, would exercise its advantages in both the economy and politics in ways which 'undermine political equality' (McChesney 2000). McChesney's argument is that news media deal extensively with issues of political education and debate, but that the media systems operating in the capitalist world do not 'exist to serve democracy'. He suggests their aim is not information, but to 'generate maximum profit to the small number of very large [media] firms and billionaire investors' (2000, p. 2). Dennis Glover (2003, p. 72) makes a similar point: by drawing attention to an alleged 'left-wing' conspiracy among the news 'elite', the conservative ideologues attempt to 'distract' citizens from 'far more important issues that involve their real interests, such as … the steady transfer of wealth to the [already] rich'. Thus in a free-market, capitalist liberal 'democracy', freedom of speech, or freedom of the press, becomes merely the freedom of the media's owners to protect their commercial interests. This points to what McChesney (2000, p. 4) calls the 'severe contradiction between a privately held media system and the needs of a democratic society'. It's yet another fault line to be explored, and one that is central to our arguments about a political economy of ethics in chapter 3.

In relation to our discussion of ethics, this aspect of ruling ideologies at play in the newsroom is best characterised by what American media sociologist Warren Breed (1997) first described in the 1950s as the problem of 'social control' in the news production process. Breed argued that the social forces that control the newsroom would also control the ideological content of the news. The concept of professionalism in journalism is an expression of these controlling social forces. However, the pushing of journalists into a mould of professionalism creates its own contradictions and paradoxes.

The paradox of professionalism and the intellectual journalist

Ian Richards (2002b) argues that journalists have an 'uncertain' relationship with the ideology of professionalism, and with notions of professional ethics. The committee that reviewed the AJA Code of Ethics in the 1990s acknowledged the problematic nature of professionalism as a category for news workers, noting that journalism 'has some marks of the traditional professions, and lacks others' (Ethics Review Committee 1997, p. 4). Michael Meadows (2001) writes that the debate about professionalism has 'disrupted' journalism's traditional association with the public, and that news is becoming a form of entertainment, or too closely resembles public relations. The public and intellectual tradition in journalism is, in the eyes of some, under pressure from these new forces of the social dialectic. Richards (1998) talks about the 'imbroglio' over journalism ethics, and points out a 'polarity' (2002b) in debates about journalistic ethics, whether in the newsroom, the living room, or the classroom. As we shall see, this polarity in ideas can sometimes get quite personal. In the United States mud slinging between 'liberal' and 'conservative' journalists has reached almost fever pitch in the past few years (Alterman 1999, 2003). In this chapter we want to explore the tensions and contradictions within the general ideologies under which journalists operate. In a sense, reporters and editors embody these ideologies, in both the relationships they form with each other, and in their work practices (Hirst 2000, 2003; Oakham 1998).

Another sense in which we need to consider the ideologies of journalists and journalism is the consideration of what Julianne Schultz (1994) calls the 'paradox' of professionalism. Put in simple terms: Are journalists wage-earning workers like most teachers, office workers, and academics, or are they professionals with different interests? We need to address this issue in any discussion of ethics, because it is an important element of a fairly common ideology among news workers, and in the academic discourse about news and citizenship (Hargreaves 2003; Henningham 1985, 1989, 1996a; Hirst 1997a; Kingston 1999b; Meadows 2001; Richards 2002b; Schultz 1994, 1998, 1999). Whether academic or journalist, the professional ideology of intellectuals stakes a claim to some degree of objectivity, and drawing logical conclusions based on 'facts'. Finally, we need to consider ideology in the context of journalists being what the Italian journalist and Marxist, Antonio Gramsci (1971), described as intellectuals: those whose work is with ideas and the creation of belief systems. In the 1920s and 1930s, when Gramsci was editing a workers' newspaper, being an intellectual meant taking sides, either for or against the rise of Fascism in Europe. George Orwell too made his choices as an intellectual and writer. Gramsci spent many years in Italian jails for his beliefs; Orwell was shot in the neck while fighting against Franco's Fascist troops in Spain in 1936. Journalist–intellectuals today are less likely to make such physical commitments, but they do play an important role in creating, disputing, and reproducing ideas in society. The intellectual work of journalists is the fashioning of ideologies, whether they are supportive of or antagonistic to the apparently common sense and mainstream views of society.

Freedom and responsibility: A clash of journalistic ideologies

If you read Sean Hannity's book *Let Freedom Ring*, you soon realise that for his brand of conservative activist journalism 'freedom' means upholding family values and the American way of life. Defending this freedom means taking a responsibility to stop the spread of 'liberal' ideas: 'Not just debate them, but defeat them' (Hannity 2002, p. 11). For John Merrill (1989, p. 25), one of the key intellectual debates about activism in modern journalism is the idea that 'many journalists therefore fear freedom because they fear to assume responsibility for decisions [and fear] ... accepting moral responsibility for actions taken'. Leonard Downie Jr and Robert G Kaiser (2002) describe the central contradiction as being between 'good' and 'bad' journalism. They argue that good journalism 'frequently changes the lives of citizens, both grand and ordinary', and is 'critical to a civilized society', while bad journalism 'can leave people dangerously misinformed', and much of it is 'just lazy and superficial'. It is not difficult to draw the conclusion that good journalism will also be free from bias, and responsible, but to whom, or what? The idea of trust is also central to the notion of good journalism, for without trust a nation is doomed (Tazreiter 2003). However, the news media is one social institution that, Tazreiter (2003, p. 9) argues, has failed the public trust: 'The media acts as taster, sifter and packager of information which most of the public consumes, even while remaining sceptical about its independence, impartiality and rigour.'

Like many of the contemporary ideas surrounding journalism ethics, the philosophical roots of free and responsible journalism go back to arguments between the Greek philosophers, Plato and Aristotle: on the one hand the concept of social responsibility, and on the other, the ideology of political individualism. For John Merrill (1989, p. 3), the most important resolution (synthesis) of the contradictions in journalism is an attempted 'merger of Platonic social responsibility with Aristotelian political individualism', which 'forms the critical dialectic in press–Government relations and in the general symbiosis between journalism and society'. Today we talk more about 'accountability' than 'responsibility', but the contradiction highlighted by Merrill has not disappeared. On the contrary, Meadows (2001, p. 40) argues that in the modern news media 'lines of accountability' between journalists, the public, and the broader society have been 'displaced'. Clearly the idea of responsibility, or accountability, raises just as many questions as it answers. Who, or what, should journalists be accountable to? While accountability is an important concept in journalism ethics, it can prove quite elusive at times (Retief 2002, p. 5).

Merrill (1989) sees the most substantial fault line in journalism ethics being between freedom on the one hand, and responsibility on the other. We can see many others, equally as substantial. In particular, these fault lines go to the core of the ideology of journalism and the concepts of accountability, objectivity, balance, accuracy, truth, fairness, and bias.

Core ideas in the ideology of journalism

As we have seen, the ideology of journalism in a western free-market liberal democracy (like the USA, Australia, South Africa, and most of Europe) is a complex and tangled set of ideas and ideals, many of which appear to be in contradiction with each other. In this section we outline what each of these competing concepts are, how they relate to each other, and how they are being revised on an almost daily basis. It is interesting in passing to note the emphasis that various authors in journalism ethics place on each of these concepts. Belsey and Chadwick (1992) make no mention of accuracy, fairness, responsibility, or accountability in their index, but they do mention bias, and objectivity; Hurst and White (1994) include accuracy, balance, bias, fairness, responsibilities, and objectivity in their index. Patterson and Wilkins (1994) mention accuracy, but not accountability, though they do include bias, balance, fairness, and objectivity. These concepts are treated here in alphabetical order, but the relationship of each to the others is constantly reinforced. The alphabetical listing also allows us to leave objectivity to last because it is perhaps the most controversial.

Accountability

In this section we have chosen to use the term accountability, but it is synonymous with 'responsibility to', or 'duty to', and in a general sense involves being accountable to the news-consuming public. Inside the concept of accountability we also find the term 'trust'. The public has to be able to trust journalists and the news media to tell the truth. However, there also needs to be a level of accountability and trust within the media organisation, particularly to the business side of the organisation, and an important responsibility towards the sources of news information. Hurst and White (1994, p. 6) also mention a moral accountability to self and society, and the contradictions inherent in conflicting loyalties.

Accountability is a vexed issue in journalism ethics precisely because of these conflicting loyalties. Should a reporter's loyalty to their employer override accountability to the public trust? Equally, should the public interest come before self-interest? This dilemma can be potentially catastrophic for a reporter caught between the wishes of their employer and the needs of the public. As Jackson (1992) points out, it becomes even more complicated in a situation where a reporter might consider it permissible to lie in order to get to a greater truth. This is the fault line between what Jackson (1992, p. 99) calls 'perfect', and 'imperfect' duties: 'the argument that those to whom the journalists would lie are themselves liars is doubtfully relevant and, in any case, not conclusive'. In this situation accountability to the source—the person being lied to—is thrown out the window, and the principle of the 'greater good' is invoked to justify dishonesty. Is this really a case of a more important duty, that of being accountable to the public? Under such circumstances it becomes difficult to discern which duty is more compelling for the reporter, and which should take precedence.

Like many issues in journalism ethics, it would seem that accountability is in the eye of the beholder, and that it might be a physical, as well as an intellectual impossibility for the news media to be accountable to every competing interest all the time. Is there also a case for being accountable to your colleagues in the newsroom to produce the best material you can, and to the journalistic fraternity in general not to bring the profession into disrepute? Johan Retief (2002, p. 2) seeks a solution in the concept of accountability in the capitalist market, but as we argue in the following chapter, this is not necessarily the best arbiter of responsibility. Nor is it necessarily the most effective guardian of accountability, given the overriding imperative of market forces to garner profit from the activities of reporters. The committee of eminent Australians who reviewed the AJA Code of Ethics in the mid 1990s was aware of this contradiction, though perhaps were not able to resolve it in terms of reconciling public interest in journalism with the private needs of media owners. However, the committee recommended, and the journalists' union adopted, a Preamble to the revised Code that attempted to deal with the issue of accountability by connecting 'power with accountability, accountability with trust, and trust with the fulfilment of the public service role of journalism' (Ethics Review Committee 1997, p. 20). In our view the success or failure of the MEAA's revised Code to finally address this issue is still open to question.

Accuracy

It would be a mistake to think that accuracy is something that we can take for granted in the news media. Reporters frequently get things wrong—most annoyingly this often means getting names wrong. In one celebrated case a senior partner in a Sydney law firm sued the *Sun-Herald* newspaper for describing him as a man who engaged in homosexual bondage games. Oops, turned out it was the wrong man and the case was sent to trial before a civil jury when Justice Levine agreed that wrongly describing a person as gay, and into sado-masochism, could be defamatory (Milligan 2003). Accuracy is also an issue of trust, and it is a trust clearly breached in cases of plagiarism. The prestigious *New York Times* became embroiled in such a scandal (the so-called Jayson Blair Affair) in May and June 2003, leading to the resignation of several top editors and reporters (Wapshott 2003). You can read our discussion of that embarrassing incident in chapter 10.

In an attempt to eliminate such problems from its newspapers, the Fairfax group (publishers of the *SMH,* the *Age* and *Australian Financial Review*, among other titles) introduced a new form of editorial management, known as 'prosecutorial editing' (Dodd 2001b). The new practice did not sit well with all *SMH* staff, with at least one senior staffer, Ben Hills, reportedly threatening to work against the new system, which was designed to identify and check all 'high risk' stories through a process of 'peer review' in the newsroom. Unfortunately, the new system did not stop the Sydney paper from further embarrassing blunders, such as wrongly identifying a man in a story about excessive drinking by workers in the finance industry. You had to feel sorry for the reporter concerned (so we'll save her from further embarrassment by not identifying her). She was following up British research that said that an alcoholic drink at lunch could have unpleasant consequences due to mid-afternoon sleepiness ('A Quick Nip and the Afternoon Dip Combine to Cut Alertness' 2003). The reporter quoted one 'Steve Renshaw, 31, a money market broker' as saying he usually had five or six schooners of beer during his three-hour lunch break and then drove home about 5 p.m. Next day, the *Herald,* in a small paragraph on page 2 said: 'The *Herald* accepts that another man, who claimed to be Mr Renshaw, made the comments and posed for the photo' (cited in Meade 2003). But somebody didn't tell the *SMH* letters column editors, because the same edition in which the 'apology' appeared also carried public criticism of 'Mr Renshaw's' drinking and driving habits (Meade 2003). The ABC's *Media Watch* identified the bragging drinker as one of Steve's mates, Mark Pisani, from the same broking firm (Marr 2003a). What's a reporter to do? Ask to see a driver's licence (or other photo ID) from every-one they interview? Whatever happened to the habit of journalists exchanging business cards with their interviewees?

It is interesting to speculate whether a system of forensic editing would have picked up this case of mistaken identity. The prosecutorial system of forensic editing was not popu-lar at the *SMH,* and former *Age* section editor Tony Berry commented on the irony of reporter Ben Hills complaining about it. According to Berry's letter in the *Australian*'s Media section the following week, Hills had instituted a similar routine in the 1970s and 'I found it possibly the stupidest idea I had encountered ... a total waste of time and insult-ing to my professionalism' (Berry 2001).

While it may seem that accuracy is a constant, and a given in news, and something that reporters should take great pride in, there are times when the pressure of competition, or just laziness, takes the edge off accurate gathering and writing of the facts (Hurst & White 1994). Accuracy is also an issue when reporters and editors wish to claim that their report-ing of a controversial or potentially defamatory issue should be privileged. For example, to claim privilege as a defence, the account given in a news story must be 'substantially accu-rate' (Pearson 2001, p. 206).

The news media cannot afford to make mistakes of fact, or accuracy. There have been cases in Australia of the media getting it wrong when racing to be first with what appears to be an important piece of news, including what Hurst and White call 'converting suggestion into fact' (1994, p. 100). A similar situation can occur when a reporter at a news event is forced to rely on eyewitness accounts from people at the scene. Eyewitness accounts can provide dramatic quotes and imagery for a news story, but they must be treated cautiously, as they can often be unreliable and inaccurate. Journalists themselves have reported that the temptation to take eyewitness accounts as gospel is primarily a response to the pressures of tight deadlines and limited research, or fact-checking resources (Schultz 1994, p. 41). Unfortunately, there is also a danger that questions of factuality and accuracy can be abused in the newsroom, or 'cynically manipulated' in a news culture that believes the facts should not be allowed to get in the way of a good story, particularly if it is an exclusive (Scott 2001, p. 144).

In a general sense it is not difficult to be accurate. The simple checking of names, places, dates, and so on (the reporter's 5W and H questions—who, what, where, when, why, and how) is the first line of defence in the newsroom. The attribution of material to named sources would also help, but on its own it does not lessen the responsibility on the reporter and editor to get things right. However, it is a different story when accuracy is deliberately thrown out the window for the sake of a good headline. When Kelvin McKenzie was editing Rupert Murdoch's *Sun* newspaper in London in the 1980s he was regularly accused of making up material for front-page stories. Sometimes the stories were relatively harmless, like the famous 'Freddie Starr ate my Hamster' story on 13 March 1986. Starr was a comedian who had pretended to eat a hamster as part of his act. The fact that no hamster was consumed did not stop McKenzie on this occasion. There were more serious consequences when the *Sun* accused fans of urinating on rescue workers when a stand at the Hillsborough soccer ground in Sheffield collapsed (Hargreaves 2003, p. 114). There is no excuse for such blatant making up of 'facts' or angles, purely for the sake of selling more newspapers, or attracting more viewers.

Balance and bias

If journalism is merely about the reporting of facts, then striving for complete accuracy would be enough. The facts would speak for themselves and journalism would be 'objective', no 'opinion' would creep in to 'slant' the news. Presented with true and accurate facts the public would be able to determine for itself an attitude towards the subject under discussion. However, journalism is more than the reporting of facts—it is also about interpretation, thus there is the potential for bias. The very existence of variety and conflict within the ideologies that journalists hold suggests that this potential is very real, and often comes into play. For a journalist the interpretation of a news story involves bringing their own emotional attitudes into play when evaluating the 'facts'. Andrew Edgar (1992) argues that any act of interpretation within journalism involves the 'selection and ordering' of the facts. This selection is part of an incomplete process, and necessarily 'biased by the horizon in which interpretation occurs' (Edgar 1992, p. 114). The concept of 'horizon' is very close to what we are calling the world view, the ideology, or the emotional attitude of the news worker. It is a dialectic arrangement of competing social forces and ideas that combine to make up 'the stock of knowledge and competencies, typically taken for granted by the journalist' (Edgar 1992, p. 117). These are the ideas and beliefs—the social values—against which the news value of an item is assessed. Thus, for us, the question of bias and balance is primarily one of journalistic ideology, and we can therefore talk about 'balance' as being the fair presentation of both sides of an argument, or conflict, and 'bias' as a definite propensity to favour one side over another. Bias is such a difficult concept to deal with in journalism, and equally difficult to pin down, primarily because the assumptions on which a reporter's views are based can be largely subconscious (Hurst 1991). There may also not be a perception of bias if the slant on the story appears to be one simply 'dictated by the perceptions of prevailing values [ideologies] in the community', or by 'the acculturation that occurs in all newsrooms' (Hurst & White 1994, p. 29).

Balance is also, at times, a question of editorial independence—independence from pressures from within, and from outside the newsroom, in particular pressures to include, or omit information in a story. Such distortions can rob the readers or viewers of the opportunity to decide for themselves about the validity of a report. One important bias that reporters and audiences are aware of (most of the time) is the tendency for news outlets to represent the views of their owners in editorials and political coverage. This is a situation in which reporters must juggle their competing loyalties. Johan Retief (2002, p. 40) points out that the context in which a news item appears is important, as well as the presentation of competing points of view. In terms of ideological bias we also have to account for the social, historic, political, and economic contexts in which the news communication occurs. Certainly we must be conscious of the political position of the journalist, and the publication/broadcaster for which they work, but we must also consider the very conventions of news reporting. This means understanding, and critiquing, the ways in which the media applies 'a narrative structure to ambiguous events in order to create a coherent and causal sense [of them]' (*Rhetorica* 2003).

Simple questions about bias in reporting

There are several questions that can be applied to news in order to detect any bias. They are not foolproof, but they will assist in most cases:

- What is the author/reporter's personal position? Does s/he belong to any professional association or political organisation that might influence how s/he reports a story?
- Does the reporter have any personal stake in the story, or the issues being covered?
- How credible are the sources or statistics that the journalist has used? Are there any obvious omissions from the data as presented? Is there another interpretation of the data that conflicts with the reporter's interpretation? Has this alternative viewpoint been fairly and accurately represented?
- What arguments does the reporter use or choose to ignore in building their case? If alternative views are presented, is the reporter's summary accurate and fair? Is the language used to describe the various viewpoints balanced, or is one side presented in a negative fashion and the other in a positive tone?
- Does the reporter have the background knowledge, the insight, self-confidence, and emotional maturity to understand the story and the consequences of reporting it in a particular way?

Fairness in reporting

The concept of balance is linked to fairness in reporting and increasingly it is being seen as the 'holy grail' for reporters, replacing the difficult and, as some would argue, outdated concept of objectivity (Krajicek n.d.; *Rhetorica* 2003). By the same token others point out that bias is in the perception of the audience. While acknowledging the fact, Ron Brunton (2002) is alarmed that such a statement implies there are no 'objective standards' by which claims of bias can be judged. He laments that bias in news is an issue usually raised by 'people who are hopelessly biased themselves' (Brunton 2002). Fairness is linked to objectivity in the same way as bias and impartiality, but also to the concept of using fair means (Retief 2002, p. 40) to obtain information for a news story. For example, it would be unfair to take advantage of a grieving mother to obtain information about a child who died under tragic circumstances.

Like the other concepts discussed in this chapter, fairness itself relies on trust, truth, honesty, and a clear representation of the facts in a story. According to Hurst and White (1994, p. 40) the duty of a reporter here is fair disclosure to the audience. It is an essential duty because if the news-consuming audience cannot rely on the reporter to be fair and accurate, how can they judge the truth of what is being reported? This issue of trust is at the heart of the relationship between journalist and citizens, and 'if that trust is misplaced then media credibility suffers' (Hurst & White 1994, p. 40). But fairness in reporting must go beyond accuracy and into the area of competing opinion. This is not just about the competing opinions of editorial writers and columnists, which are often in a narrow band of mildly conservative and conformist views circulating around a core consensus of ideas (Hallin 1994), it is also crucially about access, and who gets to have a point of view. In a period in which there has been an almost unprecedented growth in concentration of media ownership, and a simultaneous shrinking of media outlets, it is becoming harder each day for diverse voices to get a fair hearing. It was in this context that the MEAA Ethics Review Committee (1997, p. 7) commented that the 'public service role of journalism is in danger of being eclipsed by the commercial pressures of media businesses'.

The curse of objectivity

Some people will say that words like scum and rotten are wrong for Objective Journalism—which is true, but they miss the point. It was the built-in blind spots of the Objective rules and dogma that allowed Nixon to slither into the White House in the first place ... You had to get Subjective to see Nixon clearly, and the shock of recognition was often painful.

Thompson 1995, n.p.

For someone as outrageous and cynical as American gonzo journalist Hunter S. Thompson, there can be no question that objectivity is a curse for journalists. Thompson argues that by attempting to be objective, or at least by paying lip-service to the ideology of objective reporting, most news workers in fact fall back on conscious and unconscious prejudices. This is a very key fault line in contemporary journalism, and there are no easy answers.

Hunter S. Thompson is not alone in dismissing the idea of objectivity. A well-respected Australian editor of the 1950s and 1960s, Sydney Deamer, is reputed to have once counselled a young reporter, Don Whittington, to forget about objectivity, and to instead 'strive to be fair'. It was a sage piece of advice that Whittington took to heart, later using the phrase as the title for his memoir about life in the Canberra Press Gallery (Whittington 1977).

Media institutions attempt to contain the contradiction between public interest and profit within what American media critic Daniel Hallin (1994, p. 54) calls the 'sphere of legitimate controversy'. This is the limit of public debate sanctioned and tolerated by liberal–democratic elites, 'the region where [the ideology of] objective journalism reigns supreme: here neutrality and balance are the prime journalistic virtues'. At the same time the news media plays a containing role, 'excluding from the public agenda those who violate or challenge consensus values, and upholding the consensus distinction between legitimate and illegitimate political activity' (Hallin 1994, p. 54). According to such criticism, the whole point of objectivity, as a key component of journalistic ideology, is to mask, disguise, and legitimate the authority of society's powerful ruling groups over weaker sections of the population. This is a controversial idea for some, and sparks some of the most heated debates over ethics in journalism. Should reporters be observers, and recorders of events, who somehow stand outside or above social conflict, or is the concept of objectivity something that should be discarded as an 'outmoded, false and impossible ideal' (Hurst & White 1994, p. 103).

This is what we describe as the central and recurring dilemma that confronts journalists in all media organisations. The conflict over objectivity is one of the most volatile fault lines in the ideology of reporters, and in their often acrimonious relationship with the public. It was a major problem that the framers of the AJA Code of Ethics first confronted in 1944 and it clearly troubled the Code's reformers in both 1983–84 and 1994–95 (Hirst 1997a). According to the Australian media commentator and academic Keith Windschuttle, the free-market model of journalism holds that news is an objective body of truth about the world. He adds that 'the task of the journalist is to discover the events which occur and report on them in prose, or on film as faithfully as possible' (Windschuttle 1988, p. 261). British media philosopher John O'Neill ties quality and ethical reporting to the virtues of a good journalist, which he says are honesty, perceptiveness, truthfulness, integrity, and the contested virtue of 'objectivity'. However, he does have an interesting and slightly different interpretation of 'objectivity'. O'Neill defines objective journalism as a style of reporting that 'best allows the audience to appreciate the complexities of a situation [and] may be better served by non-objective presentation of events' (O'Neill 1992, p. 20).

That's a look at objectivity in the macro sense. There's also objectivity in the micro sense, as practised by individual journalists within individual stories. It is in this context that dictionary definitions of 'objective' come into play: 'external to the mind; actually existing; real' (Moore 1997, p. 922). You can see that already this might tend to contradict or clash with Orwell's 'emotional attitude'; it is hard for an individual to completely lose their personality and not bring any of their own feelings to a story. We have to ask the question: Can a story truly be reported objectively by the individual journalist?

While there are many who would argue that there are reasons why no story can be truly objective, that is no reason not to try to be as objective as possible in every story you produce. As a working journalist you will make decisions about who will give a comment, what you will use from what sources say, who you won't contact and thereby ignore (usually using the excuse of deadline pressure), etc. If these decisions are made fairly and with the best interests of the audience and the story in mind, you will be on the right track. This will not usually be difficult if the story is of the routine kind—the reporting of an accidental death, or the scores in a sporting event you have no interest in. But what about reporting the Reserve Bank of Australia's decision to lift interest rates? An objective journalist might take at face value the argument that this is in the nation's economic interest—that will certainly be the bank's spin. But what about the interests of home-buyers with mortgages, or renters in the outer urban areas, or exporters, or farmers? In this type of situation, it is vital that you talk to as many sources as you can to obtain as clear a picture as possible of the issue, research as widely as time permits to background yourself as best you can to understand the many facets of the story. Despite their differences, the authors agree that true objectivity is probably impossible to achieve on a regular basis given the pressures on modern-day journalists, but your own personal ethics should dictate that you take as much time on a story as you can in order to cover it as objectively as you can. We will return to these issues in the chapters dealing with privacy, court reporting, plagiarism, and other issues.

It is clear from our analysis in this chapter and within a framework of dialectics, that ideological positions and emotional attitudes of news workers are necessarily contradictory. The idea of determinism suggests that it is the relations of production, fundamentally economic in nature, which will ultimately shape the ideology of journalists. This argument is further demonstrated in the following chapter on economics in the newsroom and a political economy of journalism ethics. We discuss how the cultural commodity 'news' is structured as both a source of private wealth, and of public information, and the impact of this process on the fault lines in journalism ethics.

Ethical dilemmas in practice

Scenario 1: Religious and political beliefs

You are asked to cover a rally by the Right to Life organisation, but personally you believe strongly in a woman's right to choose and that abortion should be legal, freely available, and supported as a choice for women. At the rally you see disturbing images and become upset. One of the rally organisers tries to comfort you and it causes you to get angry. A scuffle develops which is noticed by other journalists and taped by a TV news crew. What will you do?

Reverse the situation. You are a strong Christian who believes abortion is murder. You are asked to cover a Right to Choose rally. To you, all the women at the rally are man-hating feminists. Would you ask your editor to take you off the story?

Discussion: We are always being advised to be cautious about discussing religion and politics. Far better in Australia to discuss sport! But what if your religious convictions, or your firmly held political beliefs, interfered with your reporting? It's probably going to happen at some stage of your reporting career. How will you handle such an ethical conflict?

Do strongly held beliefs or opinions necessarily get in the way of being a good reporter or editor?

→ ## Scenario 2: Public good versus individual harm

A public official tells you that the drinking water in a particular area of town is not fit to drink. You approach the town officials, who say yes, there is a problem, but ask you not to report it for 48 hours while they try to fix it. Their argument is that it would cause unnecessary panic. There is no way that your source, who demands anonymity, won't be implicated if you publish the story beforehand.

This is a case of the 'public good versus harm to the individual'. In this case, with the potential for panic that could be caused to a large number of people, would you write the story and 'burn' your source? Do you agree to the embargo of 48 hours with the town officials? How important would the story have to be (life-threatening?) to justify a course of action that burns your source?

Case studies

For this section we have included as case studies four short biographical sketches of historically significant Australian journalists and editors. These biographies demonstrate how reporters have been influential, famous, and infamous well beyond the newsrooms they inhabit and the titles they edit. In each case the intellectual convictions of the journalists concerned have got them into trouble, as well as earned them respect from peers.

→ ## Case study 1

Brian Penton: The 'editor–intellectual'

Historian Pat Buckridge (1999) has written a profile of the famous Australian journalist and editor Brian Penton, who for more than 20 years helped to shape arguments and practices in Australian journalism. Among many achievements he wrote the first cadets' manual for young reporters. Penton had an interesting and controversial life, which highlights many themes relevant in this chapter. Importantly, his story illustrates how a journalist's emotional attitudes to news reporting are shaped by both environment and social relationships. In particular, Penton had an interesting professional friendship with Sir Frank Packer, who was then the publisher of Sydney's *Daily Telegraph*. Penton edited the paper for a decade, from 1941 to 1951. These were years of war and post-war reconstruction. The Packer paper supported the policies of the Australian Government and Penton shaped its intellectual and ideological policies through strong editorial direction. Under Penton's editorship, the *Daily Telegraph* was a 'carefully controlled instrument of political persuasion' (Buckridge 1999, p. 189). Like other important figures in Australian journalism, such as the late *Sydney Morning Herald* editor J.D. Pringle, former *Bulletin* editor Donald Horne, and Paul Kelly of the *Australian*, Penton was a journalist and a public intellectual. That is, the sentiments and opinions he espoused in the leading articles he wrote for the *Daily Telegraph* involved 'a significant degree of social and cultural expression' of the political ideas that were in 'social circulation' at the time (Buckridge 1999, p. 185–6). Buckridge (1994, 1999) notes how hard it was to establish an intellectual tradition in Australian journalism during the 1930s because of the strong larrikin anti-intellectualism of many Australian news workers and editors. Penton helped to change this, by shifting the balance of dialectical forces in favour of a more commercially based newspaper and a belief in 'objective' reporting. Penton's *Guide to Cadets*, which he wrote to train reporters for the *Daily Telegraph*, celebrated journalism as one of the most important jobs in society, recognising the intellectual side of newspaper reporting. At the same time it also contained practical advice on the company's editorial policies and the administrative systems of the newspaper (Buckridge 1994, pp. 287–90).

Penton was an old-style Australian nationalist and anti-authoritarian, whom Buckridge suggests used his influence to promote a certain style of liberalism (Buckridge 1999, p. 198). But as a traditional intellectual of an earlier period in journalism, Penton suffered a fractured consciousness. Buckridge credits Penton with possessing a 'dialogic' mind, the ability to grapple thoughtfully with the problems of his age. In this sense he was very much an Australian George Orwell, though without the socialist politics. Ultimately Penton recognised the importance of his relationship with the proprietor Frank Packer and learned to anticipate his editorial thinking. Buckridge (1999, p. 193) says Penton regarded it as a complementary partnership and that it was 'crucial to the effectiveness of his intellectual project as editor'. Buckridge also comments on the technical and bureaucratic elements of intellectual journalism, specifically in relation to editors in their role as 'managers' of the organisation's news 'assets' on behalf of 'investors'. The economic significance of these limitations is discussed in chapter 3 and related issues are taken up in several later chapters. In particular, Penton is a significant and controversial figure in the early history of the AJA's Code of Ethics (see chapter 4).

Case study 2

Wilfred Burchett: The journalist in 'exile'

Wilfred Burchett entered the world of journalism with no formal qualifications but with a strong desire to write the truth. In his own words he had become a journalist 'for what I still consider the most important motive. I had something to say and was burning to say it' (Burchett 1969, p. 122). He wrote with a definite emotional attitude in an effort to present to the rest of the world the truth about what he saw. Burchett himself believed no qualifications were necessary for this:

> That I became a journalist without any training is a valuable lesson to others ...
> But to ensure an honourable place in future records, one has to ... shape history
> and public opinion in the best interests of humanity.

Burchett 1969, p. 137

While visiting London, just before the outbreak of the Second World War, Burchett worked at a travel agency, a job that led to his career as a foreign correspondent. In 1938. Burchett was sent to Berlin by the travel agency. During his four-month stay, Burchett witnessed a side of Germany that foreigners didn't see—a country preparing for war while arresting Jews and placing them in concentration camps. Returning to Australia in 1939, Burchett was concerned with the way the Australian press presented a rosy image of Germany. He observed that 'Newspaper readers were shown Nazi Germany as a country where order reigned, trains ran on time, everything was clinically clean and stories of ill-treatment of Jews and political opponents were grossly exaggerated' (Burchett 1969, p. 136).

As a war correspondent, Wilfred Burchett was in China shortly before it declared war on Japan and was the first Western reporter to reach Hiroshima after the atomic bomb had been dropped. He had been warned not to go there as 'everyone was dying', but he ignored this and bought a train ticket to Hiroshima. John Pilger, another leading Australian journalist, praises Burchett's courage in doing this. 'Here was a European alone in a train filled with soldiers armed and sullen and almost certainly bitter at the moment of defeat. At two o'clock in the morning he reached Hiroshima and was promptly thrown in prison' (Pilger 1986b, p. xi).

The scale of human horror that Burchett saw in Hiroshima was reported in many papers around the world under the headline 'I Write This as a Warning to the World'. Here's how Burchett's eye-witness account began:

> HIROSHIMA, Tuesday. In Hiroshima, thirty days after the first atomic bomb destroyed the city and shook the world, people are still dying, mysteriously and horribly—people who were uninjured in the cataclysm—from an unknown something, which I can only describe as the atomic plague.
>
> Hiroshima does not look like a bombed city. It looks as if a monster steamroller had passed over it and squashed it out of existence. I write these facts as dispassionately as I can in the hope that they will act as a warning to the world.

Later, back in Tokyo, Burchett was at a military briefing to hear the head of the American atom bomb project, Brigadier-General Thomas Farrell, effectively deny the 'atomic plague' remark to the rest of the press (Perry 1988, p. 13). Burchett had witnessed the true devastation resulting from the bomb in contrast to other reporters who had been kept away from clear evidence of its effects. This is perhaps Wilfred Burchett's most celebrated achievement and one that he is proudly remembered for.

After his article on Hiroshima he was issued with an expulsion order from Japan. While reporting on the Korean War, Burchett had openly criticised Australia's role as a Cold War ally of the United States. In 1955 Burchett lost his passport (which he suspected had been stolen) and applied for a replacement.

Burchett received a letter from the Minister for Immigration saying that he had 'left Australia fifteen years ago' and had 'severed all connections with Australia'. Further, the letter stated that 'his activities since his departure have been such that he is considered to have forfeited any claim he might have had ... as the holder of an Australian passport' (Burchett 1969, p. 282). Burchett had in fact returned to Australia several times and spoken at public meetings, written for Australian newspapers throughout the 15 years, and had had six books and a play published in Australia as well as corresponding with his family. The Australian Government refused to specify what 'activities since his departure' warranted refusing Burchett a passport, denying that charges against him were serious enough to require testing in a formal inquiry. At the same time however, these charges were considered serious enough by the Government to be justification for refusing him a passport.

The conservative Menzies Government portrayed Burchett as a communist and a traitor to his country, encouraging the belief that he had brainwashed and tortured Australian prisoners of war in Korea (Manne 1994; Perry 1988). It took more than 20 years for Wilfred Burchett to have an opportunity to clear his name. In the end, a civil jury in a defamation case chose to believe Burchett had been a spy, in the pay of the Soviet KGB. Burchett was unable to get this decision overturned, despite further appeals (Perry 1988, p. 229–33).

Burchett was to suffer much criticism and persecution up to his death in 1983.

Case study 3

The *Oz* obscenity trials:
Psychedelic, free-lovin' larrikins of the press

There's no doubt that when the founders of *Oz* magazine gathered in a Mosman house in January 1963, the group contained at least one or two mischievous young persons, who were good-natured, wild of spirit, and with little regard for authority. A number of them had clearly demonstrated this character flaw in the previous year: they had been associated with Sydney's vibrant student newspapers, *Tharunka* and *Honi Soit*, both of which had been condemned by the authorities (Neville 1996, pp. 18–22).

According to Richard Neville, *Oz* was chosen because it was a 'new' word and because of its association with the Wizard of Oz: 'Conjuring memories of yellow brick roads'. It was not, says Neville, because of any connection with contemporary accepted shorthand for 'Australia' (1996, p. 24).

Oz certainly fits one criterion for the new journalism then beginning to make waves in the American press—it was a 'direct confrontation' with mainstream news (Hellmann 1981). In the first issue the editors satirically deconstructed the press coverage of the Queen's March 1963 visit to Australia and uncovered the deceptive reporting of Rupert Murdoch's *Mirror* in Sydney:

> The Mirror covered The Visit. 'In Adelaide, crowds were quiet and subdued; in Hobart, they were shy, overawed ...' Two weeks later the Mirror changed its mind: 'Adelaide loved every minute of the royal visit. Crowds were enormous. In Hobart,

people stood in thousands to cheer and wave ...' Rupert Murdoch was honing his
tabloid skills. Oz picked up on the deception and headlined it as DEPARTMENT
OF FACT. We had begun to hone a few skills of our own.

Neville 1996, p. 25

This reflexive sniping at the mainstream press was to become a regular feature of
Oz magazine and continued the tradition of parody that both Richard Neville (at
Tharunka) and Richard Walsh (at *Honi Soit*) had begun in their undergraduate days.
The larrikin nature of the *Oz* venture was further confirmed by the chosen launch
date for the first issue: April Fool's Day 1963.

The first issue held an interview with a Sydney abortionist and an article about
chastity belts and apparently sold out the first print-run of 6000. It also caused a small
amount of outrage: the printers (Murdoch's *Mirror* presses) cancelled their contract; the
magazine's landlord threatened to evict them; and Richard Neville's mother wrote a letter pointing out errors of fact in the chastity belt piece (Neville 1996, p. 28).

A few weeks later the *Oz* editors had their first run-in with Australia's ancient and
derelict censorship laws: Neville, Walsh, and the third editor, Peter Grose, were charged
with publishing an obscene magazine. Magistrate E.J. Gibson said *Oz* was clearly
obscene, he fined the trio £20 each, and 'gleefully' recorded convictions against them
(Neville 1996, p. 31). The following year *Oz* magazine was again dragged into the NSW
courts on obscenity charges and the editorial offices were raided after a Lenny Bruce
satire was published. But the item that caused most offence to the police was a photograph—tame by today's standards—of three men seemingly relieving themselves into
a very urinal-like sculpture set into the wall of a prominent Sydney building:

A block away from our office stood the new headquarters of the P&O Shipping
Line, recently opened by the Prime Minister [Robert Menzies]. Set in the polished
stone wall was a bronze basin sculpture: a series of interconnecting troughs at
waist height, with water gurgling on to the pavement. I posed myself at the bronze
recess, along with two friends, and pretended to pee. 'For the convenience of
passers-by,' explained Richie's caption, 'and, despite a nominal charge, you don't
need to pay immediately: Just P&O.' We put the shot on the cover.

Neville 1996, p. 34

It seems ridiculous from our perspective today to think that this amusing pun captioning a harmless picture could have caused such outrage. The public was obviously
not too offended; Neville says *Oz* number 6 sold over 10,000 copies (1996, p. 34).
When the second *Oz* trial opened in July 1964, the Crown had radio reverend Roger
Bush set out why an article called 'The word flashed around the Arms' was obscene.
This piece was a satirical monologue about teenage culture (such as it was) in Sydney's
northern suburbs in the 1960s and it related the story of a group of young men who go
to a party, get.drunk and each have sex with a young woman, who's also drunk:

There were a few KING birds there, but they were all holding hands with these fairies—so Dennis belted them and we all got on to the birds and Frank got one of them so pissed that she passed out and we all went through her like a packet of salts—KING.

Cited in Neville 1996, p. 40

This piece, penned and illustrated by the famous artist and impresario Martin Sharp, was taken apart stanza by stanza and the argument turned on whether it was merely obscene, or did, in fact, have literary merit. Despite loquacious evidence and opinion from some of Australia's leading literary figures the magazine was declared blasphemous and obscene on several counts:

'The word flashed around the Arms' was 'filthy and disgusting', according to [magistrate] Locke's judgment. A cartoon of a clergyman squatting like a dog by a gramophone, labelled His Master's Voice, was a 'disgusting piece of blasphemy'. The Lenny Bruce item, 'Ta Ra Ra Boom Te Ay', was 'grossly offensive, blasphemous and obscene'.

Neville 1996, p. 45

Sharp, Walsh, and Neville were convicted and sentenced to six months' hard labour, later reduced on appeal. The trio was soon to split up, but their fame continued and they were briefly reunited on another journalistic adventure, *The Living Daylights,* in the last years of 'hippiedom' in Australia. Richard Walsh stayed in Australia, gave up a lucrative career in medicine and began a lifelong association with journalism, magazines, and publishing. He was founding editor of the wonderful and infamous *Nation Review*, which hosted such talented writers as Mungo McCallum, 'Sam Orr', and Bob Ellis and cartoonists Patrick Cook and Michael Leunig. Richard Neville and Martin Sharp were part of a huge Australian invasion of London in the 'swinging sixties' and a British version of *Oz* magazine got them both into even more trouble, along with lawyer and gay activist Jim Anderson. Richard Neville may be the only newspaper editor in the world to have been convicted and imprisoned on blasphemy charges on two continents.

Case study 4

John Pilger: Hero or villain?

Basically it seems to me he has taken on the great theme of justice and injustice. The misuse of power against the powerless. The myopic, stupid cruelty of governments.

Martha Gellhorn in Pilger 1992, p. x

This statement, by journalist, traveller, and writer, the late Martha Gellhorn, summarises the emotional attitudes driving the journalism of controversial Australian reporter John Pilger over many years. Pilger says he is affected by the injustice he sees all around him. This is what Pilger finds 'newsworthy'—the victims of war, of corrupt and heartless governments.

Pilger grew up in Sydney in the 1950s. At age 18 he worked as a cadet journalist on the *Daily Telegraph* before moving to London in 1962 to work on the *Daily Mirror*. His career took him around the world to report on such events as the war in Vietnam, Cambodia, the Middle East, Africa, and the Nicaraguan revolution. To Pilger, it is his 'duty' as a journalist to describe the horror he sees. John Pilger is highly critical of the news media, even though he remains passionate about his brand of partisan journalism: '… the arena in which I work, has been both a major victim of and a collaborator in the narrowing of information and ideas, although it is misinterpreted as the very opposite' (Pilger 1992, p. 2).

Pilger's work as a war correspondent further reveals his somewhat hostile attitude towards the mainstream news media. In Vietnam he became aware of the use of censorship, which made 'the news become a mockery, telling so much and explaining so little' (Pilger 1986a, p. 42). He writes of the cunning nature of censorship:

> The Vietnam war, a famous media event, was the only war fought this century by a Western power which did not impose censorship, yet it was a deeply censored war … The most common form of censorship is censorship by subterfuge. The manipulation of thought and language, such as labels and cliches that deceive and polarise ('moderates' versus 'extremists' etc.) and a conditioned deference to authority and to the 'prevailing view' in the name of objectivity. This is journalism's most insidious restrictive practice.
>
> Pilger 1986a, pp. xiv–xv

Pilger gives some examples of this. In Vietnam atrocities were reported as 'mistakes', which were 'blundered into'. 'Strategic hamlets' were concentration camps. 'Pacification', a term seldom understood and employed to 'preserve the war's façade', meant 'killing as many people as possible in a given area within a given period of time'. The Vietcong were referred to as 'communist aggressors', while the American forces were never 'invaders', they were merely 'involved' (Pilger 1992, p. 67). As Pilger writes: 'Behind this fiction the essence of war could be pursued without serious examination … In the daily flow of "news" the victims of war became almost non-existent, like phantoms' (Pilger 1986a, p. 258).

Throughout his distinguished career, John Pilger has used journalism as a tool to right wrongs and to fight for justice. This can be seen in his crusade to help British children, victims of thalidomide, gain compensation. But he is perhaps best known in Australia for his reporting of Cambodia and the reign of terror of the Pol Pot regime in which thousands of professional people and academics were either killed or expelled from the cities to work as virtual slaves in rural areas.

He says of his coverage of Cambodia that he felt like 'The Times [correspondent] at the liberation of the Nazi death camp at Belsen', with a duty 'to describe something beyond the imagination of mankind'. He continues: 'That was how I felt in the summer of 1979. During twenty-two years as a journalist, most of them spent in transit at places of uncertainty and upheaval, I had not seen anything to compare with what I saw then in Cambodia' (Pilger 1992, p. 171).

Despite Pilger's frequent visits to Cambodia and the fact that he has produced so many films about the country, his knowledge and work in that area is still criticised. Death of The Nation, another film on Cambodia, came under heavy attack from the Australian's foreign editor Greg Sheridan (1994). On 14 February, Sheridan wrote on the front page of the Australian: 'Pilger has spent the last 10 years getting Cambodia absolutely wrong and his films have been generally full of misrepresentation, half-truth, exaggerations and extreme tendentiousness.' This led to a row between Pilger and the paper's editor Paul Kelly, in which strongly worded letters were exchanged. Pilger criticised Kelly for accepting a Government appointment to the Australia–Indonesia Institute. Their correspondence continued for more than a month. In the end Paul Kelly refused to publish an article submitted by Pilger on East Timor as it did not in his mind 'meet the standard of accuracy required by this paper.' Pilger then asked Kelly to state exactly what these 'inaccuracies' were, supplying sources for each, which Kelly refused to do. (The correspondence is cited in Bacon 1994.)

Pilger gave a copy of his article on East Timor to Reportage, the media magazine published by the Australian Centre for Independent Journalism in Sydney, which decided to print it (Pilger 1994). Reportage then contacted Kelly who wrote to them on 2 June, saying 'John Pilger's mistake is his apparent belief that he has a right to be published in this paper and, if he is not published, that we are under some obligation to justify our decision. This is not so. Newspapers do not work on this basis since it is neither appropriate nor practicable' (Bacon 1994). The next day, Pilger wrote to Reportage: 'The correction of smear and untruth ought to be a fundamental right of everyone in a free society claiming to be a free press. Kelly's arrogant denial of this right is compounded by the disquieting fact that his is Australia's only national newspaper, owned by a proprietor who controls some 67 per cent of the capital city press, making the Australian press the most narrowly based in the Western world' (cited in Bacon 1994).

Issues and questions raised by case studies 1 to 4

1   Are you able to see a dialectical relationship between their various points of view?
2   Burchett's political views are less mainstream than Penton's. Why do they appear to be so extreme?
3   Can you identify any Pilger-like crusaders in the media today? Who are they and what work puts them in his class?
4   Can you think of any reporters or editors you're familiar with who could be considered intellectuals and great 'thinkers'?

5   Do you think the pranks and sexual innuendoes in *Oz* magazine would raise any eyebrows today?

6   Does an editor have a duty to support the editorial policies of the publisher, even if s/he might disagree with them?

7   How did the emotional attitudes of Penton, Burchett, Pilger, and Neville coincide with and contradict each other?

8   If you can't think of many, why do you think that is?

9   In what ways are Penton, Burchett, Pilger, and Neville all products of their day and age?

10   Isn't 'tit-for-tat' criticism between journalists all just a bit petty?

11   Pilger expected to be given specific reasons why his piece on East Timor wasn't going to be published outside the Letters to the Editor section. Should 'Joe Public' (let alone John Pilger) really expect that?

12   Pilger's comment about the 'correction of smear and untruth' being a fundamental right for everyone in a free society is a noble sentiment indeed, but do you think it happens in Australia?

13   Should reporters and editors commit themselves to political causes?

14   Why do you think Pilger attracts criticism from other journalists?

15   Would you agree that Pilger was somewhat arrogant in demanding the *Australian* give him space to attack Greg Sheridan's writings?

→   ## Case study 5
Off the Rails: The Pauline Hanson trip

Margo Kingston has been a senior political reporter with the Fairfax company for many years and *Off the Rails* is her book-length diary of the 1998 federal election campaign, or at least the part of it that she had the most to do with. At the time Margo was working from the Canberra Press Gallery and for the four weeks of the 1998 election campaign she was a virtual shadow to Pauline Hanson.

Margo Kingston copped a lot of flack for her roie in reporting the One Nation campaign. Many of her journalist colleagues in the Press Gallery and beyond were quick to blame her whenever there was an 'incident' on the campaign trail (and there were plenty). At the same time, her unconventional style also got up the noses of 'Pauline's People'—the One Nation supporters for whom Pauline Hanson represented salvation.

And, as Margo readily admits at several stages in *Off the Rails*, she sometimes blurred the lines that are supposed to separate candidates from their media 'watchers'. The first incident occurred in the first week when Victorian Premier Jeff Kennett 'happened' to be in the southern Queensland city of Toowoomba at the same time as Pauline Hanson. Kingston found herself in a position to convince Hanson that she should meet with Kennett, who had pledged to chase Hanson down every burrow. 'I took her aside. "Look, this is look-you-in-the-eye advice. It's good for you to meet Kennett. It's the big bad Southerner thing—it doesn't matter that you chase him down"' (Kingston 1999a, p. 34).

It's unlikely that the Hanson–Kennett meeting would have happened without this intervention from the reporter. Margo justifies this by suggesting that not confronting Kennett in Queensland would make Hanson look 'so politically stupid as to be beyond belief, as well as torpedoing a good story' (Kingston 1999a, p. 34). This is a value judgment that would not necessarily be shared by everyone: Kennett had vowed to destroy Hanson. What could she possibly hope to gain from a 'chance' meeting in a suburban shopping centre? It's clear from Margo's account that Pauline Hanson came to rely on the reporters in her media entourage, particularly when the more senior One Nation people were out of their political depth (which was fairly often).

Off the Rails is honest enough to acknowledge how a committed and socially aware reporter can get swept up in the emotion and rhythm of the story s/he is covering. In the end Margo's personal sympathy for Pauline Hanson may have clouded her political judgment, but it did not stop her from putting the boot into One Nation over issues and policies. During the final days of the campaign Kingston called One Nation leader David Oldfield's bluff when he refused to give promised campaign costings to the media. He was forced to back down from a threat to have the press contingent arrested.

In an interview just after the book was launched, Margo Kingston said writing it had almost been a form of therapy after the hectic pace of the campaign: 'In the end I thought the best protection is to be completely honest because hopefully that will disarm at least some critics.' Margo was also not too upset by some of the 'knife job' reviews:

> *It didn't really worry me because the review quoted slab after slab out of the book, which convinced me, not only that the book should have been written, but secondly I'm getting something out of the book that I wanted, which was a public discussion of journalism by journalists.*

> Hirst 1999

In her word-sketch of the Canberra press pack, Margaret Simons recalls seeing Margo on TV, abusing David Oldfield at a media scrum:

> *Margo's outburst made all the television news's that night. Later when people talked about the media falling out with the Hanson camp, they usually meant Margo. And yet it was clear from what she wrote that she had in a weird way come to quite like Pauline Hanson, if not Oldfield. Margo was being unmanageable again. God bless her.*

> Simons 1999, p. 109

In the end it was this love–hate relationship with Hanson that most other journalists criticised in Margo's reporting of the campaign. Kingston had broken down the Chinese wall between reporters and sources—or at least she had shattered the illusion that such a wall existed, if it ever did. It is Margo's passion and humanity that make her such an excellent and respected political reporter.

Issues and questions raised by case study 5

1   Why is it a problem when reporters become too close to controversial figures like Pauline Hanson?
2   Research other material on Pauline Hanson and comment on how the media generally handled stories about her.
3   How should reporters in the Canberra Press Gallery relate to their political sources?
4   Can a reporter accurately and fairly cover the policies of a politician s/he agrees or disagrees with?
5   Is it wrong to mix personal opinion with political reporting?

3

A POLITICAL ECONOMY OF JOURNALISM ETHICS:

OWNERSHIP, MONOPOLIES, AND FREEDOM OF THE PRESS

Objectives

When you've read this chapter and the associated case studies you will appreciate and understand the following:

- The concept of a political economy of journalism ethics.
- The influence of ownership and control over ethical media practice.
- How oligopoly and monopoly work in the Australian news media.
- How newsroom routines based on economics and social relationships can influence ethical decision-making.
- A critique of the theory that suggests there is a 'market place of ideas'.
- What causes the major economic fault line in the news media and journalism.

Introduction: A conflict of interests?

In this chapter we discuss the political economy of ethics. That is, we examine the ways in which patterns of ownership and control, alongside the social relations surrounding, or inculcated within, the newsroom, might affect ethical decision-making, and create fault lines within the ideologies of journalism. In this case the fault line is an 'inherent conflict of interest' between business interests and 'independent editorial judgments' (Hurst & White 1994, p. 238). Until now most reporters, editors, and scholars have accepted this conflict of interest, and tried to work around it, rather than confront it head-on. We argue this is the insoluble contradiction within journalism today: the drive for profit versus the media's idealised role of serving the public interest. This chapter outlines an argument that in all capitalist societies there is a clear class-nature to journalism ethics that favours private property, the free enterprise system, imperialism, and the centralised, coordinating functions of the nation state (Hirst 1993, 2001, 2003; Kim 1994; McChesney 2000).

A number of 'models' of news media political economy are discussed in relation to their ability to explain the major economic fault lines in the ideology of journalism and their influence on news ethics.

Political economy asks how Australian journalism might have developed dialectically in response to changed social conditions, the many and continuing changes in ownership and different regulatory regimes over the years.

However, political economy is not just concerned with the institutional arrangements, or the legal structures of ownership and control. By combining a study of economics with tools from the sociology of work, we can begin to understand the day-to-day implications of newsroom management procedures, or work practices. A good example to illustrate this point is the coverage of strikes in which the harm to the public is commonly emphasised. The role of management in causing or aggravating industrial disputes is hardly ever recognised, and the costs to the public of strikes are often exaggerated, while issues are rarely explained. In a similar fashion, police rounds encourage the constant reporting of crime waves that usually bear no relation to the real incidence of crime in our communities (Windschuttle 1988). There is no necessary connection between the frequency of crime reporting and the frequency of crime—the source for such information is often the police service, whose major interest is in street crime, not white collar crime. We'll come back to these issues in the context of court reporting and 'moral panics' in later chapters.

What is a political economy of ethics?

A political economy approach can help explain the central economic fault line in the news media: the contradictory relationship between media companies organised as units of commercial capital and the media as a public institution for the dissemination of critically important public and political information (Hirst 2000). The political economy technique will focus our attention on what we call the relations of production inside news companies, and the social function of news as a means of inculcating in the broader society an ideology that upholds the core social and moral values of the market system.

From the early 1980s many media scholars in the United States, and elsewhere, began to realise that there were 'deep flaws' in contemporary Western journalism, and that there was a degree of incompatibility and contradiction between the desires of a corporate news media and the information needs of ostensibly democratic nations (Bowman 1988; Cose 1989; Eldridge 1993; Franklin 1997; McChesney & Scott 2002; Windschuttle 1988). Within this perspective many scholars have argued that competition and a free market in ideas cannot adequately address the fundamental and glaring fault line within journalism; the dual nature of the news commodity. News has a sale price and is a source of profit to those who control its production and distribution. At the same time news is the circulation of public information for the benefit of the public. In effect the news media produces for sale both an ideology and a commodity. To consumers news is a source of information about the world around them, but it is also the inculcation and reproduction of particular social values. In economic terms, the news commodity has an exchange value (a price in the market place), and the ability to generate surplus value (a profit) for whoever owns the capital that employs the news workers and runs the printing presses, or transmitter (Hirst 2001, 2003; Kim 1994; Oakham 1998; Wayne 2003). Thus, a political economy approach to evaluating and understanding the news media would argue that 'competition' in the capitalist market does not produce more and better news. Instead, according to political economists, the news industry is driven by a desire to 'minimize costs and maximize profits', along the way producing 'trivial, superficial, and often inaccurate reporting' (Ehrlich 1997, p. 302).

Our argument is that this fundamental driving force—the profit motive—will eventually undercut all efforts to impose, or aspire to, ethical standards in most commercial newsrooms. In blunt terms, the ethics of a news organisation are decided, and directed, by those individuals within the organisation who control the purse strings, and the advertising sales; not by the reporters and editors in the newsroom. This implies that the institutional ethics of most media organisations will be those of the owners, not the journalists—though this statement must be qualified by the comment that there is always a contest between owners and journalists over definitions and ethical standards. As we shall see in the next chapter, the very existence of the MEAA Code of Ethics is a product of this struggle (Hirst 1997a).

John Hurst and Sally White (1994, p. 251) highlight the contradictions in the news commodity when they write: 'the business face of the news media confronts its indivisible twin, the publicly accountable social institution'.

Profits rule, OK!

Advertising money pays for most of Australia's media, and one cannot be understood without the other.

Windschuttle 1988, p. 3

This is just as true today as it was in the late 1980s. Today it is the decline in advertising revenue that drives much of the cost-cutting in newsrooms, and which eventually impacts on the quality of the news we get in print, radio, and television. It is not sales per issue that generates profits for newspaper proprietors, but the amount of advertising they attract. Circulation figures are important because the greater the circulation, the higher the charge to advertisers. The rating system in television and radio works the same way: ratings are used to set the rate card for advertisers. This is what Ehrlich (1997) calls the 'selling of eyeballs' and is why newspaper companies worry when circulation slides, or television stations complain when viewer numbers drop off for expensive programs: advertising revenues will not be far behind (Newman 2001). Commentators began to talk about a decline in newspaper advertising in the late 1990s, and tried to explain it in terms of the boom–slump economic cycle, but slowly they began to realise it was an assault by non-newspaper sources of news and entertainment (Megalogenis 2001).

Windschuttle is right to argue that 'the economics of the media put them primarily in the business of selling audiences to advertisers' (1988, p. 6). This is what drives the media—not a desire to inform, or entertain. In a nutshell, it's profit. In a more theoretical and formal sense it's the need to accumulate more capital, and more revenues, or face annihilation in the competition maelstrom of the capitalist global market. It is this dialectic process of competition and accumulation that sets the social conditions for media monopolies to be created. The social relations of news production—the work routines, lines of management and editorial control, relations with sources and audiences—are driven by the imperative of accumulation and capital 'growth'. Therefore, it is useful to see how rapidly the configurations of ownership and control in the Australian, and now global, media system have changed over the past 50 years.

The political economy approach helps us to explore a major ethical fault line for journalists: what Robert McChesney (2000) calls a 'severe contradiction' between the privately owned and controlled news media and the social, political, and ideological needs of a supposedly democratic system of government. The economic function of the news media tends to dominate, determine, and undermine any democratic function of information delivery the news media might claim for itself.

Therefore, the process of creating the ideological commodity 'news' is simultaneously a process of replacing the political identity of 'citizen', with a 'consumer identity' as an 'accepted model for political decision-making' (Thornton 1999). When a vital institution of democracy, such as the news media, is in the hands of a small group of wealthy individuals, many of whom are connected to other business owners, it does not act as a forum for debate. Instead, the news media is in danger of becoming a venue for the self-promotion and self-preservation of this elite. This is certainly the case in America, where, as Robert McChesney (2000) argues, the news media does not exist to 'serve democracy', but to 'generate maximum profit to the small number of very large firms and billionaire investors'. One of those billionaire investors is of great interest to us because his family is one of only a handful that has owned, controlled, and dominated the Australian news media for more than half a century.

Australia's media monopolies

In July 2003 Brisbane's *Courier-Mail* newspaper won the PANPA Newspaper of the Year Award. Those fortunate enough to live in Brisbane found out about this by … reading the *Courier-Mail*. The '*Curious Snail*' (as it is known by some locals) had done better than 'every other metropolitan newspaper in the country in key segments' ('Better to Best: Your Paper's Winning Year' 2003). But only one of them has much to do with actual journalism, 'news-breaking', which is not hard in a one-newspaper city. The other criteria were all about marketing, management, and sales: 'development of the editorial product, circulation, readership and advertising revenue'. On the same page readers learned that 'careerone' provides the best online job placement and advertising service on the Internet, while 'News Limited's newspapers are very well suited to recruiting specialists' ('Network Gave the Right Connections' 2003). Rupert Murdoch's company owns the *Courier-Mail* and had recently purchased the *career*one online employment classified service. It's also interesting that these two puff pieces were not by-lined in the usual manner of a news story. When you have a monopoly there's no one to show you up,'and no one for readers to complain to. Rupert Murdoch may bristle at the title 'media baron' or the suggestion that News Corporation is an 'empire' (Fallows 2003), but if the shoe fits ...

How did Rupert Murdoch become so rich and powerful in one lifetime? Through family connections, an inheritance to invest, and a ruthless mind for business is one response. A more complex answer is supplied by an historical enquiry using the methods of political economy. The twentieth century was certainly the age of media monopolies; Australia was no exception.

Fierce competition between news firms in most Australian capital cities was well under way by the outbreak of the First World War in 1914. Takeovers and circulation battles were common, particularly in the largest markets, Melbourne and Sydney. The newspaper industry was also affected by the general business cycles associated with the First World War (1914–18), and the worldwide economic depression (roughly 1927–32). This era, until the end of the 1940s, is what political scientist Henry Mayer (1968, p. 29) described as the 'toughest and most ruthless period' in Australia's newspaper history. We feel sure he would say the same about the situation today. Competition within the traditional news media is fierce, and so too is the threat posed by new platforms for news delivery. Sir Keith Murdoch won the battle for circulation and advertisers in Melbourne in the 1940s, as son Rupert did when he bought the Sydney *Daily Mirror* from Ezra Norton in 1960, to take on both Sir Frank Packer's *Telegraph*, and the Fairfax's *SMH*. At the same time in the early 1960s, the same companies were competing for greater shares of the national television market (Mayer 1968, p. 78). These days the competition for 'eyeballs' has moved online, where it is no less fierce, and just as fraught with risk.

For further evidence we can look to the industrial–political history of journalism and the news business throughout the early years of the twentieth century. Australian arbitration laws forced both employer and employee into an industrial relations system that intrinsically recognised the antagonism between bosses and workers. By 1910, the employing class and the working class had organised themselves into broadly representative political parties, and industrial associations. The newspaper industry was no exception. Like the rest of Australian society, news workers were split, and united by certain issues according to their perceived loyalties and interests: everything from votes for women, the conscription referenda in 1916–17, to the defection of the Russian spies, the Petrovs, during the Cold War, and equal pay in the 1960s. The pressure of economic imperatives in shaping the ideologies of journalists are also apparent. A history of the journalists' union until the late 1950s by former AJA General President (from 1939 to 1943) Geoff Sparrow (1960) confirms that ethics is indeed an industrial issue:

Good pay is an inducement to any worker, but to the journalist, to some extent an idealist, there is also the satisfaction in a chance to express himself by writing. If he is beaten
by frustration and disillusionment, then the money bait will catch him.

Sparrow 1960, p. 140

Sparrow was commenting on the 'poor rewards' for news work, and on the future of
journalism, noting that 'public relations work' pays better. Better still, we can add, in today's
news landscape where PR-writing can still get you on the front page of a daily newspaper.

Australian Newspapers: A family affair

At the beginning of the twenty-first century, the Australian media landscape is dominated
by two family dynasties: the Murdochs and the Packers. Both are now into a third generation, both are looking to expand and, in 2004, both had their eyes on the Fairfax group. The
Packers want to take it over and the Murdochs want to commercially defeat it. In August
2003 the CEO of Fairfax told a journalist that Murdoch has 'basically surrounded us' (Lyons
2003, p. 21). According to historian Ken Inglis (1962, p. 162), both families were driven not
just to amass great wealth, which they've done, but to fulfil a desire to 'shape human des-
tiny'. It is also about winning at all costs. John Lyons (2003) wrote that the Murdoch camp
has intentions to dominate the Australian newspaper market by becoming the 'one paper'
that people buy. Effectively, Murdoch wants to put the Fairfax newspapers out of business.
On the other hand, Kerry Packer has made it known that he is keen to buy Fairfax.

An early pioneer of Australian media history, Henry Mayer, wrote that 'it would be very
hard to find any defenders of Press monopoly'. He added that neither economists nor the
media owners had 'yet made a case for its being a good thing in the sphere of communication' (1968, p 173). But what exactly do we mean by monopoly? Usually, in economics
it refers to a situation where one supplier controls a whole market, and strictly speaking

Table 3.1 Australia's newspapers—who gets what and who owns it

City	Masthead	Ownership
National Circulation	*The Australian*	News Limited
	The Australian Financial Review	Fairfax
Adelaide	*The Advertiser*	News Limited
Brisbane	*The Courier-Mail*	News Limited
Canberra	*The Canberra Times*	Rural Press
Darwin	*The Northern Territory News*	News Limited
Hobart	*The Mercury*	News Limited
Perth	*The West Australian*	West Australian Newspapers
Melbourne	*The Herald Sun*	News Limited
	The Age	Fairfax
Sydney	*The Daily Telegraph*	News Limited
	The Sydney Morning Herald	Fairfax

this is not the case with news media in Australia. There is instead an 'oligopoly', a market controlled by only a few players, but as historian Humphrey McQueen argues, 'competition between media giants is more apparent than real' (1977, p. 6).

In the mid 1960s when Henry Mayer was writing *The Press in Australia* there were six independent owners of fourteen capital city dailies, and four dominant families: the Fairfaxes, the Murdochs, the Symes, and the Packers. By 1976 there were seventeen dailies, but only four owners (McQueen 1977, p. 36). At the time of writing this book there are ten capital city dailies (including Hobart and Darwin) and two circulating nationally, though the *Australian Financial Review* is a specialist, not a general paper. The owners are listed in table 3.1.

Today there are four companies holding all the metropolitan daily titles, and five capital cities in which there is only one local daily paper. Outside Australia's capital cities the story is much the same. The days of traditional single-owner newspapers in most regional

Monopoly and oligopoly

This is how the processes of monopoly and oligopoly work; the features match the classic merger, acquisition, and takeover strategies under conditions of monopoly capitalism:

- Concentration of production in such a way that it plays a decisive role in economic and social life (if you're the only source of news it can be pretty decisive).
- The merger of bank capital with industrial capital to form 'finance' capital (the deals that create these super-companies are funded on credit and paper transfers, rather than real wealth).
- A close affiliation between the Government and the business—a virtual blending of the functions of capital and the state. The Berlusconi Government in Italy is a prime example. The Prime Minister owns around 80 per cent of the Italian commercial media, including two important television networks.
- The export of capital in the form of money, services, or 'intellectual' property, rather than just manufactured goods (witness Murdoch's global expansion since the early 1970s).
- The formation of global cartels, and informal agreements that carve territories between erstwhile competitors and 'insider' sweetheart deals. The merger of Hollywood studios, Internet portal operators, and traditional media companies to form AOL-Time-Warner is one such deal. So too is the formation of MSNBC (Microsoft plus the National Broadcasting Company) and its affiliation with Channel Nine in Australia.
- Excessive barriers to the entry of new players (it would take several billion dollars to mount a new global media company in competition with the established monopolists).

centres and country towns have vanished. Chains of newspapers, often produced from the same news sources, and sometimes even from the same office, now dominate the rural news landscape. Both the Fairfax and the Murdoch organisations have concentrated ownership in non-metropolitan newspapers, as has Australian Provincial Newspapers (the O'Reilly group). This situation has developed over the past 100 years as companies have bought out competitors and cross-traded shares to keep other players out of the game. At various times the media companies have had to contend with legislative changes in ownership regulations. This has had an enormous impact on the print media too, as cross-media ownership laws effectively regulate in a de facto way who can own a newspaper.

All of these issues are relevant in the Australian media landscape today: financial and political imperatives, such as the 2004 free trade agreement with the United States, have placed an enormous strain on Australia's media laws, and media companies. Many business and media analysts predicted a mad rush to grab assets when, in April 2003, it was rumoured that the Howard Government had struck a deal with Rupert Murdoch about the relaxation of the cross-media and foreign ownership regulations. As Mark Day (2003b, p. 3) reported in the *Australian*'s Media section, the various players have 'run their numbers and have their targets in mind'.

The deal to 'fix' the media laws was abandoned soon after Mark Day's article appeared. Why? Precisely because non-government parties in the Senate were not satisfied that the then Communications Minister, Richard Alston, could satisfy their 'concerns about the potential concentration of media ownership', should the proposed legislation go through (Day 2003b). We can easily see how this process of concentration has slowly strangled diversity in the Australian news media. A British-based company, Daily Mail and General Trust (DMG), owns more than fifty radio stations outside metropolitan areas as well as the capital city Nova FM licences. Another radio company, RG Capital, would like to enter partnerships with regional TV networks, to cut costs, for cross-promotion opportunities, and 'complementary selling', according to boss Tim Hughes (quoted in Day 2003b, p. 3).

A history of concentration

When it comes to cataloguing the process of concentration, it is easy to illustrate in the newspaper industry. In 1903 there were twenty-one dailies and seventeen owners in Australia's capital cities. This fell slightly to twenty and twelve respectively in 1930. In the next twenty years the numbers fell dramatically, down to fifteen papers and ten owners by 1950. In compiling this list, Henry Mayer noted there was no disagreement about 'the facts of oligopoly', only about the 'consequences' (1968, p. 31). As Mayer was writing, the Murdochs and the Packers were discussing a joint venture in Sydney television station TCN-9, subject to Government approval under the then current cross-media rules. The situation has not changed much in nearly 40 years—such deals are still the daily talk of the finance pages. In March 2003 the *Australian* prematurely reported that a deal had been struck in Canberra on the cross-media ownership laws (McIlveen & Schulze 2003). In the Murdoch papers, any news about News Corp will usually take second place to blatant 'Rupert-worship', such as during the company's bid for US satellite TV company, DirecTV, in March and April 2003. The *Australian*'s media reporter Jane Schulze (2003a, 2003b, 2003d) covered the story on the front page of the paper's business section three times in just fourteen days. The *Courier-Mail*'s Belinda Tasker (2003) ensured that Murdoch's Brisbane paper carried the story, and managed to lead with a 'surge' in News Corp's share prices. In an effort to appear even-handed, during the week of Murdoch's DirecTV deal, Jane Schulze interspersed a story about Fairfax Holdings instituting a 'management shake-up' to wind back exploding costs (Schulze 2003c). When the DirecTV deal was sealed a few months later, Schulze reported Murdoch's emergence 'as media's great survivor', adding for good measure that News Corp was 'relatively immune' from the 'negative perceptions of global media business'. The success story describes Murdoch as 'the Sun King' with 'one eye on the future', backed by a 'strong management team' that gives him the ability to 'look further afield' (Schulze 2003e). Another Murdoch business writer wrote in the same issue of the *Weekend Australian* that Murdoch competitor, Fairfax CEO Fred Hilmer, is 'still stuck in a managerial time-warp', while Murdoch shows the flair of the 'owner-entrepreneur' (McCrann 2003). The Murdoch press has always been keen to belittle the opposition while singing its own praises. The other proprietors do the same, and they always have (Hurst & White 1994, pp. 248–51).

Fairfax: Rich dad, poor son

For more than 145 years the Fairfax clan owned a major interest in the *Sydney Morning Herald*. In Melbourne David Syme and his brother controlled the *Age* newspaper group first acquired by the family in 1856. The last of the Syme family sold out to Fairfax in 1973. The Fairfax family also owned other news titles, radio networks, and television stations until 1987 when Warwick Fairfax Jr attempted to buy back all the Fairfax shares that were publicly listed on the Australian Stock Exchange. He failed spectacularly, thus forever diminishing one of the longest continuous family dynasties in the Australian newspaper industry. The Fairfax family had been involved in Sydney newspapers since 1841, and from time to time in broadcasting since the early days of radio, and from the beginning of television in the mid 1950s. John Fairfax and Company is now publicly listed, though many media business analysts would regard it as a soft takeover target.

The Canadian media mogul Conrad Black briefly held control of the Fairfax papers, but bailed out in 1996. Since then the Fairfax Board has had several leaders, and the CEO in 2003 was former academic, adviser, and government regulator, Fred Hilmer. Hilmer resigned in 2004; at the same time, Fairfax also cut staff numbers. Fairfax had recently bought into a New Zealand company, INL, that owned a chain of dailies, weeklies, and free suburban papers, but that did not stop some analysts claiming that the company had 'lost the plot', or that the Melbourne *Age* newspaper was in a 'death spiral' (Lyons 2003). Though it is important to put a caveat on this—the story was in the *Bulletin*, a Packer magazine, and as we have seen, the various proprietors are not above pushing their own barrow in editorial columns. This, after all, is the freedom of the press in a market economy.

While no longer owned by the Fairfax family, the company retains the name, and the business reporters retain a loyalty to the company in ways similar to those working for Murdoch. The April 2003 trans-Tasman deal in which Fairfax secured New Zealand's Independent Newspapers by buying shares from News Corporation was very favourably reported in the *SMH* (Frew 2003).

Publishing and broadcasting ... and mobile phones, casinos, and ...

The Packer family, long-time figures in Sydney's wealthy establishment, have variously controlled newspapers and television stations in Sydney and elsewhere, and a collection of magazines. Today the main Packer media assets are the Nine Network and magazine titles. The most successful title in the Australian Consolidated Press stable is not a newspaper, it is the *Australian Women's Weekly* magazine, which the company started in 1931 and now publishes monthly.

The Packer empire now includes a casino; a resort in the Australian snowfields; and cattle properties and horse studs estimated at nearly five million hectares (Robins 2003). The family company is also in a partnership with global giants Microsoft and NBC to cross-promote the MSN Internet portal in Australia. PBL also owns a clutch of magazines, and of course the number one television network.

In 2002 the third generation Packer and Murdoch heirs decided to do business together, which must have been a shock to their parents, who a few years earlier had fought a vicious war over ownership of the Australian Rugby League, and had battled for decades over other lucrative media assets. James Packer and Lachlan Murdoch did not invest in the media business, which they knew something about, but in telecommunications, which they knew next to nothing about. Their joint venture went horribly bust under suspicious circumstances, and the young guns got their fingers very badly burnt. Life was particularly tough for James Packer, whose marriage to a catwalk model and swimsuit designer went belly up around the same time. Once the apple of his strict father's eye, James Packer was by May 2003, 'stereotyped as the idiot son—the kid who lost $375 million of Dad's money on the disastrous mobile phone company, One.Tel' (Guillatt 2003, p. 20).

In 2003 the Packers appeared to have recovered from the heavy losses incurred from the One.Tel disaster, and the family was casting around for another acquisition. The rehabilitated son, James, told his ageing father's *Bulletin* magazine that their company's 25 per cent stake in the Internet jobs portal *Seek* would position them ahead of competitors. Packer said that the migration of traditional classified advertising onto the Internet would eventually dry up the 'rivers of gold' that feed newspaper profits (Linnell 2003).

Like father, like Sun-king, like son

The Murdoch family got involved in newspapers when Rupert's editor father Keith bought into the Herald and Weekly Times group in Melbourne. The family has also owned newspapers in Adelaide and Sydney since the 1950s. HWT became the Australian launch pad for Rupert's stellar international rise to moguldom. In 1964 Rupert Murdoch launched the *Australian* as the nation's first national daily. The Murdoch family also owned Australian television stations until they were forced to dispose of them, under once-again changed cross-media ownership rules, in order to buy back into more newspapers in the 1980s.

Murdoch's empire now embraces everything from music videos to expensive coffee table editions of fine books. He makes money every time we watch a re-run of the *Simpsons*, turn on Fox cable television, or read the *Weekend Australian*. He controls similar media assets on every continent. The Murdoch family holdings include book publishing

(HarperCollins), Hollywood studios (Fox), international cable television infrastructure and content, and a bundle of newspapers, from New York to Cairns, Hobart to London, Hong Kong, and across the Pacific, from Suva to Port Moresby.

Increasingly the profits of News Corporation are generated outside Australia, and based on a global TV strategy. In August 2003, journalist Max Walsh predicted that News Corp's core assets will remain in Murdoch family hands for at least one more generation. Walsh (2003, p. 30) also noted that 'the strategically-focused Murdoch senior has locked in dynastic control of News Corp's boardroom' with about 30 per cent of voting shares.

Now, in the first decade of the twenty-first century, the two dominant media families are still acquiring assets, and still lusting after others. It is an open secret that Kerry Packer wants to buy the Fairfax papers to add to his television network and magazine empire. On the other hand, Rupert Murdoch wants a television station to sit alongside his newspapers. In the middle of 2003 it was rumoured that Packer and Murdoch might get their way. The changes proposed by Minister Alston would have allowed media companies to own print, radio, and television assets in the same market. His compromise was two out of three. In the end, that did not go through at the time. The Australian Senate under the control of Opposition parties, had other ideas. At the same time, these great and powerful media families were also suffering the roller-coaster ride of the global capitalist economy. Just like the car industry, the housing sector, retail, wholesale, mining, hospitality, travel, textiles, manufacturing, and banking, the news media industry is characterised by fierce competition, an air of uncertainty, and a boom-or-bust winner-takes-all mentality.

One reason why Australia's media families are so powerful is that they have been able to globalise and diversify their investments. The media industry has also been through several shake outs, realignments, success stories, and abject failures. In each case—the exceptions being young Warwick Fairfax, a forgetful Alan Bond, and an absconding Christopher Skase—the major family stakeholders have managed to hang on to their core assets, and continue expanding.

In the 1990s, turnovers included the industry-shaking return of Kerry Packer to Channel Nine when Alan Bond was forced to sell it back to him at a loss, and Canadian mogul Conrad Black's short, but turbulent attempt to take over the Fairfax group. In the first decade of the twenty-first century, the major catalyst seems to be the global emergence of Rupert Murdoch's News Corporation as one of a handful of extremely powerful, and unaccountable, media giants.

One reason why the oligopoly/monopoly in the Australian media has persisted for so long is the strength of bourgeois ideology, and its resilience. At the core of this ideology is a belief in the efficiency and sanctity of market forces and private enterprise. A key aspect of this ideology is the 'market place of ideas', the clever combination of notions of a 'free press', with powerful myths of 'private enterprise' as the source of both wealth and social cohesion.

The market place of ideas—myth or reality?

At the heart of the capitalist liberal–democratic system of media ethics is the notion of a 'free market' that 'increases the possibility of choice between ideas', and 'holds together' a 'theory of citizenship in a liberal-democratic society' (Horne 1994a, p. 9, 1994b, pp. 69–80). For former *Bulletin* editor Donald Horne this means adherence to a set of pluralist values, but usually 'the prevailing views in the two major political parties' (1994b, p. 70). Increasingly, this is not enough for most people, if it ever was. Donald Horne's recipe for change is a series of prescriptive pleas for the news media to reform itself. In the decade since it was written things have got steadily worse, not better. This seems to indicate that some people are not listening—those with the economic, and political power to influence media behaviour. According to Horne (1994b, pp. 69–80) there are several, simple 'fixes' available in a liberal–democratic market place of ideas: journalists should have 'at least a minimum pluralist theory of issues'; 'ideas stories should be a category in the news editors' diaries'; 'the ABC should show the way'; finally, the news media 'should present, in a popularised form, the great complex diversity of perceived problems of our post-industrial period'. All well and good in theory, but that's not how the real world market actually operates.

Pluralism has almost completely died in the black-and-white world of so-called 'global terror networks', and 'complex' ideas are reduced to manufactured sound bites, or zippy marketing slogans. News editors can no longer afford to have too many 'ideas' stories in their diaries, unless they come with funding. Even in 1994 (when Horne was writing) the ABC was suffering cuts each year in allocations from Parliament. In 2003 the ABC's funding shortage had become so severe that several programs were axed and the national broadcaster continues to suffer the death of million-dollar cuts. A senior Murdoch editor, Paul Kelly also neatly, if unwittingly, undermines the free-market thesis when he says 'most decisions are rationalised by the paper's "real" interests' (Kelly 1994, p. 82). The editors, who run their news operations 'in trust on behalf of the proprietor' don't have time to diarise 'ideas' stories; they are busy dealing with the real issues of the newsroom. This is not, unfortunately the hard news agenda; rather it is, according to Kelly (1994, p. 84), a diverse range of functions, including:

> ... marketing, promotion, circulation strategies, industrial relations, new technology, advertising, product innovation, representing his paper to the community, defamation, staff management including hiring and firing, layout, the use of colour and budget control.

The 'free-market' model is well critiqued in the Australian context by Keith Windschuttle in his pioneering work, *The Media* (1988). In economic terms the free-market ideology suggests that from the start of the twentieth century, newspapers became more commercially oriented, and less aligned to political positions, and therefore less influential in society. The free-market model suggests that because the news media is also a business, it is more focused on selling, rather than preaching to the masses. By the mid 1960s Australian media companies were sharpening their marketing skills, in particular targeting 'women as potential customers for advertisers' (Mayer 1968, p. 27). It has to be said though, that this commercial interest did not, nor can it ever, put an end to the political meddling that news proprietors like to do, and feel it is their right to do. It may be something as mild as an editorial urging a vote for a particular party, or a position in a referendum. Or it could be as serious as printing and distributing party material through the news medium. Both have been done on a regular basis in Australia.

The free-market view is represented at one level by critics such as former *Age* editor and 'elder statesman' of Australian journalism, Les Carlyon, who believes that it is the reporting that drives the newspaper business. He told *Bulletin* reporter John Lyons (2003, p. 23) that:

> Journalism drives the [news] business … If [Fred] Hilmer and the [Fairfax] board knew what they were doing, they wouldn't be worrying about costs. They'd be worried about losing an audience … about being boring and irrelevant … about sullying a wonderful heritage that goes back to 1854.

Les Carlyon may have been right once, but today the news media is run according to the rules of business, not journalism. Later in his *Bulletin* article, Lyons (2003, p. 25) notes that the mood has changed, and that there is a question over Fairfax's commitment to journalism that 'would have been unthinkable in the past'.

The liberal–democratic paradigm

According to the former journalist and eminent Australian intellectual, Donald Horne, the dominant ideas that rule a modern capitalist democracy like Australia are those of a liberal–democratic paradigm. These ideas include: a free market place of ideas; the rationality of the economic market; free speech and a free press; freedom of association; and of free choice between political parties (Horne 1994a, 1994b). The interlocking of these myths provides the basic infrastructure of understanding in which political debate in capitalist liberal-democracies takes place (Horne 1994b, p. 129). This infrastructure is such that it attempts to bridge the fault lines that cut through the news media. According to the arguments put in *The Public Culture*, these myths are no longer invested with the potential for social conflict, they are 'neutral'; they are 'the myths of modernity' (Horne 1986, p. 244). In other words, we can accept that these freedoms exist because the ideals are accepted.

The free-market model is what most people would believe to be operating in countries like Australia today—a system of media ownership based on the principles of capitalism: private ownership, wages for workers, and profits for their bosses. The system is politically stable, based on representative government and the equality of voting power—though many people recognise that the monetary value of any political action that is meaningful is way beyond what most of us can afford. In the American context the myth is that anyone can aspire to be, and can actually become, President—the reality of course is anyone with about $400 million they don't need for anything else. The rising cost of politics has also led to similar situations in Australia today.

The myth of free-market news

In a perfect news world, everything that happened in any given time frame, at any given location (at least everything of consequence, impact, and interest) would be reported as news. However, because it is technically impossible to cover everything that happens everywhere, and because many things that happen are everyday and mundane, news production is a process of selection. In the free-market model, public interest is often equated with human interest, which is mainly trivia stories (colour pieces) and a summary of the important events of the day. As Windschuttle (1988, p. 262) says of the 'theory' of a free market in ideas: 'market forces determine the selection of news and that news itself is [a] more or less objective portrayal of reality'.

The central assumptions of the free-market model are that the capitalist, free-market economic system is good and that the social/political status quo should be protected. It is clearly linked to the liberal–democratic myths of individuality/equal rights, and equal access to power through elections. The notion of objectivity in journalism plays to these ideological assumptions and reinforces them. These are the overriding dynamics driving the emotional attitudes of journalism today. Quite clearly, as McQueen (1977) has demonstrated, the intellectual dynamic of journalism, the emotional dialectic, is created and contradicted by the very nature of the news commodity. News is an important source of information, but it also has the qualities of a commercially produced commodity. It is this duality of news, and the contradiction it expresses, that drives news workers to present 'unfavourable' views of class-based issues and organisations. It is precisely these ideological assumptions that are at the heart of Julianne Schultz's argument about reviving the concept of media as the fourth estate (see chapter 5).

On the other hand, British media philosopher John O'Neill argues that 'the market undermines the relation between journalism and democracy' or, in the terms of a debate about ethics, hinders the production of 'quality' news (O'Neill 1992, p. 15). This contradiction—between democracy and profit—is insoluble in the terms that Schultz has articulated. As O'Neill points out, 'free speech' in the 'free market' immediately runs into the legal problems of ownership, control, and access. It is precisely this property right that exerts the 'limiting' influence of economic determination over the emotional dialectic of 'ethics'. In the end, the 'hidden hand' of the free market effectively prevents 'objective' journalism from existing at all. All journalism in a capitalist market economy is compromised.

Ownership, expressed through private and corporate property rights, restricts the freedom of those without property. O'Neill (1992, p.18) himself fails to bridge this contradiction, instead suggesting that the market system encourages diversity and guarantees a 'watchdog role for the news media'.

While it is possible to express some disagreements with O'Neill's (1992, pp. 22–4) argument that media outputs are consumer-driven, it can equally be argued that the idea that there is a 'sovereign' consumer is a free-market myth. In our capitalist and formal democracies the real power is in the hands of those who own the means of journalistic production—that is the whole point of ownership and control—expressed as social control over the emotional dialectic of the front-page. O'Neill is right to say that the market shapes news values, but producers, not consumers, control this process.

James Curran (1991) argues that liberal–democratic and free-market ideas have been effectively challenged in the field of journalism and media studies. Curran (1991) describes the news media as a field of ideological production in which the economic strength of capital provides a privileged position, to which subordinate social forces are denied direct, unmediated access. Ultimately it is a question of which groups have the power to influence and control news information flows. Are we being manipulated by unseen ideological 'controllers' when we watch the evening news broadcast?

The manipulative model of news production

The manipulative model of news media suggests that journalists act in the direct interests of their employers, the media owners. Hence reporters will deliberately produce propaganda, cover up the truth, and present 'the existing social order as the best of all possible worlds, and either suppress or ridicule alternative viewpoints' (Curran 1991, p. 263). Put more simply, the manipulative model suggests the news media is a giant conspiracy. The manipulative model has been popular among both left- and right-wing critics of the media for many years. It is favoured by American anarchist and media critic, Noam Chomsky, as well as some at the other extreme of the political axis, like shock-jock Sean Hannity. In the United States, and in Australia, conservative and neo-conservative commentators often lament a 'left-wing' bias in the media, even in such stalwarts of the establishment as the *New York Times*, or the *SMH* (Hirst & Schutze 2004a, b). A good example of the limitations of the manipulative model of news is the common right-wing criticism in the United States that the American media is full of 'pinko', 'queer liberals' (Hannity 2002), a charge that has been investigated and refuted by others (Alterman 2003).

Of course, the owners of newspapers, radio and television stations, magazines, and online news portals do have some level of influence over the news they relay to an audience. It makes perfect sense in a capitalist economy for the commercial interests of the capitalists to influence the selection of target audiences and the general editorial line to be taken by the news outlet they own. It follows, according to this logic, that the selection of news must conform to these same principles. In Australia there have been cases of direct intervention by two generations of the Fairfax family, three generations of Murdochs, and three generations of Packers. Despite the anecdotal evidence that owners do exercise complete control, we believe that the manipulative model greatly overstates the case for direct intervention on a day-by-day basis. For one thing, it is an inadequate account of the independent role of journalists—reporters are seen as no more than mouthpieces for owners. Most news workers would fiercely deny that they are mere pawns of the owners, others may privately acknowledge that they do curry favour, a handful are proud of their role as interpreters and popularisers of the pearls of wisdom of their company's management. The survey evidence presented over many years by John Henningham (1984, 1985, 1993, 1995a, 1995c, 1995d, 1995f, 1996a) and by the Australian results of the worldwide Media and Democracy survey (Schultz 1998) attests to the independent nature of most working journalists, and their desire to resist direct intervention from media owners.

Critics also argue that the manipulative model does not account for variations in the tastes of audiences over time, nor does it have a theory of the market for news. It shares with the free-market model the idea that there is an objective reality in which things happen, and that reporters 'report' them. The main difference is that in the free-market model, the news is there to be discovered, while in the manipulative model the 'real' news is concealed. However, rejecting the manipulative model does not mean totally discounting any form of directive control. Monopolies, oligopolies, and complex news gathering organisations need a certain amount of 'leadership'. This brings with it a necessary level of bureaucracy, and a growing number of management functions it would seem (Cose 1989; Grattan 1998; Underwood 1993).

The bureaucratic news organisation

According to Keith Windschuttle (1988, p. 265), news production is 'an organised response to a series of routine bureaucratic processes'. In this case, journalists don't just pick up news that's lying around—news is 'organised' in a number of ways, including rounds reporting, the routine inclusion of press releases to fill news holes, and the accelerating overlap between many aspects of journalism and public relations. The process is also closely managed, from both an editorial and an accounting perspective.

Journalists are still required, in most newsrooms, to select material from what's on offer, 'to fit a preconceived idea of what is newsworthy' (Windschuttle 1988, p. 266). The standard news values of journalism still apply, but in a sense, they too are a force for bureaucracy. Everybody knows what 'news' is: 'news' is what 'news' is. Always has been, always will be. Of course, no reporter of any reasonable standard would agree with that statement. News values, like any social, and professional values, are subject to change. Like emotional attitudes, news values are pushed and pulled by social forces.

However, it is true to say that in the last half of last century, a certain repetitive, standardised 'newzak' style (Franklin 1997, pp. 26–30) developed, well-suited to bureaucratic routine. There is very little variation in either news agendas, or presentation between the major networks across Australia, nor between them and the formats and news values of other Western, urbanised societies. Global similarities are also self-evident and the adoption lag is getting progressively shorter. Variations in style due to language and local 'cultural' differences are minor, compared to the almost overwhelming similarity of content, values, approach, and framing of news (Masterton 1985, 1992, 1998).

Large commercial television and newspaper concerns run along predictable and planned lines. Budgets are set, costs minimised, and a daily or nightly product is churned off the assembly line, seven days a week. The recipe changes from time to time: the new 'news lite' formula of breakfast television, and the slot-creep, to a 4.30pm news bulletin in most Australian capital cities. The Government-funded broadcasters are definitely vast bureaucracies, as both authors can attest from years of experience at both the ABC and the SBS. Despite this criticism, we are not picking on particular models—just pointing out the inherent fault lines, strengths, and weaknesses. A certain level of bureaucracy (in the sense of a functioning management and work structure) is a necessary element of any large organisation, tasked with doing just about anything. Finding, checking, producing, writing, publishing, and broadcasting the news is a complex organisational problem, and it needs to run smoothly. But sometimes highly bureaucratic ideologies can stifle imagination, creativity, and differences of opinion.

A bureaucratic routine means that in a newsroom running to a tight deadline, most news items are derived from the selective accounts of sources who themselves are players in a wider bureaucratic game. The increasing interventions of PR functionaries in the news process means that traditional newsroom gate-keeping is relegated to a second round of selection, often from public relations handouts. This routinisation of production also leads to news items that are manufactured in high volume, for high turnover. There are consequences throughout the news gathering process as a result of bureaucratic routinism. For ease of use, newsworthy information must be easily accessed from regular, predictable, and reliable sources, who then play a role in defining the process of news selection. Hence powerful and legitimate institutions further entrench their position by shaping the flow of news. This is further entrenched by the rhythm of the news cycle. The now-constant 24-hour news frame means that we get daily chunks of news, often disconnected from a time context. A fire in a southern Brisbane suburb one weekend was first reported on Saturday night. The same story, with the same grabs was still running in the Monday morning bulletins. By this time all time references had been dropped from the story, and from the reader intro. The story was recycled for more than 36 hours. In this way unusual events, like suspicious weekend fires, can be incorporated into well-known presentation formulas—not to mention how pleased the accountants are, as running the story three or four times is good value for money! There is no doubt that routines and bureaucratic management of news gathering and reporting do impact on the ethics of journalists and on the content, style, and 'shape' of the daily news agenda. However, it is important to also understand the 'glue' of ideas and shared social practices that hold the bureaucracies on their course and help individuals to internalise as 'normal' the values of the bureaucrats. There has to be some sort of agreement about common boundaries of news sensibilities and polite debate.

The ideological consensus model

The ideological consensus model of news organisation suggests that the process of news production is to a certain degree interactive between the media organisation, the audience, and events that take place in the social context of the 'real' world. In this way, the news is an ideological product. From most news sources we tend to get a certain amount of 'useful' information, so generally, what we read, hear, and see in the 'news' is broadly accurate. The IC model holds that at the same time the news is a highly selective interpretation of society, The 'objective' facts that are presented as 'news' are actually filtered through the lens of a mediating ideology. The news is 'framed' by the central ideological assumptions of the society, what Daniel Hallin (1986, 1994) calls the core ideas in the 'sphere of consensus'. In this context, the news media presents the existing economic, political, and social system as the best there is. Any attempt to move beyond the 'limits of controversy' is met with a charge of 'deviance' and the news media is engaged as an ideological border guard ensuring that deviants don't get a positive run (Hallin 1994).

From the late 1970s researchers with the Glasgow University Media Group developed and used the ideological consensus model in their work on media effects and news agenda-setting. A number of very useful papers appear in their collection, *Getting the Message: News, Truth and Power* (Eldridge 1993). According to the GUMG's interpretation of the IC model, it is the news media that defines *what* will be significant events, and then tells us *how* to interpret them using the media's own definitions and assumptions. In this way the news media places an ideological 'frame' over the news, and the assumptions, arguments, and outcomes must be defined, referenced, and reported in that context.

Keith Windschuttle (1988) argues that the ideological consensus model is just a more elaborate form of the manipulative model. The news media helps a small political elite to formulate arguments that will persuade public opinion, in Herman and Chomsky's (1988) terms, for the manufacture of public consent to follow a particular agenda—one that does not necessarily conform to the best economic, social, cultural, or political interests of the vast 'ordinary' audience, but which supports the ambitions and enrichment of the elite.

An important criticism we would make of the IC model is that it appears not to allow for any process of change or challenge from audience members (either individually or collectively), or from the people actually working for the 'manufacturers'. Not everyone employed by News Limited, Fairfax, or ACP, thinks like their bosses. But in the IC model the world of control appears as a situation of perfect closure. At some levels it can be critiqued as an idealist model, or one of implied totalitarian control with no space for any alternatives, or for opposition to grow.

The materialist model

To deal with these criticisms of the manipulative, bureaucratic, and IC models we can take a fresh look at what Keith Windschuttle calls the 'materialist' theory of news, and what in this book we are calling the political economy of news and media ethics.

In basic terms the materialist model has the following features:

- The advertising industry and the media now rely almost totally on the brand loyalty of their reading, listening, or viewing audience.
- In terms of the dialectic, it is clear that the combined economic and social forces of marketing and managerialism are driving the current changes in news formulas and the ideologies of journalism.
- Audiences do have some realistic expectation that they will get a consistent standard of news, and this has led to the application of a bureaucratic news formula.
- The news agenda, style, format and framing are fundamentally driven by economic imperatives: 'the news formula, or the personality of a newspaper [or commercial electronic media], works mainly to deliver a particular type of target audience to the advertiser' (Herman & Chomsky 1988, p. 275).

In this way, the 'news' is, for the most part, an accurate reflection of the way most people see the status quo. That is, it is the world viewed through almost the same ideological spectacles as the majority of the audience (those captured by the surveys). However, in our opinion, most Australians are not stupid, nor are they ignorant of the world around them. In some instances, but not all, the news-consuming public can see the fault lines, and recognises that there are contradictions between what the news presents to them, and the reality of their lives. News reporters and editors are subject to similar pressures, as we have seen. It is therefore not too far-fetched to suggest that both news producers and news audiences can, from time to time, challenge the dominant news paradigm as it is generally framed by, and presented through, the news media. Leading Australian historian and social critic Humphrey McQueen has provided a penetrating critique of the myth of 'market democracy', one that applies equally to the IC model, and fits with Windschuttle's materialism.

McQueen's work on media monopolies fits the materialist theory and clearly uncovers the dynamic of the 'business' of news production:

> The privately owned media are not anti-working class on someone else's behalf. They take the stands they do because of their own interests as big businesses which happen to be newspaper companies ... When the media presents unfavourable views of the working class and of socialism, they are doing what comes naturally to capitalists.

> McQueen 1977, pp. 40–1

The materialist approach of political economy allows us to explore any fault lines we can detect in the relationship between the 'free market' and 'democracy', and to take into our service the useful elements of the other models and theories reviewed here. This is useful when trying to negotiate the stress fractures around the definition, meaning, and desirability of 'democracy'. John O'Neill (1992) argues against a simple 'bi-polar' vision of the choice being between state control of the news media, along what we might call 'Stalinist' lines, and as practised in the former Soviet Union, and the 'free-market' ideal of 'consumer choice'.

The Stalinist model has self-destructed, at least in the Soviet sense, but state control over news media is a common occurrence in many nations. Some countries, like Singapore and Hong Kong, operate along Western market lines and would like to think of themselves as 'democratic', in a particular way. Regulation of broadcasting in most Western nations and throughout Africa, Asia, the Pacific, the Middle East, the Indian sub-continent, and the Americas is fraught with dangers to freedom of the media, and democracy. Is the Western, liberal model really any better?

When examined closely the market model tends to lose its appeal, once political economy uncovers the root causes of bureaucracy, monopoly, oligopoly, and subtle ideological manipulation. As an alternative we can briefly visit John O'Neill's (1992, p. 27) vision for a more democratic process of news production: 'Non-market, socialised and decentralised media serving the goals of both journalism and democracy as a forum are not a political impossibility'.

One possible solution, that would fit with O'Neill's vision, is for popularly elected editors in newsrooms (Hirst 2001). This may seem a radical alternative, but like we said at the very beginning of this book, what sounds strange and far-fetched today can easily become the common sense of the future. Who knows where tomorrow's fault lines will take news workers, the media organisations, and the news audience? The only certain thing in our increasingly uncertain world is that things are changing, including how we view the media, the practices of journalism, and the political economy of ethics. These uncertainties are highlighted in the case studies we have chosen for this chapter.

In this chapter we have described and explained the central economic fault line that runs through the news media today: the pursuit of profits versus the public's right to know. We have argued that the non-stop drive for profits, the collection and circulation of surplus value from the labour of those employed by media capital, is what creates bias in the news (Hirst 1993, 2001, 2003). This is a class bias that draws on an ideological consensus model to drive public opinion. Media capital will work to protect the values and integrity of capital generally, and in a capitalist democracy, the capitalist-run media helps churn the ideology (Wayne 2003). Further, the economics and the production relations of the newsroom hamstring critical journalism because they limit resources, availability of the news hole, and the freedom to investigate business associates of the company executives. Journalists are workers—most are employed on wage contracts—though they use brains rather than muscle-power in their labouring duties. Their conditions of employment are not that different when compared to public servants, bank staff, or clerical staff in private enterprise. Until very recently most newspaper offices had a decidedly industrial feel. Tom Wolfe (1977) once described his 1960s New York paper offices as a giant 'fact factory', painted in 'industrial' colours, and with a decidedly mechanical feel. 'Fortress Wapping', News Limited's newspaper headquarters in London, has been described in similar terms (Franklin 1997), as have countless other newsrooms around the world.

The dialectic of control over the front page and the TV news camera is a privilege of ownership that creates the class divide we have identified in the media. The owners are on one side and the vast bulk of their consumers (the general public) on the other. Journalists and other news workers are caught in the middle, in what we call a contradictory class location (Poulantzas 1975; Hirst 2003). That is, their loyalties are divided, and their emotional attitudes subject to swings and rapid changes. On the one hand, the ideological tug of the ruling-class ideas they express each day; on the other, the economic tug of proletarianisation. This is the process American political economist Harry Braverman (1974) described as the eventual de-skilling of white-collar work and the pushing of white collar labour into more restricted, and rigid employment contracts. It is a process that applies across a number of occupations, including teaching, nursing, and office-work as well as journalism. In the past 50 years it has certainly impacted on journalism, and journalism education in a number of ways. A good undergraduate degree is now almost a compulsory prerequisite for a journalism cadet, or equivalent position in most Australian newsrooms.

It is no wonder that, in this context, the growth of trade unionism among journalists throughout the twentieth century brought with it changes in newsroom organisation, better working conditions, and … better ethics. In the following chapter we will document the historical evolution of the present MEAA Code of Ethics and examine some more recent developments: Charters of Editorial Independence and various other schemes of both self-regulation, and potential legislative boundaries on journalistic independence.

Ethical dilemmas in practice

➔ ### Scenario 1

You are a junior reporter for a capital city newspaper sent to the opening of an art exhibition at a major city department store. You're in the lift heading for the store Art Gallery with the State Governor's entourage (s/he is there to open the exhibition). The lift breaks down between floors. You spend half an hour trapped in the lift with the

Governor and his/her friends, and s/he is not happy. A senior executive of the department store meets the lift when you are finally released, apologises profusely to the Governor's party, and 'warns' you that he'll pull the store's lucrative advertising contract if your newspaper publishes anything about the lift drama. Debate the pros and cons of the situation. What would you end up doing?

Scenario 2:

Your paper decides that in the run-up to the next local government elections they will offer 'free space' to any candidate who buys a package of ads. You're the one that is nominated to ring the various candidates who have been signed up by the advertising department and write stories about them. What's your reaction to that assignment?

Case studies

Case study 1
The *Courier-Mail*'s crusade against Manning Clark

The Brisbane *Courier-Mail*, under the editorship of Chris Mitchell, sparked a storm in late August 1996, when it published an eight-broadsheet-page exposé on Australia's best-known historian, the late Professor Manning Clark, claiming he may have been 'an agent of influence' working on behalf of the former Soviet Union. The *Courier-Mail* said in its page 1 lead that it had evidence from two sources that Clark had been seen in the 1970s wearing the highest honour of the Soviet Union, the Order of Lenin (Smith & Kelly 1996). In defence of their massive coverage of the story, *Courier* editor-in-chief Chris Mitchell said: 'Our extensive coverage is not a beat-up nor conclusive proof that Clark worked against the interests of his country. It seeks only to pose the questions: was Clark an agent of influence for the Soviet Union and how important might his role have been?' (Mitchell 1996).

Mitchell said that after extensive checks with their primary sources, journalist Peter Kelly and Australian poet Les Murray, the paper became convinced they were sure of their stories. He brought out some 'big guns' in pointing out that the paper had obtained ASIO files on Clark and his wife up to 1966 (admitting, though, that a lot of the material was heavily 'blacked out'). Kelly and Murray had also consulted intelligence experts, including the highest-ranking KGB double agent ever to defect to the West, Oleg Gordievsky (Mitchell 1996). Mitchell quoted Clark's cousin, Justice Robert Hope, from a 1984 Royal Commission for the definition of an agent of influence—someone who may do nothing detrimental to his own Government, but takes action to produce a beneficial outcome for the foreign power whose intelligence service operates him (Mitchell 1996). Later in his defence of the paper's stand (published in its sister Murdoch publication, the *Weekend Australian*) Mitchell posed a total of twelve questions he said the *Courier* would ask critics of the exposé. The first asked why Clark was removed in 1953 from the Department of External Affairs committee that selected all Australia's diplomatic cadets, and why the ASIO file suggested his removal was 'for security reasons' (Mitchell 1996).

The Fairfax *SMH* dismissed the evidence as hearsay, but Mitchell said his paper had legal advice that the material they published would be admissible in a court of law (Mitchell 1996). Clark's son, Andrew, who at the time was editor of the *SMH*'s sister Sunday publication, the *Sun Herald,* accused the *Courier-Mail* of suffering from editorial mad-cow disease in the companion piece to Mitchell's defence of the story (Clark 1996). Clark said the *Courier-Mail*'s year-long investigation had not uncovered any evidence of his father receiving the Soviet equivalent of a knighthood. Andrew Clark wrote: 'In fact, it ran the claim, which is based on malicious tittle-tattle, as "fact" in the first paragraph of a front-page lead which formed part of an eight-page diatribe against my father, Manning Clark, the historian, who died five years ago' (Clark 1996). Andrew Clark didn't hold back:

> *A once-proud newspaper has jettisoned its commitment to accuracy. The publication of this McCarthyist sleaze is the product of a poisonous cocktail. The ingredients include a deep malevolence springing from the enduring influence Dad has on the way Australians view themselves arising from his authorship of the six-volume* A History of Australia. *Other elements are ruthless ambition, 'trophy journalism' gone mad, a remarkable lack of sophistication, stupidity and ignorance, absence of professionalism, a reckless indifference to the facts, and secrecy. The* Courier-Mail*'s pages have been taken over by a pack of scoundrels, malcontents and no-hopers.*
>
> Clark 1996

Issues and questions raised by case study 1

1   Read the original 'exposé' in the *Courier-Mail* of 24 August 1996. What do you think of the paper's research?
2   Are the paper's conclusions justified by the evidence? If you think so, explain how. If not, explain why.
3   If you were the editor-in-chief of the *Courier-Mail* at the time, how would you have handled the story?
4   What's your reaction to Andrew Clark's defence of his father in the *Weekend Australian*?
5   Manning Clark had been dead for five years by the time the story was published. What purpose did it serve?
6   While legally you cannot defame the dead, you can damage their reputation. Was it, as son Andrew said, 'malicious tittle-tattle' or should Clark's service for the Soviet Union (if it was true) have been exposed?

7   Is it an important role of the media to 'correct' history?

8   Aside from cutting down a 'tall poppy', what purposes did publishing the story serve?

Case study 2
The ABC co-sponsorship row

In September 1994, a group of ABC staff blew the whistle on ABC co-productions that were accepting money from commercial sponsors in return for giving them favourable coverage in magazine-style programs such as *Holiday* and *Great Ideas*. The staff aired their concerns on the Nine network's *Sunday* program. The story got bigger when the *SMH* claimed that a mining company had paid $20,000, and had organised funding from other industry sources, towards the production costs for a report on the science program *Quantum,* which was initially pitched to the ABC with the title 'The magic of magnesium'. The segment went to air with the catchier title: 'Billion dollar rock' (Davies, Lecky & Norrington 1994; Guillatt 1994). This and other sponsorship deals for ABC shows appeared to be a breach of the ABC's guidelines for co-productions. A number of heads rolled as a result, including that of television boss, Paddy Conroy. Whistleblower John Millard complained that he was victimised and sent to work in ABC radio as 'payback' for his role in exposing the sponsorship deals. ABC management said another whistleblower, Tracee Hutchison, had 'an axe to grind' and implied her work had not been up to standard (Davies, Lecky & Norrington 1994).

These allegations of improper funding arrangements on so-called 'lifestyle' shows were not new in 1994. In the previous 18 months, staff-elected ABC Board member Quentin Dempster had brought these matters to public attention, but the complaints had been dismissed. An ABC spokesperson said in September that the earlier allegations had been dealt with in a sixteen-page response from the then acting director of television, Mr Kim Williams (Simper 1994).

As a result of the fresh allegations, an independent inquiry was initiated by the then chair of the ABC board, Professor Mark Armstrong, and headed by George Palmer QC. Armstrong (1994) tried to distance the ABC Board from the allegations about what he called 'infotainment' programming and said it was all in the past. At the same time West Australian Greens senator Christabel Chamarette combined with the Opposition to force a Senate inquiry. The terms of reference covered the management and organisation of the ABC and the possible impact of funding arrangements on the corporation's editorial independence (Davies 1994). The ABC's then managing director, David Hill, dismissed the Senate inquiry as a 'dog's breakfast', but it certainly gave the story legs and it continued to run in the print media for some time. Hill did find one supporter, Fairfax columnist Gerard Henderson (1994):

As managing director, Hill can be criticised for too great a commitment to ratings. But at least the time has gone when a program was deemed a hit if it appealed to a couple of yogurt-eating Stalinists in Glebe or Fitzroy.

The ABC's own editorial guidelines of the time were very strict in terms of outside funding. Section 14.1.3 of the 1993 guidelines pointed out that the 'public credibility of the ABC' was crucial; while section 14.1.5 ruled out entirely sponsorship for news and current affairs, at least on the domestic television network (ABC 1993, p. 46). Co-productions between the ABC and external funding bodies (whether private or Government) were covered by Section 15 of the *Editorial Policies* document (ABC 1993, p. 49) as well as by Section 25(5)(b) of the *ABC Act*. Section 15.6.7 of the *Editorial Policies* document deserves to be quoted in full as it made the situation crystal clear:

> The Directors of Radio and Television have an onus to review, and an obligation to reject any proposal where a public sector agency or a financier of a co-production or independent producer has an interest in the content of any program and the Director is not satisfied that the ABC's independence and integrity are fully protected. This becomes particularly important in all programs with an information, journalistic or analytical component.

ABC 1993, p. 50

The next section (s.15.7) made it clear that there should be no acceptance of free or discounted services or products if the supplier has an expectation of a quid pro quo in broadcast material (ABC 1993, p. 51).

It is exactly in this type of show where services and goods are exchanged for editorial space that the initial problem arose, mainly the *Holiday* program and *Great Ideas*.

But the ABC's *Editorial Policies*, like everything else to do with ethical behaviour, are never set in concrete. When the national broadcaster revised its *Editorial Policies* and released the next version in April, 1998, it was still concerned about the impact of 'outside funding' on its credibility (ABC 1998, p. 37). As a sign of the times, the policy indicates that the ABC would not accept advertising or sponsorship for program web sites operated by it as part of *ABC Online* (ABC 1998, p. 37).

Among the other important policies, as far as we're concerned here, the 1998 policy noted that news and current affairs would not accept offers of free or discounted products, services, or facilities—the exceptions being those occasions where coverage of an important newsworthy event is only possible by accepting such an offer, like travel to a disaster scene or a remote location (ABC 1998, p. 43). Other program-makers could only accept such offers where it could be demonstrated that the ABC's independence and integrity were fully protected (ABC 1998, p. 43)—slightly different language, but the same central sentiment. While all three versions of the policy note the ABC as being authorised under the *ABC Act* to enter outside funding arrangements for co-productions, the latest version is very clear:

> The ABC will not accept funds from such sources where it is likely that the editorial independence or integrity of the ABC would be affected.

ABC 2002

The 2002 *Editorial Policies* also introduce for the first time a nine-point Charter of Editorial Practice, with sentiments similar to those in the AJA Code (ABC 2002, p. 9). The Charter is reproduced (along with the AJA Code, the Fairfax Charter, and other sections of the latest version of the ABC *Editorial Policies*) in the Appendix.

Issues and questions raised by case study 2

1   The Special Broadcasting Service (SBS) has had commercials and sponsored programs for several years now. Is there any reason why the ABC should not be allowed to have sponsored programs?
2   What is your opinion of the actions of the ABC whistleblowers?
3   In what circumstances might you take similar risks? For example, if you worked at a commercial network would it be harder to blow the whistle?
4   What problems are there for the ABC in accepting funding from outside sources?
5   Is the ABC and/or the SBS really any different in terms of how it is run and managed?
6   Which of the models discussed in this chapter best describe the Government-funded broadcast media?

Case study 3

The super league brouhaha

The two giants of Australian media went head to head, toe to toe, eyeball to eyeball in 1995–96 over control of one of the country's most lucrative commercial sporting ventures, professional rugby league. Kerry Packer's Nine Network then owned the rights to broadcast all major fixtures of the Australian Rugby League. The ARL declined to sell these rights to Rupert Murdoch, so Murdoch established his own league and poached players from the ARL by offering huge contracts. The coverage in the Murdoch-owned press was particularly sympathetic to the 'rebel' league. The story was on the front page, the finance pages, and the sport pages. The coverage in Rupert Murdoch's papers was consistently promoting his interests, so much so that at one stage staff at Murdoch's Townsville papers, the *Townsville Bulletin* and *Advertiser* complained about their papers' coverage of Super League ('Staff Anger on Super League' 1996). The Fairfax-owned *Sun Herald* would have delighted in reporting that a front-page story in the *Advertiser*, which reflected badly on the local Super League team, the North Queensland Cowboys, had been pulled from the paper because it was feared it had the potential to adversely affect ticket sales to Cowboys games. The *Sun Herald* reported that: 'A Sub editor on the [Townsville] paper also claimed he had been approached by an advertising person saying that although there was a policy of non-interference in editorial matters he should be 'very careful' with anything 'negative' about the Cowboys ('Staff Anger on Super League' 1996).

After 12 months of trench warfare, open hostilities, and courtroom battles, Super League and the Australian Rugby League reached a compromise in May 1996. This ensured that the first State of Origin match of the 1996 season went ahead with all the star players. The atmosphere surrounding the game was that of an armed truce, rather than an end to the fighting for good. In the run-up to the origin match, which is always promoted as a grudge contest between Queensland and New South Wales, the Sydney-based *Daily Telegraph* ran a front-page story under the headline, 'Packer's Grip on League Revealed'. The story highlighted Packer's heavy financial commitment to the ARL and the influence this gave him over contracted players. Reporters Ardyn Bernoth and Bruce McDougall (1996) wrote that the ARL had given Packer's Nine network, 'unprecedented influence over the operations ... in exchange for a $50 million fighting fund.' The front page pointed to a two-page splash in the sports section. The details were highlighted in large boxed diagrams and in the text. A separate story exposed payments to ARL chairman Ken Arthurson of more than $300,000, and to NSW League general manager John Quayle of $200,000. Ever since Super League began, Rupert Murdoch's News Corporation has maintained a financial interest in the Australian Rugby League, including several individual clubs. There is an armed truce in place between News Corporation and Kerry Packer's Channel 9, which has the broadcast rights on free-to-air TV for all league matches.

Issues and questions raised by case study 3

1   Why shouldn't a media employer use their publications to promote their other financial interests?
2   Is it any different to cross-promotion on popular Australian TV programs?
3   Can you find any other examples of a media proprietor publicising their 'other activities' in their mass media publications or 'pulling' unfavourable stories?
4   Is it any different to Rupert Murdoch publications going 'all out' to publicise their employment service '*career*one'? In 2003 it was crowing about 'more than 50,000 jobs' in print and online (*Weekend Career One* 2003).
5   If you were a reporter on a Murdoch daily and were asked to do a piece on the company's annual general meeting in Adelaide, would you be prepared to report the 'bad' news as well as the 'good'?
6   Research what Australia's main media moguls (Packer and Murdoch) own, and then research the coverage given those areas in their media outlets.
7   We're not saying that this type of thing happens every day, but we wonder how often certain stories 'don't make it' because there are 'more interesting' stories to take their place. What do you think?
8   What do you think of the argument: 'It's not deliberate' (that certain stories that may be unfavourable to the media owner's other interests get dropped)? Senior management would say it just happens that way.
9   In the Townsville *Advertiser* case, how can the actions be justified?

10   Competing media organisations have a history of taking shots at each other at every oppor-
      tunity. It's just the *Sun Herald* enjoying embarrassing a commercial competitor, isn't it?
11   What does this incident tell us about the very close relationship between sport, the
      media, and big business?
12   What effect do you think stories of management interference have on the overall cred-
      ibility rating of journalists?
13   What would you do to improve that rating?

Case study 4
Sponsorship and news and current affairs shows on TV

In our second case study for this chapter we described a situation where the ABC
was caught in a minor 'scandal' about sponsorship. Ironically the allegations were
broadcast by a rival network, Channel Nine. Being a commercial network and owned
by Kerry Packer, Nine is expected to pay its way. Yes, its current affairs shows, like
Sunday, are sponsored, often by large Australian and global corporations. For this
reason alone, nowhere is the likelihood for conflict of interest more likely to arise
than in news and current affairs programs on television.

In 2003, business news on Ten was being handled by Comsec, the stockbroking
arm of the Commonwealth Bank. 'They produce the whole segment. But we have no
written agreement with them. We leave it all to them,' one Ten executive told Paul Ham
(2003) of the *Australian*. The Nine network has long had sponsorship of its flagship
current affairs programs—*60 Minutes* by Toyota and *A Current Affair* by Nissan. But
what happens if Toyota or Nissan find themselves unfavourably in the news? Paul Fenn,
Nine's News Director, told the *Australian* (Ham 2003): 'Any *sponsorship* deal is done
on the understanding that if the company involved finds itself at the centre of attention, we'd have to cover it. The sponsor would graciously withdraw their sponsorship for
the duration of the coverage'. In 2003, the *Business Show* on SBS was looking for a
sponsor, but journalists on the program were worried that having a sponsor could potentially undermine the program's independence. A bank, insurance company, or funds
manager may well pose problems for a specialist finance program. The Perpetual financial group withdrew from the *Business Show* in 2002 when a trial sponsorship coin-
cided with the presence on the program of one of its fund managers (Ham 2003).

Issues and questions raised by case study 4

1   Debate the pros and cons of sponsorship of current affairs programs.
2   What about sponsorship of the nightly news?
3   What sorts of organisations would you consider appropriate to sponsor a current affairs
     TV program? Make a list.
4   List the organisations you consider would be inappropriate to sponsor a TV current
     affairs program.

5   Would either list change if it was the nightly news?
6   Would either list change if it was a business news program?
7   What's the difference between sponsoring a program and advertising within it?
8   What's the difference between sponsorship and all the ads we see in newspapers and magazines?
9   Wouldn't a frequent advertiser, or a sponsor, expect 'preferential treatment' when stories affecting them come up in the news?

4

ON THE FAULT LINE

REGULATION, DEREGULATION, AND SELF-REGULATION IN THE WORKPLACE

Objectives

After you've read this chapter you will appreciate:

- The apparent contradictions in institutional and bureaucratic forms of self-regulation, and arguments for and against Government regulation of journalists.
- The role of the MEAA Code of Ethics in everyday ethical decision-making.
- The problems that arise in trying to apply conflicting aspects of the Code.
- The evolution of the Code through much of the twentieth century and the strengths and weaknesses of the latest version.
- The emergence of companions and alternatives to the Code, like Charters of Editorial Independence.
- The challenges facing a Code or Charter in twenty-first century journalism.

Introduction: From principle to practice

This chapter really is about being on the fault line, for it's in the everyday workplace that ethical decisions can become critical. In supporting the amended MEAA Code of Ethics, Kerri Elgar (1998, p. 10) encouraged 'critical appraisal', and urged union members to question whether each clause would 'promote good journalism, not only in principle but also in prac-tice'. The men and women who framed the first AJA Code of Ethics knew it had to be sup-ported in principle, and applied in practice by union members, in order to be effective. In the ninety or so years since the journalists' union was first organised in Australia, the AJA, now part of the MEAA, has sought to make the Code meaningful and relevant in the newsroom. What's at stake for journalists, says Kerri Elgar (1998, p. 10), is 'our credibility with the pub-lic, our self-respect as a profession, even our ability to function in a democracy'.

John Merrill (1974, 1989) argues that accountability and responsibility ultimately rest with the individual journalist. Every reporter must constantly strive for ethical perfection, in the face of all obstacles. This 'libertarian' position is applied in a slightly modified form by supporters of the free-market model (Horne 1986, 1994a, 1994b). Strong advocates of union Codes of Ethics argue that it should be a collective responsibility and that account-ability is also collective, to peers, and to the public (Apps 1985; Bacon 1996; Hirst 1997a, 2003). Finally, should someone be keeping an eye on society's watchdog? If so, who should it be? When it comes to reporting, publishing, and broadcasting, who has the right to con-trol what the news is, and what it is 'about'?

There are many possible answers to these questions; they vary in terms of ideologies, rhetorical arguments, and legislative frameworks proposed as solutions to the perceived 'crisis of credibility' we talked about earlier. In most responses, concepts like 'freedom' and 'responsibility' are usually core sentiments. As we've argued in previous chapters, the fault lines are easily visible within these 'point-of-view' frames. Dialectically, the fine and dem-ocratic ideals of media freedom, and responsibility in the news, are constantly caught in the grinding gears of the news industry.

Alongside the front line reporters and editors, news companies, Government Ministers, Opposition leaders, non-government organisations, think tanks, and nosy individuals all have something to say about the news media and ethics, or lack thereof. A particular focus of this chapter is to develop an understanding of how the social conditions under which Australian journalists work have changed over the past century, and especially how the jour-nalists' union and news workers have interacted with their employers, peers, critics, and audiences in response to complaints or breaches of the Code.

In response to public concerns and industrial pressure from the union, a range of com-mittees, reports, and enquiries have devised various documents and schemes to protect editorial freedom, or place boundaries around what is considered 'responsible' journalistic behaviour. These guidelines have been adopted over the past 30 years in various forms in many news organisations, from Fairfax to the ABC. In many instances these Charters of Editorial Practice, or 'Independence', were fought for by the union, or tightened in response to ethical challenges raised inside the organisation. This was certainly the case in the mid 1980s when *Age* journalists organised a very public campaign for an editorial Charter as a condition of any sale to the unpopular British tycoon, Robert Maxwell. In May 1988 the Fairfax board agreed to include the Charter in any contract of sale (Bowman 1988).

Mandatory and voluntary regimes of regulation vary greatly from media to media and between organisations within the same medium. In print, there is nominally 'independent' monitoring by a committee largely funded out of newspaper profits, the Australian Press Council. In broadcast there are licence arrangements and regulatory regimes that must be complied with, and industry associations with their own ethics pro formas. Regarding online journalism, it really is too early to tell who's responsible for what, though copyright issues have been addressed, along with some interesting international cases on Internet defamation. As we shall see in chapter 11, 'bloggers' also have some interesting things to say about their own, and the mainstream media's, ethics.

This chapter concludes that even good Codes of Ethics may be difficult to implement when the dominant news culture in the workplace is based on commercial production. The final aim of this chapter is to encourage further debate among media professionals, students, and journalism educators about the history and the social relations of news production. Only by radically overhauling the very foundations of the media as a commodity enterprise can the public interest achieve ascendancy over the profit motive.

Codes of Ethics, self-regulation, and mandatory regulation

Some Codes of Ethics are a form of self-regulation. They are voluntary, or apply only to members of certain groups. In some situations a collective association based on industry, or professional affiliations, will self-regulate using a Code or other instrument. Mandatory regulation implies a legal or legislative 'regime' that either replaces, or sits uneasily alongside, regimes of self-regulation. A Code can be either self-regulatory, or it can be mandated—imposed through legal sanction or moral persuasion. In Australia print journalism is almost entirely self-regulated through the MEAA Code of Ethics (applying to journalists) and the Australian Press Council (APC). Broadcast journalism is more closely regulated by a series of mandatory Codes legislatively imposed and policed by the Australian Broadcasting Authority (ABA). As we go to press the federal government has signaled that it intends to merge the ABA with the Australian Telecommunications Authority to create a new and powerful regulatory body for the broad communications industry. Several commentators have criticised the move as being fraught with contradictions; not the least of which is between the ABA's function of *content* regulation and the ATA's role as a *technology* regulator.

The APC is an industry association and similar such associations exist in both radio (CRA) and television (Free TV Australia). Each has its own Code, which is voluntarily agreed to by members and which has mechanisms for dealing with public complaints. In most cases, it is fair to say these procedures are cumbersome and not very well understood by those outside the industry. This mixed system of self-regulation and codified external regulation has created what Julianne Schultz (1999) describes as the many paradoxes of journalistic independence and media freedom.

In journalism there are almost as many written Codes and regulations as there are newsrooms around the country, and around the world. Some Codes, like the AJA's, attempt to have a wide application. From the beginning, the AJA imposed penalties for breaches of the Code by its members, including expulsion from the union. By framing the Code within its rules, the AJA sought to bind union members to its normative clauses (Sparrow 1960, p. 131). Today, all news workers, reporters, sub-editors, or producers, who are members of the MEAA, are expected to abide by the Code, and work according to its spirit. Conversely, it can't apply to non-members, as we'll see in later chapters. In some quarters today, the MEAA Code of Ethics is not well regarded. Some overly harsh critics have said it is not strong enough to deal with recalcitrants. Others claim it is a sad joke at best, or worse, a kangaroo court.

Journalism academic Mark Pearson has found that the AJA has all but given up on ethics complaints, referring them instead to the Australian Press Council (Pearson 2004b). MEAA federal secretary Chris Warren told Pearson: 'The press council can deliver something we can't, which is a published correction' (Pearson 2004b).

The lego-ethical regulation of Australian broadcasting

In broadcasting the regulation versus self-regulation fault line is a little more obvious and the industry has historically been heavily regulated by the Federal Government (Hurst & White 1994, pp. 21–4). Regulation is mandated by the Broadcast Services Act and policed by the Australian Broadcasting Authority. At the time of writing the chair of the ABA was Professor David Flint, a debonair Liberal and charming monarchist lawyer who had previously chaired the APC. In mid 2004 Professor Flint announced his resignation from the ABA after it was revealed he had been compromised by a personal relationship with broadcaster Alan Jones, then the subject of a second ABA inquiry into further allegations of 'cash for comment'. Radio and television are governed by a legal and ethical framework enshrined in legislation. This situation often leads to a blurring of legal and ethical issues and attempts to deal with the latter by means of the former.

The infamous 'cash for comment' scandal that engulfed the Sydney radio industry for several months in 1999–2000 and again in 2003–04 is a clear example of this. It also provides a textbook case of how, when self-regulation fails to stop unethical behaviour, an outside agency may be forced to step-in. While this is covered more completely in a case study (see chapter 10), it is worth noting that the relevant authorities took action (Pearson 2000) only when a sensational scoop by ABC TV's *Media Watch* program made the inaction of regulators seem inadequate (Richards 2000).

Like the various print media associations, Australia's commercial radio and television companies have their own industry associations. Both have their own published Codes of Practice, and a very drawn-out complaints process that involves first seeking 'satisfaction' from the 'offending' station, and when that doesn't work, contacting the relevant association.

In the latest (second) edition of *The Journalist's Guide to Media Law,* Professor Pearson suggests that *Media Watch* is in fact the most effective regulator of the Australian media (Pearson 2004a, p. 343). He says:

> While *Media Watch* itself has no sanctions available, the power of the program lies in the fact that ethical breaches and glaring errors are screened on national television, when journalists know their colleagues are watching.

The Australian Press Council

In the print industry, the Australian Press Council (APC) is made up of company representatives, plus a few 'independent' members. It 'adjudicates' on complaints usually made by members of the public, or advocacy groups, and can ask newspapers to print its 'findings'.

Occasionally the Press Council may suggest a printed apology, or a mild correction. Whether or not to do so is at the discretion of the offending publication's editor. In several high-profile cases the APC has disappointed many complainants, and drawn wide criticism for some of its rulings. The Press Council has for a long time been recognised as predisposed towards the free-market system (Bowman 1988) and it certainly enjoys the relative comfort of being 'self-regulated'. Economic and legal regulation of the print industry is a little stiffer (Pearson 1997), but as good business managers, these companies also comply with the letter of the law when it comes to taxes, share registers, and fair dealing in complex, competitive business arrangements (Pearson 2001).

In the early postwar years after 1945, the Australian Newspaper Proprietors' Association agreed to work alongside the union on the Australian Newspaper Board. The union continued to push for a 'Press Council or some similar body' throughout the 1950s and 1960s (Lloyd 1985, p. 234). By the late 1970s this pressure bore fruit under the leadership of AJA Federal President John Lawrence. In 1976 the Australian Press Council (APC) was formed and cooperation between employer and employee was formalised.

Almost a decade before this, media scholar Henry Mayer wrote that the Federal Council of the AJA favoured a Press Council that would have both employer and union representation. The council would be charged with preserving 'freedom of the Press', in line with the best 'professional and commercial standards' (Mayer 1968, p. 247). It was a very similar proposal that was eventually adopted nationally by the newspaper owners, with union involvement. The APC's original statement of principles began: 'The freedom of the Press to publish is the freedom of the people to be informed', which Bowman (1988, p. 70) described as a 'useful if not very literate statement'. This gentle dig to the ribs is followed up with a knockout punch: 'The pity is that in practice it is no more than a fig leaf.'

The APC began meeting and adjudicating on complaints in the late 1970s and for the first decade three journalists' union representatives sat on the council. The majority on the council has always been with representatives of the publishing companies who financially support it. The Press Council cannot enforce its rulings, nor can it punish transgressions so it is hard to see how its declared aims, the preservation of freedom of the press and maintaining high journalistic standards, can actually be met. The complaints procedure is long-winded and most complaints never make it to adjudication, and the majority of those that do are dismissed.

The fundamental fault line running through the APC processes is in the potential for conflicts of interest between the Council and the newspaper companies. The commercial and other interests of the media companies may override the public interest in the complaint being fairly dealt with. There is an inherent contradiction in having representatives of Australia's largest newspaper companies 'adjudicating' on public complaints about the ethical standards of the management and employees of these same companies. In an interesting, if contrasting parallel, one Queensland submission to the MEAA Ethics Review Committee mentioned the perception that the state's judiciary committee might be biased because the same company employed a majority of its members. While the concern of this union official was genuine, for the newspapers' management representatives on the APC the real concern is profits. In Press Council adjudications, the reputations of the employee, sometimes a 'star' columnist, and the company are on the line. This is because, as a highly tradeable commodity, reputation is fiercely protected in the mediasphere. Another 'safeguard' on the system of self-regulation is that in order for the Council to agree to adjudicate, the complainant(s) must first sign a waiver that they will not pursue further action, particularly through the courts. This makes the APC, in the opinion of many, a 'toothless tiger'.

In fact, it's fair to say that the APC was almost certainly KO'd not long after it found its feet in 1976. Henry Mayer (1968, p. 248) was right a decade earlier when he predicted: 'It is highly likely that such a council would be split on most issues.' What we attempt to explain through this account is how the contending ideological frameworks of the reporters and the proprietors have clashed in the past, and how the institutional attempts to paper over the very deep fissures have always failed, so far.

From time to time since 1976, some of these fault lines have opened up, and the AJA/MEAA has withdrawn from the APC over various disputes. Former *SMH* editor David Bowman wrote accurately, but rather cynically, about the council being a body dominated by the proprietors, but somehow also 'supposed to protect the public interest'. In 1986 Bowman (1988, p. 22) recognised the 'inherent contradiction' at the heart of the APC—the attempt to bring the unions and the bosses together to resolve disputes. At the heart of the 1986 dispute was the APC's failure to act in the face of Rupert Murdoch's takeover bid for the Melbourne Herald and Weekly Times (HWT) group. The chairman of the APC, retired judge Hal Wootten, resigned when the Council did not back his call for a Government inquiry into the takeover, and so did John Lawrence and the other AJA representatives. When the AJA finally abandoned the APC (for some 10 years), it denounced the council as a publisher's poodle.

Workplace Codes of Practice

In the past decade or so, a number of media organisations have introduced Codes of Practice occasionally in response to new technology, like digital editing of photographs (PANPA 1994a). At Rural Press and the Herald and Weekly Times the management introduced company-wide Codes of Practice that state each employee's duty to serve clients, whether readers or advertisers (PANPA 1993, 1994b). It can be seen how such a Code might entrench the contradictions we're talking about: readers and advertisers have very different, and often conflicting, interests in the contents of the newspaper or broadcast bulletin. At the Fairfax papers in Sydney and Melbourne, a 'Charter of Editorial Independence' was won through strong industrial action (Wilson 1992).

The MEAA Code of Ethics

The MEAA Code of Ethics is a form of self-regulation, this time you could say from the bottom up. Our view is that the MEAA Code of Ethics is very important, and that it is appropriate that the journalists' own union discipline its members. The real debate is about whether this is the only way to monitor Codes and behaviour, or are other 'watchdog' roles to be performed by other bodies, not directly managed by journalists themselves? It is in this area that experienced critics have worried about certain ambiguities in the 1998 revised Code and a weakening of clauses protecting against the unwelcome influence of commercial interests (Cronau 1996). Wendy Bacon (1996) outlined the new dangers posed by what she saw as the weakened language in the proposed 1998 Code. She warned that 'these surface difficulties mask much deeper problems which confront the union', adding that reporters needed more than 'aspirations'.

When the AJA sought to establish the first Australian Code for journalists, towards the close of World War II, the union believed it would help improve the public's perception of the news media by making it look more professional. At the time, the union extended an invitation to the newspaper proprietors to 'subscribe to the Code and to join with the AJA in seeing that it was observed'. Former union secretary Geoff Sparrow (1960, p. 132) records: 'They declined to co-operate, contending that the AJA was trying to interfere in their business.' Of course, if the union that represented journalists was to argue for 'freedom of the press' it could not be supported if it might then interfere with the 'freedom' of the press owners. A couple of years after the first AJA Code was adopted, several journalists, backed by the powerful newspaper and magazine publisher Frank Packer, tried to have the union's disciplinary rules declared invalid in the Arbitration Commission.

While organisations like the Press Council claim to serve a function—and certainly the public is entitled to complain and have their complaints adjudicated—the MEAA has consistently found the only bedrock for any action on its part to improve ethical standards, and behaviour, was through the Code of Ethics. Like any structure that has to stand the test of time, a Code of Ethics needs renovating from time to time. Sometimes the foundations move, usually in response to an earth tremor, or the presence of some other fault line; at other times, the brickwork, plumbing, rendering, wiring, and paintwork may need a little updating.

Since it was first adopted in the mid 1940s, the AJA/MEAA Code of Ethics has been renovated twice, usually in response to observations from within the profession, and from outside, that it might no longer be relevant. The changes can be the result of many things, a response to a legal ruling; a new technology, such as digital imaging 'cameraphones'; or a tragic event, like a farmhouse siege, or the death of a princess; or even a serious criminal investigation into unsolved serial-killings. Sometimes it might even be a series of complaints from the public. For the journalists' union, it was a feeling that the Code did not address the changing workplace practices and problems encountered by MEAA members.

Why did the MEAA want to change the Code?

Any code that is workable in this situation has to have appeal; it has to be aspirational; it has to provide signposts for the journalist of good will wanting to do the right [thing] in difficult circumstances.

Fr Frank Brennan, Preface to MEAA Ethics Review Committee 1997 *Report*, p. vi

Father Frank Brennan, of the Catholic Church's national media office, chaired the four-year review into the MEAA Code of Ethics that reported in 1997 and recommended wholesale changes to the Code. In the Preface to his report, Fr Brennan expressed a hope that the new Code would make the newsroom 'no place for cowboys', and that it would 'deserve a place on the [newsroom] wall' (Ethics Review Committee 1997, pp. v-vii). He also made a plea for news workers to be better educated, and to understand more of the world and ethics. Fr Brennan also called on journalists and news organisations to help change some less desirable habits, ingrained in newsroom culture. It seems we might be waiting a bit longer for the results Fr Brennan hoped for.

The new 1998 MEAA Code of Ethics for journalists might appear, on face value, to be an improvement on earlier versions. For example, there are now explicit references to plagiarism and chequebook journalism, and the clauses dealing with source confidentiality have been rewritten. The 1944 Code had eight points when it was adopted, the 1984 revision took this to ten and added a Preamble. The Review Committee's initial proposal from 1996–97 had shot up to twenty clauses, with a longer revised Preamble and a new short Postscript. The new Code of Ethics finally agreed to by the union's governing Conference in 1998 contained twelve clauses. It also included a version of the new Preamble and the Postscript (see Appendix).

In this chapter we mention some important changes, and in later chapters the relevant clauses are discussed in the context of the arguments and cases they relate to. It is worth noting some of the important concrete recommendations of the Review Committee, even though not all of them were adopted in the final version. For example, the proposed new Clause 2 introduced a 'right of reply' for people subject to damaging reports; Clauses 4 and 5 made direct reference to new technologies available to the media, from hidden cameras to digitally enhanced images. The proposed Clause 6 quite bluntly stated that 'Plagiarism is cheating. Always attribute fairly'. Clause 8 called for full disclosure of all cases of cheque-book journalism. Clauses 13 and 14 in the drafted Code attempted to refine the arguments about privacy for people in the news, and to improve the guidelines on grief intrusion, making the informed consent of the interviewee the central test. Clauses 16 and 17 of the longer proposed Code are of special interest. They referred to endangering people 'without informed consent', and to dealing with stories about the welfare of children. Some of these latter clauses appear to have been motivated, in part, by the controversial coverage of a siege in a farmhouse near Cangai, NSW in March 1993 (Hirst 1997a).

However, at the moment we are really more concerned with the 'big picture', a seismic exploration, and an archaeological dig around the fault lines between profitability and public interest, rather than the specific changes to clauses in the Code of Ethics. One important recognition of this contradiction is the tension between 'news' and 'entertainment' as articulated in the new Preamble: 'Journalists describe society ... They ... record, question, entertain, suggest and remember'.

While this statement is important on its own, and represents a significant change from the 1984 version, the committee's justifications are interesting:

> Good journalism has always had room for fun ... But journalists entertain with fair facts and comment. Entertainers use fiction and demagoguery, journalists show us as we are ... And journalists appreciate that public business in a participatory democracy often cannot be treated as fun, nor can making public choices be approached as if the appropriate techniques for conveying information and debating options are the same as the techniques used to entertain.

Ethics Review Committee 1997, p. 17

If this is not confusing and contradictory enough, the Committee ploughs on until it collapses exhausted on the horns of its own dilemma: 'This confusion of roles, caught in the word "infotainment", is regularly lamented in Australia'; it also highlighted contemporary tensions and conflicts, which 'can be found in earlier debates about the role of journalism' (Ethics Review Committee 1997, pp. 17–18).

The social context for a debate about media ethics

In the 1990s, when moves to update the Code first gathered steam, there had been a widespread public reaction against the 'greed is good' ethos of the 1980s and ethics became an 'issue' beyond the behaviour of the media (Smith 1992, p. 27). By the end of the century even scientists were talking about becoming more ethical. Eminent theoretical physicist, John Ziman (2001) attributed this to the 'transformation of science into a new type of social institution'. Nothing so profound happened in journalism, but the tremors from this widespread social shift in attitudes did impact on the news media. The *Australian's* acerbic media commentator, Errol Simper (1996), noted that since journalists 'have been decent and honourable enough' to review their ethics, perhaps the general community might do the same. He singled out those members of the 'public' who get caught up in court cases, or are 'named in dubious circumstances', and who commit 'murder, theft and arson'. While Simper's column is really just light relief on this occasion, he does make one strong argument about public relations and their 'bland, exploitative, boring and deliberately misleading media releases'. This 'quiet revolution', the gradual increase in the percentage of news holes filled with PR-generated and 'event-managed' stories, is starting to reach alarming proportions (Zawawi 1994). Today this process of news management extends beyond the commercial limits of public relations to encompass the information we get from governments about domestic politics and world affairs. It is more than idle speculation to suggest that the greed cycle of the 1980s has been replaced with the spin cycle of the twenty-first century.

Over the final decade of the twentieth century there was almost constant discussion of media ethics, and it tended to erupt around particular events, such as the March 1993 Cangai 'siege' (Turner 1994a); the Deborah Cornwall 'contempt of ICAC' case (Turner 1994a; *Off the Record*, 1994); *Who Weekly's* conviction for contempt over the publication of a picture of accused murderer Ivan Milat (Hirst 1997a); and trial by media (Quinn 1991).

In May 1996 important questions were raised about the media's coverage of the massacre of thirty-five people at Port Arthur, Tasmania, by a disturbed young man, Martin Bryant. In the confused days after the shootings, journalists were alleged to have stolen photographs and to have pretended to be relatives of victims to gain access to the injured. At the time one newspaper admitted tampering with a photograph of Bryant, but denied it was done to 'highlight' his alleged 'madness'. You can read about several interesting aspects of this case in later case studies in chapters 7 and 11.

The social context for the review of the MEAA Code of Ethics was a widely held perception that the world was changing rapidly and that the old Code (barely a decade old in 1994) could no longer sustain news workers confronting previously unimagined scenarios. John Hurst and Sally White (1994, p. 2) believed that the 'information revolution' that 'brought war and civil protest into people's living rooms in real time' had something to do with why media ethics could not keep up with the pace of technological change. Certainly that is an issue, but it's not the only one. As we have demonstrated in previous chapters, it is not the technology itself that causes rapid shifts in the ways that media is produced and consumed, but the changing social relations, particularly inside the newsroom.

Plenty has been written about individual aspects of the Code of Ethics, such as death-knocks (Apps 1986; Geraghty 1986; Powell 1990), chequebook journalism (Avieson 1992), and other specific issues in media ethics. We will examine these problems in the following chapters, but we believe it is preferable to tackle the problems at a level that attempts to place ethics in a dynamic social context. We also want to place them into an historical and ideological framework.

Former *Sydney Morning Herald* editor David Bowman (1983, p. 37) adopts both a philosophical and practical approach to addressing the dilemmas inherent in any discussion of ethics. He provides a point-by-point critique of the 1944 AJA Code of Ethics, including its failure to deal with increasing public concerns about privacy and chequebook journalism. Bowman (1983, p. 37) notes that ethics, like morals, depends on a person's social position and philosophical–political viewpoint, suggesting that journalists 'have no choice but to abide, by and large, by ethics accepted by the public'. In passing, Bowman notes that the rigours of commercial competition can have a bearing on ethical (or, *un*ethical) behaviour by journalists, especially in the (then) fierce afternoon tabloid market.

Professor Laurie Apps (1990) suggests that interest in media ethics began to increase in the 1980s due to both the 'trickle down' effect of events in the United States and the development of tertiary journalism courses, in which ethics are taught as a discrete subject. A major problem with ethics *codes*, according to Apps (1990, p. 70), is the relativity of truth, within 'varying religious, cultural, political and ideological frames of reference that render the truth complex, confused and even contradictory'. Under these circumstances, a Code that is fairly rigid and prescriptive cannot possibly deal with all situations in all contexts. Apps is also aware of the central contradictions between the commodity form of 'news' and its economic, political and social aspects. He notes that there are 'practical examples every day' of how news values are subverted by the political economy of the newspaper business. This is a situation in which journalistic ethics becomes the ideological support for the value system of capitalism and the 'sacred cow of journalistic objectivity' becomes the fundamental acceptance of the dominant (free market) ideology (Apps 1990, p. 73). Apps goes on to recommend the work of British media scholars Raymond Williams and Nicholas Garnham on the political economy of the media, as fresh perspectives on the processes and understanding of media ethics. What this perspective offers in terms of media ethics is a framework for describing the roles of individual and structure, based on criteria of economics, class, and power (Apps 1990, p. 78). As we have noted in the previous chapters, these elements are what constitute the grounding of the emotional attitudes of news workers, and 'ethics' is the contemporary cultural form of the dialectic that drives these attitudes.

Since the mid 1980s some attempts have been made to apply a modern political economy approach to the Australian media (Windschuttle 1988; Schultz 1994; Wilson 1989; Oakham 1998; Hirst 2001, 2003), but a discussion of ethics is usually confined to a few pages, or at best one chapter. It is significant, and perhaps embarrassing to Australian journalism, that the first book dedicated to ethics and the media in Australia did not appear until 50 years after the original Code of Ethics was adopted by the AJA. *Ethics and the Australian News Media* (Hurst & White 1994, p. xi) treats ethical issues 'by identifying the values and principles ... and examining specific cases'. Throughout the book the authors acknowledge that commercial, competitive pressures impinge on ethical discussion and decision-making. This contradiction is expressed generally in the following terms:

> ... the legitimate defence of the public right to know is, to its detriment, sometimes called upon to justify those media actions dictated solely by competitive pressures. The quest for healthy circulation figures breeds a powerful desire to scoop the opposition or to publish a story with sensational impact that titillates readers.

> Hurst & White 1994, p.15

Hurst and White (1994, p. 251) consider this theme in a chapter entitled 'The Pressure of Business' and suggest that both journalists and editors are confronted with difficult choices, 'whenever the business face of the news media confronts its indivisible twin, the publicly accountable social institution'. American news critic Daniel Hallin (1994, p. 1) expresses the problem as both an economic and ideological contradiction that is journalism's 'ambivalent identity'. It is what we call the contradictory emotional dialectic of news work. Hallin's formulation (1994, p. 4) is that this is a struggle against the internal and external limits of the 'professionalization' of journalism that threatens to upset the balance between 'the public-interest culture of journalism and the culture of commodity-production'.

The Code was 'languishing'

By the end of the 1960s a number of journalists and commentators began to think the 1944 Code of Ethics was no longer effective or relevant (Hirst 1997a). Clem Lloyd (1985, p. 235) recognised that the 'largely reactive' judiciary structures had 'inherent limitations', and only reacted when 'blatant breaches ... became apparent'. Journalist and educator John Avieson said it 'continues to languish' (Avieson 1978, p. 1). He suggested that 'there are potentially serious dilemmas for the journalist who seeks to obtain and publish the truth within the prescribed ethical framework'. Avieson highlighted two basic contradictions that the 1944 Code could not adequately deal with: protection of sources and chequebook journalism.

The first was in the formulation of Rule 3, which he said relied on imprecise definitions of the words 'confidence' and 'respect' (1978, p. 2). The protection of sources therefore relied on the following points being observed by a journalist:

a) only using the information in accordance with the wishes of the source (respect),

b) protecting the identity of the informant (confidence), and

c) how the journalist ultimately determines to use the information (Avieson 1978, p. 2).

Nearly half a century later, a 1994 Australian Senate Standing Committee's report into confidentiality and 'shield laws' also attempted to deal with this contradiction in the system of ethical reasoning—the 'necessary betrayal'. The Committee's report to the Senate, *Off the Record* (1994, p. ix), makes it clear that Australian Governments should be prepared to legislate for compulsion to disclose sources where the court considers the information is necessary to meet 'the requirements of the proper administration of justice'. Avieson's points a), b), and c) above are also very similar to the arguments Commissioner Ian Temby QC put to then *SMH* journalist, Deborah Cornwall, in attempting to induce her to reveal her police sources to the NSW Independent Commission Against Corruption (ICAC). Cornwall was eventually sentenced to jail, but this was commuted to ninety hours' community service (Buckridge 1994).

While the 1944 version of the Code mentioned bribes in Rule 5, it said nothing directly about chequebook journalism in relation to criminals. In pointing out this loophole, Avieson (1978, p. 4) wrote, 'it would be wrong to allow a rule to aid and abet a wrongdoer'. Nothing much seems to have changed. As well as addressing these 'technical' issues, the 1984 revisions altered the 1944 Code in a number of 'social' ways. Importantly this included updating the language, making it more inclusive by removing the sexist bias and acknowledging Australia's multiculturalism by removing 'gratuitous' references to the racial characteristics of 'subjects' in stories. Clauses covering 'objectivity' (4/1984) and 'death knocks' (9/1984) were included for the first time. The major structural change in the 1984 revision was to add a Preamble, which appears to be based on Clause 4 of the 1944 Code of Ethics. The 'fraternal' language of the 1944 Code was replaced in 1984, but the framing principles of respect for truth and the public right to know were enshrined (Hirst 1997a).

As Lawrence Apps (1985, 1990) and David Bowman (1990) have argued, the 1984 Preamble did not solve the contradictions in the Code of Ethics. The language is very prescriptive and dry; the 'ethical standards' are drawn up in the clauses that follow. The only intellectual principles are 'respect for truth' and the public's 'right to information'. The stiff language of the Code did not appear able to reconcile this 'overriding principle' with a central and structural reality in the media: ultimately 'freedom of expression' belonged exclusively to 'the media organisation, the corporation, the conglomerate'. In an important review of the field, Lawrence Apps (1985, p. 12) began by arguing that the recently updated 1984 Code could not adequately answer the 'simple, yet fundamental question of why a certain practice ought to be followed'. Like the 1944 Code, when it came to important issues of principle, the 1984 version tended to push the burden of proof onto a fruitless debate over semantics, and a 'straight-forward Judeo-Christian or utilitarian ethic' (Apps 1985, p. 15).

In an attempt to deal with the limitations of the 1984 version, the Preamble was further modified in the 1997–98 changes. This time the Preamble was given a complete makeover, and more principles included for consideration. The language has an almost poetic feel, and resounds with lofty idealism:

> *Journalists describe society to itself. They seek the truth.*
> *They convey information, ideas and opinions, a privileged role.*
> *They search, disclose, record, question, entertain, suggest and remember.*
> *They inform citizens and animate democracy.*
> *They give a practical form to freedom of expression.*
> *Many journalists work in private enterprise, but all have these journalistic responsibilities.*
> *They scrutinise power, but also exercise it, and should be accountable.*
> *Accountability engenders trust. Without trust, journalists do not fulfil their public responsibilities.*
> *MEAA members engaged in journalism commit themselves to:*
> * *honesty*
> * *fairness*

- *independence*
- *respect for the rights of others.*
In consultation with colleagues they will apply the following standards.

This last line is interesting because it implies some element of collective responsibility for enforcing the Code (see chapter 12). For the first time in the history of the Code, the new Preamble recognised the 'duty' of journalists to 'inform' the public, even if they work for profit-oriented media in the private sector. The wording is clear: 'Many journalists work in private enterprise, but all have these journalistic responsibilities'. But merely placing it in the Preamble does not solve the dilemma. The line was inserted at this point in an attempt to bridge the fundamental economic and social fault lines. The Review Committee's report was very clear on this point, while being careful not to endorse too warmly notions of 'public journalism':

> This recommended new preamble expressly declares the aspirations as the public responsibilities of all journalists, including those who work in private enterprise.
>
> No one has suggested that the commercial nature of most journalistic enterprises means that they are either exempt from the public service aspects of journalism, or seeking exemption. The most cynical will claim a public role for journalism, even if it is only to increase political clout, social prestige, the value of a media investment, or, more usually, to forestall externally imposed regulation.
>
> The proposed preamble articulates the ideals of the believers and calls the cynics' bluff.
>
> Ethics Review Committee 1997, pp. 19–21

While clearly wishing to sound brave, and to challenge the monopolies, the framers of the Code were unable to insert any real bite into the clauses, or into modified disciplinary procedures. The Review Committee itself was keen to make its own criticism of the 1984 Code clear: 'In effect, they adopted the "green light" approach leaving the judgment to individual journalists' (Ethics Review Committee 1997, p. 21). In 1997, the reviewers attempted to get around this problem by inserting a 'guidance clause' at the end of the Code because it recognised the inevitability of disagreements over permissible 'exceptions', over 'interpretation' of the clauses, and over its 'underlying values'. The Committee shared the view expressed in several submissions that this constituted an 'escape clause' with respect to all the other clauses. The 1998 revision rests on this tension; even 'bedrock injunctions' are 'open to interpretation' (Ethics Review Committee 1997, pp. 76–7). The new Code attempts to straddle the fault lines in news journalism. A structure built on a foundation of contradictions is sure to be unstable.

Certainly, the rhetoric of the Preamble has been 'toughened up' and now talks about lofty principles such as freedom of expression and 'animating democracy'. The new Code of Ethics appears, at first glance, to support the aims of Julianne Schultz (1998) to revive the Fourth Estate ideals in a contemporary context. The modified 1998 Preamble also declared that one function of journalism is to 'entertain', which is perhaps one of the most controversial new points. This has inserted a new contradiction, but one that recognises the growing pressure on the news genre from 'non-news' sources within highly integrated media conglomerates. In the past decade while the 'infotainment' and 'reality TV' industry has boomed, so too has another related field, entertainment journalism. The 'inform and entertain' formulation of the 1997–98 Code of Ethics recognises the ever-expanding market for so-called 'tabloid journalism' in magazines and 'infotainment' programming on television (see chapter 11).

On the other side of the ledger, the buzzwords appeared to be 'disclosure' and 'accountability'. Disclosure, as we'll see in chapter 9, can be a double-edged sword. As always, accountability is accompanied by a further question: to whom or what?

The review recommended disclosure of all relevant facts, or any interest that may lead to perceptions of bias; but also disclosure of sources, particularly in legal, and semi-judicial contexts (Ethics Review Committee 1997, pp. 26–30 and pp. 55–72). That the committee would spend seventeen pages discussing this issue of source confidentiality indicates how significant it had become. It grappled with the complexities, such as the 'key test' of 'justice' in any legal requirement to disclose a source's identity. The committee's report suggested that in 'too readily' agreeing to anonymity, reporters 'may fail their audience'. It also clearly linked reform of the MEAA Code of Ethics to the Senate report, *Off the Record*, which reviewed proposals for Australian 'shield laws'. The Senate committee was of the view that leaving decisions about confidentiality and disclosure in the hands of journalists would no longer be appropriate. In other words, the absolute privilege of the source-reporter relationship would cease to exist, and there would be legal limits to confidentiality (Senate Standing Committee on Legal and Constitutional Affairs 1994).

The MEAA Review Committee supported that view, and argued for shifting the decision about granting any 'right' of privilege onto the legal system. In the MEAA committee's report two basic reasons were presented: the public's 'lack of trust' in reporters leading to Government's 'reluctance' to grant an absolute privilege, and interestingly, an argument that by meeting the legislative onslaught half way, its effects could be ameliorated by compromise. Given the stresses already at work fracturing the Code, acquiescing to Government pressures to legislate for disclosure, *not for source protection*, would only further undermine investigative journalism, and discourage whistleblowers. It was along this particular fault line, between John Merrill's dialectically opposed libertarian doctrines 'freedom' and 'responsibility', that the 1984 Code had so spectacularly fractured in the Deborah Cornwall case, which we will study in chapter 9.

Freedom, responsibility, accountability, and 'shield laws'

In a Walkley Media Forum speech, Paul Chadwick (1999, p. 18) called 'accountability' the story that journalists 'continue to neglect'. He said it is particularly neglected by the media in a society where the concentration of media ownership is a 'given', and this poses 'special problems' when dealing with accountability (Chadwick 1999, p. 19). For the MEAA Review Committee two years earlier it appeared to contradict its stand on so-called 'shield laws'. 'Shield laws' are often described and defined as a legislative protection for whistleblowers and/or journalists who make use of them. Some form of 'shield laws' exist in parts of the United States and they have been on and off the media reform agenda in Australia for many years. In most cases the debates have centred around who should be protected: the reporter or the source?

On page 5 of the MEAA Review Committee's report, its belief in 'self-regulation' is expressed: 'journalists should be left to self-regulate without ultimate recourse to statutory sanctions'. What exactly are 'shield laws' if not statutory sanctions for non-disclosure under compulsion? In the following quotation the committee is trying to render over a massive fault line in terms of accountability and power:

> Say an owner and management granted journalists complete editorial independence. The power that comes with ownership would then shift to the journalists.

> Ethics Review Committee 1997, p. 20

This hypothetical really does provide an interesting take on our own earlier questions and it proves that you can answer a question with a question! The next statement is a logical nonsense:

> The public has no particular reason to regard journalists as more virtuous than owners or managers. Accountability is still required.

> Ethics Review Committee 1997, p. 20

One could just as reasonably suggest that 'the public' might well regard the average reporter, or sub-editor as slightly more virtuous than the 'robber–baron' image of Orson Wells's cinema masterpiece *Citizen Kane* or 'Keith Townsend', the Australian newspaper publisher in the novel *The Fourth Estate* (Archer 1996). The Review Committee appears to have conveniently ignored the power imbalances embedded in the social relations of news production in a capitalist economy. Its position on accountability also works ideologically to push the responsibility for ethical behaviour back onto individual journalists. It follows Merrill's individualistic approach to ethical reasoning by talking about 'trust'; a reporter's ability to 'fulfil their responsibilities' relies on the community trusting the individual journalist. However, this relationship is not as 'pure' as some theorists might like it to be. Hurst and White (1994, p. 33) comment that it is a sign of real 'ethical fortitude' to make a 'painful choice' to place this trust with the public ahead of one's own personal interest. They add that in the age of media concentration, and a shrinking number of employment opportunities, it is much harder for reporters to stick to their principles. It also leads to a certain degree of disorientation, even a split personality: 'Each journalist is, in effect, three people: an employee, a professional and an ordinary human being' (Hurst & White 1994, p. 6).

With accountability there is usually a regime of penalties, or guidelines for enforcement, but in arguing for the new Code, the union said very little, beyond moral persuasions, about its enforcement (MEAA 1995a; Elgar 1997, 1998). The MEAA Review Committee was charged with examining the union's complaints procedures, and its report (1997, pp. 79–96) recommended an overhaul of the union's internal disciplinary procedures.

As one architect of the new Code consistently suggested, the changes endorsed in the late 1990s were an attempt to make explicit the standards that were implicit in the 1984 Code (Chadwick 1994, 1995a, 1995b, 1996). The federal secretary of the MEAA, Chris Warren, described the revision of the Code as searching for a 'workable' ethics document for the twenty-first century (MEAA 1995a, 1995b). In this context, the Postscript to the revised Code is also worth mentioning as it attempts to make the Code workable by inserting some instructions about the 'overriding' nature of the public's 'right to know', previously contained in the 1984 Preamble. The guidance clause allows 'any standard' to be over-ridden if there is sufficient good reason:

> Basic values sometimes clash and ethics requires conscientious decision-making in context. Only substantial considerations of public interest or substantial harm to people allows any standard to be overridden.

MEAA 1998

This statement shifts the intended emphasis of the 1984 Preamble, which read: 'Respect for truth and the public's right to information are overriding principles for all journalists.' The new Postscript does more than slightly shift the ground on which these issues will be debated. It is a reversal of the onus of proof: overriding principle to principles being over-ridden in the public interest or with substantial harm to people. Any new interpretation of the Code rests on the word 'substantial'. As Wendy Bacon has pointed out, the language in the revised Code is just as vague (if not more so) than the 1984 version:

> We are now told to 'urge', 'guard against', 'disclose' but only where 'relevant' or 'improper'. (We are not told to whom the journalist should disclose or what is regarded as improper).

Bacon 1995, p. 13

The new Code does attempt to come to terms with some of the new conditions that news workers are operating in; for example, it recognises the technological ability of digital processing to alter voices and images. New forms of media technology—including satellites, digital photography, audio-editing techniques and the CD-ROM—would appear to have the potential to blur the boundaries between ethical and unethical behaviour because of the way information and images can be processed, edited, and reproduced. As production techniques and delivery systems develop, the ethics debate will have to keep pace. The rapidly growing, and popular genre of web diaries, or 'blogging' (from 'web-logging') throws down another challenge. One prominent Australian blogger, the *SMH*'s political columnist, Margo Kingston (2003), has devised her own web diary ethics code, built on the MEAA Code of Ethics. Margo's guidance clauses for herself, and for other contributors to her web diary, are a good attempt to deal with the particular issues of the Internet. Her comments cover the use of pseudonyms (acceptable with good reason); disclosure of affiliations that might affect your opinion; plagiarism; inventing 'facts'; personal attacks; writing in the first person. We will look at some of these 'information age' fault lines and debates in chapter 11.

Perhaps, at the start of a new century, the forces of production—the technologies of the Internet and digital media—have leapt ahead of the relations of production—the cultural and social forms in which journalism expresses itself. This process of dialectic contradiction, resolution, and new contradiction will inevitably cause further, unexpected fault lines to appear. One has been the rapid rise of tabloid television in the 1990s (O'Neil & Lumby 1994; Hirst et al. 1995; Langer 1998; Lumby 1999), which began to alter the boundaries of news journalism in subtle but important ways by injecting 'entertainment' into 'current affairs' television. Perhaps the inclusion of 'entertainment' as a function of journalism in the 1998 Code of Ethics was the first tremor—the one that loosened the ground, creating the initial cracks in the pavement.

Ethical dilemmas in practice

Scenario 1

You and your TV news crew are sent to a suburban hostage situation and you find it's a child custody dispute. The father has picked up his two children (aged 8 and 10) from school. He arrived at the school before his estranged wife and the staff mistakenly released the children into his care, even though it wasn't his turn to have them. He's refusing to hand them back until he is allowed to make his case for better access to the children 'on the TV'. You consult your news director and he says he's happy to cooperate with the police and 'run something' of what the father has to say, but warns he won't run it all if the father 'rambles on'. The police believe letting the father talk to your camera might diffuse the issue. What do you do? Would your decision be any different if it was a siege situation with only the father involved in a stand-off with the police?

Scenario 2

As a journalist, you're a natural to be the publicity officer for your local service club, resident's action group, or branch of the Liberal Party (or whatever). At one of your regular monthly executive meetings the treasurer resigns 'for personal reasons'. There's a suggestion that money from last year's fund-raising activities went missing 'temporarily'. The rest of the executive wants to 'hush it up' for fear of the damage it will do to the organisation on the eve of its annual major fund-raising drive. What do you do? Debate the ethical dilemma from the point of view of members of your service club, the public's right to know what happened to the money raised from them, and the chief of staff who would sense a 'good story' if you passed it on to him.

Case studies

Case study 1

Media Watch v. *60 Minutes* and Richard Carleton case

Channel Nine's flagship current affairs program, *60 Minutes,* aired a story in mid 2000 by veteran reporter Richard Carleton to mark the fifth anniversary of the massacre of 5000 Muslims (some accounts put the figure as high as 8000) by the Bosnian Serb military at Srebrenica. The ABC's *Media Watch,* at that stage hosted by Paul Barry (in

2003 he was reporting for *60 Minutes's* daily 'sister' program at Nine, *A Current Affair*), accused the program and Carleton of using the same footage and interview as an earlier BBC documentary. He accused *60 Minutes* of lifting the material 'lock, stock and barrel' from the BBC documentary (Briggs & Campbell 2002, p. 3). 'Perhaps it's plagiarism, certainly it's lazy journalism,' Barry said on *Media Watch* in July 2000. What the *Media Watch* program did not point out was that Carleton was using the BBC footage on a licence arrangement that allowed him to do so without acknowledgment.

Carleton and *60 Minutes's* producers sued Barry, the ABC, and the then *Media Watch* executive producer Peter McEvoy for defamation over two *Media Watch* programs in the ACT Supreme Court. Under cross-examination when the case came to court in early 2002, Carleton admitted he misled and lied to viewers by showing footage from another mass grave to illustrate their story ('I Misled, I Lied, Says Carleton' 2002). Carleton denied he had behaved unethically as a journalist and said the footage had enhanced viewers' understanding of the 1995 massacre. The next day he admitted he had asked his Yugoslavian researcher to find him a survivor, any survivor, for the program ('Carleton Edict: Find a Survivor' 2002). The researcher returned with Kadir Habibovic who described for the program how he was apprehended by Bosnian Serbs and managed to escape—the same story he told in the BBC documentary *A Cry From the Grave*, broadcast by the BBC and by SBS in Australia. When the judge handed down his findings on 18 December 2002, both parties claimed a victory. Justice Terence Higgins found that Mr Carleton and the *60 Minutes* producers had been defamed by the ABC, *Media Watch*, and presenter Barry. But he failed to award Carleton damages, ruling that *Media Watch* had a right to make 'fair comment' (AAP 2002b). Carleton said his reputation has been vindicated despite being denied damages. Barry said the case was a clear win for freedom of speech. Carleton said: 'This was never about money, this was about reputation from the start, the beginning and to the end' ('Defamation Row: Both Sides Claim Victory' 2002). Barry said: 'I think it goes to show that journalists shouldn't sue other journalists' (Fergus 2002).

Issues and questions raised by case study 1

1   Do you think Richard Carleton and *60 Minutes* were guilty of plagiarism?
2   What would the public think of a journalist that admitted in a court case to having misled his audience and effectively lied?
3   Carleton denied he acted unethically. What do you think? Consider both sides of the argument.
4   What's wrong with interviewing a person who has already appeared on another program talking about the same incident? Taken to its local conclusion you could argue that we'd only ever hear from anyone (the Prime Minister or Opposition leader at election time, for instance) on one channel.
5   What's your reaction to hearing that Carleton used footage from 'another mass grave' to illustrate his story?
6   Under what circumstances would you find that acceptable?

7   Should the approved use of BBC material be acknowledged to viewers of *60 Minutes*?

8   Why didn't *60 Minutes* just ignore the *Media Watch* attack? After all, how many people watch it?

9   Or alternatively, why not just attack the validity of the criticism in its own program the following Sunday night? It has a much bigger audience. That's what the *Australian* did when it took on *Media Watch* and others over their criticism of its columnist Janet Albrechtsen in a two-tabloid-page spread in its Media section in late 2003—with a pointer in the page 1 banner and an editorial (Stutchbury, 2003).

10   Both sides claimed victory after the judgment. Who had the bigger victory?

11   Do you think that journalists should sue journalists in defamation actions?

Case study 2
The Unabomber manifesto

For a period of 17 years from May 1978, the so-called Unabomber carried out a reign of terror in the United States with package and mail bombs. He sent a total of sixteen bombs, most of them through the US mail system, to academics, business executives, and other people loosely connected to one another through an involvement with science and technology. His bombs killed three people and wounded twenty-three others, some seriously (Knowlton 1997, p. 201). The FBI began to call the file on the killer the 'Unabomb' case, because early victims were associated with _uni_versities or _a_irlines. Shortly after Timothy McVeigh's unrelated terrorist attack on Government offices in Oklahoma City on 19 April 1995, which killed 168 people, the Unabomber killed a timber executive in California. Not long after, the *New York Times* and the *Washington Post,* two of the most respected newspapers in the United States, received copies of a 35,000-word treatise from the bomber who said the bombings would stop if the newspapers published his rambling manifesto and allowed for three annual follow-ups (Woods 1993). Even though the bomber gave the papers three months to respond, they still faced a major ethical dilemma: to publish or not. Would publishing encourage the bomber, or would it assist the investigation? Both papers eventually published lengthy excerpts from the document as part of a story with a legitimate news peg. The FBI announced it intended to distribute the manifesto to some fifty academics in the hope that someone might pick the style and aid in the capture of the killer. Publication did, in fact, provide the clue that led to the arrest of the brilliant, but obviously unhinged hermit Theodore J. Kaczynski. His brother read the document and thought it similar to essays written by Theodore.

Issues and questions raised by case study 2

1   Research and debate the major arguments for and against publishing the Unabomber's manifesto.

2   It's obviously a major news story. People would be interested in understanding what's in the mind of such a criminal, wouldn't they?

3   Wouldn't publishing the manifesto be giving publicity to a killer and risk copycat actions?
4   With the benefit of hindsight, publication helped police with their investigations, but how might it have backfired?
5   Who would you consult (aside from your colleagues and bosses) if such a document had dropped in your lap?
6   What weight would you put on the advice of the police, given they have such a vested interest in catching the bomber?
7   How would you maintain your paper's independence, publish what is obviously a 'great story', and yet act responsibly under the circumstances?
8   When the FBI announced they were distributing the manifesto to a number of academics, they let the papers 'off the ethical hook', didn't they?
9   Your editor decides to accompany the publication of the manifesto with a 500-word justification for the decision to publish. In dot form, what would be the main points you would make by way of justification?
10   What are the counter-arguments that need to be considered?

→ Case study 3
The BBC and journalistic transparency

The BBC sent all staff an email in mid 2003, asking them to register on an internal web site any active political involvement that they, their family, or 'close personal contacts' might have. BBC employees were also told to disclose financial holdings in media companies and in any companies where they owned more than a five per cent stake. They were also to declare business relationships with BBC customers or suppliers (Arthur 2003). Tony Lennon, the President of the broadcasting union, BECTU, described the move as 'an astonishing invasion into the privacy of people who don't have any editorial or strategic role' (Arthur 2003). The 'register of interests' used to apply only to senior editorial staff and managers able to sign purchase orders, and Mr Lennon said that although the union had agreed some changes with the BBC, it had not agreed to such far-reaching questions, or their extension to all staff (Arthur 2003).

Issues and questions raised by case study 3

1   Has a media employer the right to request all workers declare their political and financial interests?
2   Why is it any of their business?
3   Would you comply, if it was not compulsory?
4   What could you do about it if it was compulsory, and you were opposed to such disclosures?
5   How would you feel about disclosing such details?
6   What do Editorial Charters in Australia say about such disclosures?
7   It's understandable that the political journalists disclose any political affiliations (if

they have them) and financial journalists disclose their share portfolios, but why, for instance, should the person who writes the TV column or a sports reporter declare political and financial interests?

8   Why not ask the journalists to register every organisation of which they are a member, like the local service club, the local school parents' and citizens' association, or a church, cultural, or sporting organisation? Surely there's as much chance of a conflict of interest arising in those areas?

Case study 4   ←
Four Corners v. the MEAA Judiciary Committee

In May 2003, an Ethics panel hearing found the ABC's *Four Corners* journalist Sally Neighbour had breached the Code in a story involving a controversial former policeman (Jackson 2003b), but the finding was later quashed on appeal (Jackson 2003c). Former New South Wales detective Peter Thomas accused the *Four Corners* crew of acting unethically by arranging to meet him in a café without declaring who they were and filming and audio-taping without his permission (Jackson 2003b).

Sally Neighbour's program, 'Burned', examining several arson insurance investigations, was aired in October 2000. *Four Corners* was critical of Thomas's post-police force activities as an insurance investigator in Queensland. The Ethics Committee found 'the program served the public interest', but added: 'We have reservations about the methods used' (Jackson 2003b). The committee found the *Four Corners* team breached Clause 8 of the Code by failing to use honest means to obtain material, and by exploiting a person's ignorance of media practice (Jackson 2003b). At the appeal, Neighbour and *Four Corners* executive producer Bruce Belsham said the original adverse finding had been based only on Thomas's word. The Appeal Committee said it could not find that Thomas had been secretly audio-taped and on balance the conduct did not constitute dishonesty in obtaining material (Jackson 2003c). The case raised the issue of when journalists should identify themselves— an issue we will take up in the discussion of deception in chapter 10. Some on the union ethics committee said it was standard practice to disclose who they were when speaking on the phone to a potential interview subject, while others argued that not revealing their identity at that stage was a reasonable investigative journalism technique (Jackson 2003b).

Issues and questions raised by case study 4

This case highlights some crucial issues and fault lines in journalism ethics, in particular the role and effectiveness of the union's own enforcement and educational methods.

1   Do you think a program like *Four Corners* has a duty or a right to use possibly deceptive methods to uncover criminal activity?

2   Do such programs serve the public interest?

3   Can you think of similar stories that have had consequences or have led to complaints being upheld against the journalist(s) concerned?

→   ## Case study 5
    ## Queensland Premier calls for media ombudsman

The Queensland Premier, the self-confessed 'media tart' Peter Beattie, put more than a few media noses out of joint in March 2003, when he suggested that they should be answerable to an ombudsman and have their internal workings exposed under Freedom on Information laws (Parnell 2003). Mr Beattie denied he was advocating Government regulation of journalists, but said the news media should 'embrace an accountability regime similar to that imposed on Government, on Parliament, on other public institutions' (Emerson 2003). The Premier told the Queensland Parliament that the notion of an accountable, free press was out of date and needed reform (ABC Online 2003a). According to the *Courier-Mail* (Parnell 2003), Mr Beattie's comments were originally intended for the Queensland Press Forum but were withdrawn at the last minute, and read into the Parliamentary Hansard on Tuesday 25 March.

If that's true, someone forgot to tell the *Gold Coast Bulletin.* It published an edited text of what it said was the Premier's address to 'the first Queensland Press Forum in Brisbane' ('The Press-ganged Pollie' 2003). The Premier acknowledged in his speech that democracy relies on a free media and that laws and political practices reflected the shared belief that the media was a legitimate part of the political system, with a right to probe and criticise. But the Premier said:

> The cut and thrust of a thousand competing voices is long gone. Many Queens-
> landers live in communities in which there is only a single local daily newspaper
> deciding what is news, supplemented by radio and television stations. That con-
> stant, restless interrogation of policy is long gone in this age of budget-conscious,
> demographic-driven media organisations. Which is not to criticise individual jour-
> nalists or the organisations they work for. It is simply to say that to be an effective
> check on government, a free press requires intensive competition, and that such
> competition is no longer a feature of our society. Cities, such as Brisbane, that
> once hosted a dozen different newspapers, owned by competing proprietors with
> different political agendas and a sharp eye to each other's failings, are now served
> by a single newspaper. The same story can be told for much of Australia. A near
> monopoly is not a free press, at least in the traditional political sense of the term.
> Journalists do not write stories criticising each other. The Courier Mail *does not
> analyse mistaken reports in the ABC, or the ABC hold to account sloppy reporting
> in some commercial television reports. For the public, the media is the sole source*

of apparently authoritative comment about politics. But in the absence of mean-ingful competition, how can the public know whether it is getting the truth? What is it not being told?

Quoted in 'The Press-ganged Pollie' 2003

The speech received the expected reaction from local newspaper editors, political journalists, and commentators. An editorial in the *Courier-Mail,* attacking the idea in general, noted:

A fundamental flaw of the Premier's argument is the claim that there is not intense competition in the media. This assumes, wrongly, that newspapers, radio and television do not compete against one another, and that the Internet can be ignored. It is an assumption that Mr Beattie gives the lie to every day, as he uses different branches of the media to get his message across in different ways. And he is not averse to criticising reporters or their reports, particularly if they manage to reveal a truth he would rather have kept secret.

'Government and Media Accountability' 2003

Issues and questions raised by case study 5

1   Research media regulation in Australia and debate the arguments for and against it.
2   Research regulation of the media by the governments of Australia's near neighbours to the north. What affect does it have on their media?
3   What happened when the media in Indonesia was 'freed up' after the downfall of the Suharto regime in the late 1990s?
4   What's the current situation regarding freedom of the press in Malaysia?
5   Does Peter Beattie have a point about the lack of competition in some Australian cities?
6   What's your opinion of his solution?
7   Is there really competition between print and broadcast media in one-paper cities?
8   Read the *Courier-Mail* editorial on the issue on 27 March 2003. What's your reaction?
9   What are the fault lines between government regulation, economic deregulation and self-regulation by media organisations?

5

THE FOURTH ESTATE

MARKETING, CITIZENSHIP, AND THE MEDIA

Objectives

After reading and discussing this chapter you will have been exposed to:

- The strengths and weaknesses in the concept of the 'fourth estate' as society's watchdog.
- A critique of the public sphere model of journalism ethics.
- News as a consumable product versus its role in educating and informing the public.
- The changing face of twenty-first century popular journalism.
- How one television network gauges the news agenda (or audience interest).
- The idea of an alternative 'watchdog watcher'.

Introduction: The duality of the news audience

This chapter traces the fault lines evident in the model of news media commonly known as the 'fourth estate'. We noted in chapter 3 the duality of the news information commodity: a product with both market and ideological value. Just as there are two sides to the news product, there are two sides to each audience member individually, and to each market segment (the collective audience). As consumers of news, information, and entertainment via the mass media, everyone exists within this dichotomy. We are both a consuming audience and an ideological audience.

The media industries treat their audiences as 'consumers' of news, entertainment, information, sport, and associated product packaging. At the same time we are citizens, constructed as a political audience. In this latter guise we expect the news to offer us information, and political opinions about current issues. As 'citizens' we often rely on the media to provide information on which we base, at least in part, our own opinions, and our vote at election time.

As we have seen, in a market economy a diversity of views is supposedly guaranteed by having a diverse ownership base. Despite this liberal–democratic rhetoric, most news organisations today regard their readers and viewers as buyers first, and only secondly as participants in a democratic process. Respected political correspondent Michelle Grattan (1998, p. 11) says this 'revolutionary' change has taken place quietly, over the past two decades, with very little public scrutiny.

This discussion of change in the ways media constructs both a political and a commercial view of the public takes up arguments made most clearly by author and media critic Julianne Schultz (1998), in her book *Reviving the Fourth Estate*. Schultz writes that the news media's role as public watchdog over the actions of Government, business, and society has been eroded by commercialism. She adds that it can and must be 'revived' as a viable institution. Our question is really a simple one: Can the fourth estate be revived? It would seem to us that such a project might founder on the economic and ideological contradiction between 'consumers' and 'citizens'.

The fourth estate: Can it be revived?

The term 'fourth estate' is attributed to the English conservative, Edmund Burke (1729–97), who apparently used it to attack a 'self-important and braying' English press. One hundred years later, in the 1850s, English newspaper editors had turned this derision to their advantage. London *Times* editor George Reeve saw his newspaper and its peers as partners with what were at that stage the other three important 'estates': parliaments, courts, and, originally, the church. The church was later replaced in the trinity by the executive arm of government. The actuality of the modern fourth estate falls a long way short of the theory (Eggerking 1998, pp. 164–8). In fact, Kitty Eggerking suggests that the radicalism and advocacy of the English press at the time of the long revolution had dissipated by the late nineteenth century. Instead the epoch of industrial journalism saw the once radical and 'free' press become primarily commercial marketing and political process-management services for the ruling class. It is in this context that Eggerking says the problems inherent in the fourth estate mean that today it has become an 'indefensible' institution.

On the other hand, in her book, *Reviving the Fourth Estate*, former journalist, media executive, and university lecturer Julianne Schultz (1998) tries to straddle the contradiction between profitability and public interest—the contradictory dialectic of the front page. However, the underlying tensions in the news commodity mean that the fault lines today are very unstable. Many of them come together in undermining the idealism of the fourth estate. Schultz argues that journalism today can no longer 'adequately fulfil the historic role the press created for itself … as an institution of political life designed to act on behalf of the people'. Instead the news media has become 'a source of real and significant power and influence, an industry prepared to exercise and pursue self-interested commercial, political and cultural agendas' (Schultz 1998, p. 1). By her own admission, Schultz believes that attempting to revive the fourth estate is a thankless, even hopeless, task given the commercial pressures that dominate any democratic ideals that journalists, reporters, and editors might harbour about their work. Here we begin to examine the contradiction between the idealistic view of journalism as the fourth estate, and the competing view that the media is just another business.

The main reason why the news media has responsibilities to society, beyond those of other commercial organisations, is that it proclaims social responsibility as one of its aims: 'the Press actually sets out to market social responsibility' (Walsh 1970, p. 42). The 'social responsibility' theory of the press grew out of its role in the modern bourgeois revolutions of the eighteenth and nineteenth centuries—to defend and proclaim the interests of an emerging and powerful new ruling class against its enemies 'above' and 'below'. The notion of a 'fourth estate', sitting alongside the parliaments, executives, and courts that rule liberal democratic capitalism, is as old as modern journalism. It was born amid the battles for a free press that occurred in the eighteenth and nineteenth centuries (Curran 1991; Hartley 1996; Stockwell 1999).

The fourth estate model has a noble heritage, related by birth to the American War of Independence and the French Revolution (Chiasson 1995). However, like many young firebrands do with time, it has grown fat and comfortable in middle age and the fourth estate today rarely strikes fear into the hearts of tyrants anywhere. In fact, as Schultz herself concedes, the tyrants have tamed the idealism of the media through control of the purse strings. The solution, according to Schultz, is for reporters and editors to rise up, *carpe diem*, and reinvigorate the fourth estate. This is a position that is in the end little different from John Merrill's existential journalism, the triumph of individual will over the social forces compelling journalism into an ideological straitjacket.

Most journalists are indeed, at their core, idealists: they believe in the role of journalism as watchdog, but they also feel the constraints of news production that prevent them from reaching this goal. The idealism of Australian journalists was demonstrated in a 1992 survey conducted by Julianne Schultz as part of the worldwide Media and Democracy Project. The questions and results are published as an Appendix to Schultz's 1998 book, *Reviving the Fourth Estate: Democracy, Accountability and the Media*. The survey is also discussed by Hargreaves (2003).

Schultz's results show that most Australian news workers believe in investigative reporting, and a small majority are slightly 'left of centre' in terms of personal political bias. This accords with the results of several surveys by Professor John Henningham, and anecdotal evidence. Most respondents to the Media and Democracy survey blamed their organisation's leadership for a failure to pursue investigative journalism. From the results, Schultz (1998, p. 53) suggests that commercial considerations and the interests of media owners are the biggest obstacles to disclosure of unpleasant facts about the rich and powerful. From this Schultz concludes that most journalists would be predisposed to the fourth estate 'revival' project—a type of journalism that maintains a weather eye on possible 'misdeeds, questionable practices, inconsistencies and dishonesty by the powerful' (Schultz 1998, p. 55).

The fourth estate: A shifting practice?

Julianne Schultz presents a good overview of the fourth estate and notes some conflict around definitions: '... its meaning has changed over time', but further down, 'it has changed relatively little over two centuries' (1998, p. 48). According to Kitty Eggerking (1998) the first use of the term was in a satirical and cynical vein, and aimed as a barb against the press of the day. In contemporary usage it is seen as embracing positive values, a complete reversal of earlier meanings.

There can be little argument that the concept, *in practice*, has shifted over time, even if the ideal itself has remained relatively static. In terms of our fault lines thesis, these changes can be theorised as a series of discrete, but related moments of interaction: thesis–antithesis–synthesis. The idea begins with a cynical and satirical use of the term (thesis); it is then co-opted by those it was first meant to ridicule and they turn it to their advantage (antithesis); it then becomes a central element of journalistic ideology (synthesis), one that we might look upon as a 'golden age' of the past. In other words, the contradictions in the ideal of the fourth estate are practical and everyday manifestations of the emotional dialectic in journalism. The operative fault lines are evident in the concrete routines of journalism today in tension with the ideals of the news media as a fourth estate. The notion of the fourth estate itself is a set of fluid and interacting contradictory ideologies and social practices relating to doing journalism, and to the study of the news product. Sophisticated techniques of information management, commercial, marketing, and political PR practices have certainly eroded the ideals of the fourth estate, at least in their application. This is increasingly obvious, even to the layperson, in the overwhelming amount of 'news' that is sourced directly from media releases (Zawawi 1994) and in the 'dumbing down' of news values as 'infotainment' (Hallin 1994; O'Neil and Lumby 1994; Hirst et al. 1995; Langer 1998).

While we agree with Julianne Schultz that we need to do something about this, we're just not sure that *reviving* the fourth estate is the way to go. The fourth estate no longer performs a watchdog role on behalf of ordinary people; the media's policing role is performed on behalf of the system as a whole, it is used to strengthen the core ideological consensus values against 'deviance' (Hallin 1994). The news media functions as a moral, political, and ideological boundary rider that keeps in check the worst excesses, but at the same time prevents any real alternative from being seriously considered through public debate. The public sphere is kept within the sphere of limited controversy (Hallin 1994). The debate does not include anyone who can be labelled an 'extremist', only 'moderate' voices are given space and airtime. The *myth* of the fourth estate is an effective ideology—one that can mask the symbiotic relationship between the news media, corporate power, and the state. In addition, the journalistic ideology of 'professionalism' can blind reporters to the assumptions that underpin their daily practice and to their own objective situation as 'churners' of the dominant ideology. Thus, 'the media's real agenda—commercial success and maintenance of the status quo—is revealed' (Schultz 1998, p. 55) only when these ideologies are put under pressure by real world events that can shift the emotional dialectic of the front page (Hirst 2003). Such events are rare, for most of the time the news media's ideological role remains a hidden agenda (Pilger 1998).

Schultz (1998, p. 230) describes the 1980s in Australia as a decade of 'heady optimism' for investigative journalism during which time many news workers felt able to reclaim the ideals of the fourth estate. Notable in this period was the investigative reporting of journalists like Chris Masters, Paul Barry, Wendy Bacon, Brian Toohey, and the sorely missed

National Times. Schultz unhappily concludes that by the early 1990s a backlash was building against the 'journalism of disclosure'. Newspapers came under the hammer of cost-cutting, and ratings-driven television current affairs returned to the easy targets—consumer rip-offs, sexual titillation, barely disguised jingoism, crime, law and order—'the century-old standbys of popular journalism' (Schultz 1998, p. 230). The 1980s were a period of transition. Expensive investigative journalism gave way to cost-cutting (Barrass 2002). A new dialectic was beginning to exert itself, creating a new series of contradictions. An economic imperative was inserted into the mix: crusading journalism is good (thesis), but it is very expensive (antithesis). So we'll have to replace it with something cheaper (synthesis), because after all, we are running a business, and news is just another cost centre. If you've seen the wonderful movie, *Network* (MGM Pictures 1976), you will understand where these sentiments were coming from in the late 1970s. If you haven't seen *Network*, grab it on video or DVD.

By the end of the 1980s, a new breed of managers came to rule the newsroom following an economic shake-out in the industry—despite the warnings of some critics (Cose 1989; Grattan 1998; Underwood 1993). We've already noted how the late 1980s were years of trauma for the Fairfax newspapers and the last days of the afternoon editions in most capital cities (Bowman 1988). This trend has 'pushed newspapers into the business of marketing and reshaped newsrooms to dovetail with those marketing goals' (Underwood 1993, p. 15). These marketing objectives include the presentation of news in a more entertaining fashion, with a consequential reduction in actual news content and news values.

Despite the seemingly unstoppable rise of what she calls 'junk journalism', Julianne Schultz concludes that the ideals of the fourth estate have proved 'remarkably resilient' (1998, p. 231). She argues that responsibility for maintaining the fourth estate has passed 'from the news media, as a corporate institution, to the journalists, editors and producers, who produce the content of the news media' (Schultz 1998, p. 232). Unfortunately, the solution offered by Schultz (1998, p. 238) seems tokenistic and is only introduced in the very last paragraph of the book: 'If journalists were able to build more meaningful, reflective alliances with their audiences, they could become a more significant democratic force.'

This is a fine sentiment, but Schultz does not address the vital 'how' question, and given the pessimistic assessment she offers in the historical accounting of the rest of the book, it seems a little simplistic. Media proprietors and their cheer squad in the op-ed pages have argued for years that they only give readers and viewers what they want. If this basic (and false) assumption is not challenged, how can we go beyond it? The answers are not simple, good investigative reporting is expensive, and as Tony Barrass (2002, p. 29) wrote in the *Walkley Magazine*: 'Staff freezes and budget cuts have become common. The bean-counters rejoice and get promoted, the morale of the newsroom sinks'. In television current affairs the situation is the same. SBS correspondent Mark Davies (2002) believes that the cost of investigative journalism will see it gradually replaced by the less thoughtful, but cheaper '24-hour news model' that is 'just an avalanche of facts'. This model has an over-reliance on the 'regurgitation of press conferences and press releases by authoritative figures', and journalists operate with a 'robo-reporter approach', which is wrongly 'lauded as the pinnacle of professionalism' (Davies 2002, pp. 28–9). The television news programming that is supposed to make up for the lack of solid investigative work and actually break stories is built around the 24-hour news clock, and even some of those on the inside of the game call it 'news lite'. 'News lite' is a presentation of news items in the context of a chat-show, with witty and 'human' hosts, who are empathetic to and for the audience. The best way to explain it is to give an example, like Channel Seven's *Sunrise*. If you couldn't stop laughing when you saw the brilliantly funny *CNNNN* on ABC television, you will realise it was very close to 'reality'.

You've got to be up before *Sunrise* to animate democracy

One of the key directives in the MEAA Code of Ethics for journalists is that journalism should 'inform citizens and animate democracy'. This is the noble and somewhat idealistic tradition of the 'fourth estate'. While the 'watchdog' role and informative functions of journalism are important every day, they can become critical factors in the democratic exercise of public opinion during periods of social, economic, and political crisis (Chiasson 1995), and during wartime (Knightley 1975). By the same token, the news media can also be used, willingly, or unwittingly, in the manipulation of public opinion. As we shall see, there is a very fine line, but a fault line all the same, between the democratic functions of the fourth estate and the media as a tool of daily propaganda on behalf of the ruling elite. We will deal substantially with war reporting and the national interest in the next chapter; suffice to say that a news media that fails during times of relative 'normality' will most certainly be found inadequate to report accurately and fairly on hostilities between nations.

As we have noted above, traditionally the news media has strived to animate democracy through strong investigative journalism that exposed corruption or malpractice. We've also seen how this is becoming an expensive luxury. Other methods have to be found and one way is to offer readers, listeners, or viewers a chance to have their say, to let the audience express a point of view, either individually, or collectively.

Following the dominant trends in American television, the Seven network in Australia manages to do this very successfully on its morning 'news' program, *Sunrise*. In 2003–04 this program screened from 6 a.m. to 9 a.m. each weekday, and had regular news bulletins, constructed around the 24-hour news clock, and containing the usual overnight domestic compiles, sport stories, and major international events, but it also had personalities and issues. In 2004 a new SMS polling and messaging function was added to the already crowded *Sunrise* screen. It was the first application of this technology in Australia, which has been common in Europe, Asia, and the USA for some time. The experiment didn't last long—the audience apparently didn't like it.

The genial *Sunrise* hosts at 'brekky central', leading the 'dawn patrollers' are usually Seven 'personalities', Melissa Doyle and David Koch. Around its frequent news inserts and those sometimes irritating headline 'crawlies' across the bottom of the screen, the program is mostly light, and mildly entertaining, chatter. However the program also heavily promotes and campaigns for populist issues that constantly cut through the banter. Viewers are constantly invited to send in emails, and these are read out endlessly by 'Kochie' and 'Mel'. Viewers also register immediate opinions via fairly expensive phone calls, and the results are reported each day for snap opinion polls conducted on air. On a superficial viewing, *Sunrise* may seem to have lived up to its promise of being a champion for 'ordinary' Australians. There is an attempt to tap issues that the audience will respond to, and follow-ups with regular political guests, Howard Government Minister for small business Joe Hockey, and the Opposition's foreign affairs spokesperson, Kevin Rudd. They are playfully described as political 'heavyweights', though on most mornings they act like tactful opponents at a respectable bowls club. *Sunrise* also has a host of experts on everything from business, entertainment, gadgets, and movies, all the way to 'terrorism'. However you look at it, *Sunrise* is appealing to the consuming and ideological demographic that has become known as 'Howard's battlers'.

And if the reaction from Willoughby in Sydney—home of the opposition *Today* program—is any indication, *Sunrise* must be capturing a sizeable chunk of what used to be *Today's* exclusive territory. According to Brisbane's *Sunday Mail,* in a story headed 'Daggers at Dawn', Seven was (in late 2003) seeking legal advice, alleging *Today* staff approached interviewees booked for *Sunrise* to pull out and appear on the Nine show instead—or be blacklisted (Casey 2003). *Sunrise* executive producer Adam Boland was quoted as saying:

> We're out there spreading love but the *Today* bully-boys are walking down the street … trying to intimidate guests we've promoted into not appearing on our show.

The folk at Nine said it was simply tough competition (Casey 2003).

We have to ask the question of programs like *Sunrise*: Is it more 'animation' than 'democracy'? There can be no doubt that the program is carefully structured and targeted to attract an audience predisposed to respond appropriately to the populist issues regularly aired on *Sunrise*. Tax cuts, health spending, the war on terror and the war on drugs, education, crime, diet, lifestyle, and entertainment news are the staple topics of discussion on the show. The careful matching of the cast to the audience creates an easy intimacy; the gentle urging of the hosts creates a positive response to their email campaigns and frequent public stunts. Why? Because Channel Seven's marketing department has got a handle on its target demographics. How? By conducting national surveys throughout the first half of 2003 to find out what *Sunrise* audiences think about certain issues.

We survey, you believe

According to the survey booklet *Your View,* sent to households in the Brisbane area (Channel Seven News 2003), Channel Seven's news anchors, Rod Young and Kay McGrath, wanted to 'find out exactly what's on your mind in this ever-changing world'. Their appeal to encourage responses was 'tell us those issues that concern you the most'. The seven pages of questions in the *Your View* booklet were couched in terms of 'satisfaction', and attitudes to 'Government' and social institutions such as the court system, religious groups, the press, companies, the health system, banks, science, the police, and defence forces. The questionnaire asked about the respondent's 'confidence' in the 'people running these institutions'; the 'tick-a-box' answers gave a choice of 'great', 'some', and 'hardly any' confidence.

Similarly styled questions were asked about 'Government' spending on environment, health, 'quality of life' in the cities and the bush, 'dealing with drug addiction', 'dealing with crime', education, roads, 'fighting terrorism', public transport, defence, parks and recreation, unemployment, child care, and indigenous issues. The three-choice answer columns were 'too much', 'about right', and 'too little'. The inclusion of questions about attitudes to religion and the alleged threat of global terrorism is an interesting contemporary note.

Respondents to the *Your View* survey were also asked about how 'certain aspects of Australian life' should be approached. The choices were 'new approach needed', 'current approach adequate', and 'agree with old approach used in the past'. The topics were similar to those used in other questions: 'punishment for criminals', gun control, environment, indigenous issues, and education. Opinions about social versus individual responsibility were also surveyed in a question that asked if 'Government' should be doing more, or if 'people should take care of themselves more': the topics were 'improving children's discipline', 'family problems', 'underage alcohol abuse', smoking, drugs, drink-driving, and 'personal safety on public property'. These themes provide an interesting pattern to the questions and responses sought in the *Your View* survey and underline the populist nature of the exercise. They equate with typical 'family' values, and are commonly presented throughout the media as the most pressing social issues. In a sense, the framing of these issues in terms of law and order depoliticises them. What we mean by this is that they are removed from the realm of political issues, cutting across traditional political values, as if by osmosis. Instead it moves these important topics of debate onto the ground of abstract 'authority' against 'disobedience'.

Your View respondents were asked to agree or disagree on a six-point scale with a series of statements about crime, health, education, standards of living, roads, immigration and multiculturalism, TV programming, and perceptions that 'things' might be getting better, or worse.

Under the general rubric of 'crime' the following statements were presented:
- 'Criminals are not punished enough.'
- 'Car theft is on the rise.'
- 'I feel safe going out at night.'
- 'There is more crime and violence … than five years ago.'
- 'The police do not do enough about hoons.'

In the section asking questions about standards of living, the statements included the following:
- 'Things are getting better.'
- 'Work hard and you can succeed.'
- 'I am optimistic about the future in Australia.'
- 'All unemployed people should work for the dole.'
- 'The needy have a basic right to good public housing.'
- 'The laws against pornography are not strong enough.'
- 'There are too many immigrants in Australia already.'
- 'Children are exposed to too much violence and sex on the Internet.'
- 'We are not spending enough to prevent acts of terrorism.'
- 'Australia should support any war against countries that threaten world security.'

The style and tone of these 'agree', or 'disagree' statements is interesting—they postulate strong and fairly conservative positions based on massive generalisations, and no information is provided to support any proposition. The final page of the survey form is for personal information, including marital status, age, region, income and employment status, and television viewing in hours per day. Respondents are also invited to include their email address 'to receive further information from Seven'. In the accompanying fine print 'Privacy Disclosure', the network points out that email addresses will be used to compile a database 'for the purpose of contacting you in future to promote' Seven programming and 'ongoing market research'. The true purpose of the survey is thus revealed. It is the ultimate triumph of marketing over citizenship.

The timing of the survey in Brisbane during 2003 also points in this direction. Channel Seven had recently poached Rod Young from the ABC, and clearly saw a need to have his popular image linked to existing Seven personality Kay McGrath. The large photo of McGrath and Young on the cover of *Your View*, and a tailored message from them, was designed to promote the new news line-up on Seven. Clearly the responses were being used to craft and refine the news output of the station to the aspirations, fears, beliefs, interests, and opinions of respondents. Brisbane viewers were given the results of the survey in a series of nightly reports over a number of days in 2003. The survey raises interesting issues about marketing, audience research, and the shape of Channel Seven's news agenda. Will stories be dumped from the bulletin if they do not accord with the audience profiles constructed through this survey?

If the survey shows that most of the audience is in favour of tough penalties for illicit drug users, or car thieves, will these stories get preferential treatment? If responses indicate that the majority of Seven's audience is against immigration, will Kochie and Mel campaign to close the borders? If news is about the important things that are actually happening, and if the role of the news media is to animate democracy, then how can pandering to the lowest common denominator, populist opinion, be considered 'news'?

A conservative news agenda

What Channel Seven was attempting with this survey is not new. American media academic John Phelan (1991) described it over a decade ago as the process of 'selling consent' through 'integrative propaganda', largely pioneered by American television networks in the late 1980s and early 1990s. Through the *Your View* survey process Channel Seven is following the well-worn path of commercial television, which involves national networking of programs, with local windows for news and information programming, dominated by lifestyle issues. Far from being about citizenship, Phelan (1991, p. 76) argues, such campaigns are the result of media political economy, advertising, and the 'determining conditions of advanced industrial technology'. Similar forces have shaped the direction of the 'news lite' formula of *Sunrise* which is clearly striving for a demographically targeted market segment, in tune with the populist agenda it is seeking to promote through what Phelan calls 'unabashed "activist television"'. The model that was developed in the late 1980s in the United States has been successfully transplanted into Australian conditions, and the *Your View, Sunrise* formula clearly indicates this.

The formula for success in the US television morning news market was 'often exhorta-tion, about crime, drug abuse, good health practices, family conflict, education, sexual prob-lems, employment, the environment and consumer complaints'. These populist topics are 'perennial', and 'recycled regularly', and the programs have an 'overwhelming tendency … to preserve an atmosphere of upbeat optimism' (Curran 1991, p. 79). Even a cursory viewing of *Sunrise* would confirm this, and the questions in *Your View*, highlighted above, appear to fit this model perfectly. The emphasis on populist issues and solutions also has a practical, commercial side. It is a sure bet that playing safe on controversial topics, while giving the appearance of concern and wanting to do something, will not alienate too many viewers. As further security against putting off punters, *Sunrise*, and programs like it on the other net-works, also adopt another feature of the American model: the animated and charming weather reporter. This person is usually on location at an event the network wants to pro-mote, such as the Rugby World Cup in October 2003, for which Seven had the television rights. Usually the weather 'presenter' is a 'central casting type of the all-purpose warm com-munity person' (Phelan 1991, p. 79), who can be out and about in the community, visiting schools, old peoples' homes and other places sure to elicit the sympathies of the selected audience demographic. The 'weather guy' at Seven spends a lot of time with cute animals.

This campaigning style of 'news lite' programming, so evidently adapted by Channel Seven, relies on three strategic arms: the coverage of politics through personalities; the promotion of public safety, health, and welfare; and product promotion through 'con-sumer' segments. As Phelan (1991, p. 84) points out, 'the terror and the triumph are proven box-office hits', while the 'orchestrating of a campaign … can be totally explained in terms of sheer good business'.

This type of journalism, or perhaps more accurately news-marketing, is undertaken by the television networks, and increasingly the other news media, as a way of turning a profit, but this aspect can be neatly disguised by the idea that the stations are doing all this soft campaigning for the public good. The use of the survey tool appears to support the argument that the networks are only giving the audience what they want (as expressed in the survey results). The networks appear to be, and promote themselves as, good cor-porate citizens taking seriously their responsibilities to animate democracy, inform the public, and provide a forum for discussion of important social issues. However, for researchers like John Phelan (1991, p. 91), 'the contemporary television public-service/community campaign raises questions of politics and culture and thus funda-mental questions of values'.

For us it raises inevitable questions too, about the ideological framing of this 'cam-paigning' style of journalism, and about the fault lines that undermine the foundations of the liberal–democratic model of the news media, the public sphere, and the fourth estate. In this context any move towards civic responsibility in journalism is itself contradictory, and linked to a marketing function (Grattan 1998, p. 21). Symbolically this is represented at the Fairfax newspapers by marketing staff moving onto the same floor as the editorial sections in the mid 1990s (Grattan 1998, p. 18). It is possible to argue two positions in the face of this trend. The first is that it is a cynical exercise in manipulation and perception, just 'smoke and mirrors'. The second is that the news media really cares about issues of democracy, and takes its role as the 'fourth estate' and 'public sphere for debate' seriously. Unfortunately the evidence points to the former conclusion.

A critique of the public sphere model

In this chapter we examine this argument against the central contradiction between the commercial and informational/political role of the news media. In a liberal capitalist democracy like Australia, the media is widely expected to play an educative, informative, and argumentative role in politics—in particular, to be a conduit for wide debate of social issues, to be what German critical philosopher Jürgen Habermas (1990) called the 'public sphere'. The classic liberal–democratic notion of the public sphere is defined by James Curran (1991, p. 29) as:

> ... the space between government and society in which private individuals exercise formal and informal control over the state: formal control through the election of governments and informal control through the pressure of public opinion.

The news media plays a central role in conceptions of the public sphere, and can be seen as one of the 'principal institutions' of liberal democracy, 'the fourth estate of the realm' (Curran 1991, p. 29). As we noted above, the fourth estate and public sphere models of journalism ethics share some similarities. For James Curran, a basic requirement of a democratic media system is that all 'significant interests' in society are represented, differences negotiated or arbitrated, and public accountability of the political process secured. Journalism academic Stephen Stockwell (1999, p. 41) says 'political free speech' is at the heart of deliberative democracy, and the news media plays a crucial role in 'creating democracy day-to-day'. According to the deliberative theory of democracy, journalism and journalists value 'the autonomy of citizens' and 'political equality'. Deliberative theory argues that in order to be successful in meeting these ideals of democracy, and the expectations of citizen-audiences, journalists and the news media must 'confront power with hard questions', but then the news media must negotiate how that power is to be represented in the reporting (Stockwell 1999, p. 42). This seeming contradiction is confirmed by Stockwell's next line, which explains that from the deliberative perspective: 'Indeed it might be argued that journalism is at its most successful when it can negotiate with power to subvert power by revealing its excesses.'

Stockwell points to problems in the initial conception of the media as the fourth estate. In the end, the deliberative approach ends up with the normative resolutions proposed by the fourth estate and its 'incomplete account of power'. Stockwell's critique is that the media is incapable of turning its 'forensic techniques back on itself', and in this he is aligned with Schultz and others. But Stockwell takes it further, describing the fourth estate project as 'hackneyed mythology'. The reality is not the mythic Roman Senate, or Greek Agora, but the 'partisan, commercial enterprise' that cannot provide the 'free and frank' discussion required in a real functioning democracy. Instead we get the closure of the public sphere (Stockwell 1999, p. 43).

The fundamental tenets of the public sphere argument were first elucidated by the German philosopher Jürgen Habermas in the late 1950s, but not translated into English as

The Structural Transformation of the Public Sphere until 1990. Habermas (1990) wrote that in the eighteenth century, the public sphere as then constituted, served the interests of the rising class of private owners, the bourgeoisie. The printed newspapers owned by members of this class provided them with a voice against autocracy, and an organising tool for their revolution against feudalism. This worked fine for the bourgeoisie when it was a progressive social force fighting for economic and political superiority over the old system. However, once the bourgeoisie assumed the right to rule in its own name, the 'free' press became an instrument of control over other social classes. Through the printed news media, the private opinions of a wealthy, but small, bourgeois elite were reconstituted as the prevailing opinions of the broader general public. No longer was the public sphere a method of subjecting the Government to informal supervision, instead it had become an 'extension' of the state apparatus and public discourse was replaced by what Curran (1991, p. 38) calls 'power politics'. Nineteenth century newspapers were far from the ideal of the public sphere, with remnant traces of the Greek 'agora', or Roman senate. According to Curran (1991, p. 40) they were instead, 'engines of propaganda for the bourgeoisie'. Habermas argued that in order to restore the public sphere to its rightful place, public reason and openness must be reinstituted in the discourse of politics. The problem for Habermas, and for the radical liberal–democrat James Curran, is that their position is ultimately idealist—it does not account for the realities of media economics, or the birth of what we call the age of 'industrial' journalism in the mid nineteenth century. This was a time in Australia, Europe, and the United States in which increasing reliance on advertising, and mounting establishment costs, pushed out radical newspapers, and led to 'the steady transfer of control of the popular press to capitalist entrepreneurs' (Curran 1991, p. 39). Stockwell has taken this argument to its logical conclusion in the period of late industrial capitalism. He argues the way forward is not to 'circle the wagons around a claim to professionalism', which is 'patently absurd' in the face of the 'industrial practices of [Murdoch's UK news factory] Wapping' growing like a cancer over the 'entire process' of news production (Stockwell 1999, p. 43). The alternative to this defensive position, Stockwell (1999, p. 44) argues, is 'day-by-day, issue-by-issue' resistance to the 'closure of the public sphere'. Unfortunately, the call to action is not backed up by a winnable game plan. The problem is really the initial conception of the public sphere, which is flawed and ahistorical. Essentially what Habermas missed in the formulation of his theory of the public sphere is that the market system, in the news industry and other locations of production, actually prevents anyone except the economic and political elite from having anything but the most cursory access to power, debate, and decision-making. In this context the role of the news media as public forum, or as fourth estate, must be questioned.

For critics of the fourth estate model, the problem is that it misinterprets the nexus between private property and the state in a capitalist society. The free-market model assumes that the market place will provide a check and balance system on political power holders. It mistakenly believes in a fundamental separation between market economics and politics. Critics of this position argue that the state is designed, constructed, and managed to further the economic interests of the bourgeoisie; that is, it is in place precisely to manage the system on behalf of the capitalist elite. Therefore, the idea that the news media, privately owned and based on market economics, will somehow act as a watchdog over the actions of an independent state machinery is both tautologous and very wrong. In the first place the state is not independent, it is an instrument of bourgeois rule. Second, the bourgeoisie created the fourth estate to champion its cause in a revolution against feudal autocracy (Hartley 1996). The bourgeoisie is no longer revolutionary; it controls both the market place and the state machine. For the past 150 years, the bourgeoisie has had no interest in anything except its ongoing maintenance of power, and the profitability of its investments (Hirst 1993, 2001, 2003). Despite the ideological trappings of so-called media freedom, and the constant posturing in the name of liberal democracy, the bourgeois view is precisely that the news media is just another business. In the case of news, it is the business of manufacturing and selling consent, or perhaps it would be better to say acquiescence, to ruling class dominance of politics, the economy, and culture. This class divide is the fundamental fault line in the arguments about the fourth estate. The economic and political power bestowed by ownership of the means of production is translated into ideological control over the news commodity and its infusion with political ideas that validate class rule, while consistently denying its existence to the non-owning class.

Despite the shortcomings that we have identified, this free-market model persists, mainly because of its ideological strength and the support it lends to the economic, social, and political status quo. Curran too recognised these problems with the classic theory of the public sphere, which, he argued, 'has nothing useful to say about the way in which the media can invigorate the structures of liberal democracy' (1991, p. 29). However, like Schultz, Curran believes that the basic structures of the liberal democratic media system, based on private market ownership and control of the means of media production, can be reformed or revived. Curran (1991, p. 48) writes that market competition can ensure diversity, if there are limits placed on monopoly. He argues that the state should impose these limits (p. 49), but this just again highlights the circularity of this argument: an independent state should regulate a market in order to ensure that the market can watch over (regulate) the actions of the state. Stephen Stockwell (1999, p. 46) also concedes on this point: 'competition between different media organisations … may produce a diversity of editorial positions'. We think this is more hope than reality. However, we agree with Stockwell that journalists have a right, and a responsibility, to seek out the 'gaps in the media hegemony where deliberation may flourish'. Further, we agree that news workers need to examine a picture bigger than notions of the fourth estate. It should be a vision that includes 'reconsidering their work practices … beyond being mere employees', and working as advocates, consciously 'assisting in the creation of new, "active" audiences' (Stockwell 1999, p. 47).

Ethics, quality, and democracy

We agree with those who argue that reviving the fourth estate is an almost impossible undertaking, and one based on the misplaced idea that the market economy can best provide the safeguards and diversity that a vigorous democracy needs to survive and flourish. A project based on rethinking Habermas and attempting to reform the news media into a viable public sphere is ultimately doomed because it does not account for, nor does it fully appreciate, the significance of the fundamental fault line in the news commodity (see chapter 3).

From what we have argued it is clear that the fourth estate, as an ideological construct, has a chequered history. As Schultz notes, the ideal of the fourth estate is not something that has remained fixed over the past 200 years. On the contrary, it has assumed 'different guises for press barons, politicians and journalists'. Further, distortions, modifications, and new ideas have been introduced as the ideology of the fourth estate 'has been transmuted over time to incorporate a wide, and at times contradictory, set of meanings' (Schultz 1998, p. 49). The fault lines inherent in news journalism have asserted themselves to keep the ideal alive, while constantly undermining it in practice. This is the essence of the emotional dialectic: the ideas and ideology of public service, and the public interest, are constantly thwarted by the social relations of news production (Stockwell 1999; Hirst 2001, 2003). The history and popularity of the fourth estate as a model for news media has followed a trajectory that closely parallels the shifting emotional dialectic of journalism. As Schultz points out, this has included adapting to fit 'the media systems of the twentieth century' (1998, p. 49). Can it 'transmute' again to fit the media systems of the twenty-first?

The MEAA, in its attempts to modify and update the Code of Ethics, has embraced the logic of the fourth estate. But, far from solving ethical problems for journalists, the revised Code of Ethics is just one more element in what the MEAA rightly identifies as the 'continuing public debate about the power and accountability of journalists' (MEAA 1995a, p. 10). The other issues which the MEAA committee was asked to examine, such as the complaints procedures, the relationship between the Code of Ethics and media institutions, self-regulation, and the relationship between the Code and the law are not yet resolved.

Who's watching the watchdogs?

An increasingly popular suggestion in academic and critical circles (Turner 1994b) is for 'independent' watchdog bodies to oversee journalistic practice with 'appropriate powers to enforce sanctions' (Littlemore 1995, p. 11). The Senate Standing Committee (1994) that prepared the report *Off the Record* concluded that 'if the media gets out of hand ... then the need for an independent and powerful review body based on statute increases' (*Off the Record*, p. xxiii). This sanction can be avoided, the good Senators argued, only if the media (collectively) develops a system of effective self-regulation. In the Committee's view the media 'needs to satisfy the public at large that this can be done without external supervision or a legislatively imposed set of rules' (*Off the Record*, p. xxiv). Are we seeing, in effect, the creation of a possible 'fifth' estate to watch over the watchdogs?

Journalist and scholar Geoff Turner (1994a, 1994b) has argued for an independent tribunal, a 'Media Commission', to police journalistic ethics precisely because of the failure of self-regulation by both proprietors and journalists. His arguments can be summarised in the following points:
*   That such a 'Media Commission' could promote ethical standards and enforce them; that it would 'professionalise' journalism and ensure greater 'quality'.
*   That a national approach is needed to law reform.

- That the Commission would 'balance the dominance of major interests' (Turner 1994b, pp. 1–12).

Unfortunately, Turner's model has the same shortcomings as the legislative solution proposed by Stuart Littlemore. The independence of a 'Media Commission', as argued by Littlemore and Turner, is compromised. It is, in fact, Government control given that it would be 'supervised at arm's length by an all-parties' parliamentary committee' (Turner, 1994b, p.1). Keeping someone at arm's length means they are, at all times, close enough for a knockout punch. It also means there is always a hand on the leash (Hirst 1997a). 'Independent' is one of those loosely defined words that sounds democratic and principled, but in fact has no real meaning in this debate unless it means *completely* free from political interference. A second element of journalism's emotional dialectic of 'ambivalent identity' is that professional regulation brings with it a greater reliance on institutions of the state (Hallin 1994, p. 7). When this borrowed 'authority of the state' is combined with global media institutions, mainly in private hands, 'private power will increasingly eclipse the democratic process' (Hallin 1994, p. 8). There is also an obvious circularity in the arguments of those who call for 'independent' regulation of the media by Government or semi-government bodies. In a society where the weak need protection from the strong or corrupt, the role of the fourth estate is to prevent excesses of state and corporate power. Yet in an unequal society, how can the same corporate–state structures then be trusted to monitor the very group that has the responsibility to keep them honest? It is a circular nonsense to think that the Government should 'watch' the media while it 'watches' the Government.

We believe that few journalists would willingly submit themselves to a Government-sponsored media tribunal. Should the tribunal also be 'independent' of the journalist's union, or of the employers? If we were to follow Littlemore's or Turner's suggestions, there is no way that such a tribunal could be independent of legislators and bureaucrats, who themselves are accountable to virtually no one, except their party hierarchy or the Government of the day. Such a situation could easily lead to witch hunts, the persecution of unpopular journalists, blackballing, and, ultimately, a tame media. There is an argument for revamping and strengthening the judicial procedures of the MEAA, but we can see no justification for taking these matters 'out of house', or for journalists to cede such powers to any outside body.

The other question that Stuart Littlemore raises, in relation to both 'regulation' and the 'professionalism' of journalism, is: Should journalists be subject to the same regulation as medical practitioners and solicitors? This again raises the question: Are journalists professionals in the same way? As we've argued, journalism is not a profession in the same way as the law, medicine, or dentistry. Journalists do not, except in very rare cases, have a provider–client economic relationship with their audience. The economic relationship is indirect. Reporters write and analyse news events, the media outlet collates these stories into a newspaper, or broadcast bulletin, and then this is 'sold' to advertisers, who then 'present' it to the public. Most people never meet a reporter, let alone have the intimate relationship that a client has with a solicitor, accountant, doctor, or dentist.

On one hand it's easy to make an argument that journalists 'are capable of more harm than negligent chiropodists or dishonest solicitors' (Littlemore 1995, p. 11). On the other hand, licensing journalists is extremely problematic, especially for those who wish to maintain or revive the news media as a fourth estate. Medical practitioners can kill with their mistakes and fraudulent solicitors can send people bankrupt. The journalistic equivalent is perhaps to be skewered on one of the current affairs programs. The Senate Standing Committee concluded that doctors, lawyers, and priests are entitled to greater privilege because they are subject to far more rigorous selection and training than most journalists (*Off the Record*, p. xii). However, it is interesting to note that the Senate Committee stopped just short of recommending licences for journalists and appeared to endorse Paul Chadwick's opinion that:

> ... licensing journalists is fraught with risk. Such a scheme may well justly punish the bad journalist for wilful breaches of a code. But it may equally be turned against the ethical journalist when he or she does what a free society expects and unsettles the powerful with accurate disclosures.

Chadwick 1995b, p. 15

On the other hand, Stuart Littlemore is right to point out that a Code 'owned' by journalists has little power over (and holds little threat for) the likes of Alan Jones and other 'commentators' who are not technically journalists. However, Littlemore makes the mistake of lumping commentators and journalists together. The Australian Broadcasting Authority, the racial and sexual vilification laws, and other such avenues of appeal, can deal with consumer complaints against the Joneses and Lawses of the media world through the station licensing process, but a 'free' media cannot be subject to licence or whim. A Code of Ethics (no matter how well enforced by peers) can only be applied to MEAA members. Again, we can see the ways in which the relations of production govern the emotional dialectic. The application of ethics to the news production process is, ultimately, an industrial issue. Media proprietors are free to use their power in any way they like to increase circulation, ratings, and ultimately advertising revenues. As former ABC journalist and Victorian Education Minister Mary Delahunty (in Delahunty & Bacon 1995, p. 13) put it so nicely: 'The generals must also submit to an ethical edifice that demands honesty, fairness, independence and respect for the rights of others'. If only they would!

The fourth estate, crisis, and 'anarchy'

It is a comforting thought: a rule for honest, accountable, and responsible journalism that applies across the board, but it will not happen while the functions of social control rest, ultimately, with capital, rather than with news workers. What is needed is a cultural shift so great that it finally and forever undermines the function of social control and completely alters, irrevocably, the relations of production in the newsroom (Delahunty & Bacon 1995). *Sydney Morning Herald* journalist Margo Kingston (2001) believes journalists have stopped working on the fourth estate/public sphere model of journalism and citizenship. Instead reporters premise what they do on the 'consumerist' model where 'content is seen as the space between the ads'.

To remedy this failure of political communication between the reporter and the reader, Margo Kingston has called for 'anarchy' in the newsroom, and for journalists to re-connect with their readers. Journalists, she says, need to 'get back to that sense of tension between the readers' interests and the advertisers' interests'. This must be done to return the news media to the traditional ideals of the fourth estate, to be a 'provocateur' on behalf of the readers or viewing audience. This requires journalists to resist 'a rigid, hierarchical, bureaucratic management structure', and to 'restore a sense of anarchy in the newsroom' (Kingston 2001). This might sound like incendiary talk, the language of revolution, but it is necessary to raise this radical proposal to counteract the effects of another revolution in the newsroom—the trend towards overt managerialism and marketing.

One of Australia's leading political journalists calls it a secret revolution with far-reaching implications, and describes it as the convergence of editorial and commercial functions (Grattan 1998). Often this role exists in one person, increasingly the 'publisher', or 'editor-in-chief'. Michelle Grattan (1998, p. 21) argues that journalism has a 'contradictory face'; it must be connected to its audience and inevitably this means using the mechanisms of the market place to 'include the practice of democracy'. This is a difficult task at the best of times, and as we have seen, it is one that the news media often fails to deliver on. In relatively normal times the news media presents us with an homogenised, bland, and populist fare that appears to satisfy, but is in fact 'news lite'. As Lloyd Chiasson describes it, the situation is worse when there is conflict. He says the news media spends 'a great deal of time describing the most prominent trees, but we never get more than a fleeting glimpse of what the forest looks like' (Chiasson 1995, p. 221). In times of political crisis, the news media does not provide the necessary tools for citizens to make informed and rational decisions. On the contrary, the news media guides the readers through integrative propaganda, leading towards a seemingly inevitable solution that does not threaten ruling class interests. The nature of the dialectic is such however, that on rare occasions, an alternative voice is heard, or a non-elite viewpoint pushes its way through. In the next chapter we will see how these pressures operate on the media during times of military conflict, when the pressure to self-censor in the name of the national interest is even stronger.

The case studies at the end of this chapter examine some of the classic examples of where the political role of the news media—to inform the public and animate democracy—conflicts with other pressures: in some cases political, in others economic, moral, or personal.

Ethical dilemmas in practice

→ ## Scenario 1

Media organisations conduct surveys to discover what their readers or audiences are interested in. If your employer did such a survey and discovered that readers were interested in health and the environment, do-it-yourself advice and leisure activities, could, would, or should that change what the chief of staff decides the reporters will cover? Would you be willing to chase stories in the areas popular with readers? Is the media's role to inform the public about what they want to know or about what they need to know?

Scenario 2

A pressure group wants to get publicity on the TV news for their latest campaign—to save some large trees in a local park from being felled by the local council. A friend from schooldays is a senior member of the group and rings you (in your capacity as a reporter for the local TV station) to ask how to guarantee coverage. He says his members are prepared to chain themselves to the trees and refuse police instructions to leave if that is what it will take to make their point. 'Tell us what to do, and we'll do it. We really need to reverse this awful council decision and if that means breaking the law, so be it. How far would we need to promise you we'd go for you guys to come out and film us?' What do you say?

Case studies

Case study 1
The Watergate break-in

> *No other story in American history features the press in so prominent and heroic a role, inspiring a new generation of journalists to dig below the surface of events.*

> Schudson 1992, p. 103

On 17 June 1972, five men were arrested for breaking into the Democratic Party headquarters at the Watergate Apartments in Washington DC. Among those arrested were two employees of the Committee to Re-Elect the President (CRP) and a former White House aide. That day marked the beginning of what became known as the Watergate Affair. During the next two years, investigations uncovered stories of the illegal use of campaign funds, abuse of presidential powers, and political sabotage to ensure the then President Richard Nixon's re-election. After continuous denial by Nixon of involvement in the affair, the release of taped telephone calls and office conversations that took place in the White House confirmed his guilt. The President announced his resignation on 8 August 1974, the first American President to do so. The story is told in a great movie about journalism: *All the President's Men*.

The *Washington Post* received a Pulitzer prize for its coverage of Watergate. The investigative work of two *Post* reporters, Carl Bernstein and Bob Woodward, carried the Watergate story from one of a minor break-in to one of much greater significance. However, some of the methods used by the *Post* in its coverage of Watergate were far from heroic. Only after the whole truth was discovered could their ethical misconduct in any way be justified: 'At this stage they did not know the significance of their investigations or what would eventuate (Nixon's resignation). If they had known this their ethical misconduct could be considered outweighed by the enormous public benefit, but they were thinking only of protecting themselves, the *Post* and getting a story' (Christians, Rotzoll & Fackler 1991, p. 95).

In the beginning, Woodward and Bernstein would go on nightly 'fishing expeditions' in their search for information. This involved visiting the homes of campaign officials working for CRP, whose names were on a list obtained by a *Post* researcher from a friend. This list of names was considered a classified document. On these expeditions Woodward and Bernstein would identify themselves as *Post* reporters, but 'the approach that seemed to work best was less than straightforward: A friend at the committee told us that you were disturbed by some of the things you saw going on there, that you would be a good person to talk to .... that you were absolutely straight and honest and didn't know quite what to do' (Bernstein & Woodward 1974, p. 60). Of course, there was no such 'friend', and if the reporters were asked to identify this 'friend', they would argue the need to protect their sources. Thus journalistic values were used to excuse journalistic misconduct. Woodward and Bernstein were also persistent in extracting information from a person. In one case Bernstein met with a woman who worked for the CRP and told her she was being followed. After giving him some information the woman asked Bernstein never to call her. Following this meeting the same now 'hysterical' woman phoned Bernstein to tell him she had been seen talking to him and didn't want him to call her or try to see her. 'Later that night, Bernstein went to her apartment and knocked on her door' (Bernstein & Woodward 1974, p. 62), thus ignoring her requests and possibly endangering her career. An important journalistic ethic is that reporters never misrepresent themselves. However, Bernstein 'bent the rules a bit', when he failed to tell an attorney's mother that he worked for the *Post* and left a message for her son to call him. This idea was taken further when Bernstein actually identified himself as someone else when making a call:

> *Bernstein went into an unoccupied office near the newsroom. He was really going to break the rules this time and he didn't want [the Post's executive editor Ben] Bradlee, or anybody else, to walk by his desk and hear him doing it ... He closed the door and rehearsed his number: 'Gordon, this is Don Segretti. I think we've got big troubles ...' All he wanted was some sign of recognition, something like, 'What's the problem, Don?'*

Bernstein & Woodward 1974, pp. 120-1

Unfortunately for Bernstein, someone else answered the phone, but he had already lied about his identity. In October 1972, Woodward and Bernstein had written that Bob Halderman, President Nixon's chief of staff, had been personally involved in political sabotage, controlling a secret fund used for illegal activities. They had more than one source for the story, which was significant because it reached the door of the President himself. However, through his attorney, one source publicly denied giving such testimony on Halderman to the grand jury. The White

House responded with a vigorous attack on the *Post*. Senator Robert Dole delivered a 20-minute speech criticising the paper. One criticism was that: 'The *Post's* reputation for objectivity and credibility has sunk so low they have almost disappeared from the Big Board altogether' (Bernstein & Woodward 1974, p. 182).

The reporters, in an effort to find out what had gone wrong, went back to one of their sources for the story, who refused to talk to them or confirm the information he had given them. The reporters then decided to identify the source to his boss in an effort to get confirmation from him instead. Their next move represented the most difficult professional—unprofessional, really—decision either had ever made. They were going to burn a confidential source. Neither had ever done it before; both knew instinctively that they were wrong. But they justified it. They suspected they had been set up; their anger was reasonable, their self-preservation was at stake, they told each other (Bernstein & Woodward 1974, p. 190). Revealing this source most probably involved violating a promise. Following this, Woodward and Bernstein hit a dry spell with their coverage of Watergate. At the same time, the *Post* and executive editor Ben Bradlee, were being criticised for the Halderman story. There was pressure to get a story that would take the heat off the *Post*. Later, Bradlee told an interviewer that he'd been 'ready to hold both Woodward's and Bernstein's heads in a pail of water until they came up with another story. That dry spell was anguish' (Bernstein & Woodward 1974, p. 205). This pressurised atmosphere led the two reporters and their editors to the decision to seek information from members of the Watergate grand jury. Woodward and Bernstein consulted the Federal Rules of Criminal Procedure. Grand jurors take an oath of secrecy, but the burden of secrecy was on them, nothing in the law forbade questioning them.

The *Post's* lawyers agreed with this interpretation but urged 'extreme caution'. Bradlee was nervous about the situation, telling the reporters 'No beating over the head, no pressure, none of that cajoling' (Bernstein & Woodward 1974, p. 207). Woodward went to the courthouse and memorised the twenty-three names and addresses of the jurors as he had been forbidden to take this information down. The list of jurors was checked for the few least likely to inform the prosecutors of a visit. Ideally, the chosen juror would be capable of outrage at the White House or the prosecutors or both; a person who was accustomed to bending the rules. Everyone involved had private doubts about such a 'seedy' venture. Bradlee, desperate for a story, and reassured by lawyers, overcame his own … Woodward wondered whether there was ever justification for a reporter to entice someone across the line of legality while standing safely on the right side himself (Bernstein & Woodward 1974, p. 210). The procedure was deceptive, the reporters were to identify themselves to the jurors and say that through a mutual but anonymous 'friend' they understood that he or she knew something about the Watergate case. They would ask if the person was willing to talk about it and leave straight away if the answer was no. Visits to the jurors yielded no information and ended up landing the *Post* in trouble. One juror reported Woodward and Bernstein to a prosecutor who then informed Judge John

Sirica. The judge then reprimanded them in a courtroom full of reporters but did not actually identify them or the *Post*.

In seeking a story from members of the grand jury, the practices of the *Post* violated journalistic principles. Memorising of names was 'a step in the direction of misusing the grand jury system and of violating the important ethical principles on which it stands'. In deceiving the jurors by inventing a 'friend' to get them to talk, they were encouraging them to break the law and using them to get a story (Christians, Rotzoll & Fackler 1991, p. 95). Thus the role of the *Post* in the Watergate case was far from heroic:

> *Since Watergate, many of journalism's leaders have begun to question the use of deception and other 'shady' methods to get news stories. They wonder aloud how journalists can point accusing fingers at the misbehaviour of politicians and others in public life if journalism's own house is not in order.*

> Goodwin 1987, p. 139

Woodward and Bernstein went on to write the bestseller *All The President's Men*, an account of their role in the reporting of Watergate. The book and the film by the same name gave them a place in history as two heroic journalists who 'cracked' Watergate and brought the President down, creating what Michael Schudson (1992, p. 104) has called the 'myth of David and Goliath, of powerless individuals over-turning an institution of overwhelming might. The good guys win, the press saves the day'. However, this myth does not properly acknowledge the role of FBI investigations, federal prosecutions, sources who risked their careers to give information, and the grand jury. It forgets that if not for the White House tapes, the Ervin committee, Judge Sirica and other factors, there may have been no presidential resignation.

Woodward and Bernstein came out of Watergate as national heroes. *All The President's Men* sold nearly three hundred thousand copies, paperback rights were sold for a record $1,050,000. Just as the film was released, the two wrote another book, *The Final Days,* on Nixon's last days in office. All this would have made the two a lot of money, but it drew critical comment from other journalists. CBS news commentator Eric Severed said: 'Mr Nixon and his intimates did not know where to stop in their quest for power, the two reporters did not know where to stop in their quest for fame and money. A pause, at least, was in order. There is something in life called the decent interval.' In March 1974, William B. Arthur, executive director of the watchdog National News Council warned that the press must be wary of 'overkill' in Watergate (Schudson 1992, p. 114).

Around the same time as Watergate, a second scandal hit the US defence hierarchy. A secret report commissioned by Secretary of Defence, Robert McNamara, detailing US involvement in Vietnam since 1945, was leaked to the press by a Government employee, Daniel Ellsberg, who worked for Henry Kissinger on the National Security Council. The leaked documents, nicknamed the 'Pentagon Papers', were highly classified, including some 'top secret' files and it was a federal offence for Ellsberg to release the material. The US Government tried unsuccessfully to pursue an injunction preventing publication of the material.

The American press deservedly was given high marks for having helped to unravel some of the grave abuses of the American political system. It had been a rather heady period for Washington-based journalists, and the desire to trump the last big 'leak' with a bigger one was rampant. Some commentators thought at the time that there was a danger that the news media could arouse public suspicion of being power-hungry. Its investigations could come to look too much like prosecution, and some of the amazing journalistic coups could go sour, as we will see they did in later years.

Finally, a comment from Judy Wade (1974, p. 31) published in the *New Journalist* magazine offers advice to all prospective reporters: the book *All The President's Men* should be 'required reading for every cadet before a union membership card is issued. It even includes a slick new version of the old foot-in-the-door ploy.'

Issues and questions raised by case study 1

1   Before you read this case study, what was your opinion of the activities of Woodward and Bernstein?
2   Has it changed? And if so, in what way?
3   Can you justify all their actions?
4   Are some more justifiable than others? Which ones?
5   They might have caught the biggest political fish in the Western world pool, but they didn't know for much of the time where the story was leading them, so they can't really argue the ultimate good brought about by their activities, can they?
6   We'll return to questions of deception again in chapter 10, but did Woodward and Bernstein go too far?
7   Was it the same 'scent of blood in the water' that hounded Governor-General Peter Hollingworth from office in 2003 (see Chapter 8)?
8   If not, how was it different?
9   Debate the ethics of publishing material that you know has been stolen (like the Pentagon Papers).

Case study 2

Bugging the Chinese Embassy in Canberra

In 1995, the then Labor Federal Government was embarrassed by media revelations that its international espionage organisation had been spying on diplomats in Canberra by bugging the Chinese Embassy. In April 1995, the Federal Government tried to prevent publication of the story in the *Sydney Morning Herald*, first by persuasion, then by injunction. Executives at the Fairfax organisation claimed publication was in the national interest, in the same way that Foreign Minister Gareth Evans tried to insist that suppressing the story was also in the national interest (PANPA 1995d). On 25 May 1995, an item relating to the bugging of the Chinese Embassy by Phillip Williams was pulled from the ABC's prime time evening television news bulletin, apparently after intervention by then managing director, Brian Johns.

According to a report in the *Australian*, Johns made the decision to pull the item, which was to have led the bulletin, despite ABC legal advice that it did not break the law (Simper 1995a). The next day the story was broadcast and Brian Johns was reported to have acknowledged he initially pulled the item on the basis that it was subject to a Government 'D-notice'. The Commonwealth solicitor, Dr J.G. Renwick had faxed Johns seeking an undertaking from the ABC that the item would not be broadcast (Simper 1995b). The Chinese Embassy story was the subject of a five-week legal battle between media organisations and the Federal Government.

In the NSW Supreme court, Justice John Bryson dissolved temporary injunctions against Fairfax newspapers, the ABC, and 2UE, allowing them to publish the story. Foreign Minister Evans tried to get the media to adhere to a voluntary code of non-disclosure of sensitive material (D-notices) that was instituted during war time, but had fallen into disuse. Newspaper editors and electronic media representatives meet regularly with Government to review D-notices, but in this case refused to voluntarily comply with non-disclosure. As a result, Senator Evans announced he would introduce legislation to tighten the regulations. In June 1995 the Federal Government proposed amendments to the Crimes Act, giving courts the power to jail journalists for disclosing sensitive security information. The Government's proposed amendments would rule out the defence of 'public interest' and would ensure that any trial of miscreant journalists took place in secret (Lague & Wright 1995).

In December 1995 it was reported that the then Labor Government proposed to jail public officials who leaked official secrets to the press. At the same time, Defence Minister Robert Ray, was considering fines of up to one million dollars against media companies who published such disclosures (Lague 1995). The *SMH* editorial ('Unnecessary Censorship' 1995) on the same day condemned the Government's proposal as 'a threat to the public's right to information which should be made public'.

A D-notice is an agreement between the media and the Government to voluntarily suppress defence and security information in the 'national interest'. The system is administered by a committee of media representatives and defence officials, which is chaired by the Minister for Defence, and applies to the following types of information:

- Certain details of defence capability and planning.
- The whereabouts of the Petrovs (famous Russian defectors from the 1950s) until Mrs Petrov died in 2002 (her husband had died earlier).
- The activities and identities of Australian Security Intelligence Service (ASIS) agents.
- Methods of monitoring communications for intelligence purposes.

The D-notice system was initiated by the Menzies Government in 1952 and was initially supported by newspaper owners. However, for almost a decade the Australian public was not told of the existence of the D-notice system, which was itself subject to a notice. A D-notice has no legal standing, it is a voluntary system, and it is an editor's decision whether or not to abide by it. The D-notice appears to have fallen into disuse, though technically they are still on the 'books' as it were. As we discuss in the following chapter, the military establishment now has more sophisticated methods of subtle, and not so subtle, information management, such as the technique of 'embedding', which became a household term during the 2003 Gulf conflict.

Issues and questions raised by case study 2

1   Research the D-notice system. Is it a justified system of information control?
2   What sort of stories should be subject to D-notices?
3   How would you characterise its use in recent times?
4   Does it cut across the principles of a free media?
5   What can you establish about the latter years of the Petrovs, now they have both died? Was it worth being classified as a national secret?
6   Is the D-notice system any sort of problem for the fourth estate model?

Case study 3
←
The Murdoch papers and the 1975 'dismissal' election

Politicians call it bias against them, proprietors see it as their God-given right, editors see it as keeping their readers informed, the public tends not to be able to join the dots together—but get some political journalists together over a drink or three and they'll all have stories about interference in their reporting by their media masters. The classic case in Australia was the actions of Rupert Murdoch in the 1975 federal election that followed the dismissal by the Governor-General, the late John Kerr, of the Whitlam Labor Government.

Murdoch and his media outlets had supported Whitlam in the 1972 'It's Time' election, Murdoch apparently donating more than $74,000 (a tidy sum in those days) to the ALP campaign (McQueen 1977). On the twentieth anniversary of the 1975 dismissal, Murdoch is also quoted as saying, with some apparent glee, that reports of his involvement 'only tell half the story' (Wright 1995a). Murdoch's overt interference in the 1975 campaign was so bad that reporters on the *Australian* went on strike in protest and seventy-five of them wrote to their boss calling the newspaper 'a propaganda sheet' and saying it had become 'a laughing stock' (Wright 1995a). 'You literally could not get a favourable word about Whitlam in the paper. Copy would be cut, lines would be left out,' one former *Australian* journalist told Wright (1995a). Alan

Yates was a third-year cadet on the *Daily Mirror* and recalls the dismissal 'shocked the entire newsroom'. Yates was on the AJA House Committee and says that while Murdoch was not necessarily in the newsroom, 'his editors and his chiefs of staff were certainly involved in day-to-day selection of editorial content'. Alan Yates has said that he felt powerless as a 'junior reporter', but remembered his copy being altered to favour the Liberal Party's viewpoint:

> *When questioning the chiefs of staff and chief sub-editor about this I was clearly told that that was the editorial line, the editorial people had thought that it was a stronger angle. Therefore I was left not too many options to go.*

> Hirst 1997b

Respected long-time political journalist Peter Bowers claims that when Malcolm Fraser offered former Murdoch employee John Menadue the post of Australian ambassador in Japan in late 1976, it meant more than the fulfilment of a long-time interest in Japan. To Menadue the offer was 'the clincher', the proof that his old boss Rupert Murdoch 'had played an inside political role in the dismissal of the Whitlam Government in 1975' (Bowers 1995). Bowers quotes Menadue as saying: 'Dangerous then (1975), more dangerous now. America and Britain may be able to accommodate him but our country is too small to live comfortably with an interventionist the size of Rupert Murdoch'. Another long-time political journalist Alan Ramsay (1999) once noted that 'throughout 1975 Murdoch was as interfering in his newspapers' pursuit of the Whitlam Government's destruction as he had been in its election'.

However, not all journalists were necessarily against what Murdoch did to support Malcolm Fraser in 1975. David Barnett has worked in and around the federal press gallery for most of his career in journalism and in November 1975 he was on Malcolm Fraser's staff. He remembers initially being impressed with Whitlam after 1972 and generally going along with the majority in the Gallery who welcomed the Labor Government. However, Barnett's mood changed dramatically over the three years of Whitlam's term as Prime Minister:

> *As it became more and more obvious that these people had no idea of what they were doing and that the country was going down the drain, I moved my position from one of support for Gough, to the conviction that really as an Australian citizen I should do all I could to try and get rid of him.*

> Hirst 1997c.

The dismissal of the Whitlam Government in November 1975 certainly created one of the longest, deepest and widest fault lines in Australian journalism. Journalistic friendships that broke over that issue have not been mended, despite the two main protagonists, Gough Whitlam and Malcolm Fraser, having reconciled many years ago. One person who Whitlam has still not forgiven is the Governor-General who sacked him, Sir John Kerr. Whitlam's booming voice will ring forever from recordings, even when his immortal words are erased from living memory: 'Well may we say "God save the Queen", for nothing can save the Governor-General.'

Issues and questions raised by case study 3

1   Does the proprietor of a newspaper, magazine, radio, or television station have the absolute right to dictate editorial policy?
2   Would you have joined the strike against Murdoch's interventions at the *Australian* in November 1975?
3   How do you feel about reporters moving freely between journalism and jobs with political parties or lobby groups?
4   Did Alan Yates have the right to feel aggrieved when his copy was changed?
5   What do you think of David Barnett's decision to throw his support behind Malcolm Fraser?
6   What is the role of political reporting in Australia today?
7   How could it be different?

Case study 4

SBS News and the Iranian Embassy 'riot'

An SBS television crew was the only media present when a small group of demonstrators broke into the Iranian Embassy in Canberra on 6 April 1992, attacking staff and trashing the offices. The protestors were Iranians who were against the then Iranian Government. The SBS news chief in the Press Gallery, Alan Sunderland, received a telephone call from the protesters before the incident and went with a crew to cover what he thought, at the time, would be another small, routine demonstration. He was not told of the protesters' plans (one of the authors was in the office when he took the call). Alan and his crew did not intervene in the mêlée, but took video footage that was used that night in the news (Sunderland 1992).

After the story broke, SBS news was accused of staging the 'riot' and the crew castigated for not calling the police when they were told there was going to be a demonstration. The Australian Federal Police already knew something might happen as there had recently been similar protests in several countries, including an earlier Embassy occupation. However, the AFP decided not to station a squad car outside the Embassy that day. The police later used the SBS footage in its successful prosecution of the Iranian demonstrators. The footage, by experienced cameraman Mick O'Brien, showed the protesters assaulting two embassy staff, including Third Secretary Alireza Borghei Nejad; setting fire to papers; stealing videotapes; and smashing windows in the building.

In the following paragraphs we have reprinted some of Alan Sunderland's thoughts on a reporter's responsibilities under the circumstances of that day, written in the SBS staff magazine *No Names* (Sunderland 1992), a week after the incident.

Journalism is a mixture of boring routine, rat cunning and dumb luck, with the occasional inexplicable flash of insight thrown in now and then just to confuse things.

I'm not here to speculate about which combination of the above led to SBS to score its exclusive last week over the attack on the Iranian Embassy in Canberra— I'll leave that to the dozens of commentators, politicians and others who have been so quick to pass judgment on us ...

I took a phone call just before noon on Monday 6th of April. It was a man with a fairly strong Middle-eastern [sic] accent who told me there would be a protest at the Iranian Embassy in five or ten minutes and we should be there to cover it. When I asked for more information, he said it was over the Iranian Government's bombing of the Mujahadeen, and then he hung up.

It was typical of the sort of call newsrooms get all the time. Monday was a quiet day in Canberra, and there was a camera crew doing nothing at the time. I organised the crew, grabbed my coat and note-pad, and we went. Simple.

Less than a minute after we arrived ... twelve or fifteen people turned up ... and then came the six-and-a-half minute rampage ... Mick O'Brien and Justin Hanrahan ... covered the chaotic events in the most professional and fearless manner, staying with the action as it happened and providing some of the best news footage I've ever seen ....

As the attackers began to run out of the embassy grounds ... the first policeman drove up, and asked us what was happening. We told him.

That all sounds simple, but of course it's not, because ever since it happened, just about everyone in Australia has turned into an expert on morality and ethics.

Sunderland 1992

Sunderland then makes what he calls a 'couple of salient points' about the issues of morality and ethics, as he sees them:

We didn't call the police because when we left the office we thought we were covering just another protest, and then when it turned into a full scale attack we were caught up in attempting to cover the violence. We had no access to a phone, and the whole event was over within minutes.

We didn't throw down our notebooks and camera equipment and leap into the fray because, in my opinion, that would have been unprofessional, foolhardy and useless in the circumstances ... each one of us made our own gut level response at the time. In other words we behaved like normal human beings and did what we felt was right. Had any of us felt that what we were witnessing was a murderous attack, that the protestors were about to kill someone, we may well have acted differently. But we didn't feel that way, and I think we were right. Had any of us stopped reporting, stopped filming and started fighting, remonstrating or running away, it is doubtful we would have changed the chaos around us and certain we would have done a very poor job of telling our viewers what is happening in the world, which is after all what they pay us for ... If the media tries to stop events it disagrees with, or refuses to cover events it disagrees with, we will not succeed in ending the violence, the discord and the injustices of our world. What we will do is turn our news bulletins into fairy tales.

Sunderland 1992

Issues and questions raised by case study 4

1 Should the SBS newsroom in Canberra have notified the police of the pending demonstration?
2 At what stage would you have called the police, if at all?
3 Wouldn't contacting the police constitute interfering in a story?
4 Where would you draw the line?
5 Is it part of the role of the media to help uphold the law?
6 What if it is a law that you (or your media organisation) believe needs changing—like the laws that banned street marches in Brisbane under the Bjelke-Petersen Government in Queensland in the 1970s?
7 What do you think of Alan Sunderland's comments?
8 What happens when a peaceful demonstration (say against an overseas dictatorship) turns ugly? Do you still give coverage to the cause as well as the violent outcome of the demonstration?
9 What do you do when a demonstration has been 'hijacked' by professional agitators, like some of the G8 summit meetings?
10 How do you arrive at an appropriate balance between the important G8 discussions inside, and the rowdy, often violent demonstration outside?

Case study 5

The Bondi Xmas bash

Over the Christmas–New Year holiday period, it has become 'traditional' for large crowds of young people to gather on Sydney's famous Bondi beach. They usually roam up and down the promenade, and eventually many end up 'under the weather'. In 1995 this crowd scene became ugly when a mob tried to overturn a bus. The police intervened and it turned into a 'riot'. During the early hours of the morning of Boxing Day, the revellers/rioters threw beer bottles at the outnumbered police. No arrests were made. The police said this was because they feared things would escalate. As usual on slow news nights, television stations had sent crews to Bondi to 'cover' the party, and when it became a 'riot' the cameras were on the spot to record the action. The police requested, and were given, copies of the television tapes in order to identify offenders who hadn't been arrested on the night. Over the next few days a debate ensued over whether the media should cooperate with the police in such situations. The then Communications Minister, Michael Lee, said the media had a duty to help bring offenders to justice (Wright 1995b). At the time, federal secretary of the MEAA, Chris Warren, said that if people involved in such incidents knew that the tape would be given to police, news crews could be attacked. Senior news producer at Channel Seven at the time, Strath Gordon, said it was common for news organisations to give the police tape and still photographs. He added that the police might make life difficult for news crews who did not cooperate. Chief of staff in the Channel Nine newsroom, David Allender, said the media plays a public service role when it cooperates with police (all quoted in Bearup 1995). The head of the Australian Press Council at the time, Professor David Flint (1996), wrote later that the media should not gather evidence for the police that would put it at risk of attack. Professor Flint went on to say that, over time, if the media continued to give material to the police, its independence and objectivity would be jeopardised. Professor Flint (1996, p. 9) wrote that 'this case should not encourage the media to change the general principle of keeping authority at arm's length'. Professor Flint's comments provoked an angry letter from Dr Peter Robinson of Bondi Junction. Dr Robinson (1996, p. 10) suggested that if the media had refused to hand over tapes, it could be construed as 'aiding and abetting criminal activity' or 'might be construed as obstructing the course of justice'. Dr Robinson cites the media's 'very significant role in the maintenance of civil society' as a principle to be upheld in this case.

Issues and questions raised by case study 5

1   Should the media cooperate with police by providing images to help in their investigations?
2   Should there be any limits to that cooperation?
3   Do you agree with the Minister's view that the media has a duty to help bring offenders to justice?
4   What's the difference between this and showing identikit drawings of suspects, or video from closed-circuit cameras of robberies at service stations, for instance?
5   What's your reaction to the MEAA position that cooperation with the police might put the media in danger of attack?
6   Do you agree with Professor Flint, who thinks that by cooperating journalistic independence and objectivity could be jeopardised?
7   And what of Dr Robinson's assertion that not to cooperate could be construed as obstructing the course of justice?
8   Do you think police would 'penalise' news crews who did not cooperate?

9   Can you get too close to a source and become its puppet?
10   In what other ways does the media cooperate with authority in general, and the police in particular?
11   What problems do you see associated with that cooperation?

Case study 6

The video editor's dilemma—when to stop the action?

Even though television news directors would claim they are showing less violence on news programs than perhaps in the latter part of the twentieth century, viewers are still being confronted with violence on a regular basis. During the production of these case studies, one of the authors noted in one two-week period several TV news stories showed extreme violence. In one case it was against animals (horses and dogs, including one shot repeated often of a man attacked by a dog). A leading Indy car driver was shown from several angles, including slow motion, in a fatal accident, and yet another news story showed a stunt flier fatally crashing into the ground at an air show. Again the fatal crash was seen more than once. In addition, the fatal crashes were either shown in vision in the head-lines of the program, or before an ad break, encouraging the audience to stay on for the story. So, in fact, the fatal crashes were shown over and over again in the same bulletin

Television news editors face decisions almost daily on how much of a particular story will be shown. They have to decide how much of a violent or fatal act needs to be shown to make the point to an audience and when it becomes gratuitous and rat-ings-driven. Two classic cases of this dilemma were the execution of a suspected Viet Cong prisoner by the chief of South Vietnam's National Police, Brigadier General Nguyen Ngoc Loan, during the Tet Offensive of 1968, and the suicide of the State Treasurer of Pennsylvania, Mr Budd Dwyer, in January 1987.

The Tet Offensive

The Tet Offensive of January–February of 1968 was a turning point in the Vietnam War (Lipski 1993). So too was General Nguyen's course of action. The suspected Viet Cong prisoner was brought to the police chief, and was summarily executed with a bullet to the side of the head. Australian television journalist, the late Neil Davis, discussed the dilemma of how much violence to (film and) show on television in David Bradbury's video documentary on Davis, *Frontline* (circa 1980). In the film, Neil Davis says he met the police chief some time after the Tet Offensive and the Brigadier General made a pistol action with his fingers, pointed it at Davis and said 'too much violence'—mean-ing the world saw too much of the violence of war, including actions like his.

Budd Dwyer

In the case of Budd Dwyer, the Pennsylvania Treasurer called a news conference on 22 January 1987, to supposedly explain the events leading to his conviction for mail fraud, conspiracy, and racketeering. He said he was innocent and appeared to grow agitated as he read from a long, prepared statement. At one point, when a TV cameraman began to pack up his equipment, he said: 'Don't put that camera away yet, there are many important things to come' (Rowe 1987). He then took a heavy-gauge revolver from a large manila envelope and pointed it at his head. Shocked reporters called on him to stop. Aides tried to move towards him. He placed the muzzle of the gun in his mouth and shot himself through the head as the TV cameras rolled on ('Budd Dwyer, the Man Who Killed Himself on Television', 1987).

The dilemma for TV news editors in both cases was when to stop the action? In both cases the cameras kept rolling, showing the fatal action, and the audio kept going, so you heard the sounds of death.

In the case of the South Vietnamese police chief killing a suspected Viet Cong, most Australian TV stations froze the action just before the gun was fired, but allowed

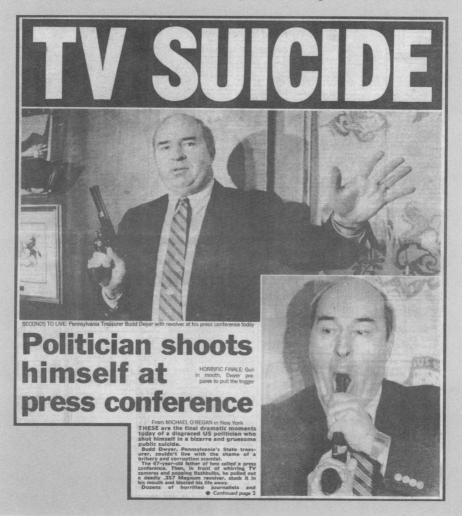

TV SUICIDE

SECONDS TO LIVE: Pennsylvania Treasurer Budd Dwyer with revolver at his press conference today

Politician shoots himself at press conference

HORRIFIC FINALE: Gun in mouth. Dwyer prepares to pull the trigger

From MICHAEL O'REGAN in New York

THESE are the final dramatic moments today of a disgraced US politician who shot himself in a bizarre and gruesome public suicide.

Budd Dwyer, Pennsylvania's State treasurer, couldn't live with the shame of a bribery and corruption scandal.

The 47-year-old father of two called a press conference. Then, in front of whirring TV cameras and popping flashbulbs, he pulled out a deadly .357 Magnum revolver, stuck it in his mouth and blasted his life away.

Dozens of horrified journalists and ● Continued page 2

the audio to continue so the sound of the gun was heard. (One of the authors had the job of editing that story for *ABC News*, Queensland, that day and that was his decision). At the disposal of editors was the complete action—seen uncut in Bradbury's *Frontline*—where the body falls to the ground as blood spurts in strong pulses from the fatal head wound. Editors at *NBC News* in the United States several times trimmed back the end of the footage, until the film was cut to only a few frames after the shooting, eliminating the most bloody scenes.

In the Budd Dwyer case, a leading public figure, now disgraced, taking his own life in front of TV cameras was news. But the decision was made that the audience didn't need to see the final seconds of his life to realise what had happened. In the United States, the public suicide took place late morning and was included in noon newscasts. Of the twenty stations with regular noon newscasts in Pennsylvania, only three showed the moment of death (Parsons & Smith 1987). One showed him shooting himself and slumping to the floor ('US Media Faced Dilemma on Coverage of Suicide', 1987). Most adopted the same practice as Australian stations did with the Saigon killing and again in this instance, they froze the action just before the shot, and allowed the audio track to continue through the gunshot.

These may be spectacular examples of the ethical dilemma facing a TV news director, but the ethics of the decision should be no different than those involved with the Indy 500 driver's fatal crash, or those of the stunt flier who got it so wrong.

Issues and questions raised by case study 6

1   Research some expert and lay-person's criticisms of violence on TV news and current affairs. What are the main issues?

2   Debate the issues from the point of view of the journalist in the field, the news editor back in the office, and the audience.

3   How much consideration should a TV news director give to the time of day that an item will be shown (prime time or late night, for instance) in deciding how much violent action an item could contain?

4   On most occasions, newsreaders will warn viewers that 'The following item contains images that may disturb some viewers'. Is that enough?

5   Is such a warning likely to be counter-productive to some elements of the audience?

6   What of the argument that the audience can 'vote with the remote' if they don't want to see violence in stories?

7   And the counter-argument that the audience is often exposed to the offending material before they have the chance to change channels?

8   Criticism of violence on TV news is not new. The BBC was criticised for the 'graphic nature' of its coverage of the Lockerbie plane disaster in Scotland in 1988. What guidelines do the main networks have in place regarding violence in news and current affairs?

9   Is violence on news broadcasts more or less acceptable than realistic violence in films or TV dramas?

→ **Case study 7**

How often do you show violence like September 11 or the space shuttle breaking up?

The shocking scenes of planes crashing into the twin towers of the World Trade Centre in New York on 11 September 2001 are forever etched in our collective memories. So are the horrific scenes at the Sari Club in Bali in October 2002, the space shuttle Columbia breaking up over the southern United States in early 2003, and the Madrid train bombings of March 2004. But how many times does the audience need to see that second plane slice through the upper floors sending a ball of flame shooting out the other side? How often do we need to see the burning nightclub and victims stumbling around, or the space shuttle debris hurtling through the atmosphere?

Journalists and their video crews and photographers were at what became known as 'Ground Zero' (and at the Pentagon in Washington, and the field in Pennsylvania where another plane headed for Washington crashed) to record the loss of life as people were either burnt to death, jumped from the collapsing towers, or were crushed to death. About 3000 people died in the 9/11 terrorist attacks, among them rescuers, police, and firemen. For weeks after the tragic events, news broadcasts repeatedly showed the impact of the planes into the twin towers, and the sickening aftermath. Equally, for days after the Bali tragedy, space shuttle disaster, and Madrid bombings, almost every news story contained that now-familiar vision of the burning nightclub, the space shuttle breaking up over Texas, and the twisted train wreckage. On the second anniversary of September 11, there were anniversary 'specials' looking back at the tragic events and there it was again, often repeated throughout each program—the second plane slicing into the tower and exploding in a ball of flame.

There is no doubt in our minds that for at least one or two future generations of news workers, the September 2001 events are a turning-point in the emotional dialectic. It is likely that the consequences of the attacks and the United States's swift responses in Afghanistan and Iraq will shape the global news agenda for the next 30 to 50 years. In this respect it will be very much a 'terror' frame, similar to the 'Cold War' frame of the 1950s and 1960s (Hirst & Schutze, 2004). There's no doubt there will be more shocking scenes of violence and death. At what stage should news editors decide (if ever) that the public has seen enough of the most shocking video images?

Issues and questions raised by case study 7

1   Could repetition of violent images lead to desensitivity on the part of the audience?
2   Research the coverage of 11 September 2001 and form your own opinions about how appropriate it was. Will some of the worst things seem less offensive with the passage of time?
3   Is it the responsibility of the media to decide when 'enough is enough'?

4   When does repeated showing of acts of gross violence become gratuitous?
5   What do you feel when you see those pictures from 9/11, Bali, or the space shuttle disaster?

Case study 8
Violent pictures in print

In the previous two case studies, we have used examples of what could be termed 'violence on television news'. Now let us turn to violent pictures in the daily newspapers. There have been a number of memorable examples in recent times, few more graphic than that in the *Weekend Australian* 'National Inquirer' section in the issue of 19–20 October 2002, less than a week after the tragic events in Bali. It was a half-broadsheet-size photograph of a Bali morgue with a line of bodies, with someone obviously gagging from the smell in the left foreground, and bodies in the right foreground where clothing may well have been identifiable ('Days of Living Dangerously' 2002). Then there was the photo on the front page of the *Age* on 17 August 1998. It was an aerial photo of the body of slain Victorian policeman, Sergeant Gary Silk, in colour, with a very obvious pool of blood near the slain officer's head. There was a public outcry about the graphic nature of the photo, and the fact that it was in colour. The Victorian Commissioner of Police at the time, Neil Comrie, in a letter of complaint to the Australian Press Council, said speculation had arisen about whether colours in the photograph had been enhanced between editions of the paper to highlight the pool of blood (Australian Press Council Case Studies 2002, p. 9). There was a similar front-page colour photo in the *Australian* on 8 May 2002, showing the body of assassinated Dutch politician, Pim Fontuyn. He'd been shot six times in the head and chest; again blood was clearly visible. Such was the reaction to the photograph that the *Australian's* editor at the time, Michael Stutchbury, in a page 2 'From the Editor' explanation the following day, said the decision to print the distressing photograph was not driven by any gratuitous desire to sensationalise. 'It was part of a genuine effort to accurately portray the reality of the human experience, from joy to horror' (Stutchbury 2002). The same issue arose in mid March, 2004, in coverage of 'Spain's September 11', the Madrid train bombings, when some Australian papers digitally removed a severed limb from the foreground of a particularly graphic shot used on many front pages. The *Weekend Australian* left it in, and it was plain to see (Day 2004b).

Issues and questions raised by case study 8

1   Are such images more disturbing in print—and therefore permanent—than on television?
2   Images such as those mentioned above offend many readers. Is that enough cause for them not to be published?
3   The *Australian*'s editor said the use of the Fontuyn photo was to 'portray the reality of the human experience'. Do you buy that rationale?

4   Should newspapers shield their readers from the grossest realities of a cruel world?

5   The AJA Code of Ethics says not to suppress relevant available facts. Could it be argued that it would be a breach of the Code of Ethics not to publish such telling photos?

6   In the case of the *Age* photo of the slain policeman, should the fact that the paper would be seen by his relatives and friends make a difference in the editor's decision?

7   Should the fact that someone might be able to identify a loved one from their clothing in the *Weekend Australian*'s Bali morgue photograph affect the decision to publish?

8   What if young children were to see the photos?

9   In the case of the *Age* photo, the paper ran letters critical of the use of the photo, and in the *Australian,* the editor wrote a page 2 justification the next day. Is that enough?

10   What's the difference between the violence portrayed in the photos mentioned above, and what you see every day at the movies?

11   What processes should the editor or pictorial editor go through in deciding to publish an obviously disturbing image?

12   Is there a public interest defence in any of the examples? In all of them?

6

THE MEDIA GOES TO WAR

Objectives

After reading and discussing this chapter you will have been confronted by:
■ The often conflicting role of the media in times of political crisis and war.
■ What happens when global media empires are caught up in the reporting of war.
■ The evolving role of the journalist in modern warfare.
■ How governments organise public (and media) support in times of major conflict.
■ The role of the media in the 'War on Terror' and the 2003 Iraq War.
■ The new form of media control—embedding.
■ The view of conflict 'from the other side'.

Introduction: War—a systemic failure?

At the height of Australian troops' involvement in the 'Coalition of the Willing' in taking on Saddam Hussein's regime in Iraq in March and April 2003, teenage schoolchildren left their classrooms and took to the streets of major Australian cities, joining others in expressing their opposition to the conflict. The 27 March front page of the *Gold Coast Bulletin* (2003a) had a large dusty-orange photo of troops supposedly in action under the banner headline 'Diggers in Hand-to-hand Combat'. Their coverage began with the story of Australian SAS troops reportedly in combat in a secret operation in 'the blinding sands of the Iraqi desert'. But cut into the right-hand bottom corner of the page was a photo of a trio of teenage girls protesting in Brisbane, all carrying placards. Two of the girls have the peace symbol painted on their faces, and one also has it painted on her exposed stomach. One of the banners reads: 'XXXX (expletive) War cause it won't stop terism (their spelling)'. Under the headline 'It's Child Abuse' (Bulletin 2003a), the *Bulletin* editorialised:

> Girls, Saddam is not a giggle. Get back to school, learn how to spell and how to express yourself without vulgarities. We have deleted the four-letter word from your poster. You have been used and abused by the rent-a-crowd organisers of the 'wagging for war' protest march in Brisbane.

Gold Coast Bulletin 2003b

So young protestors misspelled 'terrorism'. Did these high school students deserve to be ridiculed on the front page of a major regional newspaper for expressing their democratic right to oppose a Government action?

In this chapter we outline how ideological fault lines are manifest during times of political crisis. The news media is often forced into compromise and danger to bring the 'reality' of war to readers, listeners, and viewers. We describe how the values of impartiality, neutrality, and objectivity are put under enormous strain during times of military conflict. The case studies in this chapter look at these issues of 'ethics' in 'wartime' from both an historical and a contemporary perspective. In doing this we have drawn heavily on recent events, particularly those following 11 September 2001—the wars in Afghanistan and Iraq. The central dilemma news workers face in times of war is one of 'choosing' sides. As we see, this is a deep and deadly fault line.

The theoretical focus of this chapter is on the predominance of a 'national interest' frame over the reporting of conflict. This framing technique is used frequently by governments and readily adopted by the news media, not just in times of war, but in relation to most political, economic, and social issues. This chapter will argue that the national interest is one of the dominant 'ideological spectacles' (Grattan 1991) that the media wears most of the time. These glasses are so comfortable that often reporters forget they're wearing them. The thick and dirty lenses in these goggles make the inevitable fog of war even less penetrable to the gaze of the media.

The dialectic of war

...the role of war, and war-preparation, in the modern world presents us with an essential paradox. How is it that a society, which has created so much potential for human liberation—in technology, human cooperation, and ideas—can produce at the same time and with the same means such appalling danger?

Shaw 1988, p. 10

At the same time, there is always a moral and political dimension to a war or civil conflict. This is true whether the original dispute is over territory, resources, or ideologies. In each case people are asked to take sides, to 'rally around the flag', or 'defend the homeland'. In most examples we can quote from history, wars between nations are most clearly driven by economic forces. The dialectic behind many wars fought in the nineteenth and twentieth centuries was essentially a clash of economic, social, and political pressures created by the need for the capitalist system to promote 'competition' for markets and access to resources. Martin Shaw (1988, p. 22) links these deep fault lines to the global expansion of capitalism following the Industrial Revolution, which 'historically has presupposed a system of nation-states, in which warfare is the ultimate form of conflict.' It is the tension between a globalising system of economics and production and the existing system of nation states that makes the world so unstable today. In 2003 the rhetoric from the Pentagon and the US State Department was that some nation states had 'failed', that is they were not 'democracies' like the US, or indeed, like 'relaxed and comfortable', 'alert but not alarmed' Australia.

These themes are constantly repeated by the Government spin-doctors, but also by many opinion 'leaders' in the conservative media establishment. A few days after the March 2004 bombings in Madrid, the *Australian*'s Greg Sheridan (2004a) criticised fellow journalists Sandy McCutcheon and Tony Jones (both of the ABC) as 'self-obsessed intellectuals' who had 'no real understanding' of the war on terrorism in nations like Indonesia, which are on the verge of failing, or falling to the terrorists.

In fact, what these so called 'failed' states represent is the failure of the system to sort out its fundamental problems and contradictions. By resorting to 'war' as frequently as they do, the 'leaders' of the industrialised world engage in an ultimately self-defeating struggle against the historical logic of capital accumulation. As Shaw (1988, p. 23) argues, the 'enormous demands' placed on capitalist economies by preparations for implementing a war strategy, 'in the context of a permanent arms race', only serve to 'accentuate crisis'.

The military and the news media

Popular support for war is often something that has to be 'prepared' according to military timetables, alongside battle plans and supply lines. In times of war, the media's critics accuse it of being a Government propaganda tool. Others would regard support for the Government as just being patriotic. People also seek information, and some relief from the anxiety they feel about the uncertainty of war. The media can also play a role in the conflict, supporting one side or another. Most of the time the news media plays all of these roles, sometimes simultaneously. Patriotic, critical, informative and full of propaganda— little wonder it's an ethical minefield. For most of the twentieth century news organisations were expected to 'do the right thing' and report only favourable material to the public 'back home'. Phillip Knightley's excellent book, *The First Casualty* (1975), provides one of the best historical accounts of war correspondence. However, the situation has changed dramatically in the past 20 years. As we shall see from a famous case study in this chapter, much of the change in military–media relations can be traced to the post-Vietnam period (late 1970s) and the British Falklands 'war' against Argentina over possession of a few small islands in the South Atlantic.

Australian analysts and writers Young and Jesser (1997, p. 13) argue that in an age of 'limited conflict' when it is possible that 'a large part of the population might not support involvement in the conflict', journalists and editors have the opportunity to be much more critical of their own military and political chiefs. This is in line with other studies of the news media in times of crisis and conflict (Chiasson 1995; Hallin 1986, 1994; Knightley 1975; Raboy & Dagenais 1992). It is also why we stress the importance of studying the links between journalism and war historically, as we have done with other issues so far.

Ruling elites have always realised very early on, during their time in power, that if they controlled the mass media, they could influence public opinion. Historian Carole Sue Humphrey (1995, p. 3) notes that during the American war of independence: 'The revolutionary printer controlled the content of the paper, deciding what would and would not be published'. By 1775 the gate-keeping role of the press was self-evident, and the newspapers supporting the American revolution against British rule would emphasise victories in battles, 'whether that was actually the truth or not' (Humphrey 1995, p. 4). During the American civil war a leading Republican general issued an order banning the *Chicago Times* newspaper in 1863. The order also banned several other papers, which were critical of the general, from circulating in the area under his command (Reynolds 1995, p. 85). So much for freedom of the press as the land of the free was fighting to overcome the rebel Confederacy.

There's a famous anecdote in American journalism that the newspaper and movie mogul William Randolph Hearst actually precipitated a war between America and Spain over possession of Cuba, by planting a false report in his papers. According to the legend, Hearst told one of his newspaper artists in Havana, Frederic Remington: 'You furnish the pictures, I'll furnish the war' (cited in Wiggins 1995, p. 105). Whether or not Hearst actually sent the apocryphal cable to Remington is largely a moot point. It is clear that Hearst and his rival in the New York newspaper industry, Joseph Pulitzer, were both strongly pro-war and used their papers to whip up patriotic and anti-Spanish sentiment among the American public.

In every war since, according to former correspondent and journalism historian Phillip Knightley (1975), the news media has been called upon to 'play their part', to live up to a 'patriotic duty', and support the national war effort. British journalist and author George Orwell (1988) recognised this in his bleakly futuristic novel *Nineteen Eighty-four*, first published in 1949. In this story, a state of perpetual warfare between 'Oceania' and its enemies required enormous domestic resources—the production of 'hate session' propaganda, constant surveillance of the civilian population—just to keep people under a kind of ideological sedation. The main character, Winston, optimistically understands this. Even as he awaits the inevitable executioner's bullet in the neck he is able to reason: 'if there is any hope at all, it lies with the Proles'—the workers, the oppressed, and the downtrodden. This is a vital aspect of modern global conflict. Without the mobilisation of popular support for warfare, most nations would soon run out of resources to keep fighting.

During wartime, all of these pressures have a direct impact on the consciousness of journalists. For example, in Graham Greene's novel set in French-ruled Vietnam in the 1950s, *The Quiet American*, an English journalist Thomas Fowler tells the American who befriends him that as a reporter he doesn't have an opinion, and doesn't get involved. By the end of the story, Fowler is very much involved in Vietnamese politics; he even understands the need to choose a 'side'. Any reporters or editors who tell you they don't have an opinion, or that it doesn't affect their angles on stories, is blissfully ignorant, stupid, or lying. This is true of every war fought in the twentieth century, and it is continuing in the twenty-first under the chilling tag line 'the war on terror' (Hirst & Schutze 2004a, b).

An introduction to the terror frame

The framing of the news agenda around the fear of terror and terrorism is not new; it has been around since the late 1960s. The difference today is that its manifestation has global implications as well as ethical consequences for national news organisations and journalists in all media. George Gerbner's review of the literature suggests that the terror frame was common in the late 1970s and that it goes in and out of 'fashion' depending on the issues. We can reference this easily by mentioning Northern Ireland, Latin and Central America, parts of Africa, the Middle East and now, South-East Asia. What is common to each episode of 'terrorism' in the media that Gerbner (1992, pp. 84–107) describes from the late twentieth century is an ideological picture of the 'terrorist' as 'unpredictable and irrational, if not insane', and as symbolising 'a menace that rational and humane means cannot reach or control'. Writing in 1992, just after the first American-led Gulf War—which pitched George Bush Snr against Saddam Hussein after Iraq's invasion of Kuwait—George Gerbner wrote:

> Bombarding viewers with violent images of a mean and dangerous world remains, in the last analysis, an instrument of intimidation and terror … [and is] an integral part of a market-dominated system of global cultural commercialism … Only a new international movement dedicated to democratic media reform, can do justice to the challenge of violence and terror in and by the media.

> Gerbner 1992

George Gerbner's critique appears to be apt for the last decade of the twentieth century and the first of this one. The threads of the terror frame are picked up later in this chapter in a discussion of the Australian media's coverage of the Bali bombings. We believe the terror frame has become the dominant media perspective for reporting any 'military' and 'political' news. It is the new ideological sphere of limited controversy. This dominant frame allows very little room for an alternative perspective. To 'hate' terrorists is just 'common sense'. The current 'terror frame' first gained currency during and after the first Gulf War in 1991. It grew again immediately following 11 September 2001, when it was very neatly grafted onto current American policy towards the Middle East. While we were aware of it, the 'terror frame' reached Australian shores the night of the Sari Club bombing in October 2002. In the Australian context the 'terror frame' was retrospectively applied to news items about applicants for refugee status. By March 2003 the work had been done, the 'terror frame' was firmly in place, and people were starting to believe in it. Now it was sufficiently accepted and powerful enough to convince a handful of governments to back the US invasion of Iraq in March 2003. In March 2004, the contradictions in this framing were revealed. A conservative Spanish Prime Minister lost an election less than a week after the Madrid bombings. The Spanish public had overwhelmingly rejected the Government's support for George Bush and the new socialist leader promised to bring Spanish troops home from Iraq. It is the nature of this book that such an example, taken from yesterday's headlines, will be indicative and fluid. You will find plenty of material that brings this story, and its ongoing ethical quandaries, up to date.

Global media, global wars

A large-scale, long, or costly war always creates instability, anxiety, and great public concern. As Raboy and Dagenais (1992, p. 1) write, moments of crisis represent a point of 'continuity or rupture with the past', and create a framework for understanding 'the dialectics of continuity and radical change'. They argue that the contradictions of modern mass media, their 'function as agents of social discourse and their economic status as purveyors of commodified knowledge/information', mean that the news media tends to thrive on crisis situations.

The modern global media system in a sense owes its existence to wars. Control over supply routes, such as roads, sea lanes, captured territory, the route of telegraph and telephone cabling, and conquered cities are critical in warfare (Knightley 1975). Since the start of the twentieth century, we can add to the list of military and economic necessities of warfare: command of the skies, a fleet of capable submarines, a nuclear arsenal, and the ability to control 'outer space'. In the last 20–30 years the list has grown again, and become more sophisticated: biological and chemical warfare; 'battlefield' nuclear weapons; satellite and computing technology; viral and virtual warfare over the Internet; sophisticated data management; and elaborate networks of spies and informers. The one constant in the necessities of warfare has always been propaganda, and the means of creating a favourable ideological climate for war among an anxious domestic population.

The major addition to that in the twenty-first century is that the anxious population, with its own opinions and interests, is now global, rather than just national. In the 2003 Gulf War, we all knew that world public opinion was divided and that those nations whose governments supported Washington could not necessarily count on majority support in their own countries.

An Australian reporter in New York

The *SMH* correspondent in New York on 11 September 2001, Mark Riley (2002, p. 18), wrote that most Australian reporters in the city filed 'observational journalism that attempted to describe what we saw' in a way that also captured the 'fear, disbelief and sudden vulnerability filling the city streets'. It is hard, in such circumstances, for news workers not to get caught up in the emotions of the event. Riley recounts how he knew it was a moment for 'stream of consciousness narrative'. Later, he observed, it became a more arduous task of 'sifting truth from rumour', in the face of a Government that was seeking to 'control information'. However, Riley recognises that the most difficult emotional decisions for correspondents in such situations are 'in maintaining that protective professional barrier' that creates a view of 'fierce reality through the security of abstraction'. In a similar vein, *Network Ten* news producer Michael Reid (2002, p. 14) recalled that in the hours and days immediately after September 11:

> Everyone had their personal struggle with the emotional dimensions of this attack, but for me the emotive impact was unforgettable … a blend of utter horror and a certain thrill at being the first network in Australia to bring viewers an unforgettable bit of history.

Mark Riley believed that he reached a point of detachment about the story, but added that the line between his professional and personal lives in New York blurred after September 11. He notes a number of personal reasons why his family chose to display an American flag from a bedroom window and, with remarkable honesty, he writes that he is now compiling his reports from the perspective of his young son:

> My family's life has been changed profoundly by the events of September 11 … [our son] was born here in New York and is a dual US–Australian citizen. It has become clear to me now that it is his world I write about each day as I file my dispatches to Australia

... a new and uncertain world that lost a cherished element of innocence the moment the 'Up, up, up' flew overhead.

Riley 2002, p. 19

The military and the media after 9/11

Would you publish a photograph of a body falling from a building? Here's what chief pictorial editor at the *Australian Financial Review* Greg Newington said about his decision a day after the 11 September 2001 attacks:

The image of a man throwing himself from the burning tower was to me poignant, shocking and terrifying. In running it, we knew it was going to evoke exactly those emotions.

Newington 2002, p. 13

Journalism's war on terrorism began on the morning of 11 September 2001 (New York time) when it became clear that it had not been an accident when a hijacked United Airlines passenger jet slammed into the WTC tower. Less than 45 minutes later, as horrified New Yorkers panicked, another jet speared into the second tower and within an hour both towers had come crashing down. A third hijacked jet crashed into the Pentagon, a fourth went down in Pennsylvania, reportedly because 'heroic' passengers overpowered the hijackers. The immediate reaction from political sources in Washington DC was that these acts of terror were the work of a group called Al Qaeda, led by Osama bin Laden, a Saudi fundamentalist with a grudge against the United States.

Many weeks later, as rescue workers continued their search of 'Ground Zero'—for that is what Manhattan's downtown had become—the President of the United States dubbed this outrageous terrorist attack the start of the 'first war of the twenty-first century'. A significant number of American, British, and Australian media organisations, and news networks agreed and quickly fell into line. The Fox cable network in particular led a patriotic charge in the American media, eagerly denouncing those few journalists whose more 'objective', or 'neutral' stance made them 'suspect'. A much smaller number of American journalists openly criticised Washington's hardline response to September 11, which was to launch a full-scale invasion and occupation of Afghanistan, where the alleged mastermind and Al Qaeda leader was thought to be 'hiding out', under the patronage of the Taliban regime.

The memory of 11 September 2001 has created emotional tensions with global and sometimes very personal consequences for millions of people around the world. Its final impact, as yet unknown, is on potentially billions of lives. The very size of the paradox involved—the dialectic of war—has also created some new fault lines within journalism. These are manifest in arguments, disagreements, and different angles on stories between news groups, between individual reporters and editors, and between the news media and the general public.

The powerful emotional responses to the World Trade Center and Pentagon attacks washed through and over the public, and the world's newsrooms responded in unprecedented ways. When the news reached Australia, the *Herald Sun* in Melbourne made and remade five editions of the paper between midnight and four in the morning, then two afternoon editions the same day. The paper's deputy editor John Trevorrow (2002) noted how 'people turn to the media in massive numbers' when 'momentous events' occur. In this case the *Herald Sun* sold more than two million copies in three days. The 'shocking' and 'confusing', even 'chilling' events were described to *Herald Sun* readers as 'Pure Evil' in 72 point type over a full page colour picture of the first tower burning and the second plane about to hit the second tower. This clearly signalled the paper's attitude, and the editorial line that was to develop. This was how the 'terror frame' began to shape the news coverage. It is also reflected in the emotional dialectic of the front page—the framing, angles, and opinions represented in the news media (Trevorrow 2002).

Certainly there was a split in the ranks of the news media between those who were firmly behind the United States and its allies and those who dared to question the motives of those who wage 'war on terror', a point not missed by conservative columnist, Tim Blair (2001). Tim Blair's column is full of quotes from columnists of both 'Left' and 'Right', including well-known Australian journalists, who dump on each other with abandon:

> Miranda Devine's *SMH* column of September 13—which included the line 'We want that satisfying vengeance we used to get from our TV screens at the end of the last century …'—prompted a hostile email from *SMH* TV writer Ruth Ritchie: 'I just want you to know that I find your opinions and your ignorance terrifying'.

> Blair 2001, p. 13

By October 2001, it was clear to most journalists, commentators, and observers that the fault lines in the attitudes of news workers were deep, and the divisions bitter: 'The September 11 terrorist attacks … have caused deep divides where once there were mere differences of opinion' (Blair 2001, p. 12). News workers who might have considered themselves on the 'Left' also disagreed with 'fellow travellers', such was the confusion and emotion generated by September 11 (Blair 2001). For others, such as Peter Eisner, the managing director of the US Center for Public Integrity, the public questioning of American policy and patriotism, though surprising, is a good thing:

> There's been an immediate response [to September 11] that this civilisation of ours is hated in some quarters and people across a broad spectrum want to know why … And that's very positive'.

> Peter Eisener, cited in Dodd 2001a, p. 12

*Why is there such division in the ranks of the media over how the 'war on terror' is reported? Phillip Knightley believes that modern warfare—from the Falklands, the Balkans, and the Gulf War of 1990–91—has altered the bounds of what the news media *can* and *will* do, and he agues that 'no government can automatically assume that the media will be on side' (Knightley 2001, p. 37). He adds that journalists and editors 'cannot be coerced' and the media 'has to be seduced or intimidated into self-censorship' (Knightley 2001, p. 37).

Just exactly where the distinction lies between coercion and intimidation is a moot point, but the general idea is valid. We should be grateful that influential journalists like Phillip Knightley won't be easily silenced and that he has the courage to write that the 'real reason' for the US, British, and Australian Governments wanting to 'control the flow of news' about the war is that images of civilian deaths would 'shake public support for the "war on terror"' (Knightley 2001). As always, the political and ideological battle on the home front cannot be neglected:

> An attack led by two powerful industrial nations against a Third World agricultural one, already reduced to ruin and in the grip of a famine, was never going to be an easy [idea] to sell.
>
> Knightley 2001

The persuasive (seducing) actions of governments are clear in exhortations from Washington and London that the media not report statements from Al Qaeda because they are 'inflammatory propaganda and might contain coded messages to terrorists' (Jurkowitz 2001).

Bali, October 2002: The terror frame comes home

Public fears in Australia about terrorism were dramatically realised when two huge explosions ripped through Bali's resort town of Kuta in October 2002. The *Australian*'s first headline screamed 'TERROR HITS HOME', and the phrase stuck as the banner heading for all subsequent coverage. This framing of the bombings as an attack on Australia provided the key emotional link to September 11, and seemed to justify Australia's role in the 'war on terror' (Hirst & Schutze 2004a). As Errol Simper pointed out, amid the grief and outrage that ran through the Bali coverage, there was an element of wish-fulfilment:

> To deny that segments of Australia appeared to crave at least a share of the adrenalin and global media attention that accompanied September 11 is to deny the nose on your face.
>
> Simper 2002

But from the barrage of emotive journalism sprang a more serious and sinister message in the *Australian*. The news media was ideologically gearing up for war, and the Murdoch press would do its part to prepare the Australian people. Greg Sheridan (2002a) proclaimed 'The terrorist empire has struck back' and added that the 'war on terror' had moved decisively into stage two. The *Australian*'s editorial on the first day of coverage said Bali was a 'wake-up call' to the civilised world that terrorism must be defeated. In language all but transcribed from a Bush or Howard speech, the Murdoch paper proclaimed, 'Bali proves that all freedom-loving peoples are at risk from terrorism, at home and abroad' ('We Must Remain Firm in the Face of Terror' 2002). This was a decisive moment for the sabre-rattlers. Prime Minister Howard's central premise justifying action in Afghanistan and later Iraq is endorsed here—namely, that terrorism affects everyone, so it is in the national interest to fight terrorism throughout the world, Iraq included (Hirst & Schutze 2004a). From our perspective it is disappointing that sections of the Australian media have not been more critical and sceptical about the 'war on terror' and the rationale for invading Iraq. The fact that the news media was so quick to fall into line over Bali is testimony to the strength of emotional attitudes among journalists and the strong 'pull' of national ideologies—'I am, you are, we are Australian'. It seems that most reporters and editors accept this without question. One critical aspect of journalism in a confusing and 'dangerous' world is that all 'assumptions' must be questioned.

'Which side are you on?'

By October 2003 political fractures over how to fight the 'war on terror' were appearing in the American leadership. In Britain, Tony Blair's Government was reeling over allegations of cover-ups, distortions and lies, even though the Prime Minister himself was cleared of any wrong-doing. The coalition's rebuilding strategy in Iraq appeared to be unravelling, several senior officials were recalled to Washington, and policy appeared to change weekly. In this environment, the news media picked up small stories and the consequences were magnified. In one example, a leaked memo circulating in Washington DC indicated that events in Iraq had taken some administration officials by surprise. Soon after, President Bush faced his first persistently hostile media conference in more than a year. White House correspondents were beginning to ask some tough questions about strategy and policy in post-conflict Iraq. As Kevin Williams (1993, p. 306) argues in relation to Vietnam in the late 1960s, the change in the press corps' attitude to the war in Iraq was a response to the 'increasing fragmentation of official perspectives', which emboldened journalists to question things more carefully.

Despite attempts to seduce and cajole them, today's news reporters have the editorial freedom, the space, and the ability to illustrate the complexities and differences of opinion in the allied ranks in a way World War II correspondent Chester Wilmot never could in his radio broadcasts. Journalists like Gaye Alcorn can report the confusing and high-stakes politics of the war, not just the battlefield 'shoot out'. This modern phenomenon is well explained in an excellent study of the American media's fraught relationship with the war in Vietnam (Hallin 1986, 1994). Daniel Hallin explains how good journalists, reporting from the front lines *and from the corridors of power*, can take advantage of conflict among the elites over how to manage geo-political strategy and tactics. This leads to incisive analysis and open discussion of otherwise secret policy disagreements. If Hallin is right and the media becomes more difficult to manage during a crisis or conflict, one has to wonder what the reading, listening, and viewing public makes of the many and conflicting messages it absorbs.

War made for television

Much has been made of the fact that the drama of 11 September 2001 unfolded on television screens around the world—the 'first war of the twenty-first century' began live on CNN, CBS, NBC, and ABC. Hundreds of television networks around the globe (including those in Australia) relayed the American pictures around the clock for several days until they could scramble their own crews into place. Not for the first time in a modern war, 'reality' seemed to be one step behind the fictional world of Hollywood: 'It's this sense of hyper-reality—of a terror that has walked off our cinema screens—which compounds the nightmarish quality of these acts' (Lumby 2001).

A month after the attacks on New York and Washington, and one week into the air strikes against Afghan targets, Roy Eccleston's analysis (2001) in the *Australian*, headlined 'Enemy on Target in Battle of the Mind' ends with a chilling reminder of previous campaigns:

> As in the Cold War, Americans feel threatened. Keeping the [American] public committed and patient over the longer term, especially in the face of any new terrorism, will itself be a battle unlike any the US has fought.
>
> Eccleston 2001

In her *Bulletin* article on 2 October 2001, 'Hegemony over Heels', academic and media commentator Catharine Lumby comments on the Gulf War of 1991, 'infamously, the first to be fought out live on CNN', which became for many 'gripping entertainment' as TV audiences were enthralled by 'cameras on the nose cones of smart bombs … just like computer games. … There was little to remind us of the suffering the US and its allies were inflicting on the ground' (Lumby 2001). Lumby notes that the effect of this was, as we might expect, to build support for the US coalition against Saddam Hussein. This observation tends to reinforce the view that television coverage of wars is much more superficial and ideological than press coverage (Raboy & Dagenais 1992, p. 7). What television audiences didn't see very much of, during the first or second Gulf Wars, was the devastation and suffering inflicted on ordinary Iraqis. The only real taste of this in the 1991 Gulf conflict was provided by two incidents—the death of hundreds of civilians in a Baghdad bunker and the charred bodies of fleeing Iraqi soldiers incinerated by napalm on the road from Basra. The first incident was dismissed as Iraqi propaganda (unlike what Western audiences were subject to 24 hours a day); the second came too late to have much impact on public opinion in the combatant countries.

Embedding: The new way of reporting from the frontline

War correspondents have always taken risks, some more successfully than others. Many of the best, like David Brill (Little 2003), operated on the edge, without necessarily getting the sanction of the 'allied' commanders. This freelance style of operation has become more common as news demands increase on the 24-hour news clock, and equipment has become more portable. News camera journalist Jon Steele (2002) has chillingly described his 'addiction' to 'the worst places on earth' while chasing stories, interviews, and combat footage. Brill, Steele, and thousands more news reporters and their crews face this danger every day. Paul McGeough calls it the 'visa twilight zone' (2003, p. 7). Many reporters, including two Australian camera operators, were killed in Iraq between March 2003 and March 2004.

In 2003 reporters like the *SMH*'s Paul McGeough had satellite phones and many television networks kept their staff in Baghdad, providing constant pictures and updates to the 24-hour news machine that now routinely kicks into action when there's a sniff of explosives in the air. McGeough's diary (2003) *In Baghdad: A Reporter's War* tells of the constant struggle to keep lines open and the demands on his time from radio and television networks, eager to prove they too had the new toys. But this time there was an added twist: the American military started offering places with the frontline units to scoop-hungry war junkies. At a price!

Young and Jesser (1997, pp. 14–16) discuss how smaller, lighter, and faster digital technology has 'largely made the reporter independent of the military', which 'limits even further the ability of the military to block transmissions through electronic jamming'. They conclude with a blunt assessment of the first Gulf War:

> The independence and mobility conferred by such systems restricts field censorship to physical sanction. This was demonstrated during the Gulf War [1991], when [American reporter] Peter Arnett used direct satellite telephone voice communications to report from [the Iraqi capital] Baghdad.

> Young & Jesser 1997, p.15

In the second Gulf War, the 'embedding' of reporters with American and British military units took full advantage of this new lightweight equipment to put journalists in tanks and trucks. It might have seemed like giving the reporters full access, but in reality, most correspondents soon realised that like the million dollar sound-stage imported from Hollywood by the American military for its media conferences at Central Command Headquarters in Qatar, 'embedding' was cleverly designed to reduce the threat of independent reporting.

Estimates vary from 500 to 700, but somewhere in between is the number of journalists that were 'embedded' with individual combat units of the two main coalition partners, the US and Britain. The Australian military did not accept 'embedding' until fairly late in the 2003 conflict. It was the first time since World War II that journalists and in this case, perhaps more importantly, camera crews with portable satellite technology, were on the front lines with the advancing forces. It seemed like a 'win win' situation for both the military and the media. For the journalists and their camera crews there they were at the centre of the action, reporting on battles as the coalition advanced into Iraq. The military hoped that the embedded journalists, working alongside soldiers on whom their lives could well depend, would be more sympathetic to the coalition cause in their battlefield reporting. This certainly proved to be the case in many instances, such as in the book *The March Up* by reporter Bing West and his travelling companion Major General (ret'd) Ray L. Smith (2003), who rode with the 1st US marine division all the way to Baghdad, gleefully reporting Iraqi 'kills' and mourning the deaths of marines in the units they were with.

Respected American journalist Phil Nesbit (2003), commenting on embedding, said that soldiers in conflict have to operate as a cohesive unit. They are fearful, act instinctively, and watch each others' backs. 'They will be dirty, sweaty, scared, running on adrenalin and guts. "Embed" a journalist into this cauldron of emotions, fear, and sweat and you can bet some of it will rub off' (Nesbit 2003). The reporters believed their accounts were more credible because they were witnessing the events, rather than relaying military news releases and briefings (Felling 2003). By their very nature individual reporters' stories had to be one-sided as they showed only action from the point of view of the coalition forces with which they were 'embedded'. But it was a microcosm of what was happening across the battlefield.

TV audiences 'back home' were riveted to their screens, watching the advance through the desert or seeing a missile heading skywards from a warship in the Gulf and knowing it was probably bound for Baghdad. They'd never been this close to 'real' action, except perhaps in the make-believe world of the movies, or during some of Peter Arnett's reports for *CNN* from Baghdad during the first Gulf War. Incidentally, Arnett, who won acclaim for his reporting in Vietnam and was attacked in some quarters for his reporting from 'the other side' in Baghdad during the first Gulf War (to keep a warlike analogy going) 'fell on his sword' during the 2003 Gulf War by suggesting on Iraqi TV that the US war plan had failed. The Pulitzer Prize-winning Arnett, whose CV covers nineteen wars and spans 40 years, was sacked by the American NBC television network and by *National Geographic* magazine, despite an on-air apology (Felling 2003). He'd suggested that the US military had been taken by surprise by the level of Iraqi resistance and was reviewing its war plan (Cook 2003). Although the comments merely echoed what other broadcast and print journalists had been saying, Arnett's mistake was in sharing his thoughts with an Iraqi media organisation— effectively talking to the enemy. It made him appear unpatriotic while the troops were 'over there' fighting for the 'ole red, white and blue'. But all was not lost for the veteran war correspondent—the *Daily Mirror,* described by many as the British paper most opposed to the war, announced within hours of the double sacking that they'd hired him (Cook 2003).

Reporting from the frontlines has its disadvantages, too. Apart from being possibly shot at and killed, there's the discomfort, constant danger and little overall view of what's happening elsewhere in the war. War correspondents traditionally rely on information from 'head office' in crafting their stories, with input from various other staff and editors. Embedded reporters do not have that contact with their peers. Paul McGeough (2003) says it was vital for the small group of foreign correspondents in Baghdad to stick together and share information.

The embedded journalists only see what the field commanders allow them to see— from their side. They can only report back what they can deduce from what they see and what the commanders in their small area of the battlefield allow them to know. It's nigh-impossible to get 'the big picture'—that was left to the reporters covering the war from Central Command Headquarters in Qatar and the Pentagon or those trying to 'pull it all together' back in the network or newspaper headquarters, whether in New York, London, or Sydney. BBC World illustrated the dilemma in an Iraqi War edition of the program *Correspondent,* seen on pay-TV in Australia on 5 July 2003. It blamed over-eager commanders in the field and equally over-eager journalists for reporting the fall of Iraq's second city, Basra, 17 days early. The program then suggested rather dryly that the port city of Um Quasar 'seemed to fall every day' (BBC World 2003a). It was finally taken five days after the initial reports of success. More importantly, though, the BBC program traced how a battlefield report from an 'embedded' journalist, based on sketchy detail, can take on a life of its own, using as an example the suggested uprising by anti-Saddam civilians in Basra. A BBC reporter sent his field dispatch reporting some sort of uprising in the centre of the city that was being put down by Iraqi troops. The 'uprising' was given further credence by being mentioned at a briefing at Central Command Headquarters (in the million-dollar media briefing centre) in Qatar. By the evening news in London, the report was that 'British troops are firing in support of a civilian uprising'. British Prime Minister Tony Blair seized on the opportunity to tell the Iraqis: 'This time we won't let you down' re-enforcing the message of a massive leaflet drop over Iraqi cities. Support for the war was rallied 'at home' and in Iraq a domino effect was set up. As one reporter told the BBC's *Correspondent* program, the story took on a 'reality of its own, even if it didn't actually happen'. The British military maintained 'something had happened, there was a civil disturbance, it could have been an uprising' (BBC World 2003a). The Arabic language Qatar-based network Al Jazeera had the only TV crew in the city at the time, and they reported no uprising, but rather a pro-Saddam rally (Al Jazeera & BBC World 2003).

This type of confusion and lack of clarity in the basic elements of the story was common and eventually Australian correspondents complained. Some even described the conditions at the coalition-controlled media compound in Qatar as 'Operation Mushroom'.

Operating unilaterally

As well as the two groups of reporters already mentioned—those 'embedded' with the troops, and the others reporting from the Coalition Central Command in Qatar—there was another group, the so-called 'unilaterals' or independents. They were the ones who chose to report from outside the coalition's protection from Baghdad or northern Iraq. In any combat situation, the attraction of being a 'unilateral' is that you are not controlled by military 'minders'. It can be a dangerous game, especially if you get caught in the middle of heavy fighting. As Jon Steele explains in *War Junkie*, a unilateral is free to report from wherever they please, or dare:

> Stones tore over our heads and hit well-dented police shields like bulls' eyes … The rebels fell back. Their killer faces spitting in the eyes of the militia. And me falling back with them till I tripped over something big … Pull wide and watch the old man suffer for twenty seconds, waiting for just the right look on his face, then cut. I grabbed a field bandage from my body armour. 'Here! Take this!'

> Steele 2002, p. 129

In the second Gulf War, most Western journalists pulled out of Baghdad once the air attacks began, but a few remained. They were escorted by their Iraqi hosts to the scenes of devastation from coalition bombing raids, and when bombs went astray, like the two attacks on Baghdad markets, they were there to report on the civilian casualties. After the first attack on a Baghdad market place, the US military suggested it wasn't a stray American bomb, but rather it could have been the 'very old stocks' held by the Iraqis. The US military command in Qatar even suggested 'it could have been a deliberate attack' on their own people by the Iraqi military (BBC World 2003a).

Covering any war is very dangerous for the media. Of the fourteen journalists killed during the second Gulf War, more than half were 'independents' (Jackson 2003d). The first to die was Adelaide-born cameraman Paul Moran, the victim of a suicide bomber in

Northern Iraq on the second day of the war, while on assignment for the ABC. Chillingly though, five, perhaps as many as seven, were killed by coalition forces, either in 'friendly fire' incidents, or in deliberate, although apparently misguided, attacks (Jackson 2003d).

As we've seen already, and we'll see later in the case studies for this chapter, governments who send their troops to theatres of war are quick to condemn coverage not considered favourable to their cause. Australia's Labor Prime Minister at the time of the first Gulf War, Bob Hawke, attacked the ABC for what he considered biased reporting (Marr 2003b). In the 2003 Gulf conflict, the attack against the balance of the national broadcaster's coverage was led by then Communications Minister, Senator Richard Alston. He called for an investigation into coverage of the war on the ABC's morning radio current affairs program, *AM*. With the help of one of his parliamentary colleagues, Senator Alston released a 15-page, 68-point brief that he said demonstrated that 'appropriate journalistic standards may not have been upheld' (ABC Online 2003c). He was accusing the program of bias against the 'Coalition of the Willing'. The *ABC's* Complaints Review Executive (CRE) investigated the Alston dossier and concluded there was no evidence of systematic and partisan anti-American or anti-coalition reporting. It upheld only two of the sixty-eight complaints (ABC Online 2003d). ABC Managing Director Russell Balding said in a statement at the time that he was satisfied both with the process and the outcome of the investigation, and that it vindicated the *AM* program and its staff (ABC Online 2003d). But it didn't satisfy the Prime Minister, John Howard, or Minister Alston. The Government announced an independent panel to sit in judgment on political balance on the ABC (Crabb 2003). Respected Canberra journalist Michelle Grattan said the Government's attack on the ABC smacked of hypocrisy in the light of its own record (Grattan 2003). This was the Government, she pointed out, that maintained throughout an election campaign the fiction that asylum seeker children had been thrown overboard off Australia, the same Government that took Australia to war on the grounds that Iraq had weapons of mass destruction that have [as late as mid 2004] not been found (Grattan 2003). The report of the Independent Complaints Review Panel, the 'new referee' into Alston's now dwindling number of allegations, was released on 10 October 2003. It, too, found no evidence of biased or anti-coalition coverage as alleged (ABC 2003). It upheld a total of seventeen complaints, twelve for serious bias, four of 'emotional language of editorialisation' (contrary to ABC Editorial directives) and one case of sources not being identified adequately, but the latter five did not, in the Independent Panel's view, display bias against the US or the coalition (ABC 2003).

The government's attacks on the ABC's credibility didn't stop there. In July 2004, Foreign Minister Alexander Downer complained about a BBC documentary *The Third World War*, about Al Qaeda, that was promoted and shown as part of a series on the ABC. Before the screening Downer's office complained that the program was wrong about the Australian government's pre-knowledge of the October 2002 Bali bombings. The Minister demanded that the ABC broadcast a statement from his office at the end of the documentary. Thankfully, Russell Balding again refused to go along with this blatant attempt at intimidation and censorship.

Operation Mushroom: We can finally tell you about it

From very early on in the conflict Australian reporters complained about the lack of access to information from their own national military sources. The *Australian*'s staffer in Qatar, Rory Callinan, complained in print about being 'cocooned from reality by the coalition's public relations machine'. In an obvious shot across the bows of military PR, Callinan is described as 'locked into the multimillion dollar press centre… "press conference central" as he calls it.' Callinan says that the press corps is unhappy: '"We are a bit like mushrooms here, being drip fed information"' (2003). In the first few days this was a constant complaint from the media compound at Camp Doha. More importantly, the appearance of this brief piece signalled the emergence of a new genre of war stories, news, and commentary on the media's broader role.

However, it must be said that the complaints from Qatar and Canberra regarding the lack of Australian information were not the harbinger of some anti-war sentiment among the news hacks. It was really a plea for much more colour and background material to fill out the coverage and encourage a sense of Australian public 'ownership' of the conflict. From very early on there was coverage of what Australian forces were doing, including frigates 'in hunt for fleeing cronies' (Kerin 2003). Further attention was drawn to the media's role by Ashleigh Wilson's story about war coverage and comment on the Internet, 'Conflict Comes to a PC Near You' (Wilson 2003a). The Australian media wanted more information about what Australian forces were doing. In the second week the Australian military PR operation began to allow reporters to visit ships in the Gulf on search missions and mine clearing (Kerin 2003b). One ABC (Australia) news crew was allowed to 'embed' with Marines as they entered Baghdad. This led to one of the most horrific early incidents during the American occupation. A car full of civilians was raked with automatic weapons fire by US soldiers, when it tried to overtake their truck. Journalist Geoff Thompson and his crew were in the truck with the camera rolling. In the footage you can see and hear explosions and gunshots behind the accelerating car. Then there is a noise like a crash and then gunshots. All the passengers were killed. This was not the kind of story the military wanted the embedded reporters to file.

The Al Jazeera point of view

In the 2003 Gulf War it was the portable satellite communications technology that made possible live, unedited coverage from both sides of the front line for the first time. Even so, the overall coverage was very patchy and repetitive. The around-the-clock coverage pioneered by CNN in the first Gulf War is now commonplace. But it too poses its own ethical dilemmas. For example: What if the Arabic-language Al Jazeera network was broadcasting 'live' from Baghdad as Iraqis chased up and down a riverbank after a suspected downed American pilot?

This actually happened—and fascinating it was to watch, too. It was picked up by Western networks, like Skynews in England, and relayed on Sky News Australia. *SMH* correspondent Paul McGeough (2003, pp. 45–8) had a riverside view: it all happened near his hotel in the city centre. The reeds on the banks of the Tigris were being sprayed with bullets. Civilians joined the troops scouring the banks. No American pilot was found. But what if they had found a downed pilot and executed him before the cameras could be turned away?

What should and equally, what should not, be shown during wartime is a very sensitive issue. The BBC came under fire from the British Ministry of Defence for proposing to screen pictures of the bodies of two British soldiers killed in the war. The BBC planned to show the bodies as part of the special on Al Jazeera cited above and maintained that the Arab network covered the war very differently to Western journalists. It had shown material TV networks in the countries of the 'Coalition of the Willing' at least would shun—like the bodies of coalition soldiers, American prisoners of war being interrogated, and graphic footage of civilian casualties in a market bombing (ABC Online 2003b). Britain's top Gulf commander, Air Marshal Brian Burridge, attacked the channel for showing the dead British soldiers, saying the channel risked becoming a tool for Iraqi propaganda (Wolf 2003). So reporting what the military commanders on 'your side' say is reporting the facts, showing what happens in war is 'becoming a tool of Iraqi propaganda'. The 5 July version of the BBC program on Al Jazeera did contain footage of dead coalition soldiers, but to Australian eyes it was difficult to determine if they were British or American from the angles used and the 'pixilated' faces (Al Jazeera & BBC World 2003).

Al Jazeera had been a thorn in the side of the US and its allies since the early days of the 'war on terror', drawing criticism for broadcasting audio-tapes supposedly from Osama bin Laden. It was also strongly criticised for showing the coalition bodies and prisoners. Its reporters were banned from the New York Stock Exchange soon after, in what was widely seen as retaliation for their reporting (Hewitt 2003). It led to media organisations suggesting that the Americans were deliberately targeting reporters, especially after attacks that hit the Baghdad office of Al Jazeera, killing cameraman Tareq Ayyoub and damaging the nearby office of another Arab television network, Abu Dhabi TV (Hewitt 2003). In a second incident only a few days later, several foreign reporters and Iraqi staff were killed when a US tank fired on the Palestine hotel. The Americans claim to have been fired on from that location, a suggestion disputed by eyewitnesses, many of them colleagues of those who were killed. *SMH* correspondent Paul McGeough (2003, pp. 213–14) reported the reaction of many reporters who believed both incidents were deliberate attacks, despite denials from the US command.

What about the next war?

Now of course there's a whole new chapter to this story and no doubt a dozen more examples of ideological persuasion, media heroism, and media complicity in the 'war on terror'. We have briefly examined some of the issues that came up during the first two years of this conflict and a couple more get a mention in the case studies that follow. We can only speculate, so won't bother, on how this will 'play out' for reporters and the public. One thing that we are sure of, though, is that the way that wars are fought and managed in today's information environment can involve complex and sophisticated ways of manipulating 'facts' and 'figures'. If you have seen the wonderful movie *Wag the Dog*, starring Dustin Hoffman, you'll know what we mean. Otherwise, add it to the list of DVDs you need to rent one rainy weekend. This new conflict-heavy and 'target-rich' environment will also create new problems, new fault lines, and a new 'dialectic of war' that will confront good correspondents with challenges and opportunities. The ethics of war reporting and foreign correspondence is certain to remain a rich source of material for books like this.

Ethical dilemmas in practice

➔ Scenario 1: Dodgy accounting standards?

A public servant from the Department of Defence mentions over a coffee at the local squash club one day that the Department is 'throwing good money after bad' regarding a particularly expensive procurement project. The cost of the 'state-of-the-art' piece of military technology has blown out in a big way. It's now four times the original estimate, 'and we're talking about hundreds of millions of dollars', he says.

Where do you start to check out the claim? Military chiefs say there's nothing extraordinary in the costing. Sure, it's now costing far more than predicted, but they'd expected that. So they have confirmed the thrust of the story, but not the central contention that money is being wasted. Where to from there? If you can't get any further confirmation, do you run with the story?

➔ Scenario 2: Photographer gets a visit from ASIO

As a news photographer in Sydney you're always on the lookout for possible stories and one day you stumble across a police operation in a suburban street. Not knowing what's going on, you stop the car and begin taking photographs. You notice some are in overalls with 'Federal Police' on the back, others are in ill-fitting cheap grey suits and look like Agent Smith from the *Matrix* movies.

After an hour or so you leave the scene, but on the way home your housemate calls and says there's an ASIO agent in your living room and he wants to talk to you. This actually happened to a newspaper photographer in Sydney; here's what he decided to do:

> *'The agent gave me a number and a method to call to confirm his identity. I did and was told they urgently needed to speak with me. I said I would get back to him after speaking with my editor.'*

Turner 2002

The photographer hid the photographs, fearing the ASIO agent might take them. He then went home and told the agent he would listen, but not answer questions.

1   What would you do in this situation?
2   Is it necessary for a reporter, or photographer to check with an editor, or should you, as an individual, make your own decision to cooperate, or not, with the security agency?
3   It is an offence in Australia to identify ASIO agents; how would you deal with this issue if you still wanted to use some of your photographs in a story?

Case studies

We have grouped the case studies in this chapter according to a loose chronology. Therefore we start with some historic examples and then end with some more studies of particular incidents from the most recent Gulf Wars.

Case study 1
1968: The My Lai massacre

The world—and America in particular—was shocked when news leaked out of the terrible My Lai Massacre in Vietnam. What shocked people even more than the gruesome images and stories that finally emerged was that the massacre did not become a news item until 18 months after it occurred. At the height of the involvement of American troops in the ill-fated Vietnam War, on 16 March 1968, a group of about eighty soldiers from Charlie Company of the US Light Infantry Brigade, under the command of Lieutenant William Calley, marched into the village of My Lai and believing it to be a stronghold of the Viet Cong, killed its inhabitants and torched their homes. Between ninety and 130 villagers died in the bloodbath. Not one soldier was among them. Most were women and children and old men. Freelance reporter Seymour Hersch finally broke the story in *Newsweek*, under the banner headline 'AN AMERICAN TRAGEDY', but for more than a year, the 600 correspondents in Saigon could not, or would not, get it published. As John Pilger points out in *Heroes* (Pilger 1986a, p. 259), this framing 'invited sympathy for the invader and deflected from the truth that the atrocities were, above all a *Vietnamese* tragedy'. When the American public learned that their troops had massacred innocent civilians, the news had a major effect on many people's attitude to the war. By the late 1960s, much of America was disillusioned and opposed to the war.

On the thirtieth anniversary of the slaughter in 1998, two American soldiers, helicopter pilot Hugh Thompson and door gunner Lawrence Coburn, were decorated with the Soldier's Medal for landing their craft in the line of fire between the rampaging US soldiers and the fleeing Vietnamese civilians. Crew chief Glenn Andreotta was killed three weeks after My Lai and received the award posthumously (Alexander 1998).

Lieutenant Calley was the only soldier tried over the massacre. He was convicted in a military court on twenty-two counts of murder. Sentenced to life with hard labour, he served only three years under house arrest at Fort Benning, Georgia (Stewart 1998). It was not the first atrocity committed during wartime, and sadly won't be the last. But it raises a major issue about the role of the media in time of war.

The issue arose again in May 2004, with the release on American television (CBS) of pictures of American soldiers abusing Iraqi prisoners of war (see chapter 12).

Issues and questions raised by case study 1

1   Discuss how you would cope with hearing a story like My Lai. What do you think of Seymour Hersch's persistence in getting the story published?

2   Is there a moral responsibility on reporters to uncover war crimes by both sides?

3   Debate the ethical dilemma of the media in times of war exposing massacres by their own country's troops. Our troops are the 'good guys' aren't they? They wouldn't do that, surely?

4   Research the background to the international trials of alleged war criminals as a result of conflicts around the world. How does the news media in various countries frame and discuss these events?

5   It's all very well to say that the media should try to present a balanced picture of the conflict, warts and all, but could you write a story like My Lai where you accuse your country's armed servicemen of cold-blooded slaughter?

6   What effect would such a story have on your readers/viewers?

7   Some would say the public has a right to know how their troops behave, others would contend that the public needs to know, but would they really want to know?

8   The Vietnam War was not popular at home (be that in the United States or Australia). Where do you draw the editorial line in a major conflict between supporting your country's troops fighting on a foreign soil, and presenting the news if that means talking about massacres or opposition to the conflict on the streets?

9   There was robust debate in the Parliament, on the streets of Australian cities, and in the media about deploying Australian troops to the Iraq War. Once the troops are on foreign soil, should a news organisation continue to attack in editorials the reasons for their being sent?

10   Does it change things for a reporter if the war is 'unpopular'? An interesting research project would be to document the history of how various 'anti-war' movements are covered.

→   ## Case study 2

The BBC and the Conservative British Government during the Falklands conflict

The BBC was criticised during the Falklands conflict in the early 1980s for referring to 'the British' rather than to 'our' forces. Apparently, stating an obvious and fairly neutral 'fact' was not enough for some. The implication of 'our' troops is tacit support and consensus that they are somehow automatically 'right'. This emotional attitude to war reporting—the expected loyalty—was a hangover from the days of 'Imperial' England, the patriotic coverage of World War II, and the nationalist sentiment whipped up around the Suez conflict of 1956 (Harris 1983). During the Falklands conflict, the BBC felt that 'our troops' would become 'our ships' and then 'our policy', implying that the BBC was in agreement with Government decisions in the conflict, thus giving them more credibility with the public. In its defence, the BBC claimed that the Falklands conflict didn't constitute an all-out war, therefore reinforcing its claims to be offering balanced coverage. The Falklands conflict arose between Britain and Argentina over the disputed Falkland Islands in the south Atlantic.

The British Government heavily censored news reports from the Falklands and made it very difficult for television to get pictures of the conflict. It then attacked the BBC over its coverage. Conservative Member of Parliament John Page described the BBC quoting statements by Argentinian leaders about the fighting and attempts to broker diplomatic solutions as 'almost treasonable' (UPI 1982a). The 'treason' charge was levelled at BBC television anchor Peter Snow for using the phrases 'if we believe the British' and 'the only damage Britain admitted' during one program (Associated Press 1982). Another Conservative Member of Parliament, Robert Adley, formally complained to the BBC for showing funerals of Argentinian soldiers, describing the story as 'insulting propaganda' (UPI 1982b). The BBC's chairman at the time, George Howard, said BBC news reports were credible around the world because the publicly funded but independently run corporation had a reputation for 'telling the truth, however unpalatable'. 'I suppose it is inevitable that when bad news is reported the messenger will get the blame,' he added (UPI 1982b). Prime Minister Margaret Thatcher had told the House of Commons a couple of days earlier that: 'The case for our British forces is not being put over fully and effectively' by the British Press (UPI 1982b). For good measure the 'Iron Lady' added: 'There are times when it seems that we and the Argentinians are being treated almost as equals and almost on a neutral basis' (Ross 1982). The American media was smarting because neither Argentina nor Britain would allow 'foreign journalists' (for that read the big American TV networks) into the combat zone (Rothenberg 1982).

The low point for the BBC came when a British military leader, Colonel Herbert H. Jones, who later died in the conflict, threatened to sue the BBC for 'manslaughter' for allegedly reporting details of an imminent attack on an Argentinian position at Goose Green. A *Sunday Times* report claimed Col. Jones's anger stemmed from a BBC report of a statement by Defence Minister John Nott in the House of Commons that the attack was imminent. Because of the report, Argentinian reinforcements were sent to bolster forces at Goose Green. But a BBC radio reporter with the British task force denied the claim that Col. Jones had made any such threat (UPI 1982c).

Issues and questions raised by case study 2

1   What do you think of the BBC's contention that the Falklands conflict wasn't technically a war, only a 'conflict' and therefore it should be more balanced in its coverage?

2   Is there really any difference in terms of ethical decisions that need to be made?

3   Is it, in your opinion, ethically wrong to report what the 'other side' is saying? Could it be morally wrong, and yet not ethically wrong?

4   What about the terminology 'if we believe the British' and 'the only damage Britain admitted'? It's certainly emotive, but is it also tinged with disbelief?

5   Is this a case of the politicians trying to 'kill the messenger'?

6   Wouldn't the media take some comfort from Margaret Thatcher's comment that it was treating both sides as equals? Isn't that balanced reporting?

7   How would you feel if the military accused you of reporting that maybe helped 'the enemy' kill your own country's troops?

8   In this day of satellite links and Internet web sites, how could you prevent such a thing happening?

9   It would be cold comfort, would it not, that the Colonel's alleged accusation was later discredited by one of your colleagues?

→ ## Case study 3
Operation Tailwind

In 1997, a group of former American soldiers, who had fought in Vietnam and Laos with US Special Forces during the Vietnam War, were the source for an explosive piece of investigative journalism. They had witnessed the gassing of their own troops by 'friendly fire'. The veterans told reporters from CNN's *NewsStand* program that more than 25 years before, they had been eyewitnesses to the use of the deadly nerve agent sarin during an illegal military operation in September 1970. According to CNN's informants, the sarin gas was dropped from US Air Force planes onto Vietnamese and Laotian troops in a village where the military thought American deserters were hiding out. The gas may also have affected civilians in the village. The Special Forces soldiers were sent into Laos to destroy the village.

CNN's major source for the story was former soldier Robert Van Buskirk, who claimed he had recently recovered his repressed memories of what happened in Laos. He said the memories were suppressed until CNN staffers questioned him in 1997. Van Buskirk said of the raid into Laos 'All I see is bodies', after the A10 Skyraiders had dropped canisters on the enemy position. 'They are not fighting any more. They are just lying, some on their sides, some on their backs. They are no longer combatants'. The CNN reporters worked on the story for eight months before it was broadcast on 7 June 1998.

Among the Pentagon officials quoted by CNN was retired Admiral Thomas Moorer, who was Chairman of the Joint Chiefs of Staff in 1970. The story was run in the first edition of *NewsStand*, and heavily promoted to build an audience for the new current affairs program. However, CNN network executives said the story contained 'serious faults' and pointed the finger at *NewsStand* producer, Richard Kaplan. Two of the program's producers, Jack Smith and April Oliver, said they believed the story to be true.

Under a copy-sharing arrangement, the piece 'Did the US Use Nerve Gas?' (Arnett & Oliver 1998) was also run in the 15 June edition of *Time* magazine under the by-line of Pulitzer Prize-winning CNN journalist Peter Arnett and *NewsStand* producer April Oliver. According to the *Time* version of the story, several senior 'military officials with knowledge of the mission' code-named *Operation Tailwind* confirmed what the soldiers had told the reporters.

According to media reports of the case, Arnett also stood by the story, while acknowledging that CNN's subsequent investigation of its central claims had found insufficient evidence to confirm them. In the furore surrounding the airing of the story, Arnett was quoted as saying he hadn't contributed even a comma to the story, he'd only read the voiceover prepared by others. The network published an apology every half-hour in the days following its admission that the story was wrong. The president of CNN at the time, Tom Johnson, apologised to Vietnam veterans who had expressed their outrage at the sarin gas allegations. In a major understatement, the editor of *Time* South Pacific, Stephen Waterson said: 'There is an old saying in journalism that if a story looks too good to be true, it usually is. That seems to be the case here'. It would seem that perhaps *Time* magazine was caught out in the cross-promotion deal by a commercial arrangement that it would run print versions of CNN stories (Lusetich 1998; Riley 1998).

Issues and questions raised by case study 3

1   How many sources should you get to confirm a story before publishing it?
2   Is it enough, after some confirmation, to have a 'gut feeling' that the story is true, and go for it?
3   After reading this case study, how do you feel about the CNN story? Are you still prepared to believe it might be true?
4   What do you think of Peter Arnett's claim, made after the event, that he hadn't actually written the story, only read the voiceover?
5   If it is the role of the media to reveal wrongdoing by any country's military and if you believe it's true, why not 'publish and be damned'?
6   Who are the various groups in the community that would be affected by the publication of a story like 'Operation Tailwind'?
7   What lessons can we learn from its publication?

Case study 4

The US fetes its mythical heroine—Private Jessica Lynch

Among the first American soldiers taken prisoner by the Iraqis in the 2003 Iraq War was 20-year-old supply clerk, Private Jessica Lynch. Pt. Lynch was captured on 23 March near the southern city of Nassiriyah. Eleven other US soldiers were killed and nine wounded in the incident. An early report quoted unnamed US officials as saying she fought fiercely before being captured. They claimed she was shot and stabbed in the engagement with the Iraqis. It was also reported Lynch had emptied her weapon in a firefight with the enemy while her colleagues lay dead nearby. She was not among the five soldiers whose faces were shown in Iraqi television after their capture, and the US military had officially listed her status as 'unknown' (American Broadcasting Company 2003).

Residents of her home town of Palestine, West Virginia, hung yellow ribbons, held prayer services, and pulled together to support her parents after hearing that she was missing. In the land of Hollywood blockbusters, the Jessica Lynch 'story' was the stuff legends are made of, and the media lapped it up. She became a symbol of American patriotism during the second Gulf War. US commandos 'rescued' Lynch from an Iraqi hospital on 1 April 2003. Video footage shot by the commandos with a night-scope shows no Iraqi resistance and everything is eerily quiet. A doctor at the hospital told other reporters a few days later that all the Iraqi soldiers had left the area well before the American rescuers turned up. One eyewitness said that the previous day, the Americans had been told where Lynch was, including which ward she was in.

All the same, the Army made sure television stations around the world received the official video of the rescue. After it was too late to stop the 'heroism' story, a military investigation established a different story to the popular myth. Her convoy had taken a wrong turn resulting in an Iraqi attack. Pt. Lynch suffered multiple fractures and spinal compression when her military vehicle, a humvee, hit the one in front after being hit by a rocket-propelled grenade (*SMH* Online 2003). Apparently her weapon had jammed (Monaghan 2003). The BBC's John Kampfner called the Lynch story 'one of the most stunning pieces of news management ever conceived' (Kampfner 2003). But America badly wanted to believe the original version of the heroine from rural West Virginia. When Pt. Lynch returned home in a wheelchair after 102 days in a Washington military hospital, she was greeted by cheering crowds wearing 'Welcome Home' T-shirts and waving American flags (Kampfner 2003). Jessica Lynch was presented with three medals, but the myth that fuelled all the attention was far from reality. Other awkward facts were to emerge—she had survived partly due to the care she received at the Iraqi hospital. While the story of her heroism has been eroded as far as the rest of the world is concerned, to Americans she was a hero. We have put this in the past tense because by November 2003, it seemed as if Jessica Lynch's '15 minutes' were over. Her book *I am a Soldier Too* has not sold so well. The book contains a controversial statement: Lynch claims she was sodomised some time after her capture. Various media outlets reported that the Iraqi doctors at the al-Nassiriyah hospital said their examinations revealed no evidence of sexual assault. Lynch says there are three hours after the accident that she cannot remember ('Lynch Reveals Brutal Truth' 2003). US Government officials had described Lynch as a Rambo-like heroine, but in a *60 Minutes* interview with celebrity reporter Diane Sawyer, Lynch says: 'I would have been the only one ... able to say, "Yeah, I went down shooting." But I didn't. I did not ... My weapon jammed and I did not shoot, not a round, nothing' (quoted from transcript, Sawyer 2003).

Issues and questions raised by our comments on the Gulf Wars (I & II) and case study 4

1   Research the Jessica Lynch saga, particularly the early reports of her capture. A pretty young woman, fighting fiercely for her country on foreign soil, wounded and captured by the enemy. Sounds like the storyline from a movie. What do you think went through the minds of the American military when it received the first reports?

2   Do you think the American military deliberately misled reporters, or did it just not know or simply got it wrong in the heat of the battle?

3   It's virtually impossible to check some of these stories at the time, so you have to go with the 'official line' don't you?

4   What do you do when you start hearing rumours that all may not be what it first appeared?

5   The American public wanted to believe Jessica was a hero. In a time of war, would you want to be the one to burst the bubble?

6   The truth didn't seem to bother the American public. She was still a hero in its eyes. Why?

7   What lessons can the media take from the Jessica Lynch affair?

8   There's no excuse this time. The Iraq conflict was a war. So define the role of the media in times of war.

9   In what sense should the 'local' media support the Government during wartime?

10   Once troops are 'over there' fighting, what is the role of the correspondents reporting the conflict?

11   What are the problems posed by being 'embedded' with your country's forces?

12   What are the advantages?

13   Do the advantages outweigh the disadvantages?

14   Debate the ethics of showing pictures of the bodies of your country's soldiers slain in the conflict.

15   Is it any different to showing bodies of the enemy?

Case study 5

The BBC and the British Labour Government after the Iraq War

The focus changes here from reporting the military conflict of a war, to reporting the rationale for going to war. The second Gulf War had been over for some weeks when Andrew Gilligan, the BBC's defence and diplomatic correspondent, alleged that one of Prime Minister Tony Blair's aides used dubious intelligence information to 'sex up' the case for war against Iraq. The allegation was made in an unscripted 'two-way' interview between Gilligan and the (British) *Today* program presenter at 6.07 on the morning of 29 May. A throwaway line in a live 'chat' created so much political fall-out that the Blair Government looked, for a time, like it might fall.

Andrew Gilligan's allegation was that Tony Blair's aides ordered a dubious intelli-gence claim—that Iraq could deploy chemical and biological weapons within 45 min-utes of the order being given—inserted into a public dossier over the objections of intelligence chiefs. This was done, he alleged, even though the aides knew that the claim 'was probably wrong'. The report caused a furore at No 10 Downing Street, with the Prime Minister demanding a retraction. The BBC stood by the report and its reporter.

After three months of bitter dispute between the BBC and the Blair Government over the accuracy of the report, Gilligan admitted in the second round of hearings of the Hutton Inquiry (established by the Blair Government in the wake of the death of the supposed source of the story, former weapons inspector and British defence sci-entist David Kelly) that he'd made several mistakes in the story. But he didn't make this confession until after the apparent suicide of the source of the story. Kelly had been 'outed' by his own employer, the Ministry of Defence, and forced to appear before two parliamentary inquiries into the affair (which we'll discuss in another con-text in chapter 9). The now-disgraced reporter also apologised to the inquiry for send-ing an email to two Members of Parliament identifying the confidential source (Kelly) of another BBC journalist's report on Iraq. Gilligan also corrected another statement in the later broadcast in which he referred to 'my intelligence source' when in fact the late Dr Kelly was working for the MoD, not an intelligence agency (Frankel 2003a). But he stood by his central assertion that the Blair Government's former director of communications and strategy, Alastair Campbell, had 'sexed up' the report (Sengupta 2003). The admissions were a serious embarrassment for the BBC, which prides itself on responsible, accurate reporting and journalistic independence—the rationale it used 20 years earlier to justify its 'balanced' reporting of the Falklands conflict.

In a later broadcast on 29 May—at 7.32 a.m.—on the same BBC program Andrew Gilligan corrected the mistake about the claim that the aides knew the information 'was probably wrong' by saying that the intelligence involved was genuine, even if questionable. Gilligan said his error was 'the kind of slip of the tongue that does hap-pen often during live broadcasts—an occupational hazard' (Frankel 2003b). The *Scotsman* (Nelson 2003) reported that Gilligan had 'admitted to a catalogue of blun-ders in his reports on the Government's Iraq dossier—finally delivering the confession which Downing Street had demanded for the past three months'. A couple of days ear-lier, the BBC Director General, Greg Dyke, told the Hutton Inquiry there would be a wide-ranging review of the corporation's journalism, admitting 'lessons could be learned' from its reporting of the affair. Greg Dyke added that the BBC's producer guidelines would be reviewed: the use of anonymous sources, and the way they are described on air, would be looked at; and 'two-way' interviews may not in future be used to break controversial stories (Wells 2003a). He also tried to explain why the BBC had defended its reporter and his story so strongly after the initial demand by Blair's adviser, Alastair Campbell, to retract it. The Director General said that the BBC was offended by Mr Campbell's 'broadside against the whole of BBC journalism' (Wells 2003a, 2003b). Greg Dyke told another journalist that at the BBC: 'We felt that old scores were being settled, particularly in terms of the war' (Malakani 2003). He must have known something. A few days later, the Blair Government launched 'the most sweeping review of the BBC in its 80-year history'. According to Blair, the funding, structure, and role of the world's best-known public broadcaster are all 'on the table' (Wilson 2003a). Initially it looked like a Government payback for the BBC's aggressive reporting of the Government's 'dodgy dossier' on weapons of mass destruction. The report of the Hutton Inquiry, released on 28 January 2004, cleared the Prime Minister of any wrongdoing over the death of Dr Kelly, but savaged the BBC ('Blair Reigns, But Rule Under Threat' 2004). Some saw it as a 'whitewash'. Indeed, *The Independent* newspaper in London called the Hutton Report 'A Whitewash' on a white, otherwise blank front page (Simper 2004a). There were major scalps at the BBC, including the Chairman, the Director General, and Gilligan. Gilligan was found to have made 'unfounded statements' about the Government's reports on Iraq's weapons; to have wrongly presented his opinions as statements by his source; and he'd 'betrayed' Kelly by telling MPs the scientist had spoken to other reporters. 'Defective' editorial procedures allowed Gilligan to do a live, unscripted interview that prevented editors and lawyers from checking its content, and his editors did not tell senior managers they thought Gilligan was a flawed reporter with a 'loose use of language' ('Lord Hutton's Findings' 2004).

Issues and questions raised by case study 5

1   How far can you go in challenging the 'official' version of events?
2   What if you know for a fact that it is wrong?
3   How can journalists be more careful when checking sensitive intelligence information?
4   How should media organisations respond if there is a complaint by a government about a sensitive story?
5   Did the BBC and Andrew Gilligan behave honourably towards David Kelly?
6   Read the findings of the Hutton Inquiry. What's your reaction?
7   What does it do to the reputation of the world's 'most reliable public broadcaster'?
8   How does the BBC go about rebuilding its shattered reputation?
9   Given the fact that (as of mid 2004) no weapons of mass destruction had been found in Iraq, how much else of the justification for war against Iraq should the media challenge?
10   Although Gilligan may have misunderstood some of what his source was telling him, weren't he and the BBC just doing their job?
11   Where did it go all wrong? In not 'backing down' earlier?

12   There were several instances where misinformation—intentionally or unintentionally—was fed to the Western media by the American military. Do you just accept its 'spin' on the war and hope the truth will come out in the end?

→ ## Case study 6
When is the story yours?

One ethical issue to emerge from coverage of the first Gulf War was the problems it posed for reporters on the spot in the Middle East. There is no way, using their own resources, that a reporter like the Nine Network's Peter Harvey could gather the breadth of coverage either in video or words to adequately cover such a big ongoing story each day. We've already mentioned how several Australian reporters referred to the Camp Doha media compound in Qatar in the second Gulf War as 'Operation Mushroom'. The only way the bureaucratic demands of the news-clock can be satisfied in such situations is if a team of news producers, editors, and writers back in Sydney or Melbourne produced the war package for the day. This would involve writing the news script from all the information available to them, then faxing it to the Middle East for the reporter to read. This doesn't just happen during big war and conflict stories; it is common in most 'disaster' scenarios involving multiple sites and angles. The same thing happened on the Monday after the Port Arthur massacre in 1996. The Nine Network's Hugh Riminton flew to Tasmania, but since he could not be expected to 'get on top' of such a big story in a short period of time between his arrival in the Apple Isle and news-time, the 'news package' was produced in Sydney and the script sent to him to 'read back to Sydney' (Patching 1996). The practice happens almost every day in the so-called 'North American Office' or 'European desk' of the major television (and for that matter radio) stations. They monitor and for a fee are given access to the coverage of various TV news providers—like the American networks ABC, NBC, and CBS, and the BBC from Britain, and the 24-hour news channel, CNN. With access to the original script and news agency-updated reports, they produce their 'version' of that story, often suggesting with appropriate by-line and location graphics that they have covered the story. Newspapers are used to the practice of taking stories and pictures from a number of sources; television reporters are expected, somehow, to gather their own story for the nightly news bulletin. While the rationale for the practice is obvious, it still raises the ethical dilemma of whether or not it is that reporter's story.

Issues and questions raised by case study 6

1   It is accepted media practice to compile stories from a multitude of sources to make a composite story, but is it ethical?
2   Reporters covering such large events will often 'kibbutz' (share details or angles). What impact does this have on the coverage?

3   When does compiling spill over into plagiarism? What if there's a commercial fee involved and your organisation 'buys' the rights to the newsfeed?

4   Discuss the ethics of reporters simply 'reading back to HQ' the script for a major story, even though they haven't written any of it.

Case study 7
60 Minutes talks to a terrorist

On Sunday 6 July 2003, the Nine Network's flagship weekly current affairs program, *60 Minutes,* carried a report by Liz Hayes in which she talked to the terrorist who had allegedly provided the money for the bombing of two Bali nightclubs on 12 October 2002, in which eighty-eight Australians were among the 202 who died. Hayes and her crew tracked down the terrorist, an Algerian-born man, who gave his name as 'Mustafa', in Paris, and he appeared on the program heavily disguised. The startling claims made by 'Mustafa' included that there were active terrorist cells in Australia and that Australia was a target of regional terrorist groups ('Sleeper Cells Planning Terror Attacks in Australia Claim' 2003). He also said that there was a 4000-member terrorist training camp in the Abu Sayyaf stronghold in Jolo in the Philippines. Senior Philippines military were quick to deny the claim (Lyall & Jacinto 2003). During the *60 Minutes* interview, 'Mustafa' said he had met Abu Bakar Bashir, accused leader of the Jemaah Islamiah terrorist group, during his 17 days in Bali before the bombing, and Bashir was aware he was a terrorist (Hayes 2003). As *Media Watch* was to point out about three months later, *60 Minutes* had apparently found what Indonesian and Australian police had long been searching for: the miss-ing link between Bashir and the Bali bombings (Marr 2003c). But what appeared to be the investigative journalism scoop of the year attracted little attention in the rest of the media. Why? *Media Watch* approached the Australian Federal Police and the Indonesian leading the Bali investigation, General Made Pastika. Both said there was no evidence Bashir was on Bali in the 17 days before the bombings. General Pastika dismissed 'Mustafa's' claims as 'not credible' (Marr 2003c).

Issues and questions raised by case study 7

1   Would you want to interview a self-confessed terrorist who said he was associated with the Bali bombings?

2   Or anyone involved in any other terrorist attack?

3   Isn't this a case of the media giving comfort to criminals?

4   One man's terrorist is another man's freedom fighter. Should you interview freedom fighters?

5   Where do you draw the line? Do you interview them as long as you agree with their cause?

6   Or do you interview them as long as they haven't done anything *really* bad?

7   If the BBC was attacked in the House of Commons and accused of 'virtual treason' because it gave coverage to 'the other side' (see case study 2) during the Falklands dispute, aren't the actions of the *60 Minutes* crew similar?

8   If you don't think so, explain the difference.

9   Do you think that as a general rule the media should interview terrorists?

10   If you do, why should we believe anything they say?

11   Or doesn't it matter what they say, you're just lauding the fact you could find a terrorist when the authorities couldn't?

7

PRIVACY AND THE PUBLIC'S RIGHT TO KNOW

Objectives

After reading and discussing this chapter you will have been exposed to:

- The media's balancing act between the public's right to know and the individual's right to privacy.
- The dilemma of deciding how much privacy should be afforded a public figure (and their immediate family).
- Privacy versus secrecy.
- The invasion of the privacy of royalty, the rich and famous, and the 'ordinary citizen'.
- The debate surrounding 'death-knocks'.

Introduction: Whose privacy?

The colourful and flamboyant Mayor of Maroochy on Queensland's Sunshine Coast, Alison Grosse, was awarded $178,000 compensation in the District Court in June 2003, after suing a former lover and colleague Rob Purvis for breach of privacy. Ms Grosse alleged that Mr Purvis had been stalking her for years. Purvis had warned her against taking the action, saying that if he went down he would take her with him. Despite 25 years of tireless and often unpaid service to the Sunshine Coast community, the Mayor will be remembered by many people for the sensational and salacious allegations made against her during the trial—allegations that she had a string of lovers, affairs, and sexual encounters, including making love to a well-known politician on his office desk. The truth, she says, is far less exciting. 'I'm a grandmother who enjoys art and craft and working in the garden' (quoted in Passmore 2003, pp. 56–8). The Maroochy Mayor was greatly relieved when the stalking judgment went in her favour.

But not everyone was happy. In the wake of the court decision the local newspaper, the *Sunshine Coast Daily,* a long-time strong critic of Ms Grosse, which had covered its front page often with the most salacious of the evidence, continued its call for her to leave politics at the March 2004 local government elections. 'For every supporter patting her on the back, there are a hundred counting the days until next March,' a *Daily* editorial said (cited in Passmore 2003). Ms Grosse was soundly beaten in the 2004 Mayoral election.

Ms Grosse, like former Governor-General Peter Hollingworth before her, used the ABC program *Australian Story* (ABC TV 2003a) to put her side of the story. She had led successful campaigns to get a TAFE college and university for the area and established a successful apprenticeship training organisation. As Mayor of Maroochy she led one of the fastest growing regions in the country, with an annual budget of more than $200 million (Passmore 2003). But it's the salacious headlines in the *Sunshine Coast Daily* in early 2003 that will be remembered. Does anyone deserve to have his or her reputation forever tarnished? How much privacy should be granted to public figures? This chapter will attempt to draw the line at a point we think is reasonable. The 'shock-value' of sensational reporting is a valuable marketing tool for the news industry, but does it satisfy the public's *need* to know as well as it being their theoretical *right* to know?

The *Australian's* media commentator, Mark Day (who famously as co-owner and editor of the Melbourne *Truth* in the 1980s headlined a story on the death of former politician Billy Snedden, who died in the arms of a Sydney prostitute, 'Snedden died on the job') put the media's position on privacy succinctly in mid 2004 during debate over the smear campaign around Labor leader Mark Latham:

> To all those wonderful, high-minded, starry-eyed, principled folk who hold dear to the notion that our media should be scrupulously fair, ethical, above the fray and interested only in matters of national importance, I have two unhappy words of advice: get real. It's now a fact of life that if there's dirt to be dug, particularly in the political arena, it will be dug. One way or another, fairly or unfairly, deliberately and with malice, or inadvertently by accident, truth will out.

Day 2004d, p. 22

This chapter looks at one of the most contentious ethical issues facing journalists—the constant balancing act between 'the public's right to know' and the individual's 'right to privacy'. The dilemma ranges from celebrities trying to keep their affairs out of the tabloids, to the individual suddenly thrust into the media spotlight because they've become involved in a news story and who has their life 'invaded' by a 'media pack' until they are no longer considered newsworthy.

The right to privacy versus the right to know represents the most public of the fault lines in journalism ethics and is the one most likely to cause outrage. This chapter will examine how privacy of various types is 'invaded' in unequal ways, depending on privilege, power, and circumstances. The news media can sometimes seem quite callous in its disregard for the privacy of individuals, but realistically a journalist cannot do their job unless they 'invade' the privacy of people on a daily basis.

This chapter will explain why this is the case and offer some advice to reporters who wish to act ethically, but not be constrained by an over-cautious approach to privacy. We should also point out that because privacy laws are based on the common law system, it is individuals and legal entities, like companies, that gain some access to legal protection. This leads to a divide between those who are privacy 'rich' and those who are privacy 'poor'. There are several good texts in media law for journalists—each of them will help you through the legal issues, but we do not mention them, except in passing in our discussion of the ethics of privacy.

One of the most important ethical constraints on the media pertains to individuals' and groups' moral rights to privacy and confidentiality. Privacy is an ethico–legal problem in many jurisdictions. This simply means that there are legal, or quasi-legal, constraints on what the media can, and cannot, do in relation to matters of privacy. In some matters this means that the media cannot access certain forms of information that are protected by privacy laws: in most states this means medical records and other sensitive information. However, there is no general law of privacy in relation to being photographed in a public place, for instance. Some laws do protect privacy, but only as a result of actually doing something else, such as the law against trespassing on private property. For example, some telecommunications laws make it illegal to tap phones, or to record someone's voice without their knowledge—this means broadcasting someone's voice that you recorded without their knowledge, to be more precise (Pearson 1997, pp. 221–34). Governments have also attempted to deal with privacy issues through legislation, but so far in Australia without much success. This legal–ethical dilemma over the status of personal privacy has the potential to 'confound our thinking' about the issue and to destabilise both the legal and philosophic foundations of privacy (Patterson & Wilkins 1994, p. 110).

Public and private privacy

In terms of the news media's rights, a number of clear distinctions need to be made between 'public' privacy and 'private' privacy; and between 'privacy' and 'secrecy'. Andrew Belsey (1992, pp. 82–3) says 'secrecy' differs from 'privacy' in terms of its 'moral status': secrets per se are morally 'neutral' and only take on significance in particular contexts—for example, the difference between 'innocent' secrets, such as personal intimacies and 'guilty' secrets, such as when governments, or corporations, lie to the public. In such matters it is not 'legitimate' for government agencies, politicians, or business figures to claim 'invasion of privacy' in order to conceal matters that should be available in the public domain.

'Public' and 'private' privacy concerns the differences and difficulties faced by the news media in respect of the privacy of public information: the levels of privacy accorded to public figures, and the 'taken-for-granted' everyday privacy 'enjoyed' by 'ordinary' citizens. In these contexts the issue of 'consent' is also important. A person can give informed consent to be involved in a news story and there is an implied consent if people agree to talk to you once you've identified yourself as a reporter. In effect you are giving them a chance to say 'Go away'; if they do, then go. If they do not, you can fairly assume 'consent', unless of course you are dealing with children, in which case you should seek approval from someone in a position to give it, usually a parent or legal guardian. The issue of consent is important when making a distinction between the 'right' of 'Joe Average' to say 'No', and to have his privacy protected and public figures who, to a greater or lesser extent, rely on publicity and exposure for their own gain (either votes or CD sales). Belsey makes three distinctions between classes of cases involving breaches of privacy that we should bear in mind:

- For public figures 'consent can be assumed' outside any small protected [personal] domain.
- In matters of criminality or unethical behaviour by a public figure 'consent is not needed' because if a law has been broken then the perpetrator deserves public exposure.
- In cases concerning 'ordinary people ... thrust into the public eye, consent should be a requirement' (Belsey 1992, p. 89).

We must first analyse the concept of privacy in relation to autonomy, because without some degree of privacy a person's autonomy and individualism are undermined. Unwarranted invasions of privacy have the potential to cause great harm and therefore would break several of the ethical philosophies discussed in chapter 1. Privacy is also at the core of our own individual esteem, it protects us from 'ridicule and scorn', it allows us to control our reputation, and it regulates social interaction by keeping other people out of our 'personal space' (Retief 2002, pp. 152–3). Some qualifications to the right to privacy are based on the fact that an individual is a public official or otherwise in the public sphere. Other qualifications to the right to privacy are predicated on the public's need to know about certain issues that might affect them (Hurst & White 1994, pp. 112–14). But where is the line to be drawn between telling all, and minding our own business? Following our discussion in earlier chapters, the relationship between the freedom of the press and the public's right to know will be explored.

Privacy laws and public interest

Privacy laws vary greatly from country to country and in their application within jurisdictions. In Australia there are federal privacy laws protecting some forms of information that is held about us by corporations and government agencies, and the states and territories have their own privacy regimes. The debate in the Australian media context is about the privacy of individuals versus the public right to know about information that might affect their lives. Some newspaper editors and senior broadcasters believe that the right to privacy applies to ordinary people, but that once a person steps into the public arena, especially into a position of responsibility, then they lose the right to that protection. An example of invasion of privacy that is often mentioned in this context is coverage of Kerry Packer's heart attack in 1990 while playing polo at Warwick Farm in Sydney's west. This is interesting to us because it involves a media mogul whose staff are often accused of invading others' privacy, and we use it as a case study later in this chapter.

Belsey and Chadwick (1992) consider the question of statutory regulations to ensure privacy in the British context and they comment on the 1990 Calcutt inquiry into the press, which was a response to intrusions into the privacy of the royal family among others. They come down on the side of opposing legislative solutions and we agree with their statement that:

The problem [with legislation] is that it would almost certainly have a severely deleteri-ous effect on serious journalism, while leaving untouched the trivia and gossip that form the staple of the tabloids. And in general any legal restriction on the press [and elec-tronic media, authors' addition], in the absence of a constitutional guarantee of press freedom and some sort of freedom of information legislation, is a one-sided detraction, preventing the press from fulfilling a proper democratic role.

Belsey & Chadwick 1992, p. 8

Right royal privacy

It is the British royalty that appears to suffer most from what they see as the unwarranted attention of the tabloid press. After all, as we also mentioned in the introductory chapter, there are many, her brother included, who believe the media was responsible for the death of Diana, Princess of Wales. Their every public move is snapped by an 'army' of photogra-phers, the much-maligned paparazzi, who rely on saleable photos of 'the royals' for their livelihood. Often the royals will agree to the obligatory 'photo op' when they're on a skiing holiday, for instance, and everyone is happy, but let there be a hint of controversy or scan-dal and the media pack will hound them to ground, not unlike a royal fox hunt! That's why the photographers and reporters were outside that Paris hotel on the night Diana died. She had a new lover—and a very rich one at that—and pictures of them together were selling for top prices. But this sort of unwanted attention was nothing new to Diana, and other members of the royal family for that matter. And as we mentioned in the opening chapter, she is still of intense interest to the media more than six years after her death.

The British news media has for years followed the Queen's royal handbag, Prince Phillip, around to see what 'gaffe' he'll come up with next. He has had a long history of 'opening his mouth to change feet'. There is supposedly an agreement between the British media and the monarchy that the media will not follow Diana's sons around in return for selected staged media events. So when Diana's youngest son, third in line to the British throne, Prince Harry, arrived in Australia in late 2003 supposedly on a private working visit, he was duly paraded in front of the paparazzi at Sydney's Taronga Park zoo a few hours after his arrival in the country for the obligatory photo op of him meeting the native wildlife (the animals, not the media). He patted a koala, obliged by modelling the famous Australian bush hat, the Akubra, and then to the delight of the assembled media—many of them from London—was handed an echidna (a small native Australian animal with spikes on its back). Photos of the Prince grimacing as the prickly animal wriggled in the royal grip made most UK papers the next day with the *Sun* and the *Daily Express* both coming up with the witty headline 'When Harry Met Spiky' (a play on the Meg Ryan film, *When Harry Met Sally*). The conservative *Daily Mail* went with 'Ouch! Harry Gets a Prickly Reception from the Aussies'. But in the typical tabloid style that must have made Harry's grandpar-ents in Buckingham Palace cringe, the downmarket *Daily Star* ran his picture on page 3 beside a topless model under the headline; 'Harry: I feel A Bit Of A Prick'. How do we know? Because the Australian media delightedly repeated these tacky headlines for our amusement (cited in 'Spiking the Royal Guns' 2003). The 19-year-old Prince's destination was supposed to be a royal secret, but that didn't last long. The *Courier-Mail* reported that he was working on Tooloombilla, a 16,000-hectare cattle property more than 600 kilometres from Brisbane. The royal hunt was on again and the local media rushed to the area. The Sydney correspondent for Britain's *Guardian* said it could have been 'the thrill of the chase' that drove the Australian media to expose his whereabouts (cited in 'Spiking the Royal Guns' 2003). Prince Harry's minders claimed the royal was being harassed and threatened that he would head home. It should have been no surprise that the media wanted a photo of Harry in the bush. A quick photo op on the property would have been sufficient, but by crying 'harassment' the minders just complicated the issue. The *Courier-Mail* and Channel Nine got their shots (doubtless sold around the world), and others went for the local colour story. Then all went quiet 'on the western front' while the media awaited Harry turning up at a local social event and the promised royal support for the English team in the Rugby World Cup. Before we leave discussion of the media and the third in line to the British throne, the *Courier-Mail* took a cheap shot at Harry at the time in its gossipy column, 'Confidential'. It superimposed Harry's head on the body of a well-dressed young man draped around a bikini-clad model above the headline 'It's Krystal Clear Harry Would Love the Gold Coast Gals'. (The Gold Coast model in the photo was Krystal Ford.) The photo was obviously digitally manipulated—something the paper acknowledged in very small print in the bottom left-hand corner of the image. The article accompanying the photo suggested Harry should 'scout talent' in hot and friendly Queensland. It continued with Krystal suggesting where she would take the Prince on a date ('It's Krystal Clear Harry Would Love the Gold Coast Gals' 2003). There's hardly a dull moment for the 'royal watchers'. Within a few weeks of the 'Prince Harry in Australia' saga, the British royals were on the front pages again, with the tell-all (almost) book by Diana's former butler, Paul Burrell, in which he claimed the Princess had nine secret lovers, including a famous musician. It didn't take long for the musician to be identified as Bryan Adams (Lampert 2003). Then in early November 2003 came the amazing saga of Prince Charles trying to stop publication in England of more allegations of a sexual nature. In a bizarre 'pre-emptive' strike against the media, Charles's secretary made an extraordinary statement along the lines of 'We can't tell you what the allegation is, but we can categorically deny it is true'. The allegation was that Charles had been involved in some sort of sexual encounter with a male staff member at Buckingham Palace.

Celebrity, privacy, fame, and fortune

Victorian Privacy Commissioner Paul Chadwick sees at least five types of 'fame' and suggests journalists consider: 'Does the public interest in disclosure [in the various instances] outweigh the privacy interest of the persons involved?' (Chadwick 2004, p. 15). The five types are *fame by election or appointment* (politicians, judges, and others in public office); *fame by achievement* (film stars, TV presenters, sporting heroes, and business leaders); *fame by chance* (previously anonymous people randomly caught in tragedy, disaster, or good fortune), *fame by association* (those close to the famous) and *royal fame* (a category reserved for those born into, or who marry into, a royal family) (Chadwick 2004, p. 15).

The media always claim it is the public's insatiable appetite for gossip and scandal (masquerading as news) about the royals and other celebrities that fuels the paparazzi's and tabloids' fascination. The strong sales figures for the gossip magazines probably support this contention.

Following a close second in the 'unwanted attention of the tabloids' stakes are the A-list celebrities—politicians, business leaders, those at the top of their respective sports, pop idols, and film and television stars. In England, the media's A-list is headed by 'the other royal family'—soccer superstar David Beckham and his wife Victoria, the former 'Posh Spice', and their children. In the USA the A-list is whoever is this week's leading Hollywood couple, such as 'Brad and Jennifer' or the Governor of California, 'Arnie' Schwarzenegger. In Australia, it's what Russell Crowe or Shane Warne are up to, or who Nicole Kidman is currently seeing. We could go on and on, but you get the picture. It's anyone who has 'drawing power'—a public figure who draws attention because of their standing in the community, or for their sporting prowess or contribution to the arts. Or even just being famous for being famous, such as the Hilton sisters, Paris and Nicky. During a brief, all-expenses-paid-by-Channel-Seven trip to Australia for the 2003 Melbourne Cup race, Paris and Nicky were described as the 'It girls' (Munro 2003). They are the all-purpose 'existential celebrity' figures: 'Their vocation is partying in as little clothing as possible, with the apparent aim of getting arrested for public displays of soft pornography' (Symons 2003).

The material that's gathered for the social pages, the gossip columns, and the tabloid magazines is pretty much anything they do that they would prefer the public not to know about and that will titillate the audience—for example, the titbit that Paris Hilton 'stars' in a homemade video featuring 'her and [Rick Salomon] the husband of Hollywood actor Shannen Doherty' (Symons 2003). Salomon sued Hilton for claiming that she was coerced into the video performance. He is also suing a porn distributor for 'invasion of privacy' over the video ('Paris Under Siege' 2003). This is what we mean by information you might 'want' to know, but can you honestly say you 'need' to know? Next time you rush into the newsagency to buy the latest *New Idea*, *Ralph*, *Who* magazine, or *Woman's Day* to read the latest revelations about your favourite celebrity, think for a minute how you'd feel if they were writing about you. We'll return to this in a later chapter, but a lot that is written in gossip magazines is rubbish that may have begun as an atom of truth, but by the time the gossip magazines have massaged and exaggerated it, it bears no resemblance to the facts. The argument goes along the lines that person 'X' is a public figure, and therefore their life is also public 'property'. In the case of TV, film, sport, and music celebrities, the argument goes that because they make their fortunes from the public watching their TV show, going to their movies, or watching them play and buying the merchandise they endorse or CDs they produce, we have a right to know every little detail about their lives. Do we? Again, if it were you, how would you feel about people reading that sort of material about you? What would your parents or children think? This is a useful situation in which we might revisit John Rawls's (1971) 'Veil of Ignorance', behind which 'it is possible to walk in the shoes' of the person whose privacy is about to be breached. According to Patterson and Wilkins (1994, p.118–19), behind the veil of ignorance 'freedom of the press ... becomes equal to freedom from unwarranted intrusion into private life'. Is this a proposition that, as journalists, we can live with?

We'll talk about this case in the next chapter in another context, but the tragic death of former test cricketer, Victorian cricket coach and media personality, David Hookes, early in 2004 gave rise to another ethical debate over invasion of privacy. On the day of his funeral service at the Adelaide oval (attended by 10,000 and watched by many on the Nine Network), veteran radio announcer Derryn Hinch (the so-called Human Headline) told his Melbourne audience that Hookes and his wife had separated the previous year. He added: 'There is another woman, whom I have talked to off-air, who is grieving for a loved one right now' (Stewart 2004). Hinch's employer, 3AW, was the same station that employed Hookes. Hinch said he reported it because it was news and common knowledge in news-rooms. 'I did get sick of the happy family snaps of David and wife and kids on the TV news,' Hinch said (Stewart 2004). The MEAA Code of Ethics says to respect the people's right to know, but at the same time 'respect grief and personal privacy' and not to place 'unneces-sary emphasis on family relationships' (see Appendix). Hookes was very much a public fig-ure, especially in Victoria, and the row over Hinch's comments highlights the debate on how much the media should disclose about the private lives of public people.

Pursuing a 'feral' Cheryl

Now let us look at the classic Australian case of the invasion of privacy of a public figure: the case of former Australian Democrats leader and Labor politician Cheryl Kernot. Keep in mind what we have just asked: How would you feel if it was you, your mother, daughter, wife, or close friend, that all this was being said and written about?

> She is about as honest as Christopher Skase and Nick Bolkus, she is about as loyal as Benedict Arnold, and she has the morals of an alley cat on heat.

> Quoted in Wenham 2002

Liberal backbencher Don Randall made this comment about Cheryl Kernot during an adjournment speech in federal parliament on 12 March 1998 and it resurfaced in almost every major newspaper in the country during the revelations of the Kernot–Evans affair in July 2002. Journalist Laurie Oakes had revealed that Kernot had a 'big secret' that was not mentioned in her autobiography, which had just been released. The secrecy was broken when Stephen Mayne's *crikey.com* web site published the rumour: Cheryl Kernot had had an affair with Labor Senator Gareth Evans while they were both married to other people. More than 400 items appeared in the print media in the sixteen days after the 'big secret' was spilled. Why was Kernot attacked so ruthlessly? The short answer, given by Laurie Oakes and those who defended his actions, was that the affair became public property when Kernot's memoir, *Speaking for Myself Again*, was published and did not mention the liaison. This is a version of the 'public interest' argument and much of the ensuing media debate focused on the pros and cons of that position.

The most emphatic thing that one can say about this 'he said, she said' commotion is that the justification for publication is very arguable. There are no cut and dried answers when talking about media ethics. However, in Kernot's case it's fair to argue that it is basically an attitude of sexism in the media that dictated the terms of Kernot's (and Evans's) exposure over their love affair. In the ensuing hailstorm of columns and opinion pieces, the predominant tone was harsh in its treatment of Ms Kernot, but interestingly, the coverage of her equally exposed lover, Gareth Evans, was more muted. His predicament was framed as that of a 'repentant cad' and he was personified rather jokingly as "Biggles Flies Undone". Evans gained the nickname 'Biggles'—after the fictitious hero war pilot—following his decision, while federal Attorney-General, to send an Air Force jet to take photos of progress on the proposed Franklin Dam in southern Tasmania, remarking rather famously later that 'it seemed like a good idea at the time'. Cheryl Kernot was routinely portrayed as the 'scarlet woman', the 'villain' of the piece and basically deserving of the 'comeuppance' dished out by the press. Whether or not this treatment was 'deserved' is not the issue. It seems in this case that a moralistic media saw its role as putting an allegedly 'promiscuous' woman back in the kitchen (Breit et al. 2002).

The rivers of ink that poured into this story have been described by one commentator as a 'tsunami' that 'crashed over Cheryl Kernot and beached both her and her former lover Gareth Evans' (Wenham 2002). The relationship between power and sex is complex and volatile. However, this was not acknowledged by the media, which preferred to reduce it to a tawdry affair. In the process Cheryl Kernot was reduced to the sum of her sexual parts and the assumption made that she was 'horizontally recruited' to Labor by Gareth's sexual prowess, rather than it being the culmination of a process of political bonding over many months. In this version, Evans 'lured her to the Labor Party' (Murray 2002, p. 1). No one suggested that the decision-making could be sexually 'transmitted' *from* Kernot to Evans.

The dictates of the news production process and adherence to formulaic news values of drama and conflict mean that the press could not deal with the depth of human emotions involved. Kernot was described as 'increasingly erratic' (Harvey 2002, p. 21); her book was damned as an 'ill-moderated whine'(Bolt 2002, p. 13); she was said to suffer violent 'mood swings' (Shannahan 2002, p. 64) and as a result of the exposure deemed to be exhibiting 'erratic and emotional behaviour' (Ruehl 2002, p. 11). *SMH* columnist Miranda Devine (2002, p. 15) even called her 'self-obsessed and remorseless'. This kind of emotive language is rarely, if ever, used about male politicians.

The fault line here is very public, quite wide, and a certain trap for the unwary. On one side, a large percentage of the population clamour for the latest gossip about people in the public 'eye' and rationalise their fascination by saying 'We helped to put them where they are'. Across the divide others say, with equal conviction, that Cheryl Kernot 'should have known better'. Shouldn't every politician know not to mix sex and politics and as public figures shouldn't they be able to cope with the media attention? In the final analysis could anyone be expected to handle the personal attention that sees reporters gloating over the latest public figure they've skewered. We are all human—would any of us be able to handle the media attention many public figures have to endure?

Journalism academic Cathy Jenkins believes, all other arguments aside (the right to privacy versus the public's right to know about the behaviour of public figures whose salaries had been paid by the public purse), that Oakes was justified in 'outing' Kernot and Evans because Evans had originally lied to Parliament about the affair in 1998. 'One party lied, the other failed to rectify it, thereby becoming complicit in the lie' (Jenkins 2003, p. 61).

On the other hand, media attention was warranted after Australian Democrats leader Andrew Bartlett allegedly stole five bottles of wine from a Coalition Christmas party in late 2003 and manhandled and abused Liberal Senator Jeannie Ferris in the Senate chamber after she approached him about the theft (Morris 2004).

But did the new leader of the Labor party, Mark Latham, deserve some of the attention that followed his election early in December, 2003? Most of the media went to his former wife, Gabrielle Gwyther (is that an invasion of privacy or is his ex now 'public property'?), who told them he wouldn't get her vote. The *Gold Coast Bulletin* took it a step further, covering their front page with a photo of Ms Gwyther, under the headline: 'Latham's Ex-wife Tells : He Climbed Over Me'. The page 2 story recounted how the new Labor leader was 'demanding, difficult to live with' and other, similar comments ('Latham Ex Dumps on New Leader' 2003). The *Gold Coast Bulletin* gave the Latham election another four pages of coverage, including nearly an entire page devoted to the text of his opening remarks to the media after being elected ('It's All About Me' 2003). Some would say that's quite justified, that the public would be interested in his background and his vision as the new leader, but what about the *Bulletin* circling every personal pronoun in the speech, under the heading 'It's All About Me'? Was it poking a little fun at what they saw as a rather egocentric speech, or was it a piece of political nastiness? Many of these allegations were revived, and a couple of new ones raised, in the lead up to the 2004 federal election on Channel Nine's *Sunday* program and in the Murdoch-owned newspapers. It appeared to us at the time that Mark Latham was subjected to routine and hostile coverage in some sections of the news media. It had all the hallmarks of an orchestrated campaign; Latham claimed it was being 'run' by a government dirty-tricks unit that fed material to the press. We couldn't find the proverbial 'smoking gun', but given the history of news media interference in the political process in Australia it's not out of the question that the News Limited papers were actively campaigning against the Labor leader.

The private lives of ordinary people in the news

There are many circumstances when private citizens (as opposed to public figures) are suddenly thrust into the media spotlight by usually being involved in a tragic event or because a loved one has made the news. The individual could be 'in the news' for any number of reasons. Their loved one may be 'news' because they have been the victim of a flash flood, a road accident, or be one of a handful of Australian victims of a major international news event. In the context of this discussion the reason is not important. We can all think of examples. You see them almost every night on the TV news—a family appealing for information about a missing relative, or asking for help in apprehending the criminal who bashed their son, or lamenting the 'light' sentence given the killer of their loved one. It is how these people are treated by a media they basically don't understand that is our focus in this section. They are all variations on the theme of grief intrusion. But we need to make an exception here between pre-arranged publicity and 'death-knocks'.

Pre-arranged appeals to reveal and 'death-knocks'

No journalist or photographer likes doing a 'death-knock', the somewhat macabre term for the task of interviewing and filming people still in shock and grief.

Hurst & White 1994, p. 113

No one likes doing them, but they are an essential element of some stories that, at some point in your career, you will be asked to cover. There's no easy way of doing it, only ethical and unethical methods. Journalists will defend their intrusion into private grief by saying 'the public has the right to know' what happened or how the immediate family feels. They'll tell the reluctant interviewee that talking to the media about how their loved one died might save others. When they have got what they want—and usually for TV news and current affairs crews that means recording the interviewee breaking down and crying on camera—they will justify their actions to critics by claiming the relatives were 'happy to talk'. Some people want to talk—it might jog someone's memory and help find their loved one (if it's a missing relative case), they might feel flattered to be given the opportunity, or maybe feel obligated to talk about their loved one or they might just be getting their anger 'off their chest'.

On the other hand, some of the 'appeals' you see on TV have been arranged either by police to help with their investigation, or by the media negotiating with police to find an appropriate spokesperson for the family. Nowadays this negotiation process is often done through an intermediary, a family member or friend or a church or social welfare organisation representative. But sadly that is not yet the 'norm' although it is catching on and we think it's the best alternative if the media *has* to intrude on grieving relatives.

But just as there is a good side to every issue, there is also a bad side. The media is consistently attacked for being insensitive in dealing with people in grief. The best remembered in media circles was the very public brawl between reporters and relatives at the funeral of Robert Trimbole in 1987 involving the award-winning journalist Max Uechtritz, then a reporter, who later won a Walkley Award for his 1989 coverage of the Tiananmen Square massacre, and later still became the ABC's director of news and current affairs and would be involved with more battles, but more of a political nature (Simper 2003, p. 4). Then there was the behaviour of some journalists at the 1986 Moura mine disaster (see case study 4 below), and the incident in Perth in 1990, which resulted in two Channel Seven journalists being sacked for intruding on a woman's grief by showing her being informed of the death of her young child. To help his students understand the various stages of grief, Adelaide journalism educator Dr Ian Richards exposes them to what he calls 'Death Day', a one-day death awareness seminar that includes addresses by representatives of the Australian Funeral Directors' Association on a number of death-related topics, a tour of a funeral parlour, an address from a qualified grief counsellor, and a tour of Adelaide's major crematorium. The day helps the students understand some of the issues associated with grief intrusion. They learn about the eleven stages of the grieving process and a bereavement educator advises them on how to approach people in grief (Richards 1994, pp. 118-19). As Richards notes:

> Most of the ethical questions relating to intrusion into grief fall into three broad categories—Should a particular death or deaths be covered in the first place? If so, how should journalists go about obtaining material relating to the death or deaths, and how should this material be published once it has been obtained?
>
> Richards 1996, p. 101

Also at issue here is how far does the 'public's right to know' extend when it amounts to little more than the public's morbid curiosity? There's a big difference between what the public 'wants' to know and 'needs to know'. It is obvious that at a time of grief people are under considerable stress and may not in a position to answer reporters' questions in a rational manner. No one handles a personal tragedy in the same way. As we've noted above, some welcome (or at least do not object to) approaches for photographs or to talk about their loved one, but it is not the same for everyone. As Ian Richards (1996) suggests, the first question to ask is whether a death should be covered in the first place (and in this regard we talk about covering suicides in the Appendix), and once that decision is made, what is the most sympathetic way to approach the bereaved family? Nowadays, as we've noted above, it is often done through an intermediary who can approach the family on the media's behalf, rather than the 'heart-in-the-mouth' journalist knocking on the front door of the family home.

Privacy and the public interest are uneasy bedfellows in the news media. On the one hand, for the media to do its job there has to be a certain degree of transparency and sometimes intrusion is warranted. Reporters also have to operate under difficult conditions on occasion, to get an important personal story into the public arena. At the same time, the desire to get a 'scoop', particularly on an emotionally charged story of personal tragedy and anguish, can push reporters into gross breaches of privacy. Some blame must also be attached to the news organisations, particularly tabloid papers and some TV current affairs shows, which charge after such stories because they know it will boost sales or ratings.

Under such circumstances it is hard to provide solid advice, or definitive answers that will be applicable to every story. Several of the case studies below address this important fault line in journalism ethics.

Ethical dilemmas in practice

→ ## Scenario 1

You arrive at the home of the family of a person who has been killed in an accident overseas, with instructions from your editor to talk to the family, and get a picture of the dead relative. It becomes obvious from the first few words with the person's mother at the front door that she is not aware that her child is dead. What do you do?

Scenario 2

As a TV reporter you've followed the case of a Gulf War veteran who is having trouble with the Federal Government over what he believes are his rights as a returned service-man. He takes his estranged family hostage in the family home, waving a rifle at police outside. The police make contact with the man and he demands to talk to you and your crew. The police want to replace your camera-operator with one of their own in the hope of somehow subduing the man while you are interviewing him. Do you cooperate?

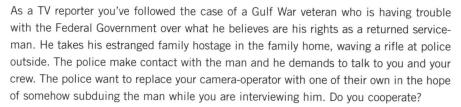

Case studies

Case study 1

The death-knock 'photo op'

In 1992, members of the NSW police force shot dead Mr Boris Milankoski on a Wollongong street. The next day, the then Channel Nine police reporter in Sydney, Steve Barrett, visited Milankoski's home to obtain a photograph of the shooting victim. The visit was captured on videotape by a news crew from Prime Television, a regional affil-iate of the opposition Seven Network. It was later broadcast on the ABC's *Media Watch*.

On the tape, Mr Barrett is seen asking Mrs Milankoski for a photograph of her hus-band, telling her 'we need the photograph for general police release'. Mr Barrett asks 'What's the best ones you've got here, madam?' and is seen removing two photographs. *Media Watch* host Stuart Littlemore suggested that the family could have mistaken Barrett for a policeman as the videotape does not show him identifying himself or his organisation (Zuel 1992). The clear implication in the *Media Watch* item was that Barrett had either 'posed' as a policeman in order to get a photograph of the dead man, or done nothing to counter the belief by Mrs Milankoski that he represented the police. Nine News says Barrett was wearing a rainproof jacket with the Nine logo clearly visi-ble, and was followed into the house by a Nine camera crew (Patching 1996).

Issues and questions raised by case study 1

1   Discuss the ethics of 'posing' as someone in authority (or at least letting the person con-cerned believe you are such a person) in order to get access to material.
2   Under what circumstances could such an action be justified?
3   Is it the same as *not* identifying yourself when gathering material for a piece of inves-tigative journalism?
4   Is it any different if someone assumes you are someone that you're not? Would ethical behaviour dictate that you correct the impression?
5   What guidelines should you employ when approaching someone who is obviously in shock after losing a loved one, or any other tragic experience?

6   Discuss how you might ethically approach doing a 'death-knock'.
7   How would you feel if it happened to you in those circumstances?

→ ## Case study 2

Cangai siege

New South Wales police were pursuing three suspected murderers and armed robbers in the north of the state in March 1993. The fugitives began their killing spree in outback Queensland, where they killed in Mt Isa and Dalby. They were wanted over the deaths of five people, including a girl of about 14, whose body was burned (Riley, Papadopoulos & Roberts 1993). The other three were killed in northern NSW (Riley 1993). With two children as hostages, the suspects eventually holed up in a farmhouse at Cangai, in northern NSW, and were trapped there by a police cordon. They threatened to kill the young hostages.

Several journalists, including a radio journalist from the ABC at Grafton, got the telephone number of the farmhouse and rang the hostage-takers to get interviews. The police had requested that the line be kept open so that they could negotiate with the fugitives. On 30 March 1993 *A Current Affair* host, Mike Willessee, recorded a phone interview with the leader of the gang, Leonard Leabeater, 41, then Robert Steele 22, and then with the children, but not before his staff had kept the fugitives on the line for the amount of time it took for the host to get to the studio. He was in his car crossing Sydney Harbour when first contact was made ('I'd Rather Have Been Killing Cops' 1993). The third fugitive was Raymond Brett Bassett, 25. The interview was broadcast that night and rated highly, but caused uproar. As the *Age* said in an editorial: 'It was a tense and highly volatile situation which could easily have gone tragically wrong. The police are right. The television reporting of the siege was intrusive and insensitive' ('Rules Are Needed To Cover Siege Reporting' 1993). The lives of the hostages could have been put in danger. Talking on the phone to the killers and children tied up the line and prevented police from making contact with the men. In another incident during the Cangai siege, an *ACA* journalist (and later host of the program), Mike Munro, flew through a police exclusion zone and tried to land inside the police cordon in a helicopter. The helicopter pilot was charged but Mike Munro said he hadn't done anything wrong.

Nearly a year later a national conference was convened by state and Federal Police and the media to try to establish ground rules about covering sieges and similar events. One of the co-authors was invited to the police-media 'summit' in Sydney on 4 March 1994. The television news representatives, perhaps realising they had overstepped the mark at the Cangai siege, seemed willing to accept a draft manifesto similar to that applying to media in Canada. Basically it said the media would report criminal activities like hostage-takings in a fashion that does not knowingly endanger lives, hamper police, or offer comfort to the criminals. It said the media would not contact either victims or perpetrators for interviews during the course of the event. For their part, the police acknowledged the media's right to report, and agreed to provide 'timely, accurate and detailed' information to the media (Patching 1994). Both the Federation of Radio Broadcasters (FARB, now Commercial Radio Australia) and the Federation of Commercial Television Stations (FACTS, now Free TV Australia) were ready to accept, with the added proviso that police would guarantee line of sight of the hostage scene. Representatives of Fairfax and News Limited, while accepting the first part of the manifesto, wanted no part of the second—they'd ring who they liked, when they liked (Patching 1994). It was a real 'bun fight'. The Police Chiefs preached responsibility, the electronic media representatives agreed to tread lightly in the future, and the print media went on about 'freedom of the press'.

Greg Lassere, the father of the two child hostages at Cangai, watched events unfold on television, like much of Australia. He was a very relieved man when he was officially told his children were safe. He had heard, on radio, that Mike Willessee had interviewed his children over the phone from the farmhouse. At the time Mr Lassere told inquisitive reporters, keen for a story, that: 'I reckon Willessee did right ... I reckon they [the media] were all right, as long as they didn't get too pushy ... I reckon the guys that rang up the house, I reckon they did right"' (quoted in O'Neil 1993, p. 11).

O'Neil reported that Channel Nine moved quickly to secure an exclusive story with the Lassere family. Its first move was to fly Greg Lassere and some relatives from Brisbane to Grafton to see the children. It backfired on Nine because a child psychologist refused to allow the children to be interviewed, despite Mr Lassere's 'kind of' consent (O'Neil 1993). From this point, Greg Lassere appears to have felt an obligation to Nine, but this did not stop *Woman's Day, New Idea,* and other media bidding for his story and access to the children. In the end Nine got the story for $1000 plus expenses. The Lasseres spent a day in Sydney and *ACA* got its exclusive. In an interesting footnote to this story, the AJA Code of Ethics Review Committee recommended changes to deal specifically with the Cangai situation (O'Neil 1993). Recommended clause 16 read: 'Never knowingly endanger the life or safety of a person without informed consent' and recommended clause 17 read: 'Exercise particular care for the welfare of children in reports involving them.' These clauses were included in the twenty recommended by the review, but were not included in the final twelve-point Code eventually adopted.

Issues and questions raised by case study 2

1   Under what circumstances would you cooperate with the police?
2   Does it make any difference if you are working for a small bi-weekly in the bush or a daily television current affairs program?
3   Under what circumstances would you consider the story to be bigger than the need to keep police contacts 'on side'?
4   Would a 'tabloid television' journalist really care about what the police thought of their actions?
5   What happens if you keep a suspected killer on the phone, antagonise him by the tone of your questions, and he kills one of the hostages?

6   As was said in the wake of the Willessee interview, unless you're a trained psychologist, how would you know how a killer might react?

7   How are siege or hostage situations handled in Australia today?

8   Is it any different in the United States?

9   What do overseas Codes of Ethics and Charters of Editorial Responsibility say about such situations?

10   Are there occasions where you would disobey police directions (or requests) to 'get the story'?

11   Where do you draw the line?

12   Research the transcript of Mike Willessee's interview with the killers, and the children ('I'd Rather Have Been Killing Cops' 1993). Debate it from the point of view of the journalist wanting a 'great story', the perspective of the editor 'back in the office', the police trying to negotiate with the killers, what psychiatrists would say about the contents of the interview, and the reaction of the public.

13   What are the lessons to be learned from this sorry chapter of Australian tabloid journalism?

14   Should the MEAA have adopted the 'Cangai clauses' in the revised Code of Ethics?

→ ## Case study 3
Mt Tambourine bus crash

In September 1990, a tourist bus crashed on a steep mountain road near the Gold Coast hinterland village of Mt Tambourine in southern Queensland. Several media crews arrived before emergency service personnel and began filming and attempting to interview survivors and witnesses. A helicopter flew close to the accident scene spraying debris over the injured and the rescue teams. An Anglican police chaplain, Father Wal Ogle, who was present at the scene, accused the media of being 'cheap ghouls with purely animal instincts' for their intrusiveness and coverage of the accident. He was critical of the media for impeding the rescue operation and for not offering assistance to the injured. He also accused a television crew of 'poking a microphone and camera in the face of a very seriously injured woman while there were dead bodies lying around her' ('Rector Slams News "Ghouls"' 1990). He was also critical of the fact that the media were asked four times to leave an area that had been set aside for the dead and the injured. On every occasion they went back into that area for pictures. In 1991, the Department of Journalism at the University of Queensland produced a series of videos titled *Dilemmas in Media Ethics* (Apps & Rexa 1991) in which cases raising ethical issues were discussed by a panel. One such case was the Mt Tambourine bus crash. Rev. Gerry Healy, a member of the violence and grief intrusion panel, emphasised the need for media personnel to consider the effects of news coverage and photographs on the bereaved. He criticised the *Courier-Mail* for its photographs of the dead passengers, which caused distress to friends and relatives, who should be able to remember the dead as they were when alive.

Issues and questions raised by case study 3

1   Lawrence Apps, then on the University of Queensland journalism staff and host of the discussion on the Mt Tamborine incident, asked: 'Is the first obligation of media personnel arriving at the scene of a disaster to get pictures, get the story, get interviews, or to assist with those who are injured or to comfort them if they have no first aid assistance?' What's your view?
2   Is it up to the individual camera crews and journalists on such occasions to decide what to shoot, and conversely, what not to shoot?
3   Isn't it the general rule to shoot now, and decide what to use in consultation with your superiors back in the office?
4   Who do you think should have the final say on what pictures go to air?
5   Does the time of the day make any difference? Should less graphic images be shown on the main news bulletins (at 6 p.m., say) than might be used in the late-night bulletin?
6   Research the Mt Tamborine incident and debate the issues involved in the coverage from the points of view of the journalist on the scene, the emergency workers trying to go about their business, the chief of staff back at the office and the relatives of the victims watching the TV coverage that night.

Case study 4
The Moura Mine disasters—1986 and 1994

After a serious accident that killed twelve men at the Moura coal mine in Queensland in July 1986, the media descended on the town and tried to get interviews with friends and relatives of the victims. A television crew, desperate for a story, knocked on the door of a miner's home at 1.30 a.m. because lights were on in the house and they thought the occupants might be relatives of a victim. They offered the miner's pregnant wife money for her story (Apps 1986, p. 12). The mine chaplain, Father Dennis Vanderwolf, exposed the journalists' actions the next day. Relations between miners, the police, and rescue officials on the one side and reporters on the other were very tense.

The local community was outraged and threatened to 'ride the journalists out of town on a rail', or to beat them up. The local police inspector warned reporters they would be arrested if they set foot on the homes of grieving families (Apps 1986). But some reporters turned up at a prayer meeting for the grieving families and were chased away by the Anglican Archbishop of Rockhampton, Bishop George Hearn, who threatened to use his bishop's staff 'in the way it was originally intended to be used' (Tate 1986). Some commentators suggested that the media became scapegoats for anger that miners and their families felt at a time of intense grief (Hurst & White 1994, p. 115).

On 7 August 1994, there was a second major explosion at the Moura mine and this time eleven miners died. Their bodies were never recovered. This time the media was more respectful of family and friends and managed to avoid incurring the wrath of locals (Lawrence 2003).

Issues and questions raised by case study 4

1   What should be your approach to someone who has just lost a loved one?
2   Would you use an intermediary, like a local church minister, or friend?
3   Under what circumstances is a grief-intruding 'death-knock' justified?
4   What do you think would be your reaction, if you were on 'the other end' of a death-knock?
5   The Code of Ethics allows journalists to decline to do a death-knock. Would you?
6   What would be the range of possible reactions by your chief of staff to your decision *not* to do a death-knock?
7   Some journalists are reluctant to knock back a death-knock for fear of what affect it will have on their career. Do you think that view prevails in newsrooms in the early twenty-first century?

→   ## Case study 5

Sharks on land: A South Australian family's grief

In June 1993, Therese Cartwright, mother of five (including quadruplets), was taken by a shark while scuba diving with her husband and some friends off the South Australian coast. Only remains of her body were recovered. The victim's husband Ian Cartwright and the five children were on the boat when the tragedy occurred. After the attack, Mr Cartwright tried to shield his family from the media to lessen their grief. The media reported his wife's demise in graphic detail, reporting which body parts had been recovered. Mr Cartwright was naturally upset by the graphic nature of the material published and requested privacy. The media that filmed the man in obvious distress at his wife's funeral ignored this. The children knew exactly what was in their mother's coffin.

The grieving husband also had to handle inaccurate reporting of issues irrelevant to the death of his wife. The media insinuated an untruth: that his wife was on an in vitro program by which she had had her quadruplets. At the funeral, the media ignored Mr Cartwright's plea for privacy. Church members had to fend off photographers, television crews, and reporters who tried to enter. As the family was driving away, camera lenses were focused on the inside of the car in an attempt to get footage of the distressed husband in tears. He received thirty to forty calls a day from the media who were trying to contact him for his story. ABC television came to his house and spoke to a lady who told them Mr Cartwright wanted no contact with the media. The television crew then left, but not before filming the washing line with the babies' nappies on it. A prominent women's magazine and a commercial television channel both offered Mr Cartwright a substantial sum of money for his story.

After being counselled that he had no right to refuse these offers for the sake of his children, he refused them on the grounds that it would feel like prostitution to make money out of his wife's death. Looking back, Mr Cartwright believes the media made the death of his wife even harder to cope with. Mr Cartwright says the media:

> ... generated pressure which made me less able to cope with my grief, and reading in the gutter press a description of how your wife has been torn apart is the most distressing thing, it aroused emotions in me I didn't know I had.
>
> Quoted in Gillespie 1993

Issues and questions raised by case study 5

1   If a person in grief doesn't want to talk to you, what can you do?
2   A death-knock is just an excuse for trying to show someone under extreme emotional distress. Discuss.
3   Is the death-knock really worth all the bother it usually causes on all sides?
4   As we've seen in an earlier context, family members at a funeral can attack journalists covering the event. What would you do under the circumstances?
5   Is there a discreet way of behaving in such trying circumstances?
6   What if a member of your family became suddenly 'famous' and was 'hounded' by the media. What could you do to help?
7   Wouldn't common decency dictate that when asked, you leave people to their grief?
8   What part of that wouldn't your chief of staff understand?
9   Is there a case for all media agreeing to leave grieving relatives alone?
10 Do you think all sections of the media would abide by the agreement?

Case study 6   ←

Are the families of politicians entitled to privacy?

Case A: Australian Prime Minister Bob Hawke appears on television and talks about proposed new laws against drug suppliers. He breaks down and cries when talking about what drugs do to people, young people in particular. Hawke's wife, Hazel, is left to reveal later that one of their daughters is suffering from a drug problem.

Case B: The *Sunday Telegraph* headlines its front page 'Senator's Tragedy' with a sub-heading 'Son, 19, Dies After Two Years of Hell'. The story details how Senator John Button, then Opposition leader in the Senate, had lost a two-year battle to save his teenage son from the grip of heroin. David Button died of an overdose. The paper quotes 'close friends' about the family's anguish and the 'senator's feelings of help-lessness, knowing that his career in federal politics kept him away from home for long periods'. While much of the story concerns Senator Button's anguish, and that of the family, it centres around the death of his son (Lynch 1982).

Here are two cases where the story hinges on a relative, not the person in the public position of accountability. Had they not had such prominent close relatives, it is unlikely the two people concerned (a daughter and a son) would have received such wide media coverage. Generally, the mass media ignores the private lives of politicians (and other prominent figures) unless the story can be linked in some way to their public life, as in the Andrew Bartlett and Cheryl Kernot/Gareth Evans cases discussed above. In the case of politicians that usually means it having some affect on their political activities.

Invading privacy doesn't seem to bother the 'downmarket' weekly tabloids and magazines. who thrive on scandal about the families of the rich and famous. Obviously there's a difference when the information becomes public, and the husband (or wife) discusses it with the media, but in the cases above, the politicians sought no public notoriety for their children.

SENATOR'S TRAGEDY

Son, 19, dies after two years of hell

By Paul Lynch

SENATOR John Button, Opposition Leader in the Senate, has lost a two-year battle to save his teenage son from the deadly grip of heroin.

With his family he endured the long months of hell trying to pull him back from the brink. But the fight ended in tragedy when 19-year-old David Button died of an overdose on May 28.

Close friends said yesterday the family's anguish was made worse by the senator's feelings of helplessness, knowing that his career in federal politics kept him away from home for long periods.

With his wife Marjorie and sons, Jamie and Nick, Senator Button — a Victorian Labor senator — is in seclusion in the country this weekend to share their grief and pick up the pieces of their shattered lives.

Yesterday a family friend spoke about the courage with which Senator Button and David confronted the heroin problem.

● Continued Page 3

Issues and questions raised by case study 6

1   Is the son/daughter/wife/husband of a prominent person entitled to any privacy?
2   When is the private life of a relative of a prominent person no longer private?
3   How prominent does the person need to be?
4   The son of the local country Mayor is picked up on a drink-driving charge. Your paper has a policy of not necessarily reporting every charge heard in the local Magistrate's Court. The police prosecutor mentions in court that the accused is a member of a prominent local family, without making the direct connection to the Mayor. Would you report the case?
5   If you do, how much would you disclose?
6   Would you identify the offender as the son of the Mayor?
7   What if it was the son of a municipal Mayor in a big capital city?
8   What if it was the daughter of your editor or owner?
9   What if the son or daughter of the Prime Minister was charged with drink-driving after a night out with some friends from university?
10   Is there a scale of prominence?

Case Study 7   ←

The family of a crooked policeman

In December 1995, the Royal Commission into corrupt NSW police officers was shown surveillance camera video of Detective Sergeant Wayne Eade discussing drug deals and the purchase of a child-pornography video with a prostitute, who was also an informer for the Commission. Royal Commissioner James Wood released copies of the tape (with some segments edited out) to the media and it was shown several times on prime time news and current affairs programs. The officer's family became embroiled in the controversy, even though Wayne Eade had separated from his wife and children some time before the video was shown. Mrs Susan Eade and her 16-year-old son, Daniel, appeared on Channel Nine's *A Current Affair*, to tell Australia how her life had been ruined by the showing of her disgraced husband's actions.

The president of the NSW police union, Phil Tuncheon, said many innocent victims would suffer as the result of such scenes being shown on television. Church groups also condemned the screening of the surveillance camera tapes. A spokesperson for the Catholic Church, Father Brian Lucas, said it was inappropriate to show when families would be watching television. The NSW Council of Churches also asked the Royal Commission and television stations to show more restraint. Commissioner Wood justified his actions on the grounds of public interest. He also said that showing such material would act as a warning to other corrupt police officers that they could not get away with cheating the public any longer (Barnsley 1995; Henderson 1996). An editorial in the tabloid *Daily Telegraph Mirror* called for sensitivity in the airing of such video evidence ('Discretion is the Key to Fairness' 1995). The editorial said it was not a question of censorship, but of taste. The editorial also said that the public value of such information was 'dubious'. However, a *Sydney Morning Herald* editorial supported Justice Wood and the public showing of surveillance material ('Police Videos' 1995). The editorial said there was an 'obvious sympathy' for Mrs Eade and her family, but that in the end 'the possibility that corrupt behaviour may be exposed to the world—and their families—may be the best weapon to beat corrupt officers into submission'.

Issues and questions raised by case study 7

1   What questions does the use of police surveillance video raise for you?
2   Given the opportunity, would you use the material on all occasions?
3   What wouldn't you show?
4   What guidelines do you think would be appropriate for the use of such material?
5   Do you think the media cares about what effects the publishing of such material will have on the families concerned?
6   Should that be a criterion? Why? Why not?

→   ## Case study 8
Port Arthur: Family privacy

Life in Tasmania was changed for ever on Sunday 28 April 1996. A man in his late 20s opened fire with a semi-automatic weapon in a crowded café at the famous Port Arthur historic site. By the time he stopped firing, thirty-five people were dead, dozens more wounded. Martin Bryant would become Australia's most deadly mass killer. The media frenzy was incredible. Facts were scarce in the early hours after the shooting. The names of those that had been killed or wounded were not released to the media, though some identifying features were known and reported. Among the rumoured dead was a tour bus driver, people from several states, and visitors from outside Australia (Dugdale 1996). Bryant was taken into custody after an all-night siege at a nearby farmhouse.

The media was kept well away from the siege and the scene of the earlier killings. The shock of the events at Port Arthur was met with several responses. The scale of the deaths meant a large number of people from around Australia, as well as overseas families of tourists killed and wounded, were directly affected. From the day after the massacre newspaper editors and artists were able to put together minute-by-minute accounts of what happened: 'He just picked them out and shot them' (Vincent 1996). There was no TV footage of the shooting, or the bodies, so graphic artists had to devise alternative representations.

For the first week after the arrest and charging of Martin Bryant, the coverage focused on the victims and the accused. There was a media-initiated debate over Bryant's 'state of mind'. Was he, or not, schizophrenic? The grieving at Port Arthur and the funerals in the following week provided many photo opportunities. On a few occasions mourners did object to the presence of cameras and journalists, however it seemed that in many cases the media was welcomed, or at least tolerated. A week after the incident, the news focus was on Bryant's mental health, but the images were of family members of victims, mourning at the site of the murders.

Issues and questions raised by case study 8

1   What problems arise from being among the first at the scene of a major story when details are sketchy?
2   What credence can you put on the recollections of eyewitnesses to such horrible events?
3   When the story is 'so big' do you just report everyone's views on what happened?
4   What are the dangers in reporting sketchy details of where the unnamed victims may have come from?
5   What is the affect of such information on people 'back home'?
6   Discuss the ethics of 'doing whatever it takes' to get the first photo of an accused.
7   Martin Bryant looked mad, didn't he? And he shot all those people in cold blood. He must be mad. Shouldn't be too hard to find someone to say that, should it?
8   You need to attend the funeral of the victims. It is a legitimate news story and follow-up to a major national tragedy. But how do you do it discreetly?
9   What would you do if the families of the victims approached you and asked you to leave?
10   Put yourself in their shoes. How would you have reacted to the saturation coverage of the tragedy and all the graphic details of what happened to your loved one(s)?

Case study 9
ACA and the unfortunate suicide

After receiving a complaint about a Sydney electrical repair shop, Nine's *A Current Affair* decided to test the claim by sending its own equipment to the shop. It had an expert damage two CD players, an amplifier, and a video recorder. After they were returned from the repair shop, they were checked again by the expert and *ACA* said it had been over-charged on each item. Reporter Jane Hansen confronted the owner of the shop, Benny Mendoza, accusing him of overcharging and in one case of not doing any work at all on the item. The story alleging overcharging went to air on Monday 18 August 1997. On Thursday 21 August, Mr Mendoza, a father of two, hanged himself in his garage. *A Current Affair* host Ray Martin read a prepared statement at the end of the following night's program in which he extended deepest sympathies to the family. That weekend's edition of the *Sun Herald* filled its front page with the story of 'TV Reporter's Pain over Suicide' (Hannan & Crittle 1997). The main page one headline read 'Sorry Will Not Bring Him Back' (Dasey 1997). Hansen was reported as saying she wished she'd never done the story, but stopped short of saying she was sorry. Mr Mendoza's relatives were quoted as demanding to know what right *A Current Affair* had to be 'judge, jury and executioner'.

The reporter said the repairman gave no hint he was suicidal during her dealings with him. *ACA* executive producer at the time, David Hurley, was quoted as saying: 'In the end, when all is said and done, no story is worth a death.'

Issues and questions raised by case study 9

1   Petty crooks are popular fare on TV current affairs programs. If they 'diddle' the public, don't they deserve to be exposed on national television?
2   The repairman in question may have not done all the repairs he charged for, but did he deserve to be 'outed' on a high-rating national program seen around the country?
3   As the family asked, who voted *ACA* judge, jury, and executioner?
4   How could the reporter (and the program's producers) possibly know that the story would have such an affect on Mr Mendoza that he would take his life?
5   Mr Mendoza had come to Australia from the Philippines 13 years before. Should the reporter have made enquiries about his cultural heritage?
6   The reporter probably knew that her story would ruin his business. Should she have thought through the ramifications more?
7   Do you think the average current affairs reporter (or news reporter for that matter) thinks about the ramifications of their stories *before* they air them?
8   What do you know about the cultures of other countries in relation to matters of public esteem and shame?

→ # Case study 10
The privacy of royals and celebrities

We've discussed in the opening pages of this book, and mentioned briefly in this chapter, the controversy surrounding the death of the 'People's Princess', Diana, and the accusation that she was hounded to her death by an over-zealous media. In the wake of Diana's death, and after calls for privacy for the Princess's two boys, Princes William and Harry, a gentlemen's agreement was reached between the media and Buckingham Palace that would keep the two boys out of the public limelight. After the death of Diana in 1997, the media in the UK agreed to allow her two boys to grow up without 'the constant hounding of the paparazzi she had to endure' ('Media Truce With Royals Falls Apart' 2003). But by mid 2003, the truce seemed to be breaking up. Since it was revealed that Harry had been caught drinking, smoking, and taking drugs, the papers and the paparazzi could hardly contain their eagerness to snap Harry with a drink or a cigarette—hopefully both—in his hand. The boys' father, Prince Charles, and his lover, Camilla Parker-Bowles, have had to contend with media attention for years. In 1999, a British tabloid published a picture of the then royal bride-to-be, Sophie Rhys-Jones, showing her breast exposed ('Sophie Print a Cruel Act, Say Palace' 1999). Buckingham Palace condemned the publication as 'premeditated cruelty'. The picture was in the

Sun, Britain's largest-selling tabloid, and had been taken by a colleague during a business trip to Spain in 1988. It showed some horseplay in which a colleague pulled up Sophie's bikini top, exposing one breast, and both Sophie and her colleague are pictured laughing ('Sophie Print a Cruel Act, Say Palace' 1999). Such is the price of fame.

Film, music, and sports stars are always having to cope with unwanted media attention and reading some truth, and much fiction, about their lives in the tabloids and gossip magazines. But in mid 2003, the rich and famous of Hollywood had something else to contend with—Los Angeles police officers selling their 'secrets' to America's supermarket tabloids ('Snooping LA Cops Sell Off Star Secrets' 2003). Australian model Elle Macpherson and actors Sharon Stone, Courteney Cox, Sean Penn, Halle Berry, Meg Ryan, and Drew Barrymore were said to be among hundreds of celebrities whose police profiles were handed over to the tabloids (McKenna 2003). Among the information kept in restricted police databases are addresses, phone numbers, driving and car records, as well as more sensitive information like restraining orders, criminal history, and arrests that did not result in prosecutions.

Issues and questions raised by case study 10

1   We've seen in case study 6 above that politicians are considered public figures and deserving of little privacy. Are members of the royal family any different?
2   'Royalty have been carrying on like this for centuries, we're just showing the public what they're like', goes the oft-used tabloid editor's justification. What do you think?
3   What makes royalty so special that we shouldn't know what they get up to?
4   Conversely, what benefit is there is seeing Prince Harry having a drink or a smoke? Or publishing a photo of a partially topless Sophie Rhys-Jones?
5   How much privacy does your average sports, film, or music superstar deserve?
6   Doesn't the public make them superstars by watching them play, going to the pictures, or a concert? Are they then public property, open to scrutiny?
7   How would you like to be one of the Beckhams?
8   'If the public didn't want to read and see this stuff, there wouldn't be a market for it' is another media justification. And they're right—*New Idea* et al. sell extremely well—so aren't they just catering to readers' needs?
9   Is it the role of the media to give its audience what it wants, however titillating, or to raise the ethical bar a bit?

Case study 11

Kerry Packer and a plea for privacy

On 6 October 1990, Australia's richest man, media mogul Kerry Packer, was playing polo at Sydney's Warwick Farm racecourse when he suffered a massive heart attack. His heart stopped for eight minutes, but he was revived by an ambulance crew using a defibrillator (which produces an electric shock to restart the heart's normal rhythm). Just six days later he was involved in a heated confrontation with television news crews and photographers at another polo match (Sutton 1990). He is alleged to have grabbed a camera from a Murdoch newspaper photographer and torn out the film. The photographer was punched twice by a Packer aide. Mr Packer reportedly scuffled with TV crews, including a crew from his own Nine Network. From the comfort of a white BMW, the 'big fella' was watching his (then teenaged) son James playing polo, until reporters (surprised to see him there less than a week after a serious heart attack) approached and asked about his condition. At first the car pulled away, but it stopped seconds later and Mr Packer walked back towards the news crews. During the following confrontation he attempted to cover the lens of a television camera, saying: 'Go away. Leave me alone' (Sutton 1990). Days after recovering from the heart attack, Mr Packer donated $2.5 million to split the cost with the New South Wales Government of fitting defibrillators into most of the state's ambulances (Cromie 1997). The defibrillators are now affectionately referred to in NSW as 'Packer Whackers'.

Issues and questions raised by case study 11

1   Does it surprise you that the owner of the Nine Network that produces several gossip magazines, the daily current affairs program *A Current Affair*, which regularly invades people's privacy in the name of a good story, and *The Bulletin,* whose columnist Laurie Oakes released details of the Cheryl Kernot/Gareth Evans affair, should be pleading for 'privacy'?

2   Shouldn't he, of all people, realise that the media is always going to follow newsmakers, and Australia's richest man almost dying and then appearing six days later to watch his son play polo has got to be a story well worth chasing?

3   Wouldn't the opposition—the other TV channels, and the Fairfax and Murdoch press—have loved it when he reacted as so many others have to unwanted attention from the media?

4.   Aside from the amusing thought of some form of payback, what reasons were there for the media to be interested in the well-being of Australia's richest man?

5   What would be the reaction be, do you think, of those who have been on the receiving end of *A Current Affair's* unwanted attention?

6   What would be the reaction on the stock market of Kerry Packer reportedly being seriously ill?

7   What was the reaction when rumours that Kerry Packer had died of a heart attack in London swept Australian stock exchanges in June 1998?

8   Does Kerry Packer deserve special treatment from the media?

9   Would your opinion about this story be different if you worked for the Nine Network?

8

THE NEWS MEDIA AND THE JUSTICE SYSTEM

Objectives

After reading and discussing this chapter you will appreciate:

- The different forms of 'trial by media'.
- Where law and ethics collide.
- How journalistic ethics are sometimes compromised through the media's interaction with the legal system.
- The media's fascination with criminal activity.
- The media excitement surrounding celebrity trials.
- How the media hounded former Governor-General, Dr Peter Hollingworth.

Introduction: Trial by media

On 22 April 2003, the partly clothed bodies of Neelma Singh, 24, her brother, Kunal, 18, and sister Sidhi, 12, were found under a blanket in the overflowing spa of the en-suite in their parents' home in Bridgeman Downs in Brisbane's north-west (Hansen 2003). They were killed while their parents, father Vijay, an auto parts importer, and their mother, Shirley, were on a business trip to Fiji. The Singh's eldest daughter, Sonia, 26, was not in the home at the time of the killings. Police said early in their investigation that they believed someone known to the family made an unforced entry into the home on Easter Sunday evening and bludgeoned two of the three children to death and strangled the other as they slept in their separate bedrooms, then dragged them into the en suite (Roberts 2003a). The bodies were found by Max Sica, 33, who said he was the former boyfriend of one of the victims, Neelma. Members of the Singh family publicly contradicted Mr Sica's claim that the pair were close, or contemplating marriage.

Police repeatedly described Mr Sica as 'a witness, not a suspect' (Roberts 2003a). In an interview with the *Australian* about five weeks after he'd discovered the bodies, Mr Sica called on police to charge him with the murders so he could clear his name. 'I want to have my day in court. The way things are right now I haven't got a life,' he said (Macfarlane 2003a). Sica said police and media harassment had made him a prisoner in his parents' home since the discovery of the bodies. 'Most of my friends won't let me in the gate. When I walk on the street people look at me funny—"is that the guy that killed those three people?"' Mr Sica added (Macfarlane 2003a).

In its search for angles on the case, the media had earlier revealed that Max Sica had been jailed for nine years in 1993 for what was described as a 'grand rampage of lawlessness'. His crimes included burning down a police station and setting fire to a school and a shopping centre. He had pleaded guilty to eighty-three offences, including arson, wilful damage, breaking and entering, endangering life, and unlawful use of motor vehicles during a six-month period in 1990 (Macfarlane 2003b). Senior detectives said they were stunned at Sica's outburst (D'Arcy 2003a). The surviving sister, Sonia Pathik, said she did not believe the 'self-confessed suspect' was the killer: 'Nobody is blaming him, so why is he doing that to himself?' (Dibben 2003). Mr Sica also spoke to the *Courier-Mail* about the suspicion he felt surrounded him. He said his criminal history had been aired prominently in the media and he thought the media was a 'willing accomplice in a case that has not been formally made against him' (Murray 2003). Mr Sica maintained a keen interest in media coverage of the investigation: 'He buys the newspaper as early as 3am when he expects a story to appear and monitors news on different television stations and from outlets as far away as the Gold Coast's local paper' (Murray 2003).

The Singh and Sica families had lived alongside each other in the Brisbane suburb of Stafford Heights for about a decade after the Singhs arrived from Fiji in 1990. Mr Sica tried to attend the slain children's funeral on 14 May 2003, but was removed by detectives at the request of the Singh family (D'Arcy 2003b). Six months after the gruesome killings, as we were writing this book, the investigation was continuing, and the police still considered Mr Sica a witness, not a suspect (Hansen 2003). At this point there are no other 'persons of interest' to the police whose identities have been made public. By his own bizarre actions Max Sica has remained in the public spotlight. He has consistently denied any involvement in the murders and has been offering to tell his story to any media outlet that will listen.

Max Sica certainly appears to be, in his own mind and in the public arena, a possible suspect in the Singh murders, in part because of the media's fascination with this gruesome case. The Singh–Sica case highlights some of the fault lines between the media and the justice system in a capitalist liberal democracy.

In this chapter we examine the phenomena of 'trial by media' from the point of view of coverage of criminal or civil matters that are, or might be, before the courts. Trial by media normally refers to the pre-judging by the media of an accused person during the *sub judice* period—that is, after they have been charged and before their case has been decided. But there's a more common, less legal, 'trial by media' where no charge has been laid against the person at the centre of media attention—such as Max Sica. There may never be criminal charges laid in this or similar cases, but the media (or individual media outlets or writers/ commentators) decides to 'try' the person in the 'court of public debate'. This chapter will focus on this lego–ethical grey area. In the next chapter we will focus on trial by media in a less formal sense in the coverage of ethnicity, race, and the criminalisation of young people.

As well as Australian examples, detailed reference is made to a landmark American case where cameras have vied with judges and juries to be centre stage in pronouncing issues of guilt or innocence. In the O.J. Simpson case, the American football star accused of murdering his wife and her boyfriend, the media had tried and convicted the high-profile athlete before his trial had even got under way.

In another case, the bashing of black motorist Rodney King by Los Angeles police officers, the 'onus of proof' was reversed. The camera caught several officers clearly beating and kicking King. The Los Angeles courts found insufficient evidence to convict most of the alleged offenders. The impact of the footage had been so powerful that the poor and black neighbourhoods of east LA erupted into days of angry street fighting and rioting. This is Case Study 4 in the next chapter.

Is it law or ethics?

Before we move on to discuss 'trial by media', we first need to distinguish between what the law says and what 'good' ethics would have us do. Though they do at times overlap (as in the issue of confidentiality of sources), 'law' and 'ethics' have different conditions and meanings for journalists. The law is indisputable: it is referred to as 'black letter'. The legal system applies to everyone, including journalists, and in theory everyone is equal before the law. The law is contestable only through the courts. Ethics, on the other hand, as we've already seen, are fuzzy, moral concepts that are often contentious and always open to debate. In this chapter we are concerned about the ethics of the news media when it is operating in the context of the legal system. This is why we refer to some issues as 'ethico–legal'. The 'black letter' legal position is 'greyed out' by the question of ethics.

The media has a fascination with reporting criminal activity, particularly if the offences involve 'sex crimes and murders'. Hurst and White (1994) have noted how this fascination has been a staple of the Australian media since at least the 1840s, while critics continue to express 'distaste and occasional revulsion'. Today crime stories tend to dominate the television news and the tabloid newspapers, despite the fact that experts constantly argue that crime rates are not 'exploding' and that Australia is not in the grip of a 'crime wave' (Grabosky & Wilson 1989; Cowdery 2001). Thus for the journalist an immediate paradox presents itself: how to balance the needs of the news media for exciting and 'gripping' stories with the needs of the community to have accurate and honest information when it comes to crime. John Hurst and Sally White outlined several areas of crime reporting that highlight the contradictions and the ethico–legal dilemmas:

- Conflict between full disclosure of facts and the 'right' to a fair trial for all accused persons.
- The glorification of criminal activity and the 'encouragement' of copy-cat crime.
- The disproportionate space that crime stories receive in the media and the actual crime rate.
- Conflicts between the needs of the police and the needs of the news media.
- Endangering public safety on one hand, or living up to an 'obligation' to the authorities to 'assist' them in maintaining law and order.
- The problem of the reporter becoming part of the story when criminal activity is under investigation.

- Presenting material in such a way that it causes distress to the audience, or to relatives of the criminal or victims of crime.
- Intrusion into privacy of victims, witnesses, and families (Hurst & White 1994, pp. 83–4).
  Hurst and White (1994, p. 110) describe crime reporting as an 'ethical labyrinth', and an area where 'journalists are most powerfully confronted with the conflicts of their profession'. We will return to these ideas later in the chapter, but for now, let us examine some of the classic 'trial by media' cases of the past 10 years.

What is 'trial by media'?

In this book we offer two definitions and discussions of 'trial by media'. In the next chapter we tackle the issues of representation and reporting and the ways in which the media informally puts 'on trial' various minority groups through stereotyping, ignorance, wilful prejudice, or through just plain sloppy and weak journalism. In this chapter we are concentrating on the interaction of the news media and the legal system (police and courts). In this sense 'trial by media' is also bound up with issues of contempt of court, but we will leave it to the legal texts to get heavily into that topic. All we will say is that in many incidents where 'trial by media' can be detected, journalists and news organisations walk very close to the line between fair comment on legal matters, the *sub-judice* rule, and contempt of court. For example, in the case of the Singh murders, if someone is eventually charged, the coverage of Max Sica and his identification with the case could be an issue for both the prosecution and the defence. Though technically the media is not in contempt for reporting of the case so far because no one has been charged (as of July 2004).

'Trial by media', while multi-faceted, often amounts to the media taking on the roles of judge, jury, and executioner in much the same way as it does in the instances of invasion of privacy recounted in the previous chapter. In the Singh case it would appear that Max Sica believes that by putting himself 'on trial' in the media he will clear his name. However, it is more usual for the media to assume 'guilt' and then to vilify the accused, regardless of the legal requirements, such as 'innocence until proven guilty'. The issue represents a very clear fault line—one that exists between the news media and the police—and one that gets stepped on regularly. In the context of 'trial by media', the cases tend to take on a life of their own. The media may defend itself by saying it reports the facts of a case, but once they are 'out in the open' the stories are churned up in the 'rumour mill' and further 'enhanced' by the utterances of radio's shock-jocks. If caught out, the media will usually offer corrections where stories are proven wrong (but rarely with the same prominence as the original story). By that time the audience largely believes 'there is no smoke without fire' (to use yet another cliché) and a person's reputation is often ruined before they have their day in court. The media's actions can also lead to contempt of court charges, as we shall see.

Human headline: Opens mouth to change feet

In April 1996, flamboyant media personality, Derryn Hinch, appeared in a Melbourne court on contempt charges. It wasn't the first time—he had been fined sums of up to

$25,000 (later reduced to $15,000 on appeal), and sentenced to six weeks' jail (also reduced in the same appeal to 28 days) on three separate occasions in the 1980s ('Hinch's Shame File' 1996). The 'human headline' was facing a possible jail sentence for naming a child sexual assault victim on his short-lived television show on the Ten Network, *Hinch*. It was Hinch's conviction on a similar charge in 1987 that led to him spending time in Melbourne's Pentridge prison, making him the first Australian journalist in 50 years to be sent to prison for contempt of court (Schwartz 1987). Hinch closed his 3AW program in Melbourne on the day of his court appearance with the comment: 'I may not be here tomorrow'. And he wasn't, heading instead to Pentridge jail after one of his famed long lunches (Schwartz 1987). The High Court had rejected his appeal against the 28-day sentence and $15,000 fine, which resulted from his on-air comments in the case of a Catholic priest charged with child sex offences. He had dwelt on priest Father Glennon's prior convictions, suggesting his guilt in advance of his trial ('The Jailing of Mr Hinch' 1987).

At the time he was facing court *again* in 1996 Hinch was also in the news after separating from his wife, actress Jacki Weaver. This time he had named an eight-year-old sexual assault victim, and was relieved to be fined $2000 and not receive the three-week jail term he had expected (Das 1996). Channel Ten was fined $1500 but the company was not convicted. Hinch had originally been acquitted the year before, but the Supreme Court overturned the ruling. Hinch lost his appeal against that decision, and appeared on 18 April to be sentenced for the offence. He had revealed the child's name in an interview with his father on 22 November 1992. Hinch said: 'I still believe I was morally right, but I've been proven legally wrong' (Das 1996). Oops, it seems that the legal system doesn't recognise moral 'right' when a legal 'wrong' has been committed. The law, too, is 'absolute'.

While we're on the subject of broadcasters flouting the law, the nation's best-known radio announcer, the man with the golden tonsils, John Laws, was given a 15-month suspended sentence in September, 2000, for interviewing a former juror on his popular morning program. He had been found guilty of breaching the New South Wales Jury Act. On 6 April 1998, Laws interviewed a woman who had been a juror in the trial of two men acquitted of murdering a computer shop owner. Laws, who had known the woman for almost 50 years, started the interview by saying: 'Tell me exactly how this whole thing transpired' (Gibbs 2000). The woman then made a series of disclosures about what happened in the jury room, including how she had unsuccessfully begged other jurors not to acquit the men.

In his summing up at the trial Justice James Wood said:

> It is obvious that Mr Laws is well able financially to pay a substantial fine, yet I do not consider that a fine, even up to the maximum available for the offence of $110,000, would of itself provide sufficient by way of personal or general deterrence or by way of punishment for this offence. By reason of Mr Laws's high profile and his well-known stand on issues of law and order, I believe that he would face a significant risk of personal injury or worse if sentenced to periodic detention. Home detention would risk attracting the derision of the community, and provide a juicy subject for lampoon by cartoonists and columnists, which would threaten respect for the law.

Cited in Gibbs 2000.

All this appeared under the headline 'Laws Too Famous To Jail, Says Judge'. The *SMH* coverage ended by noting that Laws left the court smiling (Gibbs 2002).

Putting the accused on 'parade'

One of the most insidious cooperative practices between the police and the news media is the arranged display of an accused so that the photographers and news cameras can get the shots they need to illustrate a story. Most times the accused will cover their head with a jacket (or some other piece of clothing), but the TV crews get their shots. The right to privacy, if it is to mean anything at all, must also include the rights of accused persons not to be paraded before the television cameras, particularly when this constitutes contempt of court. Despite this simple rule, police contacts still offer to 'parade' subjects for cooperative camera crews. What is perhaps worse is that many reporters and news organisations regularly accept such offers and make use of the footage or photographs obtained by this dubious method. The most famous example in recent Australian history was perhaps the case of former senior detective Harry Blackburn.

In 1989 Blackburn was still a serving officer in the NSW police service when he was falsely accused of being a serial rapist and was arrested. After being formally charged, Harry Blackburn was led through a 'media scrum' outside police headquarters in a prearranged move designed to get his face into the papers and on television. The case against Blackburn was dismissed when it was shown that there was not a shred of evidence against him. It emerged that corrupt officers within the NSW police service were intent on discrediting Blackburn, who was known to be a 'white knight' among many officers who were found to be corrupt by subsequent inquiries.

As the case studies at the end of this chapter highlight, the Harry Blackburn case was not the first, nor the last, in which these issues are raised. Australia's most sensational cases of wrong convictions being overturned, such as those of accused child killer Lindy Chamberlain, who claimed that a dingo had taken her baby, and accused conspirator in several cases involving political terrorism, former Ananda Marga sect member, Tim Anderson, are stark reminders that the news media still has much to learn on the issue of identity and respect for privacy.

The media trial of the twentieth century

American football and media personality, O.J. Simpson, was accused, tried, and acquitted of murdering his wife and her friend in a very public trial in Los Angeles, California in the mid 1990s. Simpson was subsequently found to have materially contributed to his wife's death in a civil case brought by her family. He was ordered to pay the family millions of dollars in compensation. The media circus began with the police chasing Simpson through LA and television station helicopters overhead beaming the action live around the world. When the trial got under way, a virtual television city was built outside the court (O'Connor 1994) and various media organisations tried to gain exclusive interviews with potential witnesses and jurors (Whittell 1994). Throughout the trial the major players, defence and prosecution lawyers, potential witnesses and judge Lance Ito, were not only the subject of media speculation, they in fact often gave their opinions freely in press conferences and arranged media statements.

Every minute of the trial was broadcast on 'Court TV' in America and was covered extensively in the international media. Jury members were not allowed to see any of the coverage. They were locked up in a hotel without television for the length of the trial. In the end, the public verdict was divided on Simpson's guilt, but the jury found him not guilty. Some evidence that the public was allowed to see was not presented to the jury. In an editorial at the end of the case, the *Daily Telegraph Mirror* said that 'no evidence has been advanced to suggest the trial itself was somehow compromised by the presence of cameras in court. Indeed there is a strong body of opinion to suggest the unique public scrutiny to which the trial was subjected ensured it measured up to the highest standards of legal and ethical probity' (6 October 1995: 10).

Another media circus in the making?

What was described as the largest concentration of US media outside Iraq descended on the small Colorado town of Eagle in early August 2003, for the first court hearing of a rape charge against Los Angeles Lakers basketball superstar, 24-year-old Kobe Bryant (Campbell 2003). Hundreds of reporters and television news crews (bringing with them their ubiquitous satellite trucks) were there to record the brief court appearance by Kobe, who was charged with raping a 19-year-old woman while staying at a local hotel the previous June. He publicly admitted having sex with the woman, a hotel employee, but claims it was consensual. The sports star stood to lose millions in endorsements, and if found guilty could face life in prison (Ruehl 2003). At the time of writing this book, it was shaping up as 'OJ mark 2'. As the US judicial system slowly ground along, more ethical dilemmas were arising. The tabloid *Globe* published the name and photo of Bryant's accuser in what one academic called the 'anything-goes-as-long-as-it-sells contest' (McBride 2003).

And another?

In late 2003, entertainer Michael Jackson was charged with child molestation, guaranteeing another very high profile court case. His appearance to plead not guilty to the charges in the small Californian town of Santa Maria in early January 2004 was a real media circus, with the pop star jumping onto the roof of his limousine to greet his fans (McKenna 2004). Vendors sold hot dogs, steaks, and t-shirts. Many fans had come in chartered buses and cars in a 'caravan of love' from Los Angeles and Las Vegas. After the court appearance—he was scolded by the judge for being 21 minutes late—Jackson invited the fans back to his Neverland Ranch for refreshments (McKenna 2004). Court appearances don't get much more bizarre. Earlier the giant CBS network and representatives of Jackson had denied the network paid for an interview with the beleaguered pop star for the American version of *60 Minutes*. The *New York Times* had reported that the network landed the interview by agreeing to pay $US1 million for a Jackson music special ('Jackson Interview Under Ethical Spotlight' 2004). Both sides claimed it was not a 'package deal'; the music program, a retrospective on Jackson's career, had originally been scheduled for broadcast on 26 November 2003. The show was pulled a week before its air date when Californian authorities issued an arrest warrant for the entertainer ('Jackson Interview Under Ethical Spotlight' 2004).

'Trial by media' Australian style— the hounding of a Governor-General

One of the longest-running cases of the Australian media hounding a public figure occurred at the start of the new millennium and involved the man who was then holding the highest political office in the land—the Queen's representative in Australia, Governor-General Dr Peter Hollingworth. The former Anglican Archbishop of Brisbane had earned widespread admiration for his advocacy of the underprivileged during a quarter of a century with the Brotherhood of St Laurence. As Executive Director of the Brotherhood for a decade from 1980, he championed the cause of those less fortunate, taking former Prime Minister Bob Hawke to task on child poverty, and tackling another Labor Prime Minister, Paul Keating, on social issues (Rintoul & Cameron 2003). His appointment as Governor-General was controversial from the start, blurring as it did the line between Church and State, many believing a church leader should not hold the highest office in the land. Dr Hollingworth was sworn in as Governor-General on 29 July 2001, and resigned on 25 May 2003, less than two years into his five-year term. It is perhaps fair to say Dr Hollingworth was hounded from office—but not for any wrongdoing as Governor-General. Rather it was because, as one article put it the day after his resignation, 'he was revealed as a church leader who loved the church more than he cared about child sex abuse' (Rintoul & Cameron 2003).

For nearly two years Dr Hollingworth's reputation was under almost constant attack through a series of allegations about his apparent inaction on sex abuse claims while he was Archbishop of Brisbane. In December 2001, five months after taking up the office of G-G, Dr Hollingworth was accused of failing to deal properly with complaints of child sex abuse while he was Archbishop. The accusation came after a female student of the Toowoomba (Anglican) Preparatory School and victim of serial paedophile Kevin Guy was awarded more than $800,000 (Rintoul & Cameron 2003). The former Archbishop denied involvement in a cover-up and said legal reasons inhibited his response. He was given the benefit of the doubt until 18 February 2002, when he appeared on the ABC's *Australian Story* (ABC TV 2002) to again deny a cover-up, but then imply that a 14-year-old girl had initiated a sexual relationship with a priest. He later apologised, but his successor as Anglican Archbishop of Brisbane, Phillip Aspinall, announced an inquiry into paedophilia and child abuse in church-run institutions under the Archbishop's control. The report of that inquiry, which was tabled in the Queensland Parliament, found Dr Hollingworth had made 'a serious error in judgment' in allowing a priest to continue his ministry despite knowing he was a child abuser ('Resign or be Sacked' 2003). The inquiry also found that Dr Hollingworth allowed a retired bishop to continue preaching despite knowing he had had sex with a 15-year-old girl in the 1950s ('Resign or be Sacked' 2003). The calls continued for him to resign. And the accusations kept coming.

A week after the release of the damning Anglican Church report, the Governor-General took the unprecedented step of releasing a videotaped denial that he had raped Rosemary Anne Jasmyn in Victoria in the 1960s. 'I Did Not Rape Her' screamed the front page lead of the *Gold Coast Bulletin* in a typical headline ('I Did Not Rape Her' 2003). The *Courier-Mail*'s newsagents' poster was even more blunt: 'I'm No Rapist, GG'. In his defence, Dr Hollingworth said it was a case of mistaken identity. Ms Jasmyn had died a month earlier, aged 56. TV reports suggested she had committed suicide. A former key adviser to Dr Hollingworth, Bernard Yorke, described the continuing attacks on the Governor-General as a 'modern-day crucifiction' ('A 'Crucifiction': Ex-adviser Defends His Boss' 2003). Dr Hollingworth had taken the unusual step of having a Victorian Supreme Court suppression order on the civil case against him over the allegation lifted so he could deny it ('It's a Case of Mistaken Identity: G-G' 2003). Dr Hollingworth agreed to step aside while the 40-year-old rape claims were before the court (Shanahan, Lewis & Kaszubska 2003). The civil case was dropped by the family, but the Governor-General could no longer withstand the chorus of politicians, newspaper editorials and columnists calling for his resignation. He announced his resignation on 25 May 2003, saying he was standing down in part to protect the 'dignity and integrity' of the vice-regal office (Lewis 2003). In his resignation announcement Dr Hollingworth described as 'misplaced and unwarranted' the accusations made against him (Lewis 2003). The *Australian*'s editor-at-large, Paul Kelly (2003), said the Governor-General had taken the 'only viable path open to him'. Kelly (2003) wrote that the 'Governor-General was left without any foundation of support: he incurred the hostility of the Opposition, the media, the community and finally lost the confidence of the Prime Minister who appointed him'. The example of the Governor-General is not a case of 'trial by media' in the accepted legal sense since there never was any charge against him. However, it was certainly a case that was 'tried' in the media almost daily over many months, until the weight of public opinion against Dr Hollingworth became too heavy. While not wishing to defend Dr Hollingworth's actions as Archbishop of Brisbane, we can speculate that he was a victim of the same overwhelming 'moral panic' (see chapter 9) that has come to characterise the framing of sex-related incidents involving high-profile people. We have already discussed Cheryl Kernot in this context, and one of our case studies involves the news media becoming embroiled in ethico–legal controversy around its 'capture' of a suspected paedophile in a sting operation for *60 Minutes*.

The death of David Hookes

We discussed the issue of the privacy of David Hookes's family in the previous chapter, but the incident also raises issues of 'trial by media'. Zdravko Micevic, 21, was charged with manslaughter over the assault that led to the former test cricketer's death. At a preliminary hearing, Magistrate Daniel Muling called on the media to exercise responsibility in reporting the case ('Hookes Frenzy Dismays Accused's Lawyer' 2004). *Media Watch*'s David Marr began the 2004 season with an attack on media coverage of the death commenting: 'The really heavy work the media did over the summer was to convict bouncer Zdradvo Micevic for the terrible death of cricket hero David Hookes' (Marr 2004). Marr said the media's treatment of Hookes's death was over the top 'not least in declaring Micevic guilty of an unprovoked and furious assault' (Marr 2004). He noted media databases showed 100 references in the Victorian news media to Hookes being 'bashed' and eighty-five of him being 'attacked' in the days after his death (Marr 2004). One TV station reported that the accused was already facing an assault charge, and the *Australian* published his photo on its front page. The Melbourne papers forced him out of his home by publishing the name of his street (Marr 2004). Micevic's lawyer, Brian Rolfe, said at the preliminary hearing that he had never seen such irresponsible reporting ('Hookes Frenzy Dismays Accused's Lawyer' 2004).

Bulldogs accused of pack rape

In the first half of 2004, the long-running saga over allegations of gang rape against six members of the Canterbury Bankstown rugby league team (the Bulldogs) once again pushed sex-related crime involving prominent people into the headlines (Hawse 2004). It led to acres of newsprint and hours of broadcast time being devoted to a discussion of sex crimes by sportsmen (so far no women have been accused). The allegations are shocking and if true, the perpetrators deserve to be punished. Once the story was in the mainstream media it led to many more women coming forward to claim they too had been raped and several actually named players, including AFL stars (Murphy, Denham & Davies 2004). One woman claimed that players from three clubs had been involved in raping her and that she was paid $200,000 to cover up the attack. The police charges against two players in that case were dropped. The third footballer said he contributed to the pay-out although he was never interviewed, let alone charged over the incident, 'to save my family the trauma that would have come from defending my innocence' ('Swans Star: Why I Paid "Rape" Money', 2004). Another woman came forward to claim that her mildly intellectually impaired daughter had been gang raped by four men in the Queensland city of Longreach ('Players Raped My Disabled Daughter' 2004).

While the names of most victims have been suppressed, or disguised in media reports, as required by law in sexual assault cases, some women have 'outed' themselves in the hope that by telling their stories others will be empowered to come forward. In the end, none of the Bulldogs players were charged over the incidents at Coffs Harbour and their names were kept out of the media.

While 'trial by media' is not necessarily or always about privacy, it must be considered as an issue. It is certainly an issue of individual (private) rights versus the rights of other institutions to go about their public business—the news media's right to publish facts that are in the public domain, or public interest. It's also an issue of the right of civil society (through its institutions) to conduct lawful activities in the light of public scrutiny—justice must be *seen* to be done and the legal system must be both open and accountable. However, when the news media becomes involved in high-profile legal cases, or sensational, lurid trials (such as rape cases) the rights of other individuals (family members, friends, and innocent bystanders) can get trampled in the scrum that develops around such events. Sometimes it is the news media that acts with a pack mentality, knocking out of the way anyone who stands between it and a good grab for the six o'clock news.

Ethical dilemmas in practice

→ ## Scenario 1

Covering the local Magistrate's Court, you discover a local resident has been found guilty of driving with a blood alcohol reading over the legal limit. It is your paper's policy to print the full name and address of all local drink-driving offenders. The editor believes it embarrasses the offenders and acts as a deterrent. You know the offender, Karen, has moved into the district recently to escape an abusive husband. She fears for her safety and that of her children. Do you print her name and address or should an exception be made in her case? What would you tell your editor?

Scenario 2

There has been a series of underworld murders in your capital city going back nearly a decade. Thirty crime figures have been killed, but the police have not been able to solve more than a handful of the murders. A document from the police taskforce investigating the execution-style killings is leaked to you. It contains the names of several informants and alleges that their police 'handlers' are corrupt. The material is sensational and extremely newsworthy and your gangland sources confirm it is authentic, but the police refuse to confirm its validity unless you tell them where you got the document and from whom. The police tell you that if you publish details from the report it could put the lives of several of their informants at risk. The scoop could really boost your career and several corrupt police officers could be exposed to the public. What would you do?

Case studies

Case study 1

The suspect, the body, the motive, and the coroner

This Australian case is perhaps not as well known as it should be and concerns a woman who was a journalist with SBS at the time her husband was murdered and she came under suspicion in relation to his death.

SBS executive Richard Diack's body was found in the Blue Mountains in August 1992. He had been reported missing after failing to return from a bushwalking trip. He often went alone on such walks. He had been attacked and killed. Robbery was ruled out as a motive. His wallet and watch had not been removed. His wife, SBS journalist Emilia Bresciani, was distraught. No one was charged with Richard Diack's murder after the initial police investigation. Glebe Coroner's Court was told in February 1996 by Detective Sergeant Graeme Merkel that Ms Bresciani was the only person with any possible motive to kill her husband. There was, however, the court was told, no direct evidence to show her involvement in her husband's death. Ms Bresciani responded to the allegation by saying she had been treated 'as a killer rather than as a wife' and police had been suspicious of her from the beginning. She told reporters outside the court that she was 'shattered' by the police claim. Police said Ms Bresciani had painted a very different picture of her marriage to that drawn by others, claiming it was happy when Diack's colleagues had told of his despair over the failing seven-month partnership. She told a Sunday newspaper: 'People who know me know that I didn't kill my husband. But those who don't know me will always have a doubt.' The New South Wales Bar Association's Bob Toner attacked the police in the newspaper story for failing to notify her of their suspicions so she could engage a lawyer to represent her. 'Some mud will stick,' he was quoted as telling the ABC's *7.30 Report*. 'She can defend herself in the public forum, but why should she?' (Southward, Bennett & Carmody 1996).

Issues and questions raised by case study 1

1   How would you feel under the circumstances? You've lost your partner, and a police-man tells the Coroner you're the only person with a motive?

2   Isn't it enough that she's lost a loved one? Now she has to live with the fact that police suspect her, even though she's not been charged?

3   Would you publish the police suspicions?

4   Is it a legitimate story, or were the police on a 'fishing expedition'?

5   Research what coverage the original allegation received in 1996.

6   What if the person was a professional colleague and/or a close friend? Could you write a story virtually accusing her?

→   ## Case study 2

On the hunt for 'Mr Cruel'

On 13 April 1991, 13-year-old Karmein Chan was abducted from her Melbourne home. A year later her body was found on a dump at nearby Thomastown. There were three bul-lets in her head (Daly 1996, p. 35). The Victorian police linked Karmein Chan's murder with at least thirteen attacks on other children around Melbourne from 1985 to 1988. The suspect was referred to as 'Mr Cruel' by police and media.

After her daughter's murder, Phyllis Chan would sometimes contact the parents of other abducted children. She believed that by staying in the suburb where Karmein was taken, she might be able to help the police.

The *Herald Sun* caused a stir in August 2003 when it reported that police knew who the man most likely to be Mr Cruel was, and where he lived ('Hunting Mr Cruel' 2003). Victorian police were quick to deny the report. Assistant Commissioner of Traffic, Stephen Fontana, who was one of the key investigators at the time said the claim was wrong. 'Look, we really don't know who the offender was—he could be dead, he could be interstate, he could be anywhere, we really don't know' (ABC Radio 2003). The *Herald Sun* also claimed to have discovered that police had either lost, contaminated, or destroyed vital evidence that may have convicted him (Moor 2003). The revelations came on the eve of the release of a book titled *Mugshots,* co-written by Keith Moor, who wrote a special feature on the 'Mr Cruel' case for Perth's *Sunday Times* at about the same time.

Issues and questions raised by case study 2

1   The *Herald Sun* story appeared in 2003, five years after the last death. Do you think the public would remember anything after five years?

2   Much of what was reported about this case in 2003 was based on 'hearsay' and denied by police. How would this make members of the Chan family feel after all this time?

3   Should the media report such speculation if it is not prepared to 'name names' and back up its claims?

Case study 3

Chasing down alleged paedophiles

In April 1996, it was revealed that a former Ambassador to Cambodia, John Holloway, had been charged with child sex offences, under tough new anti-paedophile laws. The former diplomat was the first Australian charged under the legislation, for allegedly procuring two Asian boys for sex. Since then several more cases have been prosecuted with varying levels of success. At the time Mr Holloway was charged by summons, one newspaper gave his name, another did not. The charges came in the same week that another alleged paedophile, Mr Phillip Bell, continued to be chased around Europe by the *Daily Telegraph*, after being named as a child sex offender by several witnesses before the NSW Police Royal Commission. The *Daily Telegraph* followed Phillip Bell from Gstaad in Switzerland to Romania, before he disappeared again, possibly for America.

Another alleged paedophile, former school teacher, Robert 'Dolly' Dunn, was seen 'perving' on young boys in a video tendered as evidence to the Wood Royal Commission. Then on 17 April, a front page 'exclusive' announced, 'Hello Dolly, We Track Hunted Paedophile To Island Hideaway' (Cater 1996a, p. 1). Having lost Bell, for now, the *Telegraph* picked up the trail of Robert Dunn and his associates, including 'former diplomat', William Stuart Brown, on the Indonesian island of Lombok. While Australian and Indonesian police were reported to be investigating Dunn, no charges had yet been laid in Australia or Indonesia. The *Telegraph* followed up with the headline, 'Charge Him' the next day (Cater 1996b, p. 1). In a companion story, the then NSW Police Minister Paul Whelan announced he'd asked the Director of Public Prosecutions to investigate the possibility of charges against him. Dunn was finally captured in a *60 Minutes* 'sting' operation in Honduras more than a year later, headed by reporter Liz Hayes (1997) and her camera crew. As one media writer commented at the time, it was a case of a well-funded TV current affairs program being able to do what 'the law' couldn't—spend up to $100,000, and several months, on an investigation that ends up netting a wanted man (Clark 1997, p. 2). Dunn was extradited to the United States and later on to Australia. The former Marist Brothers science master, then aged 60, was jailed in 2001 for 30 years after pleading guilty to twenty-four sex offences against nine boys aged as young as seven in Sydney between 1985 and 1995 (Clifton 2001). A video compiled from 250 tapes seized by police in his home was used as the main evidence against him in court (McNamara 2001). At the time of writing, it was reported that Dunn was about to appeal the 30-year sentence claiming he was double-crossed by New South Wales authorities (Barrett 2004a). He claimed he'd been given an indemnity to give evidence against three police officers (Barrett 2004a).

Issues and questions raised by case study 3

1   How could the *Daily Telegraph* track down 'Dolly' Dunn when the police seemed incapable of finding him?
2   How did *60 Minutes* track him down?
3   Is there more to this than just 'trial by media'?
4   Why is the media so obsessed with paedophilia?
5   Read the section about 'moral panics' in the following chapter and then reconsider this case study.

→   ## Case study 4

'Backpack killer' Ivan Milat on the cover of *Who Weekly* magazine

The NSW police built a careful case against their chief (only) suspect in the brutal murder of seven hitch-hikers whose bodies were found in the Belanglo state forest in southern NSW. On the day the police decided to arrest the suspect, select media outlets were informed, briefed, and escorted to the site of the arrest. They were allowed to film the man being held face down on the lawn of his house with a shotgun held to his head and to photograph both the house and the man's car. On subsequent days the media was allowed to film and report police activities at a number of properties where they were searching for evidence. Material taken from the buildings was displayed for the television and print cameras. After he was charged, the man was identified as Ivan Milat and personal details about him were released to the media. During the early stages of the trial process, the gossip magazine *Who Weekly* ('Backpacker Serial Killings: THE ACCUSED' 1994) ran a cover photograph of Ivan Milat in which he was clearly identifiable. The cover headlines read: 'Backpacker Serial Killings: THE ACCUSED', and 'The private life of road worker IVAN MILAT, the man charged with slaying 7 hitchhikers, as told by his brother Wally'. The rest of the front page was the photo of Milat allegedly 'entertaining his family the previous Christmas Eve at the home in which he was arrested'. *Who Weekly* was convicted of contempt of court for publishing the photograph on the grounds that it could prejudice or influence a jury when the question of the suspect's identity was to be an issue at the trial. *Who Weekly* was forced to withdraw the issue and re-release it with Milat's face covered with a non-removable sticker. The magazine was fined $100,000 plus costs, and the editor was fined an additional $10,000 (NSW Law Reform Commission 2000).

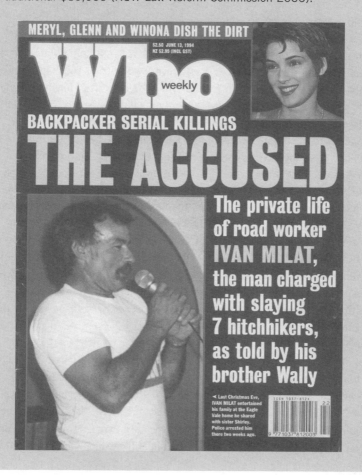

Issues and questions raised by case study 4

1   The media needs to be very careful about showing the face of a suspected criminal when identification will be an issue in their trial. What can you safely show?

2   How big does the story need to be—and the Backpacker Murders story was about as big as it gets—before you risk contempt of court and publish an accused's photo?

3   What do you think the legal advice would have been to *Who Weekly*?

4   Was the story worth $110,000 plus costs? It certainly gained the magazine temporary notoriety.

5   Isn't this a classic case of 'trial by media', only this time the media got caught?

→ ## Case study 5
TV cameras in courts

In 2003 the sight of accused Bali bombers screaming praises to their god in court, and smiling and smirking as chilling evidence unfolded, became the latest episode of the saga about admitting cameras to courts of law. Seeing justice done on television—the bombers facing five Indonesian judges—is not a familiar sight for Australians, so the Australian news crews covering the trials relished the freedom of being able to show the inside of the courtroom, rather than having to rely on 'the norm' of a reporter standing outside recounting what happened inside over shots of the main characters going in and out of the building (Smyth 2003, p. 7).

TV access to Australian courts is in the conservative British tradition, and at the discretion of the judge. The first time TV cameras were allowed to broadcast 'live' from an Australian court was the 1981 decision in the first coronial inquiry into the death of Azaria Chamberlain. Part of the reaction to the aforementioned O.J. Simpson case was that it demonstrated the dangers of allowing court proceedings to be televised (Slee 1995, p. 15). Then Federal Justice Minister Kerr said in 1994 that he saw no reason why court proceedings could not be televised only because the laws about court publications predated the electronic media (Saunders 1994, p. 4). There were some notes of caution though. Some feared people may 'play up to the cameras', and there was the danger of identifying jurors or protected witnesses, and some witnesses might feel inhibited by the presence of cameras recording their every word. Some had reservations about the accused being seen.

Broadcasters have long felt discriminated against by not being allowed to record material in courts. Imagine the outcry if the print media was banned from taking notes during trials? Australia boasts a system of open justice, where the media is allowed to observe justice 'being done'. Banning court reporting for print journalists would make the 'open justice' claim meaningless. Yet the electronic media is not allowed to bring the tools of their trade—the cameras and tape recorders—into court except on rare occasions. In May 1995, Justice Bernard Teague of the Supreme Court became the first judge to approve the televising of a criminal sentence in a Victorian court. The decision was strongly opposed by lawyers for Nathan John Avent, who was sentenced to life in front of a packed courtroom and a solitary news camera in the public gallery. The networks were allowed to use a minimum of two minutes of his sentencing on daytime and evening news bulletins (Conroy 1995). Avent appealed the sentence partly on the basis that the television presence adversely influenced the outcome (Zdenkowski 1995). The appeal judges said that the appeal was not about whether a judge should be able to allow a television camera into court. But they added that the contention that a fair-minded person might have thought that the sentencing judge had been influenced by the media attention 'was not without force' (Innes 1999). That comment from the appeals bench had the affect of stalling the move for cameras in courts until the late

1990s, when a Channel Ten camera did a pool shoot of the Court of Appeal's first electronic appeal—in which all of the documents were on computer—involving the severity
of a sentence for drug trafficking (Innes 1999). But that's all very different to allowing
TV news cameras (and radio tape recorders) into courts on a daily basis to record proceedings, or to have continuous coverage like the O.J. Simpson media 'circus'. The second 'live' broadcast from an Australian Court was of the decision by Full Court of the
Federal Court in the dispute in 1998 between the Maritime Union of Australia and
Patricks Stevedoring company over the sacking of the waterfront workforce. There was
intense interest in the result of the appeal, and it knocked *Sale of the Century* off air
temporarily (Innes 1999). In 2001 the West Australian Supreme Court allowed the filming of a full trial for an independent documentary on a drug trafficking case. The following year the WA Court of Criminal Appeal invited the media to cover the historic
overturning of the 40-year-old conviction of John Button, who was wrongly jailed for
killing his girlfriend in 1963 (Smyth 2003). Radio and television journalists still await
the same opportunities to tell their news stories afforded their print colleagues.

Issues and questions raised by case study 5

1   As a general principle should cameras and reporters' tape recorders be allowed in
    courts of law?
2   What would be some of the disadvantages of allowing cameras into courts?
3   The advantages?
4   Do the advantages outweigh the disadvantages?
5   Could you see various members of the legal system 'playing up for the cameras'?
6   Most Australians probably think the inside of a courtroom is something like a cross
    between *Judge Judy* and *Law and Order*. Visit a court, if you haven't already done so,
    and consider whether you think it would make interesting 'live' television.

Case study 6
The Scott Volkers case

If it was anybody else it would be passed through the system and be finished with,
but with me it goes on and on.

Scott Volkers quoted in Roberts 2003b, p. 3

In early 2002 the swim coach of Australian Olympic and world champions including
Sam Riley and Susie O'Neill faced court charged with sex offences against two
teenagers he allegedly coached in the 1980s (Doneman & Smith 2002). Volkers,
who was later to become Australia's head women's swim coach, strenuously proclaimed his innocence. The Australian swimming world was shocked. In September

2002, Volkers's lawyers made a submission to the Director of Public Prosecutions to discontinue proceedings against their client. The submission included what was termed 'new evidence' from other witnesses on aspects central to some of the charges, which cast doubt on the reliability of some of the girls' evidence (Barnes 2003, p. 19). It showed that the defence team believed the case against their high-profile client would not pass the critical test of being 'beyond reasonable doubt' (Barnes 2003, p. 33). The DPP accepted the statements from Volkers's lawyers and dropped the charges against the swim coach. Queensland's Crime and Misconduct Commission (CMC) investigated the DPP's handling of the case and was damning in its criticism. The DPP had accepted the Volkers's lawyers' new evidence 'on the condition that they would not interview those witnesses' (Barnes 2003, p. 19). The findings of the CMC inquiry were welcomed by Volkers's accusers—Julie Gilbert, Simone Boyce, and Kylie Byrne—as vindication of their stand that the DPP had bungled the case (Thomas & Wardill 2003). The CMC said its investigation did not disclose any evidence of official misconduct by any police or anyone in the DPP, but it did find 'serious shortcomings' in the DPP's handling of the case before the charges were dropped. In its view, the decision not to proceed with any of the charges was 'unsatisfactory' (Thomas & Wardill 2003). The only people considered for disciplinary action were two police officers involved in the case alleged to have given the *Courier-Mail* a 'tip off' about Volkers's imminent arrest. The Queensland Police's own Ethical Standards Command had already found that the two officers 'entered an arrangement' with the *Courier-Mail,* and a journalist and photographer were at police headquarters when Volkers arrived after his arrest (Thomas & Wardill 2003). The DPP announced later it was considering re-charging him. 'I would like for everything to be finished and over, but this is a never ending story,' Volkers said. 'It has stuffed my life' (Volkers 2003). It seemed that Scott Volkers would not get his wish, at least not just yet. Only a couple of months after he made this comment to the *Courier-Mail*, Volkers was to face new allegations and charges. In a statement at the time, Volkers told the *Weekend Australian*'s Greg Roberts (2003b, p. 3) that he was the victim of 'media and politically driven' efforts to ruin his life.

The Queensland DPP announced in April 2004 that no charges would be laid against Volkers over the allegations. But the story did not end here. In May and June 2004 the *Courier-Mail* began agitating again for the case to be re-opened, claiming that the legal advice given to the Queensland DPP by the NSW DPP's office was flawed. The ABC's *Four Corners* program took up the cause with damning evidence in its 5 July 2004 edition, but still the authorities were unwilling to proceed against the high-profile swim coach.

Issues and questions raised by case study 6

1   Every time anything is said about the case, the allegations against the swim coach are summarised. Is it fair to continuously draw attention to as yet unproven allegations?

2   There can be few more serious charges to level at a person; does it make any difference that the allegations concern incidents about 20 years ago?
3   What affect would the on-again off-again nature of the case have on Volkers's family?
4   What about the affect on the girls who are making the allegations?
5   Does it seem like the media is only 'doing its job', or can you detect a pattern in any of the cases presented here?
6   Research the phenomenon of 'moral panic'. How can journalists avoid getting caught up in the emotion of sexual assault cases?

Case study 7   ←
Trial by media—*Courier-Mail* style

Brisbane's morning newspaper, the *Courier-Mail,* carried the astonishing front-page headline: 'Heartless Predator' on 12 February 2004 (Doneman 2004). In smaller type above the banner headline was: 'Career criminal avoids prison despite life of robbing elderly'. Above a photo of the accused woman was the smaller heading: 'The Life and Times of Kim Scully' and then details of her criminal history dating back to 1984. Television news services had carried security footage showing a woman stealing a purse containing $400 from a 92-year-old shopper in a supermarket earlier that week. (The *Courier-Mail* also carried a still from that footage). The *Courier-Mail* story said the thief was a long-time criminal who had never been sentenced to prison. At the time of the robbery, she was serving a suspended sentence for a second crime, was on probation for a third, and on bail for a fourth (Doneman 2004). 'Kim Scully, 33, and her sister have made a living of robbing the elderly in supermarkets between Brisbane and the Gold Coast for 15 years' (Doneman 2004). Scully surrendered herself to police within hours of the publication. She was charged with the robbery caught on the security camera, and eight other similar offences over the previous 10 months (Doneman, Griffith & Moore 2004). This time the woman's face was published, with her eyes blacked out—her face was obscured for legal reasons, the paper said. Brisbane civil libertarian Terry O'Gorman called on the State Government to prosecute the *Courier-Mail* for publishing the criminal and bail history of the accused. The editor of the *Courier-Mail,* David Fagan, said the report of 12 February had demonstrated an apparent failure of the justice system to appropriately penalise repeat offenders for what were often seen by the courts as petty crimes (Doneman, Griffith & Moore 2004). 'As a newspaper we respect the civil liberties of everybody, particularly elderly people robbed of their belongings while at shopping centres', Fagan added. State Attorney General Rod Welford said it was not unlawful to disclose allegations about someone yet to be charged (Doneman, Griffith & Moore 2004).

Issues and questions raised by case study 7

1   It might not be unlawful to publish such details, but is it ethical?
2   How does such a person receive a fair trial with all that detail in the public arena?

3   In this case the evidence may seem clear-cut, but will it always be that way? Where should the media draw the line?
4   Is this a case of the local paper telling the legal system to improve its performance?
5   Or is it a case of a member of a huge international media conglomerate deciding to be judge and jury?
6   What was the point in obscuring the face of the accused the following day—everyone knew what she looked like from the page 1 photo the day before?

9

THE NEWS MEDIA AND
THE INJUSTICE SYSTEM

Objectives

After reading and discussing this chapter you will appreciate:

■ The ethical and legal minefield around promising or guaranteeing the confidentiality of news sources.
■ 'Authorised' and 'unauthorised' leaks.
■ The issues to consider before agreeing to source confidentiality.
■ The debate surrounding 'shield laws' for journalists.
■ The ethics of reporting race, ethnicity, and 'deviance'.
■ The media's role in maintaining 'law and order'.
■ How the news media can become caught up in waves of 'moral panic'.

Introduction: How far should you go?

When BBC radio reporter Andrew Gilligan ad-libbed a report on 29 May 2003, using an unnamed source to criticise an intelligence dossier produced by the Blair Government to justify going to war against Iraq, he set in train a series of events that would culminate in the suicide of his source, and an embarrassing back-down by the reporter and the BBC. Gilligan accused the Blair Government of 'sexing up' the dossier to justify the war. He said he had been told this by his source, whom he initially said was a member of the 'intelligence service', which he wasn't—he was a former weapons inspector and scientist working for Britain's Ministry of Defence (MoD).

We're not concerned here about the bitter dispute between the BBC and the Blair Government (that is discussed in a case study in chapter 6), but rather the appalling treatment of the source of the original story, Dr David Kelly. Although it was eventually the MoD that named Dr Kelly as the source for the story, Gilligan and the BBC can take little comfort from the affair. Had they not been so intent on defending their story (which was later found to contain basic errors) and taking on the criticism from Tony Blair, they may not have precipitated the events that seemed to Dr Kelly to give him no way out but to kill himself. Prime Minister Blair and his former chief aide, Alastair Campbell, heatedly denied Gilligan's report, accusing the BBC reporter of lying, and demanding a retraction. The BBC dug in its heels, releasing several statements giving full backing to Gilligan, even after Dr Kelly had told the House of Commons Foreign Affairs Committee two days before his death that he had not said some of the things Gilligan reported (Frankel 2003a). The Gilligan story triggered a major hunt for his confidential source that led to Dr Kelly. His name became public 24 hours after the MoD put out a news release saying an unnamed official had admitted meeting Gilligan. To go with the release, MoD press officers were told in a 'question and answer' sheet to confirm Dr Kelly's name if it was put to them by journalists (BBC World 2003b). The BBC only confirmed his identity as the source for the story after his death (Baldwin & Snoddy 2003). It was a tragic end to a shameful chapter in the history of perhaps the world's most credible broadcast news organisation. It also highlights in a very stark fashion how volatile and dangerous ethical fault lines can be. In this case Gilligan's agreement not to reveal the name of his source was a two-edged sword and many people ended up getting badly cut by it. A man is dead; his family distraught; Andrew Gilligan's career is in ruins; the top management of the BBC has been decimated by resignations and sackings; the organisation has been humiliated—and we are none the wiser about the Blair Government's dubious actions in justifying the 2003 attack on Iraq.

We begin by examining some of the traditional arguments about the protection of sources. Source protection, like the issues of privacy discussed in chapter 7, revolves around a grey area of legal, ethical, and philosophical issues. It is usually a legal inquiry that requires journalists to divulge sources, though in ethical terms there are difficulties with agreeing to confidentiality too readily. As we explain below, source protection has the potential to become a very important issue for journalists, one that will open up existing fault lines and perhaps create some new ones.

The discussion looks at the Australian Senate's inquiry into confidentiality of sources and proposed 'shield laws' for journalists. This is important background to the discussion of whistleblowers and the Deborah Cornwall case.

The second part of this chapter examines our second definition of 'trial by media'—the use of media power to vilify people in the news for social, ideological, and commercial reasons, not because they've committed any crime. This is another aspect of journalism and justice, or perhaps injustice, but it has little to do directly with court reporting and the regular police rounds. However, the impact on the lives of innocent people caught in the relentless roller-coaster of a news story can be just as great. In this case we are talking about the criminalisation of young people, most often on the basis of race or ethnicity.

The argument is made that some groups within society will always be harshly judged by the media, regardless of innocence or guilt. This introduces concepts of sexism, racism, ethnicity, and other forms of bias in the media. This chapter also examines the victimisation of marginalised groups that are labelled as 'deviant' by social authorities. According to the well regarded research of Ericson, Baranek, and Chan (1987), the news media plays a central and critical role in 'defining and shaping' constructions of deviant behaviour.

The final section highlights the role of the media in generally encouraging and supporting moral outrage and law and order campaigning by poll-driven politicians. These issues are highlighted by reference to coverage of indigenous affairs in Australia. We mention some codified examples in the Appendix, but here the focus is more on the ideological and political issues of a lingering racist attitude in Australia toward Aboriginal and Torres Strait Island peoples.

Source confidentiality:
The life-blood of good journalism?

Clause 3 [1998]: Aim to attribute information to its source. Where a source seeks anonymity, do not agree without first considering the source's motives and any alternative attributable source. Where confidences are accepted, respect them in all circumstances.
Clause 3 [1984]: In all circumstances they shall respect all confidences received in the course of their calling.

Which of these ethics clauses would you rather work under? As we noted in chapter 5 some critics think that the 1998 clause on source confidentiality is weaker than the one in the 1984 Code. Where would journalism stand today if there were no trust between reporters and their sources?

The first requirement in answering our questions is to look at the importance of confidentiality for sources in journalism. Serious journalism is about getting information into the public sphere that those in power would prefer was kept secret (Hurst & White 1994, p. 151). Exposure can lead to inquiries, precipitate resignations, and even bring down governments. At the very least disclosures can spark serious public concern that forces governments or private corporations or individuals into action. And it is not above governments and corporations to take measures that might protect them from exposure, such as invoking a 'national interest' or 'commercial-in-confidence' argument to prevent whistleblowers and leaks (Burnet 1992).

The quality of journalism in Australia would be the poorer if stories based on information gained from sources that need to remain anonymous were eliminated. Protecting the sources of such important information is a fundamental tenet of journalism, a principle on which serious journalists should be prepared to go to jail. A few brave souls have spent time in jail for protecting sources and many more have rallied to support colleagues who have been jailed. When *Courier-Mail* journalist Joe Budd was convicted of contempt and sentenced to 14 days' jail in March 1992, his editor, Des Houghton, spoke at a rally in his support: 'The day journalists get into the witness box and spill the beans is the day that people will stop giving us vital information about wrong-doing in public office' (quoted in Hurst & White 1994, p. 150). The sources need to be certain that the journalist will not reveal their name under any circumstance. Otherwise there will be a lot less 'whistleblowers' willing to 'blow the whistle'. David Burnet argues that without some protection in law for journalists and their sources, if they are faced with a legal challenge, reporters 'would be well advised to destroy the material in question' (Burnet 1992, p. 59). As you will see in the case studies at the end of this chapter, several journalists ended up in jail in the late 1980s and early 1990s because they refused to identify the sources of their stories. *It is not an action to be taken lightly.* It can have very serious ramifications. *It is the responsibility of the journalist not to guarantee confidentiality too readily.*

Confidentiality and the law

We hate to throw a bucket of cold water over your passion for journalism and willingness to go to prison to protect a source, but you should know that the court system feels it has equally valid reasons for demanding reporters 'give up' their sources in certain cases. The MEAA Ethics Review Committee listed some of them as partial reasons why the 'absolute' nature of the 1984 confidentiality clause should be amended. The legal contexts in which a court might demand names from journalists include:

- When a potential plaintiff is attempting to discover the name of a source so they can sue for defamation or civil damages.
- A civil or criminal trial when a source's identity may be sought from a journalist who is giving evidence on oath.
- A trial where the source is being sought in order to give evidence on their own behalf.
- In a situation where the source might be able to lend assistance to an investigation by a royal commission or similarly authorised body.

Ethics Review Committee 1997, p. 57

That's all reasonable, isn't it? We all want to do the right thing, right? The Committee suggested that the 'key test' is whether disclosure of the source's identity is necessary 'in the interests of justice' (Ethics Review Committee 1997, p. 57). The fractures over confidentiality go to the heart of journalistic ethics because the keeping of promises and trust are crucial tools that the reporter might use in the honest pursuit of 'truth', 'fairness', and 'balance'. Here we truly have fault lines with consequences. These issues were tested by the Australian High Court in the 1988 Cojuango case involving *SMH* journalist Peter Hastings. In this case the court determined that the 'administration of justice' demanded Hastings name his sources so that they could be sued by the subject of a story he had written about corruption in the Philippines. In the High Court's view, confidentiality is 'a discretionary power of the court, not a right or privilege of journalists' (cited in Ethics Review Committee 1997, p. 58). Of course, if you choose to ignore a court direction to name a source, you could end up in jail.

Confidentiality and the Code

There are many issues that need to be considered before a journalist agrees to grant confidentiality to a source—a course of action that could conceivably lead to the journalist spending time in jail. The MEAA Ethics Review Committee, in justifying its recommended change to the 'absolute' clause 3 of 1984, noted the relationship of co-dependence between journalists and sources:

The journalist needs information in order to fulfil public responsibilities; the source needs a way to disseminate information of public importance.

Ethics Review Committee 1997, p. 56

The question of maintaining confidences, it can be argued, relies on the 'public good' defence. In this case using information provided by a source on the basis that they won't be revealed is a 'greater good' than not using the material because the source is refusing to be named. On the other hand, some might argue that if a source does not have to reveal his or her identity, they might be inclined to make things up, or 'embellish' the story to make it appealing to the reporter. In such situations the confidentiality then becomes a trap, as we shall see in the Deborah Cornwall case. Because journalists are reliant on sources and some sources are reluctant to go on the record as a named source, this relationship of dependence has consequences for the reporter. The same is true for the source: if the reporter 'burns' them they too may suffer consequences. It is indeed a difficult fault line to straddle safely.

Are you authorised to leak that leak?

We need to make a distinction here about the different ways confidential information is released to a reporter by the source. This practice is referred to as 'leaking' a story. There are what can be categorised as 'authorised' and 'unauthorised' leaks. Dr David Kelly, in the case covered at the start of this chapter, was 'unauthorised' to 'leak' information to the BBC but he thought the public should know of his reservations about the British Government's reasons for going to war. On the other hand, the MoD media officers were 'authorised' to 'leak' (confirm) Kelly's name, if it was suggested to them by a journalist. 'Authorised' leaks, though, usually involve someone in authority in an organisation—for example, a company CEO, a Cabinet Minister, or Opposition Shadow Minister (or their chief media adviser) taking a journalist aside and telling them something by way of 'background', which in journalism jargon means 'information that can be used, but not attributed to the source by name'. It is used every day in Canberra to get the Government's and Opposition's messages out when the source doesn't want to be publicly named in the story. It's just another form of media manipulation, and often involves the idea of payback: 'Use this material and next time we have something good, you'll be (among) the first to know.' Or it may be what is called a 'selective leak'—the source hopes to ingratiate themself with a journalist (or small group of journalists) by leaking an important story. It appears to be a 'win–win' situation. The journalist gets exclusive access to a story in a highly competitive environment and the source can virtually guarantee favourable treatment for their story. Often it will involve the prior announcement of a policy initiative that amounts to no more than a politician 'testing the water' to gauge public reaction. If there's an adverse reaction, the politician drops the idea knowing his or her name has never been publicly associated with it. It is up to the individual journalist whether they play that game, and to what extent. It was obvious to anyone following the Blair Government's attempts to justify going to war with Iraq in early 2003 that his office and staff were leaking like the proverbial sieve. But that form of 'authorised', almost 'official' leak is very different to the 'unauthorised' leak that usually involves someone further down the 'food chain', who wants to see something their organisation is doing that they believe is corrupt, illegal, unethical, or even dangerous, exposed through the media.

Quality, motivation, and means to an end

One of the important issues to consider before agreeing to confidentiality with your source is the quality of the information. Is it an important story? Is it something that the public really needs to know about? Does it justify anonymity for the source or could you get it from other sources without having to betray the originating source? Second, can you get the same information on the record from somewhere or someone else? If you can't, then there are other issues to consider before agreeing to guarantee your source's confidentiality.

For instance, what is the motivation of the source? Ask yourself: 'What's in it for them?' Are they motivated by the highest ideals of a 'whistleblower'—seeing that important information gets into the public arena—or are they simply after revenge against an institution or individual? Is the source trying to hide behind the journalist's ethical stance that they won't reveal his/her name to ensure that they can evade any responsibility for what they have said?

As part of the process of deciding whether to agree to grant the source confidentiality, you must assess the source's motivation. If you are at all concerned, you must weigh up the decision on confidentiality, probably in consultation with your superiors. A second issue is the validity of the information—is it true? Could the source be lying? Could they be putting the best 'spin' on the story they can by ignoring relevant facts? You must always do your best to verify the information by cross-checking and trying to corroborate it with other sources. Confidential sources have been known to plant misleading information. When Lieutenant-Colonel Oliver North appeared before a US Congressional Committee in the 1980s investigating the infamous Iran–Contra scandals, he complained about leaks. The Contras were a CIA-funded opposition group in Nicaragua who trafficked narcotics into the United States. The CIA then used the profits to secretly supply weapons to Iran, which at the time was fighting a war against Iraq. *Newsweek* revealed that in some of the stories he complained of, which had appeared in their magazine, North himself had been the 'leaker' (cited in Tiffen 1988, p. 24). Other news organisations then denounced *Newsweek* for breaching the principle of confidentiality!

It is common practice for those affected by leaks (like the case of British Prime Minister Blair and the BBC above) to try to establish the identity of the confidential source by saying: 'Reveal your source or we'll know it's not true'. We have mentioned before that journalists in general don't enjoy high credibility among the public at large, and the repeated use of 'confidential sources' probably doesn't do much to enhance that reputation. You can imagine a reporter on the phone pleading with a sceptical public servant. It might go something like this: 'You can believe me, I'm a journalist.' And then in a conversation with a sceptical reader: 'Here's the information, there is a source, scout's honour, I just can't tell you who it is.' What a dilemma for everyone: the source, the journalist, and the news audience. Why should the source, or the public, believe you if your credibility isn't much better than that of the ubiquitous used-car salesman?

Another area in considering the truth of the story is that a 'confidential source' can be used by an unscrupulous journalist to inflate or exaggerate information—as we've seen with discredited BBC reporter Andrew Gilligan and the so-called 'sexing up' of the British dossier on Iraq's weapons of mass destruction. There are more cases of this type of deception in the next chapter where the journalists concerned simply made up the sources.

The *SMH* guidelines

In the wake of the BBC source suicide, and the Jayson Blair affair in the United States (see the introduction to the next chapter if the name doesn't sound alarm bells), the *SMH* introduced new draft guidelines on the use of sources. Conveniently for this discussion, the document was 'leaked' to the opposition *Australian,* and appeared in the weekly 'Media' section (Chulov 2003). The new *SMH* sourcing policy seems to follow the same logic as the 1998 MEAA Code clause 3. The *SMH* draft policy includes the following planks:

- We do not use direct quotes in stories from anonymous sources.
- We try to limit the use of anonymous sources in stories to cases where the use is essential for the integrity of the article. The use needs to be discussed with your editor.
- Our priority is to get a source on-the-record, wherever possible. We can do this by asking if they'll go public if we get official confirmation of an incident, or get it confirmed by another party or document, or if someone else goes public too, or undertake to read them back (only) their quotes plus their context.
- Always try to get a second source for material facts. At least two separate sources (or a verified document) are needed. One source may be acceptable if it's from the horse's mouth (identified to the editor).
- If we have an important story and we cannot get someone on the record it needs to be referred to the editor to determine if the story proceeds.
- We prefer to name a spokesman or spokeswoman.

The proposed guidelines continue:

Identification of unnamed source in cases where it is agreed we can use one: We can't simply say 'a source' or a 'government source'. We don't lie about a source in copy. We don't fudge on how many sources. We're precise. We don't make them sound more important or reliable than they are. We locate the source as close as possible to the action. E.g., someone who has seen the document, was at the negotiations, someone familiar with the deal. We identify in the story wherever possible where the interests of the source lie. We always explain why they will not go on the record, e.g., for fear of losing their job, life, or because of their own interests.

Cited in Chulov 2003

The draft policy then goes on to define terms like 'deep background', 'background', and 'off-the-record', and concludes with the statement: 'We don't accept conditions placed on any of our stories by sources seeking to improve their run in the paper' (Chulov 2003). As this book was being written, the policy was still in the draft—and 'leaked'—stage, and of particular interest for *Herald* reporters was going to be who would be the official 'keepers of the secrets' of the names of confidential sources.

Do we need 'shield laws' in Australia?

The protection of sources is perhaps one of the most serious areas of conflict between journalists and the law. It is one of our 'grey areas' and fraught with contradictions. Areas like defamation are covered by specific legal frameworks that set out quite clearly what reporters can and cannot do. However, in the area of a journalist's relationship to her/his sources the situation in Australia is not clearly defined. In the United States journalists have the Constitutional protection of the First Amendment and in about half the states there is specific 'shield law' legislation that protects the privilege of reporters. A 'shield law' is specific legislation that applies protective conditions to the journalist–source relationship. Unlike the whistleblower legislation, which specifically protects a source, the 'shield law' can also apply to a reporter.

A debate about 'shield laws' began in Australia in the mid 1990s. It was in the news then because of a number of court cases involving journalists (see our case study below). The most important, and one that has implications for all journalists, is the case of former *SMH* reporter, Deborah Cornwall. These cases drew attention to the sometimes weak defence that reporters have when it comes to the forced disclosure of confidential sources.

Concurrent with the MEAA's review of its AJA Code of Ethics in the mid 1990s, the Australian Senate held its own inquiry into the 'rights and obligations' of the media and documented its findings in the report, *Off the Record* (Senate Standing Committee on Legal and Constitutional Affairs 1994). The journalism profession was divided along interesting fault lines by this debate and it was surprising who lined up next to whom and where they stood. A number of people argued for some form of legislative 'shield' to protect journalists, but others were equally convinced that it could have the opposite effect, creating an offence of non-disclosure in all but the most restricted circumstances. A number of points have been raised in relation to proposed 'shield laws':

- Should there be special privileges for journalists similar to those applying to doctors, lawyers, and priests? This again raises the professional fault line argument from previous chapters.
- Unscrupulous journalists might take advantage of 'shield laws' to make unsubstantiated or malicious allegations.
- 'Shield laws' are only partial protection. They are legislatively applied and can be legislatively removed, allowing prosecution of journalists in some circumstances, or forcing disclosure on certain terms.

At the time of the MEAA Code review, prominent Melbourne-based media lawyer and commentator Paul Chadwick (1994) outlined the arguments for and against 'shield laws':

> Journalists argue that if they reveal sources then potential 'whistleblowers' will be deterred, on pain of reprisal, from airing through the media information of considerable public interest. The courts and other bodies with legal powers argue that a journalist's

commitment to their sources must yield to the interests of justice when it is necessary, for instance when a potential plaintiff wants to know the identity of a source so as to sue him or her, or when the source has breached the law or could assist the processes of the law.

Chadwick 1993, pp. 3–4

Professor David Flint (PANPA 1992, p. 6), who at the time was chairperson of the Australian Press Council, wrote a paper outlining the then current situation and a case for 'shield laws'. He said that the conflict is between the law as it stands and the journalists' ethical obligation to respect the confidentiality of their sources. Journalists' sources do not generally enjoy much protection under Australian Common Law, except in the pre-trial 'exploratory phase' in defamation trials in some states.

The ethical question in the debate about sources, confidentiality, and disclosure is not the protection of the journalist, nor the protection of information, but the protection of the source.

The Senate steps in

In October 1994, the Senate Standing Committee on Legal and Constitutional Affairs published a report of its investigations into the rights and obligations of the media (*Off the Record, 'Shield Laws' for Journalists' Confidential Sources*). Recommendation 8 of the report says in part:

> That clause 3 of the Code of Ethics [1984 version] be amended by the MEAA to remove the absolute character of the obligation it imposes on journalists to maintain confidentiality so that they can, with a clear conscience, comply with a court order made in the appropriate case to identify a source.

Senate Standing Committee on Legal and Constitutional Affairs 1994, p. xxv

The Committee's report was cognisant of the MEAA review process and made its expectation clear:

> Once the media has adopted a new Code of Ethics, and an effective disciplinary mechanism for enforcing it, it would be appropriate to enact the legislative reform of the kind recommended by the Committee.

Senate Standing Committee on Legal and Constitutional Affairs 1994, p. xxi

The Senate Standing Committee's linking of confidentiality privileges to greater accountability and more responsibility from journalists also finds an echo in the Preamble to the revised MEAA Code, 'Accountability engenders trust' (MEAA 1995a). The philosophical parallels between the Committee's report and the wording of the revised Code of Ethics are interesting. Both talk of the media's role in animating 'our democratic system' (Senate Standing Committee on Legal and Constitutional Affairs 1994, p. xvii) and giving 'practical form to freedom of expression' (MEAA 1995a).

It is quite clear that the Standing Committee wanted to legislate away any implied right of journalists to protect their sources from identification in legal proceedings, but *first* the

MEAA Code had to be changed. The MEAA review obliged the Senate by recommending that this provision (3) in the Code be amended and the change was ratified in 1998. Given that the Senate Committee signalled the possibility of legislation to entrench the court's right to insist on disclosure, it remains to be seen whether members of the Alliance will continue to resist attempts to make disclosure more a *legal* rather than an *ethical* issue.

So far journalists have shown little enthusiasm for legal intervention into their work and are already subject to (in their view) onerous defamation and contempt of court laws. As former editor of the *Australian*, Adrian Deamer, pointed out there is no guaranteed freedom of speech in Australia, it is very much at the mercy of the courts and their political masters (PANPA 1994b, p. 23). A referendum to insert such a clause into the Constitution has been a project of former Press Council chairman, David Flint, for some time (PANPA 1992, p. 6), but more than a decade later it is still not seriously on the mainstream political agenda.

While some proponents of 'shield laws' look to the situation in some American states, it is worth noting the following points about the US system:
- Only the journalist can claim privilege, not the source. This is a reversal of the Australian proposal.
- The trend is to require the journalist to share the name of the source with her/his editor. This opens up the possibility that another person, apart from the journalist, can divulge the name of the source.
- The American system makes a distinction between confidentiality and secrecy.
- Anonymous sources know that at some stage their names may be revealed, and they provide information on that basis.
- Breach of confidence through disclosure may be actionable: that is, the source may sue the journalist for breach of confidence if their name is revealed.

In the American context, Herbert Strentz (1978) talks about informing, protecting, and promoting news sources in his book *News Reporters and News Sources*. He asks two important questions:
1 How do relations with sources affect news gathering and the power of the press?
2 How do relations with sources affect the product that finally reaches the audience?

Strentz argues that reporters *inform* a news source, *protect* a source, and *promote* a source in different circumstances. The most common example of 'informing' is telling relatives of the death of a family member. This is a form of 'grief intrusion' that also raises the important question of how do you know you've got the right family? Another is when journalists become a confidant of important political figures, which raises the interesting question: 'Does this lead to the journalist being compromised?' A third example might be informing the authorities about the activities of individuals or organisations that oppose the Government of the day. This was very common during the Cold War (1945–89) when journalists worked for both sides (Knightley 1975, 1997). The fourth is the journalist's own involvement in the story. This general point is important and Strentz (1978, p. 54) has this to say about it: 'Reporters are involved in stories by the mere fact of coverage; the manner in which the reporter covers the event often shapes the news that reaches the public.' This goes beyond ethics to the very essence of the role of journalists and the way they work in our society. It addresses the fundamental fault lines of 'objectivity', 'independence', and 'distance'. Taking people into a 'confidence' is at the heart of an emotional attitude of a good journalist. It is a relationship that implies mutual 'trust'. Have you heard the cliché: A journalist is only as good as her/his sources? However, in true dialectic fashion, there are situations where a reporter might quite consciously break this relationship. Can it ever be justified? Perhaps it could be in circumstances where a source has deliberately misled a reporter. Certainly, if trust has been broken *by the source* a journalist would be justified in 'burning' that contact. The situation is not so clear if the reporter is faced with a legal requirement (a court-issued direction for example). In this situation the ethico–legal quandary is all too apparent.

A number of reasons are advanced for the continuation, or extension, of a journalist's right to protect confidential sources of information. Consider the following: How would you rank them? Can you think of any more? In this example we have related each 'reason' to an appropriate ethical 'principle'.

- Selfish reasons—protection of reputation, covering up mistakes (loyalty to self and organisations).
- Protecting the credibility of the journalist, or the source (accuracy).
- At the request of the source (loyalty to sources).
- For the benefit of the audience—the public's right to know (accuracy and balance).
- Can the source be trusted (accuracy, truth, and loyalty)?
- How do you know when a usually reliable source is giving you misleading information (accuracy, truth, and balance)?
- How should you respond if a source requests anonymity, asks to review the copy, or says certain things 'off the record' (public good, loyalty to sources, accuracy, and credibility)?
- Does professional competence and the burden of responsibility lie with the journalist and/or the organisation/publisher (responsibility)?
- Do you allow anonymity of sources for every story, or are you selective in respecting a confidence (fairness, trust, and loyalty)?
- It's not the purpose of journalism to seek to show someone in the best possible light— a source may be seeking good publicity; a journalist wants a complete (as well as a good) story (balance, truth, and fairness).
- A request by a government agency/official to vet copy might be considered censorship— it must be measured against the public's right to know (public good, truth, and trust).
- Pressure of time: checking accuracy is a journalist's responsibility (accuracy, completeness, and fairness).
- Public comments cannot be 'off the record' (public's right to know).
- Only agree to specific things under specific circumstances (trust, balance, and fairness).

Protecting 'whistleblowers'

Shielding the identity and protecting the careers of so-called whistleblowers is closely related to the issue of protecting sources. People who risk their relationships and livelihood to expose official corruption have often been hounded when their cover is blown. It is argued that potential rackets, rorts, and wrongdoings might not be uncovered if informants are silenced by fear.

Throughout the 1990s a number of legislative measures were proposed by various Australian State Governments to address the issues of sources, whistleblowers, and allegations of public corruption. Whistleblower legislation was recommended in Queensland in response to the Fitzgerald Inquiry, the WA Inc Royal Commission also recommended whistleblower protection, and the SA Parliament passed legislation in 1992. Legislatively mandated whistleblower protection regimes aim to protect people from reprisal if they report illegal, improper, or wasteful conduct to the authorities. However, recent experience in Australia shows that the 'proper authorities' may be incompetent, ineffective, or corrupt themselves and hence not the best people to investigate allegations by whistleblowers. This is why in many states special commissions have been established at arm's length from governments with a broad mandate to investigate matters in the public interest. Can it be left to the legal system, or to politicians to determine what is in the public interest, given that the very definition of public interest is in fact controlled by the state? Do corporations represent public interest? We have dealt with this argument, at least regarding media companies, in chapters 3 and 4. Equally we have seen in chapters 4 and 5 that there are a number of contradictions in the argument that what is in the interests of the Government of the day is also in the interests of the body politic.

Secrecy, privacy, and FOI: Does it work for journalists?

There is no doubt that the protection of sources—often from persecution, or even murder—is a cornerstone of journalistic ethics. At the same time the legal status of 'privacy' is itself another of our 'grey areas'. Legal protection of individual privacy is unevenly available in Australia, as are civil remedies if personal privacy is breached. Some classes of information are protected by statutes, such as tax files. Others, like medical files, are supposed to be 'confidential', but courts and other tribunals have access. On the other hand, in the name of 'transparency', a mix of state and federal Freedom of Information (FOI) laws cover statutory and corporate information. This makes it theoretically available to anyone who can pay the access fees, which can often be prohibitive. Many editors and reporters frequently complain that FOI laws have proven to be freedom 'from' information laws as far as investigative journalism is concerned.

The protection of sources, whistleblower legislation, freedom of information and the public's right to know, and the right of a reporter not to reveal their source are all important principles. However, like most issues in journalism ethics, the contradictions between these principles lead to fault lines and conflicts. Each of them must be weighed in the context of the utilitarian argument about the 'greater good' and the public benefit of disclosure or secrecy. We are also confronted again in this chapter with the problem of individual versus corporate and collective rights. As the case study below highlights, reporter Deborah Cornwall was caught in the contradiction between truth and lies, honesty and trust when she was asked to reveal a source's identity to a NSW anti-corruption commission.

Race, journalism, and (in)justice

MEAA Code Clause 2: Do not place unnecessary emphasis on personal characteristics, including race, ethnicity, nationality, gender, age, sexual orientation, family relationships, religious belief or physical or intellectual disability.

If you listen to talk-back radio for extended periods you will hear the same key phrases and code-words cropping up again and again. The most common prejudices revolve around the following simplistic slogans: 'equality for all Australians', 'Asians and crime', 'schools can't teach', 'Christian values have been lost', 'Aboriginal people are a lost cause', 'the New World Order is taking over our lives', etc. This is not to suggest that there is a control centre directing callers. There doesn't need to be. Nor is there a conspiracy in the studio necessarily (Hall 1998, pp. 45–6).

Of course there doesn't need to be a conspiracy. What the conservative radio shock-jocks tap into is the fear and distrust that are developed out of a fault line of anxiety about the present and the future. Richard Hall says it stems from most Australians not knowing the past, 'the good and the bad'. He argues that only by 'knowing the past' can we 'move on'. Hall's concern is with the history of racism in Australia and how to overcome it by tackling present-day problems. Ours is primarily with journalists and journalism. These issues are linked through the media's coverage of ethnicity, race, and crime. We need to ask ourselves: 'What role can the news media play in promoting our "knowing the past", in order that we might overcome prejudice based on mistaken ideas, or even outright "lies"?'

Crime and deviance

The problem for the news media is that 'crime' often evokes a gut reaction, an emotional response, a response that is highly ideological and built around notions of 'deviance'—that is, its ability to 'disrupt' normal routines, assumptions, and value-systems (Ericson, Baranek & Chan 1987, p. 53). In this way the news media helps to maintain the social boundaries of acceptable behaviour, at least as they are defined by the relevant 'authorities'. One way that the media participates in the social 'policing' role of authority is through the generation of 'moral panic' based on the mistaken idea that a particular and identifiable group (for example, 'Asian crime gangs') is 'dangerously deviant and poses a menace to society' (Wikipedia 2004). The term 'moral panic' was first used by a British sociologist to describe news coverage of 'Mods' and 'Rockers' in the 1960s when these teen subcultures were seen to be threatening the old order (Cohen 1972). We will return to this issue as it forms an interesting undercurrent throughout the rest of this chapter.

Like all ideological positions, the news media's emotional attitudes to criminal behaviour are caught up in this dialectic of social 'deviance' and 'control'. In such situations, the news media portrays itself as the 'objective, impartial, universal and general voice of the people ... [and] ... can rely on the same properties in the law as a cultural product to convey the image that they, too, are a neutral, objective arbiter of conflicts in the world' (Ericson, Baranek & Chan 1987, p. 53). However, the law is not 'neutral' or 'objective' and neither is journalism. The legal system in Australia (as in other capitalist nations) is the ultimate defence of private property—of the haves against the have-nots. This is why disproportionately more people of working class and lower socio-economic background are in jail. According to Frank Ferudi (1994) the media's framing of working class crime is based on the idea that it is 'undermining society's moral foundations'. It is not that the working class is intrinsically, or genetically, predisposed to crime. Rather, these people are 'criminalised' because they are poor, or ethnically different to those in positions of power, economically and politically. The MEAA Code of Ethics makes explicit in a prescriptive, normative way that journalism and journalists should be free from prejudice. In a sense a reporter or editor has to be constantly behind Rawls's 'veil of ignorance', 'objectively' looking out on the world. However, we don't think it's quite that simple. Reporters, like everyone else, are caught up in the relationships and routines that shape our ideas. They are bound up in the social relations of a divided and unjust world.

This land is our land ...

In Australia one of the most contradictory, confusing and, conflicted national ideologies is our collective emotional attitude, our national consciousness of ourselves as a people and a nation. It is incumbent on us, as responsible, honest, balanced, and fair journalists and academics to address one of the most obvious and far-reaching fault lines in ethics, the great divide in wealth, health, comfort, lifestyle, power, influence, and respect between indigenous and non-indigenous Australians. This chasm of understanding and real life experience (the core of ideologies) will not be bridged until all of us recognise and reconcile ourselves to the truth that our landmass belongs in a real and spiritual sense to the original inhabitants. This island continent that the colonial and empire cartographers eventually mapped as 'Australia' never was 'terra nulius', literally 'empty land'.

The colonial press, too, considered the continent theirs for the taking and stood up for 'squatter's rights', even if it meant supporting the murder of Aboriginal men, women, and children. The colonial press was also a vehement voice against the 'yellow peril' of Chinese immigration, believing it was foisted upon the colonies by the British Foreign Office (Hall 1998, pp. 9–48). Richard Hall's summary of nineteenth and early twentieth century racism in the Australian media may seem like ancient history now, but unfortunately some sections of the media today replicate many of the same views. Australia's 'kings' of talk-back radio, from the west coast to the east, are frequently chastised for the encouragement they give to prejudice, often adding their own strident voices to the fray (Mickler & McHoul 1998). But what of attitudes in the mainstream media today? Surely the 'bad old days' of institutional racism are over in Australia?

It would seem not. Journalists have also entered the argument on the side of Richard Hall's greater truth. As we've seen, squabbles in the news pages and over items on *Media Watch* are commonplace. What journalists and writers like Richard Hall and David Marr, along with many prominent others, have argued is that 'wedge politics' and 'wedge journalism' are today facts of life. Hall cites a litany of examples of attacks on black activists and their supporters. The Howard Government's steady and relentless attacks on the leadership of ATSIC, resulting in the agency being abolished in April 2004, were just recent examples.

Stephen Mickler (1998) has documented how the lives of ordinary indigenous families around the nation have been destroyed by 'vigilantism' on the airwaves. The Royal Commission into Black Deaths in Custody was sparked by courageous reporting of the shocking way in which the criminal 'justice' system treats far too large a proportion of Aboriginal youths and men. The Royal Commission recommended that journalism educators ensure that a 'significant component' of the curriculum should deal with indigenous issues. That was more than ten years ago, and since then we have endured the heartbreaking agony of the 'stolen generations' and the brief exhilaration of the 'reconciliation' marches that the Prime Minister, John Howard, dismissed as insignificant. John Howard's consistent refusal to issue a 'sorry' to indigenous Australians deserves to be a much bigger news story than it is.

Tampa-ing with the truth

In 2003, two years after it had shaken federal politics irrevocably, Fairfax journalists David Marr and Marianne Wilkinson, in their book *Dark Victory* (2003), carefully researched and documented the lies and distortion surrounding the well-known *Tampa* affair that clouded the November 2001 federal election. In late October that year, a Norwegian freighter, the *Tampa*, rescued a group of asylum-seekers from a leaking boat and attempted to take them to Christmas Island on Australia's western seaboard. The Federal Government used heavily armed SAS forces to storm the *Tampa* and prevent the asylum-seekers from coming ashore, in breach of many conventions of the sea. Respected *Courier-Mail* correspondent Peter Charlton (2002) was not alone in concluding that the Howard Government 'seized' on the Tampa incident to help it win the 'unwinnable' 2001 federal election. We have written plenty about 'spin' in relation to political manoeuvring over Iraq and other issues, but the real issue here is to understand the assumptions made by reporters and editors in how they cover issues of ethnicity and race. We haven't the space to document in great detail the current state of coverage, but the following short sections are important examples of the issues raised by researchers in this field. We recommend you undertake your own reading in this area, perhaps starting with *Racism, Ethnicity and the Media* (Jakubowicz 1994). Follow this up by reading some of the work of Michael Meadows and a number of others (for example, Meadows 1987, 1995, 1998a, 1998b; Meadows, Hippocrates & Van Vuuren 1997; Meadows & Oldham 1991; Castillo & Hirst 2001). This body of work supports the view that Australia's journalists could do a lot better in terms of how ethnicity and indigenous affairs are covered. More research is currently under way in this area and many journalism programs now include a specific course or unit on indigenous affairs, Aboriginal history, and reporting cultural diversity. As a guide for your own work, our appendices include some guidelines for reporters that have been prepared by community groups, reporters, editors, and journalism academics.

Covering indigenous affairs

The Royal Commission into Black Deaths in Custody, chaired by Elliott Johnston QC, issued its final report in 1991 after almost four years of hearings, submissions, and investigations. One of the key recommendations was that rates of incarceration of indigenous people should be reduced. However, Aboriginal people still face imprisonment at eighteen times the rate of non-indigenous people and human rights lawyer Chris Cunneen found in 1994 that the Commission's recommendations were being systematically ignored. He suggested this was one reason why Aboriginal deaths in custody were at their highest level since the final report was released in 1991 (Bacon & Mason 1995a, 1995b). In 1998, writing in the *Walkley* magazine, *Courier-Mail* reporter Tony Koch (1998, p. 5) lamented the fact that there were still gaps in the education of journalists about indigenous issues 'through a combination of ignorance, apathy and cultural insensitivity'. Five years later the same Tony Koch (2003a, p. 33) reported that despite many government reports and inquiries very little was actually being done to help indigenous communities cope with domestic violence, sexual assault, alcoholism, and drug abuse. As many researchers have found, the general focus of stories about indigenous affairs is entirely negative, and good news, unless it is about athletes like Cathy Freeman, hardly gets a mention. This is borne out by our random study of indigenous coverage in August 2003.

In August 2003 the release of a report by the Australian Institute of Health and Welfare 'painted a damning picture of the failure to improve indigenous health' (Jopson 2003), but the coverage did not attempt to apportion any responsibility for this 'failure'. In both the *SMH* (Jopson 2003, p. 10) and the *Australian* (Hickman 2003, p. 7) the stories were buried on the back pages of the general news section. In contrast, stories about the sacking of ATSIC chairman, Geoff Clark, were on the front page (Schubert & Rintoul 2003). Two other front-page stories on indigenous affairs in August 2003 were also framed very negatively. One concerned a 13-month-old boy who had been placed in protective custody because 'there is no safe place for him in his home town' on Mornington Island, a community 'crippled by alcohol-fuelled violence' (Koch 2003b, p. 1). A terrible picture is painted of life on Mornington Island in a feature that runs across two full pages, but again, no attempt is made to explain why this is happening. Instead there is just a litany of disturbing facts, including that more than 10 per cent of the island's adult population is in jail (Koch 2003c).

It is not enough to describe the situation—in the light of the Royal Commission's recommendations about the news media, stories such as this should also offer some perspective on solutions, on history, and on steps being taken to remedy the situation. There is no attempt to link the problems on Mornington Island to government policies or racism. Instead the problems are blamed on 'unemployment, alcohol and poor infrastructure' (O'Malley 2003). The direction that the reporting of indigenous affairs takes is neatly summed up in an editorial in the *Weekend Australian* at the start of August 2003, and one can suggest that this sets the tone for much of what followed in that month. The editorial's proposed solution to domestic violence is that indigenous communities ban alcohol, even though such bans are 'not an answer to the dispossession of indigenous Australians' ('Ban Alcohol to Save Indigenous Lives' 2003). There is implicit racism in this proposition. While alcohol may be one factor in domestic violence, it is not the only one. There is domestic violence in many non-Aboriginal communities too, but no-one suggests banning alcohol in Manly or Mt Druitt. Banning alcohol will only take away another 'right' of indigenous Australians, it will not solve the deeper issues of land rights and racism. In February and March 2004 coverage of the so-called 'Redfern riots' had the same tone. The coverage focused on one incident involving less than 100 youths throwing stones at police. The angle was 'violence' against the police rather than the endemic poverty, despair, and racism that causes young Aboriginal men to deal in drugs and engage in petty crime. This presented itself as a classic case of 'moral panic'—'These black people are out of control, do something!' Unfortunately that 'something' is usually the further criminalisation of indigenous people, particularly young men. It is an ethical issue that the news media happily (ignorantly?) participates in the creation of these 'monster' myths (Bonderson 2001). This issue must be addressed by journalists and news organisations before it's too late.

Are young people 'out of control'?

At the end of April 1999 a young Chinese–Australian man was shot during an altercation with some other youths in the western Sydney suburb of Miller. The incident was reported in the media as yet another example of the criminal nature of young western suburbs males. The *Sydney Morning Herald*'s crime reporter, Greg Bearup (1999), summed up the attitude of many mainstream reporters when he said that Miller, near the city of Liverpool on Sydney's southwest fringe, was in the news again, 'for the only thing it is ever in the news for: crime'. Bearup is right, but is he aware of the irony in writing this for the *Herald*'s mainly middle class city-based audience?

When you look closely at the headlines and content of media stories covering western Sydney and suburbs like it on the fringes of most Australian capital cities—places such as Inala in Brisbane or Broadmeadows in Melbourne—it becomes clear that young people generally, and young men of non-Anglo appearance in particular, are targets of both aggressive policing and repetitive, negative media coverage (Powell 1993; Mickler 1998; Mickler & McHoul 1998; Castillo & Hirst 2001). To a large extent this negativism involves crime and the construction of young people as somehow 'deviant' and acting against the interests of 'normal' society. Perth-based media academic Steve Mickler (1998, p. 27) quite rightly suggests that the constructed narratives of 'deviance, its control and its opposite, normality' are explicit tools of journalism and especially the police rounds. This divide is also at the heart of 'moral panic': the emotion of 'righteous vengeance' or 'cringing retreat' in the face of a perceived 'deviant' threat (Bebout 1995). We saw this spirit of outrage and revenge surface in coverage of the so-called 'Lebanese rape gangs' drama in Sydney between 2001 and 2003.

But 'deviance' is not limited to the criminalisation of young people from non-English speaking background (NESB), it often spills over into other aspects of the life of ethnically diverse communities such as those in southwestern Sydney (Castillo & Hirst 2001). It could sound like stating the obvious to suggest that there is nothing new in such negative portrayals of working class communities and poorer suburbs around our cities. As Diane Powell notes in her book, *Out West* (1998), western Sydney has been the target of negative media portrayal since the end of the 1970s and early 1980s. At the end of the day, there is nothing startling about journalists trying to get their stories from areas with a disadvantaged socio-economic background. As Powell comments, the negative reporting of working class life began with the portrayal of life in the slums of Europe and America in the late nineteenth and early twentieth century and continues today. Unfortunately, the image of working class

suburbia that has been forged in the past two decades or so in the consciousness of journalists (and some politicians, public servants, and police) will not be easily changed.

The class divide between reporters and news 'subjects'

The second issue to discuss is why negative reporting is so prevalent today. Is there a con-
spiratorial theory against people from lower socio-economic backgrounds? As we mentioned in an earlier discussion, we do not favour conspiracy theories. There is usually a
better explanation, and one that is a lot simpler to understand. In the introduction to this
chapter we suggested there might be a 'class' difference, in this case between the 'poor' and
'disadvantaged' and the more 'privileged' and 'middle class' reporters. A demographic profile developed from a survey of 1068 journalists by John Henningham (1996c) suggests their
characteristics can be distilled into one word: 'yuppies'. They are young, with a median age
of 32, predominantly of Anglo-Saxon ethnic origin and of middle-class background. Six out
of 10 come from homes in which the main breadwinner was employed in a white-collar
occupation. An *SMH* reporter told one of the co-authors that she rarely ventured any further west than the Sydney suburb of Leichhardt, famous for its Italian restaurants, coffee,
and gelato. This was on a day that she had come to Blacktown (about 40 kilometres west of
her usual journey) to chase up a story about the illegal dumping of rubbish on public land.
In the end, the story that appeared was all about the junk that was left in a laneway behind
her house in inner-city Newtown. Blacktown's problems didn't rate a mention.

For many reporters with such middle class attitudes, working under resource and deadline pressures, suburbs like Sydney's Cabramatta and Darra in Brisbane are nothing more
than a 'fertile ground' for feature stories of violence and despair. They are crafted to be read
by a faraway audience living under a solid middle class roof and inevitably reflect the limited emotional attitudes of the reporter. With a profound sense of being 'middle' class, and
with very little cultural awareness of the 'exotic' locations, they scavenge for stories that will
titillate and distress their audiences. The moral 'lessons' that the middle class audience can
draw from these reports include a sense of their own importance, the expiation of their
own 'guilt', and public pressure on the authorities to do something about it (Sands 1996;
Jenkins 1999). The 'slummer journalists' (a term coined by historians Graeme Davidson
and David Dunstan) write for an audience fascinated with the dark tales coming from the
wrong side of the tracks; what Bonderson (2001, p. 4) describes as 'fear of working-class
indiscipline and social insubordination'.

Supporting the limited choices of the news routine is the observation that most journalists rely on their own innate, or learned 'news sense' and broader system of beliefs to
make sense of the information they gather. The combination of 'dominant' news values, the
pressures of time constraints, and a dominant newsroom culture leads to the oversimplifi-
cation of news values, and complex social issues are reduced to stereotypes, myths, and
clichés. Stanley Cohen (1972, pp. 31–8) characterises this contribution to 'moral panics' as
'exaggerated attention, exaggerated events, distortion and stereotyping'.

A senior newspaper staffer commented (cited in Castillo & Hirst 2001) that in many
newsrooms 'ethnic' stories are either regarded as 'boring', particularly if they consist of
'good' news, or as a turn-off for readers. Sales figures were cited to explain why photographs of ethnic people are left off the front page and why photos of the latest pop starlet

who has come down with a slight cold might be more commercially attractive. However, news is news and the executive was quick to point out that editorial decisions are not based on purely commercial criteria. This was borne out at the launch of Castillo and Hirst's (2001) study of news reporting of western Sydney, *Look Both Ways: Fairfield, Cabramatta and the Media*. A chief of staff on a Sydney paper that circulated well in western Sydney refused to cover the launch; he said words to the effect of: 'You expect us to travel all the way out there to cover a story that bags out the news media?' Martin Hirst's reply was basically, 'Well, yeah, in the interests of balance, maybe you will!' In the end no metropolitan news media sent anyone to cover the launch, not even the ABC. The ethnic stories that do make the front page are often about crime and more importantly the social framing of the story is supplied by the police or courts; more often than not a 'law and order' perspective that reinforces the theme of 'moral panic'. In short, we believe that the news media and the 'justice' system are too close; there is a lack of critical 'distance' and journalists are too easily caught up in the heightened emotions of crime:

> Journalists visualize deviance, control remedies, and political reform in much the same way as the organizations they report on. They are one of the many agencies for policing organizational life, although with a much wider mandate and field than most other agencies. This policing is usually accomplished subtly through choice of topics, sources, frames and formulations, that transform the matter into how they want it to appear.
>
> Ericson, Baranek & Chan 1987, p. 346

It is primarily through this social organisation of news gathering routines, and the mental/emotional routines that go with the bureaucratic news model, that crime and deviance are framed by the media as a means of social control. In our opinion, journalists, editors, and news organisations should take a step back from this close relationship with the police and other justice authorities. The closeness of the relationship is problematic and symptomatic of the ideological hegemony of the state and its apparatuses (courts, security services and jails). You cannot ignore such volatile fault lines; one day they might open up and swallow you.

A brief note about moral panic

Throughout the late 1990s there appeared to be a growing 'moral panic' about paedophilia. Looking back we can say with some certainty that this was the start of what has become a decade-long campaign by interest groups to 'root out' paedophilia in Australian society. The literature on moral panic also makes the point that this was an international phenomena that has had profound consequences for many individuals caught up in the issue, and for institutions, particularly churches (Hunt 1997; Horsfield 1997; Sands 1996). The international reaction to paedophilia is a classic case of 'moral panic', complete with 'action groups' who act in a vigilante fashion to 'out' suspected paedophiles, a campaigning media 'infused with hysteria', the creation of 'folk devils', and a 'disaster mentality' (Goode & Ben-Yehuda 1994, pp. 28–9).

The problem with becoming involved in a 'moral panic' from a journalistic and ethical point of view, is that it is easy to get caught up in what appears to be a very 'worthwhile' crusade. But is this really the news media's role? Lesley Sands (1996, p. 4) points out how the British media used the tragic death of toddler James Bulger and a 'scare' about paedophiles to 'symbolise all that was wrong with Britain'. Ann Bradley (1994) pointed out that 'the [British] media pursued each new sub-plot [and] issued another little moral message for the nation to take on board: "It's an evil world and we need strict rules"'.

Media–police relations became an issue during the Wood Royal Commission hearings concerning paedophilia in the mid 1990s. In the NSW Parliament, Police Minister Paul Whelan apparently demanded that the media not obstruct the proper authorities. The head of the NSW Bar Association raised the issue of a fair trial for individuals named before the Royal Commission (Devine 1996, p. 11). Frank Devine's column carried the headline 'Child Abuse: Press Won't Be Muzzled' and included the following lines:

> A good man hounded to death by the media? Good, possibly; hounded, no. ... A tormented man sustained in a state of mortal sin by negligent supervisors? Likely. God knows how many kids the *Illawarra Mercury* saved from traumatic misshaping of their lives. Unfettered media coverage of the NSW royal commission is performing a similar service ... [Police minister] Whelan must have been driven temporarily mad by the effrontery of Sydney's *Daily Telegraph*, a modern and thus essentially serious tabloid, which solved mysteries baffling to official forces of law and order [by locating Phillip Bell and Robert Dunn, when the police said (publicly) they couldn't]. ... Royal commissioners, cops, bishops, Queen's Counsels and others would serve the public best by doing their own jobs properly and leaving the media to do theirs.

> Devine 1996, p. 11

What exactly is the media's 'job' in such situations? Is it to chase paedophiles around the world in order to make a dramatic program out of their 'capture'? Is it the media's job to publish photos of where a recently released sex offender (who has served their time for crimes committed) is living and then inviting local residents to go to the house and squirt garden hoses through the letter box? Is it the media's job to take on a tone of outrage and offence then encourage its readers, listeners, and viewers to join in an orchestrated campaign of hate against young Lebanese–Australian men, or Aboriginal youths who have been completely ignored, vilified, and marginalised by the very same media? Frank Devine might think so, but we are not so sure. In the end you will have to make these decisions for yourself.

Ethical dilemmas in practice

→ ## Scenario 1

You are granted a 'one on one' interview with an Australian pop singer who is making a comeback after a serious illness. You get on well with the singer and have interviewed her several times in the past. You notice a packet of cigarettes in her bag. She admits they are hers. She smokes up to half a pack a day as it helps her deal with stress. She begs you not to disclose her smoking habit as she sees herself as a role model for young people, particularly teenage girls. She has a clean-living image and says she has a responsibility to encourage her fans in positive ways. The Australian public has taken her to their heart, and you could turn her 'good girl' image on its head. Would you?

Scenario 2

The local police offer to take you on a high-profile raid against the home of a suspected drug dealer. It all plays out like some Hollywood movie, or a scene from *CSI Miami*. You get great pictures of police officers chasing obviously Asian-looking offenders and finding illicit drug-manufacturing equipment, and the 'finished product'. About ten people are detained and marched straight past your cameras. What limitations might you put on what you showed?

Case Studies

Case study 1

Deborah Cornwall: When a source might be lying

In March 1993, former *SMH* journalist (later Channel Nine crime reporter) Deborah Cornwall was called before the NSW Independent Commission Against Corruption (ICAC) and asked to divulge the sources for a story she had written. The story was that convicted criminal, Arthur 'Neddy' Smith, was a police informant in several serious matters. In her story revealing this information, Ms Cornwall had quoted an unnamed senior NSW police officer. Commissioner Temby said that this information was false, had the potential to intimidate witnesses, and that it put Mr Smith's life in danger. Despite this, Ms Cornwall refused to divulge the names of the allegedly corrupt police officers who gave her the information. She told the ICAC commissioner that she had given an undertaking of confidentiality to her sources and argued that it was a matter of conscience. She also said she would adhere to the AJA's Code of Ethics, which, as we have noted, in the 1984 clause made confidentiality an absolute rule.

In response, Commissioner Temby suggested that the police had given this (false) information to the reporter in order to have Smith killed in jail. The commissioner also wanted to protect the integrity of the ICAC and expose the corrupt officers behind the misinformation to the reporter. When Deborah Cornwall formally refused to name her sources, Mr Temby referred the matter to the NSW Supreme Court.

Cornwall was charged with contempt of the Commission and tried before Justice Abadee. She was convicted and sentenced to two months in jail that was suspended on condition that she undertake 90 hours of community service at Redfern Legal Centre.

According to a commentary piece by the then *SMH* legal correspondent, John Slee (1994, pp. 11–12), there was speculation in legal circles that Commissioner Temby 'hoped to bolster his inquiry by drawing Ms Cornwall into it as a witness with possibly useful information'. This would potentially have forced her to consider more serious questions such as should she help the ICAC or remain a reporter. John Slee's final comment is certainly worth discussion:

> In all, it was a clumsy and unnecessary exercise, asserting one principle to destroy another, when in truth both can and should co-exist.

Issues and questions from case study 1

1   Should Ms Cornwall have given up the names of her police contacts?
2   If the authorities say your source is lying, but they don't know their name, how do they know?
3   How would you have felt if you published such material as that mentioned above, and it led to someone being killed?
4   Is there an argument that if the information can be proven to be wrong, you would no longer feel duty-bound to respect your source's confidentiality?
5   Hasn't the source(s) just used you to spread lies, and hidden behind the veil of guaranteed confidentiality?
6   Why should you protect the source(s) when they have lied to you?
7   What principles of co-existence is John Slee talking about in his commentary?

→ ## Case study 2

Jailed for contempt

1: Tony Barrass

Perth journalist Tony Barrass served five days of a seven-day sentence in 1989 and was fined $10,000 for twice refusing to name a source. He was jailed for refusing to tell a Perth Magistrate who gave him print-outs of two tax files. He had been subpoenaed to give evidence at a preliminary hearing of a charge against a suspended Tax Department clerk who had been accused of disclosing tax information to the *Sunday Times* about former banker Laurie Connell and his wife. Barrass wrote an article in the *Sunday Times* alleging tax officers were selling confidential information for as little as $20. Barrass refused to tell the magistrate how he obtained the documents. After refusing a second time he was jailed for the maximum period of seven days (he could have been fined $175). Barrass was later fined $10,000 for again refusing to name the same source when the case came to trial in the District Court ('Contempt Law Ridiculous Says Freed Journalist' 1989; 'Jailing Reporters "Inappropriate"' 1989).

2: Chris Nicholls

Television journalist Chris Nicholls refused to reveal a source during his own trial in the District Court in 1993 for impersonation, forgery, and false pretences. It was alleged that he obtained bank statements and documents by impersonating the de facto husband of the South Australian Tourism Minister in an attempt to show her improper dealings during parliamentary debates on gaming machine legislation. Nicholls maintained during the trial that he had a confidential source who had done the impersonating and forgery. When pressed to reveal the source, he refused. The trial went for four weeks, and a jury took eight hours to acquit Nicholls of the charges. He was then charged with contempt of court over his refusal to answer the questions about the source during the trial. He pleaded guilty and was sentenced to four months' jail. On appeal, the Full Court of the South Australian Supreme Court upheld the trial judge's decision, but agreed to reduce the sentence to three months (Pearson 1993).

3: Joe Budd

Brisbane *Courier-Mail* journalist Joe Budd was jailed in Brisbane in 1992 for refusing to reveal a source during a defamation trial in the Queensland Supreme Court in which his former employer, Queensland Newspapers Limited, was the defendant. He refused to name a high-level contact in the office of former Police Minister Russell Cooper. The source had given him information about allegations of police misbehaviour at a football carnival on the condition that he would not be identified. The article contained allegedly defamatory statements about a barrister. When Budd refused to name his source, Justice John Dowsett suggested he could write the name of his source on a piece of paper and hand it to the bar table only. He refused. The court was adjourned to allow him to telephone his source and seek his permission to use his name but he was unable to make contact. When the court reconvened, and Budd again refused to name his source, Justice Dowsett charged him with contempt. Justice Dowsett called Budd's view (that he shouldn't reveal the source when he agreed he wouldn't) 'misguided', and said it was impossible to comprehend why journalists should feel entitled to conceal sources. Budd was jailed for 14 days, but served only six (Slee 1992).

Issues and questions raised by case study 2

1   This is the classic ethical dilemma—do I reveal the name of my source and avoid jail and/or a fine, or do I stand by my journalistic ethical principles and risk time behind bars?

2   Some states in the United States have so-called 'shield laws' that protect the names of sources. Such laws have been proposed for several Australian states. What is the current situation?

3   The use of unnamed sources has traditionally been the cause of mistrust of the media (the feeling being that if you don't name your source how does the public know they really exist). How do you avoid that mistrust?

4   How often could it be a case of a journalist using an 'anonymous' source because they have something to hide, rather than a source with something to lose if exposed?

5   If journalists were more credible (remember their low rating mentioned in earlier chap-
     ters) then the public might trust the need for confidentiality and legislators and the judi-
     ciary might be more open to journalists' arguments for the protection of sources. In this
     instance how could you make journalists more credible?
6   Fewer promises of anonymity to sources would be a good start, wouldn't it?
7   What do you need to consider when a source demands anonymity?
8   What alternatives are there to blanket anonymity?
9   How often are 'anonymous sources' revealing something controversial to test public
     response before adopting it officially? (And if there is an adverse reaction they can
     always wash their hands of it).
10   You have to ask why anonymity is so important in each case. Is it really justified and
     does granting it 'weaken' the story in the eyes of the public?
11   Or could it be a trade-off—a juicy bit of information about a competitor or political foe
     now, in return for some favourable publicity for the source 'down the track'?
12   What do the various media professional practice policies say about confidentiality of
     sources?
13   While it is very noble to defend the confidentiality of your source(s), would you really
     want to go to jail?

→   ## Case study 3
     ## Geoff Clark

In June 2001, the *Age* in Melbourne published a sensational story titled 'Geoff Clark:
Power and Rape', alleging the then Chairman of the Aboriginal and Torres Strait Islander
Commission had raped four women about 20 years ago (Rintoul 2002). By publishing
a story that made public allegations that were deemed by many as not fit for publication, the *Age* was criticised on the one hand for 'trial by media' and then praised for
good investigative journalism. In the article, four women—one of whom is Aboriginal—
alleged the ATSIC leader raped them. Of the four, one allegation did not survive the
courts, two did not survive police investigation, and one had not been reported.

The *Age's* editor at the time, Michael Gawenda, said the paper's legal advice was
that there was a risk attached to publishing, but his final call was that 'it was a risk
worth taking' (Rintoul 2002). The view was that where one allegation might not have
been published, four women alleging rape demonstrated a pattern of behaviour that
demanded publication. The *Sydney Morning Herald* was not privy to its sister publication's several months of investigation and was given six hours to look at the story
before publication. Both ran the story on page 1. The *SMH* had a comment from the
Victorian police, but the *Age* did not. The statement said that the police were aware
of the allegations, but 'after consultations with the Office of Public Prosecutions the
matters will not be proceeded with at this stage' (Rintoul 2002).

A year later, two of the women who had accused Clark of raping them sued him for mental and physical injuries (Rule 2002). Clarke invoked the statute of limitations to prevent the two women bringing their civil action against him. The statute says that claims for personal injury damages must not be brought more than six years after any alleged wrongdoing, but the women intended to counter-sue (Milovanovic 2003).

In mid February, 2004, a Victorian judge found that Clark had led two pack rapes against a woman 33 years previously (Rintoul & Schubert 2004). He granted the woman, Carol Anne Stingel, the right to bring a civil action for damages against Clark, the second woman to win the right to sue Clark, following his cousin Joanne McGuinness, who claimed she was assaulted in 1981 (Rintoul & Schubert, 2004). Outside the court Clark denied the alleged rapes took place and said: 'I must be the most vilified man in Australian history, thanks to you people (the media)' (Rintoul & Schubert 2004). At this stage Mr Clark was suspended on full pay (about $240,000 a year) over his conviction for obstructing police during a pub brawl.

In the middle of 2003, when Clark was being investigated over his taxpayer-funded travel, he lashed out at the *Australian* for what he called 'a dishonest campaign of reportage of indigenous affairs and, in particular, of myself' (Price 2003b). Clark went on to ask a rhetorical question: 'When is the *Australian* going to stop treating its own readers like mugs and abandon its campaign of deceit in its coverage of indigenous issues?' He had repeatedly denied allegations of travel rorts raised in the media (Price 2003b).

Issues and questions raised by case study 3

1   Why do you think the two most powerful print media organisations in Australia attacked Geoff Clark in such a major way?

2   Is this just another case—like that of Professor Manning Clark in an earlier chapter—of a tall poppy being brought down by the media?

3   Examine the *Age* newspaper's coverage of rape allegations against the Aboriginal leader. Would you have published them?

4   If the police and court system did not proceed with the allegations against Clark, what makes the *Age* think it knows more than the legal system?

5   What justification do you see for the publication of the rape allegations?

6   Research the *Australian*'s coverage of indigenous affairs in mid 2003. What is your reaction?

7   Was the *Australian* treating its readers like mugs?

8   Isn't a person presumed innocent until proven guilty?

9   Isn't this another case, like the *ACA* suicide case study in chapter 7, of the media acting as judge, jury, and pseudo executioner?

10   What do you make of Clark's claim that thanks to the media, he's the most vilified man in Australian history?

→ ## Case study 4
The Bronx in Villawood

The headline on the *Daily Telegraph* story read 'Masked in Hate' and the accompanying photograph had the caption: 'The defiant image of urban violence in Villawood'. The story began as follows:

> *He is an urban guerrilla. His face shrouded behind a shirt, his body tensed in defiance, he oozes the teenage menace that has made one place—Villawood—synonymous with everything that is wrong in Sydney's suburbs.*

> Newman 1996

Martin Newman's story was not about suburban terrorists, it was about a group of bored teenagers (and some younger children) on a housing estate in the Sydney suburb of Villawood, who lit a fire on an oval behind a row of Housing Commission homes. A woman with a young child, concerned the flames were close to her fence, called the police and the fire brigade. The fire fighters got caught up in a verbal and physical slanging match with the youths, the fire was extinguished and some stones were thrown, allegedly by both sides. The youths then turned their attention on the woman who called the firemen. Ms Jennifer James said they threatened her and her children. She said they also threatened to burn down her home. The *Daily Telegraph* very kindly allowed Ms James space to air her grievances on page 4 (James 1996). The tabloids (both print and TV) had a field day. The youths were criminalised; it was a 'juvenile crime' issue for the *Telegraph* (Newman 1996). The then NSW Police Minister, Paul Whelan, called on the police to break up the alleged 'gangs' in order to maintain law and order. He announced that anyone found to be a gang member would be thrown off the housing estate (English & Gelastopolous 1996).

Channel Nine's *A Current Affair* (naturally) sent a camera crew and journalist to the estate to talk to Ms James and the 'gang' members. According to stories told by the youths, boredom, lack of amenities, and no work opportunities contributed to their pranks. They had the obligatory shots of the youths throwing stones and acting defiantly. However, when other reporters began to probe events in a more serious and professional manner, allegations were made that the *ACA* crew and *Daily Telegraph* reporters had bribed the 'gangsters' with pizza and soft drink to pose and act tough. In a recounting of the story later given to one of the co-authors by a youth worker who had been on the estate at the time, it was alleged that a reporter on the scene had actually encouraged one of the young people present to go home to get a gun that they could pose with. In the photo, the kids covered their faces with T-shirts; the social worker said that this was done at the request of the photographer.

Issues and questions raised by case study 4

1   What is your opinion of the *Daily Telegraph*'s opening paragraph? What impression would it leave on the audience?
2   Was it a 'fair and accurate' representation of what was happening in Villawood?
3   Why would the *Telegraph* want to play the 'urban jungle' card?
4   It is common practice for the tabloid media, like the *Telegraph* and *ACA,* when they need pictures for their stories, to approach participants and ask them to 'act out' activities. Would you be comfortable approaching the teenagers in this case and asking them to recreate their antics?
5   Can the provision of pizza and soft drinks to the teenagers be justified?
6   Is it bribery?
7   If you think so, what does that say for the story?
8   What do the journalists' Code of Ethics and the various Charters of Editorial Independence say about such action?
9   Is this a case of the media promoting a moral panic?

Case study 5

Rodney King bashing

Four white police officers were videotaped beating Rodney King, a black male, in Los Angeles on 3 March 1991. The video showed King being struck fifty-six times with metal batons, kicked, and shot with a stun gun. The beating left King with a broken leg, five facial fractures, and twenty stitches in his head. The four officers (Sgt Stacy Koon, Officers Laurence Powell, Theodore Briseno, and Timothy Wind) were charged with assault and using excessive force. Despite the video evidence showing clear police brutality, all four officers were acquitted. The defence successfully argued that the officers used a 'controlled escalation of force' on a man who was drunk and resisting arrest. Michael Stone, representing Officer Powell (who struck fifty of the fifty-six blows) argued that 'the violence of the video is obvious but you don't see uncontrolled police brutality, you see a controlled application of baton strikes for the obvious reason of getting this man into custody' (ABC TV 1992). Due to pre-trial press coverage, the state trial was moved from Los Angeles to the affluent, mostly white suburbs of Simi Valley (Garneau 1992). The case was argued before a jury containing no African-Americans. Following the verdict, the streets of Los Angeles erupted in arson, looting, and shooting in what became known as the 'Los Angeles riots'.

In order to prevent another 'riot', at the subsequent federal trial of the four police officers on charges of violating King's civil rights, televised coverage was forbidden. Permission to provide audio coverage of verdicts from the courtroom was withdrawn at the last minute. This made little difference; media technology overcame the problem.

CNN set up an information relay that provided fast transmission of the verdicts as they were being read out: 'the television viewer could hear the words of judgment from the courtroom just a few seconds before the CNN reporter repeated them more clearly. When the viewer got the news, it was about three seconds old' (Stahel 1993, p. 16).

With the acquittal of the four officers the issue of police brutality was no longer such an issue. The media therefore 'ever resourceful ... quickly switched themes from police brutality to suburban racism' (O'Sullivan 1992). The jury, which had contained an Asian and an Hispanic, suddenly became an 'all white jury' (O'Sullivan 1992). O'Sullivan writes that the mainstream media all followed the same themes in its reports:

> Watching network TV in particular was rather like living in a one party state whose vast propaganda apparatus was ultimately dependent upon the talents of one overworked clerk. Dissenters were allowed a say on discussion programs. But news reports were ideologically uniform.

O'Sullivan believes the theme of 'the urban crisis' (a sub-set of 'moral panic') was so ingrained in the media that it was reported, rather than what was actually happening. There is no doubt that news is often distorted to make it more 'appealing' to the viewer. As Stamm and Bowes (1990, p. 93) write in *The Mass Communication Process*, 'TV news tries for visually exciting stories to attract audience interest. But these needs may distort (or ignore) what is of central importance, or they may change the emphasis considerably.' Thus in the Rodney King coverage, the emphasis was 'changed considerably' from police brutality to suburban racism in order to make the news more 'appealing'.

Media coverage of the Rodney King case, from the videotaped beating to the last trial, was extensive. Yet the media seems to only pay attention to the issue of race relations when things turn nasty and therefore become 'newsworthy'. At the American Newspaper Publishers' Association Convention in 1992 a panel of mostly minority journalists discussed the media coverage of Rodney King. They concluded that: 'The racial violence unleashed in Los Angeles caught America by surprise because news organisations ignore the bitter racial lines dividing America, in part because they lack a minority perspective' (Garneau 1992, p. 11). *Washington Post* columnist Dorothy Gilliam believes the media must carry some of the blame for stereotyping blacks into the role of aggressors:

> Most Americans learn about other races and cultures from the media, which often show 'images' of minority groups without 'context'—pictures of blacks looting stores and attacking whites without the reporting of long-term social, economic, and racial problems that led to such a violent eruption of frustration and outrage.

Gilliam cited in Garneau 1992, p. 12

Issues and questions raised by case study 5

1   So-called 'high profile' cases always pose problems for the media. How do you adequately cover the pre-trial stories without jeopardising the accused's right to a fair trial?

2   Do you care whether they get a fair trial?

3   In the Rodney King case they had to shift the trial to a different area because of the pre-trial publicity. Could such a situation occur in Australia?

4   Research where Australian media organisations and journalists have been charged with contempt of court. What sort of things did they do?

5   The Rodney King trial became a trial about racism and repression as much as it was about police brutality. How can you prevent being swept up by public anger over such events?

6   What is your reaction to the media talking about an 'all-white' jury (that contained an Asian and an Hispanic)?

7   What of the criticism that the media all followed the same line on the story? Where were the alternative views?

8   Are alternative views expressed in the Australian media?

9   Could the TV stations that broadcast live pictures of the rioting be accused of inciting it?

10   Do you accept the criticism that the media only covers race relations when things turn nasty?

11   Research the Australian media's record on reporting issues of race.

12   Are there any similarities in the way the Australian and US media handle issues of race?

Case study 6
The poor old Paxtons

This is one of the modern-day classics of 'tabloid media' attacks. Initiated by the Nine Network's *A Current Affair*, it snowballed into a media frenzy and the 'poor old' Paxtons got hammered. It was clearly a story designed to generate 'moral panic' about unemployment and to stereotype young people as 'dole bludgers'. It contains the classic element of 'moral panic', the creation of an opportunity for Government intervention, 'incorporation into legislation and social policy' (Cohen 1972, p. 9).

Three Melbourne teenagers and their mother, the Paxton family, had been on welfare for some time. *ACA* reporter Mike Munro offered them an opportunity to go with him to an island on the Great Barrier Reef where they would be offered work. The two boys and their sister accepted the offer. When they arrived on the island, the work offer evaporated into a series of conditional promises. The first was that the job would only be there if the boys agreed to get their (long) hair cut. They refused. Their sister was told she would have to wear a uniform—she refused, because it was too 'unstylish' for her taste. Mike Munro and Ray Martin were outraged. On Monday 4 March 1996, the story aired on *ACA* and was unflattering to the Paxton family. They were portrayed as 'no-hopers', 'dole bludgers' who didn't want to work and were not prepared to make small sacrifices like moving more than 3000 kilometres from Melbourne to the Barrier Reef ('paradise', according to Mike Munro), get their hair cut, or wear a uniform. Munro told the *Daily Telegraph* that Channel Nine received hundreds of calls after the Paxtons were exposed. *A Current Affair* even dragged new Prime Minister John Howard into the debate. The tabloid papers picked it up and eventually, after manufactured public outrage, the Paxtons lost their entitlement to unemployment benefits.

Just three days after the 1996 federal election, the *Daily Telegraph* reintroduced 'dole bludger' into the Australian vernacular (Akerman 1996a). The paper used strong, emotive language to attack the Paxtons, using front-page headlines like 'Stop their Dole'; reinforced by sub-heads, 'The Kids Who Refused Jobs in Paradise' and 'Community Outrage' (Hilferty, Lalor & Dunlevy 1996). The lead story also reinforced the new Government's 'get tough' attitude towards 'dole recipients who were not really looking for work' (Hilferty, Lalor & Dunlevy 1996, p. 4). The *Telegraph*'s senior columnist, Piers Akerman (1996a, 1996b), poked fun at the Paxtons, suggesting they were somehow 'New Age' and invoking 'hippy' images. The *Telegraph* editorial on 6 March branded the Paxtons as 'lazy'. It ended, 'For their own sake, and for the sake of all our children they must be ordered to take a job - or lose their unemployment handout' ('Take Job or Lose Dole' 1996).

Media Watch's then host, Stuart Littlemore, took a swipe at *A Current Affair* and the *Daily Telegraph*, over their coverage of the Paxton's story. Piers Akerman gave himself the 'right of reply', describing *Media Watch* as 'the essence of the whining, self-congratulatory envy journalism' (Akerman 1996b). Once the initial 'outrage' had cooled, the *SMH* ran a column by broadcaster Jaslyn Hall. Hall (1996) criticised the media's preoccupation with attacks on young people and youth culture. In his *Sun-Herald* column, Brian Toohey (1996a) linked the attacks on the 'vilified' Paxton family to 'a spectacular error made by well-paid economists in the Treasury and Finance departments'.

Issues and questions raised by case study 6

1   The Paxtons deserved everything they got, didn't they? That was the feeling on talk-back radio and in the pubs around the time.

2   There was *ACA* offering them a shot at a job in 'paradise' and they couldn't even cut their hair or wear a uniform. *ACA* was serving up the stereotypical 'dole bludger' for the hard-working Aussie battler in the living rooms of the outer suburbs to abuse, weren't they?

3   How would you justify the *ACA* approach?

4   And the *Daily Telegraph*'s follow-up?

5   'Bashing a dole bludger' has always been popular sport in tabloid media (print and TV). Why do you think they always take such an attacking approach to those on unemployment benefits?

6   Many university journalism students know how hard it is to get even part-time work during their studies. Would they have sympathy for the Paxtons?

7   Investigate what the life of an unemployed young person is really like.
8   Research the current media treatment of unemployed youth in the tabloid and serious media. Is it any different to during the 'Paxton Affair'?

Case study 7

The exposure of John Marsden

In May 1996, after a long legal battle and at the height of the 'moral panic' about paedophilia, Channel Seven's *Witness* program ran a story about prominent gay lawyer and civil rights activist, John Marsden. Eventually the story backfired on Seven and John Marsden won a remarkable defamation battle in which he represented himself. *Witness* employed actors to re-enact scenes it alleges were from Mr Marsden's 'life' as a paedophile. At the time the story was being prepared, the Wood Royal Commission into the NSW Police Force had been hearing evidence of paedophile networks operating in the Sydney–Wollongong region and overseas. The NSW Supreme Court refused to block screening of the story on *Witness,* but in a strange judgment, the court noted that the material might be defamatory, suggesting that, 'it would be verging on the perverse for a jury to find otherwise' (cited in Akerman 1996c, p. 11). Piers Akerman described the *Witness* report as 'sensationalist' and 'inaccurate', suggesting it might be prejudicial to Mr Marsden getting a fair trial, should he ever be arraigned on charges resulting from police and Royal Commission inquiries.

Marsden sued the Seven Network for defamation over allegations contained in broadcasts on *Today Tonight* (in March 1995) and later on *Witness,* in what would became the longest running defamation case in Australian history to date (Lloyd 2001). He was awarded $525,000 in damages plus costs, substantially less than he had hoped for. Marsden declared outside the court that, despite his win, his reputation had been forever tainted (Lloyd 2001). A *60 Minutes* item on Marsden titled 'The price of a reputation' and aired on 8 July 2001 said Marsden's five-year battle to clear his name had cost him $6 million (Lyons 2001). The program detailed how Marsden had first been 'outed' as a suspected paedophile under Parliamentary privilege by a Labor member of the New South Wales Parliament on the basis of a statement by a convicted paedophile, Colin Fisk (Lyons 2001).

Issues and questions raised by case study 7

1   Was John Marsden a victim of 'moral panic'?
2   Should the *Witness* program have taken more care with the information supplied by its informants?
3   Why do paedophilia and homosexuality become so mistakenly entwined in the media's coverage of such issues?
4   Do you agree with Marsden that his reputation is 'forever tainted'?
5   What affect do such revelations have on his family and friends?

10

ISSUES OF DECEPTION

PLAGIARISM, CHEQUEBOOK JOURNALISM, FREEBIES, AND FALSEHOODS

Objectives

After reading and discussing this chapter you will have been challenged by:

- The principles of honest reporting.
- The reasons behind the pressure to deceive in news gathering.
- The pros and cons of chequebook journalism.
- The ethical dilemmas associated with investigative journalism.
- Whether it is ever justifiable to deceive news sources 'for the greater good'.

Introduction: Sensational stories, too bad they ain't true!

One of the most respected newspapers in the United States, the *New York Times,* the so-called 'journal of record' carries on its front page the slogan 'All the news that's fit to print'. Yet on 11 May 2003, the *NYT* was forced into an embarrassing admission. Under the headline: 'CORRECTING THE RECORD', the paper's front page lead admitted:

> A staff reporter for the *New York Times* committed frequent acts of journalistic fraud while covering significant news events in recent months, an investigation by *Times* journalists

has found. The widespread fabrication and plagiarism represent a profound betrayal of trust and a low point in the 152-year history of the newspaper.

'CORRECTING THE RECORD: *Times* Reporter Who Resigned Leaves Long Trail of Deception' 2003

In this way the *Times* revealed what has become known as 'the Jayson Blair affair'. Twenty-seven-year-old Jayson had resigned from the paper earlier after it was discovered he had plagiarised parts of a story of the Texas family of a soldier missing in the Iraq War. A team of five reporters and two researchers spent a week looking at stories filed by Blair over the previous seven months. The resulting four-page, 7000-word investigation showed errors in half the seventy-three articles Blair had written since October 2002 (Dalton 2003). The embarrassing exposé also invited *Times* readers to point out any other errors that might have occurred in Blair's stories.

The African–American reporter had habitually filed stories from places he never visited, quoted people he never talked to, and described details he never saw (Rosen 2003). Blair had selected details from photographs to create the impression he had been somewhere or seen someone, when he had not. The *New York Times* investigators said 'his tools of deceit were a cellphone and a laptop computer—which allowed him to blur his true whereabouts—as well as round-the-clock access to databases of news articles from which he stole' ('CORRECTING THE RECORD: *Times* Reporter Who Resigned Leaves Long Trail of Deception' 2003, p. 1). The *NYT* web site carried examples of Blair's deception. One example is a 6 April 2003 story, headed 'Family Begins Trip to Rejoin Freed Soldier'. In the article, Blair described the decision by the parents of rescued Iraq War prisoner Jessica Lynch to fly to Germany to see her while she was undergoing treatment. The *Times* investigation found that, although the story carried the dateline of Charleston, West Virginia, 5 April, hotels in the area had no record of Blair checking in. An editor in the national department of the *Times* said he saw Blair in the newsroom in New York at 4 p.m. that day. The editor, who had been under the impression Blair was in Charleston when he spoke to him late that morning, asked the reporter how he had returned to New York so quickly. Blair said he had taken the 2 p.m. flight. There does not appear to have been such a flight that day. The article stated that Lynch's family had flown to Germany on a commercial flight. But Brandi Lynch, Private Lynch's sister, said in a telephone interview that the H.J. Heinz Company's private jet had been made available to the family ('Case Studies—When Truth Becomes a Casualty' 2003).

Blair had been a *Times* prodigy who had charmed and dazzled the right people on a rapid rise from cocky college student to *NYT* national reporter—a position that enabled him to 'create' the stories the way he did (Rosen 2003). Some suggested his rapid rise was Affirmative Action in action—what appeared to be minor errors at first were overlooked. Blair had started as an intern five years previously and had been previously disciplined for errors in his articles. At one stage in 2002 the newspaper's editor, Jonathon Landman, sent an email to news administrators urging them to stop Blair from writing for the paper (Cock 2003). By an amazing twist of fate, it was another former *NY Times* intern, Macerena

Hernandez, who was also on the paper's Affirmative Action intern program with Blair, who was to help bring him down. Both were offered jobs at the paper after their three-month internships. But Macerena decided to move back to Texas to live with her mother (who didn't speak English or drive) after her father was killed in a car accident. She wrote a story for the *San Antonio Express-News* in mid April about Edward Anguiano, the last American soldier missing in action in the Iraq War (Hernandez 2003). After reading Blair's version of the same story, she became convinced he had 'stolen' her story—the similarities were too blatant. Hernandez dismisses suggestions that Blair's misdeeds were about race, diversity in the newsroom, and affirmative action:

> His story is that of a guy who disrespected his profession, cheated his readers and deceived his editors. Period. Any other way of looking at it lets Jayson Blair, a man who stole from me and many other journalists, off the hook.

> Hernandez 2003

In one of those 'it could only happen in America' postscripts to the Jayson Blair affair, four weeks after the scandal broke, after Blair had spent time in rehabilitation to kick a cocaine habit and appeared on the cover of *Newsweek,* he had an agent 'selling' a book proposal and was fielding offers to sell his story to Hollywood (Jackson 2003e). Blair's is perhaps the most spectacular recent case of plagiarism, but it happens all too often, not just in the United States, but in Australia as well. We are continually amazed at the seniority and public profile of journalists who get caught plagiarising other people's work, or passing off barely disguised media releases as their own work. If there is one lesson that all journalism students should learn from the Jayson Blair fiasco and from ABC television's *Media Watch* program (Marr 2003d), it is that if you plagiarise, you will get caught out.

This chapter outlines the basic principles of honest reporting and the major transgressions. The argument will be clearly made that the pressures to deceive, to plagiarise, and to engage in chequebook journalism are part and parcel of the dominant journalistic culture and typify the fault lines discussed in earlier chapters.

Examples will be taken from Australian and international cases to illustrate the themes of honesty, cultural interpretation, when it is OK to accept 'contra' deals, and the grey areas of debate about 'good' or 'bad' cases of deception in journalism.

This chapter examines the 'public good' argument and the utilitarian principle of the 'greater good' in relation to journalism ethics—in particular, paying for stories that are in the public interest or of interest to the public, and deceptions to expose wrongdoing. A central question in this essay is: Are there ever times when deception is permissible, or justified?

Fair and honest means ...

> MEAA Code Clause 1: Report and interpret honestly, striving for accuracy, fairness and disclosure of all essential facts. Do not suppress relevant available facts, or give distorting emphasis. Do your utmost to give a fair opportunity for reply.

The opening point of the MEAA/AJA Code of Ethics says it succinctly—journalists should be honest, accurate, fair, and should disclose all facts. Clause 8 of the Code reminds us that reporters should use honest means to obtain material. Much of the rest of this chapter is a litany of at best suspect, at worst dishonest and unethical, practices used by journalists to gain stories.

It is our contention that it is the pressure of competition, deadlines, and individual egos that lead a small minority of journalists into compromising positions that may lead them to cut ethical corners. Not all journalists are so inclined. Far from it. Most journalists go about their daily routine never once in their career faced with a situation where they might cross the line into suspect behaviour. Others face the ethical dilemma, and take a stand against it. But a small minority, as we have said, give in to the temptation of taking others' work without acknowledging it, inventing sources, accepting a free trip or other 'freebies' that might lead to a compromising position in the future, or engage in suspect activities (like pretending to be someone they aren't) in order to get that 'scoop'.

It is undoubtedly the pressure of competition and the need to lift ratings or sales that drives chequebook journalism. But in most cases of suspect actions, the first thing to ask is whether you really want the story, and is there any other way of getting it that doesn't involve subterfuge or payment?

Freebies, junkets, and compromising positions

> MEAA Code Clause 4: Do not allow personal interest, or any belief, commitment, payment, gift or benefit, to undermine your accuracy, fairness or independence.

The issue of gifts and inducements offered to journalists is covered in the AJA Code of Ethics, but in practice the rules are set and broken *in house* by journalists and their editors. Many journalists see nothing inherently wrong with accepting some forms of 'freebies' from sources. After all, they take their sources to lunch from time to time to 'pump them' for information, and will often send them a 'bottle of something' (usually at office expense) along with the corporate Christmas card as an annual 'thank you' for services rendered. So why not let a source offer the same hospitality? Why not accept the fancy folder or conference participants' satchel along with the speech handouts? Or the pen, the notepad, the free use of the phone? These 'freebies' seem petty, but there is not a big jump between that and the free tickets to the footy or live theatre, the autographed copy of the star's new book, and down the spiral to cheap holidays or free trips.

The Melbourne *Age* newspaper, under the editorship of Creighton Burns, had the policy that there had to be an executive clearance for people to accept free travel. If the offer was accepted it was on the basis that the reporter was under no obligation to write a favourable story and the paper declared in its pages that a story had been prepared with the assistance of certain parties. Creighton Burns's argument was that newspapers cannot afford the luxury of virtue. He claimed that the Arts and Travel pages of every major newspaper would be blank if journalists were not allowed to accept the hospitality of commercially interested parties (cited in 'Ethics and the Media' 1987). But it raises serious questions about just how far this relationship should go and how watertight are the claims that the journalist/editor will not be influenced by a debt of gratitude felt to the sponsor? When does this sort of sponsorship cross over into advertising copy and become an *advertorial?* In the 1970s one of the co-authors was given a free flight on a State Government-chartered plane to cover the opening of a natural gas pipeline. He was also given a cigarette lighter containing natural gas. If the State Government hadn't offered the flight, then the ABC would not have been able to send a crew from Brisbane to the event. It's not an issue nowadays with TV stations all having helicopters, but then (and perhaps among less affluent regional media still) it was a case of accept the offer or don't cover the story, or have it covered by a freelance journalist and a part-time camera crew.

The argument is that if journalists accept 'freebies' and other favours, like junkets, they place themselves under some form of obligation to those handing out the 'freebies'. They run the risk of losing their independence. Their job is to tell the news, good or bad, and they might feel reluctant to write a 'bad' story because they feel in some way indebted to the source because of the favours they have accepted. This is also an argument against getting too close to contacts, too: It is hard to write an unfavourable story about someone who has become a friend. The chief motive of those handing out the 'freebies' is to obtain 'good' publicity or at least reduce the instances of 'bad' publicity. As journalism educator and ethics author John Hurst suggests:

> Rarely are strings attached to the benefits they [sources] confer, and seldom is it explicitly stated that they want something in return. Rather, it is suggested that the real aim is to provide a good story, and the junket is merely to assist the journalist carry out the job.

> Hurst 1992a

Journalists will admit privately that the gifts, however small, are probably intended to 'buy' their goodwill, but would never admit they were influenced, or that their independence had been compromised in any way. Regardless of what they believe, journalists must be vigilant that their news gathering activities are not compromised by any favour from a source, however seemingly insignificant.

At the 'top end of the "freebie" scale' you might be offered a flight to the site of the company's latest venture (overseas perhaps, or near a fashionable resort, where you'll be housed 'for convenience sake') just so you can see the scope of the project for yourself. Or you are writing travel features and end up somewhere new every weekend at your host's expense. At what stage does the quality or quantity of the hospitality start to influence your stories?

Most news organisations have very strict rules about what can be accepted by their news staff—usually it amounts to accepting nothing over the value of a few dollars. Some in-house policies state that 'freebies' must be handed in and given to charity. The safest course of action is probably to accept virtually nothing without first clearing it with a superior.

Chequebook journalism

MEAA Code Clause 7: Do your utmost to ensure disclosure of any direct or indirect payment made for interviews, pictures, information or stories.

The MEAA Code of Ethics does not preclude chequebook journalism, though the 1990s Review Committee did suggest that disclosure of payments to sources should be automatic (Ethics Review Committee 1997, p. 40). Chequebook journalism has been around for as long as the modern newspaper, at least 250 years. The late John Avieson, one of the founders of journalism education is Australia, noted that while the media trumpets the cause of freedom of the press and the public's right to know:

> When they pay people to keep that information out of rival media, they are using their wealth to subvert the rights of the people they are supposed to champion.

> Avieson 1992 p. 45.

In a very public way, the practices of chequebook journalism highlight the centrality of the economic fault line in modern journalism—the quest for greater profits will cause editors and proprietors to override the public functions of the news media. Chequebook journalism taints the information that it buys and distorts the news picture. As John Hurst and Sally White (1994, p. 195) wrote, chequebook journalism 'sometimes encourages greed on the part of the seller and a frantic, unseemly scramble between buyers to outbid their rivals'. There's also no doubt that some media companies see chequebook journalism as just another business expense.

Aside from the odiousness of 'paying for exclusive rights to tell', there are a number of issues associated with the practice that warrant consideration. The practice is widespread, particularly among gossip magazines, tabloid newspapers, and television current affairs programs. Magazines in the highly competitive women's or gossip market are continually engaging in chequebook journalism as is the Nine television network in its flagship pro-grams, *A Current Affair* and *60 Minutes,* and Seven on *Today Tonight.* Often the gossip mag-azine and the television interests will join forces, and the person at the centre of media attention will appear on one of the TV current affairs shows, and their story will also appear in a gossip magazine. How much they are paid for their 'exclusives' is rarely released publicly, but most figures quoted in the media by their opposition are highly educated guesses, in some cases because they had been involved in the bidding war, too.

There have been plenty of examples of chequebook journalism in Australia in recent years. The following were mong the more celebrated:

- James Scott, the 23-year-old Brisbane medical student and mountain climber who sur-vived 43 days in a Himalayan snow cave eating only chocolate bars, who told his story to *60 Minutes* for a reported $100,000.
- Tony Bullimore, the British yachtsman rescued in the southern ocean in 1997 at a cost to the Australian taxpayers of $200,000 was paid $10,000 by the Seven Network for his account of the drama. Another account at the time put the Bullimore figure at $150,000, but the *Today Tonight* exclusive proved not to be worth it—the story was out-rated on the night by arch rival *A Current Affair* (Freeman 1997).
- Bob Hawke and Blanche D'Alpuget, who pocketed an estimated $120,000 from *Women's Day* and *60 Minutes* for sharing their love story.
- Sally Carey, wife of two-timing husband Aussie Rules football star Wayne, who was said to have been paid a five-figure sum for sharing her hurt with readers of *New Idea* (Callaghan 2003).

- Lindy Chamberlain apparently banked $250,000 for telling her story ('a dingo took my baby') to *60 Minutes* after her release from jail (Wilmoth 1997).

No sooner had the lone survivor of the Thredbo disaster, Stuart Diver, been pulled from the rubble on that fateful Saturday afternoon in early August 1997, after being trapped for 65 hours, than the media was clamouring for his exclusive story. Eighteen people, including Diver's wife, Sally, died in the tragedy. Diver hired celebrity agent Harry M. Miller to handle negotiations with the media. This was the same Harry M. Miller who was quoted in the *Sunday Age* the day after the rescue as saying: 'It would be ghoulish and disgusting if any used-car dealer agents or any of the media tried to buy or sell this man's story. This is all so tragic and awful that if anyone goes sniffing around this story it would be just awful' (quoted in Freeman 1997). The Seven network won Stuart Diver's story not by offering a lump sum there and then, but rather a job as a 'special commentator' whose work, the network said at the time, would include covering the Winter Olympics in Japan in early 1998. This time the story on Seven's short-lived *Witness* program rated well. It averaged a little more than two million viewers in the five mainland capitals (Oliver & Russell 1997).

But the news isn't always that good. Consider the relatively recent case when chequebook journalism backfired in England. 'WORLD EXCLUSIVE We stop crime of the century POSH KIDNAP' screamed the headlines on the front page of Britain's bestselling Sunday paper, *News of the World*. It was a tabloid editor's dream story. In November 2002, the paper exposed what it said was a plot to abduct Victoria, the former Spice Girl and wife of soccer superstar, David Beckham (Britain's 'other' royal family), and their children. The paper claimed the plotters planned to kidnap Mrs Beckham (Posh Spice) and her two sons for a ransom of $12,500,000 (Este 2003). Five men were arrested, four Romanians and one Kosovo Albanian. But the case collapsed when prosecutors discovered their prime witness, a parking attendant with a criminal record for forgery, was paid about $25,000 by the *News of the World* for the story ('Kidnap of Beckham Trial Axed' 2003). The *News of the World* reporter on the Posh kidnap story was Mazher Mahmood, known as the 'fake sheik' because he once posed as a wealthy Arab and recorded a conversation with Sophie, Countess of Wessex. In the interview, Sophie, the wife of Prince Edward, made several indiscreet remarks about the royal family and British Prime Minister Tony Blair. The lawyer for one of the men accused of the kidnapping plot claimed his client had been the 'victim of a set-up by Mahmood' ('Kidnap of Beckham Trial Axed' 2003).

Another memorable overseas case involved the Government-funded Italian television station RAI3 paying $40,000 to former SS officer, Erich Priebke, for an exclusive interview in August, 1995. At the time Priebke was facing extradition from Argentina to stand trial for his alleged role in the massacre of 335 Italian civilians near Rome in June, 1944. Priebke admitted to playing a role in the murders, but argued that he was only obeying orders. He had been living in Argentina since 1948. RAI3 was not planning to disclose the fee, but news of the pay-off was leaked to the Italian press. Politicians, Jewish groups, and other journalists condemned the TV station. The news director at RAI3, Daniela Brancati, defended the payment. She said RAI3 paid for exclusives all the time and the Priebke interview had already been sold to French and German television stations. Brancati also defended the interview, saying: 'The search for truth about a still shady historical event is for me the primary consideration' (quoted in Gumbel 1995, p. 21). In the end the money was never paid. The governing body at RAI3 blocked the payment.

The biggest case of chequebook journalism in Australia in 2003 centred on runaway Rockhampton schoolgirl Natasha Ryan, and we have used her as our first case study at the end of the chapter. Then there was cricketer Shane Warne's alleged affair with Melbourne stripper, Angela Gallagher, 38, who was reported to have been paid $80,000 to tell of her three-month relationship with the trouble-prone spinner on Seven's *Today Tonight* and in *New Idea* ('Woman Tells of Lie Test Over Shane' 2003). It came as no surprise, given his earlier (s)exploits, that the affair began after the two exchanged phone numbers at a Melbourne nightclub, and Warne sent her a series of explicit text messages to her mobile phone ('Warne's Affair' 2003). As 2003 was drawing to a close, there would be one more public chequebook journalism episode involving controversial One Nation leader, Pauline Hanson. Hanson had been jailed for electoral fraud and after spending seventy-eight days behind bars she was released when her conviction (and that of One Nation co-founder David Ettridge) was quashed on appeal. There was a media frenzy again for the exclusive post-prison interview with the controversial politician. And again the big chequebook of *60 Minutes* carried the day—this time for somewhere between $120,000 and $150,000 (Whiting 2003).

Whatever spin you put on it, chequebook journalism compromises honest and ethical journalism. Karen Sanders (2003, p. 115) suggests it can lead to 'embellishment'—the addition of material that may not be entirely accurate, or exaggeration of claims—and that it can 'stifle the free flow of information'. The main offenders are the television current affairs programs and the gossip magazines. Most newspapers, particularly broadsheets, don't pay for stories. The *Sydney Morning Herald*'s Code of Ethics says unequivocally: 'No payment shall be proffered to sources for interviews or access' (2003). This Code is reprinted in the appendices. Surprisingly, the ABC's guidelines in 1998 appeared to condone chequebook journalism, but only in 'certain circumstances':

> (S. 4.10.1) The ABC, as a matter of policy, will not enter into financial competition with other media for access to sources of news (commonly called 'chequebook journalism'). Occasionally, modest payments to individuals will be appropriate when they are inconvenienced because of the ABC's news gathering requirements, or when the public interest and right to know are involved and access to information can be gained by no other means.
>
> ABC 1998

But in the latest version of the guidelines (ABC 2002), the ABC has tightened its policy considerably—dropping the 'modest payments' paragraph from the 'chequebook journalism' section (S. 6.6.1). Under an earlier directive on 'Payment for Interviews' the guidelines state that:

> (S. 6.5.2) Interviewees whose contribution has required research, travel, a substantial commitment of time or other inconvenience may receive modest payments by way of compensation.
>
> ABC 2002

How do we know that what is being delivered 'exclusively' is the whole truth, and nothing but the truth, as they say in TV court dramas? Once a person is being paid a fee for their story, they will feel an obligation to 'perform' to earn the money. Who's to say they won't 'gild the lily' or exaggerate their story to give the paymaster value for money?

It is another nail in the coffin of journalistic credibility. We have mentioned often enough in this book the low level of credibility journalists 'enjoy', and chequebook journalism does nothing to enhance it. Reporters and editors need to ask themselves a number of questions about the use of payments to sources before they embark on this road:

- How important is the story, and do we need it to beat the opposition? This is basically a commercial decision that should be made by the executives of the news organisation. Under the Code of Ethics journalists are not obliged to accept editorial directives that they feel compromise their integrity or commitment to the Code.
- Is the source accurate, or is this an invitation to be ripped off? In recent years there have been occasions where newspapers have paid for allegedly good stories only to find out later that they'd been sold a dud, or a pack of lies. The so-called *Love Boat Affair*, involving allegations by a prostitute that she was present at floating sex parties with leading politicians, could be such a story, though it might also be the case that the real story was buried by an even more elaborate cover-up. Either way the photographs that were said to exist of these activities have yet to be published.
- How much should news organisations and individual journalists be allowed to make undercover enquiries in personal, business, or political affairs of people in the 'public eye'?
- Do the rights of so-called 'ordinary people' differ from those of public figures and celebrities?

A former editor-in-chief for the Herald and Weekly Times group, Harry Gordon, once said that editors learn to live with chequebook journalism in a competitive market. But he added that responsible editors also have to be aware of the harm that it can cause ('Ethics and the Media' 1987).

The MEAA Ethics Review Committee outlined four chequebook journalism scenarios in its report, but could not reach a 'consensus' on whether or not the practice is, in itself, unethical. The committee's report suggests that paying 'wrongdoers' who then 'profit from their wrongdoing' is 'clearly unethical'. Payments to witnesses in current or pending court cases would be unethical and might also be a legal problem (Ethics Review Committee 1997, p. 39). The third problematic category of chequebook journalism is payments to celebrities, which the committee felt constituted 'entertainment' and does not necessarily constitute unethical behaviour if an 'habitual' celebrity is paid for an exclusive interview. The committee added an important rider to this statement: 'It goes without saying that public officials, in office or seeking it, are not celebrities in that sense' (Ethics Review Committee 1997, p. 40). The committee's final category was payments for 'non-celebrities who are associated with a newsworthy event, often a tragedy'. However, the committee (1997, p. 40) also posed a question in relation to 'ordinary' people caught up in news events: 'So long as other relevant ethical standards are met, have people a right, in effect, to "commodify their suffering"?' This is a mercenary way of viewing this issue and one, unfortunately, which seems to dominate the thinking of news executives, editors, and reporters.

In our view it undermines any argument against chequebook journalism because, after all, don't we all have this dubious 'right'?

Investigative and undercover reporting

MEAA Code Clause 8: Use fair, responsible and honest means to obtain material. Identify yourself and your employer before obtaining any interview for publication or broadcast.

There is a very fine line between legitimate investigative reporting and using illegitimate methods to get a story. Definitions and practices will vary from organisation to organisation, but in general 'dubious' methods include disguising your journalistic identity and the use of undercover techniques. Some of these methods are in fact illegal. One method of researching major stories for newspapers is for a journalist to pose as something they are not for a specific period of time, virtually living *undercover,* and then writing up the story once they are back at head office. Examples include journalists living with street kids, or in Housing Commission flats, to get the story about hardship in these circumstances. In the case study example at the end of this chapter, a journalist pretended to be a senior high school student to write about their activities.

The justification that is often given is that there is no other way for the reporter to gain the trust of the people who are the subjects of the story, or that they would refuse access to a journalist if s/he identified her/himself before trying to get the story. We have seen in an earlier chapter in relation to an MEAA inquiry into the actions of a *Four Corners* team that some journalists see it as a legitimate tactic in investigative journalism not to identify themselves from the outset. The justification in such circumstances is the argument of the 'greater good', using the overriding principle of the public's 'right to know' to justify their deception. But can't it be argued that by denying the 'subjects' the right to refuse (or agree), that we are at the very least misleading them?

This is an issue on which the authors have a slight disagreement. One believes there is almost no circumstance (nothing is absolute in a discussion of ethics) that justifies journalists misleading sources by either not identifying themselves, or pretending to be someone they're not, in order to get stories. He has heard the arguments about the 'greater good' in exposing wrongdoing, that there might be no other way to get the story, and the overriding principle of the public's right to know, but feels that stories gained by deception are 'tainted'. Roger acknowledges that some of the biggest investigative stories have involved some form of deception, but still questions whether the end result justified the deceptive means that were used to get it. Roger knows many will disagree with him—especially those of the investigative journalism club—but that is his ethical stance. On the other hand, Martin believes that deception is acceptable if it leads to the exposure of a larger 'lie', such as government deception, significant criminal activity, or corporate fraud. He says that using subterfuge to trap a lying politician or to expose a commercial scandal is obviously in the public interest and crusading journalists are not being unethical if they use deception to gather evidence.

On one point the authors agree: deception used against ordinary people who have no chance to give informed consent to being questioned by a journalist, or who might be unnecessarily embarrassed by exposure, is not justified. How would you like everything you said to someone in a casual conversation to appear in a newspaper? If you knew what you were saying was being recorded for later use, you might answer questions quite differently, certainly not with the flippancy people sometimes employ. In the British case of chequebook journalism mentioned above, the reporter concerned had earlier posed as a sheik to entrap a relatively new member of the royal family (by marriage) and report her ill-advised remarks. You can bet she wouldn't have said what was reported if she knew she was talking to the *News of the World*! So was the deception justified for a few cheap shots at the royal family and Tony Blair? We doubt it.

The use of deceptive technologies

What about the use of hidden cameras, so popular with TV current affairs programs? The authors would obviously have different views on this too. Roger might say 'No, never'; Martin might say 'If the story warrants it and there's a strong public interest angle, go ahead.'

The crew conceals a camera and then records some wrongdoing, like a drug sale to the reporter—'See how easy it is to buy drugs in …' the voiceover tells you. Is it deception? The reporter is only trying to buy drugs for the story, so they are deceiving the 'pusher' in order to get a story. Is it entrapment? Some would say so. Is it ethical? The story is probably interesting in a small way, but it's not like most people wouldn't know that drugs are readily available in certain areas of big cities, and it's not the calibre of story that will win a Walkley Award. Small-time street pushers are not the real issue, though in 'moral panic' terms they are an easy media target. On the other hand, international criminal gangs are a different matter. Investigative journalists say hidden cameras are necessary for them to do their job in exposing wrongdoing. But theirs is not to aid in the commission of crimes by soliciting the sale of drugs in the 'fictitious' case mentioned above, is it? What happened to the journalist as independent observer and reporter of facts? Under what circumstances should a journalist take such an active (and deceptive) role in getting a story?

Other cases where not revealing the truth becomes an issue is in deciding not to run a story because of a request by someone in authority. In the example given above of a journalist posing as a street kid, there would be no thought that the 'subjects' could request that the story not be run, but the police regularly ask reporters not to publish material that might harm an investigation.

Under Creighton Burns's editorship, the *Age* would not run details of suicides because of fears about the so-called *copycat effect* on other potential suicides. A similar policy is followed by the ABC in its editorial policies (ABC 1993, p. 33). Nor would the *Age* print bomb hoax stories if the police asked them not to. The then editor Creighton Burns felt that this was serving a public interest ('Ethics and the Media' 1987). Many media organisations have policies covering the reporting of suicides and kidnapping, where publication of details may interfere with police procedures.

Plagiarism and fabrication

MEAA Code Clause 10: Do not plagiarise.

As we saw in the cautionary tale of Jayson Blair at the beginning of this chapter, the advent of the Internet and almost unlimited access to material from other media sources have made plagiarism easier to perpetrate and harder to detect. Plagiarism is where a reporter 'lifts' major parts or all of another journalist's work and publishes it as their own. It is lazy journalism and it is unethical journalism, and sadly there have been some memorable cases in Australia.

The *Sydney Morning Herald* computer editor at the time, Gareth Powell, left the paper after Stuart Littlemore exposed on *Media Watch* how he'd extensively plagiarised material from an American publication for the section of the *SMH* he edited. Littlemore was also responsible for drawing the public's attention to one of broadcaster Alan Jones's memorable transgressions—he plagiarised extracts from a Frederick Forsyth novel, *The Negotiator,* for a column he wrote in the *Sun Herald* (Clark 1998). In another incident a senior foreign correspondent was caught lifting sections from a recent book and incorporating them verbatim into his own by-lined stories from Sarajevo and other parts of the former Yugoslavia. *Media Watch* has maintained its strident anti-plagiarism campaign over the years. You'll recall from chapter 4 the court battle with *60 Minutes* and Richard Carleton over what it considered plagiarism in his year 2000 program on the anniversary of the massacre of thousands of Muslims at Srebrenica.

In 2003, in *Media Watch*'s first edition for the year, presenter David Marr 'outed' right-wing Sydney *Daily Telegraph* columnist Piers Akerman for quoting verbatim slabs of an Israeli Defence Force news release, and in another story extracts from the web site of the Arlington National Cemetery in the United States, both without acknowledgment (Marr 2003d). The program has an annual award titled the 'Campbell Reid Perpetual Trophy' named after the editor-in-chief of Akerman's paper for what it calls the 'brazen recycling of other people's work'. And Campbell Reid himself was the winner in 2003 for a feature the paper published titled '50 Things To Do Before You Die', which had been reprinted virtually word-for-word from a BBC TV program and web site (Marr 2003d).

Just plain falsehoods

Before the Jayson Blair affair, the best-known case of fabrication involved another of the most respected newspapers in America, the *Washington Post*. The *Post's* investigations into the Watergate Affair played a major role in forcing President Nixon to resign—a high point in modern American journalism. But it was also a *Post* reporter, Janet Cooke, who wrote a story in late September 1980 titled 'Jimmy's World' in which she looked at the drug problem among young children (Leo 1999). Cooke claimed to have interviewed an eight-year-old heroin addict called Jimmy. The story caused a furore, and she won a prestigious Pulitzer Prize (the American equivalent of the annual Walkley Awards in Australia) on 13 April 1981, for her 'fine investigative journalism'. No sooner was the ink dry on the Award testamur than she and her very embarrassed newspaper had to announce they were returning the award—the story was a fabrication. On 15 April, the paper admitted there was no 'Jimmy', he represented a composite of child addicts, and Cooke's story was fiction (Marr 2003d).

Another US serial fabricator is Stephen Glass from the *New Republic*, whose story is told in the 2003 movie, *Shattered Glass*. It's another DVD worth renting, though the story is actually quite sad and you are left wondering whether Stephen Glass might have a mild social disorder given his propensity for big lies!

If you think a similar incident couldn't happen in Australia, we're here to tell you it can, it has, and it most likely will again. In 1996 Stuart Littlemore drew his *Media Watch* audience's attention to a 'Special Report' in the Melbourne newspaper, the *Herald Sun*. It told the story of four single mothers in Victoria each with twelve children who were being paid a total of about $3300 a week in welfare payments—four women with forty-eight children between them. The Federal Department of Social Security, which makes welfare payments in Australia, consulted its computer records, Littlemore reported, and could find no record of any Victorian woman on welfare with twelve children. According to Littlemore, the DSS wrote to the *Herald Sun* asking it to correct the story, but the paper didn't formally correct the apparent fabrication (Littlemore 1996).

We have had a lot to thank *Media Watch* (and its unheralded army of informants) for over the years. In 1997, while Stuart Littlemore was still at the helm, the program revealed that Seven's *Today Tonight* had faked footage in a story about fugitive businessman, Christopher Skase. The program claimed that Skase had so much clout with local police in Majorca in Spain that he had them put up roadblocks against reporters trying to track him down. *Media Watch* revealed that the 'Skase roadblocks' in Majorca were actually traffic barriers put up quite innocently by police in distant Barcelona (Clark 1998). It was another case of pure fabrication.

There can be no excuses for fabrication in a news item—news is fundamentally about truth and accuracy. Perhaps the notion that news must also be entertaining has been around long enough now that it is making it easier for unscrupulous reporters and editors to cross the line without the fear of being caught, or at least being punished too severely. In terms of Merrill's dialectic it would seem that the most prominent contradiction in journalism at the start of the twenty-first century is between information and entertainment. We will look more closely at this in the next chapter.

Ethical dilemmas in practice

→ ### Scenario 1

You are at the school oval watching your son playing soccer. You strike up a conversation with another parent, who tells you he's a local doctor (you don't know him, and he doesn't know you). He lets it slip that he's treating a high-profile local sportsman who has a career-threatening injury. The injury is not publicly known. What would you do with that information?

Scenario 2

You are at a news conference. Included in the media pack is a pen to help you take down the answers (on the note pad provided) to the questions you and others ask. In the corner is a bar and after the conference the media is invited to have a drink and some nibbles before heading off. Has your objectivity been compromised? A visiting author hands out autographed copies of his latest book to the assembled media. An actor gives you a copy of their latest fitness video (in case you want to include a few shots in your story) or invites you to a special screening of their latest movie. Visiting celebrities want you to sample the food at their latest theme restaurant. Would you still pan the book, video, film, or food if you didn't like it? When does the 'gift' become too big?

Case studies

Case study 1
Chequebook journalism: The Natasha Ryan case

The most celebrated case of chequebook journalism in Australia in recent times involved Natasha Ryan, the Rockhampton (Queensland) teenage runaway who spent about four-and-a-half years in hiding with her milkman boyfriend. She had gone missing in Rockhampton in September 1998. A local man, Leonard John Fraser, was charged with her murder and the deaths of several other women. It was in the middle of his trial that Miss Ryan was found alive and well at her boyfriend's home. The charge of murder relating to Natasha Ryan was dropped, but Fraser was sentenced to three consecutive life terms on two charges of murder and one of manslaughter. He was already serving an indefinite term for the murder of a nine-year-old girl (Watt 2003).

This story had everything that current affairs producers love: drama, pathos, romance, mystery, and a pretty young woman. The dramatic announcement at the murder trial that one of the 'victims' had been found alive was just the start. Natasha's mother had long thought her daughter was dead. Natasha was found crouched and shivering in a cupboard. Her skin was pale for lack of sunlight and she told police she had only been outside the house six times since her disappearance ('Why She Did It' 2003).

Naturally the media was clamouring for the story of the girl it said had 'come back from the dead'. She hadn't, obviously, but since her mother thought she had been killed, and the police had spent an estimated $300,000 on the case, and charged someone with her murder, it was just too good a line not to use. One of the better headlines in this context was the *Australian*'s '"Murder victim" to sell her story' (Wilson A. 2003b). There was a public outcry and some locals demanded that the girl and her boyfriend be charged and forced to pay the cost of her murder investigation. A celebrity agent, Max Markson, handled the sale of Natasha's story, for a figure widely reported as between $200,000 and $250,000, to *Woman's Day* and *60 Minutes.* The TV version of the Natasha Ryan story was held back a week so that it could go head-to-head with the opening night of the new season of the reality show *Big Brother* on the rival Ten network. The ratings for the Natasha Ryan story were described as 'lacklustre' and *Woman's Day* reported no 'circulation spike' the week her story appeared (Callaghan 2003). Some 2.3 million viewers in the five mainland capital cities watched the latest group of under 30s move into the camera-infested house on the Gold Coast, while only about two-thirds of that number (1.6 million) watched Natasha tell her story (Simmons 2003). But *60 Minutes* got their money's worth in other ways—for more than a week almost every newspaper photo of Natasha 'returning to normal life' and every piece of video of the runaway featured *60 Minutes* reporter Tara Brown prominently. She was sticking to her costly talent like glue.

In early 2004, Natasha's boyfriend, Scott Black, was waiting to be tried for perjury. He could be facing up to fourteen years' jail for telling police he had no knowledge of Ms Ryan after her disappearing act in 1998 (Meade & Macfarlane 2003). By this time Natasha was pregnant and she told (should that be sold?) her story exclusively to *New Idea* (Smethurst 2004). 'Some people have said that we have fallen pregnant in the hope the judge will be lenient with Scott, to keep him out of jail. That sort of gossip is really hurtful and totally untrue', she told *New Idea* (Smethurst 2004). Why tell it to a gossip magazine, then?

Issues and questions raised by case study 1

1   What are the advantages and disadvantages of paying for stories?
2   Would chequebook journalism cease if every arm of the media agreed not to pay anyone for their story?
3   In the competitive news and current affairs market, what would it take for that to happen?
4   We usually hear about the big dollar payments for major stories, but is there anything ethically wrong in meeting a source's out-of-pocket expenses?
5   What about paying to fly a source from a regional centre to the capital city, putting them up in a city hotel and paying all their expenses while you interview them for a series of features. Is that chequebook journalism?
6   At what point does 'meeting out-of-pocket expenses' become chequebook journalism? Can you put a dollar figure on it?
7   Is there an argument that it is 'OK' for some sections of the media to pay for stories (the gossip magazines, tabloids, and TV current affairs programs, for instance) while the 'serious media' maintains the moral 'higher ground' and refuses to pay?
8   Should there be qualifications on who should get paid? What if the source is a criminal?
9   What does paying for stories do for journalism ethics and integrity?

10 Obviously those who win the chequebook battle for exclusivity are happy about the result, and those that miss out not so happy. Aren't stories about how much was paid for exclusive rights to a story just 'sour grapes' on the part of the losers?

11 There was an amusing episode of the TV current affairs satire program *Frontline,* where the team was banking on getting exclusive rights to a story about survival in the outback. They are all positive about the 'amazing story' until they learn they have lost the story to the opposition. Then they immediately change tack and look for angles that will destroy the survivor's story. How close to the truth do you think that approach is?

12 If you were on the Natasha Ryan story, how could you get around the exclusivity deal done with *60 Minutes* and get a story?

Case study 2
Cash for comment

The 'cash for comment' scandal that engulfed several talkback radio 'stars' began with a bang, but ended with an unfortunate whimper 5 years later. On 12 July 1999, the ABC-TV program, *Media Watch* (Ackland 1999) alleged a financial arrangement between the so-called 'man with the golden tonsils', Australia's King of Radio, 2UE's John Laws, and the Australian Bankers' Association. The Australian Broadcasting Authority mounted an inquiry into the *Media Watch* allegations and other financial arrangements involving Laws's 2UE colleague Alan Jones, 6PR's Howard Sattler, 5DN's Jeremy Cordeaux, and 3AW's Bruce Mansfield. It became known as the 'cash for comment' inquiry and was held in the second half of 1999 and early 2000. It found that Laws had financial arrangements with nine different organisations, and Jones five. Basically, the broadcasters were paid large amounts of money—above their handsome salaries—by various organisations, like Qantas, Optus, the State Bank of New South Wales, Foxtel, RAMS Home Loans, and the Star City Casino, in return for favourable treatment 'on air'. The inquiry found that there was 'a causal link between the existence of an agreement and the on-air conduct' of both broadcasting superstars (ABA 2000). The ABA final report, and the newspaper reports of the era provide fascinating reading about how the nation's top commercial broadcasters were able to 'line their pockets' by entering financial arrangements with companies to virtually promote their interests. As we mention briefly in the final chapter, 'round two' of the 'cash for comment' scandal came to a head in 2004. The ABA determined that allegations of breaches by Alan Jones were not sustainable and that the allegations against John Laws should be referred to the Commonwealth DPP. In the end there was no prosecution over 'cash for comment 2', as the DPP determined there was little chance of a conviction being obtained on the evidence.

In the orginal inquiry, lawyers for John Laws and the radio stations argued that the ethical constraints on those who work in radio only relate to the professional codes of practice for journalism. Those who are not journalists—as we have said earlier—are not covered by those constraints. According to their legal advisers, broadcasters like Laws and Jones are 'entertainers' and so are not bound by ethical considerations like not accepting money for saying nice things about a product or service. But that fine legal distinction would be lost on most people. When John Laws interviews the Prime Minister during an election campaign and grills him about his policies and proposals, isn't that journalism? The traditional dividing lines between journalism (and with it accuracy, balance, and fair play) and show business are becoming blurred. Is John Laws interviewing the Prime Minister entertainment masquerading as journalism, or journalism masquerading as entertainment? In the wake of the first cash for comment inquiry, journalists were forced to examine some of their practices. Was it ethical, for instance, for some of the nation's top interviewers to accept money to teach politicians or 'captains of industry' how to handle tough television interviews? And what of the political journalists who 'cross over' to become political advisers to Cabinet Ministers, then return to journalism a couple of years later? Or the journalist who 'moonlights', writing public relations material? Most media organisations have policies about what their staff can and can't do 'out of hours', and there are major ethical issues involved in such activities.

Issues and questions raised by case study 2

1   Debate the ethical ramifications for journalists of the 'Cash for Comment' scandal.
2   What do the Code of Ethics and the various Charters of Editorial Independence have to say about the issue?
3   What do you make of the 'Laws defence' that he is not a journalist, so he is not bound by the Code of Ethics?
4   Should a journalist make extra money by training people how to handle TV interviews?
5   What happens when that interviewer has to interview one of their former high-profile clients?
6   Discuss the ethics of political journalists becoming political advisers for Government Ministers or Opposition Shadow Ministers.
7   What about when that political adviser wants to return to the media? Can s/he claim to be unbiased?
8   Why would media employers want to give such a person a job?

→   ## Case study 3
Rural Press: The farmer's friend

Rural Press newspapers dominate a number of regional and rural markets outside the capital cities. In 1996 the then managing director of Rural Press, Brian McCarthy, told the ABC that the company was:

... committed to serving the needs of country people all around Australia. We don't own newspapers or radio stations in metropolitan areas, and we believe we understand country markets. We believe we have something to offer for our readers and listeners, and we believe that we can further push the country identity better as a company.

Warren 1996a

On ABC radio's *Media Report*, broadcast on 14 March 1996, presenter Agnes Warren challenged Brian McCarthy's statement with documents and interviews with former Rural Press journalists. Warren reported that between November 1995 and March 1996, the Victorian Department of Agriculture paid $40,000 for a series of advertorial features in *Stock and Land*, a Rural Press weekly. Agriculture Victoria directly supplied some of the editorial material for these features. The *Media Report* item revealed that the editor of *Stock and Land*, Mark Patterson, had written to the Department, assuring it that the stories would be presented as news, 'so they're not perceived as advertising features'. The material was to include an interview with a senior official from Agriculture Victoria. If this were a 'one-off' incident at Rural Press it would be questionable enough, but Agnes Warren presented evidence that over a number of years it had been policy at Rural Press to service the needs of advertisers in its editorial pages. Warren quoted from an internal bulletin called *Rounds,* which circulates within Rural Press. The following comments were allegedly written by Mr Ian Law, a senior Rural Press manager:

We've once again put the Hereford Society offside. The Land's otherwise excellent report of the Wodonga White Face Sale was tarnished by another negative headline.

Rounds, 29 May 1995, quoted in Warren 1996a

In another extract it was revealed that other commercial deals had been struck for editorial copy:

The company has signed a significant advertising contract with the Poll Dorset Association and there is an obligation on us as a result, to run some editorial material relating to the breed over the next few months. It is company policy for editors to support these commercial activities.

Rounds, 4 September 1995, cited in Warren 1996a

When Agnes Warren's story went to air, Rural Press owned 126 rural publications, fifteen printing presses, and twenty-seven radio stations. In the next few months this empire grew when Rural Press bought newspapers in the central west of NSW from John Amati. Within months of taking over the *Western Advocate* in Bathurst, the *Central Western Daily* in Orange, and papers in Lithgow, Blayney, and out to Dubbo, Rural Press had changed both the management structure and the 'look' of its new papers. Rural

Press also now owns the *Canberra Times* and undertook a similar campaign of changes after buying the masthead. Rural Press holdings in Australia are also complemented by media assets in New Zealand, and the United States. According to media law expert, Paul Chadwick, Rural Press was doing what many more media organisations have done before: 'acquire more and more publications so they can exploit the economies of scale that come with it' (quoted in Warren 1996a).

Issues and questions raised by case study 3

1   Discuss the advantages for a newspaper or magazine of running advertorials.
2   How do advertorials work in the electronic media? Do you know of any examples?
3   What are the arguments against the practice put forward by journalists?
4   How widespread is the practice? Do some research in state and regional newspapers and popular magazines.
5   What is the difference (if there is one) between an advertorial, a special supplement, say, previewing the Rugby World Cup in 2003 (as was included in most major Australian newspapers), and the weekly IT, Higher Education or Media supplements in the *Australian*?
6   How should advertorials be identified in a newspaper or magazine?
7   What are the ethical implications of not labelling advertorial material?
8   Most daily newspapers are full of supplements these days, mainly about health, lifestyle, and the public's fascination with do-it-yourself. It's a spin-off from the so-called 'infotainment' television programs. Are newspapers blurring the lines between editorial and advertising?

Case study 4
SMH reporter in high school

In 1988 the *Sydney Morning Herald*'s education writer posed as a high school student to write a series on the drug/sex culture of NSW suburban high schools. He encouraged other students to supply him with drugs and deceived the principal of the school. After writing the stories and upsetting everyone in NSW education, the reporter was forced to apologise. The *SMH*'s Tony Hewitt (1988), had posed as a Year 11 student in August/September 1988 and enrolled at the Glebe High School to research teenagers and their attitudes to various aspects of their education. He told the principal he had moved to New South Wales from Western Australia. Due to family circumstances his school records were unavailable, and his enrolment was accepted. He spent five weeks at the school and the principal, teachers, and students welcomed him as they would any new student ('Students Are Betrayed for the 'Truth' in Classroom'

1988). A five-part series titled 'Classroom' and subtitled 'The Inside Story' was published between 17 and 22 September 1988.

When the ruse was revealed and the articles published, the then NSW Education Minister, Terry Metherell, told State Parliament that another *Herald* journalist, Margo Kingston, had signed the enrolment form as Mr Hewitt's purported sister and guardian. The Education Minister described the project in Parliament as a 'Fairfax stunt' and a 'tawdry exercise'. The then editor-in-chief of the *Herald*, John Alexander, said: 'Our over-riding aim was a discussion of what a representative group of high school students are thinking, the sorts of issues they regard as important, how school life in Australia has changed, and what their hopes are for the future'. He added, in apparent self-justification: 'Unfortunately, having a reporter pose as a student was the only way we believed a truly accurate picture could be drawn' ('Metherell Accuses Herald of Breach of Ethics' 1988; Hurst & White 1994, pp. 177–8). The President of the NSW Teachers' Federation at the time, Jennie George, said the *Herald* had breached the Code of Ethics, adding that she was surprised the paper would condone such behaviour. The students had shared their thoughts with a fellow student, not knowing he was a *Herald* journalist ('Inside the Classroom: Our Readers Reply' 1988).

In a similar scenario, Michael Gawenda, then a reporter with Melbourne's *Age* newspaper, moved into a public housing high-rise block to research a series of undercover stories about violence in the area. The *Age* newspaper paid the expenses of a tenant to move out so the reporter could live in the block for a period of nearly two weeks. At first he didn't tell anyone who he was and befriended several people. Before the stories were published, the reporter went to each of his sources and told them who he really was. He sought their permission to use material they had supplied to him. The article won the Walkley award for best feature and Michael Gawenda went on to become the editor of the *Age*. After the event Michael Gawenda told John Hurst that he felt the ruse had been 'a bit dicey' (cited in Hurst & White 1994, p. 179).

Issues and questions raised by case study 4

1   Search out the series of Hewitt articles and read them. What did you think of the series?
2   In this case, does the end justify the means?
3   Clearly the *SMH* would not have been able to get the raw material for the series if the reporter had identified himself to the year 11s from the start and told them what he was going to be writing about. Does that justify his actions?
4   Is the Michael Gawenda case any different, given that he later went back to the flats to explain himself to the tenants?
5   What does the Code of Ethics say about identifying yourself to your sources?
6   Are there occasions when it is necessary to maintain anonymity in order to get a story?
7   Do the ends always justify the means?

8   What examples can you think of where you would feel justified in not identifying your-self as a journalist—in other words, in deceiving your sources?

9   Where would you draw the line—how important would the story need to be for you to deceive your sources?

10   Should you alone make that call?

→ ## Case study 5
Plagiarism and the Internet

Educational writer and consultant Dale Spender (2003) raised the issue of plagia-rism in the tertiary education system in August 2003, when she asked, in an article in the *Australian*'s Higher Education supplement: 'What's the difference between Internet process and plagiarism?' She suggested that there was nothing wrong with searching the Internet for material, cutting and pasting it to come up with something new, and calling it your creation. As she rightly pointed out, cutting and pasting is the *modus operandi* of the Internet, but without suitable attribution it is classic pla-giarism. She maintained that it was only what she called 'print-primed professionals' who considered the action an offence. She wrote that by continuing to apply 'the old rules' they have 'failed to recognise that the medium has changed from print to dig-ital' (Spender 2003). In a remarkable piece of logic, Ms Spender continued: 'So instead of declaring that the sky has fallen in, it might be more helpful for profes-sional educators to do some thinking, for the Internet is here to stay and yesterday's plagiarism is today's way of earning a living.'

Issues and questions raised by case study 5

1   The Spender article says: 'The Internet is here to stay, and yesterday's plagiarism is today's way of earning a living'. Do you agree?

2   Do you see anything wrong with the 'cut and paste' method of academic essay pro-duction? What about using this technique in journalism?

3   Do you need to differentiate between simply 'cutting and pasting' someone else's work and calling the composite 'your work', and traditional academic research?

4   Is there a difference (in degree or substance) between academic and journalistic plagiarism?

5   We have seen in the introduction to this chapter—the sad tale of Jayson Blair—just how easy it can be to plagiarise material from other reporters and get away with it. When does taking a story idea from another source become plagiarism?

6   How much of another's work can you use without it being considered plagiarism?

7   How can you guarantee that you won't be accused of plagiarism in 'following up' another writer's work?

8   How do the AJA Code of Ethics or the various Charters of Editorial Independence sug-gest you handle the issue of plagiarism?

Case study 6

Media behaviour at Port Arthur and Thredbo

As we have mentioned, the tragic events at both Port Arthur and Thredbo were big stories—arguably the biggest 'tragedy' stories in Australia from the 1990s. But the behaviour of the media covering these events at times left a lot to be desired. A total of thirty-five people were shot dead on 28 April 1996, at the Port Arthur historical site in southern Tasmania, the highest number to be killed by a lone gunman (Simpson 2001). We have discussed aspects of the coverage of the convicted killer, Martin Bryant, elsewhere. Here we are concerned with the behaviour of the journalists covering the story.

Aside from the accusations that journalists 'stole' photos of Bryant and posed as police officers or other officials (Bilboe 1998), there was the suggestion that soon after the massacre had begun, one photographer struck up a conversation with some locals in a bar near Port Arthur and got them to take him overland to the site of the massacre, ignoring a police roadblock several kilometres from the site. As the Public Affairs spokesman for the Tasmanian police at the time, Geoff Easton, was to tell ABC radio: '... that's just stupidity. At the time there was a person there with a high powered rifle firing bullets all over the place' (cited in Warren 1996b).

A little over a year later, a landslide at the Carinya Ski Lodge at Thredbo in southern New South Wales on 31 July 1997 claimed a further eighteen lives and one miracle, the rescue after several days of lone survivor Stuart Diver (Bolton 1997). But in this instance, there was much more documented evidence of the media behaving badly. Wendy Bilboe (1998, pp. 88–110), in her research on journalists' behaviour at Thredbo, notes that although the number of verified unethical incidents may appear low, given there were 250 journalists, camera operators, and sound recordists there during the rescue, 'there are indications that many more journalists actually attempted some form of unethical behaviour'. Among the incidents reported by Bilboe were:

- Two journalists, dressed in orange State Emergency Services overalls, attempted to enter the area of the land slip and were escorted off by police.
- Police removed two photographers from the Thredbo church during the first memorial service, when they attempted to go around the back of the church to photograph grieving relatives through large plate glass windows. (A pool camera was allowed inside the church less than a metre from relatives.)
- A Sydney broadsheet journalist burst into a Thredbo hotel room at 11 p.m. where a rescue worker was talking to grieving family members. He told the rescue worker: 'I am not leaving until you give me a story.'
- A journalist believed to be from a Sydney media organisation rang the Carinya Lodge management and announced he was 'a police officer' and said the list of guests in the lodge that night had been mislaid and asked for the details to be read again over the phone.

- Head of police rescue operations, Charlie Sanderson, was aware that a journalist was at the back of the first staff rescue briefing, which was closed to the news media, and Sanderson's comments to his team were reported 'word for word' in a Sydney paper.
- A journalist purchased one victim's photographs from the Thredbo photographic shop.
- Many journalists failed to identify themselves when they approached grief counsellors and Thredbo village residents.
- One resident threw a jug of beer over the head of a national television reporter who was talking to another resident. The resident claimed the journalist had identified himself as a doctor.

Issues and questions raised by case study 6

1   We all want to 'scoop' the opposition, but how far would you go to get that exclusive?
2   Surely stories like the Port Arthur massacre and the Thredbo disaster are big enough in themselves, without the media having to resort to 'dirty tricks' to get material?
3   What's your opinion of the various incidents detailed above? Would you be prepared to do similar things if the story was 'big enough'?
4   The argument for either not identifying yourself to a source, or pretending to be someone else, is that you wouldn't get the story you wanted if you said you were a reporter. What does that say about the reputation of journalists?
5   What alternative methods can you think of to gain information on important stories without resorting to deception?
6   If the main sources are too upset by what has happened to want to 'tell all' to the media, how else might you get access to their story?
7   While the litany of unacceptable behaviour detailed above would make an ethical journalist's blood boil, are there occasions when a 'little deception' may be necessary to get a story? Can you think of such a scenario?

11

CREATING THE STORYLINE

INFOTAINMENT AND DIGITAL DILEMMAS

Objectives

After reading and discussing this chapter you will have been exposed to:
- The blurring of news and entertainment into infotainment.
- Politics reported as a sporting contest.
- The 'dumbing down' of the news agenda.
- The uneasy relationship between journalists and 'spin doctors'.
- The ethical dilemmas of the changing media landscape of the twenty-first century.
- Blogging.

Introduction: 'We report, you believe'—*CNNNN* slogan

> When I heard Jessica Lynch had been released I remember thinking: 'I hope she's good looking'. Then when I saw her I knew we had our lead story.

Reucassel 2003a

Craig Reucassel is a very clever satirist, one of the brains behind the comedy program *Chaser Non-stop News Network* (*CNNNN*) that aired on ABC television in 2002–03. His comment quoted here is a great spoof of those made at the time on the very patriotic American Fox network. It highlights a major concern of this chapter (and indeed of both authors) that news information is being steadily diluted with entertainment values. On some commercial television and radio networks and in many Sunday newspapers, it is diluted almost to the point that it is becoming impossible to tell where news ends and entertainment begins.

We are all familiar with the term 'infotainment', the blending of information with entertaining words and pictures. The writers and producers of the ABC's satirical 'news' broadcast, *CNNNN*, have taken this to its logical conclusion, 'newstainment'. In 2003 they often presented their comedy as a news game show, complete with audience participation in events such as 'body count' bingo. Like all good satire, *CNNNN* cut very close to the bone. New forms of media technology, such as cable, satellite, and the Internet have two things in common. The first is that they share a digital platform that makes them convergent and interactive. And they share the potential to blur the boundaries between ethical and unethical behaviour because of the way in which information and images can be processed or reproduced.

In the past couple of years we have noted an increasing and alarming trend to put stories *about* entertainment into the news. We now expect the latest gossip about who is having plastic surgery, an affair, a baby, a divorce, treatment for cancer, a date with a stripper/toy boy, or going into rehab for their addiction to 'pain-killers'. To a certain extent if people put themselves into the public spotlight for their own purely commercial reasons then really, so what? Why else do 'habitual celebrities' pay all that money to an expensive publicity agent? They shouldn't get too upset if occasionally a tabloid, a gossip rag, or an Internet site goes overboard. But what about ordinary, unknown people who, through no fault of their own, get pushed into the public consciousness?

On a more serious note, it is possible to argue that news is being depoliticised. By this we don't mean that there's no news about 'politics'; there is and often too much of it. Rather, what we mean is that the style of news presentation is no longer 'political'—that is, it is not focused on issues of importance and citizenship, but on being *entertaining*. Political scientist Rod Tiffen first wrote about this in his book *News & Power* (1989), in which he demonstrated how politics is reported very much like a sporting contest with winners, losers, victories, and defeats. This is a situation in which a politician's hunger for publicity will be inversely proportional to the substance of the issue (Tiffen 1989, p. 179). We are also very familiar with the 'presidential' style of political campaigning that now dominates everything from mayoral elections to federal polls. Ian Ward's (1995) careful study of media effects avoids the pitfalls of 'technological determinism', but concludes that television has impacted significantly on the shape and feel of Australian electoral politics. John Langer (1998) has written about the ways in which politics is stripped out of the nightly bulletin in favour of what he calls the 'other' news; human interest, 'celebrity lifestyle', and the 'heroic acts of humble people'.

Creating the storyline #1: 'Newstainment'

Not surprisingly, John Langer's book is called simply *Tabloid Television*. However, the depoliticisation of the news does not mean that there isn't an ideological agenda involved. Langer's 'other' news categories still contain 'ideological cues' which make news 'items' understandable 'in terms of preferred readings with the repertoire of dominant ideologies' which, in televisual terms, are linked to 'stable visual images' that act 'within preferred referential contexts' (Langer 1998, p. 147). Significantly Langer recognises that with this new form, which we now call 'infotainment', comes new contradictions, in particular, tensions between the news media's functions of social control and its 'pleasure' functions:

> ... it might be suggested that it is around the site of pleasure, as it is located in the 'other news', where some of these instabilities and contradictory tendencies get layed out where paradoxically ideology ... [can be] ... forceful ... [but] ... the struggle over meaning is never a settled affair.

> Langer 1998, pp. 153–4

As John O'Neil and Catharine Lumby (1994, p. 153) point out, the rapid rise of tabloid TV, which began in the early 1990s, had by the middle of that decade already begun to alter the boundaries in subtle but important ways by injecting 'entertainment' into 'current affairs'. By the mid 1990s this was beginning to appear mainstream. Most current affairs programs on commercial television followed a tried and true 'infotainment' formula (Hirst et al. 1995).

Today so-called 'reality TV' is commonplace. But it too, has further diluted the once immutable boundary between information-rich documentary-style programs and those made purely for entertainment. It seems, at one level, that our voyeuristic tendencies have won the struggle against our better judgment. At another level, it might be that both authors are too old to appreciate how the 'fly-on-the-wall' reality show, *Big Brother*, became such a cult show with teenagers and twentysomethings in the 'noughties'! Lastly, could it be that the average television viewer is tiring of the nightly diet of death and destruction on the TV news? Whatever the cause it appeared throughout 2003 that the 'infotainment' programs were winning the ratings battle, but the genre hit the proverbial 'brick wall' in early 2004, when ratings for 'reality' shows began to decline.

Creating the storyline #2: Spin doctors

Alastair Campbell was British Prime Minister Tony Blair's chief 'spin doctor' in the lead-up to, during, and in the immediate aftermath of the 2003 Iraq War. You have met him before—in chapter 6 on the media and war. When he resigned during the Hutton Inquiry into the suicide of British arms inspector David Kelly, the page 1 headline in London's *Daily Mirror* said: 'The most powerful man in Britain quits' (Wilson 2003b). It was an overstatement, but only just. While Campbell was never as powerful as Blair, his political master and friend, political insiders in Britain had long called him 'the real deputy prime minister' (Wilson 2003b). It was Campbell at the centre of the row between Blair and the BBC over the so-called 'sexing up' of the dossier on Iraq's weapons of mass destruction used by Blair to justify going to war. His resignation quite rightly led to some serious thinking in political circles from London to Washington and even in Canberra about the role of 'spin' and the presentation of information to the public in modern politics and government. 'Spin' is nothing new. In the context of this chapter on the creation of news, it is the 'spin doctors' who create the image of their bosses. Public relations officers or private consultants have been around as long as there have been journalists chasing politicians and leading public figures for comments. Quite often it is former journalists, well schooled in the techniques of the newsroom, who emerge as the best spinners—not only do they know how the newsroom works, they know how to manipulate and side-step and shuffle around the bureaucracy too. They are there to suggest the 'spin' that should be put on a particular announcement or reaction in order to show their bosses in the best possible light. Alastair Campbell's critics said it was the 'spin', the emphasis on presentation over substance, that became the hallmark of the Blair Government in the early years of this century (Wilson 2003b).

There is an uneasy relationship between journalists and public relations people, the 'spin doctors'. Both need the other, and the journalists accept that the 'spin doctors' are going to put the best light they can on anything affecting their clients. It is when they deliberately mislead the public, by feeding if not incorrect, then incomplete, information to journalists, that the battle lines are drawn between those advising the politicians or private clients, and the journalists. We say it is an uneasy relationship, because journalists now move freely between the two areas—working for a Cabinet Minister for a while, and then returning to daily journalism. Time was when senior journalists left the hectic pace of daily journalism for the relative peace, and much higher remuneration, of a public relations position. The 'hacks' would say their former colleague had gone over 'to the dark side of the force' (invoking the *Star Wars* imagery). Nowadays it is not uncommon to see relatively young former ministerial media advisers 'coming back' to daily journalism. Much pub talk involves often heated discussion about how a person who had represented a State or Federal Cabinet Minister can return to daily journalism without carrying with him/her some bias from their previous position. One such figure had worked for a Labor leader and then, when his boss lost office to the conservatives, returned to the press gallery for a television network. It was obvious to other reporters that the new Prime Minister had cut him dead. For about 18 months the network could not get a much sought after 'one on one' with the PM. When media organisations employ former Ministerial staffers it is the reporter's prior knowledge and contacts that they are buying. But if they are so used to 'creating the news' with carefully crafted statements and photo opportunities, how do they stop 'playing the game' when they rejoin the ranks of media workers? Maybe they're better political journalists because they have seen 'spin doctoring' from the inside, and can see through it. It is a lively debate.

Reflections and criticisms of journalism

One positive to emerge through the 1990s, as television journalism became a form of entertainment, was greater public scrutiny. Through programs like the ABC's *Media Watch*, *Frontline*, and more recently *CNNNN* adding its own brand of news satire, the practice of journalism has become more accessible to the audience—if they care to look. Radio has also done its bit to lampoon the news, dating back to journalist and broadcaster Mike Carlton's early efforts in the 1980s with *Friday News Review with Brian Hambone* (presumably satirising Nine's former longstanding Sydney newsreader Brian Henderson). Carlton's characters included reporter 'Peter Gravy' reporting with his gravel voice and drawn-out sign-off from Canberra (a thinly disguised Peter Harvey, then reporting from the national capital). More recently, there is *How Green is my Cactus?* (with its Friday version of *Cactus National News*) poking fun at national political figures and heard regularly on commercial radio around the country. Most of the programs are about national politics, but Friday's program is usually a satirical review of the news.

But it's the satirical TV programs that have exposed some major fault lines in the media to public scrutiny. Before the advent of television, the public had to rely on newspapers for their accounts of 'instant history', supplemented by radio news and current affairs (such as it was in the first half of the twentieth century). Television news and current affairs came to the fore in the second half of the twentieth century, particularly through the ABC's *This Day Tonight*, an early pioneer in this field. From the mid 1970s, the public could 'see' the news happening in colour, usually with equally colourful comments from the reporters, who were beginning to break out of a stilted and formal 'BBC' mould (Peach 1992). But still it was the journalists and producers showing the audience what they decided the public needed to see.

Satirical television in Australia has a proud history, from the *Mavis Bramston* and *Aunty Jack* shows of the 1960s to *CNNNN* in 2003. These shows and programs like *Media Watch* meant that, for the first time, the public could be 'in the know', getting glimpses behind the journalistic screen. The ABC's comedic current affairs send-up, *Frontline,* showed with biting satire how such television is produced. For those in the industry it became compulsory viewing, and the following day was spent deciding who was 'done over' in that week's program, what specific stories they were satirising, and who had 'dropped a bucket' on their workmates to provide the storyline for the program. But for the general public it meant they saw the conflicts played out in the program's fictitious current affairs show. We believe this has had the effect of making some in the audience more sceptical of what they see on television news and current affairs programs.

Media Watch, particularly during its early years with founding host Stuart Littlemore QC, gave viewers plenty of reasons to question the media. Some of the celebrated case studies used in this book—including Michael Willessee and the Cangai siege, Steve Barrett posing as a policeman to get a photo from a grieving family, and various cases of plagiarism—were first aired on *Media Watch* (Clark 1998). *CNNNN*, as the opening comment to this chapter demonstrates, in satirising coverage of supposed Iraqi war casualty Jessica Lynch, has picked up where *Frontline* left off. But it is even more cutting in its attacks on journalists' motives and news gathering practices. Among the written 'sign-offs' before supposed ad breaks in the program of 28 August 2003, were 'CNNNN: embedded in your heart'; 'CNNNN gives you both sides' (against background photos of President Bush and British Prime Minister Tony Blair); and our favourite: 'CNNNN: We don't just cover wars, we win them' (Reucassel 2003b).

The public is generally now more 'streetwise' to the activities of the news media. People are more wary of the news media, and with the aid of examples from *Media Watch* and a healthy scepticism heightened by watching *CNNNN*, the public is now more able to critique the performance of reporters and editors. Where in the past they may have had to accept what the media was reporting as 'gospel', the public now regularly criticise the media—just ask any journalist. Before the advent of the Internet, there was only the way stories were reported—in the mass media. Now those who want to know more about a news item of interest have a wealth of information to seek out. But the downside is that *CNNNN* is right—'newstainment', as they characterise their program, is becoming very popular and is dumbing down the serious news agenda. Gossip magazines have been 'doing deals' with television current affairs programs to bring the latest scandal to the small screen and into your local newsagency using the 'technique' of blatant chequebook journalism.

So far we have discussed the print media, radio, and television, but what of the Internet and digital production techniques? As digital production techniques and delivery systems develop further in the years ahead, the ethics debate will have to keep pace. For now let's take a quick look at an incident in which the 'new' media fed back into the 'old' media, highlighting some inherent contradictions and ethical dilemmas.

Ever heard of the 'Star Wars Kid', Ghyslain Raza? In July 2003, this very ordinary Canadian junior high school student, from Trois-Rivieres in Quebec, videotaped himself playing around with a golf-ball retriever, pretending to fight like a *Star Wars* Jedi with a light sabre. The tape was made purely for the enjoyment of Ghyslain and his family, but his fooling around inadvertently made him instantly famous as an international laughing-stock. Several of his classmates at school got hold of the tape and uploaded it to a web site. You can imagine what happened next—within days the images had travelled far and wide and people began getting interested in the young boy. Ghyslain felt that his privacy had been invaded and that he had been humiliated. He told Canada's *National Post* newspaper that he wanted his life back (Associated Press 2003).

When the *SMH* ran the AP story in late August 2003, it illustrated it with four stills from the tape and also gave the URL for a site where the video was available to download. Under the guise of reporting the story about how the Raza family was now attempting to sue the families of the children who had taken Ghyslain's tape and uploaded it to the Internet, the *Herald* was now almost guaranteeing another few thousand hits on the site it mentioned, thus further internationalising the humiliation and hurt.

This case highlights just how easy it has become in the so-called 'information age' to get your 15 bytes of fame, infamy, or humiliation and have it transmitted around the globe in a blink. Not only that, it's also able to be infinitely copied and amended. Ghyslain's gyrating image has now been digitally incorporated into a myriad movie backgrounds, including *Hulk* and *The Matrix* (Associated Press 2003).

Digital Dilemmas #1: Image-shifting

As we mentioned above, Ghyslain Raza was an unfortunate victim of digital circumstances and his pain was compounded by the news media, who showed the footage and reported the story, complete with details of where curiosity seekers could download the images. Then the manipulation continued as the 'Star Wars Kid' was digitally enhanced and added to other backdrops. These same technological innovations are now available to reporters and news organisations. What tempting mischief do they offer to the unprincipled and ill-disciplined?

The new technologies now available to journalists—miniature digital audio recorders, the 'prosumer' video gear, and tiny digital cameras—are almost daily creating new ethical dilemmas for the media. One important area of change is in privacy laws (remember the ethico–legal dilemmas of this issue?). The changes, in place since late 2001, have made it harder for journalists to get access to information held by public institutions and corporations (Brook 2001). A new problem arose a couple of years later with the introduction of a new generation of mobile phones that could take and transmit photographs. The YMCA has banned the phones from its showers, swimming pools, and dressing rooms because of the fear that someone would take pictures and post them on the Internet (Hoare 2003). It really is becoming tricky to negotiate these new technologies.

Even before the technology improved remarkably in the 1990s, 'wire photos' as they were called—pictures sent from overseas of news events—often had to be enhanced so the picture could be seen. And the physical manipulation of images has been around a long

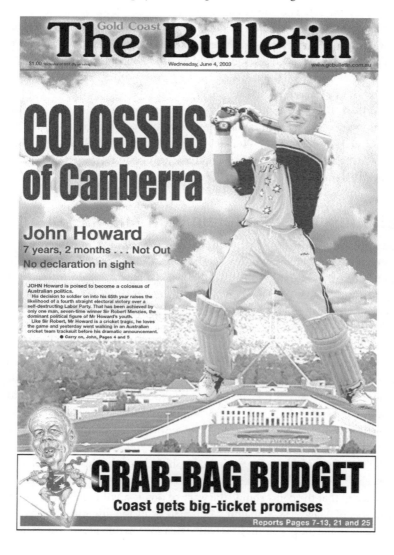

time. But that's a far cry from so enhancing the picture as to introduce distortion, or blatant fabrication. Sir Donald Bradman, talking to Ray Martin in a memorable interview titled '87 not out' on the Nine Network on 29 May 1996, said a photo of him walking with King George during one of his tours of England had been 'doctored' to omit others, who, like him, were walking with the King with their hands in their pockets. 'The Don' drew criticism for 'insulting' the King by walking alongside him with his hands in his pockets, and as they say in royal circles 'he was not amused' (Martin 1996). A similar instance was the *Gold Coast Bulletin*'s coverage of Prime Minister Howard's announcement that he would 'bat on' past his 64th birthday in the nation's top job. Under a banner headline 'Colossus of Canberra' on page 1, the paper depicted the Prime Minister, a self-confessed cricket tragic, in Australian one-day cricket gear, astride Parliament House having (it appeared) struck the ball either to the boundary or for six. The sub-head on the front page read: 'John Howard 7 years, 2 months … Not Out, No declaration in sight'. The paper reported that the Prime Minister had gone walking in an Australian cricket team tracksuit before his dramatic announcement ('Colossus of Canberra' 2003). This, too, would be defended as a 'bit of fun' and a clever representation of the essence of the story, given the Prime Minister's love of the 'gentlemen's game' ('Colossus of Canberra' 2003).

The *Gold Coast Bulletin* example might seem like a harmless bit of fun, but what about more serious issues of digital manipulation, for example putting someone in a photograph who wasn't originally there just to make a 'more attractive' news photograph? Two very prestigious American newspapers were caught out doing this during the 2003 Gulf War. We have outlined this incident in case study 5 below.

Digital Dilemmas #2: Defamation and the Internet

A decision by the High Court of Australia on 10 December 2002 sent collective shivers down the spines of media executives worldwide. The High Court decided 7-0 that mining magnate and Orthodox Jewish rabbi Joseph Gutnick could sue the New York-based news service Dow Jones in the Australian state of Victoria for defamation for a story about him that was put on its web site in the US (Jackson & Fitzsimmons 2002). The headlines over two of the *Australian*'s reaction pieces to the decision indicated the scare the High Court had given media proprietors. 'High Court has unleashed a jurisdictional nightmare' said the headline to media commentator Mark Day's reaction, and 'High Court throws a spanner in the global networks' said the headline to an opinion piece by Glenn Harlan Reynolds (2002), who at the time taught Internet law at the University of Tennessee. Mark Day (2002) said the decision meant that publishers must 'take responsibility for their words in every one of the 300-odd legal jurisdictions around the world'. The *Australian*'s editorial called the decision 'a dark day for the Internet' ('A Dark Day for the Internet' 2002). The editorial turned the issue back on the High Court judges, suggesting they should now be more careful what they say in their speeches on the High Court web site ('A Dark Day for the Internet' 2002). The editorial also warned that the court should 'be wary of saying anything derisory of Zimbabwe's Robert Mugabe, of Malaysia's Mahathir Mohamad or of the litigious-happy ruling elite in Singapore'. Four of the judges wrote: 'It is where that person downloads the material that the damage to reputation may be done. Ordinarily, then, that will be the place where the tort of defamation is committed' (quoted in 'A Dark Day for the Internet' 2002).

The offending article had appeared in the American financial magazine *Barron's* in October 2000. It suggested that Mr Gutnick used religious charities to manipulate stock prices in the US. Publisher Dow Jones sold more than 300,000 copies of that issue of *Barron's* and the offending article was also available to 550,000 subscribers to the *Wall Street Journal* on its web site wsj.com. Basically, *Dow Jones* had failed to prove that the offending article had not been 'published' in Victoria, and was therefore not subject to that state's defamation laws (Pearson, Proud & Willcox 2003). The story was written in New York, uploaded to a Web server in New Jersey, and downloaded by subscribers around the world, including Victoria. It was proven in the High Court case that only five copies of the offending *Barron's* magazine made their way to Australia. Of the more than half a million worldwide subscribers to the Internet version of the *Wall Street Journal*, 1700 had Australian-based credit cards (Pearson, Proud & Willcox 2003). The Gutnick decision probably has more implications for publishers outside Australia—like the British tabloids and some of the more racy American 'supermarket trashies'—than local publications, because Australian publishers have long realised the legal minefield of the nation's defamation laws that differ from state to state. In one state the defence against defamation may be truth, in another truth and the public interest, and in another truth and the public benefit. So Australian proprietors publish realising they have to meet the 'lowest common denominator' for defamation cases—truth and the public benefit (Pearson 1997). An important aspect of the High Court decision was the realisation that Internet publications, although often merely copies of printed versions, are separate legal entities (Pearson, Proud & Willcox 2003, p. 111). Federal Attorney-General Phillip Ruddock announced in March 2004 that he would once again put debate about uniform national defamation laws on the public agenda. This was first suggested a decade earlier by then South Australian Attorney-General Dean Wells. Given the political differences between states in Australia it is, in our opinion, unlikely that things will change inside the next decade.

One thing that is clear in the digital age of international electronic 'publishing' is that newspapers publishing Internet versions will need to assess them legally in their own right for each edition, rather than just duplicate the print edition online (Pearson, Proud & Willcox 2003, p. 109). As Pearson et al. (2003) point out, smaller publications who host 'shovelware' web sites (online clones of their print versions) need to be very careful in light of the Gutnick decision. 'Newspapers choosing to continue with their Website publishing need to take special note of the place of residence of the individuals mentioned in their stories and think through the defamation defences available in the states where their predominant reputation resides' (Pearson, Proud & Willcox 2003, p. 109).

Internet journalism: Get used to it

The Internet is here to stay and it is only one of a long line of big improvements in news gathering techniques, like the invention of the typewriter, the telegraph, telephone, tape recorder, and personal computer. Journalists are quite rightly using it as an additional resource for information-gathering. Kieran Lewis undertook a survey into how journalists use the Internet in 2003 as part of his doctorate at the Queensland University of Technology. His initial findings were that journalists used the Internet to trawl for story ideas from the sites of established media organisations and download material from the web sites of their traditional 'official' sources—government, university, and research institutions (O'Regan 2003). Lewis told the ABC's Mick O'Regan that rather than using the billions of web sites available to access a more diverse range of opinions, journalists were not using those sites because they didn't trust the information on them, or it was too hard to verify the information.

American academic and writer, Nora Paul, who has published extensively on computer-assisted reporting (CAR) and the Internet, says in the fourth edition of *Computer-Assisted Research: A guide to Tapping Online Information* (Paul 1999):

> The Internet did not invent mis-information or disinformation. The Internet did not create rumour mongering. The Internet did not spawn propaganda. The Internet is not responsible for dirty data and stupid statistics. All of these have been around forever. They just have a new distribution outlet. The Internet DOES make it possible for the mis-information, disinformation, rumour-mongering, dirty data and stupid statistics to be distributed more quickly and widely than in the past.
>
> Paul 1999, cited from Poynter Institute web site

So how do you evaluate information gained online? As journalists have the 5 Ws and the H of news gathering (who, what, when, where, why, and how), librarians have the two As, two Cs, and an O—authority and accuracy, currency and coverage, and objectivity—as questions to ask about web sites (Paul 1999). Under each criteria (and they were developed for a news web site) there are several questions to ask, and the more questions that can be answered 'yes', the more likely it is that the source is of 'high information quality' (*Evaluating Web Resources*). You can look at the web site for yourself, but let's take one criterion—accuracy—as an example. These are some of the questions you might ask:

- Are sources for factual information clearly listed so they can be verified in another source?
- Are there editors monitoring the accuracy of the information being published?
- Is the information free of grammatical, spelling, and typographical errors? These kinds of errors not only indicate a lack of quality control, but also can actually produce inaccuracies in information.

Evaluating Web Resources

The University of Albany Libraries (library.albany.edu/internet/evaluate.html) use slightly different headings (purpose, source, content and style, and functionality), but cover similar ground. Let's look at their comments under 'accuracy':

- Don't take the information presented at face value.
- Web sites are rarely refereed or reviewed, as are scholarly journals and books.
- Look for point of view and evidence of bias.

- Source of the information should be clearly stated, whether original or borrowed from elsewhere.

Cited at Evaluating Web Resources

The ethics of blogging

'Bloggers' are people who write and upload to the Internet a virtual diary of information and commentary on the news and events that may be in the news. 'Blog' is a shortening of 'weblog' and is a form of electronic diary of personal insights and comments on events. One of the most famous blogs of 2003 was the lone voice of 'Salam Pax'. 'Pax' was in Baghdad during the 2003 Gulf War and he provided what the *Weekend Australian* ('Chronicler of Chaos' 2003) called a 'ground zero account … that attracted a huge following around the world'. London's *Guardian* newspaper found the young Iraqi, a 29-year-old architecture graduate living with his family. According to the *Weekend Australian* 'Pax' started the blog for 'his best friend Raed', a student in neighbouring Jordan ('Chronicler of Chaos' 2003). The Baghdad blogs were published in book form in September 2003 (Pax 2003). The 'Pax' blog is at times very personal; he mentions coffee and pastry with his family and the death of 'Raed's' aunt. At other times 'Pax' makes his strong feelings about the war known: 'Let me tell you one thing first. War sucks big time.' And he gives interesting details of the constant air attacks on the city: 'As one of the buildings I really love went up in a huge explosion I was close to tears.' However, in the end, 'Pax' agrees that getting rid of Saddam Hussein was absolutely necessary. On 7 May 2003 he diarises an exchange with a Baghdad taxi driver who 'grumbling and mumbling' would say 'something like: "Well it wasn't like the mess is now when we had Saddam."' 'Pax' then writes:

> This is usually my cue for going into rage mode. Then the question that would shut them up: 'So dear Mr Taxi Driver, would you like to have your Saddam back?' End of conversation.

Pax 2003, 7 May 2003. Cited in 'Chronicler of Chaos' 2003

What can we reasonably make of the 'Pax' blog? In May 2004 Salam Pax gave up his blog on the Internet, but had begun writing a column in Britain's *Guardian* newspaper instead. Visiting Australia for the Sydney Writers' Festival, he told Elisabeth Wynhausen that he preferred 'the printed stuff', but understood the attraction of the weblog that is 'just immediate' (Wynhausen 2004).

The Pax case and other blogs also raise questions about a Code of Ethics for bloggers. Journalist Margo Kingston's *SMH* blog has a very clear Code of Ethics for those who contribute to her site, but what about the anonymous and 'non-journalist' blogs? Where do they sit on the responsibility–accountability scale?

The *CyberJournalist* web site (www.cyberjournalist.net) has posted a Code for bloggers that lists several principles: 'Honest and fair; Minimize harm; Be accountable'— none of which is too difficult or remarkable. But interestingly there are some additions for the digital age: 'Never distort the content of photos without disclosing what has been changed'; 'Invite dialogue with the public'; and 'Expose unethical practices of other bloggers' (*A Bloggers' Code of Ethics* 2003). That last point is interesting; no other Code we've come across encourages that level of accountability between reporters.

According to their own definition, bloggers are the 'mavericks of the online world', with a 'widely dispersed' audience. Bloggers also see themselves as mainly outside the mainstream media, working to their own 'quirky criteria' (Blood 2003, p. 1). Rebecca Blood presents a strong argument in favour of blogging, but she is aware of its central contradiction. The greatest strength of blogging is its 'uncensored, unmediated, uncontrolled voice', but according to Blood it is also a source of weakness. She argues that unlike the mainstream news media, blogs do not have the accountability of the market place. Mainstream news must maintain ethical standards 'so that readers keep subscribing and advertisers keep buying'. Blood says this provides 'incentives' for journalists and media owners to act ethically. On the other hand, for bloggers, 'the lack of gatekeepers and the freedom from all consequences may compromise their integrity and thus their value' (Blood 2003, p. 2). As a solution, Rebecca Blood suggests a blogger's Code to promote 'transparency', not to necessarily be 'even-handed', but 'to be forthcoming about their sources, biases, and behavior'. At the same time she is careful to point out that these are not the standards of 'a professional journalist'. This is truly a twenty-first century fault line.

Ethical dilemmas in practice

→ ## Scenario 1

Nowadays just about every home has a video camera. Every time there's a news event down the street, someone is there before the TV crews and offers their coverage recorded earlier to the highest bidder. You see it all the time—grainy footage from the back door of hailstones 'the size of golf balls', a school fire, or road accident. Sometimes the private camera even captures the actual news event (like some did on 11 September 2001). If you were the TV news director would you use such material regardless of the quality? If the pictures would normally be rejected as unusable, would the importance of what's been captured override the lack of quality in the images?

→ ## Scenario 2

You are compiling a story about the latest research into potential flooding of a local area (floodplain, river, whatever is appropriate), and the Premier makes a comment during his daily news conference. You're not there to report it, but your station's political reporter is at the news conference, and his camera crew records it. Is it ethical to use that 'grab' in your story, even though you weren't there?

The 'opposition' carries a particularly important exclusive on its main news bulletin. It carries the caption 'exclusive', and the station's 'water-mark' logo. Is it ethical to use its images without acknowledging the opposition station?

Newspapers often use quotes from newsmakers from the round of Sunday morning talk shows on TV without acknowledging their source. Consider the ethics of such a practice.

Scenario 3

A previously unknown group, calling itself Australian Jihad, claims on its web site that several high-ranking military personnel have been engaged in the torture of terror suspects at a secret location near Perth.

The group's web site says that the young men, who are all Australian citizens, were arrested in Pakistan, secretly flown to Australia on an American military flight, and have been kept in isolation for the past four weeks.

The web site names the fictitious men as Abdul Isham, Malek Yousson, Mohammed Dashir, and Ahmir Taisan. Photographs of the men are available for download from the website.

The army public relations office has issued a statement denying that any terror suspects are being held in Western Australia and that the web site is a hoax.

You are assigned to write the story. Where do you begin?

Case studies

Case study 1
The global gossip magazine industry

We're all used to taking stories in the so-called 'supermarket tabloids' of the now defunct *National Inquirer* genre with the proverbial grain of salt. After all, only so many people can be kidnapped in flying saucers. Even though they are not 'tabloid' in size, the women's magazines and gossip rags follow a similar format. Quotes are sourced to 'friends of the star' and so on, rarely does the actual celebrity go on the record in such 'stories'. In general they can be characterised as harmless pieces of fun, which probably wouldn't qualify for inclusion in the *Guinness Book of Records* or *Ripley's Believe It or Not*. But what about when a glossy magazine like *New Idea*, with a circulation of about 400,000, or *Woman's Day*, which sells about 540,000 copies each week, tells you the latest on the private life of your favourite celebrity? Do you believe it? After all, they are carefully written to read like plausible stories. According to media commentator for the *Australian*, Mark Day, it happens every week in Australia's popular glossies. Much of what they report is made up, says Day (2003a, p. 2): 'If you're reading about Jennifer and Brad, Liz Hurley, Ben and J. Lo, Madonna and Guy, Nicole, Tom and Penelope or Melanie and Antonio, don't believe it.' Not only are the sources unreliable, says Day, most of the time they're non-existent: 'It is not merely a case of putting the egg-beater into a few facts and concocting an appealing confection for the cover. It is worse—it is pure, unadulterated bullshit, without any basis in truth' (Day 2003a). Mark Day said he made the claims after years of observing his wife, who acts as Australian publicist for Nicole Kidman and Russell Crowe, trying to hose down the made-up nonsense surrounding her clients' lives. He recounted a litany of stories that had appeared in *New Idea* and *Women's Day* in 2002 when Nicole faced a *cancer scare*, signed the *richest* movie deal ever, went to hospital after suffering a *terrifying panic attack*, had a *secret affair* with Russell Crowe in Mexico, followed by a *shocking love triangle* involving Ben Affleck, Crowe, and Tobey Maguire, had the *holiday from hell* with former husband Tom Cruise and his new woman, Penelope Cruz, *dated* Vin Diesel while at the same time agreeing to an *astonishing secret pact* with Tom and Penelope and (as Day suggests) presumably the *New Idea* reporter who quoted every word of it. All that in a year. And, according to Day, not a skerrick of truth in any of it (Day 2003a, we added the italics to the story lines). Nearly a year later, and, according to Day (2004a), nothing has changed. 'The mags continued to beat up non-stop nonsense and feed their readers a diet of in-their-dreams goss.' 'Yet people lap it up. Market research indicates that readers don't care if it is made up' (Day 2004a).

Issues and questions raised by case study 1

1   Do you buy gossip magazines, or peruse them at the newsagent or doctor's surgery? Why? Is it 'guilty pleasure', 'escapism', or are you hungry for 'news' of the stars?
2   Do you believe what you read in the weekly gossip magazines?
3   Why do you think people buy them?
4   What is the role of gossip magazines in the mass media spectrum?
5   We can all tell the difference between fact and fictional drama on TV, but how do you differentiate in a gossip magazine?
6   Should gossip magazines be likened to soap operas on television—there just for pure entertainment?
7   Should all gossip magazines carry a warning on their cover—'Don't believe all you read inside'?
8   What damage does the performance of the glossy gossip magazines do to journalistic integrity?
9   Is it just the financial 'bottom line' that encourages media proprietors to allow this form of dishonesty to abound?
10 Would you work for one of the 'glossies'?

Case study 2

When *Australian Story* helps set the news agenda

Time was when *Sunday* and *60 Minutes* (Nine), *Meet the Press* (Ten), and *Insiders* (ABC) helped set the news agenda for at least Monday, and sometimes later into the week. *Four Corners* (ABC) over the years has had its fair share of scoops and set the news agenda for days. Nowadays some of the infotainment shows have become the most quoted TV programs, like the latest eviction from the *Big Brother* house or the latest wannabe to be voted off *Australian Idol*. But in recent years, the ABC's documentary series *Australian Story* has been making news. The producers often release details of who is on the program (seen on Monday nights) to the weekend newspapers, thus drumming up additional viewers. The former Governor-General, Dr Peter Hollingworth, chose *Australian Story* in February 2002 to defend himself against allegations he had covered up child abuse claims while Anglican Archbishop of Brisbane (see chapter 8). The Mayor of Maroochy on Queensland's Sunshine Coast, Alison Grosse, chose *Australian Story* in September 2003 to tell 'her story' in the wake of salacious evidence against her in a stalking case (see chapter 7). Later that year (November, 2003) the wife of former Australian Prime Minister Bob Hawke, Hazel, publicly revealed she was suffering from Alzheimer's disease on the program. But it hasn't been all plain sailing for the flagship program. A Queensland District Court judge condemned the program for depicting the so-called 'postcard bandit', Brenden Abbott, as 'not such a bad chap'. A judge was handing down a decision in Southport Court when he slammed the program in which the convicted bank robber and serial jail escapee was portrayed as a misunderstood political prisoner. 'The television station that produced that nonsense for public consumption should be thoroughly ashamed of itself', the judge said. Abbott, 41, at the time was serving a 23-year sentence in a maximum security prison for armed hold-ups and a series of jail escapes. He reportedly robbed about 100 banks of about $5 million.

Issues and questions raised by case study 2

1   Why do you think the likes of the Governor-General and Alison Grosse chose *Australian Story* to tell their story?
2   Would they expect a sympathetic hearing from such a program?
3   Is it, perhaps, because they feel they will be able to express themselves in more than a news sound bite, and not be badgered by over-zealous daily current affairs interviewers?
4   What do you think of the style of current affairs interviewing today?
5   Do you ever feel sorry for the interviewee, trying to get an answer in between the badgering of the long-winded questioner?
6   What is the role of such personality/documentary programs like *Australian Story*?

7   Are they entertainment programs that often make news, or extended news programs that entertain? Is there a difference?

8   What were the benefits of someone like Hazel Hawke talking about her illness on TV?

9   Research the reaction to the Brenden Abbott program. If you were the executive producer of *Australian Story* how would you respond to the judge's criticism?

Case study 3
Martin Bryant: 'Wild in the eyes'

Early on the afternoon of Sunday 28 April 1996, a man in his late 20s got up from a table and opened fire in a crowded café. By the end of the day, thirty-five people were dead, dozens more wounded. That day at the site of the historic Port Arthur penal colony in south-east Tasmania, a quiet and 'strange' local, Martin Bryant, became Australia's most deadly mass killer. The suspect, Martin Bryant, was taken into custody after an all-night siege at a farmhouse near the site of the Port Arthur ruins. Bryant is alleged to have set fire to the house in which he was holed up, randomly firing at the surrounding police. Badly burnt, Bryant was taken to a Hobart hospital under a heavy police guard. There was a media-initiated debate over Bryant's 'state of mind'. People who knew Bryant were cross-examined by journalists and several conflicting stories emerged (Paget 1996). Bryant quickly became the 'world's worst killer'.

It wasn't until Tuesday 30 April that the first picture of Martin Bryant was splashed across most front pages around the country (Sutton, Gilmore et al. 1996). The *Australian* 'enhanced' the photograph to emphasise the whiteness of Bryant's eyes. This had the effect of giving him an eerie, 'spaced out', 'mad' look that fitted a favoured media image of the suspect. Once pictures of Martin Bryant began appearing in the papers, it became a flood. In the 6 May 1996 edition of ABC's *Media Watch* it was suggested that the first photographs were taken from Bryant's house by journalists, while the police guard was distracted. However, distant relatives of Martin Bryant provided an album full of photographs. Two of his ex-girlfriends also supplied more recent pictures.

Issues and questions raised by case study 3

1   What guidelines should be in place when 'altering' images for production purposes?

2   Discuss the ethics of so 'enhancing' a photo that it changes it.

3   Did changing the photograph by whitening Bryant's eyes have any emotional impact on the issue and how people may have perceived the tragedy?

4   Under what circumstances do you think it is permissible?

5   Does the AJA Code of Ethics address this issue?

6   Do any of the other Codes or Charters of Independence have anything to say about 'digital' enhancement?

7   Haven't daily newspapers had a history of 'touching up' photos to enhance important aspects of the image?

8   You have a great picture, but it's at a distance and not very clear. Do you 'enhance' it so your readers can see the critical part(s) of the shot?

9   Where do you draw the line? What is acceptable?

10 Who makes that decision?

Case study 4

Kennett on the cover: Digital nudity

Good Weekend, the magazine published by the Fairfax organisation and included in the weekend editions of the *SMH* and the *Age*, thought it would have some fun at the expense of Victorian Premier Jeff Kennett on 31 July 1993, when it published a front cover photo of him supposedly addressing a street crowd in the nude, under the headline 'Unreal, Jeff'. The paper explained how the 'reconfigured' Jeff Kennett image was

created by merging a slide and a print using a Quantel Graphics Paintbox XL, an image retouching system. It replaced the 'fully clothed' body of the Premier with a naked body of a male model. Harmless fun, it thought, although the Premier was not amused. But it drew attention to a then-new area of ethical dilemma for journalists and photographers. How much digital manipulation should there be of an image before the line is crossed?

In 1993 the science of digital imaging was so new to Australian newspapers that the issue of ethical guidelines was still to be addressed. The pictorial editor of the *Sydney Morning Herald* at the time of the Kennett image enhancement incident, Peter Morris, said the paper had set no formal guidelines, but he considered 'to distort reality would place us all in grave danger in terms of credibility'. Three years later, the 'touching up' of Martin Bryant by the *Australian* (the case study above) to the point where many felt the eyes made the accused look positively evil, shows that the ethical discussion hadn't gone very far. Newspapers have always 'touched up' photos to highlight the appropriate person or part of the image, and dulled, painted out, or cut out parts of the picture not considered important to the central focus of the shot.

Issues and questions raised by case study 4

1 Would you have allowed the 'doctored' photo of former Premier Kennett to be published?
2 How would you defend the decision to publish?
3 Was there any harm done by the 'digitally enhanced' photo of self-confessed 'cricket tragic' John Howard in the *Gold Coast Bulletin* mentioned in the essay? And what about the Prince Harry and the Gold Coast model 'picture' mentioned in chapter 7?
4 Can you recall any other photos that have obviously been 'enhanced' or 'doctored'?
5 Is it that offensive when it's really only a 'bit of fun'?
6 Surely those complaining are a bit thin-skinned? Surely public figures can expect gentle ribbing from time to time?
7 How would you feel if it was you?

Case study 5

Los Angeles Times photographer fired over altered image

The 2003 Gulf War threw up all the usual ethical dilemmas, and then some, as we've seen in chapter 6, but we have saved this one until now, because it has much in common with the previous two Australian case studies on photo manipulation. *Los Angeles Times* photographer Brian Walski, on assignment covering the war in Iraq, was fired on 1 April 2003, for deliberately altering an image to enhance its impact. The offending photo (of a British soldier and a group of Iraqi civilians, one a male clasping a young child) was submitted from the battlefield on Sunday 30 March. Other members of the *Tribune* group (of which the *LA Times* is part) had access to the photo via Newscom, the company's internal picture distribution service (Irby 2003). Both the *Hartford Courant* and the *Los Angeles Times* used the photograph prominently on Monday 31 March. The *Courant* published it over six columns, taking up about half the front page, and the *LA Times* used it over three columns top left of page 1. A *Courant* employee noticed what appeared to be duplication in the picture and drew it to the attention of senior staff. Walski, by telephone from southern Iraq, acknowledged that he had used his computer to combine elements of two photographs, taken moments apart, in order to improve the composition. In an email to the photography staff of the *Times,* Walski admitted his lapse in judgment and accepted responsibility for it. In part, his apology read: 'This was after an extremely long, hot and stressful day but I offer no excuses here' (cited in Irby 2003). Interviewed by Poynter Online via satellite phone from Kuwait City, *LA Times* staff photographer Don Bartletti recounts seeing Walski after he returned from the desert on 1 April. 'When I saw him, I really did not recognise him. He was sunburned, had not eaten in days, not slept in 36 hours, his clothes were filthy, his beard—all over the place. And he smelled like a goat' (quoted in Irby 2003). On Tuesday 1 April, the *Los Angeles Times* posted an editor's note on its web site notifying readers about the breach of its photographic ethics policy, the investigation, and the subsequent firing of Walski for altering the photo. By way of a belated apology to their readers, the *Times* and the *Courant* published all three photos—the two originals and the altered composite—on 2 April 2003.

Issues and questions raised by case study 5

1   What's so wrong with what Walski did?
2   Should there be a different set of rules for war coverage?
3   Research the case of Paul Walski and put the case in his defence?
4   Find the relevant part of the *Los Angeles Times*'s ethical policy and evaluate it.
5   Do Australian Codes of Ethics and Practice have similar clauses?

Case study 6

Urban myths and the Internet: Did you read the one about exploding mobile phones?

Before the Internet, urban myths circulated by word-of-mouth. The Internet just speeds up the process and gets a 'good story' worldwide in no time. Here is a salutary tale in *not* trusting online sources.

In July 2003, the *Daily Telegraph* (Sydney) warned its readers not to use their mobile phones while filling their cars with petrol because there had been explosions at service stations overseas ('Switch Off Mobiles at Fuel Pumps' 2003). The story had been doing the rounds of the Internet for years—like those lists of amazing law suits in America, or the frightened Nigerian diplomat's son who wants to give you $400 million. Yeah, he never calls back! The 'exploding phone' yarn got its first run in December 1996 (Marr 2003e). According to *Media Watch* it first appeared in the Melbourne *Herald Sun* when it reported that a woman suffered burns to 50 per cent of her body when her car burst into flames while she was using a mobile phone ('Mobile Phone Fire Threat' 1996). The official report blames the car's exhaust for igniting the fuel. According to *Media Watch,* the story emerged again in 1999 in Taiwan's *China Post* quoting a report from Shell Chemicals as saying a driver in Indonesia suffered burns and his car was severely damaged when petrol vapour was ignited by static electricity from his mobile phone ('Mobile Phones An Explosive Risk At Gas Stations, 1999). The *Bangkok Post* added to the story with some details from Australia: '...a serious fire at a gas station in Adelaide, Australia, three years ago was likely caused by a mobile phone' (Bangkok Post 17 May 1999, cited in Marr 2003e). A representative of the South Australian Metropolitan Fire Service told *Media Watch* there never had been an explosion or a death caused by a mobile phone in that state. Variations on the theme have been circulating around the Internet for years. *Media Watch* discovered that the *Australian Financial Review* had printed the one about the 'dead unlucky' driver who was at the bowser when a mate phoned him, the call sufficient to cause an internal spark in the phone and trigger the explosion that killed him ('Petrol Heads: Switch Off the Mobile for Safety' 1999). The *Daily Telegraph* had become another victim of an urban myth and was forced to admit as much by publishing a letter from the Australian Mobile Telecommunications Association six days later ('Blasts Were Phony' 2003). And as if that wasn't enough, four weeks later, the ever-vigilant *Media Watch* ('Blasts Were Phony' 2003) reported that the bogus email had found its way into the New South Wales Rural Fire Service and from there to the *Coonamble Times:* 'The phone was placed on the car boot during refuelling; it rang and the subsequent fire destroyed the car and the petrol pump' ('Warning About Mobile Phones at Petrol Stations' 2003). A sceptical journalist will always say: If it sounds (or reads) too good to be true, then it probably is!

Issues and questions raised by case study 6

1   Where would you go to check a possible urban myth?
2   Do you know of any others 'doing the rounds'?
3   How do you verify information in general on the Net?
4   How would you react if your editor told you to rewrite a media release that you thought was bogus, or might be a hoax?

Case study 7

Influence of television stations like Al Jazeera

Every night, thousands of Arab speakers across Australia, and far more in the United States, tune into satellite television stations from the Middle East, like Al Jazeera. Even before it made world headlines by showing pictures of destruction in Baghdad and bodies of coalition soldiers during the 2003 Iraq War, Al Jazeera had been broadcasting confronting images of the ongoing Arab–Israeli conflict. 'The images are bloody and brutal. Palestinian children throw rocks at Israeli tanks, Israeli soldiers shoot back. Innocent people die' (Karvelas 2003). But while Al Jazeera has been criticised for anti-Western bias, the lesser-known, but increasingly popular A-Manar is, according to the *Australian,* blatant about its anti-Israeli agenda (Karvelas 2003). It is the mouthpiece of the Hezbollah party in Lebanon, an organisation that has been placed on Australia's list of terror groups (Karvelas 2003). Al-Manar's web site says it provides coverage 'in support of the oppressed Palestinian people' (Karvelas 2003). In 2003 there were ten Arab TV channels available in Australia via subscription.

Issues and questions raised by case study 7

1   What is the role of stations like Al Jazeera in Australia?
2   What reaction is their coverage likely to provoke among Australian Arabs who subscribe to such services?
3   In a multicultural society like Australia, how should governments and individuals react to overseas news services?
4   How do you feel about news services in languages other than English broadcast on SBS radio and television?

12

THE LAST WORD?
THE FUTURE OF
JOURNALISM ETHICS

Objectives

After reading and discussing this chapter you will have been challenged by:

- Our reflections on the industry you are entering and our hope that it may some day change for the better.
- Some crystal-ball gazing into the future of ethics in the twenty-first century.
- Our views about the changing culture in newsrooms and a radical suggestion for worker control of the news process.

Introduction: Towards an alternative news culture

This is the final chapter, so our objectives are very simple: to wind up our discussion of some of the current arguments, cases, and fault lines in journalism ethics. What will be the final outcome of some of the case studies and debates we haven't been able to resolve at this point? We don't know, but if, after reading this chapter, you are more familiar with the current fault lines in journalism ethics, we have done all we can.

Our final objective is to point you towards a discussion of changing newsroom cultures and to look forward in a hypothetical, though positive way, to an alternative to the control exercised over journalism by the social relations and economic forces of news production. Ultimately, we'll be satisfied if you can take away from this text the idea that you and your peers will have to take some of the responsibility for the future shape of news reporting. Our purpose is simple: to help you get to know yourself, the industry you want to work in, and the organisation you might one day work for. Only then will you be in a position to reflect critically on your own journalism and help change things, hopefully for the better.

No last word in journalism ethics

Black or white; shades of grey, fine lines, and fault lines; there's no such thing as the last word in a discussion about journalism ethics. Every answer suggests another question. The resolution of one contradiction opens up the space for further tensions and conflict. When one ethical dilemma appears to be resolved another emerges. That's the nature of the dialectic; the process of history informing today's events and laying the foundations for the future. As we put the finishing touches to this text a number of things have happened that clearly demonstrate our central thesis: the fault lines in journalism ethics can never be finally healed or sealed while the central contradiction remains. That contradiction is the private ownership of what are essentially public informational resources deployed and employed for the pursuit of profit, rather than to enhance the public good. In the following few pages we want to revisit some of our examples and case studies from previous chapters to show you what we mean.

Don't mention the war

'Our view is that you can't have security compromised just a bit. Once it's over it's over. So the reporting can begin from the time the Prime Minister is in Baghdad,' said one Defence official.

Shanahan 2004

In response to September 11 and the 2002 Bali bombing the Australian government granted far-reaching new powers to the spy agency ASIO in the context of the war against terrorism. Under the laws a journalist who is thought to have information about terrorists or terrorist activities can be detained and questioned. This undermines the fundamental ethical principle of protecting sources, on the grounds of a threat to the so-called national interest. It also inhibits the news media's ability to tell the public about dangers and compromises to civil liberties in the name of the 'war on terror'. While news organisations have offered some mild criticisms of the ASIO powers, generally they are prepared to wear the restrictions in the name of national security.

To celebrate ANZAC Day 2004 (25 April) Prime Minister Howard decided to pay a surprise and top secret visit to Australian troops serving in Iraq (Shanahan 2004). The media knew he was going, but agreed to keep it secret in case 'terrorists' heard Howard was on his way to Baghdad and shot down his plane (Maiden 2004). The visit was a stunning propaganda coup for John Howard (did anyone mention that 2004 was an election year?) and the media got a story through the pool system that allows a small number of TV crews, photographers, and a couple of print journalists to cover the events for everyone. Why was it deemed so sensitive that we couldn't know beforehand that Howard was going to Iraq? After all, his defence minister and others had visited the city several times in the weeks previously;

these were all well-publicised trips. One positive, though, is that the news media did manage to make a few complaints about access and deadlines. When it was all over, those of us who read the Media section of the *Australian* got to hear about it. The views of the journalists involved were mixed: some thought the news blackout was a good idea, others were annoyed that there were delays and interference in the filing process (Maiden 2004).

In May, as we were finishing this final chapter, the war in Iraq claimed the scalp of British newspaper editor Piers Morgan. He was forced to resign when it was confirmed that pictures published in the *Daily Mirror* were fake (Wilson 2004). The pictures allegedly showed British soldiers torturing Iraqi detainees, including one image of a solider urinating on a prisoner. The British government admitted some abuse had taken place, but denied the evidence of the photographs. The war against terror also claimed another victim—the Internet (Harris 2004). A group of Islamic militants videotaped the gruesome decapitation of an American civilian, David Berg, they had kidnapped in Baghdad and it was then broadcast from a web site. This outrage prompted one commentator to remark that the Internet had now become unsafe and was a recruiting ground for terrorists who then sent coded messages about imminent attacks:

> Terror experts say the internet is now an online training camp … 'The internet has become a virtual Afghanistan,' says Clive Williams, director of terrorism studies at the Australian National University.
>
> Harris 2004, p. 15

The solution, according to the 'experts' quoted by Trudy Harris, is for security forces around the world to crack down on terrorists using the Internet. More surveillance and resources for 'counter-terrorism' agencies. By generally limiting our freedom of communication, we are somehow made safer and more free. Where's the logic in that? However, the freedom-loving American troops in Iraq found a use for the Internet that also, eventually, got them into trouble. Guards at the American-controlled Abu Grhaib jail in Baghdad had been emailing copies of their own abuse photographs around the world. According to news reports at the time, members of the American Congress were shown videotapes and other images of American guards engaging in group sex, sexually abusing Iraqis, and attacking them with dogs. War has truly become the new pornography.

In this instance there were no claims that the images had been faked and several US service men and women were court-martialled for their part in the abuse. It became clear that sexual degradation, painful beatings, and ritual humiliation of Iraqis in the jail were a systematic element of psychological operations. Even the pro-war columnist Greg Sheridan (2004b) was moved to admit that the material bordered on the pornographic, while at the same time trying to argue that what Berg's killers had done was worse:

> The beheading of the young American civilian David Berg, proudly displayed on the internet by his murderers, does serve in all its pornographic exhibitionism to underline the difference between the US and its enemies … The horrible abuses carried out by some US soldiers … are a long way down the line of cruelty compared with the murder of Berg.
>
> Sheridan 2004, p. 13

Remember the 'Hutton affair' and the accusations of bias at the BBC during and just after the 2003 invasion of Iraq? The BBC sought to address the problems by sending reporters to a series of 'impartiality seminars' to counteract the influence of a perceived 'left-leaning liberal' bias at the British state-funded broadcaster. According to a report in the *Sunday Times* newspaper (Cracknell & Brooks 2004), the BBC has now imposed a rule that only 'the most senior journalists' should be able to express opinions in their news coverage. No doubt they will first have to be psy-oped to remove any trace of partiality or liberal sentiment. It is not clear from our information whether the Australian government will attempt to institute a similar policy at the ABC, but the Communications Minister [at the time, Richard Alston] decided that the ABC's own investigation of alleged anti-American bias in the Iraq war coverage should be further investigated by the Australian Broadcasting Authority on the grounds that the ABC inquisition didn't provide the right answers. The person who was to head the ABA's inquiry was forced to remove himself from the panel when it was revealed that he had previously made public comments to the effect that he too believed the ABC was a nest of left-wing traitors who regularly exhibited pro-republican and anti-US sentiment (Charlton 2004a). The man in question was the then chairperson of the ABA, Professor David Flint. Even conservative editorialists were calling for Flint to be sacked. 'The Prime Minister should sack him but probably won't,' argued the *Courier-Mail* ('Howard Must Act to Sack Biased Flint', 2004) after revealing that Howard and Flint were classmates at law school in the late 1950s (McIlveen 2004).

Australia had its own mini version of the BBC–David Kelly source affair involving Melbourne's *Age* newspaper. Just like the infamous British case, it involved a journalist writing about the strength of information on weapons of mass destruction in the lead-up to the 2003 War in Iraq. The source was 'outed' in a dramatic fashion, and in early 2004 there was the prospect of an independent inquiry.

In the Australian case, the unnamed source was contained in a report by *Age* defence writer Mark Forbes. The 14 February article quoted one of Australia's most senior intelligence officers as having told the Federal Government in the weeks before the war that some of the Bush Administration's claims were exaggerated. Forbes got the information from a seminar he attended as a Masters student—not a journalist—at the Strategic and Defence Studies Centre at the Australian National University the previous September.

The seminar was under the 'Chatham House rule', which allows students to use the information, but not attribute it. Insiders said the source was obvious to people working in the area. Five days after the story appeared, the director of the Defence Intelligence Organisation, Frank Lewincamp, told a Senate Estimates Committee that he believed he was the unnamed official, but denied he ever said the Iraqi weapons claims were exaggerated, and took issue with some parts of the *Age* report. The *Age* stood by the accuracy of the report (McLean 2004).

Oops, they did it again

Professor Flint's troubles didn't end with his removal from the ABC inquiry. Do you recall the 'cash for comment' case study from chapter 10? Just as we were finishing this book 'cash for comment mark 2' exploded in David Flint's face when a verbal brawl erupted between two high-profile radio announcers (Charlton 2004b). According to newspaper reports

(Leys 2004) the *Media Watch* program received a tip-off about a draft ABA report into broadcaster Alan Jones that alleged he had breached the guidelines (and perhaps broken the law) by accepting sponsorship from Telstra in return for favourable on-air comments. The ABA's final report had cleared Jones and this was at odds with the draft. Then it got dramatically worse.

While Jones had been cleared in the ABA's mind, his rival over at 2UE, John Laws had not. Laws was annoyed that one rule seemed to apply to Alan Jones and another to himself. Laws took advantage of having a high-rating radio show at his disposal and went on air to drop a bucket on Jones, accusing him of using his considerable political influence with the Prime Minister to ensure that David Flint remained as chair of the ABA. Laws called Jones a 'vicious old tart' (cited in Charlton, 2004b) and told his morning show audience that at a dinner party he had heard Jones boasting of going to visit John Howard at his Sydney residence, Kirribilli House, to put pressure on him to reappoint Flint.

Both the Prime Minister and Alan Jones denied any such conversation had taken place (Elliott, Maiden & Higgins 2004). Then it got even more interesting. *Media Watch* got hold of a copy of a personal and very glowing letter written to Jones by David Flint just months before the first 'cash for comment' inquiry in 1999. Not surprisingly the rest of the ABA board was upset about the actions of their chairman, but there was little they could do about it. It seems Jones and Flint had exchanged several letters over the years. On the ABC's *7:30 Report* Flint denied any wrongdoing and claimed he would not have written the letters to Jones had he known there would be an inquiry. According to Sally Jackson (2004b), it was money that fuelled whatever civility there was between Laws and Jones and money that ripped their relationship to shreds in the wake of 'cash for comment'.

After the revelations by Laws and *Media Watch*'s exposure of his letters to Jones, David Flint was hopelessly compromised for the last few months of his leadership of the ABA; Jones and Laws continued their on-air duelling and the 'cash for comment' affair rolled on. A small, but quite humorous side bar to this tawdry story of jealousy and money emerged when it was revealed that Government Minister Danna Vale sent Jones a herogram, but mistakenly faxed it to the wrong Sydney radio station. The cheesy note, signed by Vale and her staff, urged Jones to stay 'brave and true' in the face of the unfair flack he was copping. On a serious note this incident indicates just how close and unhealthy (for Australian democracy) the relationship is between powerful radio announcers and our political leaders. One of the factors motivating Laws in his fight with Jones is that John Howard is a regular guest on the Jones show, but tends to ignore John Laws (Jackson 2004b).

The second round of 'cash for comment' opened up a massive fault line, right under the ABA chairman, Professor Flint. Once again *Media Watch* led the way, but this time the disclosures forced everyone involved to go glaringly public. 'Cash for comment' is the San Andreas fault of Australian journalism and media ethics; it exposes the fundamental nature of the profit motive. Alan Jones devised a clever scheme to get around the ABA's code of conduct: he became a shareholder in his employer and could fairly claim that he wasn't directly paid for his opinions, even though it was clear that this is precisely what his customers paid for, including Telstra. Finally, as we go to press it was announced that John Laws would not face charges over his alleged breaches of the 'cash for comment' rules and

Professor Flint resigned as chair of the ABA. However, both Alan Jones and David Flint refused an FOI request to release copies of their correspondence, claiming it was personal and private (Maiden & McKinnon 2004).

From accuser to accused

The saga of rape allegations against several members of the Canterbury Bulldogs rugby league team, discussed in chapter 8, came to a closure of sorts just as we were finishing this book. At the end of April 2004, the NSW police investigating the allegations declined to lay charges because of inconsistencies in the woman's story and contradictory accounts from several witnesses. What is clear is that there was sexual contact between the woman and several Bulldogs' players over a period of several days, including the night and morning of the alleged rape. The police said there was physical evidence, but that it did not prove rape (Warne-Smith & Barrett 2004b). However, it was clear that the young woman at the centre of the scandal was traumatised by the whole experience. In statements given to the police and in the media's reporting she was portrayed as a sexually promiscuous young woman who enjoyed frequent encounters with members of the Bulldogs team whenever they were in Coffs Harbour. At one point a Bulldogs player is said to have called her a 'slag' in an interview with the *Daily Telegraph* in Sydney. Once the police case was dropped, the media moved in seeking to buy the young woman's story and reporters swooped on her friends and acquaintances seeking comments. The *Sunday Mail* reported that the woman's actions had 'divided' Coffs Harbour, but actually provided no evidence to back the claim. Instead the story cast doubt on the woman's credibility: 'So was she a victim of gang rape later that morning—or is she a conniving villain?' (Jameson, 2004)

It seems she might, at least, be a victim of media frenzy as celebrity agents Harry M. Miller and Max Markson offered to represent her in dealing with interview requests from all the major TV tabloid current affairs shows (Symons 2004). Her credibility was also on the line here, with *Daily Telegraph* editor Campbell Reid (cited in Symons 2004) suggesting she should not accept any chequebook blandishments, so that her credibility could not be questioned. It's worth speculating that Reid was merely trying to cut the price through this negotiating tactic; no doubt he's actually fully aware of the dollar value of such an exclusive. Thus far she had resisted such offers, tempting though they might be. However, what's actually most intriguing and disturbing about the media's coverage of this story is the glossing over of any apparent conflict of interest between the Murdoch stable of newspapers and News Limited's deep financial commitment to the National Rugby League (NRL) and in particular to the Canterbury Bulldogs club.

As the scandal began to grow in February 2004, a News Limited executive was appointed to lead the Canterbury club's business operations and to head the club's internal investigation into the gang-rape allegations, which included hiring private detectives to do their own snooping. According to some accounts, this and other events led to delays in interviewing the Bulldogs players and in the collection of evidence from them. Some rival publications actually speculated that the police investigation had been compromised by the presence of the club's own investigators. It also leads to questions about how the Murdoch newspapers were able to secure 'scoops' on the story, particularly when they were favourable to the club, or cast doubt on the woman's version of what happened. For example, how did reporter Steve Barrett (2004b) get access to police and lawyers' copies of statements from witnesses who gave 'a very different picture of what is alleged to have happened', including that there appeared 'nothing unusual about the woman's manner'. Finally, it was reported that several Bulldogs' players demanded apologies from the media for the way they were treated. Fortunately most sensible people treated this with the contempt it deserved, including Tony Koch (2004) writing in the *Courier-Mail*:

> It struck me this was a strange response from these civic-minded citizens whom I have noted have sometimes been described as 'heroes' for feats they performed on the football field.
>
> The same people making those calls did not, to my knowledge, use their heroic profiles to take the opportunity to express concern about the plight of the young woman victim who obviously was treated—apparently by unidentified persons—like a piece of meat.
>
> Abused, degraded, passed around, then discarded.
>
> Koch 2004, p. 27

Koch makes the valid point that 'once again' in this story, 'the media becomes the demon', and he continues in a strong defence of journalists who display 'great courage and responsibility' in doing a job 'which has aspects that many people would run a mile to avoid'. Certainly there are journalists who do not take any ethical responsibility for their work and stories such as this one often attract the worst kinds of journalistic behaviour, but Tony Koch is essentially correct, the media does not owe any Bulldogs player an apology for uncovering some of the less savoury aspects of professional sport in Australia.

These foolish celebrities, won't they ever learn?

We've discussed celebrities and the invasions of privacy that they have to endure in several chapters and case studies, but when the damage is sexually transmitted and self-inflicted, we have little sympathy. Take the talented and very wealthy soccer star, Mr David Beckham, one half of a fabulous celebrity couple. Beckham appears to have fallen victim to 'Shane Warne syndrome'—sending suggestive text messages to a woman who is not your lawfully wedded wife. Unfortunately, Beckham was called 'offside' by two women who felt jilted by his apparent 'love 'em and leave 'em' attitude. Was it about revenge (and the small fortune for selling a story to *News of the World*)? Of course, in the usual way these stories are treated, once it was in the public domain via a sleazy publication like *News of the World*, the more 'respectable' papers couldn't leave it alone. One of the women who claimed to have had an affair with Beckham was revealed as a high-class prostitute who had worked for a Sydney escort agency and suitably raunchy photos of her were splashed across the papers (Crawford 2004). A second woman who claimed to have loved Beckham was paid over $200,000 for her story and she too became a 'scarlet woman' trying to 'steal' the world's most beautiful soccer player from his spouse. The Brisbane tabloid *Sunday Mail* got into the act by publishing advice for people who wished to indulge in adulterous cybersex or those who might wish to catch a cheating spouse:

Credit card records are the infallible guide to infidelity. The redial button can be as incriminating as a lipstick stain on the collar.

Lydon 2004, p. 56

Of course any recap about the news media's fascination with celebrity and sex would not be complete without noting that the adorable Paris Hilton once again made the news pages, just for being who she is. Her April 2004 visit to a night club, while on Queensland's Gold Coast making a movie, was given half a page in the *Courier-Mail*, including a side bar on her allegedly pornographic video, *One night in Paris*, going on sale in Australian 'adult stores' (Heffernan 2004). Celebrity culture and tabloid journalism also appeared to be an element in the continuing scandal about Australian footballers and sex. Rape allegations against high-profile players in other codes made the news in the wake of the Bulldogs story, leading one columnist to the conclusion that 'celebrity corrupts and absolute celebrity corrupts absolutely' (Wiseman 2004).

Though not really a celebrity like the Beckhams, Annita Keating, the former wife of ex-Prime Minister Paul Keating, did feel it necessary to defend herself from rumours about why and how her marriage fell apart. Annita took the unusual step of outing herself in an interview with the *Bulletin* magazine. Of course this then provoked a frenzy as the other media outlets, who had till then merely gossiped among themselves, felt the story was legitimised by the *Bulletin* piece. The Keating marriage was then dissected from every angle and no-one got any privacy. Writing in the *Weekend Australian*, Kate Legge (2004) argued that the story had 'touched our fascination with political glamour'. The question is whose fascination—that of the reporters and editors, or a wider public fascination?

But we will never satisfy our appetite for stories of private lives. Even as I reach for *New Idea* or *Who Weekly* at the supermarket checkout counter, I know the lurid promise of peeking at Posh and Beck [sic], Di and Charles, Nic and Tom is a glossy lie.

Legge 2004 p. 19

Finally, we predicted that the Michael Jackson child-sex charges and subsequent trial would become a media circus; well, as of April 2004, it seems we were right. It appears that Jackson's lawyers wanted to boost his defence by turning the trial into a 'carnival':

Celebrity justice—after high profile cases such as that of ex-footballer O.J. Simpson—has become its own genre, with a formulaic choreography played out by prosecutor and defendant.

McKenna 2004

This carnival comes complete with a 'sea of parents with children in their arms' gathering outside Jackson's Neverland home and the defendant 'dancing on a four-wheel drive outside court' (McKenna 2004). While the news media is fascinated with this high-profile case, we must remember that Michael Jackson is facing serious sexual assault charges and could spend the rest of his life in jail (Seamark & McKenna 2004). The media's interest in this case is fuelled by Jackson's celebrity status, but at the end of the day, he's a guy facing serious charges and he does have a right to a fair trial. In a case like this, though, we have to question whether there is a direct motive in the defence exploiting Jackson's profile. Or is he just playing to the cameras?

One celebrity who loves the camera did have a small win in a court case. Model Naomi Campbell won her privacy action against the British tabloid *Daily Mirror*. Ms Campbell won over $800,000 as a settlement for 'breach of confidence' ('Tabloids Fear Naomi's Court Win Will Spell End for Exposés' 2004). The court ruled that the newspaper was entitled to describe Campbell as a drug addict 'because she had always made a point of distancing herself from drugs', but the paper was not entitled to reveal confidential information about her treatment for addiction, or her attendance at a Narcotics Anonymous meeting. One judge in the case, Lord Hope of Craighead, outlined his reasons for backing privacy over freedom of expression:

> 'Despite the weight that must be given to the right of freedom of expression that the press needs if it is to play its role effectively, I would hold that there was here an infringement of Miss Campbell's right to privacy that cannot be justified.'

> Cited in the *SMH* 8 May 2004, p. 15

While we have to leave this matter here, it's still not necessarily the last word. The *Daily Mirror* is reported to be considering an appeal to the European Court under the auspices of the European Union. The Campbell case has once again opened up the fault line between personal privacy and freedom of the tabloids to report the lives of celebrities. Reporters too fall under fame's spell. Robert Lusetich (2004) argued that some 'misguided journalists pursue stardom' and 'become a celebrity as much as a journalist'. Inevitably this affects the quality of their reporting, leaving the public thinking journalists are biased, immoral, dishonest, and 'harmful to democracy' (Project for Excellence in Journalism, cited in Lusetich, 2004).

He's not a suspect, just a very naughty boy

In mid 2004 it seemed that any time soon Max Sica's strange and fanciful world might come crashing down. You'll remember Mr Sica as a key figure in the mystery surrounding the murders of three children from same Brisbane family. As of our to-press date Sica has not been charged with the Singh family murders, though the Queensland police did question him extensively, take DNA samples and other materials from his house, and then name him as a 'person of interest' to their investigation. Then in April 2004 the *Courier-Mail* followed a virtual trail leading them to Max Sica's since-abandoned web site that included a password-protected section of 'strange pictures' including of himself 'semi-naked' with 'skin irritations' (Black, Lill & Doneman 2004). This was very damaging to Max Sica's reputation and left the impression that he could be a sociopath, or worse. If he is ever charged with the Singh murders this kind of reporting will have to stop. Mr Sica has always maintained his innocence and we can't help but wonder if he wouldn't be relieved to be charged so that he can clear his name and so that this kind of cheap-shot reporting doesn't continue. The other lesson from this is that even when you think no one is watching, your virtual trail on the Internet is never completely cold. You have been warned.

And speaking of crime, privacy, and public interest, the news media in Queensland complained when the police decided to introduce a new radio network to make it secure against terrorist infiltration (Parnell 2004). The reason for the complaints? For years newsrooms around the country have illegally listened in to the police frequencies on scanners. While this was technically against the law, most police services ignored it. When the *Courier-Mail* and Channel 9 in Brisbane heard about the change in police equipment they complained:

> Digital radios, which were to be introduced without public consultation, would prevent the media from monitoring police communications. In turn that would hinder the media's ability to report on crimes and the subsequent actions of police as it happened.

Parnell 2004, p. 8

As a result, the Queensland Crime and Misconduct Commission (CMC) called for public submissions on the issue and the news media was of course pushing hard for access to the new digital police network. Should the media have this access? Probably, it can be argued that it helps keep the police honest, but in reality it's just a cheap way of gathering news of crimes and perhaps it distorts the news agenda. If newsrooms didn't have someone monitoring the police radio all day, it might mean extra resources for chasing other stories. We have already mentioned that there's a disproportionate focus on the news values of crime in many cities and Brisbane is no exception. There is also the issue of privacy in relation to people who come in contact with the police, particularly around sexual assault and domestic violence cases. There is a strong case to be made that much of the news generated by the police scanner falls under the heading of gossip, rather than real public-interest news. It seems that the CMC will not agree to allow media access to digital police communications, forcing journalists out of the office and back into police 'rounds' and old-fashioned cultivation of sources.

A grab bag of new cracks

We can't cover everything here, so it's time to wind up the review of major ethical dilemmas. But before moving on we can spend a few lines mentioning a couple of interesting new fault lines. One potential crack is the expansion of Kerry and James Packer's empire into more casinos and non-media assets. How will this acquisition impact on the Packer family's long-held desire to have newspaper assets? It is always interesting to follow the business end of the media. The Packers paid themselves a $40 million dividend on the back of the Burswood deal (Schulze 2004a). This might go into the fund to buy more shares in Fairfax. The same week, Fred Hilmer announced his departure after five years as CEO of the Fairfax corporation, which will no doubt bring an interesting new chapter to life and yet more concerns for some senior staff, like Michelle Grattan. Grattan has publicly criticised the bean-counter mentality at Fairfax under Hilmer and no doubt she will have plenty to say about the new regime too. Hilmer resigned in the same month that Fairfax offered forty or so senior reporters a redundancy package; a move that the MEAA said would 'gut the Fairfax newspapers' (Stapleton 2004).

Over at the ABC there has also been change: the broadcaster has hired conservative columnist and publisher, Michael Duffy, to host an afternoon talk program called *Counterpoint*. Duffy has been described as the 'right-wing Phillip Adams' (Simper 2004b) and no doubt his appointment is meant to counter the perception that the ABC is a hotbed of left-wing activism. We have always argued that the ABC only appears to be 'left' because the rest of the media is so conservative and Duffy's appointment to Radio National does nothing to undermine our position. Duffy already has a column in the Murdoch press, so it can hardly be seen as the ABC offering a greater range of opinion. The marketing slogan for Duffy could easily be: 'New *Same* with added *More*'. Duffy is no doubt going to stir things up at 'Aunty'; he is a critic of the network and has advocated advertising, as well as partial privatisation of the ABC. In our view Duffy's appointment represents another attempt by ABC senior management to appease conservatives in the Howard government; it is not a move to diversify the range of political opinion.

Speaking briefly of marketing, it seems that Channel Seven's *Sunrise* has been enjoying 'extraordinary success' through its 'flexible and loose' format that, according to Seven's Peter Meakin, is 'a bit more personable and certainly more local than Nine' (cited in Meade 2004). *Sunrise* also came under fire for launching a competition to find independent candidates to stand in the federal election, due by March 2005. The program sought audition tapes from viewers, who were then vetted by a panel of experts. The winner in each state was to be given air time on the Seven network and some funds towards their election campaign. Politicians and commentators said the *Sunrise* stunt was fraught with dangers and could undermine support for the political system.

There's also the possibility that the federal government will have another go at easing cross-media and foreign ownership restrictions again, with a bill now before the Senate. But there are still big 'ifs' about any such changes. It seems as if the Communications' Minister's office must have a revolving door and a hot seat. After the departure of Richard Alston, Daryl Williams got the job in a reshuffle, but he announced he would be retiring at the federal election due before March 2005. Media commentator Mark Day (2004c) described Williams as a lame-duck minister and said there is a 'leadership vacuum' at the federal policy level in broadcasting and media. Perhaps the many fault lines running through the administrative (ABC & SBS), regulatory (the ABA) and policy (cross-media laws and foreign ownership) arms of the portfolio are just too deep and too wide, leading to exhaustion of the Minister. Mark Latham's Labor Opposition also released a media policy for its next term in office: a fourth free-to-air television network. Perhaps the new station's slogan could be 'New, real *More* with extra *Same*'.

The future of reflexive journalism

> We have shareholders. Equally I'm totally aware of my responsibility and the responsibility of the editors, to present a viewpoint that isn't beholden to any commercial point of view. So balancing that is something that I think this company has shown in the past to find vitally important, but equally to find that we do that very well.

> John Hartigan, CEO of News Limited, cited in O'Regan 2001

This is a rare public comment from a man at the heart of the News Limited empire. John Hartigan is a former journalist and editor who, at the time of this interview on Radio National's *Media Report*, was the CEO of News Limited. In a wide-ranging discussion,

Hartigan was prepared to comment on the internal working of Murdoch's papers, something that would not have happened a generation ago. A scan of news columns reveals an almost continuous commentary about media ethics, scandals, industry gossip, media law, economics, and policy. Journalists, academics, audiences, media institutions, and governments are taking an active interest in the performance of news and current affairs providers. We mentioned how some television programs have pushed the envelope for journalism. This reflexivity is a fairly new and important development of the emotional dialectic of journalism. It has been going on now for just over a decade and is a long way from any final resolution. However, it is an important indication that some of the long-standing shibboleths, such as 'objectivity', are beginning to crumble under the pressure of new social relations of production. For example, journalists are now turning their attention to questions about the value of trust in the sciences and the media and the extent that trust has given way to spin-doctoring in relationships between political figures and reporters (Coleman 2004; Hargreaves 2003). It's also interesting that journalists are now talking about the issues. To some extent this is due to the influence of programs like the ABC's *Media Watch* and publications like the *Walkley* magazine, which has many fine contributors who are also working journalists. In the United States too, organisations like Fairness and Accuracy in Reporting (FAIR), the Pew Centre, and the Committee of Concerned Journalists are leading the way in exposing some of the fault lines in journalism. There is more openness and discussion among reporters, editors, and audiences, which can only lead to better journalism in the long run.

At an April 2004 forum hosted by the School of Journalism and Communication at the University of Queensland (where one of the authors was working) the *Australian*'s senior correspondent Paul Kelly was surprisingly forthcoming about his relationship with Rupert Murdoch and the process of his appointment several years earlier as editor-in-chief of the paper. According to Kelly, he was flown to Los Angeles for a series of meetings with Murdoch that took place over several days and involved a frank exchange of opinions. In the end Kelly realised, or came to understand, that it was Murdoch's paper and that to be comfortable as editor, he would have to adopt something close to Murdoch's view of the world. Kelly went on, in his remarks, to outline his philosophy of the right of ownership. That is, because it is Murdoch's paper, he has the right to set the editorial position and to expect his editors to endorse it through the leading articles that express an editorial viewpoint. That Kelly was comfortable with this is not the point. That he was prepared to talk about it openly in a public forum is more remarkable. In an interesting counterpoint, Michelle Grattan, a senior reporter at the *Age*, outlined how the lack of a clear 'owner' of the Fairfax group meant that there was no one individual setting the editorial tone for the group's publications, the *AFR*, the *SMH*, and the *Age*. In fact, Grattan was once again highly critical of the corporatised nature of newspapers today—the problem at Fairfax is not the imposition of an owner's editorial line, but rather the ascendency of the bean-counters over the newshounds. Again it is Grattan's honesty and openness, her willingness to question and criticise that stands her apart from many reporters.

Just a week before Kelly and Grattan spoke at the UQ seminar there was a graphic reminder that the *Australian* really is Murdoch's paper. Murdoch had been briefly in

Australia to attend the News Limited annual general meeting in Adelaide. Incidentally, one of the major decisions made at that meeting was to formalise the 'offshore' nature of Murdoch's control by moving News Limited's corporate HQ from Adelaide to New York. Of course, as we've mentioned earlier, the Murdoch papers were again full of glowing accounts of the meeting and the decisions taken. Jane Schulze (2004b), writing in the newly rebadged 'Media and Marketing' lift-out in the *Australian*, could hardly contain herself:

> The bright lights of Hollywood first lured Rupert Murdoch 19 years ago but unlike many who have tried and failed to crack the US market, Murdoch's success has seen his initial engagement become a full-blown marriage.

> Schulze 2004 p. 17

Unusually, Murdoch decided he would give his old buddy John Laws an exclusive interview while he was in Australia. Murdoch was asked his opinion of the Iraq conflict. A slightly rewritten transcript made a page 2 story in the following day's *Australian*: ' "It's clear we have no alternative—we've got to see the job through," Mr Murdoch told Sydney radio' (Kerin 2004). Does Rupert Murdoch's view of the war in Iraq really matter to readers of the *Australian*? Just because he owns a newspaper and is one of the richest individuals in the world doesn't mean his opinion about American and Australian foreign policies are worth more than anyone else's. At the same time his wealth and power mean Rupert Murdoch has special access to the corridors of power in Washington, London, Canberra, and many other nations. His commercial interests are also aligned with US foreign policy in the Middle East.

From fine line to fault line

The greater self-reflexivity of journalists in the news media these days was nicely illustrated in 2004 through a series of programs made for SBS television by reporter Ellen Fanning. Fanning herself had a meteoric rise at the ABC, hosting the *PM* program among other things, but she was attracted to the fame and fortune of commercial television and at the time she wrote and produced *Fine Line* was contracted to Channel Nine. Fanning (2004) describes her project as an attempt to reveal the 'secret life of journalists'. The premise of the series was excellent—to get journalists and editors talking about those times when self-doubt and reflexivity kick in around daily editorial decisions. Fanning recalls that nearly all of her subjects (about sixty in all) were clearly unnerved by the experience of being questioned about their ethics and decision-making. Fanning makes a very good point about 'doing ethics' in journalism. She rightly says it is 'about knowing the right questions to ask yourself in the hope of ending up with a good answer'.

Copies of the series are available from SBS and you should check to make sure it is in your nearest library. We're sure that the 30-minute episodes will be screened repeatedly in ethics classes over the next few years and they should be compulsory viewing. Whether we agree with Ellen's position or not, we think the programs and the process of recording the interviews were themselves an important indicator of the reflexive trend in journalism. And, as we have said all along, the major fault lines in journalism ethics often started out as fine lines. Ellen Fanning has made an important contribution to the discussion of journalism ethics in Australia.

Changing newsroom culture

The news media is now a vast business with its own economic, political, technological and social priorities. The scale and power of the news media threatens to undermine its continued viability as the Fourth Estate. If the ideal is to retain contemporary relevance, the locus of struggle must become a contest within news organisations over editorial independence, commercial priorities, political relevance and the public interest.

Schultz 1998, p. 233

This is the problem in a nutshell. The contest within news organisations can be no less than news workers involved in a fundamental contest with capital over the very issues of social control. The four 'grounds' over which this struggle must be waged—editorial independence, commercial priorities, political relevance, and public interest—are at the very terrain of the emotional dialectic and the dialectic of the front-page. The problem is how to resolve this contradiction and it cannot be done within the framework that Schultz endorses: the liberal–democratic free-market model. This whole system of a supposed 'market place of ideas' is itself a hegemonic ideological construct that masks an imbalance of economic and political power. So, while the terms of the debate revolve around 'reviving' the discredited Fourth Estate, news workers cannot win. Having said that, it is important to qualify this statement by observing that, ultimately, the battles will be fought initially over these issues. It is only when the emotional dialectic of the newsroom coincides with a more general level of social unrest that real change can occur.

The *Australian*'s resident media commentator Errol Simper (1996) was right to suggest that the culture of journalism needs to change and that the pressure of newsroom deadlines means that rules are bent in the name of expediency. It is also relevant to ask if an alternative news culture is possible. For our part we have argued that an important first step is to show how the news culture inside media organisations is ultimately dependent on the economic and social relations that govern news gathering as a daily production process.

There is a solution that could help solve ethical dilemmas in the newsroom, but which in the current political climate some critics would argue is immensely impractical: our suggestion of collective responsibility. This might, for instance, involve having elected editors in charge of the newsroom (perhaps elected by the journalists themselves). There is no reason why journalists' house committees in each workplace cannot act as a place of review and discussion on ethical questions. The Media Alliance might consider developing a short course for in-house training. Unfortunately, with news budgets being so tight, it is not likely that on-the-job mentoring or postgraduate training will be a high priority in the future. Pamela Williams (2000, p. 20) rates this as one of the biggest challenges facing journalists.

The 'house committee' proposal is radical because it consciously involves creating a greater level of workers' control in newsrooms. We argue this case here briefly based on three considerations: first, that we need to celebrate the role of important figures from the rich history of radical and alternative journalism—famous reporters such as John Reed and Louisa Bryant, George Orwell, Martha Gellhorn, Anne Summers, Brian Toohey, Wendy Bacon, Mike Moore, and John Pilger (among many others). Second, that in journalism courses it is possible to promote a series of universal humanist values and also to ground young journalists in the emotional dialectic in ways that will increase their ability to 'read' the news from a more self-conscious and critical perspective. Finally, it comes from our experience of working in news organisations where ethical behaviour is reinforced by peer pressure and where commercial considerations are more likely to surface as ethical problems.

In order to achieve such changes, the culture of the newsroom would be altered by a fundamental shift in the power relationships that are central to the production process (Williams 2000; Hirst 2003; McChesney 2000; McChesney & Scott 2002). If such a shift were to occur, the exercise of social control would shift from capital to labour. However, such a shift will not be easy as it involves a frontal assault on the business interests of the media owners. It is more likely to happen in a situation of social crisis affecting all relations of production.

John Hargreaves (2003), in his book *Journalism: Truth or Dare?* takes up some of these issues, but he too ultimately falls back on the old Fourth Estate model, arguing that 'market mechanisms' and 'competition policy' will sort out the reliable and trustworthy from the dross of poor journalism. And if the market doesn't work? In Hargreaves's view (2003, pp. 265–7) there is room for 'intelligent regulation', which seems like an oxymoron; but how can journalism 're-absorb the values of democracy into its own self-conduct'?

Instead of trying to revive the discredited idealism of the fourth estate we should give it a decent burial and move on. We have always favoured a more radical approach based on shifting the power in the newsroom towards rank and file journalists, away from the corporate cowboys, whose real fascination is with the 'bottom line', not the 'public interest'. Ultimately, Julianne Schultz and John Hargreaves do not rise to the challenge of arguing for an alternative, which spoils an otherwise interesting and important thesis that they both believe in—the revival of engaging and radical journalism. Such new cultural forms of reporting can only emerge in response to changes in the newsroom; positive steps towards creating the conditions under which good, investigative, and democratically motivated journalism might occur. It requires a new emotional dialectic of the front page.

A new dialectic: Workers' control?

> What might happen if a system of 'workers' control' became the norm in newsrooms and if journalists controlled the newsgathering process itself? A newsroom in which news values, angles, and stories are democratically decided on the 'shop floor' might be a very different place to a newsroom where Warren Breed's social control is exercised by managers more in tune with the commercial needs of the organisation (as a capitalist enterprise) than with the needs of a working-class audience.
>
> Hirst 2001, p. 68

On a day-to-day basis the news that the public receives would be noticeably different if journalists were more critically aware and more class-conscious. There would be less news about the 'big end' of town and more about the daily lives of real people in the suburbs, factories, and offices. There might also be a shift in the types of stories considered for investigation and certainly there would be a change in the way politics and economics are covered.

It is possible to argue that a fully developed working-class journalism—that was animated by the emotional dialectic of the 'grey-collar intellectual' (Hirst 2001, 2003)—would be more of a public service and lead to more public good than the journalism that passes for informed public critique today.

We argued in chapter 3 that journalists are economically members of the working class. But we have also shown how the ideologies of professional journalism often blind news-workers to understanding their contradictory class roles. Certainly the survey data from most Western countries tends to support this view; journalists see themselves as being mid-dle class, fairly privileged, and 'liberal' in their attitudes (Hargreaves 2003, pp. 227–33, Schultz 1998). Despite this fairly progressive world view, journalists as a group tend not to move beyond the realm of individual consciousness when it comes to ethics. Many writers in this field end up by plaintively arguing for a conscience clause that binds individuals to a code of behaviour that is ethical, sound, and moral (see for example Christians, Rotzoll & Fackler, 1991; Ethics Review Committee, 1997; Hendtlass & Nichols, 2003; Merrill, 1974, 1989; Sanders, 2003). John Hargreaves (2003, p. 227) calls this individual conscience the reporter's 'moral compass' that is learned 'outside journalism'. He argues that individuals must preserve this guide 'to be true to their own and their community's values … don't expect your employer, or the news industry, to do if for you'. John Merrill (1989, p. 241) is right to say that 'being a dialectical journalist today is not easy'. But it is not made any eas-ier by his prescription for achieving a moral balance through a 'slow process of self-libera-tion' towards 'negative freedom—freedom from constraints'. For Merrill it is an individual process, akin to a religious conversion: 'When the journalist accepts positive freedom, he or she becomes truly free and ethical' (1989, p. 241). As we mentioned earlier, Merrill follows Hegel's idealism, rather than the materialist dialectic of Marx and Engels (Norman 1980). It is this idealism that leads to seeking individual solutions to what is essentially a social and collective problem.

We take a slightly different view: certainly individuals have a responsibility to behave eth-ically, but the collective social relations of the newsroom often push individuals into unethi-cal behaviour (deadline pressures, commercial imperatives, etc.). Media theorist Mike Wayne (2003) suggests possible sources of contradiction are the 'division of labour within the cul-tural industries,' including journalism, and the fact that 'creative labour' is difficult to bring under the 'command and control' of traditional capitalist enterprises. The wage-labour eco-nomic structure of news production means that the 'real but variable autonomy [of journal-ists] is under constant threat'. The fault lines are active and the emotional dialectic emerges in news work because there is 'no necessary fit between the economic imperative and cultural values and, indeed, there are good reasons why they often diverge' (Wayne 2003, pp. 20–1).

So if there is collective pressure to go against one's own moral compass, why don't we look for a collective solution, such as a group-based behavioural pattern that reinforces pos-itive moral and social values and recognises the contradictions inherent in journalism. Such collective responsibility would certainly help reinforce positive, reflexive behaviours and overcome the pressures pushing reporters towards unethical practices. After all, journalism is 'a domain of moral choices, sometimes involving a melodramatic interplay between good and evil' (Hargreaves 2003, p. 206), but it is also a set of collective work practices that lend themselves to ethical team-work. In order to get anywhere near such ideal conditions the newsroom culture of individual bravado must change.

Mike Wayne (2003, p. 249) describes this 'class dialectic' as having at its core a 'normative argument for the emancipation of labour, for the free association of producers'. He takes this a step further to argue for media and news values to be established on the basis of class consciousness, a 'critical and dialectical social alignment' of the interests of media workers with those of the vast working-class audience. He writes that this process 'requires expanding our imaginative horizons far beyond what a capitalist public sphere can accommodate' (Wayne 2003, p. 256).

It is hard, from our current vantage point, to predict the ultimate impact of such a far-reaching cultural shift in the newsroom on the nature of news work, but one might argue that class-conscious journalism could be *better* journalism. Such a change is possible, the very nature of a dialectic—tension, conflict and resolution—guarantees it and as we have demonstrated the dialectic is very strong in modern journalism. While most writers do not mention it explicitly, it is embedded in their comments, such as this statement from John Hargreaves:

> The confusion of the times arises from the fact that so many apparently contrary things are happening at the same time ... these phenomena can be explained as reactions to each other, all part of the restless churning of the news media, as they resist confinement by old technologies, old establishments and old certainties.
>
> Hargreaves 2003, p. 260

As we have said from the beginning, the only certainties are change and uncertainty.

The future of ethics in journalism

> Journalism is under pressure in a way we have not seen before. Almost every journalistic outlet—be it television news and current affairs, radio, newspapers, or magazines—is stretched out like a piece of string.
>
> Williams 2000, p. 19

One of the most controversial, intense, and hard-to-close fault lines in journalism today is to define exactly just who is a journalist. As we have seen, for some, like John Laws, it is a day-to-day proposition. Laws and Jones do not consider themselves to be journalists when it comes to 'cash for comment', but they sure act like it when interviewing politicians and generating the news agenda for the day. One of the authors spent an interesting couple of years working for various government departments as a media manager. He was initially surprised at how seriously one CEO took the morning radio shock-jocks. After a 'roasting' by Alan Jones, the agency concerned spent days hosing down a potentially embarrassing situation. Jones and Laws are simply 'journalists of convenience', no more than a sideshow really. However, a new fault line is emerging in relation to just what defines journalism on the Internet these days. It usually starts with the question: 'Why can't everyone be a journalist?' It appears at first to be an argument about greater democracy in information flows.

But if we had more democracy in dentistry would we all want to pull our own teeth? It's not about keeping journalism for the elite; it's really a debate about journalists taking sides. It's about recognising the ideological, intellectual, and moral trap of objectivity and embracing greater self-awareness and humanism in reporting. We can call this alternative to elitism a journalism of engagement—others call it 'partisan'. It's certainly controversial, but in our view, it's more honest.

Just who or what is a journalist on the Internet is a question raised by the blogger of Baghdad, Salam Pax. He was eventually 'weighed down with the responsibility of it' and quit to then move 'in the opposite direction', writing a column in a print publication (Wynhausen 2004). This is a clear case of the blurring of boundaries between blog-opinion and journalism. But which way? If Salam Pax wasn't a journalist when he was just blogging, is he a blogger-journalist now he's writing for the *Guardian*?

On that note it might now be time to drag up that hoary old cliché, which we've all heard from acquaintances and even relatives on occasion: 'Ethics in journalism, isn't that an oxymoron?' Hopefully, if you have read the arguments in this book and discussed the cases, you will realise that it is not impossible to act ethically and still be a very good journalist. We have shown consistently how the cultures, dynamics, and relationships of the newsroom shape the ideologies of journalism, of which 'ethics' is but one component.

Ethics: An endless conversation?

While a number of advances can be made through reform, the history of ethical debates among journalists and media proprietors suggests that such issues will not be dealt with quickly or painlessly (Lloyd 1985). In part the answer is for journalists, the Media Alliance, editors, and journalism educators to get together and discuss how the culture of newsrooms can be improved. This is part of the greater reflexivity that can kick-start this process of change. In tertiary programs where ethics is taught as a discrete subject or course, there also has to be an emphasis on integrating the norms and principles of ethical journalism into the practical aspects of the course. There must also be more debate about the history, culture, and politics of the newsroom. The MEAA, working journalists, and journalism educators have a lot more to do in this area. In that sense there needs to be a shift in the way that journalism education is conducted—the contradictions between public interest and profitability cannot be ignored any longer, or simply glossed over with 'if only' statements.

American journalism educator Brian Richardson (1994, p. 109) argues that in too many instances journalists are taught 'negative ethics', that is a list of 'don'ts', and he suggests that this practice be changed using a four-point guide. The teaching of ethics should be 'affirmative', 'systematic', 'integrative', and 'definitive'. In short, ethics subjects should teach 'what we should do rather than what we should not do'. It should 'offer a workable, flexible and defensible way to proceed to make ethical decisions'. This to us sounds like a plea to fundamentally alter the emotional dialectic that operates in the newsroom. But, as we have suggested throughout this book, this cannot be done without a radical shift in the relations of production (Hirst 2001, 2003)—the physical and social conditions that set the limits to the emotional dialectic.

Richardson argues that ethical practice should be 'inseparable from doing good journalism' and through the use of case studies the teaching of ethics should 'show not only that ethics is a systematic process, but also that there are right and wrong answers' (Richardson 1994, p. 110). There is no problem with the first three of Richardson's points, but the fourth—the concept of right and wrong answers—is debatable. Australian journalism is perhaps more daring and more adversarial than that practised in the USA today and we are not sure that there actually *are* 'definitive' solutions to complex situational and contextual problems.

In the best possible world, journalists would never have to consider unethical behaviour, because the culture of the newsroom and beyond would be such that to behave unethically would be unthinkable. Instead, we are all thinking about it: about the moral, legal, ethical, political, social, and philosophical limits on the methods and outcomes of the journalistic process. It's important that you don't feel alone and that you realise most ethical issues have surfaced before in most newsrooms. Our final piece of advice would be that you don't operate as an 'ethical orphan' in the newsroom. An important first step in 'collectivising' responsibility for ethics is that when confronting an ethical dilemma you seek advice. In the first instance this might mean asking your news editor or chief of staff for their opinion. Or, if that sounds too daunting, try approaching your colleagues. Ask them if they have ever encountered a similar problem, or simply engage them in a conversation. The key thing is not to just ignore an ethical issue. If you do, it may return to 'bite' you later; you won't learn anything and could end up being 'doomed' to repeat the same mistake again and again.

At each step of the way there are pitfalls and pressure points, numerous real and potential fault lines. Despite what John Merrill might have been thinking when he wrote *The Dialectic in Journalism*, history did not stop in 1989 and the process of change, contradiction, argument, and resolution continues. As new technologies come into being, and improvements occur in those existing today, many more fault lines will reveal themselves. We can't prepare you for all of them: the incidents that will eventually become case studies in future years haven't even happened yet.

Instead, what we have tried to do in this volume is give you some 'ethical armour': the arguments and references to the classics of the last 50 years, as well as a guide to some mundane, but important examples from the everyday world of news reporting. The principles that can be distilled from this text will, hopefully, stand you in good stead to confidently move into your twenty-first century career in the media, wherever it may lead. Finally: Good luck.

Appendix

Codes of Ethics and examples

AJA CODE OF ETHICS (Adopted 1998)

Respect for truth and the public's right to information are fundamental principles of journalism. Journalists describe society to itself. They convey information, ideas and opinions, a privileged role. They search, disclose, record, question, entertain, suggest and remember. They inform citizens and animate democracy. They give a practical form to freedom of expression. Many journalists work in private enterprise, but all have these public responsibilities. They scrutinise power, but also exercise it, and should be accountable. Accountability engenders trust. Without trust, journalists do not fulfil their public responsibilities. MEAA members engaged in journalism commit themselves to

Honesty
Fairness
Independence
Respect for the rights of others

1. Report and interpret honestly, striving for accuracy, fairness and disclosure of all essential facts. Do not suppress relevant available facts, or give distorting emphasis. Do your utmost to give a fair opportunity for reply.

2. Do not place unnecessary emphasis on personal characteristics, including race, ethnicity, nationality, gender, age, sexual orientation, family relationships, religious belief, or physical or intellectual disability.

3. Aim to attribute information to its source. Where a source seeks anonymity, do not agree without first considering the source's motives and any alternative attributable source. Where confidences are accepted, respect them in all circumstances.

4. Do not allow personal interest, or any belief, commitment, payment, gift or benefit, to undermine your accuracy, fairness or independence.

5. Disclose conflicts of interest that affect, or could be seen to affect, the accuracy, fairness or independence of your journalism. Do not improperly use a journalistic position for personal gain.

6. Do not allow advertising or other commercial considerations to undermine accuracy, fairness or independence.

7. Do your utmost to ensure disclosure of any direct or indirect payment made for interviews, pictures, information or stories.

8. Use fair, responsible and honest means to obtain material. Identify yourself and your employer before obtaining any interview for publication or broadcast. Never exploit a person's vulnerability or ignorance of media practice.

9. Present pictures and sound which are true and accurate. Any manipulation likely to mislead should be disclosed.

10. Do not plagiarise.

11. Respect private grief and personal privacy. Journalists have the right to resist compulsion to intrude.

12. Do your utmost to achieve fair correction of errors.

Guidance Clause
Basic values often need interpretation and sometimes come into conflict. Ethical journalism requires conscientious decision-making in context. Only substantial advancement of the public interest or risk of substantial harm to people allows any standard to be overridden.

ABC CODE OF PRACTICE
[This is the print version of www.abc.net.au/corp/codeprac.htm]

Contents
1. Preamble
2. General Program Codes
3. Specific Program Codes
4. News and Current Affairs
5. Factual Programs
6. Promotions for Programs
7. Warnings
8. Television Program Classifications
9. Complaints

1. Preamble
The ABC's place in the broadcasting system is distinctive because of its Charter, which gives the Corporation unique responsibilities, and because of other provisions under the Australian Broadcasting Corporation Act, 1983, which give the Corporation particular responsibilities, for example, the provision of an independent news service.

The ABC Act guarantees the editorial independence of the Corporation's program services. The ABC holds its power to make programming decisions on behalf of the people of

Australia. By law and convention neither the Government nor Parliament seeks to intervene in those decisions.

2. General Program Codes

The guiding principle in the application of the following general program codes is context. What is unacceptable in one context may be appropriate and acceptable in another. However, the use of language and images for no other purpose but to offend is not acceptable.

The code is not intended to ban certain types of language or images from bona fide dramatic or literary treatments, nor is it intended to exclude such references from legitimate reportage, debate or documentaries. Where appropriate, audiences will be given advance notice of the content of the program.

2.1 Violence. Particular care must be taken in the presentation or portrayal of violence. The presentation or portrayal of violence must be justifiable, or else the material should not be presented.

In news and current affairs programs, violent events should never be sensationalised or presented for their own sake.

In drama programs, the aim is not to see how much violence will be tolerated, but how little is necessary to achieve honest ends without undue dramatic compromise.

2.2 Language. Variations of language favoured by different groups of Australians are valid and have their place in programs. On occasions, the language of one group may be distasteful to another. Use of such language is permitted provided it is not used gratuitously and provided the language can be justified in the context of, for example, news and current affairs reporting, fiction, documentary, dramatisation, comedy and song lyrics.

2.3 Sex and Sexuality. Provided it is handled with integrity, any of the following treatments of sex and sexuality may be appropriate and necessary to a program:
- it can be discussed and reported in the context of news, information or documentary programs;
- it can be referred to in drama, comedy, lyrics or fictional programs; and
- it can be depicted, implicitly or explicitly.

2.4 Discrimination. To avoid discrimination programs should not use language or images in a way which is likely to disparage or discriminate against any person or section of the community on account of race, ethnicity, nationality, sex, marital or parental status, age, disability or illness, social or occupational status, sexual preference or any religious, cultural or political belief or activity. The requirement is not intended to prevent the broadcast of material which is factual, or the expression of genuinely-held opinion in a news or current affairs program, or in the legitimate context of a humorous, satirical or dramatic work.

2.5 Privacy. The rights of individuals to privacy should be respected in all ABC programs. However, in order to provide information which relates to a person's performance of public duties or about other matters of public interest, intrusions upon privacy may, in some circumstances, be justified.

3. Specific Program Codes

3.1 Children's Programs. While the real world should not be concealed from children, special care will be taken to ensure programs children are likely to watch unsupervised will not cause alarm or distress.

3.2 Religious Programs. Religious programs include coverage, explanation, analysis, debate and reports about major religious traditions, indigenous religions, new and innovative spiritual movements as well as secular perspectives on religious issues. It does not promote any particular belief system or form of religious expression.

3.3 Indigenous Programs. Program makers and journalists should respect Aboriginal and Torres Strait Islander cultures. Particular care should be exercised in the coverage of traditional cultural practices such as the naming or depicting of the deceased.

3.4 Avoidance of Stereotypes. Programs should not promote or endorse inaccurate, demeaning or discriminatory stereotypes. Programs will take care to acknowledge the diverse range of roles now performed by women and men. Irrelevant references to physical characteristics, marital status or parental status will be avoided. In programs using experts, interviewees and other talent to present opinions, program makers should ensure a gender balance of commentators and experts where possible.

3.5 Closed Captioning for People who are Hearing Impaired or Deaf. Closed caption programs will be clearly marked when program information is provided to the press or when captioned programs are promoted. Where possible, open captioned advice will be provided if technical problems prevent scheduled closed captioning.

Television programs broadcast in prime time (6pm–10.30pm) and news and current affairs programs broadcast at any time are captioned in accordance with the Broadcasting Service Act (1992 as amended). Addresses to the nation and events of national significance will be transmitted with closed captioning. The ABC will endeavour to increase the amount of closed-captioning programming, as resources permit.

3.6 Accessible Television for People who are Blind or Have a Visual Impairment or Limited Reading Comprehension. Where material appears in text format on the screen, the ABC will endeavour to provide it in audio as well, subject to availability of resources and considerations of creativity, editorial integrity and immediacy.

4. News, Current Affairs and Information Programs

This section applies to all programs produced by the News and Current Affairs Division of the ABC and other information programs that comprise both news and information relating to current events. ABC programs with significant factual content which do not comprise both news and information relating to current events are dealt with in section 5 below.

4.1 Every reasonable effort must be made to ensure that the factual content of news and current affairs programs is accurate. Demonstrable errors will be corrected in a timely manner and in a form most suited to the circumstances.

4.2 Every reasonable effort must be made to ensure that programs are balanced and impartial. The commitment to balance and impartiality requires that editorial staff present a wide range of perspectives and not unduly favour one over the others. But it does not require them to be unquestioning, nor to give all sides of an issue the same amount of time.

4.3 Balance will be sought through the presentation, as far as possible, of principal relevant viewpoints on matters of importance. This requirement may not always be reached within a single program or news bulletin but will be achieved as soon as possible.

4.4 Editorial staff will not be obliged to disclose confidential sources which they are entitled to protect at all times.

4.5 Re-enactments of events will be clearly identified as such and presented in a way which will not mislead audiences.

4.6 If reported at all, suicides will be reported in moderate terms and will usually avoid details of method.

4.7 Sensitivity will be exercised in broadcasting images of or interviews with bereaved relatives and survivors or witnesses of traumatic incidents.

4.8 News Flashes. Care will be exercised in the selection of sounds and images used in news flashes and consideration given to the likely composition of the audience.

4.9 News Updates and News Promotions. Television news updates and news promotions should not appear at inappropriate times, especially during programs directed at young children. They should include very little violent material and none at all in the late afternoon and early evening.

5. Factual Programs

This section applies to all ABC programs with significant factual content which do not comprise both news and information relating to current events.

5.1 The ABC is committed to providing programs of relevance and diversity which reflect a wide range of audiences' interests, beliefs and perspectives. In order to provide such a range of views the ABC may broadcast programs which explore, or are presented from, particular points of view.

5.2 Every effort must be made to ensure that the factual content of such programs is accurate and in context and does not misrepresent viewpoints.

5.3 Demonstrable errors of fact will be corrected in a timely manner and in a form most suited to the circumstances.

5.4 Editorial staff will not be obliged to disclose confidential sources which they are entitled to protect at all times.

6. Promotions for Programs

Program promotions will be scheduled so as to be consistent with the nature of surrounding programs.

7. Warnings

Where appropriate, the audience will be given advance notice of programs or program segments which some viewers or listeners could find distressing or disturbing.

8. Television Program Classification

This system of television program classification applies the Guidelines for the Classification of Films and Videotapes issued by the Office of Film and Literature Classification and current at the time of publication of this Code of Practice.

Programs having a particular classification under the Office of Film and Literature Classification Guidelines may be modified so that they are suitable for broadcast or suitable for broadcast at particular times.

8.1 Classification

G - General (suitable for all ages)
G programs, which include programs designed for pre-school and school age children:
− are suitable for children to watch on their own;
− may be shown at any time.

PG - Parental Guidance (parental guidance recommended for persons under 15 years)
PG programs:
− may contain adult themes and concepts which, when viewed by those under 15 years, may require the guidance of an adult;
− may be shown between 8.30 a.m. and 4.00 p.m. on weekdays
    7.30 p.m. and 6.00 a.m. on any day of the week.

M - Mature Audience programs; and
MA - Mature Adult Audience programs
− are programs which, because of the matter they contain or because of the way it is treated, are recommended for viewing only by persons aged 15 years or over.   ·
M programs may be shown between:
− noon and 3.00 p.m. on weekdays that are school days
    8.30 p.m. and 5.00 a.m. on any day of the week.
MA programs may be shown between:
− 9.30 p.m. and 5.00 a.m. on any day of the week.
    While most adult themes may be dealt with, the degree of explicitness and intensity of treatment will determine what can be accommodated in the M and MA Classifications—

the less explicit or less intense material will be included in the M classification and the more explicit or more intense material, especially violent material, will be included in the MA classification.

X programs and unmodified R programs (not suitable for television)
– contain material which cannot appropriately be classified as G, PG, M or MA because the material itself or the way it is treated renders them unsuitable for television;
– must not be shown at all.

8.2 Implementation Guidelines. The time zones for each program classification are guides to the most likely placement of programs within that classification. They are not hard and fast rules and there will be occasions on which programs or segments of programs appear in other time-slots, for example, a PG program or segment of a program designed for teenage viewers could appear before 7.30 p.m. if that is the time most suitable for the target audience, or a PG segment in an arts program could appear during a weekend daytime program.

There must be sound reasons for any departure from the time zone for a program classification.

Programs which are serious presentations of moral, social or cultural issues, may appear outside their normal classification period provided that a clear indication of the nature and content of the program is given at its commencement.

8.3 Television Classification Symbols. The classification symbol of the PG, M or MA program (except news, current affairs, sporting and general information programs other than documentaries) being shown will be displayed at the commencement of the program.

The classification symbol of the PG, M or MA program (except news, current affairs, sporting and general information programs other than documentaries) being promoted will be displayed during the promotion.

8.4 Consumer Advice. Audio and visual consumer advice on the reasons for an M or MA classification will be given prior to the commencement of an M or MA program.

9. Complaints

9.1 This Code of Practice does not apply to any complaint concerning a program which is or becomes the subject of legal proceedings or any complaint which is made to the ABC more than six months after the broadcast to which it refers.

Complaints that the ABC has acted contrary to this Code of Practice should be directed to the ABC in the first instance. Phone complainants seeking a written response from the ABC will be asked to put their complaint in writing. All such written complaints will receive a response from the ABC within 60 days of their receipt.

The ABC will make a reasonable effort to provide an adequate response to complaints about Code of Practice matters, except where a complaint is frivolous, vexatious or not made in good faith or the complainant is vexatious or not acting in good faith.

9.2 Independent Complaints Review Panel. The ABC Board has established an Independent Complaints Review Panel (ICRP) to review written complaints which relate to allegations of serious cases of bias, lack of balance or unfair treatment arising from an ABC broadcast or broadcasts.

If a complainant making such an allegation does not receive a response from the ABC within six weeks or is not satisfied with the response, the complainant may ask the Convener of the ICRP to accept the complaint for review. Further information can be obtained from the Convener, Independent Complaints Review Panel, GPO Box 688, Sydney, NSW 2001 or by phoning (02) 8333 5639.

If the Convener rejects the complaint or if the complainant is dissatisfied with the outcome of the review and the complaint is covered by the ABC Code of Practice, the complainant may make a complaint to the Australian Broadcasting Authority about the matter.

9.3 Australian Broadcasting Authority. If a complainant:
    does not receive a response from the ABC within 60 days; or
    the complainant is dissatisfied with the ABC response; or
    the complainant is dissatisfied with the outcome of the ICRP review (as mentioned above); and
    the complaint is covered by the ABC Code of Practice;
    the complainant may make a complaint to the Australian Broadcasting Authority about the matter.

Contact Addresses
Australian Broadcasting Corporation
GPO Box 9994, in the capital city of your State or Territory

Independent Complaints Review Panel
GPO Box 688, Sydney, NSW, 2001

Australian Broadcasting Authority
PO Box Q500, Queen Victoria Building, NSW 1230

ABC EDITORIAL POLICIES
2002 EDITION

ABC Editorial Policies were updated in 2002. Only relevant excerpts are provided here.

AUGUST 2002

Excerpts:
2. Editorial principles
Key values

The ABC aims to follow four key values in all its activities:
* Honesty
* Fairness
* Independence
* Respect

Honesty requires integrity and accuracy. Program makers should be enterprising and questioning in perceiving, pursuing and presenting issues that affect society and the individual. They must make every effort to ensure that the factual content of programs is correct and in context. If errors occur, the ABC will accept responsibility and respond promptly.

Fairness calls for balance and impartiality in news and current affairs and programs that comprise both news and information relating to current events. All program makers should present a wide range of perspectives, and must not unduly favour one over others. In programs of opinion and comment, every effort must be made to ensure the content does not misrepresent viewpoints.

Independence demands that program makers not allow their judgement to be influenced by pressures from political, commercial or other sectional interests, or by their own personal views or activities. There must be no external interference in the presentation or content of programs. For its part, the ABC accepts legal responsibility for what it publishes, and program makers are responsible for the editorial decisions they make.

Respect for the rights of others is extended to subjects, program participants and audiences. It requires careful handling of sensitive issues such as violence, sex, grief, trauma, privacy and children's programming, and understands the need to avoid stereotypes and other prejudicial content.

5.1 The Charter of Editorial Practice

A Charter of Editorial Practice for news and current affairs sets the following standards. It should be read in conjunction with the policy of 'upward referral', which applies to all types of programs.

1. The ABC takes no editorial stand in its programming.
2. Editorial staff will avoid any conflict of interest in performance of their duties.
3. Every reasonable effort must be made to ensure that the factual content of news and current affairs programs is accurate and in context. Demonstrable errors will be corrected in a timely manner and in a form most suited to the circumstances.
4. Balance will be sought through the presentation, as far as possible, of principal relevant viewpoints on matters of importance. This requirement may not always be reached within a single program or news bulletin but will be achieved as soon as possible.
5. The commitment to balance and impartiality requires editorial staff to present a wide range of perspectives and not unduly favour one over the others. But it does not require them to be unquestioning, nor to give all sides of an issue the same amount of time. News values and news judgements are a material consideration in reaching decisions, consistent with these standards.
6. In serving the public's right to know, editorial staff will be enterprising in perceiving, pursuing and presenting issues which affect society and the individual.
7. Editorial staff will respect legitimate rights to privacy of people featuring in the news.

8. Authority for editorial directions and decisions will be vested in editorial staff.
9. Editorial staff will ensure that coverage of newsworthy activity within the Australian community is comprehensive and non-discriminatory.

THE SYDNEY MORNING HERALD CODE OF ETHICS

Our editorial management shall be conducted upon principles of candour, honesty and honour. We have no wish to mislead; no interest to gratify by unsparing abuse— or indiscriminate approbation.

The Sydney Morning Herald, April 18, 1831

These values, set out in the Herald's first editorial, have guided the paper for more than 170 years. Our most valuable asset is our integrity, and it is this that the code is designed to protect.

The code reflects the Fairfax group's corporate values statement and incorporates the code of ethics of the Australian Journalists Association.

It is to apply to the editorial staff of The Sydney Morning Herald and, where relevant, its casual employees, freelancers and contributors. In interpreting and applying the code, the interests that shall always be paramount are those of the public. Community values evolve, and the code will be reviewed from time to time to ensure it reflects what our readers expect of us.

HONESTY
Herald staff will report and interpret honestly, striving for accuracy, fairness and disclosure of all essential facts. They will not suppress or distort relevant facts. They will do their utmost to offer the right of reply, and they will separate comment from news.

IMPARTIALITY
Staff will not allow personal interest, or any belief or commitment, to undermine their accuracy, fairness or independence.

FAIRNESS
Staff will use fair, honest and responsible means to obtain material. They will identify themselves and the newspaper before obtaining interviews or images.

INDEPENDENCE
Staff will not allow advertising or other commercial considerations to undermine accuracy, fairness or independence, or to influence the nature of the Herald's coverage. Advertising copy which could be confused for editorial should be marked 'special promotion'.

PRIVACY
Staff will strike a balance between the right of the public to information and the right of individuals to privacy. They will recognise that private individuals have a greater right to protect information about themselves than do public officials and others who hold or seek power, influence or attention. They shall not exploit the vulnerable or those ignorant of media practices.

RESPECT

Staff will respect private grief. They have the right to resist pressure to intrude.

RELEVANCE

Staff will not place unnecessary emphasis on personal characteristics, including race, ethnicity, nationality, gender, age, sexual orientation, family relationships, religious belief or physical disability.

PLAGIARISM

Staff will not plagiarise.

ATTRIBUTION

Staff will seek to attribute information to its source. They will always declare the use of pseudonyms in their work. They will seek to avoid being compromised by a source and to use multiple sources wherever possible. Where a source seeks anonymity, the journalist shall first consider the source's motives and seek alternative attributable sources. Quotes not attributed to a named source will be used only with a section editor's approval. Where confidences are accepted the journalist will respect and protect them in all appropriate circumstances.

HONEST PRESENTATION

Staff will present pictures and sound that are true and accurate. They will disclose manipulation that could mislead.

COMPLAINTS AND CORRECTIONS

Complaints shall be dealt with promptly and respectfully. Material errors in the paper and its related publications will be corrected or clarified publicly as soon as is practicable.

Findings by the Australian Press Council or the defamation courts involving the Herald will be reported promptly.

PUBLIC ACTIVITIES

Herald staff shall avoid any prominent activity in partisan public causes that compromises, or appears to compromise, the journalist or the newspaper. Membership of organisations or activity that may compromise the journalist's or the paper's reputation shall be declared to their section editor. Those responsible for coverage of news, current issues and opinion shall not be members of a political party nor stand as a candidate in an election for public office.

Staff shall not produce material for use in the paper or its related publications when they are a member of an organisation with an active interest in that issue.

Columnists and contributors writing on an issue where they have a direct or indirect interest are to declare that interest to readers after receiving approval from their section editor to write on that topic.

If it is possible that the activities of a member of a journalist's immediate family may compromise the journalist or the Herald, the staff member shall inform their section editor.

FINANCIAL INTERESTS

Herald staff shall avoid taking a specific financial interest, or participating in financial activities and arrangements, that could conflict with their obligations of fairness and integrity, or that could be perceived to do so.

They will avoid writing about issues in which they have a financial interest, either directly or through their immediate family. If they do write about such issues they shall first obtain permission from their section editor, and that interest will be declared where their section editor deems it necessary.

Staff shall maintain an up-to-date file of their interest in any securities. A register of such files will be maintained by the editor-in-chief.

In addition, the Corporations Act 2001 requires financial journalists to maintain a more detailed register and to disclose their register to the Australian Securities and Investments Commission, and it is the journalists' responsibility for doing so.

Staff responsible for stories about securities of public companies shall not trade shares or other financial products within three months of acquiring them, except with the permission of their section editor.

ENDORSEMENTS

Staff shall not give paid endorsements for any product, service, political party or other lobby, nor shall they provide advertising copy, public relations services or media training on a commercial basis.

CONTESTS

Staff will submit work only to contests whose central purpose is to recognise journalistic excellence, and not to competitions designed primarily to promote a product, an industry or a lobby. The decision on which competitions are entered will be made by the editor or the editor-in-chief.

CHEQUE-BOOK JOURNALISM

No payment shall be proffered to sources for interviews or access.

PERSONAL ADVANTAGE

Those working for the Herald shall not use their position with it to seek any benefit or advantage not afforded to the public. Such advantages include discounts, priority bookings, access to venues, retail or wholesale sales, restaurant bookings, real estate queues and upgradings.

GIFTS

Gifts shall not be accepted, other than those of a small and inconsequential nature. Those known or estimated to be worth more than $10 will be donated to charity.

HOSPITALITY

Staff shall ensure that accepting hospitality does not oblige them or the Herald to their hosts. Invitations to attend a lunch or dinner should be repaid where possible. Accepting invitations for corporate hospitality where the purpose of the visit or the event is to develop contacts will be permitted, but staff shall inform their section editor before accepting such invitations.

TRAVEL AND ACCOMMODATION

The Herald shall pay its own way. It will not accept free or materially subsidised travel and accommodation. However, in exceptional circumstances the editor may approve subsidised travel. Travel will be accepted when it is included in a recognised education scholarship, where the editor is satisfied that neither the journalist nor the Herald will be compromised. Where it is not possible to buy tickets on commercial services the unpaid portion of the travel shall be declared.

TICKETS AND EVENTS

Staff shall not solicit tickets. Complimentary tickets may only be accepted by a staff member who is covering or reviewing that event. Sports journalists may also accept tickets for events for which they are accredited, as may reviewers for events that are designated as media only (for example, media screenings of films). All other tickets will be paid for.

WORKING FOR OTHERS

Staff journalists wishing to undertake outside work shall first seek the approval of their section editor. They shall not work for direct competitors. Staff offering work to other publications, or seeking, or being offered, commissions from them, will first ascertain that the Herald does not wish to publish the work.

Staff having their work published elsewhere shall require an acknowledgment that they work for the Herald, if it so wishes. Where the Herald does not want such acknowledgment, the journalist shall ensure its wish is met. Such work must not compromise this code, or other Herald standards.

Staff shall provide the editor or the editor-in-chief with an annual register of their regular paid outside work.

Staff wishing to accept or undertake speaking engagements, or to represent the paper in other media outlets, shall first seek approval from their section editor. Before undertaking such activities, staff shall satisfy themselves that in doing so they are not compromising themselves or the Herald.

CASUAL EMPLOYEES, FREELANCERS AND CONTRIBUTORS

All casual employees, freelancers and contributors shall abide by this code when on assignment for the Herald and should avoid any conflict of interest which would harm the integrity of the Herald.

They shall declare to the Herald all relevant circumstances under which a story has been written or edited or any other conflicts which should be disclosed .

For Herald commissions they shall not accept materially subsidised travel or accommodation.

No casual employee, freelancer or contributor shall represent themselves as working for the Herald without an express commission from it.

Resources for ethical thinking and checking

As well as the various Editorial Charters and the MEAA's Code of Ethics, some useful resource packages are available to help journalism students handle reporting in sensitive areas. Equally, research has been undertaken by academics to help journalism students prepare for the moral and ethical minefield ahead. Here we have included a brief mention of some of the resources around specific issues that often crop up in newsrooms.

The reporting of mental health and suicide

In 1999, the Commonwealth Department of Health and Aged Care released *Achieving the Balance—A Resource Kit for Australian Media Professionals for the Reporting and Portrayal of Suicide and Mental Illnesses,* containing booklets and quick reference guides on both areas. The *Life Promoting Media Strategy* booklet for the responsible reporting and portrayal of suicide encourages the media to:

- Report and portray suicide in the media responsibly to minimise the capacity for imitation suicide, or for normalising or glamorising suicide.
- Present balanced images of diverse groups of young people and, where relevant and appropriate, encourage their participation and inclusion in the broader community.
- Always provide information about sources of help when reporting on potentially distressing material and encourage young people at risk and their families to seek assistance. (*Life Promoting Media Strategy: A Positive Approach* 1999)

The companion booklet on accurate reporting and portrayal of mental illness states as its two main aims:

- To promote mental health literacy throughout the media environment and media workforce.
- To improve the reporting and portrayal of mental health issues and people with mental illness.

Secondary aims are to promote mental health literacy in the community, to reduce the stigma and discrimination, to promote recovery and understanding about mental illnesses, and to increase appropriate early help-seeking behaviour for mental health problems and illnesses (*Mental Health Promoting Media Strategy: A Positive Approach,* 1999, reprinted with changes 2000). Most university libraries, particularly those with journalism faculties, would have copies of the resource kit. The Department of Health and Aged Care also funded, as part of its 'National Mental Health Strategy', research into Australian media coverage of suicide and mental illness (Blood et al. 2002). In its conclusions, the report suggested that future guidelines to the media should give more attention to the wide use of the word 'suicide', and the inappropriate uses of medical terminology about mental health and illness. 'One danger is that the word suicide is becoming popular in media discourse, when used to mean something other than suicide. This type of usage may contribute to the normalizing of suicide' (Blood et al. 2002, p. 127). Copies of the four-volume report are available from the Mental Health and Special Programs Branch, Commonwealth Department of Health and Aged Care, GPO Box 9848, Canberra, ACT, 2601.

In August 2002, the second edition of *Achieving the Balance* (National Media and Mental Health Group 2002) was released after consultation with the peak media organisations, mental health professionals, consumers, and after testing with media professionals. The main handbook, *Reporting Suicide and Mental Illness: A Resource for Media Professionals*, is a much-expanded version of the original booklets and contains useful sections on facts and statistics on suicide and mental illness, and suggests possible contacts. The useful quick reference guides have been expanded to two-page back-to-back A4 cards and include facts and statistics, issues to consider when reporting suicide or mental illness, and a page of useful contacts in the areas of 'help-lines', statistics and research, Health Departments, and non-governmental suicide or mental health organisations. Its web site is www.mindframe-media.info. The primary focus of these materials is the working media, but copies are being used by journalism educators.

The Hunter Institute of Mental Health, through its *Response Ability* project, has produced a resource package for journalism students on reporting mental illness and suicide. It is a comprehensive teaching resource designed to introduce tertiary journalism students to the issues associated with mental illness and suicide and to provide suggestions for appropriate reporting. As well as a constantly updated web site (www.responseability.org), the project resources include dramatised hypothetical case studies on CD and video, examples of recent Australian reporting on suicide and mental illness, and guides to reporting on mental illness and suicide. The Hunter Institute works closely with journalism educators around the country in the continuing development of these resources, and has ensured all institutions with journalism programs have copies of the resources. A number of journalism programs include discussion of the hypotheticals in their ethics classes.

Indigenous reporting

The 1991 Royal Commission into Aboriginal Deaths in Custody noted that the media is 'a principal source of information for the public and is generally considered to play an important part on forming—or at least influencing—public consciousness and public opinion' (Media and Indigenous Australians Project 1998). Among the Royal Commission's recommendations relevant to journalism education was the request that staff ensure that courses contain a significant component relating to Aboriginal affairs, and consider, in consultation with media industry and media unions, the creation of specific units of study dedicated to Aboriginal affairs and their reporting (MIAP 1998). The Media and Indigenous Australians Project (MIAP) began consultations in 1995, and produced a series of teaching resources four years later. The materials provide teaching modules on the main journalism areas of news values, lead writing, research, interviewing, news-writing, sub-editing, using statistics, ethical decision-making, news sources, feature writing, investigative journalism, advanced news writing, and statistics, and specialist rounds written from an indigenous reporting perspective. Each module has a structure of introduction, goals, strategies, tasks, process, and resources.

The various modules are aimed at stimulating student thinking about indigenous issues and encouraging critical reflection on how Aboriginal affairs are presented in the media. We noted earlier that journalists come into the media industry with a set of values that influence the way they report. The MIAP team wrote that the learning materials 'are not designed as an exercise in telling students what they *ought* to think about Indigenous issues, but rather are intended to help students identify what they already think, the basis of that thinking and how such views might impact on their professional practice' (Media and Indigenous Australians Project 1998). Copies of this resource package should also be in the libraries of universities where journalism is taught. Griffith University academic and journalism educator Dr Michael Meadows has researched the Australian media's reporting of Aboriginal issues since white settlement and he concludes: 'The picture that emerges ... is a long history of media *misrepresentation* of indigenous Australians. Several clear patterns emerge: either they are omitted or reported as problems, deviants, linked with crime and disruption. There are exceptions, of course, but the overriding images are negative' (Meadows 1995, p. 24). The April 1999 version of the Commercial Television Industry Code of Practice contains several 'advisory notes'. One is on the portrayal of Aborigines and Torres Strait Islanders. It urges Commercial Television Australia (CTVA—formerly FACTS) members to produce programs 'which treat the Aboriginal and Torres Strait Islander peoples as an integral and important part of contemporary Australia, and which respect the dignity, traditions, diversity and contemporary achievements of these peoples' (CTVA Code of Practice, p. 41). It warns reporters to be conscious of their own preconceptions, to avoid stereotyping, and to be aware of the cultural norms and experiences of indigenous people. It calls on journalists to give a balanced portrayal of indigenous affairs and avoid misrepresentation, to respect local social protocols, not to use language offensive to indigenous people, and not use paintings and symbols without permission. It also addresses the widespread prohibition among indigenous people on displaying images of the dead or naming them during periods of mourning (CTVA Code of Practice, p. 41). If the period of mourning cannot readily be ascertained it suggests preceding the use of images of recently deceased with an appropriate oral warning. There are other advisory notes on the portrayal of cultural diversity, people with disabilities, the portrayal of women and men, and privacy. In 2004 CTVA became Free TV Australia.

Cross-cultural reporting

As we have seen already in this book, the media is constantly attacked for wielding power or influence with scant regard for truth, objectivity and the impact its work has on the public. The *All-Media Guide to Fair and Cross-Cultural Reporting* (Stockwell & Scott 2000) notes that media workers who inflict unfair treatment are rarely aware of the harm their work may cause: 'They are surprised, and sometimes offended, by community criticism.' The booklet is a practical guide for media workers and journalism students on how to write about the diverse communities in Australia. It contains useful mini-chapters on subjects like finding contacts in a diverse society, effective cross-cultural communication, and covering ethnic communities. It also covers issues associated with indigenous reporting.

After the introduction of the Racial Hatred Act in 1995 as an amendment to the then 20-year-old Racial Discrimination Act, the Human Rights and Equal Opportunity

Commission released a booklet titled *The Racial Hatred Act: A Guide for People Working in the Australian Media* (Human Rights and Equal Opportunity Commission 1996) as a guide for journalists in covering issues of racism. The report of the National Inquiry into Racist Violence in 1991 had concluded:

> … the perpetuation and promotion of negative racial stereotypes, a tendency towards conflictual and sensationist reporting on race issues and an insensitivity towards and often ignorance of minority cultures can all contribute to creating a social climate which is tolerant of racist violence.

Cited in Human Rights and Equal Opportunity Commission 1996

It contains advice on how to cover issues of race and draws upon case studies that look at an Australian Muslim's experience of the media, the stereotyping of indigenous Australians, and comments on Pauline Hanson's famous maiden speech to Parliament in September 1996. It, too, is a useful guide and can probably be found in most university libraries.

Reporting on the aged

There are any number of annual awards for Australian journalists, from the prized Walkley Awards administered by the MEAA to everything from business to health reporting, but one of the more creative is the national and Queensland awards coordinated by the *Older People Speak Out* group in Brisbane (www.opso.com.au). These awards recognise excellence in the portrayal of older people and their issues, through newspapers, television, radio, photography, newsletters, and advertising. The aim is to break down the stereotypes of older people held by the community—stereotypes that lead to elder abuse, mature age unemployment, and lack of self confidence in older people. The awards encourage the community to view ageing positively for the benefit of all. Bond University's Mark Pearson, with the help of media professionals, students, and the Positive Ageing Foundation of Australia, has produced an interactive web-based tool to help journalists deal with issues of ageism (agekit.bond.edu.au). As Pearson notes: 'Rather than being an exercise in political correctness, this resource aims to challenge perceptions and raise awareness about age and how it is represented in electronic and print media' (Pearson 2003, p. 236). It provides editors, news producers, journalism educators, and students with relevant information to help them in reporting ageing.

Reporting on disabilities

A group of Australian journalism educators is also looking at the problems faced by organisations like Special Olympics Australia in getting publicity for their activities (Tanner, Haswell et al. 2003 p. 85). Nearly one in five Australians has a disability that affects them in their daily lives. Of those, 9 per cent have an intellectual disability (cited in Tanner, Haswell et al. p. 85). 'Add to this family, friends, carers and other people who work in the disability field and the number of people who stand to be "interested" in stories involving disability potentially becomes much larger' (Tanner, Haswell et al., p. 85). The group surveyed Special Olympics Australia office-holders across the nation on their reaction to media coverage of people with an intellectual disability, the tone of the reporting, and the focus of different groups of sportspeople. Those surveyed were very negative about media reporting of an intellectual disability; felt the tone of most reporting was either how they had 'overcome the odds to succeed' or were 'inspirational'; and believed that the focus of media coverage was on elite sportspeople—those without a disability (Tanner, Haswell et al., p. 90–1). The researchers say that the media has an enormous responsibility to present disability issues in an informed and empathetic manner (Tanner, Haswell et al., p. 99). The research is ongoing.

Trauma and journalists

Just as members of the public may be suddenly thrust into the media limelight because of a personal tragedy, and find it difficult to cope, journalists, too, can be affected by what they see and hear when reporting death, tragedy, or disaster. In times past, when a journalist had to report on a particularly horrific accident and told the boss he (or she) was 'feeling crook', they were advised to 'have a few beers and forget about it'.

Queensland University of Technology journalism academic Phil Castle, who completed a Masters on journalists and trauma, offers the following advice on how to avoid trauma in the workplace:

> Since the mid 1980s many Australian employers working in the trauma fields such as medical, police, fire, ambulance, search and rescue have adopted sound management and self-care programs to ensure their staff are not adversely affected by what has become known broadly as Post Traumatic Stress Disorder. While the military became aware of 'war neurosis' much earlier, particularly following the Vietnam conflict of the 1960s, the media has been slower to accept it as a genuine concern in its industry. This is changing for the better.
>
> While PTSD is rather narrowly defined clinically it is sufficient in this context to accept that many journalists have and can become 'troubled' by covering and engaging in certain stories. Classical PTSD is a persistent, on-going unwanted recall of the events and circumstances which lead to an unhealthy state sometimes manifested in discernable medical reactions such as high blood pressure, accelerated pulse rates and sleep disorders. Most journalists, except war correspondents, suffer vicarious PTSD in that they do not directly experience the trauma but report on the aftermath.
>
> Some journalists (used in its widest sense to include photographers, sub-editors, producers etc) have felt isolated when dealing with difficult traumatic stories and traditionally the antidote has been to get thoroughly drunk or, worse still, abuse other drugs. There can be a small positive role in having a few quiet drinks with colleagues and friends but there are other ways in which troubled journalists can deal with the aftermath of their coverage of the 'horror' stories. The best way to deal with traumatic stories is to act professionally, do the story really well and accurately and look to your own well being, ie self-care. There is nothing to equal good self-care and that includes preparation at the training level, having the appropriate skills, equipment and support, good diet and sleep and showing genuine courtesy and empathy. That's the prefect world, in

the real world, often during and after covering a trauma story many aspects change or go wrong. So it's important to remember that as journalists we have to make tough and ethical decisions, it's wise to always try to adopt the adage of treating others as you would like to be treated and you can't fake compassion.

Based on research in Australia and overseas, talking with sympathetic colleagues has been found to be an excellent early step in dealing with troubling and traumatic stories. This is important as a colleague can often identify with the story and understands the newsroom culture which can sometime exacerbate the problems. All journalists researched have shown their concern about confidentiality when expressing their troubles. They do not want their management to know when a story has badly affected them (they fear losing their job or rounds), but they do expect their managers to accept that at times their work can be troubling and even dangerous. Most major media organisations now have supportive counselling services available and provided they are confidential, they should be used, if appropriate. Often an experienced colleague can refer to an effective counsellor/clinician.

Some stories become traumatic because the journalist later realises they may have behaved unfairly, unethically, or without due care. Do no further harm is contained in some overseas codes of ethics and should have been included in the AJA code. It is important for journalists to recognise they can do harm and should not do further harm. There are too many stories of journalists having left the subjects of their stories and their family and friends hurt by the media experience. Good journalism plays an important social role in society and can be very helpful to individual people as well as the journalist.

A few tips: try to prepare when interviewing a person who has suffered, using an appropriate intermediary can help everyone, don't ever say you know how they feel, listen, be accurate in your reporting, ask permission for photographs if you can and try to explain as much as you know about the media process and how the story is likely to be used. If you get it wrong, correct it. Some trauma stories can be painful to everyone involved but doing them well can be enormously rewarding and enhance the profession of journalism.

Castle 2003

A QUT project team, which completed its work on 10 September 2001, the day before the terrorist attacks in the United States, also proposed a series of organisational and individual guidelines for handling trauma among the media workforce (QUT 2001). It suggested media organisations should have trained peer support staff, have debriefing sessions, counselling, staff training, survey retiring staff, and give special training for those involved in foreign assignments or inter-cultural contacts. For individual journalists it suggests they maintain safe living and healthy habits, be taught how to recognise stress, share mentoring and support with others, be ready to talk about their feelings in private, call for professional help where appropriate, and consider the effects of their work on others (QUT 2001).

The Dart Center for Journalism and Trauma is a global network of journalists, journalism educators, and health professionals dedicated to improving media coverage of trauma, conflict, and tragedy but also addresses the effects of such coverage on those working in the media. Its web site (www.dartcenter.org) contains resources to help journalists cope with covering tragedies.

'Trauma in the Newsroom' is a collaborative project between the University of Canberra, the University of South Australia, Fairfax Media Limited, and the Dart Foundation, looking at journalists' practices when reporting on traumatic events and the effects of those practices on victims, their families, and the journalists themselves (Sykes, Embelton et al. 2003, p. 73).

Bibliography

AAP. 2001. 'Nurses Top Honesty Poll' [cited 12 December 2001. Available from www.smh.com.au/news/0112/10/national/national103.html.]

——. 2002a. 'List of Professions Ranked by Honesty and Ethics' [AAP Newsfeed (wire); cited 12 September 2003].

——. 2002b. '60 Minutes Journo Fails to Win Damages from Media Watch' [AAP Newsfeed; cited September 14 2003].

AAP. 2004. 'Ambulance officers Australia's most trusted' [AAP Newsfeed; cited 27 May 2004].

ABA. 2000. 'Key Findings of the Investigations into Radio Stations 2UE, 3AW, 5DN and 6PR.' Australian Broadcasting Authority 2000 [cited 13 October 2003]. Available from www.aba.gov.au/radio/investigations/projects/commerc_radio/report/html/key_findings.htm.

ABC. 1993. *ABC Editorial Policies*. Australian Broadcasting Corporation, Sydney.

——. 1998. *ABC Editorial Policies*. Australian Broadcasting Corporation, Sydney.

——. 2002. *ABC Editorial Policies*. Australian Broadcasting Corporation, Sydney.

——. 2003. 'ICRP Review of Minister's Complaint.' ABC media release, 10 October.

ABC Online. 2003a. 'Beattie Calls for New Laws to Regulate the Media' [cited 26 March 2003]. Available from www.abc.net.au/news.

——. 2003b. 'BBC Under Fire Over Footage of Dead UK Troops', [cited 27 May 2003]. Available from www.abc.net.au/news/newsitems/s863120.htm.

——. 2003c. 'Richard Alston Calls for Investigation into ABC's AM Program', 28 May 2003 [cited 27 June 2003]. Available from www.abc.net.au/pm/content/2003/ s866825.htm.

——. 2003d. 'AM Found to be Unbiased by the ABC's Complaints Review Executive' [cited 25 July 2003]. Available from www.abc.net.au/pm/content/2003/s906924.htm.

ABC Radio. 2003. 'Police Reject Claim of Child Rapist "Mr Cruel" Known.' In *ABC Radio News*. Melbourne.

ABC TV. 1992. 'LA Law—the King Trial.' In *Four Corners*.

——. 2002 'The Gilded Cage—Peter Hollingworth'. In *Australian Story*. 18 February.

——. 2003a 'Madam Mayor—Alison Grosse'. In *Australian Story*. 15 September.

——. 2003b 'The Big A—Hazel Hawke'. In *Australian Story*. 11 November.

Ackland, Richard. 1999. 'Cash for Comment.' In *Media Watch*, ABC Television.

——. 2001. 'We Regret Rupe's Rant Merchants.' *The Sydney Morning Herald*, 9 November, 10.

Akerman, Piers. 1996a. 'Taxpayer-funded Idleness Experts Escape Workforce by a Hair's Breadth.' *The Daily Telegraph*, 6 March, 4–5.

——. 1996b. 'Little More Than Stale Whine.' *The Daily Telegraph*, 21 March, 11.

——. 1996c. 'Ethics Not in the Script in News Theatre.' *The Daily Telegraph*, 9 May, 11.

——. 2001. 'Bordering on the Ridiculous.' *The Daily Telegraph*, 8 November, 22.

Al Jazeera & BBC World. 2003. Al Jazeera TV excerpt. In *Correspondent,* London.

Alexander, P. 1998. 'My Lai Memorial Recalls a Village with Blood, Fire, Mass Graves', Associated Press newsfeed.

Alterman, Eric. 1999. *Sound and Fury: The Making of the Punditocracy.* Ithaca, NY: Cornell University Press.

——. 2003. *What Liberal Media: The Truth About Bias and the News.* New York: Basic Books.

American Broadcasting Company. 2003. 'Lynch Family is Elated Over Daughter's Imminent Return to US.' In *ABC News* (US).

Apps, Lawrence. 1985. 'Where Ideology Intersects Media Ethics.' *Australian Journalism Review* 7: 12–18.

——. 1986. 'Deathknocks: The Code of the Ethics.' *Australian Journalism Review* 8: 10–13.

——. 1990. 'Journalism, Ethics and Ideology.' In *Issues in Australian Journalism,* ed. J. Henningham. Melbourne: Longman Cheshire.

Apps, Lawrence & Heidi Rexa. 1991. 'Dilemmas in Media Ethics.' Department of Journalism, University of Queensland, St Lucia, Queensland.

Australian Press Council. 2002. *Australian Press Council Case Studies.* Sydney, Australian Press Council.

Archer, Jeffrey. 1996. *The Fourth Estate.* HarperCollins, London.

Arlington, K. 2004. 'Nurses Earn Public's Trust.' *The Courier-Mail,* 8 January, 3.

Armstrong, Mark. 1994. 'ABC Always True to Values of Charter.' *The Australian,* 26 September, 11.

Arnett, Peter & April Oliver. 1998. 'Did the US Drop Nerve Gas?' *Time,* 15 June, 33–5.

Arthur, Charles. 2003. 'BBC Accused of Intrusion After Ordering Staff to Register Political and Financial Ties'. *The Independent* [online newspaper], 6 June. Available from news.independent.co.uk/ uk/media/story.jsp?story=412803.

Associated Press. 1982. 'Row Erupts Over British Media Coverage of Falklands Crisis' (PM cycle), 8 May 1982 [cited July 10 2003].

——. 2003. 'Lone Jedi Now a Reluctant Star Lighting Up a Million Hearts.' *The Sydney Morning Herald,* 23–24 August, 21.

Avieson, John. 1978. 'The Code of Ethics: Problems and Dilemmas.' *Australian Journalism Review* 1: 1–5.

——. 1992. 'Chequebook Journalism: A Question of Ethics.' *Australian Journalism Review* 14 (1): 44–50.

'Backpacker Serial Killings: THE ACCUSED.' 1994. *Who Weekly,* 13 June, 1.

Bacon, Wendy. 1994. 'A Media Dustup: Pilger and The Australian.' *Reportage: Media Bulletin,* Winter, 20–1.

Bacon, W. 1995. 'Market Control of the Media.' In Stuart Rees & Gordon Ridley (eds) *The Human Costs of Managerialism: Advocating the Recovery of Humanity,* pp. 69–83, 308–11. Sydney: Pluto Press.

——. 1996. 'The Code of Ethics: When Aspirations are not Enough.' *Reportage,* 8–9.

Bacon, Wendy & Bonita Mason. 1995a. 'Aboriginal Deaths in Custody: A Dead Issue?' *Reportage,* Autumn, 17–22.

——. 1995b. 'Deaths in Custody: A Timeline.' *Reportage,* Autumn, 17–22.

Baldwin, Tim & Raymond Snoddy. 2003. 'BBC Admits Errors on Sex-ed Source.' *The Australian,* 24 July, 8.

'Ban Alcohol to Save Indigenous Lives.' 2003. *The Weekend Australian,* 2–3 August, 16.

Barnes, Michael. 2003. 'DPP Flaws Must Be Addressed.' *The Courier-Mail,* 9 April, 19.

Barnsley, Gail. 1995. 'Turn It Off: Demand for Ban on Police Videos.' *The Daily Telegraph Mirror*, 20 December, 1–2.

Barrass, Tony. 2002. 'Expenses Before Exposes?' *The Walkley Magazine*, Summer, 29.

Barrett, Steve. 2004a. 'I Was Double-crossed: Dolly.' *The Weekend Australian*. 7–8 February, 4.

———. 2004b. 'Bulldog Witnesses Deny Rape Allegations.' *The Weekend Australian*, 24–25 April.

BBC World. 2003a. 'The Iraqi War.' In *Correspondent*. London.

———. 2003b. *MoD Officials Defend Kelly Treatment*, 18 September [cited 19 September 2003]. Available from news.bbc.co.uk/2/hi/uk_news/politics/3118174.sm.

Bearup, Greg. 1995. 'Media Warned Against Working with Police.' *The Sydney Morning Herald*, 28 December, 3.

Bebout, Rich. 1995. *Gerald Hannon, the Media, and Moral Panic: 1977–1995* [Internet]. Canadian Lesbian and Gay Archives, 14 December [cited 20 March 2004]. Available from www.clga.ca/Material/Records/docs/hannon/ox/essay.htm.

Belsey, Andrew. 1992. 'Privacy, Publicity and Politics.' In *Ethical Dilemmas in Journalism and the Media*, ed. R. Chadwick. London: Routledge.

Belsey, Andrew & Ruth Chadwick, eds. 1992. *Ethical Dilemmas in Journalism and the Media*, ed. R. Chadwick. London: Routledge.

Bernoth, Ardyn & Bruce McDougal. 1996. 'Packer's Grip on League Revealed.' *The Daily Telegraph*, 9 May, 1, 84–5.

Bernstein, Carl & Bob Woodward. 1974. *All the President's Men*. London: Secker & Warburg.

Berry, Tony. 2001. 'Reporters on the Ropes. *The Australian*, 22–28 November, 15.

'Better to Best: Your Paper's Winning Year.' 2003. *The Courier-Mail*, 9 August, 4.

Bilboe, Wendy. 1998. 'The Thredbo Landslide: Was It Only Media Ethics That Came Tumbling Down?' *Australian Journalism Review* 20 (2): 88–110.

Bita, Natasha. 2003. 'Tanned Blairs Returning to Storm.' *The Weekend Australian*, 23–24 August, 2.

Black, A., J. Lill & P. Doneman. 2004. 'Triple Murder Suspect's Personal Interests: Cars, Girls and Death.' *The Courier-Mail*, 10 April, 3.

Blair, Jayson. 2004. *Burning Down My Masters' House*. Beverly Hills, CA: New Millennium Press.

Blair, Tim. 2001. 'When Columnists Take to the Barricades.' *The Australian*, 4 October, 12–13.

'Blair Reigns, But Rule Under Threat.' 2004. *The Weekend Bulletin*. 31 January–1 February, 37.

'Blasts Were Phony'. 2003. *The Daily Telegraph*, 27 July, 28.

A Bloggers' Code of Ethics 2003. [Internet]. CyberJournalist 2003 [cited 25 August 2003].

Blood, Rebecca. 2003. *Weblog Ethics*. Rebecca's Pocket 2003 [cited 25 August 2003]. Available from www.rebeccablood.net/handbook/excerpts/weblog_ethics.html.

Blood, R.W. et al. (2002). *The Case Studies: How the Australian Media Report and Portray Suicide and Mental Health and Illness*. Canberra, Commonwealth of Australia.

Bolt, Andrew. 2002. 'Privacy Depends on Who You Are.' *Herald Sun*, 11 July, 21.

Bolton, Robert. 1997. 'Media Coverage of the Thredbo Disaster.' In *The Media Report*: ABC Radio.

Bonderson. 2001. 'Monsters and Moral Panic in London.' *History Today*, May.

Bone, J. 2004. '"Sex and Drugs" as the Presses Rolled.' *The Weekend Australian*, 6–7 March, 17.

Bowers, Peter. 1995. 'Revealed: Murdoch's Role in 1975.' *The Sydney Morning Herald*, 4 November, 1.

Bowman, David. 1983. 'Ethics in Journalism.' *Australian Journalism Review* 5: 36–48.

———. 1988. *The Captive Press: Our Newspapers in Crisis and the People Responsible*. Melbourne: Penguin.

———. 1990. 'The A.J.A. Code.' In *Issues in Australian Journalism*, ed. J. Henningham. Melbourne: Longman Cheshire.

Bradbury, David. Circa 1980. *Frontline*. Ronin Films, Canberra.

Bradley, Ann. 1994. 'A Morality Play for our Times.' *Living Marxism* (63).

Braverman, Harry. 1974. *Labor and Monopoly capital: The Degradation of Work in the Twentieth Century*. New York: Monthly Review Press.

Breed, W. 1997. 'Social Control in the Newsroom: A Functional Analysis.' In *Social Meanings of News*. D. Berkowitz. Thousand Oaks, Cal.: Sage 107–22.

Breit, Rhoda, John Harrison, Martin Hirst, Trina McLellan & Desley Bartlett. 2002. 'Ethics in Journalism and Cheryl Kernot: A Colloquim.' *Australian Studies in Journalism*, No. 10/11, 2001–02, 33–57.

Briggs, Richard & Roderick Campbell. 2002. 'Carleton Happy to Lose Defamation Case: Judge Finds Against Reporter Who Claims ABC Damaged Reputation.' *The Canberra Times*, 19 January, 3.

Brook, Stephen. 2001. 'The Privacy Bar.' *The Australian*, 20–27 December, 2–3.

Brown, Phil & AAP. 1992. 'Judge Jails Journalist for Contempt.' *The Weekend Australian*, 21–22 March, 1.

Brunton, Ron. 2002. 'Bias Depends on Point of View.' *The Courier-Mail*, 19 January, 28.

Buckridge, Patrick. 1994. *The Scandalous Penton: A biography of Brian Penton*. Brisbane: University of Queensland Press.

——. 1999. 'Editors as Intellectuals.' In *Journalism: Print, Politics and Popular Culture'*, ed. J. Schultz. Brisbane: University of Queensland Press.

'Budd Dwyer, the Man Who Killed Himself on Television.' 1987. *The Sydney Morning Herald*, 24 January, 1.

Bullock, Alan & Stephen Trombley, eds. 2000. *The New Fontana Dictionary of Modern Thought*. Third edn. London: HarperCollins.

Bunning, Cliff. 1991. 'Turning Experience into Learning.' *Training & Development in Australia* 18(4).

Burchett, Wilfred. 1969. *Passport: An Autobiography*. Melbourne: Thoman Nelson Australia.

Burnet, David. 1992. Freedom of Speech, the Media and the Law.' In *Ethical Dilemmas in Journalism and the Media*, ed. R. Chadwick. London: Routledge.

Byrne, Fiona & Chris Tinbler. 2003. 'Warne's Off to England.' *The Sunday Mail* (Qld), 24 August, 17.

Callaghan, Greg. 2003. 'Selling Ryan's Privacy.' *The Weekend Australian Magazine*, 24–25 May, 26.

Callinan, Rory. 2003. 'Journalists Kept in Dark'. *The Weekend Australian*, 22-23 March, 2.

Callinicos, Alex. 1995. *Theories and Narratives; Reflections on the Philosophy of History*. London: Polity Press.

Campbell, Duncan. 2003. 'US Media Scents a New OJ Trial as Basketball Star Faces Rape Charges.' *The Guardian*, 7 August, 3.

'Carleton Edict: Find a Survivor.' 2002. *The Weekend Bulletin*, 2–3 March, 19.

'Case Studies—When Truth Becomes a Casualty.' 2003. *The Courier-Mail*, 13 May, 11.

Casey, Marcus. 2003. 'Daggers at Daybreak—The Bitter Feud That Has Split Morning Television.' *The Sunday Mail* (Qld), 2 November, 23.

Castle, Phil. 2003. Personal communication with authors.

Castillo, Antonio & Martin Hirst. 2001. '"Look Both Ways": Fairfield, Cabramatta and the Media.' In *The Other Sydney: Communities, Identities and Inequalities in Western Sydney*.

Cater, Nick. 1996a. 'Hello Dolly.' *The Daily Telegraph*, 17 May, 1, 4.

——. 1996b. 'Charge Him.' *The Daily Telegraph*, 18 May, 1, 4.

Chadwick, Paul. 1993. 'Why We Need a Shield.' *The Alliance*, June–August, 3–4.

———. 1994. 'Creating Codes: Journalism Self Regulation.' In *Not Just Another Business: Journalists, Citizens and the Media*. Sydney: Pluto Press.

———. 1995a. 'Cracking the Code.' *Eureka Street* 5 (9): 15–17.

———. 1995b. 'Licensing Journalists is Fraught with Risks'. *The Australian*, 6 September, 15.

———. 1996. 'Ethics and Journalism.' In *Codes of Ethics and the Professions*.

———. 1999. 'Time to be Called to Account.' *The Walkley Magazine*, 18–19.

———. 2004. 'Privacy on Parade: The Investigators.' *The Walkley Magazine*, 14–15.

Channel Seven News. 2003. *Your View*. Brisbane: Seven News.

'Charles in Kill Probe'. 2004. *The Gold Coast Bulletin*, 8 January, 3.

Charlton, Peter. 2002. 'Tampa: The Triumph of Politics.' In *Howard's race: Winning the Unwinnable Election*, ed. D. Solomon. Sydney: HarperCollins.

Charlton, P. 2004a. 'Flint Forced Out of Inquiry into ABC Coverage.' *The Courier-Mail*, 1 May.

Charlton, P. 2004b. 'Radio Wars Get Nasty.' *The Courier-Mail*, 1 May, 31.

Chiasson, Lloyd, ed. 1995. *The Press in Times of Crisis, Contributions to the Study of Mass Media and Communications*. Westport, CT: Praeger.

Christians, Clifford G., Kim B. Rotzoll & Mark Fackler, eds. 1991. *Media Ethics: Cases and Moral Reasoning*. New York: Longmans Inc. Original edition, 1983.

'Chronicler of Chaos.' 2003. *The Weekend Australian*, 30–31 August, 22–23.

Chulov, Martin. 2003. 'Fairfax Code of Conduct Could Muzzle News Scoops.' *The Australian*, 30 October–5 November, 10.

Clark, Andrew. 1996. 'Battle of the Editors.' *The Weekend Australian*, 1 September, 19.

Clark, Pilita. 1997. '"Dolly" Scoop Also Poses a Question of Ethics.' *The Sydney Morning Herald*, 15 November, 2.

———. 1998. 'Littlemore's Legacy.' *The Sydney Morning Herald*, 31 January, 34.

Clifton, Brad. 2001. 'Pedophile "Dolly" Dunn Smiles at 30-year Term.' *The Hobart Mercury*, 8 December 2001 [cited 24 September 2003]. Available from gateway.library.qut.edu.au: 2684/...b08_md5=0327a9bc48/aa55883a1623551760eca.

Cock, Anna. 2003. 'This Reporter's News Just Not Fit to Print.' *The Courier-Mail*, 13 May, 11.

Cohen, Stanley. 1972. *Folk Devils and Moral Panics*. London: MacGibbon & Kee.

Coleman, P. 2004. 'Spin Takes on Trust.' *The Weekend Australian*, 17–18 April, R12.

'Colossus of Canberra.' 2003. *The Gold Coast Bulletin*, 4 June, 1.

Conroy, Paul. 1995. 'Justice Being Seen to be Done.' *The Age*, 6 October, 18.

'Contempt Law Ridiculous Says Freed Journalist.' 1989. *The Weekend Australian*, 16–17 December, 16.

Cook, Anna. 2003. 'Networks Muzzle Their Star Reporters.' *The Courier-Mail*, 2 April, 6.

'CORRECTING THE RECORD: *Times* Reporter Who Resigned Leaves Long Trail of Deception.' 2003. *The New York Times*, 11 May, 1.

Cose, Ellis. 1989. *The Press: Inside America's Most Powerful Newspaper Empires—From the Newsrooms to the Boardrooms*. New York: William Morrow.

Cowdery, Nicholas. 2001. *Getting Justice Wrong: Myths, Media and Crime*. Sydney: Allen & Unwin.

Crabb, Annabel. 2003. 'ABC and Fair Play: PM and Alston Want New Ref.' *The Sydney Morning Herald Online*, 26 July 2003 [cited 26 July 2003]. Available from www.smh.com.au/cgi-bin/common/popupPrintArticle.pl?path=/articles/2003/07/25/1059084192233.html.

Cracknell, D. & Brooks, R. 2004. 'Besieged BBC Sends Journalists on "Impartiality Seminars." ' *The Australian*, 22 April, 16.

Crawford, B. 2004. 'Becks Girl a "Scammer" Who Worked as Escort.' *The Australian,* 15 April, 6.

Cromie, Ali. 1997. 'Australia's Most Generous.' *Business Review Weekly*, 1 June, 36.

Cronau, Peter. 1996. 'Ethical Journalists Deserve a Better Code of Ethics.' *Reportage*, 6–7.

'A "Crucifiction": Ex-adviser Defends His Boss.' 2003. *The Gold Coast Bulletin*, 9 May, 4.

Curran, James. 1991. 'Rethinking the Media as a Public Sphere.' In *Communication and Citizenship: Journalism and the Public Sphere*, ed. C. Sparks. London & New York: Routledge.

CTVA. 1999. Commercial Television Industry Code of Practice, CTVA.

Dalton, Rodney. 2003. 'NY Times Comes Clean on Reporter Who Made Up the News.' *The Australian*, 15–21 May, 10.

Daly, Martin. 1996. 'Still Searching for Mr Cruel.' *The Sydney Morning Herald*, 13 May, 35.

D'Arcy, Steve. 2003a. 'Singh Probe Team Baffled By Witness.' *The Weekend Bulletin*, 31 May–1 June, 17.

——. 2003b. 'Torn Apart by Tragedy.' *The Weekend Bulletin*, 24–25 May, 16.

'A Dark Day for the Internet.' 2002. *The Australian*, 11 December, 14.

Das, Sushila. 1996. 'Hinch Grateful to Escape Jail Sentence.' *The Age*, 16 April, 3.

Dasey, Daniel. 1997. 'Sorry Will Not Bring Him Back.' *The Sun-Herald*, 24 August, 1.

Davies, Anne. 1994. 'Time to Talk of Money, Friends.' *The Sydney Morning Herald*, 20 September, 2.

Davies, Anne, Sue Lecky & Brad Norrington. 1994. 'ABC Ads Inquiry Widens.' *Sydney Morning Herald*, 20 September, 2.

Davies, Mark. 2002. 'Joining the Dots.' *The Walkley Magazine*, Summer, 28–9.

Davis, Mark. 2002. 'Great White Noise.' *The Sydney Morning Herald*, 12–13 January, 4–5.

Day, Mark. 2002. 'High Court Has Unleashed a Jurisdictional Nightmare.' *The Australian*, 11 December, 4.

——. 2003a. 'Lies, Damn Lies and Women's Mags.' *The Australian*, 9–16 January, 2.

——. 2003b. 'Media Players Eye Up New Suitors While Alston Woos Hard-to-get Independents.' *The Australian*, 3–9 April, 3.

——. 2004a. 'Bulldust Mocks Hot Goss Gloss.' *The Australian,* 1–7 January, 2.

——. 2004b. 'Madrid Photo Too Gruesome, Some Say.' *The Australian,* 18 March, 19.

——. 2004c. 'Williams' Departure Leaves Policy Leadership Vacuum.' *The Australian,* 8 April, 24.

——. 2004d. 'Truth Will Out, Dirt Will Be Dug, But Slathering Frenzy's Not On'. Media & Marketing, *The Australian*, 8 July, 22.

'Days of Living Dangerously.' 2002. *The Weekend Australian,* 19–20 October, 19.

'Defamation Row: Both Sides Claim Victory.' 2002. *The Gold Coast Bulletin*, 19 December.

Delahunty, Mary & Wendy Bacon. 1995. 'Ethics Code—More Than Just Aspirations?' *The Sydney Morning Herald*, 1 September, 13.

Department of Journalism, University of Queensland. 1998. 'Media and Indigenous Australians Project', Department of Journalism, University of Queensland.

Devine, Frank. 1996. 'Child Abuse: Press Won't Be Muzzled.' *The Australian*, 22 May, 11.

Devine, Miranda. 2002. 'A Man's Best Friend, But Feminism's Worst Enemy', *The Sun-Herald*, 7 July, 15.

Dibben, Kay. 2003. 'Nobody Blames Him—So Why Do That to Yourself?' *The Sunday Mail* (Qld), 29 June, 2.

'Diggers in Hand-to-hand Combat.' 2003. *The Gold Coast Bulletin*, 27 March, 1.

'Discretion Is the Key to Fairness.' 1995. *The Daily Telegraph Mirror*, 20 December, 10.

Dodd, Andrew. 2001a. 'Strikes a Defining Moment in US Journalism.' *The Australian*, 4 October, 12.
———. 2001b. 'Reporters Grilled by the Prosecution.' *The Australian*, 15 November, 5.
Doneman, Paula. 2004. 'Heartless Predator.' *The Courier-Mail*, 12 February, 1.
Doneman, Paula & Wayne Smith. 2002. 'Top Swim Coach Charged.' *The Courier-Mail*, 27 March, 1.
Doneman, P., C. Griffith & T. Moore. 2004. 'Woman Surrenders to Face Stealing Charges.' *The Courier-Mail*, 13 February, 3.
Downie Jr., Leonard & Robert G. Kaiser. 2002. *The News About the News: American Journalism in Peril*. Knopf.
Dugdale, Lynda. 1996. Victims 'From All Corners of the Country.' *The Daily Telegraph*, 29 April, 5.
Eccleston, Roy. 2001. 'Enemy on Target in Battle of the Mind.' *The Australian*, 11 October, 2.
Edgar, Andrew. 1992. 'Objectivity, Bias and Truth.' In *Ethical Issues in Journalism and the Media*, ed. R. Chadwick. London: Routledge.
Eggerking, Kitty. 1998. Review of Schultz (1998), 'Reviving the Fourth Estate.' *Australian Journalism Review* 20 (2): 164–8.
Ehrlich, Matthew C. 1997. 'The Competitive Ethos in Television Newswork.' In *The Social Meaning of News: A Text-reader*, ed. D. Berkowitz. Thousand Oaks, CA: Sage. Original edition, *Critical Studies in Mass Communication*, 1995, Vol 12, pp. 196–212.
Eldridge, John, ed. 1993. *Getting the Message: News, Truth and Power*. London, New York: Routledge.
Elgar, Kerri. 1997. 'Code of Ethics Under Review.' *Alliance*: 10–17.
———. 1998. '12 Points to Consider.' *Alliance* (Autumn): 10–11.
Elliott, G., S. Maiden & E. Higgins. 2004. 'Radio Hams Brawl Over Howard Watchdog.' *The Australian*, 29 April, 1–2.
Emerson, Scott. 2003. 'Beattie Calls for Media Scrutiny.' *The Australian*, 27 March, 14.
Ericson, Richard V., Patricia Baranek & Janet B.L. Chan. 1987. *Visualizing Deviance: A Study of News Organization*. Milton Keynes: Open University Press.
Este, Jonathon. 2003. 'Shabby Sheik's Chequebook Heist Fails to Add Up for NoW.' *The Australian*, 12–18 June, 10.
'Ethics and the Media.' 1987. ed. Department of Journalism, Deakin University.
Ethics Review Committee, MEAA, AJA Section. 1997. *Ethics in Journalism: Report of the Ethics Review Committee, MEAA, AJA Section*. Melbourne: Melbourne University Press.
Evaluating Web Resources [cited 31 July 2003]. Available from www2.windener.edu/Wolgram-Memorial-Library/webevaluations/news.htm.
Fallows, James. 2003. 'The Age of Murdoch.' *The Weekend Australian*, 30–31 August, 24.
Fanning, E. 2004. 'Telling Tales Reveal Home Truths.' *The Australian*, 22 April, 16.
Felling, Matthew T. 2003. 'Embedded in Danger.' *The Courier-Mail*, 31 March, 13.
Fergus, Shiel. 2002. 'Carleton to Pay the Price for Plagiarism Victory.' *The Age*, 19 December, 3.
Ferudi, Frank. 1994. 'A Plague of Moral Panics.' *Living Marxism* (73): November.
Flint, David. 1996. 'The Wrong Arm of the Law.' *The Sydney Morning Herald*, 3 January, 9.
Frankel, Glenn. 2003a. 'BBC Reporter Admits Errors on Iraq: Story Claimed Blair Aides Had Misled the Public on Danger Posed by Saddam.' *The Washington Post*, 18 September, C04.
———. 2003b. 'BBC Staffer Admits Errors, Apologizes; False Statements Not Corrected, Inquiry Told.' *The Washington Post*, 18 September, A16.
Franklin, Bob. 1997. *Newszak and News Media*. London, New York: Arnold,.
Freeman, Jane. 1997. 'The Selling of Heroes.' *The Sydney Morning Herald*, 17 August, 11.
Frew, Wendy. 2003. 'Fairfax $1.1bn NZ Purchase.' *The Sydney Morning Herald*, 15 April, 27.
Garneau, George. 1992. 'Bearing The Burden of Blame.' *Editor and Publisher*, 9 May, 11.

Geraghty, Andrew. 1986. 'Deathknock: A Reporter's View.' *Australian Journalism Review* 8: 8–9.

Gerbner, George. 1992. 'Violence and Terror In and By the Media.' In *Media, Crisis and Democracy: Mass Communication and the Disruption of Social Order*, ed. B. Dagenais. London: Sage.

Gibbs, Stephen. 2000. 'Laws Too Famous to Jail, says Judge.' *The Sydney Morning Herald*, 6 September, 1.

Gillespie, Iain. 1993. 'Without Fear or Favour.' SBS TV.

Glass, Stephen. 2003. *The Fabulist*. New York: Simon & Schuster.

Gledhill, Matthew & Christopher Henning. 1997. 'Diana: Court Acts Over Seven Paparazzi.' *The Sydney Morning Herald*, 3 September, 1.

Glover, Dennis. 2003. *Orwell's Australia: From Cold War to Culture Wars*, Scribe Short Books. Melbourne: Scribe.

Goldenberg, S. 2003. 'Fox Sees Red After Some Joker Pinches Its Slogan.' *The Sydney Morning Herald*, 16–17 August, 13.

Goode, Erich & Nachman Ben-Yehuda. 1994. *Moral Panics: The Social Construction of Deviance*. Oxford: Blackwell.

Goodwin, H. Eugene. 1987. *Groping for Ethics in Journalism*. Ames, Iowa: Iowa State University Press.

'Government and Media Accountability.' 2003. *The Courier-Mail*, 29 March, 24.

Grabosky, Peter & Paul Wilson. 1989. *Journalism and Justice: How Crime is Reported*. Sydney: Pluto Press.

Gramsci, Antonio. 1971. *Selections from the Prison Notebooks of Antonio Gramsci*. Trans. G. Nowell Smith. New York and London: International Publishers and Lawrence & Wishart.

Grattan, Michelle. 1991.' Ideological Spectacles; Reporting the "Ratpack"'. *Media Information Australia* (60): 7–10.

——. 1998. *Editorial Independence: An Outdated Concept?* Ed. J. Henningham. Vol. 1, *Australian Journalism Monographs*. Brisbane: University of Queensland.

——. 2003. *The First Casualty of Alston's War*. The Age Online, 1 June 2003 [cited 10 June 2003]. Available from theage.com.au/articles/2003/05/31/1054177766535.html.

Griffith, C., C. Jones, et al. 2003. 'We Got Him.' *The Courier Mail*, 15 December, 1.

Guillatt, Richard. 1994. 'Mine Firm Backed Film with $22,000.' *The Sydney Morning Herald*, 20 September, 2.

——. 2003. 'Shadow on the Son.' *Good Weekend*, 3 May, 20–7.

Gumbel, Andrew. 1995. 'Nazi Gets $40,000 for Scoop.' *The Sydney Morning Herald*, 2 September, 21.

Habermas, Jürgen. 1990. *The Structural Transformation of the Public Sphere: An Inquiry Into a Category of Bourgeois Society*. Trans. T.B. &. F. Lawrence. Cambridge: Polity Press.

Hale, Brian, Helen Shield & Chris Henning. 1998. 'When the Owner of News Becomes an Item of News.' *The Age*, 22 April, 3.

Hall, Jaslyn. 1996. 'Media Mounts a Witch-hunt on Teenagers'. *The Sydney Morning Herald*, 23 March, 17.

Hall, Richard. 1998. *Black Armband Days: Truth from the Dark Side of Australia's Past*. Sydney: Vintage.

Hallin, Daniel C. 1986. *The Uncensored War: The Media and Vietnam*. New York: Oxford University Press.

——. 1994. *We Keep America on Top of the World: Television Journalism and the Public Sphere, Communication and Society*. London; New York: Routledge.

Ham, Paul. 2003. 'Sponsorship of Finance Shows Turns Out to be a Tricky Business.' *The Australian*, 19–25 June, 12.

Hannan, Liz & Simon Crittle. 1997. 'Why Did Angel Die?' *The Sun-Herald*, 24 August, 3.

Hannity, Sean. 2002. *Let Freedom Ring: Winning the War of Liberty over Liberalism*. New York: ReganBooks.

Hansen, Peter. 2003. 'We'll Catch the Killer by Christmas.' *The Sunday Mail* (Qld), 19 October, 21.

Hargreaves, Ian. 2003. *Journalism: Truth or Dare?* Oxford: Oxford University Press.

Harlan Reynolds, Glenn. 2002. 'High Court Throws a Spanner in the Global Networks.' *The Australian*, 11 December, 15.

Harris, T. 2004. 'Virtual Camp for Killers.' *The Australian*, 13 May, 15.

Harris, R. 1983. *Gotcha! The Media, the Government and the Falklands Crisis*. London: Faber & Faber.

Hartley, John. 1996. *Popular Reality: Journalism, Modernity, Popular Culture*. London: Arnold.

Harvey, Michael. 2002. 'The Cheryl Kernot Bombshell: Secret Lovers?' *Herald Sun*, 1.

Hawse, Adam. 2004. 'Pull Your Socks Up, Dogs Told.' *The Sunday Mail* (Qld), 14 March, 7.

Hayes, Liz. 1997. 'Capture of Dolly Dunn.' In *60 Minutes*. Sydney.

——. 2003. 'The Bagman of Bali.' In *60 Minutes*, Sydney: Nine Network, 6 July.

Heffernan, R. 2004. 'Everyone Loves Paris in Autumn.' *The Courier-Mail*, 24 April, 5.

Hellmann, John. 1981. *Fables of Fact: The New Journalism as New Fiction*. Chicago: University of Illinois Press.

Henderson, Gerard. 1994. 'It's Not the Time to Hoist Hill out of Aunty.' *The Sydney Morning Herald*, 27 September, 17.

——. 1996. 'When the Named are Shamed.' *The Sydney Morning Herald*, 2 January, 11.

Hendtlass, Jane & Alan Nichols. 2003. *Media Ethics: Ethics, Law and Accountability in the Australian Media: With Case Studies for Classes and Groups, Ethics in Daily Life*. Melbourne: Acorn Press.

Henning, Christopher. 1997. 'Driven to her Death.' *The Sydney Morning Herald*, 1 September, 1.

Henningham, J. 1984. 'Australian Television Journalists' Professional Values and Audience Orientations.' St. Lucia. Doctoral thesis.

——. 1985. 'Journalism as a Profession: A Re-examination.' *Australian Journal of Communication* (8): 1–17.

——. 1989. 'Why and How Journalists Should be Professionalised.' *Australian Journalism Review* 11: 27–32.

——. 1993. 'Australian Journalists' Attitudes to Education.' *Australian Journalism Review* 15 (2): 77–90.

——. 1995a. 'Australian Journalists' Religious Views.' *Australian Religion Studies Review* 8 (2): 63–77.

——. 1995c. 'Journalists' Perceptions of Bias.' *Australian Journalism Review* 17(2): 28–31.

——. 1995d. 'Political Journalists' Political and Professional Values.' *Australian Journal of Political Science* 30(2): 321–34.

——. 1995f. 'A Profile of Australian Sports Journalism.' *ACHPER Healthy Lifestyles Journal* 42 (3): 13–17.

——. 1996a. 'Australian Journalists' Views on Professional Associations.' *Asia Pacific Media Educator* 1(1): 144–52.

——. 1996c. 'Australian Journalists' Professional and Ethical Values.' *Journal of Mass Communications Quarterly* (73): 206–18.

Herman, Edward & Noam Chomsky. 1988. *Manufacturing Consent: The Political Economy of the Mass Media*. New York: Random House.

Hernandez, Macerena. 2003. *He Stole a Lot More Than My Words*, 25 May 2003 [cited May 27 2003]. Available from http://www.latimes.com/news/printedition/opinion/la-op-hernandez25May,1,76609.

Hewitt, Giles. 2003. 'Stock Exchange Kicks Arab Reporters Off the Floor.' *The Courier-Mail*, 27 March, 7.

Hewitt, Jennifer. 1998. 'Scandal Puts Media in the Dock.' *The Sydney Morning Herald*, 31 January, 19.

Hewitt, Tony. 1988. 'Five-part "Classroom" series.' *The Sydney Morning Herald*, 17, 19, 20, 21, 22 September.

Hickman, Belinda. 2003. 'Lifespan of Blacks Still 20 Years Less.' *The Weekend Australian*, 30–31 August, 7.

Hilferty, Tim, Peter Lalor & Sue Dunlevy. 1996. 'Stop Their Dole.' *The Daily Telegraph*, 6 March, 1, 4–5.

'Hinch's Shame File.' 1996. *The Age*, 19 April, 3.

Hirst, Martin. 1993. 'Class, Mass News Media and the 1993 Election.' *Australian Journal of Communication* 20 (2): 28–43.

——. 1997a. 'MEAA Code of Ethics for Journalists: An Historical and Theoretical Overview.' *Media International Australia* (83): 63–77.

——. 1997b. Where were you on November 11? Interview with Alan Yates.

——. 1997c. Where were you on November 11? Interview with David Barnett.

——. 1999. Off the rails: Interview with Margo Kingston, October.

——. 2001. 'Journalism in Australia: Hard Yakka.' In *Journalism: Theory in Practice*, ed. C. Varley, pp. 55–70. Melbourne: Oxford University Press.

——. 2003. 'Grey Collar Journalism: The Social Relations of News Production', School of Social Sciences and Liberal Studies, Charles Sturt University, Bathurst, NSW.

Hirst, Martin & Robert Schutze. 2004a. 'Allies Down Under: The Australian at War and the Big Lie.' In *Global Media Goes To War: Role of News and Entertainment Media During the 2003 Iraq War*, ed. Ralph D. Berenger, Spokane WA, Marquette Books, 171–87.

——. 2004b. 'Getting the Story Straight: Greg Sheridan in the Shifting Sands of Iraq'. *Overland* (176): 18–25.

Hirst, Martin, Tiffany White, David Chaplin & Justine Wilson. 1995. 'When Too Much Entertainment is Barely Enough: Current Affairs Television in the 1990s.' *Australian Journalism Review* 17 (1): 79–98.

Hoare, Daniel. 2003. 'Don't Look Now, Privacy Laws are Changing.' *The Australian*, 12 June, 3.

'Hookes Frenzy Dismays Accused's Lawyer'. 2004. *The SMH Online*. Available at: www.smh.com.au/articles/2004/01/22/1074732545444.html. [cited 23 January 2004].

Horne, Donald. 1986. *The public culture: The triumph of Industrialism*. London: Pluto.

——. 1994a. 'A Marketplace of Ideas?' In *Not Just Another Business: Journalists, Citizens and the Media*, ed. J. Schultz. Sydney: Pluto Press in Association with Ideas for Australia, National Centre for Australian Studies, Monash University.

——. 1994b. 'But That's Not the Issue.' In *Not Just Another Business: Journalists, Citizens and the Media*, ed. J. Schultz. Sydney: Pluto Press in Association with Ideas for Australia, National Centre for Australian Studies, Monash University.

Horsfield, Peter. 1997. 'Moral Panic or Moral Action? The Appropriation of Moral Panics in the Exercise of Social Control.' *Media International Australia* (85).

'Howard Must Act to Sack Biased Flint.' 2004. *The Courier-Mail*, 1 May, 26.

Human Rights and Equal Opportunity Commission. 1996. 'The Racial Hatred Act: A Guide for People in the Australian Media.' Sydney.

Humphrey, Carol Sue. 1995. 'Selling the American Revolution.' In *The Press in Times of Crisis*, ed. L. Chiasson Jr. Westport, CT: Praeger.

Hunt, Arnold. 1997. '"Moral panic" and Moral Language in the Media.' *The British Journal of Sociology* 48 (4): 629–48.

Hunt, Ian. 1993. *Analytical and Dialectical Marxism, Avebury Series in Philosophy*. Aldershot, UK: Avebury.

'Hunting Mr Cruel.' 2003. *Herald Sun*, August 5 2003 [cited September 25 2003]. Available from heraldsun.news.com.au/printpage/0,5481,6864536,00.html.

Hurst, John. 1991. 'Journalistic Objectivity and Subjectivity in News Reporting and News Selection.' *Australian Journalism Review* 13 (1–2): 23–30.

——. 1992. 'Freebies, a Conflict of Interest?' *Australian Journalism Review* 14 (1): 33–43.

Hurst, John & Sally White. 1994. *Ethics and the Australian News Media*. Melbourne: Macmillan Education.

'I'd Rather Have Been Killing Cops.' 1993. *The Sydney Morning Herald*, 31 March, 1, 4.

'I Did Not Rape Her.' 2003. *The Gold Coast Bulletin*, 9 May, 1.

'I Misled, I Lied, says Carleton.' 2002. *The Gold Coast Bulletin*, 1 March, 9.

Inglis, Ken S. 1962. 'The Daily Papers.' In *Australian Civilization: A Symposium*, ed. P. Coleman. Melbourne: F.W. Cheshire, pp. 145–75.

Innes, Prue. 1999. 'Jury is Still Out.' *The Australian*, 1–7 April, 2.

'Inside the Classroom: Our Readers Reply.' 1988. *Sydney Morning Herald*, 24 September, 8–9.

Irby, Kenny. 2003. *L.A. Times Photographer Fired Over Altered Image*. Poynter Institute 2003 [cited 17 June 2003]. Available from poynteronline.org/content/content_view.asp?id=28082& sid=32.

Irving, Mark. 1989. 'Perth Journalist Jailed for Protecting his Source.' *The Australian*, 12 December, 5.

'It's All About Me.' *The Gold Coast Bulletin*, 3 December, 8.

'It's a Case of Mistaken Identity: G-G.' 2003. *The Gold Coast Bulletin*, 9 May, 5.

'It's Child Abuse.' 2003. *The Gold Coast Bulletin*, 27 March,1.

'It's Krystal Clear Harry Would Love the Gold Coast Gals.' 2003. *Courier-Mail*, 25 September, 32.

'Jackson Interview Under Ethical Spotlight.' 2004. ABC News Online, 1 January. Available at www.abc.net.au/news/newsitems/S1018928.htm [cited 1 January 2004].

Jackson, Jennifer. 1992. 'Honesty in Investigative Journalism.' In *Ethical Dilemmas in Journalism and the Media*, ed. R. Chadwick. London: Routledge.

Jackson, Sally. 2003a. 'History's Fault Line.' *The Weekend Australian*. 28–29 June, 25.

——. 2003b. 'Four Corners Outrage at MEAA Ruling.' *The Australian*, 10–16 July, 9.

——. 2003c. 'Four Corners Ruling Thrown Out on Appeal.' *The Australian*, 7–13 August, 7.

——. 2003d. 'Journalists the First Casualties in Reporting the Truth of War.' *The Australian*, 17–23 April, 7.

——. 2003e. 'No Times for Blair Rich Project.' *The Australian*, 29 May–4 June, 9.

——. 2004a. 'Reality's Vital First Step.' *The Australian*, 18 March, 17.

——2004b. 'Radio Men Behaving Badly.' *The Weekend Australian,* 1–2 May, 22.

Jackson, Sally & Caitlin Fitzsimmons. 2002. 'Gutnick Decision Spooking Internet.' *The Australian*, 11 December, 4.

'The Jailing of Mr Hinch.' 1987. *The Sydney Morning Herald*, 15 October, 10.

'Jailing Reporters Inappropriate.' 1989. *The Australian*, 20 December, 6.

Jakubowicz, Andrew, ed. 1994. *Racism, Ethnicity and the Media*. St Leonards, Sydney: Allen and Unwin.

James, Jennifer. 1996. 'My Year of Terror in a Dream Home.' *The Daily Telegraph*, 5 January, 4.

Jameson, J. 2004. 'Villain or Victim? How One Young Woman Has Divided a Town.' *The Sunday Mail* (Qld), 2 May.

Jasmen, Lill. 2001. 'Firefighters Top Trust Ladder in Jobs Survey.' *The Courier-Mail*, 25 July, 9.

Jenkins, C. (2003). 'Private Lives, Public Interest: Did We Need to Know about the Kernot/Evans Affair?' *Australian Studies in Journalism* (12): 48–63.

Jenkins, Henry. 1999. 'Lessons from Littleton: What Congress Doesn't Want You to Hear about Youth and Media.' *Harper's*, August.

Jopson, Debra. 2003. 'Report Finds Indigenous Health Still in Sorry State.' *The Sydney Morning Herald*, 30–31 August, 10.

Jurkowitz, M. 2001. 'Media Asked to Think Before Airing Al Qaeda Statements.' *The Sydney Morning Herald*, 13 October, 26.

Kampfner, John. 2003. 'America Lynches Truth.' *The Weekend Australian*, 24–25 May, 5.

Kant, Immanuel. 1959. *Foundations of the Metaphysics of Morals*. Translated by L.W. Beck. New York: Macmillan. Original edition, 1785.

Karvelas, Patricia. 2003. 'Arabic Channels Bring the War Back Home.' *The Australian*, 26 June–2 July, 7.

Kelly, Paul. 1994. 'Bound for Disappointment on the Highway from Heaven to Hell.' In *Not Just Another Business: Journalists, Citizens and the Media*, ed. J. Schultz. Sydney: Pluto Press in Association with Ideas for Australia, National Centre for Australian Studies, Monash University.

——. 2003. 'The Only Viable Path.' *The Australian*, 26 May, 1.

Kerin, John. 2003. 'Frigates in Hunt for Fleeing Cronies.' *The Weekend Australian*, 22–23 March, 4.

Kerin, J. 2004. 'See it Through in Iraq, says Murdoch.' *The Australian*, 8 April, 2.

'Kidnap of Beckham Trial Axed.' 2003. *The Gold Coast Bulletin*, 4 June, 2.

Kilborn Richard, W. 1997. 'Fly on the Wall Documentarists: A Dying Breed?' *Continuum (Perth)* 11 (1): 43–53.

Kim, J. 1994. 'Diversifying Marx: Communication Labor and the Origin of Information Society.' Paper read at International Communication Association, July, at Sydney.

Kingston, Margo. 1999a. *Off the rails: The Pauline Hanson trip*. Sydney: Allen & Unwin.

——. 1999b. 'Journalistic Independence: Holding the Line.' *The Walkley Magazine*, Aug: 33–4.

——. 2001. 'Anarchy in the Newsroom.' *The Walkley Magazine*, Spring 2001, 35.

——. 2003. *Webdiary ethics* [Internet]. Sydney Morning Herald online 2003 [cited 23 July 2003]. Available from www.smh.com.au/articles/2003/07/23/1058853117710.html.

Knightley, Phillip. 1975. *The First Casualty: The War Correspondent as Hero and Myth Maker*. London: Quartet.

——. 1997. *A Hack's Progress*. London: Jonathon Cape.

——. 2001. 'When the Media are a Menace.' *The Sydney Morning Herald weekend edition*, October 27–28, 27.

Knowlton, S.R. 1997. *Moral Reasoning for Journalists*. Westport, CN: Praeger.

Koch, Tony. 1998. 'A Gap in Our Education.' *The Walkley Magazine*, July, 5.

——. 2003a. 'Hurry Up and Do Nothing.' *The Courier-Mail*, 9 August, 33.

——. 2003b. 'Next Stop Jail for Child Escaping Island of Fear.' *The Courier-Mail*, 30 August, 1.

——. 2003c. 'A People Diseased by the Delivery of Grog.' *The Courier-Mail*, 30 August, 16–17.

——. 2004. 'Barking Up the Wrong Tree.' *The Courier-Mail*, 1 May, 27.

Krajicek, David. 2003. 'Journalism Ethics' [Internet]. 'Justice Journalism' n.d. [cited 25 August 2003]. Available from www.justicejournalism.org/crimeguide/chapter06_pg02.html.

Lague, David. 1995. 'Media Chiefs Baulk at Crackdown on Secrets.' *The Sydney Morning Herald*, 14 December, 3.

Lague, David & Tony Wright. 1995. 'Jail for Journalists Who Reveal Australia's Secrets.' *The Sydney Morning Herald*, 2 June, 1.

Lampert, Nicole. 2003. 'Rock Singer Linked to Diana.' *The Courier-Mail*, 6 November, 11.

Langer, John. 1998. Tabloid Television: Popular Journalism and the 'Other News.' Ed. J. Curran, *Communication & Society*. London & New York: Routledge.

'Latham Ex Dumps on New Leader.' 2003. *The Gold Coast Bulletin*. 2 December, 3.

Laurie, Victoria. 2003. 'Rite of Damage.' *The Weekend Australian*, 8–9 November, 20.

Lawrence, Jessica. 2003. 'Oasis Helps a Town to Remember Its Own.' *The Sunday Mail* (Qld), 11 May, 52.

Legge, K. 2004. 'Spouses Caught in the Spotlight.' *The Weekend Australian*, 24–25 April, 19.

Leo, John. 1999. 'Bloopers of the Century.' *Columbia Journalism Review*, Jan/Feb (37) 5, pp, 38–41.

Lewis, Steve. 2003. 'Hollingworth Resigns as G-G.' *The Australian*, 26 May, 1.

Leys, N. 2004. 'Pot Plant Tip-off in ABA Affair.' *The Australian*, 22 April, 17.

Life Promoting Media Strategy: A Positive Approach. 1999. Commonwealth Department of Health and Aged Care

Linnell, Garry. 2003. 'The Packer View.' *The Bulletin*, 26 August, 32–3.

Lipski, Sam. 1993. '1968: The Year That Changed the World.' *The Australian Magazine*, 27–28 March, 38–9.

Little, John. 2003. *The Man Who Saw Too Much: David Brill, Combat Cameraman*. Sydney: Hodder.

Littlemore, Stuart. 1995. 'Wrong Solution for Media Code-breakers.' *The Australian*, 11 September, 4.

——. 1996. 'Fictional Single Mother Story.' In *Media Watch*, ABC Television.

Lloyd, Clem. 1985. *Profession: Journalist. A History of the Australian Journalists' Association*. Sydney: Hale & Iremonger.

Lloyd, Peter. 2001. *Marsden Wins Defamation Case*, 27 June 2001 [cited 25 September 2003]. Available from www.abc.net.au/worldtoday/s319864.htm.

'Lord Hutton's Findings.' 2004. *The Australian*, 30 January, 9.

Lumby, Catharine. 1999. *Gotcha: Life in a Tabloid World*. Sydney: Allen & Unwin

——. 2001. 'Hegemony Over Heels.' *The Bulletin*, 2 October, 49.

Lusetich, Robert. 1998. 'A Big Scoop of Humble Pie.' *The Weekend Australian*, 4–5 July, 17.

Lusetich, R. 2004. 'Truth a Casualty of the Fame Game.' *The Australian*, 8 April, 23.

Lyall, Kimini & Al Jacinto. 2003. 'Manila Court Airs Hambali Charges. *The Australian*, 8 July, 13.

Lynch, Paul. 1982. 'Senator's Tragedy.' *The Sunday Telegraph*, 6 June, 1.

'Lynch in $1.5m Book Deal.' 2003. *The Sydney Morning Herald Online* [cited 3 September 2003]. Available from www.smh.com.au/articles'2003/09/01/1062515427558.html.

'Lynch Reveals Brutal Truth.' 2003. *The Weekend Australian*, 15–16 November, 12.

Lyndon, N. 2004. 18 April. 'A Lesson for All You Txt Maniacs.' *The Sunday Mail* (Qld), 56–7.

Lyons, John. 2001. 'The Price of a Reputation.' In *Sunday*, 8 July, Nine Network. Sydney.

——. 2003. 'Stop Press.' *The Bulletin*, 26 August, 21–6.

Macfarlane, Duncan. 2003a. 'Please, Charge Me with Murder.' *The Australian*, 30 May, 3.

——. 2003b. 'Mother Collapses During Public Plea.' *The Australian*, 1 May, 5.

Maiden, S. 2004. 'Howard's Iraq Dash a Testing Event.' *The Australian*, 29 April, 15.

Maiden, Samantha & Michael McKinnon 2004. 'For My Eyes Only, Says Flint on Jones Letters.' *The Australian*, 8 July, 4.

Malakani, Gautam. 2003. 'BBC Head "Regrets" Not Launching Full Probe.' *The Financial Times*, 16 September, 4.

Manne, Robert. 1994. *The Shadow of 1917: Cold War Conflict in Australia*. Melbourne: Text Publishing.

Marr, David. 2003a. 'In Vino Veritas.' In *Media Watch*. ABC TV. 25 August.

——. 2003b. 'The Minister's Complaint.' In *Media Watch*. ABC TV. 3 November

——. 2003c. '60 Minutes' Bali Bagman.' In *Media Watch*. ABC TV. 22 September.

——. 2003d. 'Piers' Plagiarism.' In *Media Watch*. ABC TV. 10 February.

——. 2003e. 'The "Exploding Phone" Yarn.' In *Media Watch.* ABC TV. 28 July.

——. 2003f. '"Exploding phone" Update.' In *Media Watch.* ABC TV. 25 August.

——. 2003g. '50 Things to do Before You Die'. In *Media Watch.* ABC TV. 3 November.

——. 2004. 'Trial by Media.' *Media Watch*, ABC TV. 9 February.

Marr, David & Marianne Wilkinson. 2003. *Dark Victory.* Crows Nest, Sydney: Allen and Unwin.

Martin, Ray. 1996. 'Sir Donald Bradman, 87 Not Out'. The Nine Network.

Masterton, Murray. 1985. 'What Makes News: And Do the World's Journalists Agree?' *Australian Journalism Review* 7: 96–100.

——. 1992. 'A New Approach to What Makes News News.' *Australian Journalism Review* 14 (1): 21–6.

——. 1998. 'A Theory of News.' In *Journalism: Theory and Practice*, ed. M. Breen. Sydney: Macleay Press.

Mayer, Henry. 1968. *The Press in Australia.* reprint ed. Melbourne: Landsdowne Press.

McBride, Kelly. 2003. *Tabloid Publishes Prom Picture of Kobe's Accuser.* Poynter Ethics Journal 2003 [cited 31 October 2003]. Available from www.poynteronline.org/column.asp?id=53 &aid=53231.

McChesney, Robert. 2000. 'Journalism, Democracy ... And Class Struggle.' *Monthly Review* 52 (6).

McChesney, Robert & Ben Scott. 2002. 'Upton Sinclair and the Contradictions of Capitalist Journalism.' *Monthly Review* 54 (1).

McCrann, Terry. 2003. 'Yesterday's News for Fuddy-duddy Fairfax Mob.' *The Weekend Australian*, 12–13 August, 42.

McGeough, Paul. 2003. *In Baghdad: A Reporter's War.* Sydney: Allen & Unwin.

McIlveen, L. 2004. ' PM Studied with Professor at Uni.' *The Courier-Mail,* 1 May.

McIlveen, Luke & Jane Schulze. 2003. 'Deal Done for Media Shake-up.' *The Australian*, 27 March, 1, 10.

McKenna, Michael. 2003. 'LA Police Face Probe After Stars' Secrets Sold.' *The Courier-Mail*, 26 June, 12.

McKenna, M. 2004. 'Legal Carnival as Jackson Faces First Court Hearing.' *The Courier-Mail*, 1 May.

McLean, S. 2004. 'Spooked by the Seminar Spy.' *The Australian,* 26 February, 23.

McNamara, Denise. 2003. *Dunn Handed 30 Years Jail for Depravity Against Young Boys.* AAP Newsfeed, 7 December 2001 [cited 24 September 2003]. Available from gateway.library.qut. edu.au:2684/...b&_md5=11fc620af85351214033eb6573139427.

McQueen, Humphrey. 1977. *Australia's Media Monopolies.* Melbourne: Widescope.

MEAA. 1995a. 'A Code for the 21st Century.' *The Alliance*, September, 7–10.

——. 1995b. 'A Code for the 21st Century.' In *Media Release*, edited by C. Warren. Sydney: MEAA.

Meade, Amanda. 2003. 'The Diary', Media. *The Australian*, 28 August–3 September, 2.

——. 2004. 'Sun Rises on Seven News.' *The Australian*, 6 May, 15–16.

Meade, K. & D. Macfarlane. 2003. 'Runaway's Partner on Perjury Charge.' *The Weekend Australian*, 13–14 December, 9.

Meadows, Michael. 1987. 'People Power: Reporting or Racism?' *Australian Journalism Review* 9: 102–12.

——. 1995. 'Sensitivity Not Censorship: Reporting Cultural Diversity in Australia.' *Australian Journalism Review* 17 (2): 18–27.

——. 1998a. 'The Media and Indigenous Affairs.' In *Urban Life, Urban Culture: Aboriginal/ Indigenous Experiences: Proceedings of the Goolagullia Centre,* University of Western Sydney, 27–29 November, ed. George Morgan.

——. 1998b. 'The Media as Cultural Resource.' *Australian Journalism Review* 20 (2): 1–23.

——. 2001. 'A Return to Practice: Reclaiming Journalism as Public Conversation.' In *Journalism: Theory in Practice*, ed. C. Varley. Melbourne: Oxford University Press.

Meadows, Michael, Cratis Hippocrates & Kitty Van Vuuren. 1997. 'Targeting the Media. Comparing Print and Television News Coverage of Indigenous Affairs.' *Australian Journalism Review* 19 (2): 73–87.

Meadows, Michael & Cheyenne Oldham. 1991. 'Racism and the Dominant Ideology: Aborigines, Television News and the Bicentenary.' *Media Information Australia* (60): 30–40.

'Media Policy is Still a Shambles.' 2003. *The Weekend Australian*, 28–29 June, 16.

'Media Truce With Royals Falls Apart.' 2003. *The Weekend Bulletin*, 10–11 May, 28.

Megalogenis, George. 2001. 'Rivers Run Dry.' *The Australian*, 13–19 December, 6-7.

Merrill, John C. 1974. *The Imperative of Freedom: A Philosophy of Journalistic Autonomy*. Ed. A.W. Blueam, *Studies in Public Communication*. New York: Communication Art Books.

——. 1989. *The Dialectic in Journalism: Towards a Responsible Use of Press Freedom*. Baton Rouge: Louisiana State University Press.

'Metherell Accuses Herald of Breach of Ethics.' 1988. *The Sydney Morning Herald*, 16 September, 2.

Mickler, Stephen. 1998. *The Myth of Privilege: Aboriginal Status, Media Visions, Public Ideas*. Freemantle, WA: Freemantle Arts Centre Press.

Mickler, Stephen & Alec McHoul. 1998. 'Sourcing the Wave: Crime Reporting, Aboriginal Youth and the WA Press, Feb 1991/ Jan 1992.' *Media International Australia Incorporating Culture & Policy* (86): 122–52.

Milligan, Louise. 2003. 'Gay Artist Error Ties Fairfax Up in Court.' *The Weekend Australian*, 28–29 June, 3.

Milne, Glenn. 2002. 'There Can Be Nothing to Gain from the Pain.' *The Australian*, 8 July, 11.

Milovanovic, Selma. 2003. 'Civil Rape Case Too Late: Clark', 11 March 2003 [cited 25 September 2003]. Available from www.theage.com.au/c.../articles/2003/03/10/1047144918544.html.

Mitchell, Chris. 1996. 'Battle of the Editors.' *The Weekend Australian*, 1 September, 19.

'Mobile Phone Fire Threat.' 1996. *Sunday Herald Sun*, 8 December, 1.

'Mobile Phones an Explosive Risk at Gas Stations.' 1999. *China Post*, 4 April.

Monaghan, Elaine. 2003. 'US Fetes Its Mythical Heroine.' *The Australian*, 24 July, 8.

Moor, Keith. 2003. '"Mr Cruel" Rapist Creeps Among Us', 4 August 2003 [cited 25 September 2003]. Available from www.sundaytimes.news.com.au/printpage/0,5942,6860726,00.html.

Moore, Bruce. 1997. *The Australian Concise Oxford Dictionary*. Oxford University Press, Melbourne.

Morris, S. 2004. '"Teetotal" Bartlett Back in Saddle.' *The Australian*, 27 January, 6.

Munro, Peter. 2003. 'When You've Got It.' *The Sydney Morning Herald*, 8–9 November, 31.

Murphy, Damien. 1996. 'Facts and Friction.' *The Bulletin*, 28 May, 14.

Murphy, Padraic, Greg Denham & Michael Davies. 2004. 'Saints Train on Amid Sex Crisis.' *The Australian*, 18 March, 3.

Murray, David. 2003. 'Murder Mystery Sideshow.' *The Courier-Mail*, 17 May, 31.

Murray, Paul. 2002. 'Hypocrisy Adds to Torrid Affair.' *The Sunday Times*, 7 July.

Narain, Harsh. 1973. *Evolution of Dialectic in Western Thought*. Delhi: Motilal Banarsidass.

National Media and Mental Health Group (2002). 'Achieving the Balance: Reporting Suicide and Mental Illness: A Resource for Media Professionals', Commonwealth of Australia.

Nelson, Fraser. 2003. 'The Hutton Inquiry: Gilligan's Day of Humiliation.' *The Scotsman*, 18 September, 1.

Nesbit, Phil. 2003. 'Are the Media Afraid of "Embedded" Journalists?' American Press Institute 2003 [cited 27 March 2003]. Available from www.americanpressinstitute.org/news.cfm?id=939.

Network. 1976. MGM Pictures.

'Network Gave the Right Connections.' 2003. *The Courier-Mail*, 9 August, 4.

Neville, Richard. 1996. *Hippie, Hippie Shake: The Dreams, the Trips, the Trials, the Love-ins, the Screw Ups— the Sixties*. Melbourne: Minerva. Original edition, Bloomsbury Publishing, London 1995.

Newington, Greg. 2002. 'They Were People Not Numbers.' *The Walkley Magazine*, 13.

Newman, Geoffrey. 2001. 'Down, Not Out.' *The Australian*, 25–31 October, 5.

Newman, Martin. 1996. 'Masked in Hate.' *The Daily Telegraph*, 5 January, 1, 4.

NSW Law Reform Commission. 2000. *Law Reform Commission, Discussion Paper 43 - Contempt by Publication, Appendix C: Table of penalties* 2000 [cited 25 September 2003]. Available from www.lawlink.nsw.gov.au/lrc.nsf/pages/dp43appC.

Norman, R. 1980. 'On the Hegelian Origins.' In S. Sayers & R. Norman (eds), *Hegel, Marx and Dialectic: A debate* (pp. 25–46). Brighton, Sussex: The Harvester Press.

Oakes, Laurie. 2003. 'Kernot-Evans "secret"'. In Channel Nine News.

Oakham, Katrina Mandy. 1998. 'Kick it Karl: A Jump Start for Journalism.' *Australian Journalism Review* 20 (2): 24–34.

O'Connor, Mike. 1994. 'OJ's Trial Under Way.' *The Daily Telegraph-Mirror*, 28 September, 28.

Off the Record. 1994. *See* Senate Standing Committee on Legal and Constitutional Affairs.

Oliver, Robin & Matthew Russell. 1997. 'Ratings Soar as Thredbo Survivor Relives Ordeal.' *Sydney Morning Herald*, 28 August, 3.

O'Malley, Brendan. 2003. 'Paradise is Lost with No Sign it Will Come Again.' *The Courier-Mail*, 30 August, 17.

O'Neil, John. 1993. 'A Family Under Siege.' *The Independent Monthly*, July, 11–13.

O'Neil, John & Catharine Lumby. 1994. 'Tabloid Television.' In *Not Just Another Business: Journalists, Citizens and the Media*, ed. J. Schultz. Sydney: Pluto Press in association with Ideas for Australia, National Centre for Australian Studies, Monash University.

O'Neill, John. 1992. 'Journalism in the Market Place.' In *Ethical Dilemmas in Journalism and the Media*, ed. R. Chadwick. London: Routledge.

O'Regan, Mick. 2001. 'John Hartigan, CEO News Limited.' In *The Media Report*: ABC Radio.

——. 2003. 'Journalism and the Internet and Improving Media Literacy.' In *The Media Report*: ABC Radio.

Orwell, George. 1984. 'Why I Write.' In *The Penguin Essays of George Orwell*. London: Penguin. Original edition, *The Collected Essays, Journalism and Letters of George Orwell v.1-4*, edited by Sonia Orwell & Ian Angus.

——. 1988. *Nineteen Eighty-four*. Penguin Books, with an Introduction by Richard Hoggart and a Note on the text by Peter Davison ed. London: Penguin in association with Secker & Warburg. Original edition, 1949.

O'Sullivan, John. 1992. 'Riots, Lies and Videotape.' *National Review*, 25 May, 4.

Paget, Dale. 1996. 'He Was Trying to Beat Dunblane Toll.' *The Daily Telegraph*, 30 April, 2.

PANPA. 1992. 'Professor Flint Presses for Referendum.' *PANPA Bulletin*, June, 6.

——. 1993. 'Editor-in-chief Establishes a Journalists' Code of HWT.' *PANPA Bulletin*, December, 9.

——. 1994a. 'Rural Press Releases New Manual Stating Its Staff's Moral Obligations to Its Communities. *PANPA Bulletin*, July, 54–55.

——. 1994b. 'Ex-Australian Editor Says Freedom of Speech Not Guaranteed.' *PANPA Bulletin*, August, 23.

——. 1995. 'Australian Government Backs Away From Plans to Stop Security Leaks.' *PANPA Bulletin*, August, 59.

'Paris Under Siege.' 2003. *Who*, 1 December, 68–9.

Parnell, Sean. 2003a. 'Honestly, People Trust Press Over Politicians.' *The Courier-Mail*, 2 April, 3.

——. 2003b. 'Premier Calls for Media Ombudsman.' *The Courier-Mail*, 27 March, 10.

Parnell, S. 2004. 'Media Fights for Access to Police Action.' *The Courier-Mail*, 8 May, 8.

Parsons, P. & W. Smith. 1987. 'R. Budd Dwyer: A Case Study in Newsroom Decision Making.' Paper read at AEJMC Annual Conference, at San Antonio, Texas.

Passmore, Daryl. 2003. 'I Had Sex Six Times and They Painted Me as a Sort of Scarlet Woman— A Prostitute.' *The Sunday Mail* (Qld), 22 June, 56–8.

Patching, Roger. 1994. Personal notes on National Media Forum, 4 March.

——. 1996. Paul Fenn interview about journalism ethics, 24 May.

Patterson, Philip & Lee Wilkins. 1994. *Media Ethics: Issues and Cases*. 2nd edn. Dubuque, IA: Brown & Benchmark.

Paul, Nora. 1999. *Computer-Assisted Research: A guide to Tapping Online Information*. Fourth edn. St Petersburg, Florida: Poynter Institute/Bonus Books.

Pax, Salam. 2003. *The Baghdad Blog*. Melbourne: Text.

Peach, Bill. 1992. *This Day Tonight: How Australian Current Affairs TV Came of Age*. Sydney: ABC Enterprises.

Pearson, Mark. 1993. 'Australian Journalists, Confidential Sources and the Court Room: Toward an Evidentiary Privilege for Reporters.' Paper read at Association for Education in Journalism and Mass Communication Convention, 12 August, at Kansas City, USA.

——. 1997. *The Journalist's Guide to Media Law*. Sydney: Allen & Unwin.

——. 2000. 'Advertorials and the Trade Practices Act: Why the "Golden Tonsils" Saga Might Prove Costly in the Long Run.' *Australian Journalism Review* 22 (1): 57–67.

——. 2001. 'A Question of Legality.' In *Journalism: Theory in practice*, ed. C. Varley. Melbourne: Oxford University Press.

——. 2003. 'Sensitive or Sanitized? Guidelines for Reporting Age.' *Australian Studies in Journalism* (12): 229–39.

——2004a. *The Journalist's Guide to Media Law: Dealing with Legal and Ethical Issues*. Crows Nest, Sydney: Allen and Unwin.

——2004b. 'AJA Finds Ethics Too Hard to Enforce.' *The Australian*, 15 April, 20.

Pearson, Mark, Carolyn Proud & Peter Willcox. 2003. 'The Cyberboundaries of Reputation: Implications of the Australian High Court" Gutnick Decision for Journalists.' *Australian Journalism Review* 25 (1): 101–14.

Perry, Roland. 1988. *The Exile: Burchett: Reporter of Conflict*. Melbourne: William Heinemann Australia.

'Petrol Heads: Switch Off the Mobile for Safety.' 1999. *The Australian Financial Review*, 17 May.

Phelan, John. 1991. 'Selling Consent: The Public Sphere as a Televisual Market-place.' In *Communication and Citizenship: Journalism and the Public Sphere*, ed. C. Sparks. London & New York: Routledge.

Pilger, John. 1986a. *Heroes*. Revised edn London: Pan Books. Original edition, Jonathon Cape.

——. 1986b. Preface. In *Burchett: Reporting the Other Side of the World*, ed. B. Kiernan.

——. 1992. *Distant Voices*. London: Vintage.

——. 1994. 'The Evidence Suggests.' *Reportage*, Winter, 22–3.

——. 1998. *Hidden Agendas*. London: Vantage.

'Players Raped My Disabled Daughter.' 2004. *The Australian*, 18 March, 3.

'Police Videos.' 1995. *The Sydney Morning Herald*, 21 December, 10.

Potter, Deborah. 1998. 'The President, the Intern, and the Media: Journalism Ethics Under Siege.' www.poynter.org/content/content_view.asp?id+5633.

Poulantzas, Nicos. 1975. *Classes in Contemporary Capitalism*. Trans. D. Fernbach. NLB edn London: New Left Books. Original edn: Editions du Seuil, 1974.

Powell, Diane. 1990. 'Media Intrusions into Grief.' *Media Information Australia* (57): 24–9.

——. 1993. *Out West: Perceptions of Sydney's Western Suburbs*. Sydney: Allen and Unwin.

'The Press-ganged Pollie.' 2003. *The Gold Coast Bulletin*, 27 March, 25.

Price, Matt. 2003b. 'Clark Lashes Out at Media Critics.' *The Australian*, 21 July, 4.

'A Quick Nip and the Afternoon Dip Combine to Cut Alertness.' 2003. *The Sydney Morning Herald*, 22 August, 3.

Quinn, Michael. 1991. 'Courts Should Take Strong Action to Stop Trials by Media.' *Australian Journalism Review* 13 (1-2): 45–51.

QUT. 2001. 'Trauma and Media.' School of Media and Journalism.

Raboy, Marc & Bernard Dagenais. 1992. 'Media and the Politics of Crisis.' In *Media, Crisis and Democracy*, edited by B. Dagenais. London: Sage.

Ramsay, Alan. 1999. 'Sparring with Citizen Murdoch.' *The Sydney Morning Herald*, 6 November, 49.

Rawls, John. 1971. *A Theory of Justice*. Cambridge, MA: Harvard University Press.

'Rector Slams News "Ghouls".' 1990. *The Courier-Mail*, 1 October, 3.

Reid, Michael. 2002. 'First With an Apocalypse.' *The Walkley Magazine*, 14.

'Resign or be Sacked.' 2003. *The Gold Coast Bulletin*, 2 May, 5.

Retief, Johan. 2002. *Media Ethics: An Introduction to Responsible Journalism*. Cape Town: Oxford University Press.

Reucassel, Craig. 2003a. 'Chaser National Non-stop News Network.' In *CNNNN*: ABC Television.

——. 2003b. 'Chaser National Non-stop News Network.' ABC TV.

Reynolds, Donald. 1995. 'Words for War.' In *The Press in Times of Crisis*, ed. L. Chiasson Jr. Westport, CT: Praeger.

Rhetorica 2003. [Internet] n.d. [cited 28 August 2003].

Richards, Deborah. 2000. 'A Watching Brief.' *The Walkley Magazine*, Autumn, 11–13.

Richards, Ian. 1994. 'Encountering Death for the First Time.' *Australian Journalism Review* 16 (1): 115–20.

——. 1996. 'Dealing with Death: Intrusion into Grief and Journalism Education.' *Australian Journalism Review* 18 (1): 99–105.

——. 1998. 'Searching for a Way Out: The Imbroglio in Journalism Ethics.' *Australian Journalism Review* 20 (1): 72–81.

——. 2002a. 'Adjusting the Focus: Levels of Influence and Ethical Decision-making in Journalism.' *Australian Journalism Review* 24 (2): 9–20.

——. 2002b. 'Leading Parallel Lives: Journalism and Professional Ethics.' Paper read at IIPE/AAPE 2002 Conference: Reconstructing 'the Public Interest' in a Globalising World: Business, the Professions and the Public Sector.

——. 2003. '"Trust Me, I'm a Journalist": Ethics, Journalism and Journalism Education.' *Asia Pacific Media Educator*, 14, December, 140–6.

Richardson, Brian. 1994. 'Four Standards for Teaching Ethics in Journalism.' *Journal of Mass Media Ethics* IX (2): 109–17.

Rieder, R.A. 1998. 'A Verdict Without a Trial.' *American Journalism Review*, May.

Riley, Mark. 1993. 'Trail of Blood that Led to Cangai.' *The Sydney Morning Herald*, 31 March, 1, 4.

——. 1998. 'This is the News: Er, Well, It's Like This, Sorry.' *The Sydney Morning Herald*, 4 July, 17.

——. 2002. 'That Day in September.' *The Walkley Magazine*, 18–19.

Riley, Mark, Nick Papadopoulos & Greg Roberts. 1993. '"It's Time to Die," Say Gunmen.' *The Sydney Morning Herald*, 31 March, 1.

Ringle, K. 2003. 'West Still Shies Away From Violent Images of War.' *The Sydney Morning Herald*, 26–27 July, 17.

Rintoul, Stuart. 2002. 'Violation, But of Whom?' *The Australian*, 21–27 June, 3.

Rintoul, Stuart & Stewart Cameron. 2003. 'How the Mighty Fall.' *The Australian*, 26 May, 10.

Rintoul, S. & M. Schubert. 2004. 'Judge Says Clark Leader of Rape Pack.' *The Weekend Australian*, 14–15 February, 3.

Roberts, Greg. 2003a. 'A Puzzling Murder Where the Pieces Just Don't Fit.' *The Sydney Morning Herald*, 3–4 May, 13.

——. 2003b. 'Swim Coach Faces Fresh Abuse Case.' *The Weekend Australian*, 6–7 September, 3.

Robins, Brian. 2003. 'A Big Part of the Packer Family Farm.' *The Sydney Morning Herald*, 30–31 August, 34.

Robinson, Peter. 1996. 'Media Obliged to Help Police.' *The Sydney Morning Herald*, 2 January, 10.

Rood, David. 2002. 'Car Salesmen Get a Lemon Rating.' *The Age*, 20 December, 6.

Rosen, Jill. 2003. 'All About the Retrospect', *American Journalism Review*, June 2003 [cited 27 January 2004]. Available from www.ajr.org/Article.asp?id=3020.

Ross, Jay. 1982. 'Warfare on Fleet Street: Some Media Accused of Lacking Patriotism.' *The Washington Post*, 9 May, A20.

Rothenberg, Fred. 'British Accent to Networks' Falklands Coverage' (PM cycle). Associated Press, 4 June 1982.

Rowe, D. 1987. 'TV Deaths are a Part of Life.' *The Sydney Morning Herald*, 29 January, 10.

Ruehl, Peter. 2002. 'Car Nuts and Crazy Prices to Boot.' *The Australian Financial Review*, 9 July, 64.

——. 2003. 'How to Screw a Perfectly Good Career.' *The Australian Financial Review*, 7 August, 64.

Rule, Andrew. 2002. 'Accusers Sue Clark Over Rape Suffering.' *The Age*, 21 August, 1.

'Rules Are Needed to Cover Siege Reporting.' 1993. *The Age*, 2 April, 13.

Sanders, Karen. 2003. *Ethics & Journalism*. London: Sage.

Sands, Lesley. 1996. 'Moral Panics.' [Internet] 1996 [cited 20 March 2004]. Available from www.aber.ac.uk/media/Students/lcs9603.html.

Saunders, David. 1994. 'Televising of the Courts Wins Cautious Approval.' *The Age*, 31 January, 4.

Sawyer, Diane. 2003. Jessica Lynch interview – '60 Minutes'. In *60 Minutes* (USA).

Schubert, Misha & Stuart Rintoul. 2003. 'Ruddock Suspends Clark.' *The Australian*, 14 August, 1.

Schudson, Michael. 1992. *Watergate in American Memory: How we Remember, Forget and Reconstruct the Past*. New York: HarperCollins.

——. 1997. 'The Sociology of News Production.' In *Social Meanings of News*, edited by D. Berkowitz. Thousand Oaks, Cal.: Sage. Original edition, *Media, Culture & Society*, 1989, Vol. 11, pp. 263–82, Sage.

Schultz, Julianne. 1994. 'The Paradox of Professionalism.' In *Not Just Another Business: Journalists, Citizens and the Media*, ed. J. Schultz. Sydney: Pluto Press in association with Ideas for Australia, National Centre for Australian Studies, Monash University.

——. 1998. *Reviving the Fourth Estate: Democracy, Accountability and the Media*. Melbourne: Cambridge University Press.

——. 1999. 'The Many Paradoxes of Independence.' In *Journalism: Print, Politics and Popular Culture.*

——. ed. 1994. *Not Just Another Business: Journalists, Citizens and the Media, Ideas for Australia Program.* Sydney: Pluto Press in association with Ideas for Australia, National Centre for Australian Studies, Monash University.

Schulze, Jane. 2003a. 'DirecTV Back in News Picture.' *The Weekend Australian,* 29–30 March, 39.

——. 2003b. 'News Circles Pay-TV Globe.' *The Australian,* 3 April, 21.

——. 2003c. 'Fairfax Wields Axe at the Top.' *The Weekend Australian,* 5–6 April, 21.

——. 2003d. 'News Sweats on DirecTV.' *The Australian,* 10 April, 21.

——. 2003e. 'Last Man Standing.' *The Weekend Australian,* 12–13 August, 39, 42.

——. 2004a. 'Family Gets $40m in Extra Divvies.' *The Australian,* 29 April, 23.

——. 2004b. 'It's Good News Week.' *The Australian,* 8 April, 17.

Schwartz, Larry. 1987. 'Hinch Goes to Jail for Month (or Four Days).' *The Sydney Morning Herald,* 15 October, 3.

Scott, Paul. 2001. 'On the Fringe: Journalism, Representation and Cultural competence.' In *Journalism: Theory in Practice,* ed. C. Varley. Melbourne: Oxford University Press.

Seamark, M. & M. McKenna 2004. 'Jacko Could Die in Jail.' *The Sunday Mail* (Qld), 2 May, 5.

Senate Standing Committee on Legal and Constitutional Affairs. 1994. *Off the Record: Shield Laws for Journalists' Confidential Sources.* Canberra: Parliament of the Commonwealth of Australia.

Sengupta, Ken. 2003. 'Gilligan Maintains: I Got It Right Over 45-minute Weapons Claim.' *The Independent,* 18 September, 6.

Shanahan, D. 2004. 'Daring Dash That Delivered PM.' *The Weekend Australian,* 1–2 May, 1–2.

Shanahan, Dennis, Steve Lewis & Gosia Kaszubska. 2003. 'G-G Considers Resignation.' *The Weekend Australian,* 24–25 May, 1.

Shannahan, Angela. 2002. 'The Role of Victim Will Suit Kernot.' *The Australian,* 9 July, 13.

Shaw, Martin. 1988. *Dialectics of War: An Essay in the Social Theory of Total War and Peace.* London: Pluto Press.

Shawcross, W. 1997. 'Patron Saint of the Global Village.' *The Sydney Morning Herald,* 6 September, 32.

'She Kissed Me'. 2003. *The Gold Coast Bulletin,* 15 August, 3.

Sheehan, Paul. 2003. *The Electronic Whorehouse.* Sydney: Macmillan.

Sheridan, Greg. 1994. 'Dili Massacre Claims Need to be Scrutinised.' *The Australian,* 14 February, 1–2.

——. 2002. 'A Threat We Ignore at our Peril.' *The Australian,* 14 October, 11.

——. 2004a. 'Curiosity Won't Kill These Cats.' *The Australian,* 18 March, 13.

——. 2004b. 'The Buck Stops with Rumsfeld, Who Should Resign.' *The Australian,* 13 May, 13.

Sheridan Burns, Lynette. 1994. 'Hypothetical: Better Than the Real Thing?' *Australian Journalism Review* 16(1): 108–14.

——. 1995. 'Philosophy or Frontline? A Study of Journalism Educators about Teaching Ethics.' *Australian Journalism Review* 17(2): 1–9.

——. 1996. 'Blocking the Exits: Focus on the Decision in Ethical Decision-making.' *Australian Journalism Review* 18(1): 87–97.

——. 1997. 'Problem-based Learning (PBL) and Journalism Education: Is It New Jargon for Something Familiar?' *Australian Journalism Review* 19(2): 59–72.

Sheridan Burns, Lynette & Alan McKee. 1999. 'Reporting on Indigenous Issues: Some Practical Suggestions for Journalists.' *Australian Journalism Review* 21(2): 103–16.

Sheridan Burns, Lynette & T. Hazell. 1998. 'Response ... Ability: Youth Suicide and the National University Curriculum Project.' *Australian Journalism Review* 20(2): 111–28.

Sheridan Burns, Lynette, L. Reardon, et al. 2001. 'Are Journalism Educators "Response Able"?' *Australian Journalism Review* 23(2): 105–17.

Simmons, Lisa. 2003. 'Ratings Showdown.' *The Gold Coast Bulletin*, 29 May, 14.

Simons, Margaret. 1999. *Fit to Print: Inside the Canberra Press Gallery*. Sydney: UNSW Press.

Simper, Errol. 1994. 'ABC Staff Condemn Management Action.' *The Australian*, 27 September, 5.

——. 1995a. 'ABC Pulls ASIO Item.' *The Australian*, 26 May, 1.

——. 1995b. 'Free speech - right or wrong?' *The Weekend Australian*, 22–23 July, 72.

——. 1995c. 'Ban on Claims We Bugged China.' *The Weekend Australian*, 27-28 May, 1.

——. 1996. 'Who Monitors Community Ethics.' *The Weekend Australian*, 9–10 September, 76.

——. 2002. 'Tragedy Calls for Responsible Media.' *The Australian*, 17 October, 6.

——. 2003. 'The Max Factor—To the Max.' *The Australian*, 21 August, B01.

——. 2004a. 'Spin that Killed the Doctor.' *The Australian*, 5 February, 24.

——. 2004b. 'ABC Hires Duffy as Its "Right-wing Adams".' *The Australian*, 6 May, 15.

Simpson, Lindsay. 2001. 'Reporting Port Arthur: A Personal Account.' *Australian Journalism Review* 23 (2): 191–9.

Singer, Peter. 1991. *A Companion to Ethics*. Oxford: Basil Blackwell.

Slee, John. 1992. 'Journalist's Jailing Has Hurt the Law.' *The Sydney Morning Herald*, 27 March, n.p.

——. 1994. 'Jailing Deborah Cornwall Was Clumsy and Unnecessary.' *Free Speech* 1 (2): 11–12.

——. 1995. 'Jury's Still Out on Issue of TV Trials.' *The Sydney Morning Herald*, 15 October, 15.

'Sleeper Cells Planning Terror Attacks in Australia Claim.' 2003. *The Cairns Post*, 7 July, 2.

Smethurst, Sue & Paul Broben. 2004. 'Saving Private Ryan.' *New Idea*, 14 January, 10–12.

Smith, Michael. 1992. 'Accountability: The Writing on the Wall.' *Australian Journalism Review* 14 (1): 27–32.

Smith, Wayne & Peter Kelly. 1996. 'A Question of Influence.' *The Courier-Mail*, 24 August, 1.

Smyth, Chris. 2003. 'Televised Trials Reveal Justice.' *The Australian*, 12–18 June, 7.

'Snooping LA Cops Sell Off Star Secrets.' 2003. *The Gold Coast Bulletin*, 26 June, 5.

'Sophie Print a Cruel Act, Say Palace.' 1999. *The Gold Coast Bulletin*, 27 May, 9.

Southward, Jane, Margory Bennett & Kathleen Carmody. 1996. 'Media, Murder and Mystery.' *The Sun-Herald*, 11 February, 29.

Sparrow, Geoff, ed. 1960. *Crusade for Journalism: Official History of the Australian Journalists' Association*. Melbourne: Federal Council of the A.J.A.

Spender, Dale. 2003. 'Where's the Disgrace if You Cut and Paste?' *The Australian*, 20 August, 36.

'Spiking the Royal Guns.' 2003. *The Courier-Mail*, 25 September, 4.

'Staff Anger on Super League.' 1996. *The Sun-Herald*, 11 February, 22.

Stahel, Thomas H. 1993. 'CNN Does It Again.' *America*, 1 May, 16.

Stamm, Keith & John Bowes. 1990. *The Mass Communication Process: A Behavioral and Social Perspective*. Dubuque, Iowa: Kendall/Hunt Publishing Company.

Stannard, Bruce. 1989. 'Why are Australia's Media on the Nose?' *The Bulletin*, 14 November, 54–60.

Stapleton, J. 2004. 'Fairfax Job Cuts to "Gut Papers".' *The Australian*, 19 May, 6.

Steele, Jon. 2002. *War Junkie: One Man's Addiction to the Worst Places on Earth*. Sydney: Bantam Press.

Stepp, Carl S. 1999. 'A Powerful Warning for the Media.' *American Journalism Review,* October.

Stewart, Cameron. 1998. 'My Lai Heroes Live Down US Shame.' *The Weekend Australian*, 14–15 March, 17.

——. 2004. 'Privacy or Truth Sparks Radio Row.' *The Australian,* 5 February, 20.

Stockwell, Stephen. 1999. 'Beyond the Fourth Estate: Democracy, Deliberation and Journalism Theory.' *Australian Journalism Review* 21 (1): 37–49.

Stockwell, Stephen & Paul Scott 2000. 'All-Media Guide to Fair and Cross-Cultural Reporting', Australian Key Centre for Cultural and Media Policy.

Strentz, Herbert. 1978. *News Reporters and News Sources: What Happens Before the Story is Written.* Ames: Iowa State University Press.

Strickland, K. 1998. 'Impeach the Media.' *The Australian,* 27 November, 13.

'Students are Betrayed for the "Truth" in Classroom.' 1988. *The Weekend Advocate,* 1 October, 8.

Stutchbury, M. 2002. From the Editor. *The Australian,* 9 May, 2.

——. 2003. 'Gang Attack—Crime and Punishment.' *The Australian,* 1 November, B01.

Suich, Max. 2003. 'And Who Asked For Your Opinion.' *The Sydney Morning Herald,* 8–9 November, 14–15.

Sunderland, Alan. 1992. 'InterOffice Memo: The Iranian Embassy "Affair".' Canberra: Special Broadcasting Service.

Sutton, Candice. 1990. 'Packer, TV News Crews in Scuffle.' *The Sun-Herald,* 13 October, 2.

Sutton, C., H. Gilmore, et al. 1996. 'Bungling Let World's Worst Killer Go Free: He Could Have Been Stopped.' *The Sun-Herald,* 5 May, 1.

'Swans Star: Why I Paid "Rape" Woman.' 2004. *The Sunday Mail* (Qld), 21 March, 4.

'Switch Off Mobiles at Fuel Pumps.' 2003. *The Daily Telegraph,* 21 July.

Sykes, J., G. Embleton, et al. 2003. 'Covering Trauma: Suggestions For a More Collaborative Approach.' *Australian Journalism Review* 25(2): 73–83.

Symons, Emma-Kate. 2003. 'The Existential Celebrity.' *The Weekend Australian,* 8–9 November, 23.

——. 2004. 'Victim Resists the Media Frenzy for her Story.' *The Australian,* 29 April, 4.

'Tabloids Fear Naomi's Court Win Will Spell End for Exposes.' 2004. *The Sydney Morning Herald,* 8 May, 15.

'Take Job or Lose Dole.' 1996. *The Daily Telegraph,* 6 March, 10.

Tanner, S., S. Haswell et al. 2003. 'Breaking Down the Barriers: Trying to Convince the Media That Disability is Newsworthy.' *Australian Journalism Review* 25(2): 85–102.

Tasker, Belinda. 2003. 'News Shares Surge on New DirecTV Bid Rumours.' *The Courier-Mail,* 29 March, 70.

Tate, Alan. 1986. 'Grief: The Media Overwhelmed.' *The Sydney Morning Herald,* 19 July.

Tazreiter, Claudia. 2003. 'The Things We Rely On.' *The Sydney Morning Herald,* 3–4 May, 8–9.

'The Numbers Game.' 2003. *The Australian.* Media, 14–20 August, 12.

Thomas, Hedley & Steven Wardill. 2003. 'Volkers Faces New Threat of Prosecution.' *The Courier-Mail,* 3 April, 1.

Thompson, H.S. 1995. *Better Than Sex: Confessions of a Political Junkie Trapped Like a Rat in Mr Bill's Neighbourhood.* New York: Ballantine Books.

Thornton, Alinta. 1999. 'Does Internet Create Democracy?' Masters, Journalism, University of Technology, Sydney.

Tiffen, Rodney. 1988. 'Confidential Sources in the News: Conventions and Contortions.' *Australian Journalism Review* 10: 22–7.

——. 1989. *News and Power.* Sydney: Allen & Unwin.

Toohey, Brian. 1996a. 'The Blue That Cost $4 Billion.' *The Sun-Herald,* 21 April, 39.

Trevorrow, John. 2002. '36 Hours Non-stop.' *The Walkley Magazine,* Issue 15, Summer, 13–14.

Turner, Geoff. 1994a. 'Frontline Ethics: The Australian Media's Siege Mentality.' *Australian Studies in Journalism* (3): 24–38.

——. 1994b. 'Journalistic Ethics in Australia: Raising the Standards.' *Australian Journalism Review* 16 (1): 1–12.

Turner, Grant. 2002. 'The Spy Catcher.' *The Walkley Magazine*, 12.

'TV Reporter Admits Jail Release Forgery.' 1995.*The Daily Telegraph Mirror*, 11 July, 2.

Underwood, Derek. 1993. *When MBAs Rule the Newsroom: How the Marketers and the Managers are Reshaping Today's Media.* New York: Columbia University Press.

'Unnecessary Censorship.' 1995. *The Sydney Morning Herald*, 14 December, 12.

UPI. 1982a. *Our Job is to Report Events* (AM cycle) [News Wire], 9 May 1982 [cited].

——.1982b. *British Press Debate Truth and Treason in Falklands Coverage* (PM cycle), 10 May 1982 [cited].

——. 1982c. *Reporter Denies Slain Commander Threatened Suit* (AM cycle), 6 June 1982 [cited].

'US Media Faced Dilemma on Coverage of Suicide.' 1987. *International Herald Tribune*, 24–25 January.

Verrender, Ian. 1996. 'The Pack That Hunts Diana.' *The Sydney Morning Herald*, 2 November, 36.

Vincent, Nigel. 1996. 'He Just Picked Them Out and Shot Them.' *The Daily Telegraph*, 29 April, 4–5.

Volkers, Scott. 2003. 'Quotes of the Week.' *The Courier-Mail*, 17 May, 30.

Wade, Judy. 1974. 'Hacks into Heroes.' *New Journalist*, September, 31.

Walsh, M. 1970. 'The Social Responsibility of the Press.' Paper read at The Sixth Summer School of Professional Journalism, at Canberra.

Walsh, Max. 2003. 'The Show Goes On.' *The Bulletin*, 26 August, 29–30.

Wapshott, Nicholas. 2003. 'NY Times Editors Quit Over Plagiarist.' *The Weekend Australian*, 7–8 June 2003, 12.

Ward, Ian. 1995. *Politics of the Media.* Melbourne: Macmillan Education.

'Warne's Affair.' 2003. In *Today Tonight*, 26 August, Seven Network.

'Warne's Woes.' 2003. *Herald Sun*, 12 February, 2–3.

'Warning About Mobile Phones at Petrol Stations.' 2003. *Coonamble Times*, 13 August.

Warne-Smith, D. & Barrett, S. 2004. 'Accuser Admits Previous Group Sex with Players.' *The Australian,* 29 April, 4.

Warren, Agnes. 1996a. 'Advertorials.' In *The Media Report*: ABC Radio, 14 March.

——. 1996b. 'Port Arthur Massacre—How Were Journalists Affected?' In *Media Report*, ABC Radio, 21 November.

Watt, Amanda. 2003. 'Runaway Returns to her Former Hideout.' *The Courier-Mail*, 27 June, 1.

Wayne, Mike. 2003. *Marxism and Media Studies: Key Concepts and Contemporary Trends.* London: Pluto Press.

'We Must Remain Firm in the Face of Terror.' 2002. *The Australian*, 14 October, 14.

Weekend Career One. 2003. *The Weekend Australian*. 13–14 September. 1.

Wells, Matt. 2003a. 'Hutton Inquiry: Dyke to Review Rules After 'Unacceptable' Gilligan Email.' *The Guardian*, 16 September, 5.

——. 2003b. 'BBC Chief: Lessons in Reporting to be Learned from Iraq Dossier Row.' *The Guardian*, 16 September, 5.

Wenger, E., R. McDermott, et al. 2002. *Cultivating Communities of Practice: A Guide to Managing Knowledge.* Boston, Mass.: Harvard Business School Press.

Wenham, Margaret. 2002. 'A Lot of Hot Air?' *The Courier-Mail*, 5 July, 17.

West, Bing & Ray L. Smith. 2003. *The March Up: Taking Baghdad with the 1st Marine Division.* London: Pimlico.

Whiting, Frances. 2003. 'Pauline Signs Deal for TV Interview.' *The Sunday Mail* (Qld), 9 November, 5.

Whittell, Greg. 1994. 'Simpson Team Seeks the Ideal Juror.' *The Australian*, 28 September, 12.

Whittington, Don. 1977. *Strive to be Fair: An Unfinished Autobiography.* Canberra: Australian National University Press.

'Why She Did It.' 2003. *The Weekend Bulletin*, 12–13 April, 1.

Wiggins, Gene. 1995. 'Journey to Cuba: The Yellow Crisis.' In *The Press in Times of Crisis*, ed. L. Chiasson Jr. Westport, CT: Praeger.

Wikipedia. 2004. 'Moral Panic' [Internet]. Wikipedia 2004 [cited 20 March 2004]. Available from en.wikipedia.org/wiki/Moral_panic.

Williams, Kevin. 1993. 'The Light at the End of the Tunnel: The Mass Media, Public Opinion and the Vietnam War.' In *Getting the Message: News, Truth and Power*, ed. J. Eldridge. London: Routledge.

Williams, Pamela. 2000. 'A Question of Identity.' *The Walkley Magazine*, Summer, 19–20.

Williams, Raymond. 1989. *Keywords: A Vocabulary of Culture and Society.* Flamingo revised and expanded, 1983 edn London: Fontana Press.

Wilmoth, Peter. 1997. 'Diary of a Deal.' *The Sun-Herald*, 17 August, 47.

Wilson, Ashleigh. 2003a. 'Conflict Comes to a PC near You.' *The Weekend Australian*, 22–3 March, 4.

——. 2003b. '"Murder victim" to Sell her Story.' *The Australian*, 14 April, 3.

Wilson, Bruce. 2004. 'Editor Sacked Over Fake Abuse Photos.' *The Sunday Mail* (Qld), 16 May, 3.

Wilson, David. 1992. 'Charters of Editorial Independence.' *Australian Journalism Review* 14 (2): 31–36.

Wilson, Helen, ed. 1989. *Australian Communication and the Public Sphere: Essays in Memory of Bill Bonney.* Melbourne: Macmillan.

Wilson, Peter. 2003a. 'BBC to Go Under Blair Microscope.' *The Weekend Australian*, 20–21 September, 14.

——. 2003b. 'Spin King's Fall Heralds Blair's New Order.' *The Australian*, 1 September, 16.

Windschuttle, Keith. 1988. *The Media: A New Analysis of the Press, Television, Radio and Advertising in Australia.* Third edn Ringwood, Vic: Penguin. Original edn, 1984.

Wiseman, N. 2004. 'The Power and the Gory in Celeb City.' *The Sunday Mail* (Qld), 18 April, 57.

Wolf, Jim. 2003. 'Gulf Commander Denounces Arabic Network.' *The Courier-Mail*, 29 March, 11.

Wolfe, Tom. 1977. *The New Journalism: With An Anthology Edited by Tom Wolfe and E.W. Johnson.* London: Picador (published by Pan Books). Original edn, 1975.

'Woman Tells of Lie Test over Shane.' *The Gold Coast Bulletin*, 26 August, 3.

Woods, Keith. 1995. 'Unabomber Case Holds Lessons for All Journalists' [Internet]. Poynter Institute CHECK [cited 17 June 2003. Available from poynteronline.org/content/content_view.asp?id=5639.

Wright, Tony. 1995a. 'On the Wrong Side of Rupert.' *The Sydney Morning Herald*, 13 October, 23.

——. 1995b. 'Media's Duty to Help Police: Lee.' *The Sydney Morning Herald*, 29 December, 3.

Wynhausen, E. 2004. 'Salam Pax Succumbs to the Unbearable Weight of Blogging', *The Australian,* 20 May, p. 17.

Young, Peter & Peter Jesser. 1997. *The Media and the Military: From the Crimea to Desert Strike.* London: Macmillan.

' "You're kidding"—Warne Answers Phone-sex Claim.' 2003. *The Courier-Mail*, 11 August, 1.

Zawawi, Clara. 1994. 'Sources of News: Who Feeds the Watchdogs?' *Australian Journalism Review* 16 (1): 67–71.

Zdenkowski, George. 1995. 'Cameras in Court: Justice Must Stay in the Picture.' *The Sydney Morning Herald*, 22 June, 19.

Ziman, John. 2001. 'Why Must Scientists Become More Ethically Sensitive Than They Used To Be?' Review of Accessed Online 23 April 2001. *Science*.

Zuel, Bernard. 1992. 'Row Over Ethics of TV Reporter's Photo Request.' *The Sydney Morning Herald*, 12 August, 11.

Index